THE ANARCHISTS
IN THE SPANISH
CIVIL WAR

THE ANARCHISTS IN THE SPANISH CIVIL WAR

ROBERT J. ALEXANDER

JANUS PUBLISHING COMPANY
London, England

First published in Great Britain 1999
by Janus Publishing Company Limited,
Edinburgh House, 19 Nassau Street,
London W1N 7RE

www.januspublishing.co.uk

A CIP catalogue record for this book
is available from the British Library.

ISBN 1 85756 400 6

Phototypeset in 11 on 13.5 Sabon
by Keyboard Services, Luton, Beds

Cover design Creative Line

Printed and bound in Great Britain by
Athenaeum Press Ltd, Gateshead, Tyne & Wear

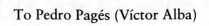
To Pedro Pagés (Víctor Alba)

Contents

Preface

Perhaps one can say that this book has been nearly 60 years in the writing, since my first visit to Spain, during the first month of the Civil War. Although at the time of that visit I was certainly not fully aware of what was going on, the experience aroused in me a lasting interest in the Spanish Civil War, which was one of the crucial events of the twentieth century.

Furthermore, the Spanish Civil War presented one of the two events that determined my lifelong political convictions – which made me an anti-Communist from the days of Stalin to the days of Gorbachev. This was the way in which the Communists behaved in Spain during the Civil War, when they strove ruthlessly to try to establish there a replica of the Stalinist regime in the Soviet Union. The other factor that determined my life-long political outlook was going on at the same time – the Great Purge in the Soviet Union, during which Stalin destroyed virtually all of the other leaders of the Russian Revolution, in addition to millions of other people.

There is reason to believe that these two events – Stalin's ruthless purge in the USSR and his servants' drive to establish a similar kind of regime in Spain – alienated vast numbers of people from Marxist-Leninism who had originally had sympathy with it, not only in the United States but in many other countries. I recall a talk with Carlos Lacerda, in the 1930s head of the Brazilian Young Communists and in the 1960s a supposedly Right-wing political leader in that country. When I asked him what had alienated him from the Communists, he mentioned the Great Purge and the way the Stalinists had behaved in Spain during the Civil War.

Just out of high school, I spent the summer of 1936 in Europe. My father had received a few months earlier his share of the First World War veterans' bonus, and had given me half of it to go to Europe on 'the grand tour'. However, my parents had certain worries about my taking that trip, since for several years I had already been active in the Young People's Socialist League (YPSL) So they gave me strict instructions: I could not go to the Soviet Union under any circumstances; I could only go to Nazi Germany with friends of theirs who were going there that summer; I could only go to Mussolini's Italy on a conducted tour. But they did not tell me that if a civil war broke out in Spain I could not go there. So I concluded that silence gave consent. I went.

When I got to Port Bou, the Spanish town at which the railroad from France ended, it was very late at night. There was little evidence of life. But the next day, I found my way to the headquarters of the local revolutionary militia. When I presented then the Spanish visa, which I had received in Marseilles, the militiamen told me that it was not valid, since the consul had gone over to the Franco forces. But they did accept as a valid 'visa' a letter of introduction I had from the New York representative of the Spanish Socialist Party daily *El Socialista*. I concluded that, together with that letter, my great difficulties in answering them in Catalan, Spanish or French had convinced the militiamen that I was too ignorant to be a spy, if that was my intention, and they allowed me to proceed to Barcelona,

I arrived in the Catalan capital at sunset. I was informed that the city's hotels were no longer functioning, having been taken over by various revolutionary parties and other organizations. I just didn't know what to do. However, issuing from the railroad station, I encountered a man with a visor cap, who looked like someone in authority, and who turned out to be a professional guide of the city of Barcelona, Since 'guiding' was not a prosperous occupation at that point, he agreed to show me around the revolutionary city, and also said that he knew a family who would take in a boarder. He served as my guide during my several days in the Barcelona of August 1936.

My guide took me to see the 'sights' of revolutionary Barcelona. These included the Ataranzanas barracks where anarchist leader Francisco Ascaso had died in trying to take one of the last strongholds of the army rebels, the headquarters of the General Council of the Militia, and the plant where buses were being constructed in a firm which had been taken over by its workers.

Unfortunately, I was not old enough at the time to know what questions to ask. So I did not learn as much from the experience as I should have done. However, I did feel the exuberance and exhilaration that was still prevalent in Barcelona a few weeks after the suppression of the military insurrection and the consequent Revolution and, in retrospect, I know that I saw ample evidence of the anarchist control of Barcelona in that period.

Upon returning home, I entered Columbia University and immediately became involved in the Columbia Socialist Club, the local group of the Young People's Socialist League. As a member of the YPSL and the Socialist Party, I followed closely the evolution of the politics of the Spanish Civil War, and my sympathies were with the Spanish left Socialist leader Francisco Largo Caballero and his followers. I lamented what the Communists did to him and to the Partido Obrero de Unificación Marxista (POUM) but was relatively unaware of what was happening to the anarchists.

In spite of my short visit to wartime Barcelona, I was hardly more conscious than most other Left-wing Americans of the role the anarchists were playing in the Spanish Civil War. However, in subsequent years I learned much more about this and decided that I wanted to investigate it. In the summer of 1960 I received a grant from the Rutgers University Research Council to go to France and Spain to look into this question. I was able to interview a considerable number of those anarchists who had played more or less important parts in the Civil War and to attend a congress of one of the factions into which the Spanish anarchist movement in exile was then divided. Also, over the years, I was able to talk with other anarchist leaders in other places, including New York, Mexico and Caracas.

Finally, in 1984, my wife and I returned to Spain to seek out some of the old-time anarchists who had returned home after the death of dictator Francisco Franco, as well as some of the newer recruits to the movement. By that time, too, it was possible to obtain a good deal of printed material – memoirs and other papers – which had been published in the post-Franco period. We were able to acquire some items published during the Civil War and some manuscript material written by anarchist and other participants in the conflict.

No one writing about as controversial a subject as that of the present book can honestly maintain that he/she has no preconceptions or prejudices in approaching it. It is therefore appropriate that I state mine.

In the first place, I think that what the anarchists did during the Spanish Civil War is one of the most interesting social experiments that has taken place in the twentieth century, replete as it is with social experiments. It is the only case where anarchists held considerable power for an appreciable amount of time, during which they put into effect in the economy, the society and polity of much of Loyalist Spain, the ideas that they had been developing and preaching for three-quarters of a century.

Secondly, what the anarchists did in Republican Spain half a century ago is not without relevance to the closing years of the twentieth century. There is today considerable interest in 'community control', workers' self-management, and other proposals to allow decentralization of decision making, an essential element in the thinking and practice of the anarchists.

Therefore, the efforts of the Spanish anarchists between 1936 and 1939 are of contemporary relevance in the 1990s.

In the third place, in the political conflicts in which the anarchists were engaged during the Civil War, my sympathies were with the anarchists rather than with their principal enemies, the Stalinists. However, I hope that this has not blinded me to the weaknesses, errors and even outrages of the anarchists.

A great deal has been written about the Spanish Civil War. Its military campaigns, its importance as a runner-up to the Second World War, and many other aspects of the conflict have been written about in many different languages. However, one phase of the Civil

War that has received almost no serious study abroad, either during the war or since (except by the anarchists themselves), has been the revolution which the anarchists brought about, and their overall role in Republican Spain during the Civil War. For the most part, when the participation of the anarchists has been noted by others, that role has tended to be disparaged. An exception to these generalizations is the book by Walther Bernecker, a German scholar who, although concentrating on anarchist collectives, also deals in some degree with their role in politics.

The anarchists themselves have written a good deal about their part in the Spanish war. However, with the exception of the three volumes of commentary and documents of José Peirats, most of what has been written has been episodic, in the sense of dealing with particular incidents, such as the military insurrection of July 18–19, 1936 or the May Days of 1937, or discussing particular rural and urban collectives or other specific activities of the anarchists. There are also a few autobiographical and biographical studies. In the present volume, I am seeking to present a total view of the role the anarchists played in the Spanish Civil War.

Obviously, I owe many debts of gratitude to people who have helped me gather the material I have used in this volume and have otherwise encouraged me in the writing of it. First are those who, over the years, allowed me to interview them and tell me about their personal experiences during the conflict. The names of most of them are to be found in the segment of the Bibliography dealing with interviews.

Special thanks are due to Pedro Pages, generally known by his *nom de plume* Victor Alba. He was very helpful over the years in putting me in contact with Spanish exiles, anarchists and others, and made available to me some unpublished material of his own on various aspects of the subject at hand.

Several Spanish anarchist veterans have been very cooperative in my search for information for this volume. Two of these, Ramón Alvarez of Asturias and Enrique Marco Nadal of Valencia, were very kind in answering at considerable length letters from me asking about particular aspects of the anarchists' behavior during the war.

They have also sent me very useful printed and manuscript material for which I am grateful.

Similarly, Antonia Fontanillas, an anarchist youth leader during the Civil War, was very helpful when I met her in Barcelona in 1984 in making available to me periodicals and pamphlets published during the conflict. Gaston Leval, the late French/Spanish anarchist leader, when I visited him in 1960, not only let me interview him at length but also allowed me take extensive notes on original manuscript material in his possession.

George Esenwein of the Hoover Institution, a fellow researcher on Spanish anarchism, has been exceedingly cooperative in making available to me key material from Hoover's extensive collection of material on the Spanish Civil War.

As always, I owe my wife a debt for her tolerance of my frequent preoccupation with the Spanish anarchists when perhaps, from her point of view, I might better have been paying attention to something else. Also, her companionship, and her acute observations, during our trip to Spain in 1984, contributed much to this volume.

Finally, my thanks are also due to Ronald Ross Stanton and to his editor for help in arranging the publication of this work.

Of course, the usual disclaimer is in order. Whatever the people I have mentioned have contributed to this volume, they are not responsible for the judgments made here and the errors committed – those are mine alone.

Rutgers University
New Brunswick, N.J.
February 1998

Introduction

The Spanish Civil War has been one of the major events of the twentieth century, being seen by many people as a 'warm-up' for the Second World War. It is certain that the Nazi Germans and Fascist Italians backed one side militarily and Stalin's Soviet Union supported the other. It is also clear that some of the weapons which were used in the Second World War were given trial run in Spain during the Civil War.

But what was little recognized in the reporting to the Civil War at the time, and has gone almost unnoticed in most of what has been written since, is the social revolution that occurred behind the Republican lines with, the onset of the War. When the history of the twentieth century is finally written, that may turn out to be the most important fact about the Spanish Civil War.

Victor Alba has underscored the importance of this revolution. He has written that 'the Spanish revolution of 1936, with all the limitations imposed by the fact that it occurred only in one part of a third-rate country and lasted a few months, was the only workers' revolution that history has known ... if one reflects on it, free of the popular clichés, he will see that there was not before, nor has there been since, any workers' revolution.'[1]

Xavier Paniagua has also noted the uniqueness of the revolution which took place during the Spanish Civil War. He wrote that 'Spain is converted into the only place where there is attempted a model of libertarian structure of society. Catalonia, the Valencian Country,

Aragón and some zones of Castille and Andalusia, were to be the places where for the only time in history it would be attempted to live in anarchy, although its practical realization has been interpreted in many different ways.'[2]

Reasons for Hiding the Revolution

There were reasons for this silence about the Spanish Revolution. News of it was purposely suppressed by those in the Spanish Republican government who were responsible for publicising the Loyalist side in the War, to the end of winning support abroad for the Republican cause.

Liston Oak, an American Communist journalist who worked for the Spanish Republican propaganda apparatus early in the War, and broke with the Stalinists because of what he observed there, wrote in September 1937:

> The fact is concealed by the coalition of the Spanish Communist Party with the Left Republicans and the right-wing Socialists, that there has been a successful social revolution in half of Spain. Successful, that is, in the collectivization of factories and farms which are operated under trade union control and operated quite efficiently.
>
> During the three months that I was director of propaganda for the United States and England under Alvarez del Vayo, then Foreign Minister for the Valencia Government, I was instructed not to send out one word about this revolution in the economic system of Loyalist Spain. Nor are any foreign correspondents in Valencia permitted to write freely of the revolution that has taken place.[3]

The principal leaders of the Spanish Republic were anxious not to 'frighten' the governments and dominant economic interests of Great Britain and France, hopeful to almost the end of the war that those governments would finally came to the aid of the Republic, at least to the degree of allowing it to purchase arms and equipment in those countries. On a broader scale, they were anxious to avoid having the 'legitimacy' of the Republican regime undermined by any frank portrayal of what had happened within the Republic in the first weeks and months of the conflict.

Thus the Civil War was presented officially by the Republican government as simply a struggle for political democracy and Spanish national sovereignty. President Manuel Azaña probably presented as well as anyone this line of the Republican government in a speech he gave in Valencia in January 1937:

> I hear it said by biased sources of propaganda, although for my mental health I refrain from listening to these daily, that we are fighting for communism. That is utter folly, if it were not wickedness. If we were fighting for communism, only the communists would be fighting; if we were fighting for syndicalism, only the syndicalists would be fighting; if we were for left or centre or right-wing republicanism, then only the republicans would be fighting. That is not the case; we are all fighting, the worker and the intellectual, the professor and the bourgeois – the bourgeoisie are fighting, too – the syndicates and the political parties, and all we Spaniards who are gathered under the republican flag, are fighting for the independence of Spain and for the liberty of Spaniards, for the liberty of Spaniards and our native land.[4]

Furthermore, it was certainly not in the interest of Stalin and his followers, in Spain and elsewhere, to have a frank picture presented of the Revolution that had happened in the Republic after the outbreak of the Civil War. For one thing, that Revolution was not carried out by Stalin's followers, and so by their definition was not a revolution at all. (In their book on the War, Communist leader Dolores Ibarruri and her colleagues refer to it as a 'pseudo-revolution.')[5] For another, Stalin, too, was not anxious to frighten the British and French ruling groups, hoping that, until at least mid-1938, they might get involved on the Republican side, which might provoke the British and French into war with Germany and Italy, a war that would deflect Hitler's attention from the East.

There are indications that after he began in 1938 to lay his plans to divert Hitler's attention to the West (which culminated in the Stalinazi Pact of August 1939), Stalin lost further interest in Spain, except to have the war there continue if possible until the inevitable outbreak of the Second World War.

Another reason why little publicity was given to the Spanish Revolution during the Civil War and later was that the Revolution was largely led by the anarchists, seconded by the small Partido Obrero do Unificación Marxista (POUM) and by the left wing of the Partido Socialista Obrero Español, Spain's Socialist Party. Unlike the Communists, the anarchists had no powerful international organization, or the support of any powerful foreign government, which could disseminate news of the Revolution that had taken place in Republican Spain.

Distortions of the Anarchists' Role in the Civil War

Those who have written the most widely read books about the Spanish Civil War since its end and have similarly paid little attention to the role which the anarchists played in it. Thus, Hugh Thomas, in his large volume on the conflict, all but ignores the part the libertarians played in the Republican military, and at best gives glancing reference to their economic political role.

The book about the war which is certainly most widely read, Ernest Hemingway's novel *For Whom the Bell Tolls*, similarly slights and distorts the role of the anarchists. It leaves the impression that the Communists, both Russian and Spanish, were the only ones really doing any fighting. The only Spanish commanders and units mentioned with any approbation are those of the Communists Lister, Modesto and El Campesino. The Russians for the most part are a jovial and competent crowd. There is absolutely no indication of the way in which the Communists, both Russian and Spanish, were using the war in order to establish their own dictatorship. Even in the case of André Marty (who masquerades under the name of André Massart), the only Communist whom Hemingway thoroughly condemns, his passion for 'purging' the Republican ranks is pictured as a personal idiosyncrasy, not having any really political motivation.

The references to the anarchists scattered throughout the novel are all bad. In the scenes of the massacre in Pablo and Pilar's village after the defeat of the uprising there, the drunks and sadists are pictured as those wearing red and black kerchiefs. The military patrol of the anarchists which André meets on his way to Golz's headquarters are 'screwy' characters who would as soon shoot one of their own as one of the enemy.

Hemingway's treatment of the anarchists is typified by the following: '"No, man," André said, relieved. He knew now he was up against the crazies; the ones with the black-and-red scarves. "*Viva la Libertad. Viva la FAI. Viva la CNT*," they shouted back at him from the parapet, "*Viva el anarcos-sindicalismo* and liberty."'

In one other reference to the anarchists, Hemingway accepts the Communists' story that Buenaventura Durruti 'was good and his own people shot him there at the Puente de los Franceses. Shot him because he wanted them to attack. Shot him in the glorious discipline of indiscipline...'

When notice was taken of the crucial role of the anarchists in the Spanish Civil War by contemporary observers and subsequently by those writing the history of the conflict, it was usually for the purpose of deprecating and maligning that role. This was particularly the case with the Stalinists and their sympathizers.

Typical of this line of attack upon the anarchists was the history of the Civil War written by Dolores Ibarruri and her colleagues in the exile leadership of the Spanish Communist Party more than a quarter of a century after the end of the conflict. 'La Pasionaria' and her comrades first divided the anarchists into two groups, those who, 'As the necessities of the combat conflicted with anarchist principles ... with difficulties, resistances, vacillations and even pain, were putting aside some of those principles and accepting the imperatives of the war,' and a 'second group'. According to Ibarruri *et al.*

In the second group one can include the men who considered it their principal mission to carry forward the 'anarchist revolution'. For this group, the war against fascism was secondary;

they were interested in it above all as 'an occasion' to seize arms and implant 'libertarian communism'. These anarchists considered the various democratic parties, and above all the workers' parties – and in first rank the Communists – not as allies, but as their principal enemies...

This attitude responded, in general, to the policy of the leadership of the FAI. An essential part of that policy was the accumulation of arms behind the lines – with a view to armed struggle against the other antifascist forces – taking them from the republican camp. Among the components of this second group there were people with little connection with the working class, elements of the 'lowest depths', declassés, Spanish and foreign adventurers, professional gangsters, which made up the bulk of the ranks of the FAI and a part of those of the CNT...

In addition to the two groups indicated so far, which apart from their positive or negative values were defined by political and ideological characteristics, it is essential to point out the enemies and camouflaged fascists who had infiltrated the anarchist organizations... The infiltration of these enemy elements in the anarchist ranks was not difficult. After the first defeats of the rebels in the principal Spanish cities, in Barcelona there concentrated the representatives of the various anarchist currents coming from the different countries of Europe and America, among whom there were not a few agents of the secret services of the different imperialist groups...[6]

A couple of comments are appropriate at this point concerning this kind of attack on the anarchists, which was widely diffused by the Stalinists during and after the War, and was picked up not only by Communist fellow-travellers, but also by other observers who should have known better. In the first place, the 'accumulation of arms behind the lines' was most notably achieved by the Stalinists and their allies, not only in their militia units, but also in the re-established police forces, the Civil Guard and Assault Guards, which within a few months came largely under Communist control. Most notorious of all was the case of the *carabineros*, under the control of the Communists' ally, Juan Negrín, from the beginning to the end of the War, and which was converted from a small border patrol unit into a force with ten times the pre-war personnel, under circumstances in which they had almost no borders to patrol, and were used mainly to try to destroy the Spanish Revolution.

A second thing to note is that it was the Communist ranks which expanded most and most rapidly with the onset of the Civil War. Furthermore, as we shall see in the pages that follow, it was exactly the Stalinists who recruited most ardently among those middle-class and even upper-class ranks whose loyalty to the Republic was most doubtful.

Rebel Ignoring of the Anarchists' Role in the War

For their own reasons, the supporters of the Franco Rebellion also sought to cover over the anarchist nature of the social revolution which had occurred on the Republican side, seeking rather to picture their 'crusade' as a struggle against 'Communism'. Typical was the Letter of the Spanish Bishops endorsing the Rebels' cause. It spoke of 'the scrupulously prepared scheme of the Marxist Revolution.'[7] It also claimed that on the Republican side in the War was 'the materialist tendency, be it called Marxist, Communist or Anarchist, which wanted to substitute for the old civilization of Spain with all its factors, the ultra-new "civilization" of the Russian Soviets.'[8] Finally, it cited with approval comments of 'clear-sighted' observers, to the effect that 'it is a race of speed between Bolshevism and Christian civilization', and 'an international struggle on a national battlefield: Communism wages in the Peninsula a formidable battle, on which depends the fate of Europe.'[9]

Foreign propagandists for the Franco cause also pictured the Spanish struggle as a crusade against Communism. Thus, Edward Lodge Curran, the American priest who was one of the most active defenders of the Rebel cause in the United States during the Civil War, wrote in one of his many pamphlets on the subject: 'There is no longer any mystery about the Spanish Revolution. It is a struggle between civilization and Communism.'[10] A bit further in the same work he wrote: 'There is no longer any mystery about the aims of the opposing parties in the Spanish Revolution because the leaders on either side have declared themselves. The former premier of the Red Spanish Government, Francisco Largo Caballero, has openly declared himself for the establishment of an association of Soviet Socialist Republics in the Iberian Peninsula. That means Russia and Moscow and Communism with all their blasphemous and anti-democratic tyranny.'[11] Finally, Curran claimed: 'Plans for a Communist Revolution had already been prepared in May 1936, under the direction of Ventura, a delegate of the Third International. The people of Spain rallied behind General Franco just in time.'[12]

The Rebels and their supporters certainly had at least two good reasons for picturing their cause as a 'Crusade against Communism'. On the one hand, that line of propaganda was designed to rally support abroad among those wide elements of public opinion in the democratic countries who, with or without real reason, feared the growth of Communism.

However, there was also certainly another reason for the Rebels not to present a true account of what had happened behind the Republican lines in the first phase of the War. Had the Rebels drawn an accurate picture of the taking over of factories and other enterprises by their workers, and of the land by the peasants, this would certainly have had the effect of sowing discontent behind their own lines.

Nature of the Anarchists' Role in the Civil War

But the fact is that a major Social Revolution did take place in Republican Spain, with the suppression in more than half of the country's territory of the rebellion of Franco and his colleagues. The workers seized control of their factories and put them back to work under leaders chosen by themselves. Anarchist, and Socialist peasants seized much of the country's rural land, and organized a substantial part of it on the basis of spontaneous collectives. The maintenance of law and order in most of Republican Spain was taken over by committees composed of trade unionists and members of the parties supporting the Republican cause. A new military force was organized, by those same trade unions and parties, to oppose the regular army which had arisen in revolt against the Republic.

Overall, the anarchists played a major role in the Republic during the Civil War. They ran much of the economy. They made up the largest single element in the rank and file of the Loyalist army, and developed from within their ranks important military commanders, who played key roles in the defense of the Republic, but did not get the international publicity obtained by such Communist commanders as El Campesino (Valentín González), Modesto and Lister but, none the less played a significant role in leading the Republican forces, in their few significant victories as well as in their defeats.

The anarchists also played a major role in the politics of Republican Spain. From the onset of the Civil War they were faced with the basic contradiction between their traditional repudiation of the State and political power, and the fact that at the beginning of the War they had power thrust upon them because of their crucial role in defeating the military Rebels in more than half of the country. Throughout the War they had to continue to participate in politics and government in order to defend the Revolution as much as possible, and to defend the very existence of their own organizations.

Père Ardiaca, a wartime leader of the Stalinist United Socialist Party of Catalonia (PSUC), commented several decades later to Ronald Fraser, speaking particularly of the first phase of the war, 'The CNT had real power but it didn't know what to do with it; it had great revolutionary will but lacked a revolutionary consistency ... Even if it had taken power it lacked a program which would have won the support of the majority of the Catalan people. Meanwhile, it continued to act much of the time as though it had taken power (without actually saying so) while at the same time, apparently, sharing that power with the petty bourgeois Catalan parties and us...'[13]

Juan Domenech, one of the principal anarchist leaders in Catalonia, who served in the *de facto* and then the *de jure* government of the region for nine months, made much the same point about the CNT leaders not being prepared for a government role. He asked, 'How could we be? Our revolution had always been conceived of as abolishing all governments. Now all of us had to learn. We CNT ministers didn't have a "line" like the Communists. As long as we had no great problems, the CNT imagined that each of us was doing his job; the organization didn't discuss our work. Only if there were a serious problem – and it hardly ever got to that – would there be a meeting of militants to discuss the organization's position...'

Ronald Fraser, to whom Domenech was talking, added: 'Of course, the CNT would have been a lot stronger if it had had a defined line.' But, he thought, it would not have been the CNT in that case. 'The CNT was like that – you loved it with all its defects or you left it. There could be no such things as "party discipline"...'[14]

The anarchists were faced from the outset with an increasingly powerful Spanish Stalinist apparatus, backed by Soviet and Comintern 'advisers' of all sorts, and by the Stalin government's blackmail of the Republican government, with threats to cut off the military aid which was essential to the conduct of the War if the Republican government didn't help the Spanish Stalinists. In contrast to the anarchists, who didn't know what to do with power, the Stalinists – both Spanish and foreign – knew very well what to do with it, and how to acquire more power, with the ultimate objective of establishing a replica of Stalin's regime in Republican Spain.

The anarchists were unprepared for the role which was thrust upon them by the Civil War. For three-quarters of a century, they had developed extensively their analysis of the evils of capitalism, the State, political parties. But they had no clear blueprint of what they wanted to establish to replace those institutions, if they got a chance to do so.

So, when the anarchists suddenly had power in their hands at the beginning of the War, they functioned more on the basis of improvization than of precise doctrine. Their rank and file members in the cities took over control of their factories and other enterprises, which had been largely abandoned by their owners. In the countryside, they also took over the land, and organized their own style of collective farms.

Their efforts to reorganize the economy on the basis of workers' and peasants' control were hampered by the fact that the structure of their own mass organization, the Confederacion Nacional del Trabajo, was largely lacking the national industrial unions which might have provided the framework within which the anarchists could have organized the whole Spanish Republican economy. By the time these national unions had been established, it was too late.

Furthermore, getting power in the midst of a civil war, the anarchists were immediately forced to begin to compromise their principles in order to fight the War. Less than a week after the beginning of the conflict, the anarchists of Catalonia, with political and economic power almost completely in their hands, decided not to exercise it by themselves, but rather to share authority with all of the other trade unions and parties which were supporting the Republic.

This process of compromise never ceased so long as the Civil War continued. It brought widespread demoralization within the rank and file of the libertarians, and ultimately led to a bitter conflict within their leadership. It also resulted in bitter controversies between the Spanish anarchists and their foreign colleagues in the International Workingmen's Association.

In this volume, I present all aspects of the anarchists' participation in the Spanish Civil War. I begin with an introductory section. It includes a presentation of the ideological background of Spanish anarchism, both within the context of the international anarchist movement, and the way it had been developed within the Spanish movement during the more than half-century preceding the Civil War, as well as a chapter on the organizations which constituted the Spanish anarchist or Libertarian Movement.

The second section deals with the anarchists' participation in putting down the Rebellion in much of Spain in July 1936, and their subsequent role in the Republican armed forces. I look at their role in recruiting and organizing the militia, who were the first armed forces to undertake the confrontation with the regular army which had revolted against the Republic. I survey particularly the anarchist-led troops in the Aragon–Catalonia front, in the defense of Madrid, and in their role in other fronts during the War. Finally, I look at the issue of 'militarization' of the militia, converting them into another regular army to confront the one with which they had to carry on the War, and the consequences of this militarization.

I then turn to a survey of the anarchists' organization of much of the rural economy of Republican Spain. I pay attention to this process in Catalonia, Aragon, the Levante (the Mediterranean coastal area south of Catalonia), and in Castille, Andalucia and other parts of the Republican area. These libertarian experiments were particularly interesting from an ideological point of view.

The fourth section deals with the workers' assumption of control of factories, public utilities, and other segments of the urban economy of the Republic. I look at the way these seizures were legalized in Catalonia, as well as the way they were organized in other parts of the Republic. I also note the process by which the Stalinists and their allies worked to undermine the anarchist collectives in both the urban and rural parts of the Republic.

I likewise look at the anarchists' participation in the political life of Loyalist Spain. This discussion not only involves looking at the spontaneous establishment of revolutionary authority at the beginning of the War, but also the attitude towards the participation of the anarchists in the re-establishment of legal organs of government in various areas of the Republic. I look particularly at the anarchists' participation in the governments of Catalonia, in other regional authorities, and in the Republic itself.

Although in the first phase of the Civil War–Revolution, the anarchists played a major role in the politics of the Republic, after May 1937, they were on the defensive, trying to maintain their role in the economy and their position in the country's politics, in the face of the Stalinists' ruthless drive to obtain total power within the Republic. I consider the Communists' drive to destroy all of those elements in Spanish Republican politics which stood in their way, leaving the anarchists as the only major force impeding their drive for absolute power, and the anarchists' reaction to this Stalinist campaign. I also look at the impact of this long struggle on the unity of the Libertarian Movement. Finally, I study the role of the anarchists in the coup against the government of Juan Negrín less than a month before the end of the War, and their participation in the National Defense Council established by those who ousted the Negrín regime.

There are three appendices which do not fit into the general organization of this volume. One deals with the question of the anarchists' use of violence, particularly towards the Catholic Church, during the Civil War. The second concerns the question of the Spanish anarchists' relations with the international organization to which they belonged, the International Workingmen's Association. The third lists a number of the leading anarchist figures during the Civil War.

This study has a significance that extends beyond the Spanish Civil War. The Revolution which occurred at the beginning of the War was the only case in which, for any extended period of time, the anarchists had a chance to attempt to reorganize the economy, society and polity of any country. It is therefore of certain historical importance.

In addition, the experience of the anarchists in the Spanish Civil War has had certain relevance since the Second World War. On the one hand, the Yugoslav regime of Marshal Tito, after the break with Stalin in 1948, adopted a kind of workers' control and it may be suggested that since several people who later were leaders of the Tito regime were in Spain during the Civil War, their experience there may have had some influence on that development.

Finally, after the severe disturbances in several European countries in 1968, there was a renewed interest in self-government of workers in their enterprises. As a consequence, there was also a renewed interest on the part of people advocating these ideas in what had happened in Spain during the Civil War. This would seem to indicate that, in spite of the fact that the Spanish anarchists did not revive as a major force in Spain in the post-Franco era (as I have indicated in my postscript), their experience in the 1936–39 period has by no means lost all relevance at the end of the twentieth century.

Part One

The History and Nature of Spanish Anarchism and the Outbreak of the Civil War

1

The Ideological Roots of Spanish Anarchism

One of the major problems which the Spanish anarchists had to face when power was suddenly thrust upon them at the commencement of the Civil War was that there was really no clear consensus among them concerning the kind of society they wanted to create. Although the movement had existed in Spain for almost three-quarters of a century, it had not sought until about two months before the War began to spell out in detail the kind of society it wanted to substitute for capitalism, and the kind of political organization it wanted to put in place to supersede the State. But even the document adopted at the Zaragoza congress of the Confederación Nacional del Trabajo in May 1936 by no means reflected unanimous agreement among the Spanish anarchists. (I will discuss the Zaragoza document in the next chapter.)

The Spanish anarchists had been part of a broad international movement. The principal theoreticians of that movement were not Spanish, although some Spanish libertarian thinkers had made significant contributions, and certainly national experiences and traditions in Spain going back as far as the Middle Ages had helped to mold the thinking of the Spanish anarchists, both leaders and rank and file, before and during the 1930s.

With the outbreak of the Civil War, and the disintegration of existing authority on a local, regional and even national level, anarchist groups in various parts of Loyalist Spain, where they found themselves suddenly in power or had more or less extensive influence, began to put into effect anarchist ideas, as they interpreted them. As we shall see in this volume, there was a wide diversity in these interpretations.

Also, faced with the double task of trying to rebuild society under circumstances in which they were only one of several competing forces – even in regions where their supporters constituted the majority – and of organizing the defense of the Loyalist region against the armies of General Franco, the anarchists were forced from the outset to compromise some of the most cherished parts of their philosophy and ideology. Indeed, from one point of view, the history of the anarchists during the Spanish Civil War is an account of the accumulation of compromises they agreed to in an effort to defend the bases of a libertarian society which they had established during the first days and weeks of the conflict.

As a background to a study of both what new in institutions the anarchists put in place at the beginning of the War, and their increasingly disastrous retreats subsequently, it is certainly necessary to paint, if only in a rather cursory fashion, a picture of the kind of Revolution that the Spanish anarchists were trying to achieve. To this end, in this and the following chapter, I shall first look at the intellectual origins of anarchism. I shall then sketch the principal currents of thought in the anarchist movement during the century preceding the outbreak of the Spanish Civil War, and their modifications and elaborations within Spain. Finally, I shall summarize and comment on the fully fledged statement of the objectives and program of Spanish anarchism adopted by the movement just before the advent of the Civil War.

The Earliest Roots of Anarchist Ideas

Peter Kropotkin, Rudolf Rocker and other anarchists who have sought the remote origins of the ideas they have espoused, have professed to trace their roots to ancient times. Both Kropotkin and Rocker agree that the Chinese philosopher Lao-tze and the Greek philosopher Zeno were among the earliest exponents of essentially anarchist concepts.[1] Of the latter, Kropotkin wrote that 'the best exponent of anarchist philosophy in ancient Greece was Zeno ... who distinctly opposed the conception of a free community without government to the state-Utopia of Plato.'[2]

Similarly, anarchist tendencies were to be observed in 'certain Christian sects of the Middle Ages,'[3] and particularly among the Hussites and the Anabaptists, the immediate precursors of the Protestant Reformation. Both Rocker and Kropotkin also argued that anarchist ideas were to be found in the writings of Rabelais and of Diderot.[4]

Peter Kropotkin insisted quite strongly that the medieval city states of Europe, stretching from England to Russia, were the nearest historical models for the kind of polity and society the modern anarchists were seeking. He wrote in *Mutual Aid* '. . . a medieval city was not a centralized State. During the first centuries of its existence, the city hardly could be named a State as regards its interior organization... Each group had its share of sovereignty... The medieval city thus appears as a double federation: of all householders united into small territorial unions – the street, the parish, the section – and of individuals united by oath into guilds according to their professions, the former being a product of the village community origin of the city, while the second is a subsequent growth called to life by new conditions.'[5]

Kropotkin's great predecessor, Michael Bakunin, did not share his enthusiasm for the medieval city states as a model for modern anarchist reorganization of society:

... between the commune of the Middle ages and the modern commune there is the vast difference which the history of the last five centuries wrought not just in books but in the morals, aspirations, ideas, interests, and needs of the population. The Italian communes were, at the beginning of their history, really isolated centers of social and political life, independent of one another, lacking any solidarity, and forced into a certain kind of self-sufficiency. How different that was from what is in existence today! The material, intellectual, and moral interests created among all the members of the same nation – nay, even of different nations – a social unity of so powerful and real a nature that whatever is done now by the States to paralyze and destroy such unity is of no avail...[6]

Whatever the relevance of medieval thought and politico-economic organization to the ideology and philosophy of nineteenth- and twentieth-century anarchism, there is virtually universal agreement that the first modern anarchist was William Godwin. Peter Kropotkin wrote of him: 'It was Godwin, in his *Enquiry Concerning Political Justice*, who stated in 1793 in a quite definite form the political and economic principles of anarchism. He did not use the word "anarchism" itself, but he very forcibly laid down its principles, bodily attacking the laws, proving the uselessness of the State, and maintaining that only with the abolition of courts would true *justice* – the only foundation of all society – become possible. As regards property, he openly advocated communism.'[7]

Pierre Proudhon

William Godwin organized no political movement to seek the establishment of the kind of society that he advocated in his *Enquiry*. Pierre Proudhon did take an active part in revolutionary politics and can be said to have been, therefore, the real founder of modern anarchism.

Peter Kropotkin noted that Proudhon was the first person to use the word 'anarchy with application to the no-government state of society'. In his first pamphlet, *What Is Property?*, Proudhon explained that 'property is theft'. However, Kropotkin argued that Proudhon 'meant only property in its present, roman-law, sense of "right of use and abuse," but that, understood in the limited sense of *possession*, he saw the best protection against the encroachments of the State.' He sought to 'dispossess the present owners of land, dwelling-houses, mines, factories and so on ... by rendering capital incapable of earning interest; and this he proposed to obtain by means of a national bank, based on the mutual confidence of all those engaged in production, who would agree to exchange among themselves their products at cost-value, by means of labor checks representing the hours of labor required to produce every given commodity... Besides, such a bank would be enabled to lend money without interest, levying only something like 1 per cent, or even less, for covering the cost of administration...'[8]

Rudolf Rocker explained: 'This form of economy makes superfluous all coercive political machinery. Society is converted into a league of free communities, ordering their affairs according to their needs, by themselves, or associated with others, and in which the freedom of the individual doesn't have limitation in the equal freedom of the rest, but rather its confirmation and security... This organization of federalism had no limits as to the possibilities of future development and offers the most ample perspectives to each individual and all social activity.[9]

Surprisingly enough, in spite of Proudhon's condemnation of the state, he served as a deputy in the constitutional assembly of the Second French Republic in 1848, and vainly sought to get it to approve his project for a national labor bank and, when that failed, he tried unsuccessfully to establish such an institution on a private basis.[10] Of these efforts, Michael Bakunin later remarked that they 'might have prospered under more favorable circumstances.'[11]

Although the ideas of Proudhon did not for the most part have any direct influence on Spanish anarchism, they did help mold the thinking of a leading Spanish politician, whose strong endorsement of federalism served to reinforce and perhaps somewhat legitimize the anarchists' insistence on that principle. That man was Francisco Pí y Margall.

Pí y Margall was the major spokesman for republican federalism in Spain during the latter half of the nineteenth century. He was a deputy on four occasions and minister of interior and then president during the short-lived First Spanish Republic in 1873. Carlos Rama has noted: 'From the point of view of his intellectual formation, the most pronounced influence is that of Pierre Joseph Proudhon,' and that he translated into Spanish several of the principal works of Proudhon.[12]

The influence of Proudhon on Pí y Margall is reflected in the

Spaniard's comment in a book he published in 1854: 'All power is an absurdity. An y man who puts his hand on another man is a tyrant. He is more; he is sacrilegious. Between two sovereigns there can be nothing but pacts. Authority and sovereignty are contradictory. Authority as the basis of society must, therefore, give way to the social contract.'

Elsewhere, Pí y Margall wrote: 'Federalism results not from humanity, but from the individual man. From the man there arises as a spontaneous and natural development (that is to say, by pacts) the family, the local community, the province, the nation, groups of nations, and since it is falacious to believe that collectivities don't have the essential characteristics of the elements which make them up, since the individual is autonomous, societies are recognized and declared autonomous. Autonomous is the nation, autonomous the province and the municipality, and each is autonomous by virtue of itself, of its own right.'[13]

George Esenwein has observed: 'Both as a devoted apostle of Proudhon and as a theoretician in his own right, Pí helped to shape the ideas of several generations of anarchists, including such outstanding figures as Juan Serrano y Oteíza, Rafael Farga Pellicer, Gaspar Sentinón, Fermín Salvochea, Anselmo Lorenzo, Ricardo Mella and Fernando Tarrida del Marmol.'[14]

Another foreign observer of Spanish anarchism, the German Helmut Rudiger, has also stressed the importance of indigenous Spanish federalism, which was reflected in the thinking of Pí y Margall in explaining the importance of anarchism in the country. Writing during the Civil War, he said:

Spanish anarchism is nothing more than an expression of the federal and individualist traditions of the country. That explains the big influence of Spanish anarchism and the fact that Marxism has not been able to absorb the libertarian movement in Spain as in other European countries. But we need to observe that Spanish anarchism is based on simple instincts of the people, something that is both its strength and its weakness. It is its strength, because the wide people's movement is not an outcome of abstract discussions, or theories cultivated by a few intellectuals, but an outcome of a social dynamic force that often is volcanic, and the tendency towards freedom in it can always count on the sympathy of millions of people...[15]

However, the young Spanish anarcho-syndicalist movement, which had been founded just over four years before the advent of the First Republic, did not support the republic or Pí y Margall. Anselmo Lorenzo, the first major figure of Spanish anarchism, wrote many years later: When the republican party was in the opposition ... and seduced and flattered the worker, assuring him that within the republican-federal political form he would find completely guaranteed the practice of individual rights, we always answered that knowing the principle of authority made us understand that their promises were not true and that the highly conservative mission of all government, call it what one will, convinces us that, on the contrary, individual rights must be attacked by the federal republicans as they had been by the reactionaries... The facts proved us right...'[16]

However, in retrospect, the Spanish anarchists had a high regard for Pí y Margall. Ricardo Mella, another leading thinker and activist of Iberian anarchism, in an obituary for the federalist-republican leader, who died in 1901, wrote that he was 'the wisest of the federalists, almost an anarchist, almost just among the just ones.'[17]

The Importance of Michael Bakunin to Spanish Anarchist Ideology

Without question, one of the two anarchist theoreticians who had most influence on Spanish anarchism was Michael Bakunin. He was the one who sent an Italian follower to Spain to win the incipient labor movement there over to anarchism, first in Madrid, and then in Barcelona, giving rise to the Spanish anarchist movement. Apparently, on two occasions he contemplated going to Spain himself, but did not do so.[18]

Although Bakunin did not appear to visit Spain, he was in personal contact with his followers there and his correspondence with a number of his disciples was extensive.[19]

As Professor Bert Hoselitz has said, 'Without Bakunin anarchist syndicalism, such as existed for a long time notably in Spain, is unthinkable. Without Bakunin, Europe probably never would have witnessed an organized anarchist political movement...[20]

Bakuninist anarcho-syndicalism was predominant in the anarchist urban labor movement and influenced the unions of the Confederacion Nacional del Trabajo (CNT), when they took over most of the industries of Catalonia, many of those of the Valencia region, and others in various parts of Republican Spain after July 18 1936.

Michael Bakunin was a Russian aristocrat, the oldest son in a family of eleven children. He had a short military career and, subsequently, both in Russia and abroad, was a student of philosophy. His first political allegiance was to Pan Slavism, but as an exile he was also a participant in the Revolutions of 1848–49 in Germany. He did not adopt his anarchist philosophy until the early 1860s.[21]

Bakunin was, of course, Karl Marx's great opponent within the First International (International Workingmen's Association, IWMA) and, when he was expelled from it by the Marxists in 1872, he organized his own version of the 'real' IWMA. Some of Bakunin's Spanish followers, particularly Anselmo Lorenzo, personally participated in Bakunin's struggle within the IWMA and in his breakaway faction of the organization.[22]

In most regards, the Spanish anarchists in the labor movement adhered to the ideas of Michael Bakunin. However, as we shall see, in several ways, the Spaniards diverged from his theories and prescriptions.

Bakunin's Ideas on the State

Like all advocates of anarchism, Michael Bakunin was a strong enemy of the State, He argued: 'Historically, it arose in all countries out of the marriage of violence, rapine and pillage – in a word, of war and conquest... From its very beginning it has been – and still remains – the divine sanction of brutal force and triumphant iniquity.'[23]

Furthermore, said Bakunin, 'It is evident that all the so-called general interests of society supposedly represented by the State, which in reality are only the general and permanent negation of the positive interests of the regions, communes, associations, and a vast number of individuals subordinated to the State, constitute an abstraction, a fiction, a falsehood, and that the State is like a vast slaughterhouse and an enormous cemetery, where under the shadow and the pretext of this abstraction all the best aspirations, all the living forces of a country, are sanctimoniously immolated and interred.'[24]

One of the many evils of the State, he argued, was that it gave rise to property: 'The doctrinaire philosophers, as well as the jurists and economists, always assume that property came into existence before the rise of the State, whereas it is clear that the juridical idea of property, as well as family law, could arise historically only in the State, the first inevitable act of which was the establishment of this law and of property.'[25]

Therefore, Bakunin argued, 'The State has always been the patrimony of some privileged class: he sacerdotal class, the nobility, the bourgeoisie – and finally, when all the other classes have exhausted themselves, the class of bureaucracy enters upon the stage and then the State falls, or rises, if you please, to the position of a machine. But for the salvation of the State it is absolutely necessary that there be some privileged class interested in maintaining its existence.'[26]

Even a democratic State was not exempt from the noxious qualities inherent in the institution: 'No State, democratic though it may be in form ... can give the people what they need, that is, the free organization of their own interests, from the bottom upward, with no interference, tutelage, or violence from above, because every State, even the most Republican and most democratic State – even the would-be popular State conceived by M. Marx – are in their essence only machines governing the masses from above, through an intelligent and therefore a privileged minority, allegedly knowing the genuine interests of the people better than the people themselves.'[27]

Nor is universal suffrage any protection against the evils of the

State. Bakunin noted: 'So long as universal suffrage is exercised in a society where the people, the mass of workers, are ECONOMICALLY dominated by a minority holding in exclusive possession the property and capital of the country, free or independent though the people may be otherwise, or as they may appear to be from a political aspect, these elections held under conditions of universal suffrage can only be illusory, anti-democratic in their results, which invariably will prove to be absolutely opposed to the needs, instincts, and real will of the population.'[28]

Bakunin's Spanish supporters followed his condemnation of the State. The first national congress of Spanish anarcho-syndicalists in Barcelona, in June 1870, adopted a resolution which proclaimed that 'Sealed in blood there are in history the laudable aspirations of the peoples for their welfare; but based constantly on the conservation of the State, all efforts to fulfill these objectives have been sterile. The State does not permit changes in systems, or reforms.'[29]

Similarly, the so-called Comic Theater Congress of the Confederación Nacional del Trabajo in December 1919, adopted a Declaration of Principles which reiterated the anti-state and generally anarchist position of the movement: '...taking into account the tendency manifested with most force in the workers' organizations of all countries is that marching towards the complete, total and absolute liberation of Humanity in the moral, economic and political spheres, and considering that that objective cannot be achieved without socialization of the land and instruments of production and exchange, and without disappearance of the absorbing power of the state ... the Congress ... in accordance with the essence of the postulates of the First International of Workers, declares that the objective sought by the Confederación Nacional del Trabajo of Spain is anarchist communism.'[30]

Down to the outbreak of the Civil War, the Spanish libertarians never varied from their denunciation of the State, and from their determination to eliminate it at the onset of the Revolution. However, the most striking compromise with their basic ideology which they made during the conflict was their agreement to participate, first in the official government of Catalonia and then in that of the Spanish Republic itself. Even after they were removed from both of these regimes, they continued to hold posts as mayors, municipal council-lors and other positions in various levels of the State until the final loss of the Civil War.

Bakunin's Opposition to Political Parties

Consistent with his total opposition to the State, Bakunin was also against all political parties: 'It is not true then to say that we completely ignore politics. We do not ignore it, for we definitely want to destroy it. And here we have the essential point separating us from political parties and bourgeois radical Socialists. Their politics consists in making us – of, reforming and transforming the politics of the State, whereas our politics ... is the total *abolition* of the State, and of the politics which is its necessary manifestation ... he who wants to pursue politics of a different kind, who does not aim with us at the total abolition of politics – he must accept the politics of the State, patriotic and bourgeois politics...'[31]

Bakunin argued that workers' deputies in a State parliament would cease to be revolutionaries: 'The inevitable result will be that workers' deputies, transferred to a purely bourgeois environment and into an atmosphere of purely bourgeois political ideas, ceasing in fact to be workers, and becoming statesmen instead, will become middle class in their outlook, perhaps even more so than the bour-geois themselves.'[32]

Even a totally labor government controlling the State would not be exempt from such pressures: 'I can express without fear of being contradicted the conviction that if there should be established tomor-row a government or a legislative council, a Parliament made up exclusively of workers, those very workers who are now staunch democrats and Socialists will become determined aristocrats, bold or timid worshippers of the principle of authority, and will also become oppressors and exploiters.'[33]

From the beginning Spanish anarchists echoed this position of Bakunin. In 1870, the first national congress of the Spanish anarcho-syndicalists in Barcelona passed a resolution declaring that 'all participation of the working class in governmental politics of the middle class will be unable to produce any results except consolidation of the existing order of things, which necessarily, will paralyze the revolutionary socialist action of the proletariat. The Congress recommends to all sections of the International Workingmen's Association to renounce all operative action which has as its objective effectuating social transformation by means of national political reforms...'[34]

In 1877, the Spanish Federation of the International Workingmen's Association (IWMA) similarly passed a resolution to the effect that 'Considering that the conquest of power is the natural tendency that all political parties have, and that this power has no other object than the defense of economic privilege; considering, in addition, that in reality, present society is divided, not into political parties but into economic situations; exploited and exploiters, workers and employers, wage earners and capitalists... The Congress declared that it makes no distinction among the various political parties, whether or not they call themselves socialists; all of these parties, without distinction, form in its eyes a reactionary mass, and it believes it its duty to combat all of them...'[35]

However, although over succeeding decades other anarcho-syndicalist gatherings continued to reiterate a general opposition to all political parties, in fact the relations with the parties of the Left, particularly with the Socialist Party, continued to be an issue of controversy in the ranks of the Spanish libertarians. More often than not, this controversy centered on whether the anarchist leaders should urge their followers to abstain from voting in elections, or should allow them to be free to vote for whosoever they wished. As we shall see in a later chapter, this problem became particularly acute just before and after the establishment of the Second Republic in 1931. Some anarchist leaders on an individual basis joined a coalition of Socialists and Republicans to seek the removal of the monarchy in 1930.[36] Subsequently, the anarchist workers tended to vote en masse for the Left parties in the 1931 elections; their abstention in 1933 largely determined the victory of the Right; and in February 1936, when the CNT leadership first formally gave their followers freedom to vote or not to vote, it was undoubtedly the ballots of the anarchists that were the margin of victory for the Popular Front.

The issue was particularly acute in Catalonia during the Second Republic. There, the question was the anarchists' relationship with the Catalan Left Party, led by Luis Companys. As in the republic as a whole, the libertarians' relations with the Catalan Left zig-zagged considerably in the five years of the Republic preceding the outbreak of the Civil War.[37]

Shortly before the outbreak of the Civil War, a small group of anarchists, under the leadership of Angel Pestaña, broke with the anti-party tradition of the movement, and established their own party, the Partido Sindicalista. Finally, during the Civil War, one of the most important 'concessions to reality' made by the anarchists was the virtual conversion of one of the principal elements of the libertarian movement, the Federacion Anarquista Iberica, into a political party.

Bakunin's Emphasis on the Revolutionary Role of the Organized Workers

Intransigent opposition to the State and to political parties are ideas common to all schools of anarchism. However, the distinctive characteristic of Bakuninist anarcho-syndicalism was its particular emphasis on the revolutionary role of the urban worker, of the proletariat.

It seems not unlikely that this all-important strain in Bakunin's thinking came from his association with Karl Marx, which was a long one. He met Marx as early as 1847 in Paris, where they had extensive discussions and debates. Although, according to Max Nettlau, Bakunin 'greatly disliked' Marx and had a 'final break' with him early in 1848, many years later he referred to Marx as 'the illustrious leader of German Communism', and called *Das Kapital* 'his magnificent work.'[38]

Certainly in his analysis of the evolution of capitalism, Bakunin accepted many of the key elements of Marx's critique. He insisted on the economic factor being the determining one in all societies,[39] on the growing immiseration of the working class under capitalism,[40] on the ultimate and rapid crushing and disappearance of the small capitalists,[41] the iron law of wages,[42] and on the inevitability of the class struggle.[43]

Similarly, he agreed with Marx that the urban working class was the true revolutionary element in modern society. However, he gave his own interpretation to this theme:

> States do not crumble by themselves; they are overthrown by a universal international social organization. And organizing popular forces to carry out that revolution – such is the only task of those who sincerely aim at emancipation. The initiative in the new movement will belong to the people – in Western Europe, to the city and factory workers – in Russia, Poland and most of the Slavic countries, to the peasants. But in order that the peasants rise up, it is absolutely necessary that the initiative in this revolutionary movement be taken by the city workers, for it is the latter who combine in themselves the instincts, ideas and conscious will of the Social Revolution. Consequently, the whole danger threatening the existence of the States is focused in the city proletariat.[44]

Bakunin argued that the workers are learning their revolutionary ideas from their own personal experiences, in their unions and the solidarity among them:

> The workers in every trade and in every country – owing on one hand to the material and moral support which in the course of their struggle they find among workers in other trades and other countries, and on the other hand, because of the condemnation and the systematic hate-breathing opposition with which they meet not only from their own employers but also from employers in other, even very remote industries, and from the bourgeoisie as a whole – become fully aware of their situation and the principal conditions necessary to their emancipation. They see that the social world is in reality divided into three main categories: 1. The countless millions of exploited workers; 2. A few hundred thousand second- or third-rank exploiters; 3. A few thousand, or, at the most, a few tens of thousands of the larger

beasts of prey, big capitalists who have grown fat on directly exploiting the second category and indirectly the first category, pocketing at least half the profits obtained from the collective labor of humanity.

Upon understanding this, Bakunin argued, the worker 'must soon realize, backward though he may be in his development, that if there is any means of salvation for him, it must lie along the lines of establishing and organizing the closest practical solidarity among the proletarians of the whole world, regardless of industries or countries, in their struggle against the exploiting bourgeoisie.[45]

Finally, insisted Bakunin, proletarian solidarity must lead to revolution. He said that solidarity:

... produces everything else; the most sublime and the most subversive principles of the International, the principles most destructive of religion, of the juridical right of the State, of divine and human authority – the most revolutionary ideas, in a word, being from the Socialist point of view the necessary, natural development of this economic solidarity. And the immense practical advantage of the trade union sections ... consists exactly in that this development, and those principles are being proved to workers not by theoretic reasoning but by the living and tragic experience of a struggle which is becoming wider, deeper and more terrible with every day, so that even the most ignorant, the least prepared, the most submissive worker, ever driven on by the very consequences of the struggle, ends up by avowing himself a revolutionist, Anarchist, and atheist, very often being unaware as to the process whereby he became such.[46]

The Bakuninist Secret Society: The Alliance of Socialist Democracy and the FAI

Bakunin saw a special role in this process of developing proletarian solidarity and its conversion into revolution for:

17

... an aristocracy not by virtue of position but by that of conviction of revolutionary class-consciousness and of rational, energetic passion and will ... they are the best people, not only among the working class but in society as a whole... They would find it quite easy to rise above their own class, to become members of the bourgeois caste ... but the desire for that kind of personal advancement is foreign to them. They are permeated with the passion for solidarity, and they cannot understand any other liberty and happiness but that which can be enjoyed together with all the millions of their enslaved human brothers. And it stands to reason that those men enjoy a great and fascinating, although unsought, influence over the masses of workers. Add to this category of workers those who have broken away from the bourgeois class, and who have given themselves to the great cause of emancipation of labor, and you get what we call the useful and beneficent aristocracy in the international labor movement.[47]

Presumably, Bakunin considered that the Alliance of Socialist Democracy, which he organized in 1868, consisted of such an 'aristocracy'. George Esenwein has noted: 'Bakunin believed that the formation of a secret body of devoted radicals within the International was absolutely necessary for it to maintain a revolutionary orientation. The Alliance itself was to be used as a vehicle for transforming the International – and all the popular masses outside it – into a power which could effectively destroy the capitalist system.[48]

Paul Avrich has noted:

... for all his assaults on revolutionary dictatorship, Bakunin was determined to create his own secret society of conspirators, subject to 'a strict hierarchy and to unconditional obedience'. This clandestine organization, moreover, would remain intact even after the revolution had been accomplished, in order to forestall the establishment of any 'official dictatorship'. Thus Bakunin committed the very sin he so bitterly denounced. He himself was one of the originators of the idea of a closely knit revolutionary party bound together by implicit obedience to a revolutionary dictator, a party that he likened at one point to the Jesuit order... His ends pointed towards freedom, but the means – the clandestine party – pointed towards dictatorship.[49]

Although the Alliance of Socialist Democracy was officially dissolved as the price of admission of the Bakuninists to the First International, its affiliate in Spain persisted for several years after the ending of the Bakuninist group as an international organization. Its principal leaders, according to George Esenweign were the medical doctor José García Viñas and Tomás González Morago, an engraver.[50] The alliance was very active in the Federación Regional Española, the anarchist trade union group of the early 1870s and apparently did not go out of existence until the early 1880s.

The anarchist urban labor movement in Spain generally agreed with Bakunin that the labor union was the fundamental revolutionary organization. However, it was periodically torn between the exigencies of the day-to-day struggle of the unions to gain immediate benefits for their members and remaining loyal to the ultimate goal of total revolution.

During much of the history of the Spanish anarchist labor movement there existed groups of activists, usually called 'groups of affinity', which thought it their mission to see that the unions remained loyal to that revolutionary goal. In the late 1920s those groups were brought together in the Federación Anarquista Iberica (FAI) and the struggles between FAIistas and those whom they accused of being 'reformists', brought controversy and schism to the anarchist labor movement during the Second Republic, a schism that was only mended two months before the outbreak of the Civil War.

Although some similarity may be seen between Bakunin's concept of a secret revolutionary society and the FAI, there were substantial differences between them. The 'affinity groups', which were the basic organizations of the Federación Anarquista Iberica until the Civil War, enjoyed a wide degree of autonomy. There did not exist the kind of hierarchical discipline within the FAI that Bakunin had advocated, there were numerous different tendencies within the FAI, and there certainly was no 'revolutionary dictator' within the organization.

Bakunin and Forms of Trade Union Organization

There was one position taken by Bakunin with regard to the labor movement, which his Spanish followers were late in accepting and another which they rejected. These were the problems of organizing national industrial unions and of the maintenance of strike funds by the unions.

Bakunin pictured the progression of organization of the workers as moving from the establishment of a union of workers in a particular 'shop', followed by the joining together of all of the unions in a particular trade or industry in a single country, followed by an international organization of the unions in that particular branch of economic activity, and ultimately all of those international organizations joining the International Workingmen's Association.[51]

Bakunin apparently did not make a distinction between a 'craft' and an 'industrial' union, using the words 'trade' and 'industry' interchangeably. However, he quite clearly did favor the establishment of national unions of workers of a particular category. The Spanish anarchists were very slow in accepting that notion.

It was not until after the proclamation of the Second Republic that the Confederación Nacional del Trabajo gave its approval to the formation of national industrial unions (federations). However, the December 1919 Congress of the Comedy Theater in Madrid did debate the question of forming industrial unions on a local scale. According to Comín Colomer: 'It had been proposed to form single unions of branches or industries in the large population centers, and single unions of workers in small urban nucleii, the old system of federations thus disappearing...' According to him, the vote in favor of these *sindicatos unicos* was 681,437 in favor out of the total of 714,028 votes recorded.[52] Each delegate cast a vote in accordance with the number of members he/she represented.

However, the establishment of national unions (or federations) was the subject of very long controversy. One of the early anarcho-syndicalist national organizations, the Spanish Regional Federation of the International Workingmen's Association, at its congress in Seville in 1882, had declared that its basic units were 'the Craft Section ... the Local Federation ... County Federations and Unions of Similar Crafts...' This last type of group was described as being made up of all the Craft Federations which exist in the region... These Unions are essentially technical...'[53]

However, when it was organized nearly thirty years after the Seville congress, the Confederación Nacional del Trabajo did not have any such national affiliates organized either by craft or industry. It was organized on the basis of local unions (mostly craft groups) brought together on a municipal basis, with those municipal groups joined into county federations, which were joined in wider federations for Catalonia, Levante and other parts of Spain, coming together to form the CNT.

However, from the inception of the CNT, there were prominent anarchist leaders who urged the establishment both of industrial unions on a local level and their federation on a Spanish-wide level. For instance, Palmiro Marba, an anarchist publicist, who wrote usually under the pseudonym of Fructidor, as early as 1911, cited with approval the argument of the French syndicalist Georges Ivetot:

> The national federation of crafts brings together all the unions of the same craft, such as Mechanics in the Federation of Mechanics; as the unions of Painters, etcetera, etc. The national industrial federation brings together all the unions of Metallurgical workers in the Federation of Metallurgical Workers; all the unions of Construction in the Federation of Construction...
>
> As will be easily understood, the Federation of industries will take the place of the Federation of crafts. Why? Because, first of all, industry, with the aid of machinery has so simplified things in its development that craft workers are giving way rapidly to industrial workers... From the organizational point of view, it is also more logical for workers in the small town to form, for example, a construction union, composed of bricklayers, carpenters, painters, glass window workers, etc., than to form unions of sixteen bricklayers, 15 carpenters and 12 painters...[54]

However, it was not until the Extraordinary Congress of the CNT in June 1931 that Bakunin's idea of organizing the workers nationally by industry was finally accepted, at least formally, by a vote of 342,303 in favor to 90,671 against. The resolution on the subject said:' ... the national industrial federation has for its mission to bring together all the unions of the industry which it represents and to coordinate their industrial action technically, economically and professionally, without it being permitted to invade other zones of trade union activity of a general nature, which functions are completely within the competence of the *sindicatos* and the non-industrial federal and confederal organizations.[55]

Bakunin's Advocacy of Strike Funds

Although the Spanish anarchists finally officially adopted Bakunin's model of organization, they never did come around to his endorsement of strike, or resistance, funds. Bakunin had written: ' "The emancipation of the workers should be the task of the workers themselves," says the preamble of our general status. And it is a thousand times right in saying so. This is the principal basis of our great association. But the world of workers is generally ignorant, it is almost innocent of any theory. Consequently, there remains only one way, *the way of practical emancipation.* What is and what should be that method? There is only one way: that is complete solidarity in the struggle of the workers against the employers. It is the organization and federation of workers' resistance funds.'[56]

The Spanish anarcho-syndicalists did not support Bakunin's endorsement of resistance funds. A clear statement of their position was that of Palmiro Marba, who wrote soon after the establishment of the CNT: 'The resistance fund has failed ... there remained for the workers, therefore, only one resource, which is the most powerful and the most effective: solidarity, or mutual support in the struggle... The resistance fund ... is absolutely useless for modern struggles. Using such an antiquated procedure, conflicts are eternalized and the employers win; their resources are always superior to those which the workers can collectively possess. In contrast, the use of solidarity among them constitutes the most powerful resource for triumph ... solidarity must be active and rapid.'[57]

Bakunin's Endorsement of Cooperatives

Another idea that Bakunin supported, and that most Spanish anarchists did not, was the establishment of cooperatives by the workers.

> Let us organize and enlarge our Association, but at the same time let us not forget to strengthen it in order that our solidarity, which is our whole power, may become more real from day to day... Let us rally our forces in common enterprises in order to render existence somewhat more tolerable and less difficult; and let us form everywhere, and as far as it is possible, consumers' and producers' cooperatives and mutual credit societies, which, though unable to free us in any adequate and serious manner, under present conditions, are important inasmuch as they train the workers in the practice of managing the economy and prepare the precious germs for the organization of the future.[58]

The early Spanish anarchists also endorsed the idea of consumers' cooperatives. In the April 1872 congress of the Spanish section of the IWMA, a resolution was adopted outlining the statutes for a 'consumer cooperative federation to contribute to the emancipation of the workers, relieving them from the exploitation exercised over them by the avarice of the middle class in the commerce of basic needs, with falsification, excessive prices and fraud in weights and measures.'[59]

However, many of the later Spanish anarchists were at best sceptical about cooperatives of either producers or consumers. Thus, Palmiro Marba, writing at about the beginning of the First World War, damning consumers' cooperatives with faint praise, cited with approval a comment that 'consumers' cooperation has produced modest results, and has facilitated a useful means of bringing together publicly a considerable number of workers.' But he totally condemned producers' cooperatives, saying that they 'only produced a few more bourgeois and a few less pesetas.'[60]

However, one Spanish anarchist leader who believed thoroughly in cooperatives was Juan Peiró. He had helped to organize, and had led, a glass workers' producer cooperative in Mataró, near Barcelona, where he worked from 1923 until the end of the Civil War, except for the seven months that he was a minister in the Largo Caballero government.

Peiró also supported consumers' cooperatives: '...as in capitalist society commerce has as much importance as industry and agriculture ... the distribution of products in the future society will also have to be as important as the organization of production ... because organized distribution will be an element of orientation of the people from the first moment of the revolution insofar as the distribution of food is concerned ... and because, furthermore, the cooperative has inevitably to be the means of distribution of the new society redeemed from capitalism and the State.'[61] He also saw cooperatives as a means of financing 'rationalist' schools pending the revolution.[62]

But, Peiró added, 'Clearly, the cooperativism which we support is not the restricted, egotistical, degenerate cooperativism which is popular today. We consider that the cooperativism which limits its objectives to eliminating intermediaries, to credit and aid in cases of strikes, unemployment or illness, and to the distribution of dividends appears to us as something poor, without emancipating possibilities...'[63]

With the outbreak of the Civil War, the Spanish anarchists established many consumers' cooperatives in areas in which they had influence. Most of the rural collectives in Aragon and other areas in which anarchist-led peasants took over the land, organized cooperatives of one kind or another. Also, in many of the urban industrial collectives these were also established to facilitate the distribution of goods to the workers belonging to those organizations.

Bakunin on the Road to Power

For Bakunin, the strike was the principal instrument for carrying out the Revolution. Each strike was in effect a school of revolution, and the culmination of the process would be the general strike:

Every strike is the more valuable in that it broadens and deepens to an ever greater extent the gulf now separating the bourgeois class from the masses of the peoples and in that it proves to the workers in the most perceptible manner that their interests are absolutely incompatible with the interests of the capitalists and property-owners. Strikes are valuable because they destroy in the minds of the now exploited and enslaved masses of people the possibility of any compromises or deals with the enemy; they destroy at its roots that which is called bourgeois Socialism, thus keeping the cause of the people free from any entanglements in the political and economic combinations of the propertied classes. There is no better means of detaching the workers from the political influence of the bourgeoisie than a strike... Yes, strikes are of enormous value; they create, organize, and form a workers' army, an army which is bound to break down the power of the bourgeoisie and the State, and lay the ground for a new world.[64]

But it was the general strike that was to be the crowning act of revolution: 'When strikes begin to grow in scope and intensity, spreading from one place to another, it means that events are ripening for a general strike, and the general strike coming off at the present time, now that the proletariat is deeply permeated with ideas of emancipation, can only lead to a great cataclysm, which will regenerate society. Doubtless we have not yet come to that point, but everything leads towards it. Only it is necessary that the people should be ready, that they should not permit themselves to be eased out of it by chatter-boxes, windbags, and dreamers...'[65]

The Spanish anarcho-syndicalists agreed with Michael Bakunin on the significance of both strikes of particular groups of workers and the general strike. However, the early Spanish anarchists' own experience taught them that revolutionary general strikes should not be undertaken lightly. Thus, Tomás González Morago wrote in 1873 that such a walkout required 'a long period of preparation and of propaganda that would have to precede it, the latter being the fundamental task of the movement at hand.'[67]

Although there was some controversy over the utility of partial strikes, they too were generally supported by the Spanish anarchists.

Typical was Palmiro Marba's comment that 'Partial strikes are ... an exercise, a healthful school which fortifies the proletariat, preparing it for the supreme struggle which will be the revolutionary general strike...[67]

The founding congress of the Confederación Nacional del Trabajo in 1910, after adopting a resolution saying that the purpose of the organization was to 'hasten the integral economic emancipation of the entire working class through the revolutionary expropriation of the bourgeoisie as soon as syndicalism is strong enough numerically and intellectually prepared to carry out the expropriation ... and provide them for subsequent direction of production,' adopted another resolution about the general strike. That document argued that 'A general strike should not be called to win an increase in wages or a slight reduction in the working day, but only to achieve total transformation... The strike will be general in the true sense of the term, when all the workers of the entire country lay down their tools at the same time.'[68]

Bakunin's Vision of the Anarchist Society

On various occasions, Bakunin put forward – albeit in quite general terms – his proposals for the anarchist reorganization of society. Three of these presentations may be cited. At one point, he wrote:

> All classes ... are bound to disappear in the Social Revolution, with the exception of two – the city and the rural proletariat – who will become owners, probably collective owners, under various forms and conditions determined in every locality, in every region and every commune... The city proletariat will become the owner of capital and of implements of labor, and the rural proletariat of the land which it cultivates with its own hands, both, impelled by their needs and mutual interests, will organize, and naturally and necessarily balance each other in an equal and at the same time perfectly free manner.
>
> [Society would be organized] through a free federation of workers' associations – industrial and agricultural as well as

scientific, artistic, and literary – first into a commune; the federation of communes into regions, or regions into nations, and of nations into a fraternal international union. The land belongs to those who have cultivated it with their own hands – to the rural communes. The capital and all tools of labor belong to the city workers – to the workers' associations. The whole organization of the future should be nothing else but a free federation of workers – agricultural workers as well as factory workers and associations of craftsmen.[69]

On another occasion, Bakunin listed five specific attributes of an anarchist society:

Abolition of the right of property inheritance.

Equalization of the rights of women – political as well as socio-economic rights – with those of men. Consequently, we want abolition of the family right and of marriage – ecclesiastical as well as civil marriage ... inseparably bound up with the right of inheritance.

The land belongs only to those who cultivate it with their own hands, to the agricultural communes. The capital and all the tools of production belong to the workers; to the workers' associations.

The future political organization should be a free federation of workers, a federation of producers' associations of agricultural and factory workers.

And therefore, in the name of political emancipation, we want in the first place abolition of the State, and the uprooting of the State principle, with all the ecclesiastical, political, military, bureaucratic, juridical, academic, financial, and economic institutions.[70]

In a somewhat different form, Bakunin presented these same major points elsewhere:

1. Political, economic and social equalization of all classes and all people living on the earth.

27

2. Abolition of inheritance of property.

3. Appropriation of land by agricultural associations, and of capital and all the means of production by the industrial associations.

4. Abolition of the patriarchal family law, based exclusively upon the right to inherit property, and also upon the equalization of man and woman in point of political, economic and social rights.

5. The upkeep, upbringing, and educating of the children of both sexes until they become of age, it being understood that scientific and technical training, including the branches of higher teaching, is to be both equal for and compulsory for all.[71]

The early Spanish anarchists largely followed Bakunin's concept of the post-revolutionary anarchist society. One of the earliest statements along those lines was adopted by the Zaragoza congress in 1872 of the Spanish Federation of the IWMA. Interestingly enough, the co-authors of the resolution were Anselmo Lorenzo and Paul Lafargue, a son-in-law of Karl Marx who subsequently took a leading role (although a Frenchman) in establishing a Marxist party in Spain. The Zaragoza document proclaimed:

All the great instruments of labor joined today in a number of idle hands, might be transformed from night to day by a revolutionary force and put immediately in use at the disposition of the workers who today make them productive. These workers, by only organizing themselves in an Association, if they don't have one already, and offering necessary guarantees to the local Councils, would enter into full use of the instruments of work... Our local Councils, which would then be the legitimate representation of all the producers, transformed into Councils of administration, would be responsible to the county Councils for all that belongs to the collectivity; these to the regionals, and those to the international, constituting the true economic federations...

This resolution also had a passage which is of particular interest, in the light of what was actually carried out by some CNT unions in Barcelona and elsewhere after July 18 1936. It said: 'There are small workshops of sewing, shoemaking, carpentry, hat making etc., etc. ... which might be inventoried and transferred provisionally to the churches and the princes' palaces ... where the workers organized in a society could receive the full product of their work without leaving anything in the grasp of any bourgeois.'[72]

Many years later, the anarchist publicist Palmiro Marba presented a variation on Bakunin's description of the post-revolutionary organization of the society and economy which presaged what was to become an issue of consequence among the Spanish anarcho-syndicalists during the Civil War. This was the question of the relationship between the group of workers in a particular local enterprise, and the larger union to which they were affiliated. Marba wrote:

After the general and definitive movement ... the unions will take possession of their respective means and elements of labor, each continuing the function appropriate to it. The unions of railroads will take over everything affecting transport of general traffic; those of Posts and Telegraphs all relative to communications; those of teachers all related to teaching; those of engineers and architects will take care of all concerning the construction sector ... the doctors, within their sphere will take care of general hygiene and the conservation of health; the agricultural unions will take possession of the cultivable land ... and thus successively with the unions of the other industries and professions.[73]

It would seem that Marba who, it will be remembered, was a strong advocate of the formation of national industrial unions, was assigning to these organizations the key role in reorganizing the economy. Although Marba makes no mention in this discussion of the Industrial Workers of the World (IWW) – and there are some indications elsewhere in his volume that he was not very well informed about the IWW[74] – this prescription for post-revolutionary economy would appear to be closer to the IWW's concepts than to those of Bakunin.

The Industrial Workers of the World proposed the organization of workers into eight great national industrial unions, which would conduct the struggle against the capitalists until the Revolution and be the basis of the reorganization of the economy thereafter.[75]

José Peirats, the Spanish anarchist historian, has said that those favoring control of industries by the national industrial unions drew their inspiration from the IWW, as well as from the ideas of German and Swedish anarcho-syndicalist unions.[76] Xavier Paniagua has argued that the Spanish defenders of the role of national unions in administering the post-revolutionary economy were particularly influenced by the French anarcho-syndicalist Pierre Besnard, who wrote detailed analyses of an anarcho-syndicalist form of libertarian communism.[77]

Bakunin on the Peasants as Allies of the Proletariat

We have already noted that Bakunin felt that, even in what were still predominantly peasant societies, the urban proletariat would inevitably take the lead in bringing about anarchist reorganization of society. However, he was equally insistent that the peasants were the natural allies of the urban workers, and frequently stated that the latter should not try to dominate or impose upon the peasantry.

Bakunin's attitude towards how the peasantry should be brought into participation in the Revolution derived from his general belief that Revolution must be inspired, not imposed. He asked the question, 'What should revolutionary authorities – and let us try to have as few of them as possible – do in order to organize and extend the Revolution?' and answered thus: 'They must not do it themselves, by revolutionary decrees, by imposing this task upon the masses; rather their aim should be that of provoking the masses to action. They must not try to impose upon the masses any organization whatever, but rather should induce the people to set up autonomous organizations...[78]

Bakunin recognized the current devotion of the peasants to the idea of owning their own piece of land. He warned: 'It is necessary to lay down a line of revolutionary conduct which will obviate the difficulty of proselytizing the peasants and which will not only prevent the individualism of the peasants from pushing them into the camp of reaction but, on the contrary, will make it instrumental in the triumph of the Revolution...[79]

Bakunin therefore concluded: 'Since revolution cannot be imposed upon the villages it must be generated right there, by promoting a revolutionary movement among the peasants themselves, leading them on to destroy through their own efforts the public order, all the political and civil institutions, and to establish and organize anarchy in the villages.'[80]

Although he recognized that such a movement might provoke civil war in the countryside, Bakunin argued that one should not fear:

> that the peasants, once they are not restrained my public author-
> ity and respect for criminal and civil law, will cut one another's
> throats. They may at first try to do it, but they will not be slow
> in convincing themselves of the practical impossibility of con-
> tinuing such a course, following which they will endeavor to
> come to a mutual understanding, with the view of putting an
> end to their strife and forming some kind of an organization.
> The need of eating and providing for their children – and
> consequently the necessity of cultivating the land and continuing
> work in the fields, the necessity of securing the safety of their
> houses, families, and their own lives against unforeseen attacks –
> all that will necessarily compel them to enter into some kind of
> mutual arrangements.[81]

The issues raised concerning the imposition of collectivization on the peasants were of great importance to the Spanish anarchists during the Civil War. Although there was a great deal of action by peasants in several parts of Republican Spain to establish collectives, the anarchists' enemies – and a few more or less impartial observers – claimed that in Aragon militia columns of anarchist city workers, especially from Barcelona, imposed collectivization in some areas as they reconquered half of that region from the Franco troops. Certainly, fear of anarchist collectivization was a major factor in making it possible for the Communists to establish a strong peasant federation in the

Valencia area, composed principally of people who had supported right-wing parties in the past.

Philosophical Background of Peter Kropotkin's Anarchism

The second great foreign theorist whose influence was felt extensively among Spanish anarchists was Peter Kropotkin. Not untypical
was the comment of Fidel Miró, who led the Libertarian Youth
during the Civil War, that Kropotkin was 'my first theorist'.[82]

Kropotkin, like Bakunin, was a Russian aristocrat. He was an
army officer, who had spent a five years' assignment in Eastern
Siberia. A man of scientific training, he used much of his time to
study the geography, the geology and the flora and fauna of that part
of the Russian Empire. Returning to St Petersburg, he was offered the
post of secretary of the Geographical Society of the Russian Academy
of Sciences, but turned it down.

Turned revolutionist and ultimately anarchist, Kropotkin was
soon exiled, and spent three decades or more in Western Europe,
particularly in England. After the Bolshevik Revolution, he finally
returned home, but he soon became deeply disillusioned with the
Bolshevik regime. He died in 1921.[83]

Although Kropotkin agreed with Bakunin in his condemnation of
the State, law, religion and the existing educational system, he did
not put major emphasis on the role of the proletarians as the
leading revolutionary force or of the unions as the major vehicle of
change.

Also, the philosophical base from which Kropotkin started was
markedly different from that of Bakunin. Herbert Read, the leading
British anarchist of a later generation, wrote: 'Kropotkin gave
fresh direction and coherence to a doctrine which, though as old as
philosophy itself, still lacked a formulation in the terms of modern
science and thought.'[84] Read added: 'There was no aspect of sociology which Kropotkin did not study with scientific thoroughness –
system of land tenure, methods of cultivation, housing, public
health, education, crime and punishment, the evolution of the
state...[85]

The starting point of Kropotkin's anarchist philosophy was his concept of 'mutual aid', which he saw as a fundamental principle of not only all of the animal kingdom, but of mankind itself. He started his book on the subject by noting that in his travels in Siberia he did not encounter 'that bitter struggle for the means of existence, *among animals belonging to the same species*, which was considered by most Darwinists (although not always by Darwin himself) as the dominant characteristic of struggle for life, and the main factor of evolution.'[86]

Nor did he think that the rule of 'survival of the fittest' in the terms of Herbert Spencer and others applied to mankind. Kropotkin wrote: 'When my attention was drawn ... to the relations between Darwinism and Sociology, I could agree with none of the works and pamphlets that had been written upon this important subject. They all endeavored to prove that Man, owing to his higher intelligence and knowledge, *may* mitigate the harshness of the struggle for life between men; but they all recognized at the same time that the struggle for the means of existence, of every animal against all its congeners, and of every man against all other men, was 'a law of Nature'. This view, however, I could not accept, because I was persuaded that to admit a pitiless inner war for life within each species, and to see in that war a condition of progress, was to admit something which not only had not yet been proved, but also lacked confirmation from direct observation.'[87]

Kropotkin starts his study of mutual aid by considering its existence among animals: 'As soon as we study animals ... we at once perceive that though there is an in immense amount of warfare and extermination going on amidst various species, and especially amidst various classes of animals, there is, at the same time, as much, or perhaps even more, of mutual support, mutual aid, and mutual defense amidst animals belonging to the same species or, at least, to the same society ... if we resort to an indirect test, and ask Nature: "Who is the fittest: those who are continually at war with each other, or those who support one another?" we at once see that those animals which acquire habits of mutual aid are undoubtedly the fittest.'[88]

The same applies, Kropotkin argued, to the human species.

Although he said: 'It is not love and not even sympathy upon which Society is based in mankind,' he continued, 'it is the conscience – be it only at the stage of an instinct – of human solidarity. It is the unconscious recognition of the force that is borrowed by each man from the practice of mutual aid; of the close dependency of every one's happiness upon the happiness of all; and of the sense of justice, or equity, which brings the individual to consider the right of every other individual as equal to his own. Upon this broad and necessary foundation the still higher moral feelings are developed.'[89]

After discussing mutual aid among 'savages', 'barbarians' and in the medieval city, Kropotkin devoted two chapters to 'Mutual Aid Amongst Ourselves'. In those he argued that in spite of the centralizing tendencies of the State, mutual aid has continued in innumerable forms. He lays particular stress on the persistence of mutual aid in the village community, but also recognizes it in the labor union and other 'free associations for various purposes'.[90]

The 'Communalist' Anarchism of Kropotkin

The emphasis of Kropotkin on the community rather than the labor union as the major center of both pre-revolutionary agitation and post-revolutionary reconstruction of society gave rise to what might best be labelled the 'communalist' school of anarchist thought. Indeed, at one point, Kropotkin himself referred to his ideas about the nature of the future anarchist society as being 'communalistic'.[91]

Although Kropotkin apparently never expounded at great length on the exact nature of the post-revolutionary society, at various places he indicated its general contours. Thus, in *Modern Science and Anarchism*, he wrote: '*This was the form that the social revolution must take* – the independent commune. Let all the country and the world be against it; but once its inhabitants have decided that they *will* communalize the consumption of commodities, their exchange, and their production, *they must realize it among themselves*.

Kropotkin went on to say, 'More than that. We made one step more. We understood that if no central government was needed to rule the independent communes, if the national government is

34

thrown overboard and national unity is obtained by free federation, then a central *municipal* government becomes equally useless and obnoxious. The same federative principle would do within the commune.'[92]

One essential element in Kropotkin's communalist approach to anarchist reorganization of society was his insistence that the communes engage in both agriculture and manufacturing. At one point, in *Fields, Factories and Workshops*, he wrote: 'The moral and physical advantages which man would derive from dividing his work between the field and the workshop are self-evident, But the difficulty is, we are told, in the necessary centralization of the modern industries. In industry, as well as in politics, centralization has so many admirers.'[93]

Although conceding that some industries, such as shipbuilding, for instance, 'must be surrounded by a variety of workshops and factories,' he asked, 'why, in a rationally organized society, ought London to remain a great centre for the ham and preserving trade, and manufacture umbrellas for nearly the whole of the United Kingdom? Why should the countless Whitechapel petty trades remain where they are, instead of being spread all over the country?'[94]

Kropotkin concluded: 'The scattering of industries over the country – so as to bring the factory amidst the fields, to make agriculture derive all those profits which it always finds in being combined with industry ... and to produce a combination of industrial with agricultural work – is surely the next step to be made, as soon as a reorganization of our present conditions is possible... This step is imposed by the very necessity of *producing for the producers themselves*; it is imposed by the necessity for each healthy man and woman to spend a part of their lives in manual work in the free air...'[95]

At another point in the same volume, Kropotkin presented a hypothetical case of the kind of mixed agricultural-industrial commune he was advocating. Presuming a group of two hundred families of five persons each settled on a thousand acres of land, he concedes that if each family cultivated only its smallholding, the result would be failure. However, he says:

The same two hundred families, if they consider themselves, say, as tenants of the nation, and treat the thousand acres as a common tenancy ... would have, economically speaking, from the point of view of the agriculturalist, every chance of succeeding, *if they know what is the best use to make of that land* ...

In such case they would first of all associate for permanently improving the land which required immediate improvement... On an area of 340 acres they could most easily grow all the cereals – wheat, oats, etc. – required for both the thousand inhabitants and their livestock... They could grow on 400 acres, properly cultivated, and irrigated if necessary and possible, all the green crops and fodder required to keep the thirty to forty milch cows which would supply them with milk and butter, and, let us say, the 300 head of cattle required to supply them with meat. On twenty acres, two of which would be under glass, they would grow more vegetables, fruit and luxuries than they could consume. And supposing that half an acre of land is attached to each house – for hobbies and amusement (poultry-keeping, or any fancy culture, flowers, and the like) – they would still have some 140 acres for all sorts of purposes: public gardens, squares, manufactures, and so on. The labor that would be required for such an intensive culture would not be the hard labor of the serf or slave. It would be accessible to everyone, strong or weak, town bred or country born; it would also have many charms besides...[96]

Like Bakunin before him, Kropotkin insisted that in an anarchist society recompense to all would be in accordance to need. From this belief, Kropotkin drew the conclusion that in such a society, there would be no place for money of any sort.

'Services rendered to society, be they work in factory or field, or mental services, *cannot be* valued in money. There can be no exact measure of value (of what has been wrongly termed exchange value) nor of use value in terms of production. If two individuals work for the community five hours a day, year in year out, at different work which is equally agreeable to them, we may say that on the whole their labor is approximately equivalent. But we cannot divide their work, and say that the result of any particular day, hour, or minute of work of the one is worth the result of one day, one hour, or one minute of the other.'[97]

He applies this idea to the working of a coal mine, and concludes:

> All those who are engaged in the mine contribute to the extraction of coal in proportion to their strength, their energy, their knowledge, their intelligence, and their skill. And we may say that all have the right to live, to satisfy their needs, and even their whims, when the necessaries of life have been secured for all. But how can we appraise the work of each one of them?
>
> ... It is utterly impossible to draw a distinction between the work of each of those men. To measure the work by its results leads us to an absurdity; to divide the total work, and to measure its fractions by the number of hours spent on the work also leads us to an absurdity. One thing remains: to put the *needs* above the *works*, and first of all to recognize *the right to live*, and later on *the right to well-being* for all those who took their share in production.[98]

In a system in which each was paid according to his needs, there would be no place for any kind of money, according to Kropotkin. He develops this argument by criticizing the ideas of Marx and others whom he labels 'collectivists':

> This system for the remuneration of labor ... comes very much to this: Everyone works, be it in fields, in factories in schools, in hospitals, or what not. The working day is regulated by the state, to which belong the soil, factories, means of communication, and all the rest. Each worker, having done a day's work, receives a labor note, stamped, let us say, with these words: *eight hours of labor*. With this note, he can procure any sort of goods in the shops of the state or the various corporations. The note is divisible in such a ways that one hour's worth of meat, ten minutes' worth of matches, or half-an-hour's worth of tobacco can be purchased. Instead of saying 'two pennyworth of soap,'

after the Collectivist Revolution they will say, 'five minutes' worth of soap'.[99]

Kropotkin noted that, following Marx's own distinction between skilled and unskilled labor, some Marxists are willing to make distinctions between the 'hour-value' of hours spent on different kinds of work. 'Their principles are: collective property in the instruments of labor, and remuneration of each worker according to the time spent in productive toil, taking into account the productiveness of his work.'[100] He concludes: 'The nation or the commune which should give to itself such an organization would be forced either to return to private property or else to transform itself immediately into a communist society,'[101] that is, one organized along anarchist lines.

Kropotkin's Influence on Spanish Anarchism

The influence of Kropotkin's version of anarchism upon the Spanish movement was substantial. Unlike Bakunin, Peter Kropotkin personally visited Spain in 1878. At least one important early Spanish anarchist leader, the teacher Severino Albarracín, had already spent several years working with Kropotkin in Switzerland during the mid-1870s.[102] Enrico Malatesta, the Italian who was a close ally of Kropotkin within the international anarchist movement, also visited Spain, lecturing widely.

The ideas of Kropotkin and his allies contributed to the ideological struggle within Spanish anarchism in the 1880s and 1890s. José Peirats has noted that at the end of the nineteenth century there was a conflict among Spanish libertarians between the collectivist school led by Ricardo Mella, and the anarchist communism tendency headed by José Prat. The collectivist group argued that in the new society each worker should get the full value of what he produced, that surplus value should be eliminated, and the full value of what was turned out should be distributed among the workers who created it.

The anarchist communist school, on the other hand, argued that in the anarchist society everyone should receive according to his needs. Peirats described this idea as being 'the great pile' theory of Kropotkin, that all should take from the total pile of goods the things which they needed.

According to Peirats, José Prat and the anarchist communist school won out in that struggle.[103] However, as we shall see, there was no unanimity on this subject among the workers, particularly those in the urban areas, who took over industries at the onset of the Civil War.

Kropotkin's communalist version of anarchism was particularly relevant to the actions of the Spanish anarchists in the rural parts of Republican Spain during the Civil War. Hundreds of peasant collectives were formed in those areas, which to a greater or less degree applied Kropotkinesque ideas. In many cases, they organized small industries as complements to their agricultural activities. In a substantial proportion of them money was formally abolished and members of the collectives were allowed to take things from the common store, at least to some degree, in terms of their needs. At first, goods were exchanged among the collectives, and between them and anarchist-controlled factories in the cities, through a process of barter, presumably determined by the needs of the parties involved. Subsequently, federations of collectives were organized to conduct exchanges on a somewhat more formal basis.

The Kropotkinist abhorrence of money, with which the Spanish anarchists were very much imbued, had one unfortunate result for them, as Cesar Lorenzo, son of the one-time National Secretary of the CNT, Horacio Prieto, has noted. He observed that in the early days of the War, when most of the factories in Catalonia were seized by the workers, and where some of the land was collectivized by the peasants, while commerce was organized under anarchist control, the banks were left untouched: 'Only the banks escape seizure and remained at the disposition of the government of the Generalidad, and their employees formed the nucleus of the small Catalan UGT. The libertarians did not understand the importance of the banking system and its long-term impact on socialization; thus they did not touch this fundamental sector of the economy.[104] As we shall see later, this disregard for the banking system, rooted in the deep anarchist aversion to money, had very serious negative consequences for the worker-controlled industries, not only in Catalonia but also in some other parts of Republican Spain.

Luigi Fabbri's Summation of Anarchism

Perhaps the Italian anarchist Luigi Fabbri, whose writings were widely circulated by his Spanish colleagues, has best summed up in general philosophical terms the kind of society which anarchists were seeking to bring into existence. Writing about the turn of the nineteenth century, he said:

> There is a certain authority which comes from experience, science, which it is not possible to reject and would be crazy to reject, as it would be crazy for the nurse to rebel against the authority of the doctor in the curing of a sick person, or a bricklayer who did not want to follow the instructions of the architect in the construction of a building, or a sailor who wished to steer the ship against the instructions of the pilot... The nurse, the bricklayer and the sailor respectively obey the doctor, the architect and the pilot *voluntarily*, because they have in advance freely accepted the technical direction of these people. Fine; when there has been established a society in which there is no other form of authority than the technical, the scientific moral influence, without the use of violence of man against man, no one could deny that it would be an anarchist society.[105]

Conclusion

From its inception, Spanish anarchism was part of the larger international movement. Its philosophy and doctrines were profoundly influenced by ideas of Proudhon, Michael Bakunin and Peter Kropotkin. The general condemnation of the State, political parties, any kind of collaboration between revolutionaries and reformists, which they all shared were accepted by virtually the whole of the Spanish movement. But the different approaches of Bakunin and Kropotkin – the anarcho-syndicalism of the former and the communalist approach of the latter – had their impact principally on the Spanish urban and rural anarchist movements, respectively.

2

Spanish Anarchist Sketches of Libertarian Society

Although the Spanish anarchists endorsed different aspects of the Bakunin and Kropotkin versions of anarchist philosophy at various times, they did not officially present a detailed picture of the kind of society they wanted to create to displace capitalism until May 1936, two months before the outbreak of the Civil War. As early as 1919 the Confederación Nacional del Trabajo had gone on record as favoring libertarian communism, it was not until the Zaragoza congress of the CNT in May 1936 that they adopted a long resolution setting forth their ideas concerning the details of the reorganization of the Spanish economy, polity and society.

There were those in the Spanish libertarian movement who were strongly opposed to any attempt to sketch the future libertarian society. For instance, Federica Montseny wrote in August 1931: 'Anarchism is an ideal without boundaries. It cannot be enclosed within the confines of a programme.'[1]

Most sketches by Spanish anarchist leaders of the future libertarian communist society tended to be general and vague in terms of specific post-revolutionary institutions and how they would function. Xavier Paniagua has noted that many, if not most, of them saw the anarchist society as being overwhelmingly rural and basically communalist.' A number of them were specifically anti-industrial in their thinking.[2] Some were even vocally anti-urban.[3] At least a few

---

42

wrote nostalgically about a 'return to the Middle Ages' of agrarian communities.[4]

However, during the decades preceding the Civil War, a number of anarchist leaders and intellectuals had presented more or less detailed accounts of their concepts of the kind of anarchist society they wanted to create. Before recounting at some length the outline of the Zaragoza resolution, it is therefore worthwhile to discuss a few of these concepts.

La Nueva Utopia of Ricardo Mella

Ricardo Mella was one of the outstanding Spanish anarchist leaders of the late nineteenth and early twentieth centuries. Other anarchist writers, including Juan Díaz del Moral, Diego Abad de Santillán and Max Nettlau, called him 'the most gifted of anarchist thinkers'.[5] He wrote about many aspects of anarchist theory and policy, and summed up his vision of the future libertarian society of Spain in a novel, *La Nueva Utopia*. As the name of the work implies, it had a good deal in common with the ideal societies characteristic of the Utopian Socialists of the nineteenth century. George Esenwein noted:

> The social system of *Nueva Utopia* is grounded on two fundamental principles: liberty and equality. Natural resources – that is, the forests, oil, gas, iron ore as well as the bountiful fruits of the soil – now belong to everyone ... The citizens themselves are related through a system of reciprocally binding pacts ... These vital links, which are the only means by which individuals form economic and social relations, are highly flexible in that they can be rescinded or annulled at any time ... Another unifying force in society is the general feeling of social solidarity. No longer plagued by political, religious and other sources of social friction which formerly divided society into opposition factions, the people of *La Nueva Utopia* have only to worry about the general welfare of society...[6]

The society that emerges in Mella's tale is one which in nearly every way conforms to the principles of all anarchist schools. It is not, for example, dominated by a particular kind of economic system – although Mella makes it clear in the story that collectivism is without question the superior form of economic arrangement. Men and women are free to choose whatever form of exchange they are predisposed to: 'if the worker wishes to reserve the right to exchange the products of his labour, no one will impede him, if he wishes to donate his products to the community at large, no one will stop him, if he wants to turn them over to a cooperative, he is free to do so.[7]

Orobón Fernández's Version of Libertarian Society

Valeriano Orobón Fernández was one of the leading figures of the CNT in the pro-Civil War period who died soon after the War began. In 1925, he provided a sketch, although an abbreviated one, of the post-revolutionary libertarian society:

The most elemental manifestation of this regime would be the 'Unity Production Cooperative', in lightly populated areas. This organism would include all the people of the Commune capable of working. The Sindicato of today is potentially tomorrow's producers' cooperative. Consequently, where the former exists, the second will be viable ... In more heavily populated areas, the a most adequate economic organism would be the 'Specific Industry Cooperative'. Its purpose would not be different from the other, except that in the circumstances it would confine itself to its specialty. Generally, its mission would be the same: taking over the means of production, establishing the conditions and methods for a new organization of labor, etc. The simple transformation of our Industrial Unions ... would give us this second type of cooperative...

On organization of the economy beyond the local level, Orobón Fernández wrote:

The connection among the cooperatives could be the establishment of the two groups: 1. That of 'specific nature' through the creation of Federations of Industry which would group the specific cooperatives of the cities and specialized sections of the communal cooperatives. Their purpose would be to apply measures of a general nature to improve the industry, regularize the administration of raw materials, etc. 2. That of 'general relations' of all the active organisms through the constitution of a General Intercooperative Confederation, the mission of which would be inter-industrial collaboration of firms on a national level. Also, it would assume representation of the country in its international relations...[8]

Higinio Noja Ruíz's View of Post-Revolutionary Anarchism

Higinio Noja Ruíz, an anarchist professor at the University of Valencia and contributor to the libertarian periodical *Estudios*, published in 1933 an extensive pamphlet discussing, among other things, the future organization of libertarian society. He argued:

With the triumph of the revolution, each locality will take possession within its municipal limits of the exploitation in common of its riches. In so far as possible, parcelization and the development of small property should be avoided as one of the most serious impediments to the installation of a communist regime. But where this cannot be entirely avoided, it must be established that all production, both that resulting from individual cultivation and collectivized cultivation must pass through the administration and distribution of the Commune, free Municipality or Committee of the Local Trade Union Federation, depending on which each locality adopts.

This prescription was followed in most of the rural collectives set up by the anarchists during the Civil War, particularly in those of Aragón.

Noja Ruíz went on to argue: 'In the large population centers, production must be in the hands of the Sindicatos, whose committees, aided by Workshop Committees and Factory Councils, in accordance with the workers of local units and general necessities, will undertake to regulate it. General administration would seem most likely to be carried out by the Committees of the Local Federations, formed by one or more representatives of each *Sindicato*.'

This anarchist writer appended to his article several charts outlining various phases of the future libertarian economic organization. These charts are reminiscent of the structures sketched by the Industrial Workers of the World of the United States a quarter of a century earlier.

Noja Ruíz's charts indicated the relationship of the individual factory committee to the local industrial union, to the respective national industrial union; alongside a structure leading from the local commune, to regional federations of communes, to a national confederation of communes. Similarly, Noja Ruíz sketched a national organization of agricultural production, starting with a local committee of exploitation, to an agricultural *sindicato*, to the national agricultural federation. Finally, he joined factory councils through their respective local unions and federations of unions, as well as their national industrial federations and regional union confederations, to the Confederación Nacional del Trabajo, which would have a national labor council to coordinate all of the economy. On each level there would be specific dependencies for collecting statistics and other purposes.

Noja Ruíz summed up his notion of the future libertarian economic organization thus: 'In all these graphs it is seen that all organization begins with the individual, to the collective invariably. The autonomous individual in the autonomous section; the autonomous section in the autonomous *sindicato*; the *sindicato* in the Federations and Confederations, also autonomous.'[9]

Isaac Puente's Version of Libertarian Society

A year before the publication of Noja Ruíz's pamphlet, Dr Isaac Puente had published his own interpretation of the future libertarian society. Puente was a medical doctor who was one of the principal Spanish anarchist intellectuals in the period before the Civil War. He died during the conflict.

Isaac Puente started out by defining libertarian communism: '...the organization of Society without the State, and without private property. For this, there is no need to invent anything, or to create any new organism. The nuclei of organization, around which the economic future will be organized are present in today's society: they are the Sindicato and the Free Municipality.'[10] He added: 'Social organization has no other objective than to make *common* everything which constitutes social wealth, that is to say, the means and factors of production and the products themselves, to make common also the obligation of contributing to production, each according to his ability and aptitude, and to undertake then to distribute products among all, in accord with individual need.'[11]

Puente outlined the principles for organization of both urban regions and rural communities. He set forth several basic points with regard to the former, which included the following:

> Considering that each professional group is capable of organizing its own affairs, tutelage is not necessary, and the State is superfluous. Initiative passes to professional organizations. Control of teaching to the teachers. Health to health professionals. Communications to its employees. The internal regime of a factory is decided by the technicians and workers meeting in assembly, and the Federation of Sindicatos controls production...

> Men are grouped by the identity of their preoccupations and needs in the *Sindicato*, and for convenience of location and community of interests in the free Municipality ... All citizens are made equal only as producers. Officers are administrative, temporary, without allowing exemption from production, and always at the disposal of the decisions of the Assemblies ... In

economic organization, the hierarchy goes from the base. Accords of a Committee can be revoked by a Plenum; those of the latter by the Assembly, and those of the Assembly by the People.[12]

Isaac Puente added:

The *Sindicato* brings together individuals, associating them by their type of work ... Workers of a factory or workshop, constituting the smallest cell, with autonomy in what is peculiar to it. These cells, brought together with their counterparts, form the section within the Sindicato of Craft or Industry ... The *Sindicatos* of the locality are federated, constituting the Local Federation, which has a Committee chosen by delegations of the Sindicatos to a Plenum, made up of all the Committees and by the General Assembly, which is what has maximum sovereignty ... The Free Municipality is the Assembly of the workers of a small locality, village or hamlet, with sovereignty to take care of locality.[13]

It is in the countryside that the realization of Libertarian Communism is easiest, since it means only putting into practice the Free municipality. The Free Municipality or Commune is the meeting in Assembly of all the neighbors of a village or ward, with sovereignty to administer or order all local matters, but first of all production and distribution. There will not exist private property except in the use of what each needs, such as housing, clothing, furniture, tools, the garden left to each neighbor and small animals or chickens which he might want for consumption. Everything beyond what is necessary can be taken over at any time by the Municipality, after agreement of the Assembly, since all that we accumulate without needing it does not belong to us, since we take it from others.

All neighbors will be equal: 1. To produce and cooperate in maintenance of the commune, except for differences in aptitude ... 2. To participate in administrative decisions in the Assemblies, and 3. To consume in accordance with their needs or rationing.[14]

Puente saw distribution of consumer goods as being organized by 'the producing *sindicatos*, using Cooperatives or the buildings of stores and markets.' Each *sindicato* member would have a producer's card which would give its possessor the following rights: '1. To consume in accordance with rationing or his need, all the products distributed in the locality. 2. To have the use of a decent house, indispensable furniture, yard fowl or a garden if the collective decides so. 3. To use public services. 4. To take part in the voting decision of the factory or workshop of the Section, the *Sindicato* and the Local Federation.'

The local federation 'will take care of providing the needs of the locality and developing its specific industry, either for better distribution or for meeting national needs.'[15]

In so far as the organization of the national economy was concerned, Puente argued that 'above local organization, there is no need for a superstructure, except those with a special function which cannot be undertaken locally. Congresses are the only things which interpret the national will and will carry it out in passing and transitionally, the sovereignty which is given them by the votes of the assemblies.' The only exceptions to this rule, Puente argued, were national union federations of communications and transport workers, which are clearly in need of national organization.[16]

Alfonso Martínez Rizo's Version of Libertarian Society

Another version of the post-revolutionary society was presented in 1933 by Alfonso Martínez Rizo, vice-president of the CNT's *sindicato* of Intellectual Workers. Like the other writers we have discussed, Martínez sketched the libertarian organization of both urban and rural parts of the economy, but placed special emphasis on the importance of the disappearance of money, and dealt with other problems not always touched upon by all anarchist theorists.

Beginning his detailed description of post-revolutionary society, Martínez argued:

The norm and guide can and must be the present functioning of the Confederación Nacional del Trabajo, since it is governed by the same principles. With proclamation of libertarian communism, and the *Sindicatos* taking over all economic activities, its organisms would take over general administration. In those organisms ... offices are of six-month duration, those holding them being eligible for re-election. Of those, the president, secretary and treasurer, are elected in the Assembly by all the members. Each autonomous section has its Administrative Junta and elects delegates to the Plenum of the Committee. The Plenum elects among its members the vice-president, vice-secretary, accountant, and librarian. All these posts are carried out without pay. It will also be logical that the present trade union jurisdiction and federal organization continue...[17]

Martínez argued that the reorganization of the economy along the lines he suggested would be undertaken immediately on a national basis: 'On Libertarian Communism being proclaimed there would meet a National Congress, which would establish the points, fundamental and secondary though basic, of a federal pact of all local communities...'[18]

Martínez went into some detail on the reorganization of the urban economy: 'The workshop committees will take the place of the bourgeois specialists ... the factory council that of the administrators. The industrial union that of the employers groups. The local, regional federations and national confederation, the place of local, regional and national capitalist conglomerates, the national labor economic committee that of the national economic council. The industrial federations and the labor economic council will have only technical functions, and the other organism will have both technical and social ones.'

Martínez went on to say:

All these will be subject to a Committee or Council named in general assembly of workers or by representatives of these meeting in National Congress. This National Committee or Council, charged with executing the accords of the assemblies or congresses, will be revocable at any time, and consequently will be submitted to permanent control of the workers, not exercising delegated authority...

The National Confederation will also have a technical council formed by representatives of the industrial federations and that will be the Labor Economic Council ... This Labor Economic Council will inform the regional economic councils which will distribute work to the local economic councils and these to their respective industrial unions, thus connecting production with exchange and consumption. This Labor Economic Council will be controlled by the National Committee of the CNT, responsible to the Sindicatos. The Labor Economic Council would also control international trade, seeking to maintain the country's balance of payments.[19]

In so far as the rural economy was concerned, Martínez said: 'Given the basic autonomy of our system, the local agrarian communities can decide, in accord with the indications of the Labor Economic Council and supported by the agreements of the national congresses, what class of cultivation and what kind of crops should be grown, and then the products will be exchanged for industrial products of equal value in terms of hours of work. In these conditions, with the agrarian workers receiving the full product of their labor, or its equivalent, the level of all will be improved under the new regime...'[20]

Martínez stressed the suppression of traditional money, and the substitution of another means of distribution, with some similarity to the ideas of Proudhon. 'The new money will be evaluated and denominated in hours of work. It will consist of bonds emitted by the unions, equivalent to the hours of work of every worker. These bonds will be issued weekly and only will have value during the following week. So that each can meet his needs, the workers who have children or a wife who cannot work, once this is indicated to his union, will receive, on collecting his weekly bond, others to meet the needs of his family members. Invalids will receive forty-eight hours of work per week from the social assistance offices.'

Prices of goods would be set in hours-of-work' terms, by each locality, so as to clear the market, in the light of the value of the bonds issued to the members of the community. The bonds would be valid only in the local community.[21]

As for commerce among various communities, Martínez wrote: 'For ... exchange among different autonomous communities, products will be evaluated in hours of work, payment being in tokens which will then be exchanged to equalize sales and purchases. Thus, then, there will be two prices: one representing the exact number of hours of labor invested in production and which will be used for exchange between different autonomous municipalities; the other, which will be the same multiplied by a variable factor, which will serve in each locality to facilitate the sale to the public of all goods.'[22]

Martínez also dealt with two problems which were not economic. These were crime and the armed forces. In relation to crime, Martínez wrote:

With the disappearance of yours and mine and authority attributed to anyone, there will disappear automatically almost all kinds of crime. The criterion that no one can exercise authority suppresses the posts of magistrates and judges. That is not to say that justice will disappear, that will be carried out by plebiscite by the collective ... We consider the delinquent of passion as disturbed, and we only feel that he merits treatment as a sick person. In our peculiar concept, in libertarian communism there will only continue one punishment for the only crime which can continue in such a regime. The crime is disobedience to the agreements of the collective or to the principles of libertarian communism. The only punishment that the author conceives of is exile to bourgeois countries, so long as those continue; when one no longer exists, exile from the collective, which will force him to live alone at the cost of individual work.[23]

In the face of the attack on a revolutionary libertarian Spain by capitalist states, which he expected would take place, Martínez admitted that military defense would be necessary, in spite of the anarchists' traditional anti-militarism. However, his solution to the problem was one which was undoubtedly widespread in anarchist ranks, and was to raise serious problems for the libertarians with the outbreak of the Civil War. He wrote:

> Many times I have heard the objection that libertarian communism is incapable of war, since it requires that there be those who command and those who obey, which is contrary to its principles. This objection comes from confusing two different things, the exercise of authority and technical direction. Also in the workshop the worker will have to work as the technician indicates and not as he pleases, and the technician will neither be an authority nor will command; he will be a working companion and his way of working will be precisely that of studying how the manual worker must work to get the best output...
>
> Equally, in the units of the proletariat in arms, power will always be the result of decisions of the collective which puts in the workers hands the arms to defend it. The organic units will have the mission of fulfilling and seeing fulfilled the agreements of the collective, and in that, as in anything else, there will be the workshop committee and the technicians, who will be the officers. The latter will decide in every case how the soldiers should operate to obtain the hoped-for triumph over the enemy. The committee will supervise his action. The soldier who does not behave as the officer indicates will be guilty of the same fault that the worker does who refuses to follow the indications of the technician.[24]

The Libertarian Society According to Gaston Leval

Another significant sketch of the post-revolutionary libertarian society by an anarchist theoretician was that of Gaston Leval. Although he was by birth a Frenchman, Gaston Leval (real name, Pierre Filler) was a member of the Spanish Confederación Nacional del Trabajo from at least the First World War. He was a member of the CNT delegation to Russia in the early 1920s, and was one of those who strongly opposed affiliation of the CNT to the Red International of

Labor Unions. During the Civil War, Leval was one of the most important publicists of the achievements of the anarchists after July 18 1936. He spent some years in Argentina before returning to Spain a couple of months after the Civil War began.[25]

Leval's sketch of the future libertarian society appears to have been published in Barcelona in 1936, shortly before the outbreak of the Civil War. It was revised and reprinted in 1937.

Leval started out by attacking several ideas in anarchist thinking which he thought were either excessively emphasized or were mistaken. One of the over emphasized was autonomy:

There has been repeated and there has been written ... the mentioned formula: 'the individual is free within the group, the group is free within the federation'. We have always, on hearing it, our mental reservation ... If we are really free, if we can or not fulfill a resolution taken, if for every debated problem there is formed a minority in rebellion, what other practice could be carried out, how is it possible to live together? Malatesta has already insisted on the necessity of fulfilling the accords taken by the majority, and this necessity is being accepted by those who understand that without compromise collective and individual existence is not possible...

On entering a group, I do not consider myself free. I am subject to a common norm, to a responsibility, to a task from which I cannot flee. I am not autonomous. I abdicate part of my autonomy to contribute to the welfare of all, that may or may not react in my favor. Unless one wants to play with words, subtle philosophy of different dialectics separated from truth, when a revolutionary joins with others, he is not going to exercise his freedom, but to fulfil a social duty, forgetting about himself.[26]

Gaston Leval also attacked the argument which Kropotkin put forth in one of his books in favor of national autarchy: 'It is not an ideal that each region is sufficient unto itself; as an aspiration, much superior and much more noble is a vast and permanent cooperation throughout the earth...'

Gaston Leval also opposed the degree of heterogeneity for the libertarian economy which Ricardo Mella had advocated. 'How can one conceive of economic relations among communist producers' groups and collectivist ones? Some offer money in exchange for products. Others want products for products. The eases multiply. How can one reach understanding? Hundreds of entities will practise a concept opposed by hundreds of others. Economic life would deteriorate quickly.' He said that only the kind of local self-sufficiency advocated by Kropotkin would make this kind of system viable, and added: 'This is completely impossible, and as soon as one observes the multiplicity of articles necessary for civilized life, and the productive possibilities of each region, province or corner of whatever part of the world, he imposition of exchange and general cooperation is obvious; to carry out this exchange, the regime of relations must be the same.'[28]

Leval sketched the hierarchy of organizations which would conduct economic affairs under libertarian communism: '1. The workers considered as individuals; 2. The craft sections formed by these workers; 3. The industrial unions composed of the related craft sections; 4. The federations of industry made up of industrial unions; 5. The Industrial Confederation made up of the industrial federations.'

He described the way in which the levels of organization would function:

1. Each craft section names a technical delegate, and the craft delegates constitute the Administrative Committee – generally this representation appears to us more necessary than that of the factory or workshop Committees – more revolutionary than technical, while we must look at organization from the point of view of production; that is to say, with an eminently technical criterion. 2. The Congress of the Industrial Federation names a Committee composed of delegates of certain industrial zones, in accordance with their importance and special characteristics; this would permit the Central Committees to maintain more direct contact and know better the general reality of the country. 3. The Confederation Congress would in their turn name a

> Central Federal Commission and without doubt various regional ones, made up of delegates of the various industrial federations, in proportions dictated by the circumstances (numerical importance of each federation, intensity and characteristic of the work to be carried on, etc...[29]

In so far as the organization of the rural economy was concerned, Leval argued:

> The peasants must organize themselves communally – and not be organized in unions – in accordance with their traditions... This form would respond to the objectives sought. The objectives of peasant activity are the provision of the cultivated products of the land, the chicken coops, the meat and other animal products, skins, wool, etc...
>
> The work of the peasant must respond to general need, not to his caprice or particular interpretation of things... It is a dangerous norm, and false to affirm, as is done too often, that the peasants will give for exchange, after keeping what they need, the excess products. It is equally false to think that way about any kind of production.
>
> ...As in industry the administrative mechanism would be federalist, the decisions taken in the congresses, and the work determined by the permanent commissions would come from the wishes expressed by the rank and file, by congresses ranging from specialized regional federations, to the General Congress of Agriculture and Grazing...[30]

Distribution of both industrial and agricultural products, according to Leval, would be through cooperatives:

> There would be circulation of products, from productive zones to consuming zones. The cooperatives would be charged with carrying it out...
>
> To their central deposits would come, in the cities, the excess product of local industrial production. These cooperatives would not distribute haphazardly, or according to the sporadic

demand of each locality. Each would specialize in one or various types of articles, each would have its own district to supply; a certain number of small cities or localities. The inhabitants of that district would be directed to it according to a generally established order. Thus there would be formed a vast network whose activities would cover all points and all consumption of the territory...

These cooperatives would transmit them to the centers of the productive organisms diverse requests, which would permanently reflect oscillations of demand. And they would become the sources of information of the federations and the Industrial and Agricultural-Grazing Confederations, contributing to the direction of productive activities.'[31]

Leval proposed union membership as the basis of distribution of goods to consumers: 'The best form that occurs to us consists of creating a network of distributive organisms in connection with the producing organisms... There could exist, in parallel, a general cooperative associated with the same union, which would have sections in contact with sections in the neighborhoods. The workers, or their families, will go to the sectional cooperative of their union to look for consumer articles. The presentation of the trade union card would be enough to accredit the producer with the right to consume.'[32]

The Ideas of Diego Abad de Santillán

Finally, Diego Abad de Santillán, who earlier had been opposed to trying to sketch the future libertarian communist society, published early in 1936 *The Economic Organization of the Revolution*, which did just that. Gómez Casas has noted of this work:

The author condemns economic separatism and supports the idea of federal organization of the economy, beginning with factory councils or local trade or industrial unions and moving up to local and regional councils, assisted by technical and statistical data, and up to the national or federal economic council. The local council, coordinator of local organizations, would replace municipalities and elected bodies... According to Santillán, the federal economic council would replace the State. There would be no political power, only an economic and administrative regulator... Since decisions would be based on figure's and statistics, compulsion by any organization would be counter-productive and impossible. Such a coordinating body would guarantee a free society of producers and consumers, would coordinate the plans developed by all the organizations, and would respect the relative autonomy of all the federated bodies.[33]

Nature of the CNT Zaragoza Resolution

All of the sketches which we have so far discussed represented the opinions of individual anarchist leaders and theorists. However, in May 1936, the Confederación Nacional del Trabajo adopted an official outline of the kind of society which it wanted to establish after the hoped-for revolution.

César Lorenzo, the son of one-time CNT national secretary Horacio Prieto, said of this document: 'After sixty-seven years of tests and many experiences rich in lessons, it presents an idyllic program ... in which puerility and Utopia are given free rein, with total disregard of the peculiarities of Spain, the international situation, the historic moment and the means of attaining the new promised land.'[34]

The CNT's Zaragoza resolution seems to reflect considerably more the Kropotkin version of anarchist ideas, and even that of Pierre Proudhon, than that of Michael Bakunin. Certainly there seemed to be relatively little room in the document for national industrial unions as the center for the reorganization of the national economy and society. Rather, the emphasis was on the kind of communal organization that had been suggested by Peter Kropotkin.

Although the Zaragoza resolution conceded that '... to construct with mathematical precision the society of the future would be absurd, since often there exists a real chasm between theory and practice...' it did in fact sketch in considerable detail how the future society would be organized.

However, before doing so, the resolution noted: 'The revolution cannot be based either on mutual aid, on solidarity or on the archaic idea of charity. These three formulas ... must be recast and perfected in new norms of social relations which find their clearest interpretation in libertarian communism: to give to each human being that which his needs require, without the satisfaction of these having other limitations than those imposed by the needs of the newly created economy.'

Details of the Zaragoza Resolution

The CNT's Zaragoza resolution then began to describe the new society:

> With the violent aspect of the revolution terminated, there will be declared abolished: private property, the State, the principle of authority, and consequently, classes which divide man into exploiters and exploited, oppressed and oppressors. Wealth socialized, the organization of the producers, now free, will undertake direct administration of production and consumption. With establishment in each locality of the Libertarian Commune, we shall put into place the new social mechanism. The producers of each branch of trade, united in their Unions and in their work places will freely determine the form in which these will be organized...

The resolution set forth a general principle for the reorganization of the economy: 'the economic plan of organization, throughout national production, will adjust to the strictest principles of social economy, directly administered by the producers through their various organs of production, designated in general assemblies of the various organizations, and always controlled by them.'

In the urban areas, the resolution established 'as the organ of relations within the Commune and in the workplace, the workshop or factory Council, reaching pacts with other labor centers. As organ of relations of Union to Union (association of producers) the Councils of Statistics and Production, which will federate among themselves, forming a network of constant and close relations among all the producers of the Iberian Confederation.'

In the rural areas, the resolution provide:

As the base, the producers of the Commune, which uses all the natural riches of its political and geographic area. As organ of relations, the Council of Cultivation, which will include technical elements and workers belonging to associations of agricultural producers, charged with orienting the intensification of production, indicating the land most appropriate to that, in accord with its chemical composition. These Councils of Cultivation will establish the same network of relations as the Workshop, Factory Councils and those of Production and Statistics, complementing the free federation represented by the Commune as a political entity and geographic subdivision.

The resolution set forth not only how production would be organized, but how consumption would be determined. It provided that 'letters of the producer, issued by the Workshop and Factory Councils will be sufficient for them to acquire what is necessary to fulfil their needs. The producer's letter constitutes the basis of exchange, which will be subject to these two regulating elements: First, that it be intransferable; second, that there be adopted a procedure through which the letter indicates the value of labor by days of work and that this value have at most a year of validity to acquire products. For dependent elements of the population, it will be the Communal Councils which issue the letters of consumption...'

This provision would seem to be more like Pierre Proudhon's labor banknote scheme than like the 'to each according to his need' preached by Peter Kropotkin. It perhaps introduced a note of confusion, when two months later the CNT's members set about establishing peasant collectives and organizing manufacturing firms which they had seized. The former tended to follow the Kropotkin formula, whereas the factory workers often more nearly approached the Proudhon prescription.

For dealing with national economic problems, the resolution provided that 'Both the Associations of industrial producers and Associations of agricultural producers will federate nationally ... if, carried to this point by the process of work to which they are dedicated, they esteem it convenient for the most fruitful development of the Economy; and similarly there will be federated those services needed to facilitate logical and necessary relations among all the Libertarian Communes of the Peninsula.'

The resolution also set forth the basis of the political reorganization of post-revolutionary Spain. 'The political expression of our revolution must be based on this trilogy: The Individual, the Commune, and the Federation ... The basis of this administration will consequently be the Commune. Those Communes will be autonomous and will be federated regionally and nationally to carry out objectives of a general character. The right of autonomy will not exclude the duty to fulfil agreements of collective convenience.'

On the political form of the new society the resolution stated:

The Communes will federate on a county and regional basis, fixing voluntarily their geographical limits, when it will be convenient to unite in a single Commune small villages, hamlets and places. Together these Communes will constitute an Iberian Confederation of Autonomous Libertarian Communes...

For the function of distributing production and so that the Communes can better supply themselves, there can be created supplementary organizations for the purpose. For example: a Confederal Council of Production and Distribution, with direct representatives of the National Federations of Production and of the annual Congress of Communes.

The resolution insisted that 'the Commune must take care of what interests the individual.' More specifically, 'It must take care of all the tasks of ordering, regulating and beautifying the locality; of the housing of its residents; of the articles and products put at its service by the Unions or Associations of producers. It will also take care of health, of community statistics and collective needs; of teaching; of the sanitary and conservation establishments, and perfection of the local media of communication.'

There was also strong insistence on decentralization of power, and resistance to bureaucratization of public authority:

> The procedure for election of the Communal Councils will be established in conformity with a system in which differences of population require, taking account of the political decentralization of the metropoli, establishing in them Federations of Communes. None of these organs will have executive or bureaucratic character. Except for those people who carry out technical or statistical functions, the others will carry out their mission as producers, meeting after the work day to discuss questions of detail which don't require the decision of the communal assemblies...
>
> Assemblies will meet as often as needed by the interests of the Commune, on petition of the members of the Communal Council, or by the desire of the inhabitants of each of them... The inhabitants of a Commune will discuss among themselves their internal problems: production, consumption, instruction, health and anything necessary for moral and economic development. When problems are dealt with which affect a county or province, it must be the Federations which deliberate, and in the meetings and assemblies all Communities will be represented, and the delegates will bring the points of view previously agreed upon.

Certainly, this prescription for the organization of the post-revolutionary polity was approached to some degree after the outbreak of the Civil War in rural areas where the anarchists were predominant, most notably in Aragón. However, there was no effort – or even possibility – of establishing that pattern in the urban parts of the country.

There was similar provision for dealing with problems of wider geographical scope. The resolution provided that 'in matters of regional character, it will be the Regional Federation which puts agreements into practice, and these will represent the sovereign desires of all the inhabitants of the region. Thus, it begins with the individual, passes then to the Commune, from there to the Federation, and finally to the Confederation. Similarly, we shall come to discussion of all problems of national scope, since our organisms will be complementing one another. The national organization will regulate relations of international character...'

The Zaragoza resolution also dealt with social reorganization. It proposed:

> The disappearance of the present system of judicial correction, and so, of the instruments of punishment (jails etc.) This Statement presumes that social factors are the principal cause of so-called crimes in the present state of things, and thus, with the disappearance of the causes which bring about crime, in most cases it will cease to exist...
>
> Libertarian Communism, then, will base its 'corrective action' on Medicine and Pedagogy, the only preventive measures which modern science justifies. When any individual, victim of pathological phenomena, acts against the harmony which must exist among men, therapeutic pedagogy will cure his disequilibrium and stimulate in him the ethical sense of social responsibility that an insane heritage naturally denied him.

The CNT resolution also dealt briefly with problems of the family and sexual relations: 'The revolution should not operate violently against the family, except in those cases of mismatched families, in which case these will be recognized and their dissolution supported... Libertarian Communism proclaims free love, without any regulation but the free will of the man and the woman, guarantees the children the safeguards of the collectivity, and saving the latter from human aberrations by the application of eugenic biological principles...'

The anticlerical traditions of Spanish anarchism were confirmed in the Zaragoza document: 'Religion, purely subjective manifestation of the human being, will be recognized so long as it is confined to the individual conscience, but never can be considered as a form of public orientation or moral or intellectual coercion. Individuals will be free to conceive of whatever moral ideas they deem convenient, all sects disappearing.'[35]

Special attention was paid to the educational needs of the masses.

> We have a pedagogical task to fulfil immediately after the social revolution. Culture will be provided for those deprived of it... The immediate task will be to organize among the illiterate population an elementary culture, consisting, for example, of teaching to read, write, accounting, physical culture, health, historical process of evolution and revolution, theory of the inexistence of God, etc. This can be carried out by a large number of educated young people who, during one or two years, controlled and oriented by the National Federation of Teachers which, immediately after the proclamation of Libertarian communism, will take charge of all teaching centers.

> We regard as a fundamental function of pedagogy aid to the formation of men with their own judgement – noting that in speaking of men, we do so in a generic sense – for which it will be necessary for the teacher to cultivate all the faculties of the child, to achieve the complete development of his possibilities...

Finally, the Zaragoza resolution dealt with what was to become one of the most bitter issues, both within the CNT and between it and other elements in Republican Spain, during the Civil War, that was the role and nature of the military. It proclaimed:

> A permanent army constitutes the greatest danger for the revolution... The armed people will be the best guarantee against all attempts to restore the destroyed regime by interior or exterior forces. There are thousands of workers who have been in the barracks and know modern military techniques...

> Each Commune should have its arms and elements of defense, until the revolution has been definitively consolidated, and these will not be destroyed to convert them into instruments of work... If the moment arrives, the People will mobilize rapidly

to confront the enemy, the producers returning to their work-
places as soon as they have completed their defensive mission. In
this general mobilization all persons of both sexes capable of
fighting will be included to carry out the many different combat
missions.[36]

The Inadequacy of the Zaragoza Document

In spite of adopting this long document indicating what they hoped
to do after the revolution, the delegates to the Zaragoza CNT
congress 'did not adopt any analysis of the political situation...' As a
result, César Lorenzo insisted that the anarchists 'were obliged on
July 19 to improvise in total incoherence.'[37]

Certainly, it is notable that this document gave at best a very
secondary role in the future society to the national industrial unions
(federations) of the CNT. The emphasis in the CNT program was on
the individual, the commune and the regional federation, with little
reference to the hierarchy of CNT unions as having any role in the
reconstruction of the national Economy.

Perhaps this 'oversight' is due to the fact that the Zaragoza
Congress of the CNT, which among other things brought about the
reunification of the radical and moderate factions of the organization, was dominated by the former, which had always viewed the
national industrial unions with scepticism. This division in the
Spanish anarchist forces was of long duration, before, during and
even after the Civil War.

Fidel Miró described this long-lasting split among the Spanish
anarchists:

The most notable discrepancies have been more virulent in the
tactical area than in the theoretical ... the 'ultras' or maximalists
are partisans of propaganda by the deed – direct action badly
understood – if the permanent revolutionary high school; that is
to say, continuous violent action and the immediate revolution;
while the possibilists have always been more cautious, always
so in the use of violence, without discarding it totally, when

they considered that violence was the necessary reply to un-limited repressive action of the bourgeoisie or of the public powers.[38]

While the maximalists almost always confused tactics with principles, considering them inseparable parts of the same body, the possibilists judged that tactics must always be circumstantial, depending on the exigencies and needs of the moment and place, but never in contradiction to principles.[39]

One of the principal leaders of what Fidel Miró referred to as 'the possibilists', Juan Peiró, who was to serve as an anarchist member of the Largo Caballero government in 1936–7, had some years earlier expressed opposition to the CNT's adopting the kind of ideological document that was endorsed by the Zaragoza congress: '...the CNT being characteristically an economic class organization, of hetero-geneous composition, it cannot and must not have a permanent ideological objective or an airtight set of ideas...'[40]

Peiró had also made an observation which would seem to be directly pertinent to the Zaragoza document:

The realities which economic-social problems present to the peoples are much more complex than the pseudorealities seen by the ultrarevolutionary sectors which have prevailed in recent times. The life of the peoples is no longer conceivable in that primitive form, rural, simple, very appropriate for peasants and shepherds, but incompatible for life in the great cities, where life, in contact with the extraordinary progress of science and new expansions of civilization, necessarily has a corresponding org-anization, disciplined, which takes care of the needs of life...[41]

There is no doubt that in the society emancipated from the tutelage of capitalism and the State, the organization of pro-duction, if only transitorily – and we presume that the transition will have to be extended for a long time – will be in the hands of the unions, and we admit that these have within them sufficient elements with the capacity for this, as we suppose that likewise the superior organizations – which hopefully will be suppressed as soon as possible – will have the capacity to organize relations among the different industries, etc., in so far as the exchange of raw materials and social necessities are concerned...[42]

We have no indication whether Peiró and other CNT leaders associated with him raised any serious objections to the adoption of the Zaragoza Congress resolution. However, Eduardo Comín Colomer says that, together with two maximalists, Juan García Oliver and Federica Montseny, Juan López, a possibilist and CNT leader from Valencia, was one of those sponsoring the resolution.[43]

Within about two months of the Zaragoza congress, the anarchist transformation of Spanish society was to be converted from a theoretical proposal into a practical possibility, at least in certain parts of Republican Spain. The CNT in Catalonia, where in the days following the suppression of the military uprising there, power was almost completely in the hands of the anarchists, held a regional plenum which debated whether to go ahead and establish libertarian communism. The plenum decided overwhelmingly against doing so, in the face of the need for cooperation with a wide range of other groups in the military struggle against the France forces.

Only in that part of the Aragón region, which was largely recaptured from the rebellious army by anarchist militiamen from Catalonia, was anything approaching libertarian communism actually installed during the first year of the Civil War. Anarchist rural communes there were brought together under the Council of Aragón, which corresponded more or less to the pattern established in the Zaragoza resolution.

3

The Spanish Libertarian Movement

The political current in Spain that espoused the ideas of anarchism and anarcho-syndicalism consisted of several different organizations before and during the Civil War. These groups played their own peculiar roles, had more or less varying ideologies, and enjoyed different degrees of popular support both before and after July 18–19 1936.

The mass organization of Spanish anarchism was the Confederación Nacional del Trabajo (CNT). It was the oldest part of the movement, and was a trade union organization, with particular strength in Catalonia, one of the two major centers of Spanish industry, but with a following also among the peasants and agricultural laborers of Andalusia, Murcia and Extramadura, as well as among the industrial workers and peasants of Aragón, Asturias, the Levante, and several other parts of Spain. After the establishment of the second Republic in April 1931, it grew particularly rapidly in the center, that is, Madrid and New Castille, which had been a major center of Socialist strength.

The second oldest element in Spanish anarchism was the Federación Anarquista Ibérica (FAI). As its name indicates, it was an anarchist ideological group. It would have rejected the definition 'political', although that is in fact the correct categorization of the organization. During the Civil War, the FAI, in fact, adopted the form of organization of a political party, and perhaps had the conflict turned out differently, they would have ended up as an anarchist political party, however incongruent that idea might at first appear.

The third part of the Spanish Libertarian Movement was the Juventudes Libertarias (JJLL), the youth organization. It was recognized during the Civil War as an official part of the Movimiento Libertario (Libertarian Movement), and played an important role, particularly in trying to provide an alternative to the Communist-controlled Juventud Socialista Unida (JSU) in the ranks of youth in Loyalist Spain.

Fourth, there was the Mujeres Libres. This was an organization established after the beginning of the Civil War, and sought to rally the women of Spain for the anarchist movement and the defense of the Revolution and the Loyalist cause. Unlike the other three anarchist groups, the Mujeres Libres was never fully recognized as a constituent part of the Libertarian Movement.

Fifth, there was the Solidaridad Internacional Antifascista, also established after the War began, as a service and propaganda group for the movement as a whole.

Finally, there were many local groups which were an integral part of the Libertarian Movement, but were not organized on a national or even regional basis. These included a large number of *ateneos*, local groups which were centers principally of adult education, but also featured debates and discussions of interest and concern to the anarchist movement. These had been features of the movement virtually from its inception. There were also local cooperatives and mutual benefit societies in which the anarchists participated.

Before proceeding with a discussion of the libertarian revolution which took place in much of Spain at the outset of the Civil War, and of the fate of that revolution subsequently, it is important to have at least some understanding of the nature and trajectory of the groups which made up the Libertarian Movement. The rest of this chapter will deal with that subject.

Nineteenth-Century Spanish Anarchism

The origins of the Spanish labor movement go back at least to the

1830s and 1840s. The country's first general strike took place in May–June 1855 in Barcelona, in response to the civil governor's ban on strikes and lockouts, thus beginning a long history of antipathy between the labor movement of Catalonia and the region's civil and military authorities.[1]

The formal introduction of anarcho-syndicalist ideas into Spain is generally attributed to Giuseppe Fanelli, sent to the peninsula in 1868 by Michael Bakunin, already engaged in his struggle in the First International with Karl Marx. More or less directly as a result of Fanelli's efforts, there was established in Madrid the Committee of the International Workingmen's Association, among whose founders was Anselmo Lorenzo, who was to become one of the major spokesmen and theoreticians of Spanish anarchism. This organization ultimately became the Federación Obrera Regional Española (FORE), and affiliated with the Bakuninist faction of the First International.[2]

The Federación Obrera Regional Española was relatively short-lived. It held two conferences in 1872. At the second one, in December, there were reportedly 849 local groups represented.[3] Five years later, it was reported that there were ten regional federations in the FORE, with 73 local federations.[4] According to Gaston Leval, the Spanish section was, by 1871–72, 'the best organized of all of the sections of the First International'.[5]

During the First Republic, which lasted from February 1873 to January 1874, the FORE reached the apogee of its influence. By the end of 1873 it is estimated to have had between 50–60,000 dues-paying members, and perhaps as many as 300,000 who considered that they belonged to the organization even though they were not regular dues payers.[6]

The anarcho-syndicalists were participants in the series of *cantonal* uprisings which took place during the short life of the First Republic. These were seizures of control of villages, towns and cities in various parts of the country by groups of workers and peasants, who organized local revolutionary juntas and proceeded to confiscate the belongings of the clergy, tax the rich, and even distribute land among the landless agricultural workers. These revolts had all been suppressed by the fall of the First Republic.[7]

With the re-establishment of the Bourbon monarchy under Alfonso XII in 1874, the FORE was driven deeply underground and largely dispersed. It suffered severe persecution not only from the government, but also from extraofficial organizations, the most famous of which was known as the Black Hand.[8]

It was not until 1880 that the movement revived as the Federación de Trabajadores de la Región Española (FTRE). It held two more congresses, in Barcelona in 1881, and Seville in 1882.[9] At the 1881 meeting there were reportedly 140 delegates present of whom 110 voted for 'anarchism as their ideal'.[10] The largest number of groups represented were in Andalusia, with somewhat smaller numbers in Catalonia, and considerably fewer in Valencia.[11]

The revival of the movement in the 1880s was marked by bitter struggles between the collectivists, based in Catalonia, who were trade unionists and followers of Bakunin, and the anarcho-communists, particularly strong among the illiterate peasants of Andalusia, who looked for inspiration to the ideas of Kropotkin and the Italian anarchist Malatesta, who visited Spain in 1892. The former believed in building a strong labor movement, both as a revolutionary instrument to seize power through a general strike, and as a basis for the organization of the post-revolutionary society. The latter favored spontaneous insurrections whenever the opportunity presented itself and the resort to personal terrorism against representatives of authority. The struggle between these two groups was largely responsible for the final dissolution of the FTRE at its congress in Valencia in October 1888.[12] The two tendencies within Spanish anarchism which appeared in the 1880s persisted in modified forms for the next half century.

Juan Gómez Casas has sketched the evolution of Spanish anarchism during the two decades before the establishment of the Confederación Nacional del Trabajo. 'After a period of dispersion, the Workers Federation of the Spanish Region disappeared, to be replaced by the Anarchist Organization of the Spanish Region... This organization then changed, in 1890, into the Solidarity and Assistance Pact, which was itself dissolved in 1896 because of repressive legislation against anarchism and broke into many nuclei and autonomous workers' societies... The scattered remains of the

FRE gave rise to Solidaridad Obrera in Catalonia in 1907, the immediate antecedent of the Confederación Nacional del Trabajo.'[13]

One other major event was to occur before the emergence of the Confederación Nacional del Trabajo (CNT). This was the *semana tragica* (tragic week) late in July 1909. This was a period of demonstrations and rioting in Barcelona provoked by calling of conscripts to the colors to fight in the endless war in Morocco.[14] The rioting was blamed by the government on the city's anarchist elements. Several months after it ended, Francisco Ferrer Guardia, one of the most important intellectuals associated with the anarchist movement, and founder of a series of modern schools in various parts of Catalonia, was executed by the authorities, as being responsible for the *semana tragica*.[15]

The Founding of the Confederación Nacional del Trabajo

The mass organization of the Spanish Libertarian Movement, the Confederación Nacional del Trabajo (CNT), was established at a congress in Barcelona, October 30–November 1 1910. The meeting was summoned by Solidaridad Obrera, the Catalan labor organization which had been founded a few years before, and was both the second congress of Solidaridad Obrera and the founding congress of the CNT. Among those who played a major role in planning the meeting was the old anarchist unionist, Anselmo Lorenzo, although he did not actually participate in its sessions, except through a letter of greeting which he sent.[16]

There were delegates present not only from various parts of Catalonia, but also from Zaragoza, Gijón (Asturias), Valencia, Alcoy, Murcia, Málaga, Seville, Algeciras, Palma de Mallorca, and La Coruña (Galicia), among others. Adolfo Bueso gives the names and affiliations of 96 delegates.[17] Only three represented rural workers' organizations.[18]

After considerable discussion, it was decided to establish a new national labor organization, and after further debate, it was agreed to call it the Confederación Nacional del Trabajo. Neither decision was unanimous; there were delegates belonging to the Socialist Party who argued that a new national central labor body was not needed in view of the existence of the Socialists' Unión General de Trabajadores (UGT), and urged Solidaridad Obrera to join the UGT as its Catalan affiliate.[19] But the vote in favor of establishing the new group was 84 in favor, 14 against, and three abstaining. Similarly, there were some delegates who thought that the new group should be called a 'federation', rather than a 'confederation', although a consensus seems to have finally been reached about the new organization's name.[20]

The founding congress of the CNT supported the craft union as the most favored form of organization. However, it did go on record as supporting the establishment of national federations of such groups.[21]

The anti-intellectual bias of many of the workingmen who were the delegates to the founding congress of the CNT was shown by a resolution which was introduced, proclaiming that 'only the manual workers are really interested in the abolition of all privileges, all exploitation and all forms of oppression', and could belong to the organization. However, that resolution was not approved by the delegates.[22]

A special resolution was passed dealing with women workers. It opposed women being forced to do work 'superior to their physical powers', but strongly supported the idea of women joining the labor force, and urged a special effort to recruit them into the CNT. During the discussion of this motion, several delegates denounced the exploitation of wives by their husbands.[23]

There was an extended discussion of the efficacy of the general strike. A resolution was passed proclaiming that a general strike should be 'essentially revolutionary', and ought to be carried out on a national basis. However, there was also a proviso recognizing that in certain circumstances the workers might be forced to declare a general strike on a local or regional basis with objectives short of total revolution.

Finally, the founding congress agreed that the CNT should have two basic functions. One should be the immediate improvement of the economic situation of its members, the other the longer-term objective of 'revolutionary expropriation of the bourgeoisie'.[24]

Throughout the discussions of the meeting it was emphasized that the new Confederación should be federalist in its form of organization, with each constituent organization maintaining a high degree of autonomy. This principle was adhered to generally until the Civil War when, under the dire pressures of the latter part of the conflict, the principle of federalism came to be honored more in the breach than in practice.

The one postulate of the 1910 congress which the CNT subsequently changed was its commitment to craft unionism. At its national Confederance in Sans in June 1918, the organization went on record in favor of industrial unionism, with skilled and unskilled workers belonging to the same base organization, the *sindicato unico*, although within that group, each craft should have as wide a degree of autonomy as circumstances permitted.[25]

History of CNT Before the Civil War

The history of the CNT between its founding in 1910 and the outbreak of the Civil War in July 1936 was a stormy one. From its inception, it was the predominant labor group in Catalonia and Aragón. It also developed considerable influence in the Levante area centering on Valencia. In the early years, it was very active among the peasants, particularly in the southern part of the country, although Robert Kern has argued that it did not pay as great attention to the Andalusian and other peasant groups during the Second Republic (1931–6) as it had done during and just after the First World War.[26]

The relations between the CNT and the Socialists' UGT were generally very competitive and antithetical. Although the two organizations cooperated in general strikes in 1916 and 1917, and subsequently there were many cases of local cooperation between the two union groups (particularly in Asturias), latent or blatant hostility was more often the case. Relations were particularly bad during the Primo de Rivera dictatorship of 1922–30, when the UGT cooperated with the dictator and the CNT was particularly severely persecuted; and during the first two and a half years of the Second Republic, when the CNTers felt that Francisco Largo Caballero, head of the UGT, was exploiting his position as minister of labor to favor his own organization.

José Peirats has noted that the Asturian delegation to the 1919 CNT Congress 'fought an epic battle' for unity between the CNT and the UGT.[27] However, the Asturians failed there, and during the years following there was little sentiment in the anarchist labor group for unity with the Socialist rival. Only in the Zaragoza Congress of the CNT in May 1936, two months before the Civil War began, was there a call for 'unity of action' with the UGT.[28]

The CNT grew, in spite of considerable government persecution, during the First World War. However, in the immediate post-war years it was subjected to particularly brutal persecution. This came not only at the hands of succeeding civil and military governors of Catalonia, but also from employers groups, with the support of the Church and governmental authorities. 'Free' unions were organized by these forces as supposed rivals to the CNT, and employers' groups employed substantial numbers of gangsters to assassinate leaders and rank and file members of the anarcho-syndicalist labor group. José Peirats has argued that these free unions had their roots in the very conservative Carlist movement, which at an earlier time had had considerable support in Catalonia, particularly in the rural areas.[29]

The most important anarchist figure to be murdered by the employers' *pistoleros* was Salvador Seguí, a major leader of the more moderate faction of the CNT. His colleague Angel Pestaña was also severely wounded. Scores, if not hundreds, of lesser figures were assassinated by the professional killers. During this period, the CNT and those associated with it met violence with violence; their most famous victim was Prime Minister Eduardo Dato.

Manuel Buenacasa, one of the principal Catalan anarchist leaders of the period, described the CNTers' situation in the immediate post First World War years. He wrote: 'The best of our cadres are faced with this dilemma: to kill or be killed, to flee or to wind up in prison. The violent ones defend themselves and kill; the stoics die, as do the brave, who are assassinated in betrayal; the cowards or prudent flee and escape; the most active who don't worry about what will happen to them waste away in jail.[30]

75

With the advent of the Primo de Rivera dictatorship late in 1923, the CNT was virtually obliterated as a national organization. Many leaders were forced into exile or underground, its press was largely closed down, it could not maintain any open headquarters.

At one point, when the national committee headed by Angel Pestaña resigned as the result of an internal dispute with a faction led by Juan Peiró, the committee formally proclaimed the dissolution of the organization. However, in fact, a simulacrum of national leadership was maintained until the political situation turned for the better in 1929–30.[31]

For at least part of this time, the headquarters of the CNT was established outside of Catalonia, where persecution of the anarchists was most intense. For instance, in 1925 a new national committee, headed by Avelino González Mallada, and made up mainly of people from Asturias, was set up in Gijón.[32]

However, during the Primo de Rivera regime one very important event for the future of the CNT had taken place. This was the bringing together of the dispersed groups of anarchists at a conference in Valencia in July 1927, to form the Federación Anarquista Ibérica (FAI). The principal center of attention and action of the FAI came to be the unions of the CNT, and FAI influence during the first years of the republic proved to be very disruptive of the Confederación.

With the forced resignation of General Primo de Rivera in January 1930, it became possible to reorganize the rank and file organizations of the Confederación Nacional del Trabajo, to re-establish its press, and to begin to open legal headquarters. This was particularly the case immediately following the proclamation of the Second Republic in April 1931.

Although the anarchists widely voted for Left candidates, in Catalonia, particularly for those of the Catalan Left Party, apparently, in the elections for a constituent assembly held soon after the proclamation of the Republic, relations between the CNT and the Republic rapidly degenerated. Under FAIista leadership, portions of the CNT attempted three revolutionary general strikes and uprisings in 1932–3, and libertarian communism was proclaimed in a number of localities for short periods of time.

Within the CNT itself, FAI influence brought about a split. On September 1 1931, 30 moderate CNT leaders (*los Treintistas*) protested against the FAI tendency to promote 'simplistic revolution', and denounced the growing influence of the FAI within the CNT itself. Among the signers were Angel Pestaña, Juan Peiró and Juan López, the principal CNT leader in the Valencia region.[33] In the months that followed, unions supporting the Treintistas were either thrown out of or withdrew from the CNT. They formed the Sindicatos de Oposición. This split was not healed until two months before the outbreak of the Civil War.[34]

Frank Mintz summed up the relative importance of the FAI-dominated CNT and the opposition *sindicatos* thus:

> Provinces where the CNT was majority: Coruña and Pontevedra in Galicia; Seville, Cádiz, Málaga and Almería in Andalusia, Murcia in Levante; Gerona, Barcelona and Tarragona in Catalonia; Huesca and Zaragoza in Aragón. There were centers of important minorities in Asturias; in New Castille in Madrid; in Old Castille in Logroño; in the Basque Country in Alava; in Catalonia in Lérida; in Aragón at Teruel; in the Levante at Castellón, Valencia, Albacete and Alicante; in Huelva in Andalusia, Cordoba and Grenada. There was no or little anarchist influence in Lugo and Orense in Galicia; in Jaén in Andalusia; in the provinces of León, Extremadura, Old Castille (except Logroño), New Castille (except Madrid), and the Basque area (except Alava). Treintism was widespread in Huelva, in the Levante (Valencia and Alicante) and in Catalonia (metallurgical workers of Barcelona).[35]

In spite of considerable persecution at the hands of successive republican governments, the CNT expanded rapidly during the Second Republic. For the first time, it even began to have serious influence in the trade union movement of Madrid, which has always been a major stronghold of the Socialists' UGT.

In the election of November 1933, the CNT and FAI both strongly urged their followers to abstain. This was undoubtedly a major factor in the victory of the Right in that election. Subsequently, when the Socialists and Catalan Nationalists attempted a national general strike and uprising against the entry of the far-Right (CEDA) party into the government, the CNTers did not participate in this movement, except in Asturias, where their relations with the UGT were closest and the revolt lasted the longest, being put down there only by Moorish and Foreign Legion troops, among whose commanders was General López de Ochoa.

When elections were once again held in February 1936, both the CNT and FAI refused to mount campaigns for abstention from the polls, as a result of which the Left, now organized in the Popular Front, once again won.[36] The overriding issue in that election was support of an amnesty for all the political and trade union prisoners jailed since the advent of the Rightist government, many of whom were members of the CNT and/or the FAI.

The last important event in the history of the CNT in the period before the outbreak of the Civil War was its congress in Zaragoza in May 1936. This not only reunited the CNT and Sindicatos de Oposición, but also drew up a detailed description of the kind of libertarian society that the CNT sought to create, some of the details of which we have noted.[37]

Structure and Functioning of the CNT

By the outbreak of the Civil War, the Confederación Nacional del Trabajo had a well-established structure. At its base was the local *sindicato unico* or industrial union group, or in rural areas, the *sindicato de oficios varios* (union of various trades). The *sindicatos* in the larger towns and cities formed a local federation. Above it was a provincial committee, and the country was divided into seven regions, each of which had a regional committee. Finally, there was the national committee, consisting of a full-time national secretary and a part-time assistant secretary and members representing each of the seven regions.

On each level of the organization there was a representative body. In the *sindicato unico* or *sindicato de oficios varios* this was the general assembly, made up of all members in good standing. On each level above this there would meet from time to time congresses, to which each *sindicato unico* within the local, provincial, regional or national organization was entitled to representation, In addition, there were *plenos*, or plenums, on the several levels, which were smaller meetings which met more frequently than congresses, and in which local *sindicatos unicos* were represented indirectly rather than directly. National plenums met at least once every three months.[38]

Finally, there were national federations of industry. The establishment of these organizations, grouping together all of the *sindicatos unicos* in a particular industry, had been rejected by the CNT in 1918, but was accepted by its Congress of 1931, the first held after the establishment of the Republic.[38] Robert Kern has noted that their 'tasks included forming wage policies for various industries, general strike planning, studying working conditions, negotiating with employers on an industry-wide basis, and making general socio-economic studies.'[40]

In spite of the decision by the 1931 Congress of the CNT favorable to the establishment of national industrial unions, the group which controlled the organization during most of the period from then until the outbreak of the Civil War was not, in fact, in favor of such organizations. The upshot was that only a handful of national industrial federations had been set up before the War began. This fact was to present a major handicap to the anarchists in their efforts to reorganize the national economy along anarcho-syndicalist lines during the conflict.

As anarchists, the Spanish libertarians rejected the idea of authority even within their own organizations. This had been made clear as early as 1882 in the Seville congress of the Spanish regional federation of the International Workingmen's Association, one of the predecessors of the CNT. In a manifesto, that congress declared that the federation's federal commission,

> ... is not a power or an authority which is imposed on our organization; it has no means or regulatory faculties for that; it is simply a center of statistics, an office of communications among the organizations ... with its own purely administrative functions, limited and determined by our Statutes. It is not a

government, nor is it a directive force which we, as anarchists, could not permit in our midst ...

Neither in the Section Committees, nor in the Local Federations and Union of Similar Trades Councils, nor in our Assemblies and Congress are permanent presidencies known or used. We are not partisans of such authorities. When we meet in deliberative assemblies ... we authorize a comrade to direct the discussion within the limited rules agreed to among ourselves ... in which role he ceases as soon as, in fulfillment of his duty, he has adjourned the session.[41]

Until the outbreak of the Civil War, the Confederación Nacional del Trabajo and its affiliated groups operated in much the same manner as had been described in 1882. With their rejection of authority, the CNT insisted before the Civil War on the autonomy of each constituent part of the organization to behave as it wished to. José Peirats has noted: 'The almost unlimited autonomy which the *sindicatos* enjoyed to declare conflicts difficult to solve, which presented problems of obligatory solidarity as a *fait accompli*, greatly undermined the prestige of the organization with the defeats which such vehemence and lack of forethought provoked.'[42]

The manner in which the CNT conducted its meetings, particularly its congresses and plenums reflected this anarchist rejection of authority. Although I was too young to ever have attended any such sessions in pre-1939 Spain, I did have an opportunity to attend a congress of the hard faction of the exiled CNT, held in Limoges, France, in August 1960. Excerpts from my notes on that meeting may serve to give the flavor of such CNT proceedings, whether in exile or in Spain itself in earlier times:

The emphasis was on 'democracy' in the extreme. Debate was never cut off, so long as there was a delegate who wanted to talk about the matter at hand, the floor was open to him or her – there were perhaps half a dozen women delegates. The surprising thing about this was the lack of long speeches. Very few took advantage of the situation to speak at great length, and most of those who did, had something to say.

The emphasis was also on anonymity. A delegate was almost never referred to by name, but rather as 'the delegation from such and such a place'. Once, one delegate made personal reference to Federica Montseny, and there was a chorus of shouts that 'There is no Montseny!' and 'The delegation from—!' Also, in choosing officers for the various sessions, it was the delegation which was proposed, not the individual in the delegation.

All delegates seem to have come instructed on the various points on the agenda. The procedure is for the agenda to be drawn up by the secretary-general asking each local group for its suggestions. Everything thus suggested is supposed to be included in the agenda, which is sent out to the local groups with considerable anticipation, so that they can decide their positions on the various items to be discussed...

Associated with the passion for anonymity was the lack of applause. Although there were some very fierce battles, only once was there applause, when one delegate suggested that there was a great deal of time being wasted – which was eminently true. Shortly afterwards, when that particular session ended, one delegate got up and asked the rhetorical question whether there had ever before in the history of CNT congresses been applause. There was a unanimous shout of 'No!'...

A few words on how the meeting was conducted. All those delegations who wanted to speak on a given issue were asked to give their names. The various delegations then spoke in the order listed – but this didn't prevent others from asking for the floor later on, if they wanted to do so. When nominations for committees, and for the presiding officers of a session were taken, they first asked for the names of all those delegations who wanted to nominate another delegation. When there were no more of these, each delegation was asked whom it wished to nominate. Then acceptances and declinations were asked for. Several times there were so many declinations that the process had to be done over again. Once, to end an impasse, one delegation nominated itself, since it was willing to accept...[43]

The Anarchist Grupos de Afinidad

Since long before the foundation of the CNT there had existed *grupos especificos* or *grupos de afinidad* among the Spanish anarchists. These were more or less small groups of activists, usually made up of friends who agreed not only in their adherence to anarchist ideas, but also on strategy and tactics, and who did not necessarily live in the same area.

The *grupos de afinidad* (or *grupitos*) first appeared in the 1880s, when they were among the strongest proponents of the anarchist communist ideological trend in Spanish anarchism. George Esenwein has said of these early organizations:

> The *grupitos* themselves consisted of nothing more than a small circle of ardent radicals, numbering between five and ten members. Their activities were organized around the *tertulia*, which usually met at one of the numerous cafés found in every working-class neighborhood. There the workers belonging to a *grupito* met to debate politics, to hear the latest news – which was especially significant for those who were illiterate – or to plan their next act of reprisal against the bourgeoisie ... Patently rejecting the collectivist heritage of the FRE and FTRE, when a formal bond of union existed among the respective federations, the anarchist communists argued that it was enough for each group to decide for itself what to do ... they gave primacy to violent revolutionary acts, believing that their most urgent task was to bring down the capitalist system.[44]

After the formation of the Confederación Nacional del Trabajo, the *grupos de afinidad* had no organic connection with the CNT. However, the more important members of the affinity groups usually worked within the unions affiliated with the CNT.

The *grupos de afinidad* had a rather different interpretation of direct action than did the CNT. For them it meant not only barring the State from having any role in labor-management relations, but also the calculated use of violence. This might take many forms, from robbing banks to finance revolutionary and even trade union activities, to assassinations of particularly oppressive employers or public or Church officials deemed to be aligned with reaction, to attempts at armed revolt to establish, it was hoped throughout the nation, but at least for a time in some locality or other) libertarian communism.

The most famous of these *grupos de afinidad* in the pre-Civil War period was known as Los Solidarios, formed in the early 1920s by, among others, Francisco Ascaso, Buenaventura Durruti, Juan García Oliver, Miguel García Vivancos, Alfonso Miguel, Ricardo Sanz and Aurelio Hernández. They took part in the violence and counter-violence preceding the establishment of the Primo de Rivera dictator-ship. However, that regime forced Los Solidarios to disperse. Most of them went into exile, and Ascaso and Durruti spent considerable time not only in France and Belgium, but also in several parts of Latin America. Ricardo Sanz was virtually the only figure in the group who was able to stay in Barcelona.

The Los Solidarios group did not immediately join the Federación Anarquista Iberica when it was founded. They regarded the FAI's most prominent leaders, Diego Abad de Santillán (pseudonym of Sinesio García Fernández), Federica Montseny and Fidel Miró as radicalized liberals. However, when, after the fall of the Primo de Rivera dictatorship it again became possible to hold public meetings, they did appear on platforms with the FAI leaders. Finally, in 1933, finding that another newer *grupo de afinidad* had appropriated their name, they renamed their group Nosotros, and joined the FAI.

Members of the Los Solidarios–Nosotros group gained Robin Hood-like reputations in the decade and a half before the outbreak of the Civil War. In the early 1920s, their most famous operations had been a robbery of a courier of the Banco de Bilbao, which netted 300,000 pesetas, and the assassination of the Cardinal Archbishop of Zaragoza Juan Soldevilla Romero, a particularly reactionary mem-ber of the Church hierarchy. Buenaventura Durruti was involved in both of these events.

With the end of the Primo de Rivera dictatorship, followed soon afterward by the establishment of the Second Republic, the Nosotros group no longer engaged in personal violence. Rather, they were at the center of various attempted anarchist insurrections, particularly between 1932 and 1933. Their line at the time was, according to Juan García Oliver, that these were 'revolutionary high schools', and that even if any particular insurrection didn't succeed, it gave its participants, and the anarcho-syndicalist movement in general, valuable experience for the ultimate insurrection which would succeed.[45] José Peirats has described the Nosotros group as representing 'revolutionary romanticism'.[46]

The association of the Nosotros Group with the FAI was by no means complete. Gómez Casas has noted that the Nosotros Group 'was never active in the FAI, preferring to participate in the conspiratorial activities of the CNT, together with other defense groups'.[47] Later on, he noted, in relation to the January 1933 anarchist uprising.

> The central force for this revolutionary attempt was the Nosotros Group, according to Juan Manuel Molina and Abad de Santillán. It would be more appropriate, however, to credit the anarchist sector of the CNT, which identified itself with the FAI at times and sometimes acted as a sort of super-FAI. Peirats tells us that he represented the local federation of the FAI in Barcelona at that time, and that Molina served as secretary of the Peninsular Committee; 'When I tell you that there was another FAI above the organization we represented officially, I am referring to Ascaso, Durruti, and, especially García Oliver, the real Robespierre of the Revolution...[48]

Some anarchist leaders were very critical of the *grupos de afinidad*. Among these was Juan Peiró, several times national secretary of the CNT, and for a period in 1936–7 an anarchist minister in the government of Francisco Largo Caballero.

Peiró wrote that ideally these groups should be 'a place of study. The most outstanding ethical, economic, political and social problems must be dealt with and put on the table for analysis, to develop profound knowledge of what is being analyzed and from that to reach as real and exact a judgment as possible, so that the result of the study can be beneficial for the cause of human emancipation as possible.'[49]

However, in the judgment of Peiró, the anarchist affinity groups did not fulfill what should have been their role:

> Generally speaking, one can say that the specific groups of our time ... have been more secret revolutionary clubs than classrooms for the cultivation of knowledge. We would say that they have no attributes of a class room, but have great narrowness and puerility ... the contemporary anarchist groups are nothing more than exponents of solemn ingenuousness which resolve nothing and can resolve nothing. Without denying the good intentions and abnegation of the members of these organizations, it is necessary to say that most of them are ignorant of the general ideas of Anarchism and of the mission of the anarchists...[50]

Several efforts to bring together the specific anarchist groups on a regional or national basis were made before the establishment of the Federación Anarquista Iberica. National anarchist conferences were held in Barcelona in 1918, and in Zaragoza in 1921.[51] Finally, in April 1923 a National Federation of Anarchist Groups was formed.[52] Abroad, a Federation of Spanish Language Anarchist Groups was established in France in June 1925. In Catalonia, a Regional Committee of Anarchist Groups, and a plenum of that group laid the basis for the founding congress of the FAI.[53]

The Federación Anarquista Iberica

Most of the scattered anarchist *grupos de afinidad* were brought together in the Federación Anarquista Iberica (FAI) in 1927. There were reportedly some 50 delegates (including two from Portugal) present at the conference near Valencia which established the organization.

Robert Kern has noted of this founding meeting: 'No exiles attended the conference. As a result, most of the delegates were relatively unknown villagers from Aragón, Valencia and Catalonia. The more intellectual, urban and volatile anarchists remained in exile, jail, or hiding. This made the FAI, at the very beginning, an organization with surprisingly deep roots in local society.'[54]

Juan Gómez Casas has noted the groups which were represented at the Valencia conference. There were delegates from groups in the Levante, Andalusia, Catalonia, Alicante, the Portuguese Anarchist Union, as well as regional organizations of the CNT in Catalonia and the Levante. The National Federation of Anarchist Group's liaison secretariat was also represented.[55]

The base organizations of the FAI continued to be *grupos de afinidad*. However, until the fall of Primo de Rivera it, like its affiliates, remained deeply underground. Thereafter, with the revival of the CNT, in which the FAIistas became very active, the FAI began to grow, and also to change.

Between the end of the Primo de Rivera dictatorship and the outbreak of the Civil War, the FAI held only two national meetings. These were the plenum of October 1933 and that of January–February 1936. The latter was particularly notable because of its prediction of a military insurrection, and its indications to the FAI and CNT membership of how to deal with such an eventuality.[56] The CNT adopted a similar resolution on the day of the February 1936 election.[57]

Concerning the size of the FAI in the pre-1936 period, Gerald Brenan has noted: 'As the FAI was a secret organization, no figures of its strength have been published. One may assume however, that from 1934 to 1936 its membership lay round about 10,000.'[58] José Peirats, on the other hand, estimated the FAI membership at the outbreak of the War at 30,000.[59] However, Juan Gómez Casas has concluded that there were less than 5,000 members of the FAI in February 1936.[60]

The nature of the leadership of the FAI changed after 1930. Journalists, such as Federica Montseny and Diego Abad de Santillán, and CNT trade union activists, such as the members of the Nosotros group had become, became its principal figures. As we have noted earlier, the FAI soon gained predominant influence in the CNT. Although FAIistas participated in the 1931 CNT Congress as delegates with only informative status, their influence led to a split late in 1931, with the dissident Sindicatos de Oposición only returning to the CNT fold in May 1936.

In 1930, Juan Manuel Molina returned from exile to become the secretary of the Peninsular-Committee of the FAI, and remained in that post for several years.[61] Then, in 1935 the Nervio Group in Barcelona was designated to be the Peninsular Committee. It included Diego Abad de Santillán, Pedro Herrera, Ildefonso González, Germinal de Souza, Fidel Miró, and several others. Juan Molina then became editor of the FAI newspaper *Tierra y Libertad*.[62]

With the outbreak of the Civil War, any differences in outlook which might have existed between the leaders of the CNT and those of the FAI were not apparent, at least for the first year of the conflict. Posters, graffiti and banners emblazoned 'CNT–FAI' were seen everywhere in Loyalist Spain. However, the existence of the FAI served to provide the anarcho-syndicalists with double representation, in the name of the CNT and the FAI, whether in the Central Milita Council or the government of Catalonia, or in the numerous other official and semi-official bodies which were formed during the first months of the War.

Juan Gómez Casas has noted the apparent identity between the CNT and FAI in this period: '...the people turned the combined name CNT–FAI into a myth. For a long time they were regarded as merely two aspects of one indissoluble reality ... This identification of the two organizations with each other led to a dissolution of their differences...'[63]

José Peirats has written that right after July 19, the Peninsular Committee of the FAI was reorganized, 'reinforcing it with distinguished militants'.[64]

Certainly during the first months of the Civil War, the membership in the FAI increased dramatically. In its Circular No. 3, issued on October 25 1936, the Peninsular Committee of the FAI noted that because of its role in directing the economy, 'the *sindicatos*, converted into hybrid organisms from the political point of view ... cannot impose on their activities more than that professional function which is assigned them. And it is therefore necessary that there exist the motor producing the quantity of fabulous energy needed to move therm ... This motor can be no other than the specific organization, that is, the FAI. Therefore, the FAI had to grow rapidly.' The circular said: 'We must seek out the comrades with capacity of living in anonymity ... The trade union organization can be an inexhaustible quarry for militants...'[65]

The *Tierra y Libertad* boasted in its issue of July 17 1937: 'Our specific organization has more than 164,000 members ... In the FAI a member is not just another number, because each one of its members is an anarchist, which is to say, a militant.'[66]

However, after the fall of the government of Francisco Largo Caballero, with its four CNT–FAI ministers, the situation of the FAI as a partner of the CNT in public and semi-public bodies seemed to be in danger. This danger served to provoke a fundamental change in the structure and organization of the FAI.

José Peirats has noted: 'Minister [Manuel] Irujo, in eliminating it from the Popular Tribunals, was the first to underscore the juridical irregularity which the FAI represented as an organization not subject to law but participating nonetheless in State organisms.' As Peirats observed, the Marxist parties also had double representation through the UGT trade unions. But, 'the presence of the FAI alongside the CNT was rather a matter of fact, first imposed and then tolerated. But as events developed, if the criterion of the Minister of Justice, which was undoubtedly the criterion of the Government, prospered, the FAI might from one moment to the next be vetoed in representative organizations and declared a "clandestine" or non-existent organization.'[67]

Even several months before Manuel Irujo's move against the FAI, the federation had begun to feel the need to change its form of organization. Circular No. 3 of the organization, in dealing with the rapid growth of the FAI after July 19, cautioned that the *grupos de afinidad* type of structure left it susceptible to being infiltrated by undesirable elements, and suggested that, 'We must renovate the present forms of our organization.'[68]

After the fall of the Largo Caballero government, this change in the structural nature of the FAI could not be postponed. Peirats commented: 'The circumstances therefore impelled the FAI, making it willing either to accept with all its consequences, its transformation into a species of political party, or to prepare to abandon part of the positions acquired because of its revolutionary merit.[69]

The decision was taken at a plenum of the FAI in Valencia from July 4–7 1937. The major resolution adopted there noted: 'The *grupo de afinidad* has been during more than fifty years, the most efficient organ of propaganda, of anarchist interrelations and practice. With the new organization adopted by the FAI the organic mission of the *grupo de afinidad* will be annuled.'[70] This resolution constituted the statutes of the reorganized FAI. César Lorenzo has said emphatically that until then the FAI had never had formal statutes.[71]

The resolution set forth an organizational structure starting with a base group in a small population center or a city ward; local federations of these base groups, provincial federations 'so long as the present political divisions persist', regional federations, and finally Federación Anarquista Iberica, 'to which belong all the geographically natural regions of the Iberian Peninsula'.

Each local group was instructed to set up a membership committee, new applicants for membership had to be vouched for by two existing members and time should be taken to ascertain the political reliability of the applicants. Meanwhile, all those who belonged to the FAI at the time of the July Pleno were declared to be in good standing, and all those who 'acted as militants of trade union etc. organizations related to anarchism' before July 1936 could become so on application. Any other applicants for membership would have to wait six months after joining before they could hold posts in the FAI or by its nomination.[72]

This reorganization of the FAI was not adopted without controversy within its ranks, particularly in Catalonia. One of those who most strongly opposed this was José Peirats, leader of the Juventudes Libertarias in Lérida, and also a member of the FAI. After the change was adopted, Peirats dropped out of further activity in the FAI.[73]

Although both the Barcelona and Catalan plenos of the FAI following the Valencia meeting voted in the majority to accept the reorganization, the Catalan Pleno, in early August (when faced with a schism over the issue) agreed to allow those *grupos de afinidad* which wanted to do so to stay in existence, but with the proviso that for purposes of representation in *plenos* and congresses they should have only the proportion of the total which their own membership represented.[74]

After the overthrow of the Largo Caballero government, relations between the FAI and the CNT began to diverge. As we shall trace in another part of this work, the FAI became increasingly critical of the government of Juan Negrín, and particularly of the growing tendency of the CNT leadership to collaborate with that regime and in so doing to compromise with the principles on which it was based.

Perhaps because it had long been a secret organization, and also because it was clearly a political group, the FAI was, during the Civil War and afterwards, a favorite target of the enemies of the libertarian movement, particularly the Stalinists. Whereas, the Communists might hesitate openly to attack the CNT, which was, after all, a trade union organization, they felt no such compunctions with regard to the FAI.

Perhaps not untypical were these comments in the more or less official Communist account of the Civil War, published 30 years after the conflict began: 'In that situation it was difficult to impede the emergence of declassed elements, including common criminals, who succeeded in infiltrating the anti-fascist organizations, principally the FAI...[75] 'In Catalonia and Aragón the FAIistas held back the re-establishment of an antifascist order.'[76]

The Juventudes Libertarias (JJLL)

The youth wing of the Spanish libertarian movement was the Federación Ibérica de Juventudes Libertarias (more frequently referred to as the JJLL), established in 1932.[77] In its declaration of principles adopted at the funding congress, it proclaimed: 'This Group will fight against property, the principle of authority, the State, politics and religion.'[78]

Juan García Oliver observed that the JJLL 'were not controlled in their activities by the CNT or the FAI. Rather, the Youth intervened in the life of the trade union and specific organizations with permanent delegates in the regional, national and peninsular committees. The CNT and FAI could not adopt any accord without the delegate of the Youth being informed and in agreement.'[79]

The Juventudes Libertarias, although like the FAI a political rather than a trade-union organization, had a different form of organization from that of the FAI before July 1937. They had more or less large neighborhood groups as their base organizations, in each part of Barcelona and in the other cities where they were organized. The group in Barcelona to which Fidel Miró, the JJLL's principal spokesman during the War, belonged had several hundred members.[80] At the outbreak of the Civil War, the Federación Ibérica de Juventudes Libertarias had an official newspaper which appeared in Madrid, *Juventud Libre*. Subsequently, in October 1936, the Catalan branch began publishing another periodical, *Ruta*.[81]

José Peirats, himself a leader of the JJLL of Catalonia during the Civil War, has written:

> Almost at birth the Libertarian Youth showed two tendencies. Among the young libertarians of Catalonia there predominated the criterion opposed to a national federation. These young people conceived of the Juventudes as affiliates of the *sindicatos* and the anarchist federations. They understood their mission as limited to the tasks of culture and propaganda, training and self-training, thus carrying out what the groups and *sindicatos*, absorbed by the heat of the economic and revolutionary struggle, could not do...
>
> In the anarchist and confederation milieu themselves, the idea of a national federation of this type, with independent organized personality, not only was considered a deviationist danger, but revived the old polemic over the inconvenience of dividing the militants between older people and the youth, a polemic which really brought confrontation between representatives of the older and younger generation, with their jealousies and petulance.[82]

As a consequence of these disagreements, the Catalan youth groups did not join the Federación Ibérica de Juventudes Libertarias until after the beginning of the Civil War. At a congress of the Federación in Barcelona on November 1 1936, there was debated 'the proposal made by the Juventudes Libertarias of Catalonia ... that they join the FIJL', and a resolution was adopted to the effect that 'On the proposal of the FIJL, the congress decides unanimously in favor of the entry of the same, reserving full autonomy for the Catalan Regional group, permitting it to maintain its relations with the FAI.'[83]

The JJLL remained relatively small before the outbreak of the Civil War. However, like all of the other segments of the Libertarian Movement, it grew rapidly once the conflict had begun. Fidel Miró claimed in May 1937 that the organization at that time had 'about 170,000 members'.[84]

The Juventudes Libertarias played an important role both in the Revolution and the Civil War. During the early months of the War they were particularly active in recruiting for the militia columns at a time when the Loyalist forces were made up almost exclusively of volunteers.[85] One of the columns, Los Aguiluchos (The Eaglets), was organized specifically by the Catalan JJLL. In the beginning this unit was commanded by Juan García Oliver but, after a short while, its leadership was turned over to Gregorio Jover, another member of the Nosotros grupo de afinidad.[86]

Both behind the lines and among the anarchist troops, the JJLL carried on an extensive program of propaganda and indoctrination, holding classes, meetings and conferences on a wide variety of subjects. They also carried on an extensive campaign urging 'arms to the front', at a time when very well-armed militarized police groups, for the most part under Communist influence, were being kept in the rearguard, while military units, particularly on the Aragón front, were starved of arms and munitions.

The Juventudes Libertarias played a particularly key role after the collapse of the Aragón front early in 1938, accompanied by heavy bombings of Barcelona. There was panic in Catalonia, and particularly in Barcelona, which spread not only to the government but to the CNT. Leaders began not to come to meetings, went into hiding, began packing their bags. Rank and file citizens sought shelter, particularly in the subway system.

At that point, the Libertarian Youth, without consulting other anarchist groups, put out a manifesto to the population, urging people to go back to their homes and to work, saying that the danger was not as great as the people thought it was, and that in any case, life in the city had to go on. They also organized groups to go into the subway stations to harangue the people to go home. One night they painted the walls and streets of Barcelona with simple slogans, denouncing those who left their jobs as traitors. Finally, they organized flying squads to go to businesses which had shut their doors, forced them to open and told those in charge that if they found them closed the next day, there would be reprisals. These actions did much to re-establish a degree of normality in the Catalan (and then Spanish Republican) capital.[87]

At least two national meetings of the Juventudes Libertarias took place during the War. The first was a national plenum in July 1937. Representatives were present from all regional organizations except those of Extramadura and the North, where the process of the war impeded their attendance. A new peninsular committee of the JJLL was formally installed, headed by Fidel Miró.[88] In fact, Miró had been acting as secretary-general since March 1937, when his predecessor had mysteriously disappeared.[89]

The other national meeting of the JJLL was the second congress, which met in February 1938, with delegations present from the center, south, Levante, Aragón and Catalonia regions, and including people from the various anarchist-controlled military units. There was extensive discussion there of the opposition of a sizeable part of the Catalan youth organization to establishment of a centralized National Libertarian Movement, including the CNT, FAI and JJLL. The congress also chose a new national leadership, headed by Lorenzo Iñigo of Madrid.[90]

The Libertarian Youth played a major role in the May events of 1937, the outbreak of armed opposition to Communist aggression against the anarchists and POUMists, manning most of the barricades raised throughout the city. However, they finally obeyed the directives of CNT and FAI leaders to lay down their arms.[91]

The JJLL formed several alliances with other youth groups during the War. The first of these was a pact with the youth group of the Partido Socialista Unificado de Catalonia in November 1936. It provided for establishment of a liaison committee, 'as the first step to bringing about close collaboration of all the antifascist and revolutionary youth...' It was signed for the Libertarian Youth by Alfredo Martínez, Fidel Miró and Juan Bautista Aso.[92]

In February 1937 in Catalonia, as tension mounted between the anarchists and the Stalinists of the PSUC, the JJLL joined with the youth group of the anti-Stalinist Partido Obrero de Unificación Marxista and several other organizations to establish the Front of Revolutionary Youth. It held a number of large public meetings throughout Catalonia, most notably one in Barcelona on February 14, addressed by Fidel Miró and Alfredo Martínez for the JJLL and Wildebaldo Solano for the POUMist youth.[93]

This meeting precipitated an open break between the young libertarians and the Catalan Stalinist youth. Although the PSUC youth were invited to participate in the meeting, they refused because of the participation of the 'Trotskyist' POUM youth. (As José Peirats stated, 'All non orthodox Communists were Trotskyist' for the Stalinists.[94])

Subsequent to the suppression of the POUM, the Juventudes Libertarias came under intense pressure to join in another alliance, this time with the Comintern-affiliated United Socialist Youth (JSU). Near the end of 1937, the Alianza Juvenil Antifascista (AJA) was established. García Oliver described it as consisting of 'the Federación Iberica de Juventudes Libertarias, the Juventudes Socialistas Unificadas (communists), Juventudes de Izquierda Republicana (philo-Communists), Juventudes Sindicalistas (non-existent), Juventudes Federales (non-existent), Unión Federal de Estudiantes Hispanos (with philo-Communist leadership.'[95] Fidel Miró insisted that the AJA had few functions except holding a series of public meetings in various cities of Loyalist Spain.[97]

One major organizational problem the Juventudes Libertarias faced after the advent of the Negrín government in May 1937 was getting draft exemption for those conducting the work of the organization. As one of the JJLL leaders of the wartime period said many years later, although the Juventudes Socialista Unificadas got such exemptions for everyone from their president to the porter in their headquarters, the government refused to concede exemption to

JJLL leaders. As a consequence, in the latter part of the war most of the active leaders of the Federación de Juventudes Libertarias fell into three categories: 4-fs, war cripples and women.[97]

When the executive committee of the Libertarian Movement was established in Catalonia in April 1938, the Federación de Juventudes Libertarias was one of its three component parts, along with the CNT and the FAI. Fidel Miró was the JJLL representative in that body.[98]

The Union de Mujeres Libres

Unlike the CNT, FAI and Federación de Juventudes Libertarias, the Federación Nacional de Mujeres Libres was established only after the Civil War started. Also, in spite of efforts on its part, the Mujeres Libres was not able to achieve the status of co-equal organization in the Spanish libertarian movement.

The Mujeres Libres had its origins in a magazine of that name, established in 1934 by three women, Lucia Sánchez Saornil, Mercedes Compaposada and Amparo Poch. Then, soon after the War began, a group of anarchist women, who had encountered a hostile attitude when they participated in classes run by the Federación Local de Sindicatos of the CNT in Madrid, formed a local group which they named Mujeres Libres, with the declared objective 'to achieve training and feminine personality ... to be able to acquire any position within the organization and, thus, remove this stamp which it appears to bear, that character of for men only...' The organization referred to was the CNT. In September 1936 a similar women's group, the Grupo Cultural Femenino, was established in Barcelona. Between them, the two organizations had about 500 members by that time.[99]

The movement spread rapidly, and its focus of activity changed with the intensification of the War. Mary Nash noted that its objective came to be 'to orient the spontaneous activities of women and raise their social conscience to make them understand the significance of the moment in the struggle for the Social Revolution.' It spread rapidly to all parts of Loyalist Spain, and although estimates of the total membership of the Mujeres Libres groups varied widely, Mary Nash concluded that it probably came to have 20,000 or more women in its ranks.[100] Lola Iturbe put the membership at 38,000.[101]

In August 1937 the first national conference of Mujeres Libres took place in Valencia, with delegations present from Barcelona, Gerona, Tarragona, Lérida, Guadalajara, Horcha, Yena, Mondejar, Valencia, Elda, Almería, Igualada, Sadurni de Noya, Alcoy and Madrid. Those delegates present in many cases carried additional mandates from other local groups, and Nash estimated that about 115 groups were in fact represented at the conference.

The major business of the meeting was to establish the Federación Nacional de Mujeres Libres, and to name a committee to write the final statutes of the new organization, which were issued a month later. The statutes set forth its purpose as being 'a. To create a conscious and responsible feminine force that will act as a vanguard of progress; b. To establish for this purpose schools, institutes, lectures, special courses, etc., to train the woman and emancipate her from the triple slavery to which she has been and still is submitted: slavery of ignorance, slavery of being a woman, and slavery as a worker.'

Article 2 of the statutes stated: 'For fulfilling these objectives, it will act as a political organization identified with the general objectives of the CNT and the FAI, since its aspiration for feminine emancipation has its supreme objective that women can participate in human emancipation with acquired knowledge, enriched with their own characteristics, to build the new social order.'[102]

Lola Iturbe commented: 'The groups of Mujeres Libres established general and vocational schools in all of the localities in which they were organized... Mujeres Libres aided in organizing agricultural collectives and worked in them with great enthusiasm. They engaged in distributing propaganda at the combat fronts. They created many child-care centers. Their publishing work was also very important.'[103]

Mujeres Libres urged the full incorporation of women in the war effort, particularly behind the lines. The May 1938 issue of its periodical presented the following seven-point program to that end:

1. Suspension of all urban construction works and use of those materials for fortifications. 2. Suspension of all activities not useful for the war, agricultural production and education of the people. 3. Displacement of all able men, under 45 years of age, to the fronts. 4. Incorporation of the rest, until 55 years of age, in fortification battalions, with the only exception being technicians of war and war-related industries. 5. Incorporation of women in all mechanical activities in the war industries and in all production in general. 6. Creation of child care centers to give freedom of action to mothers. 7. Opening of Popular Dining Rooms for all workers of both sexes who present their credentials as such?[104]

The Mujeres Libres met considerable resistance from other parts of the libertarian movement. It was argued by some that recognition of the organization as a constituent part of the movement would split the country's anarchists.[105]

The Mujeres Libres were particularly criticized by the Juventudes Libertarias. Undoubtedly some of the younger female members of the CNT and FAI saw the Mujeres Libres as consisting mainly of older women with whom their younger counterparts didn't have very much in common.[106] However, Mary Nash has argued that the Juventudes Libertarias were very much afraid that the women's group might raid their constituency. As a result, she says, the youth group established female secretariats in their various local and regional organizations. They also worked to end all support by the CNT for the Federación de Mujeres Libres.[107]

The Mujeres Libres sought to have their organization accepted as the fourth constituent part of the libertarian movement. However, when they presented this idea to a plenum of the whole movement in October 1938, it was only tentatively accepted, being made subject to a referendum of the other elements of the movement.[108] There is no clear indication of the result of that referendum, if it was held, but at the last joint meeting of the movement in February 1939, after the fall of Catalonia, the Mujeres Libres were still complaining of the lack of recognition they had received.[109]

Although the Mujeres Libres were put under great pressure by other political groups during the War to participate in the broader feminine organization led by the Communists, the Agrupación de Mujeres Antifascists (AMA) they rejected this pressure. This was in spite of the fact that on a local and regional level some female anarchists did participate in AMA groups.[110]

As late as August 1938, the AMA sought to get the Mujeres Libres to join its ranks. But Mary Nash noted: 'In this polemic Mujeres Libres constantly reiterated their anarchist orientation and insisted on the right of each organization to follow its own ideology without any interference. The lack of revolutionary content was another motive to reject unity with the AMA... The AMA was an organization of ambiguous composition without clear tendency and thus easily manipulated...[111]

Solidaridad Internacional Antifascista

The anarchists had long had *comités de presos* (prisoners' committees) to help those of their number who were imprisoned for one reason or another, as well as to help to take care of the families of those in jail. This tradition of aiding their less fortunate members found wider expression during the Civil War with the establishment in July 1937 of Solidaridad Internacional Antifascista (SIA). Its purpose was to assemble and disperse humanitarian aid both to the anarchist troops at the front and to civilians behind the Loyalist lines.

According to one anarchist source, the SIA had 'the participation of numerous figures in the field of letters and politics,' both in Spain and abroad. Foreign branches of the SIA were organized. That in France included in its ranks not only anarchists such as Sebastian Faure, but the Socialist politician Marceau Pivert and trade union leader Leon Jouhaux. Branches were also established in the United States and Great Britain. The US unit, with its headquarters in New York, and local groups in at least nine states, sponsored a tour of

Spanish anarchists to raise funds for the SIA activities. The British branch contributed not only food and medicine, but also 123 ambulances and £360,000.[112]

Local Anarchist Organizations

In addition to the five nationwide organizations, the Spanish libertarian movement before and during the Civil War included numerous local organizations serving a wide variety of different purposes. These groups dated at least from the last decades of the nineteenth century.

George Esenwein, discussing the anarchist movement during this time, observed that their activities 'mostly centred around the broadly based social institutions of the workers, the *circulos* (circles), cafés, clubs, *ateneos* and *centros obreros* found in the *barrios* of the cities, towns and countryside throughout Spain. By working through these institutions as well as their own, the anarchists eventually became permanently integrated into the fabric of working-class society.'[113]

Esenwein also commented on the particular importance of the neighborhood bar, or café, whose significance had by no means entirely disappeared by the outbreak of the Civil War:

A vital component of the worker's milieu in late nineteenth-century Spanish society was the café or bar. This was true not least because of the miserable home life that the overwhelming majority of workers had to endure... The bar or café provided the most convenient and perhaps only escape from this bleak existence. In the morning the worker would go there on his way to work in order to take his meagre breakfast... At the end of the day, he would return to the tavern in order to drink wine, converse with his friends, or while away the evening by playing games like cards, chess, and checkers.[114]

Recognizing the significance of the bar and café as socializing agents, the anarchists sought to alter qualitatively these institutions so that they reflected anarchist values. In an anarchist café, then, one might find workers not only playing games but also educating themselves by reading books, periodicals and pamphlets. It should be noted here that the immense rate of illiteracy among the workers did not prevent the anarchists from using the café as an educational centre. On the contrary, there was usually one or more *obreros concientes*, or enlightened workers, whose role it was to read the latest anarchist paper or lead discussions on political and educational topics.[115]

It was such more or less informal anarchist centers – as well as CNT unions' headquarters – which served as rallying points for the workers when the military insurrection began on July 18 1936. Through them, news was quickly spread as to what was taking place, recruits were rapidly mobilized to besiege barracks or to confront the insurgent military in the streets of the major cities and smaller urban centers. Similarly, during the May Days in Catalonia in 1937, it was to a large degree through the informal anarchist centers that, within a few hours of the events in the Plaza de Catalonia, the anarchist workers of the Catalan cities had been mobilized to confront the Communist-controlled police and the paramilitary elements of the Partido Socialista Unificado de Catalonia, with the construction of barricades throughout the working-class wards and central part of Barcelona and other cities. Throughout much of the Civil War, too, it was through the informal network, as well as the trade union apparatus, that workers were recruited for service in the militia and for construction of fortifications in Madrid and elsewhere.

Spanish Anarchists and the AIT

Both before and during the Civil War, Spanish anarchism was part of an international movement. This was the International Workingmen's Association (Asociación Internacional de Trabajadores), usually referred to in Spain by its Spanish initials, AIT.

Immediately after the Bolshevik Revolution, the CNT had been very sympathetic to the regime which the Leninists installed. The 1919 Congress of the CNT passed by acclamation a resolution providing that the CNT 'declares that it adheres provisionally to the Communist International'.[116]

In pursuance of that resolution, a CNT delegation headed by Angel Pestaña, attended the second congress of the Comintern in July 1920. Pestaña 'immediately objected to Lenin's strong stress on the role of the communist party in Third International activities.' He associated in Moscow with a number of European and American anarchists, including Emma Goldman, Alexander Berkman and Augustine Souchy, who were already becoming disillusioned with the Bolshevik regime.[117]

In any case, the Comintern was an organization of political parties, which meant that the CNT, as a trade union group, could not belong to it. But when the Communist International (CI) decided to set up the Red International of Labor Unions (RILU), invitations were extended to the CNT to send delegates to its founding congress. At a clandestine plenum of the CNT in April 1921, at which time Andrés Nin was acting as secretary following the assassination of the elected secretary, Evelio Boal, and the arrest of most of the other veteran leaders of the organization, it was agreed to send Nin, Joaquín Maurín, Hilari Arlandís and Jesús Ibáñez as delegates to the RILO congress. All were strong supporters of the Bolshevik regime and the Comintern.[118] The anarchist specific groups exercised their right to add another member of the delegation, and named the young French anarchist, Gaston Leval. Unlike the four pro-Communists, he aligned himself in Moscow with Russian and foreign anarchists and returned to Spain hostile to Bolshevism.[119]

This decision was subsequently repudiated by another CNT plenum, The CNT congress in Zaragoza in June 1922 reached a final conclusion on the question of international affiliation. García Oliver wrote: 'With regard to entry into the Trade Union International of Berlin, that is, the International Workingmen's Association, it was decided to go along with the reports of the National Committee, Pestaña, Gaston Leval. The agreement was unanimous. That is, that we cease definitively to belong, to the Red Trade Union International, and join that of Berlin, which would include the CNT of Spain, the SAC of Sweden, the FAUD of Germany.'[120]

The AIT continued to be a small and relatively weak organization.

By the time the Spanish Civil War broke out, its affiliate in Germany had been destroyed, and that of Argentina had been sadly reduced in numbers and significance.

Although the AIT did not succeed in mobilizing much aid for their Spanish colleagues during the War, they were able to cause then considerable annoyance and inconvenience. Foreign anarchists, and the AIT itself, were highly critical of the collaborationist positions and actions of the CNT–FAI and, in December 1937, Juan García Oliver and Federica Montseny went to an AIT congress in Paris to explain and defend the Spanish anarchists' behavior. The details of this controversy will be dealt with elsewhere in this book.

Conclusion

Anarchism in Spain had a 75-year-old history before the outbreak of the Civil War. At the time the War started, it had the largest following of any political tendency in the country. It remained the largest, although not the most powerful, popular movement in Republican Spain until the end of the conflict.

Different parts of the libertarian or anarchist movement had different functions. The Confederación Nacional del Trabajo was a trade union group and played the most significant part in the socio-economic revolution which occurred at the outset of the War and continued in an attenuated form until its end, as well as playing a significant political role. The Federación Anarquista Ibérica was the political arm *par excellence* of Spanish anarchism, and was virtually transformed into a political party during the War. The Federación de Juventudes Libertarias sought to rally the widest possible number of young people to the anarchist cause, and played an important role both among the anarchist military units and in the rearguard. Two new groups, the Federación de Mujeres Libres and the Solidaridad Internacional Antifascista, appeared during the War; the first seeking but not obtaining the rank of a co-partner of the CNT–FAI–JJLL in the libertarian movement, the second being a specialized service unit for all elements of the movement.

The rest of this book will seek to trace the inter-relationships among these elements of Spanish anarchism, and the relations of each and all of them with other elements within the shrinking Spanish Republic, in all aspects of the society of Loyalist Spain, including the military, economic, social and political spheres during the Civil War.

4

The Advent of the Civil War

The origins of the Spanish Civil War can be traced back at least to the proclamation of the Second Spanish Republic on April 14 1931. That event, which occurred while Spain was undergoing the effects of the Great Depression, was relatively painless, but subsequently gave rise to increasingly great tensions within the Spanish body politic.

The overthrow of King Alfonso XIII and the proclamation of the Republic was a relatively smooth operation. The King had been so discredited by his association with the Primo de Rivera dictatorship between 1923 and 1930, that at the moment of truth he had few supporters. When municipal elections produced Republican majorities in the country's principal cities, the monarch interpreted these results as a repudiation of him and of the monarchy, and so went abroad, although never formally abjuring the throne.

The proclamation of the Republic, after the flight of the King, was carried out not only by traditional republicans but also by those who had until recently been monarchists and ministers of the king, such as Miguel Maura, who was the republic's first minister of the interior. Indeed, the first president of the Republic, Niceto Alcalá Zamora, had been a monarchist until shortly before the proclamation of the Republic.

Some anarchist leaders had participated in the conspiracies to overthrow the monarchy which had preceded the downfall of Alfonso XIII. With the advent of the Republic, there was at first considerable support for the new regime among the anarchist workers of Catalonia and other parts of Spain.

On the day the Republic was proclaimed, the CNT issued a statement to the effect: 'We are not enthused by a bourgeois republic, but we will not consent to a new dictatorship. If the Republic is to be consolidated, it will undoubtedly have the backing of the labor organization, otherwise it will not [be consolidated].'[1]

The Communists, then in the midst of the so-called Third Period of extreme sectarianism, were totally hostile to the new Republic. José Bullejos, at that time secretary general of the Spanish Communist Party has indicated that the party received instructions from the Comintern to the effect that, 'The Communist Party must not, under any circumstances, make pacts or alliances, even momentarily, with any other political group. At every moment, and with regard to every other political group, it must maintain its entire political independence and complete freedom of action. In no case must it defend the republican government or support it.'[2]

Economic Situation of the Republic

One aspect of the tragedy of the Second Spanish Republic was the fact that it came into existence when the Great Depression was sliding into its deepest crisis. And recovery from the Depression had not yet really started by the time the country became caught up in the Civil War.

The Depression elsewhere impacted on the demand for Spain's agricultural and mineral exports. In rural areas, this helped intensify the exploitation to which the agricultural laborers had historically been subjected, and to make precarious the situation of small producers. The country's industries, although enjoying strong tariff protection, also suffered severely. Closing down of manufacturing plants and of mines was commonplace in those years. Unemployment was very widespread. Frank Jellinek reported during the Civil War that before it began the government 'had to admit a minimum of 79,000 part-stopped and 178,000 totally unemployed industrial workers, 154,000 part-stopped, 168,000 wholly unemployed peasants, a total of 579,000 unemployed.' He added that '...it was known that agricultural unemployment was in fact far higher, that there were nearly a million unemployed altogether...'[3]

Those were the years before the Keynesian Revolution and the Spanish Republican government did not know any better than most other governments of the time about how to deal with the national catastrophe which was the Great Depression. However, the inability of the Republican regime to deal adequately with the country's economic problems tended to intensify the polarization of politics and to reinforce the long-term tendency of Spanish politicians to resolve their problems through the use of violence.

The First Phase of the Second Republic

Soon after the proclamation of the Republic, there were elections for a new constituent assembly, to write a constitution for the new Republic. In those elections, the anarchists did not strongly insist on electoral abstention as would have been in conformity with their ideology. Undoubtedly, many anarchists voted, and David Cattell has noted that, 'Because of close rivalry, the Anarchist vote was not generally in favor of the Socialists whose program was nearest to their own. They chose rather to vote for the Republicans, thereby swelling the ranks of the Republicans in the Cortes by their ballots.'[4] To a considerable degree as a result of anarchist support, the Left won those elections, that is to say, the Socialists and Left-wing Republicans in much of Spain, and the Catalan Left in Catalonia.

As a consequence, for a bit more than two years, a government of Left Republicans and Socialists was in office. It elaborated a new republican constitution, but moved very cautiously in bringing about basic changes in the economy and society of Spain. Although it enacted a number of anticlerical measures, and passed an agrarian reform law, it did little in fact to carry out any fundamental program of land redistribution.

Manuel Azaña, the Left Republican, was the dominant political figure in this first phase of the Republic. He was largely responsible for a measure designed to reduce the size of the armed forces, by encouraging retirement of officers under favorable terms. It proved counter-productive when many officers who were fundamentally in favor of the Republic sought retirement.

Another significant political development during those first two years was the enactment by the Spanish parliament of an autonomy statute for the region of Catalonia. It granted an elected government there some powers over the police, education, and social questions. Control of the new regional regime in Catalonia passed to a new Catalan Left Party, which had been first organized in exile by retired Colonel Francesc Macía, and had appeared in Catalonia after the proclamation of the Republic. Macía was elected first president of the new Catalan regime, and when he died in December 1933, he was succeeded by Luis Companys, until then head of the Catalan parliament, and a one-time lawyer for the CNT, as well as president of the Unión de Rabassaires, the organization of most of the region's tenant farmers.[5]

Francisco Largo Caballero, secretary-general of the Socialist-controlled Unión General de Trabajadores, was minister of labor during this first phase of the Second Spanish Republic. He instituted a procedure whereby labor disputes were submitted to conciliation and arbitration tribunals, which the anarchist labor movement was totally unwilling to accept. They interpreted his actions as being designed to strengthen his own Unión General de Trabajadores and to weaken the anarchists' Confederación Nacional del Trabajo. Thus, during the first period of the Republic, the anarchists became particularly antagonistic towards Largo Caballero. José Peirats has written that as minister of labor, Largo Caballero was not only partial to his own organization, 'but provoked in the rival organization a sectarian rancor'.[6]

Another factor intensified the opposition of the anarchists to the Left Republican-Socialist government. This was the regime's violent suppression of the spontaneous uprisings of the agricultural workers in considerable parts of central and southern Spain to bring about a grassroots redistribution of the large landholdings of those parts of the Republic. The culminating case was the Casas Viejas incident in which Civil Guards murdered peasant rebels in cold blood. That event contributed strongly to the government's downfall.

During this first phase of the Second Spanish Republic, the anarchists, who were dominated after 1931 by the extreme elements of the Federación Anarquista Iberica, engaged in a series of local uprisings in various parts of the country, which established libertarian communism in the areas involved. In no case did these insurrections last more than a few days, and as we have noted earlier, they were regarded by the FAIistas as schools of revolution. In any case, they intensified the feud between the anarchists and the Republican regime.

The other major far-Left element in Spanish politics, the Communist Party, underwent an important change during this first period of the Second Spanish Republic. José Bullejos, secretary-general of the party in the early 1930s, described this many years later. He said that when the revolt of General Sanjurjo took place in 1932, and the Communist Party raised the slogan 'Defense of the Republic', instead of the current Comintern slogan of 'Workers' and Peasants' Government', he and other party leaders were accused of being opportunists and capitulators, since in the opinion of Moscow, the principal danger for the Republic and democratic revolution consisted not in the monarchists and the parties of the Right ... but in Azaña, Largo Caballero and Prieto, representatives of reactionary capitalism.'

The result was: 'In the face of our intransigent refusal to change a position which we thought inconvenient for the working class, the Comintern resolved to separate us from the Party to impose its points of view and tactics.' Bullejos and his colleagues were succeeded by 'the new leadership of the Communist Party, composed of José Díaz Hurtado, Vicente Uribe, Antonio Mije, Jesús Hernández and Juan Astigarrabía', who 'accentuated the attacks on the Socialists, without that being changed until the eve of the revolution of October 1934.'[8]

The Second Phase of the Second Republic

With the resignation of the Left Republican-Socialist regime, new elections were called in November 1933. In those elections, the anarchists called upon their supporters not to vote, in conformity with traditional anarchist ideas. The result of this was a victory of the Right. (However, the anarchists apparently voted for the Catalan Left in regional elections held two months after the national poll, assuring the Left Catalan victory.)[9]

The two principal forces of the Right after the 1933 elections were the Confederación Española de Derechas Autonomas (CEDA), which was in fact a federation of parties, led by José María Gil Robles; and the Radical Party, headed by Alejandro Lerroux, who earlier in the century had been a populist-type demagogue, but by the 1930s had moved to the Right of Center.

Other Right-wing parties which were minor factors in the 1933–6 period, but were to become of great significance in the months leading up to the outbreak of the Civil War and during the War itself, were the Falange Española, headed by José Antonio Primo de Rivera, the son of the old dictator; and the Partido Tradicionalista. The former was a fascist party, a few of whose leaders had come out of the anarchist movement. The Tradicionalistas, or Carlists as they were popularly known, were a conservative party with origins in the civil wars of the nineteenth century. They were particularly strong in the north – Navarre and the Basque provinces – but also had some following in Aragón, and the Mediterranean coastal provinces. Both the Falangistas and the Carlists had paramilitary groups. Dolores Ibarruri *et al.* have noted that in the period preceding the Civil War, Colonel Varela, a fellow conspirator with General Sanjurjo in the 1932 revolt in Seville, who was restored to his rank in the army by the Right-wing government of 1933–5, was active in training the Carlist paramilitary group, the Requetes.[10]

Another party which had been allied with the Right during the first phase of the Republic changed its alignment during the 1933–6 period. This was the Basque Nationalist Party. José Bullejos has described this process: 'Although Basque nationalism, because of its strong Catholicism, its conservatism and devotion to tradition, formed part of the Right bloc in the Constituent Cortes, it did not satisfy their autonomist aspirations, and the project of a Statute was not even presented in the new Parliament. Due to this, the Basque

Nationalists began to move towards the Left... The Rightist government also refused to allow municipal elections in the Basque country, as provided for in the Republican constitution.'[11]

The logic of parliamentary arithmetic after the elections of 1933 would have indicated formation of a government of the CEDA and Radicals. However, the Left was most violently opposed to participation of the CEDA (which it labelled 'fascist') in the government, threatening insurrection if this occurred. So it was not until October 1934 that Prime Minister Lerroux invited Gil Robles to become minister of defense, and other members of CEDA also to join the cabinet.

As the Socialists and some of the Left Republicans had promised they would do, the Socialists Unión General de Trabajadores launched a revolutionary general strike. At the same time, President Luis Companys, the Catalan Left Party head of the autonomous government of Catalonia declared that region 'independent within a Spanish Confederation.' Also, the general strike called by the Alianza Obrera, was effective in Barcelona, where the unions controlled by the POUM and smaller elements belonging to the UGT were able to close down public transport, most commerce, and some key factories of the city. This was in spite of the fact that a representative of the regional committee of the CNT got on the radio and announced that no general strike had been called.[12]

However, within a few hours, Companys had surrendered to army troops which had marched out of the barracks to quash his move. One lasting result of this move of the Catalan autonomists was that the anarchists were able to gather a substantial number of weapons, which Catalan nationalist paramilitary groups abandoned when Companys's independence movement collapsed.

The only part of Spain in which there was a real insurrection in October 1934 was in the Asturias region. That was the only area in which the anarchists collaborated with the Socialists, not only in the general strike, but also in seizing control of the region. It took two weeks for units of the army, led by General López de Ochoa, and consisting largely of Moorish and Foreign Legion troops, to put down the uprising. The military operation in Asturias was under the supervision of General Francisco Franco, who was brought to

Madrid from the Balearic Islands, where he had been commandant general and was made the real boss of the ministry of war and general staff.[13]

After these events the Rightist government cracked down very strongly on all elements of the Left. Tens of thousands of workers, peasants, politicians and others were jailed. A number of important political figures were put on trial, including Francisco Largo Caballero, leader of the UGT, who was sentenced to death, but was released after a year and a half. The continuing imprisonment of tens of thousands of anarchists, Socialists, Left Republicans and others generated great bitterness on the Left and became a major factor in the downfall of the Right government.[14]

In the year following the October 1934 uprising, the Right wing government suffered deterioration from within. The Lerroux administration, and particularly Lerroux's own Radical Party, was plagued with a series of corruption scandals which finally forced Lerroux to withdraw from the prime ministership. Another significant result of these scandals was the splitting away from the Radical Party of a considerable faction, headed by Diego Martínez Barrio, to form the Unión Republicana, a party of the moderate Left.

Another significant change among the middle-class Republican parties took place early in 1934. This was the merger of Acción Republicana and the Partido Radical Socialista, the two Republican parties which had participated in the government throughout the 1931–3 period, to form the Partido de Izquierda Republicana, headed by Manuel Azaña, Marcelino Domingo and Alvaro de Albornoz.[15]

Burnett Bolloten cited the Madrid moderately liberal newspaper *El Sol*'s description of government policy during the two year or more of the Right-wing government: 'During the second biennium we fell into the other extreme. Within a few months wages declined sharply from ten and twelve pesetas a day to four, three, and even two. Property took revenge on labor, and did not realize that it was piling up fuel for the social bonfire of the near future. At the same time many landlords who had been forced on government orders to reduce rents devoted themselves to evicting tenant farmers...'[16]

111

In September 1935 Lerroux was succeeded as prime minister by Joaquín Chapaprieta, a one-time minister under the monarchy. However, his government lasted only about three months before it was brought down by another scandal. At that point, President Niceto Alcalá Zamora, rather than turning to the CEDA for a new prime minister, named Manuel Portela Valladares, head of a small centrist party. When Portela Valladares was unable to rally a majority in the Cortes the president authorized him to dissolve parliament and call new elections, those of February 16 1936.[17]

The Popular Front

In the election of 1933, the Left had been split, with Socialists, various republican parties and others running separate tickets; while the Right was for the most part united. In the election of February 1936, the reverse was the case. Virtually all of the Left, except the anarchists, were united in the Popular Front.

The idea of forming some kind of unified front of elements on the Left had its origins soon after the victory to the Right in November 1933. The Bloque Obrero y Campesino (predecessor of the POUM) first suggested the establishment of a Workers' Alliance of all trade union groups and labor–based parties. In December, such a group was established in Catalonia and it included the Bloque, the unions under its influence, the CNT faction of the Treintistas, the Catalan UGT, several other parties and the Unió de Rabassaires, the regional share croppers organization. During 1934, workers' alliances were formed throughout much of Spain. The only region in which the CNT majority participated was in Asturias.

As the disintegration of the Right government proceeded in the last half of 1935 and the prospects of new elections grew, the Socialist Party and republican parties began conversations about an alliance for those elections. Given the recent change of the Comintern to support popular fronts, the Communists asked to be included in those discussions, and were. So were the Catalan leftist parties, the new Partido Sindicalista, recently formed by CNT leader Angel Pestaña, and finally (over the objections of the

Communists) the Partido Obrero de Unificación Marxista (POUM) was admitted to what by then was being called the Popular Front. The Front allotted candidacies among the participating organizations, so that the parties in the Front would not compete with one another.

To a considerable degree the success of the Popular Front depended on what attitude the anarchists would adopt in the election. That was a matter of considerable discussion within the CNT ranks. The anarchists finally decided to leave their members free to decide individually whether or not to vote, rather than taking the traditional anti-electoral position.

There was undoubtedly one overriding consideration which made the anarchists decide as they did. This was the problem of the tens of thousands of political prisoners who were still in jail, a considerable percentage of whom were from the anarchists' ranks. So long as the Right remained in power, those prisoners had little prospect of being released, whereas a new government of the Left would have as one of its first obligations the opening of the jail doors for the political prisoners. In any case, Gómez Casas has indicated that 'there was practically no abstention from voting' on the part of the anarchists.[18]

The victory of the Left in the February 1936 election was close enough that the votes of the anarchists in its favor were probably decisive. The Popular Front received 4,540,000 votes and the Center and Right received 4,300,000. However, the Popular Front parties received 271 seats in the new Cortes, parties of the Center got 52, and parties of the Right received 129.[19]

The Pre-Revolutionary Situation, February–July 1936

The months between the February election and the outbreak of the Civil War in the middle of July were marked by increasing and rapid political polarization, growing violence, and threats of insurrection from both Right and Left. It was truly a pre-revolutionary situation.[20]

One fundamental problem during those months was the weakness of the government. During the whole period from February to July the cabinet consisted only of members of the middle-class Republican parties. The Socialists, who had the largest representation in the Cortes, and at that were under-represented, since, due to the apportionment of candidacies among the parties of the Popular Front, it was undoubtedly working class and peasant Socialist votes which in fact elected many of the deputies of the Republican parties, refused to join the government.

One of the first acts of the new Cortes was to depose President Niceto Alcalá Zamora, and to elect in his place Manuel Azaña. Although Azaña had had a reputation as a strong man during the earlier years of the Republic, he was unable to handle the increasingly splintered and chaotic political situation with which he was faced, first as prime minister (he took office as that immediately after the election) and then as president.

Another problem of the period was the deep division within the Socialist Party. There were two major factions within it, the Left headed by Francisco Largo Caballero, whose forces controlled the Unión General de Trabajadores, and the Center, headed by Indalecio Prieto, which controlled most of the party apparatus, at least on a national level. This deep rivalry was to persist virtually until the end of the Civil War, although the two factions would reverse during the War the positions they held in the months just preceding its outbreak. This was particularly the case with regard to the attitude to be taken towards the Communists.

Following the end of the Republic's first phase, and the defeat of the Socialists and Left Republicans in the 1933 elections, Francisco Largo Caballero had become radicalized. He came to the conclusion that close Socialist collaboration with the Republican parties had been an error, and had prevented the government of that period from making drastic reforms which were long overdue (which was true). He had begun to preach the need for a 'dictatorship of the proletariat', without very carefully defining just what he meant by that. In the months before the outbreak of the War, it was largely due to his influence that the Socialists did not enter the government. In those months he was talking of the need for a workers' revolution. José Peirats has suggested that at least one motive for Largo

Caballero's radicalization was his worry about the rapid growth of the CNT in the Madrid area, one of his own principal centers of support.[21]

In these attitudes, the Communists strongly encouraged Largo Caballero's leftism, at least publicly, although Burnett Bolloten has argued that privately they tended to be very critical of his 'infantilism'.[22] Their press referred to him as 'the Spanish Lenin', a title which Luis Araquistain has said 'came from Moscow'.[23] Upon occasion, Largo Caballero himself used this sobriquet. The Communists supported Largo Caballero because they hoped to profit from his positions – and indeed they did so.

An early step from which the Communists were to profit very much was the agreement of the leadership of the UGT to accept into its ranks the handful of unions which had belonged to the Communists' 'unity' labor confederation. The Communists liquidated that confederation in December 1935, in pursuance of the new policy of the Comintern to put an end to Communist dual unionism around the world, as part of the Comintern's new Popular Front line. Although its future importance certainly was not seen at the time, the merger of their unions into the UGT gave the Stalinists for the first time in many years at least a small base in one of the country's two mass labor organizations.

The Communist Party undoubtedly grew in the months preceding the outbreak of the Civil War. The more or less official Stalinist account of the War claimed that between February and July 1936 its membership rose from 30,000 to 102,000.[24] Although these figures may be somewhat exaggerated, there is no doubt that Communist membership and influence grew in the period following the February 1936 election.

One of the things which was much discussed in the pre-war months was the possibility of merging the Socialist and Communist parties, to form a single workers' party. Largo Caballero ostensibly favored pushing this idea, probably being convinced that the Socialist Party, which was many times the size of the Communists, could absorb and neutralize them. The Communists, of course, had quite different ideas.

What these ideas were was indicated by an event that occurred in

April 1936. This was the merger of the Socialist youth group, with an estimated 200,000 members, and the Communist youth, with a membership of 'no more than 50,000', to form the Federación de Juventudes Socialistas Unificadas (JSU).[25] Largo Caballero favored this idea, at least at first, and the Socialist youth group, the Socialist Youth Federation, had been a strong supporter of Largo Caballero within the Socialist ranks.

However, the way this merger was brought about, and the kind of organization which resulted from it, were certainly not to Largo Caballero's liking. Negotiations were conducted in the apartment of Julio Alvarez del Vayo, then supposedly one of Largo Caballero's principal supporters in the Socialist Party, but who later became a bitter enemy. In that apartment, the Socialist Youth leaders had long discussions with Victorio Codovila, then the Comintern's principal agent in Spain, and Codovila arranged for the Socialist youth leaders to take a trip to Moscow to confer, among others, with Dmitri Manuilsky, a major leader of the Comintern. Without doubt, it was out of those conversations the nature of the new 'unified' youth movement was determined.[26] When the unification took place, the new group immediately joined the Young Communist International. During the Civil War the JSU was to be one of the key parts of the Stalinist apparatus in Spain. Most of its top national leaders joined the Communist Party a few months into the War.

However, during the Civil War, there were tendencies within the JSU for the Socialist and Communist elements within it to break apart. Palmiro Togliatti, the principal Comintern agent in Spain, noted a split-away of pro-Caballero young Socialists from the JSU in the province of Murcia as early as May 1937.[27] About a year later, he accused Socialist Party National Secretary Lamoneda of organizing Socialist groups within the JSU, and that the Socialist Party leadership was demanding a reorganization of the JSU leadership on the basis of parity between Socialists and Communists, a demand which the Communist Party politburo rejected.[28] David Cattell has also noted that local Socialist Party units in Jaén, Albacete, and Almería, supported 'unofficial "Socialist youth" organs closely associated with the Socialist Party in their locality.'[29]

Indalecio Prieto's faction of the Socialist Party was strongly opposed to any talk about possible Socialist-Communist unity and was generally opposed to the whole line that Largo Caballero was taking these months. Prieto was a seasoned parliamentary politician, had the reputation of being a very good orator and, among other things, was a businessman. He got along quite well with the politicians of the Republican parties, and was at one point considered by them to become prime minister, a move which Largo Caballero strongly opposed.[30] He had strong control of the machinery of the Socialist Party in those months. Gabriel Jackson has claimed that Prieto's victory in internal Socialist Party elections in June 1936 was 'the first tangible evidence that the revolutionary tide within the Socialist Party was beginning to ebb'.[31]

Whereas the Socialist Party was bitterly divided during the pre-war period, the anarchists were overcoming the serious split in their ranks which had taken place in the first years of the Republic. At a congress in Zaragoza in May, the Treintista (anti-FAI), opposition) unions which had withdrawn or had been expelled from the Confederación Nacional del Trabajo, were readmitted, and took full part in the meeting, and thereafter shared in the leadership of the anarcho-syndicalist union movement.

If there was great polarization on the Left between February and July 1936, there was a similar process going forward on the Right of Spanish politics. Although the CEDA had come out of the elections with the second highest number of deputies in the Cortes, and overwhelmingly the largest party of the Right in the new parliament, this position of pre-eminence was swiftly undermined in the months that followed.

Within the CEDA, Gil Robles lost ground to more extreme elements, particularly José Calvo Sotelo. In fiery speeches inside and outside of the parliament, Calvo Sotelo castigated the Left, denounced the weakness of the incumbent government, and predicted impending disaster. He almost certainly was also involved in the plotting within the military which led to the Civil War.

At the same time, the CEDA was losing ground to more extremist elements on the Right. Both the Carlists and the Falangistas carried the struggle into the streets, where they had constant clashes, particularly with the Socialist and Communist youth groups. Falange leader José Antonio Primo de Rivera was jailed by the government.

The Falange grew particularly rapidly during this period. Large numbers of the younger people, until then affiliated with CEDA, went over to Primo de Rivera's organization. In those months, it was converted from a small fringe group into a serious actor on the Spanish political scene.[32]

Increasingly, elements on both sides of the political spectrum were resorting to violent action against their opponents. Numerous deaths resulted from this resort to violence. Stanley Payne has cited police statistics to the effect that political violence between February 17 and July 17 resulted in 215 deaths and 537 people injured.[33]

Two of these violent acts gained particularly wide publicity just a few days before the Civil War began. A young Assault Guard officer, who was loyal to the Republic, was murdered, presumably by Right-wing elements. Several of his colleagues then decided to take their own revenge for this, and to that end sequestered and murdered José Calvo Sotelo, who would probably have been the civilian head of the Rebellion had he survived. Although some have argued that the murder of Calvo Sotelo was the act which provoked the uprising of July 17, this was certainly not the case – the Rebellion was organized and ready to go considerably before Calvo Sotelo's, assassination.

Socio-Economic Developments

The months between February and July 1936 were marked by widespread upheavals both in the countryside and the cities. In the central and southern parts of the country there was extensive seizure of land by the tenants and agricultural workers and, at the same time, the official Institute of Agrarian Reform moved in to carry out a substantial number of legal expropriations of land and transferred them to peasants. According to one report, the institute took over 600,000 hectares of arable land and settled 100,000 landworkers on it in four months.[34] According to Edward Malefakis, 'Far more land was redistributed from March to July than in the entire previous history of the Republic.'[35]

At the same time, in other places, there were extensive strikes of agricultural workers. Edward Malefakis has written: 'In the two and one-half months between 1 May and the outbreak of the civil war on 18 July, the Ministry of Labor recorded 192 agricultural strikes, as many as during the whole of 1932 and almost half as many as during that entire year of trouble, 1933.'[36]

There was equally serious upheaval in the cities:

> If the unrest in the countryside was a source of acute disquietude to the government, no less so were the labor disputes in the urban centers. From the end of May until the outbreak of the Civil War, the Republic had been convulsed by strikes affecting almost every trade and every province. Despite the censorship, the columns of the press abounded with reports of strikes in progress, of old strikes settled, of new strikes declared, and of others threatened, of partial strikes and general strikes, of sit-down strikes, and sympathetic strikes. There were strikes not only for higher wages, shorter hours, and paid holidays, but for the enforcement of the decree of 29 February compelling employers to reinstate and indemnify all workmen who had been discharged on political grounds after 1 January 1934.[37]

Perhaps the most serious strike of all was that of the construction workers of Madrid. It started out as a joint movement of UGT and CNT unions, but after the UGT settled, the CNT construction workers were unwilling to do so, leading to serious clashes between anarchist and Socialist workers, and to the arrest of the principal CNT construction workers' union leaders. They were still in prison when the Civil War began, when they were finally released and, under the leadership of Cipriano Mera, organized a militia column which retrieved the Cuenca area for the Republic.[38]

The Military Conspiracy

Against this turbulent background in civilian politics, important elements in the leadership of the nation's military forces were plotting the insurrection which was to be the starting point of the Civil War. They did so with amazingly little interference from the government of the day.

José Bullejos, one-time secretary-general of the Spanish Communist Party, has argued: 'The historic truth is, not that the uprising was improvised in the early months of 1936, or that it resulted from the policy of the Azaña and Cásares Quiroga government, but began to be organized in 1933, when a group of high military chiefs, in their majority monarchists, founded the Unión Militar Española, an essentially reactionary organization proposing to restore the monarchy ... According to fascist sources ... the sedition against the Republic began to be organized in March of that year, in frequent meetings in which also participated distinguished military and political leaders, among them Generals Franco, Queipo de Llano, Villegas and Colonel Yague.'[39]

Some civilian elements of the far Right reportedly approached a number of leading generals, including Franco, Fanjul and Goded, even before the February 1936 election, proposing a coup to prevent a victory of the Left.[40] Right after the results of the election became known, not only General Franco, who was chief of the general staff, but also the political leaders Calvo Sotelo and Gil Robles, reportedly tried to get Prime Minister Portela Valladares and President Alcalá Zamora to declare a state of war, which would have effectively turned power over to the army. Both the prime minister and president refused these demands, and agreed to the immediate installation of a government of the forces which had won the election, under Prime Minister Manuel Azaña.[41]

Dolores Ibarruri and her colleagues, citing Francoist sources, maintain that the basis of the conspiracy which finally led to the outbreak of civil war was established late in February, before Franco left to take up his post as military commander of the Canary Islands: 'The first Junta of generals was established, charged with organizing the uprising, and made up of Mola, Varela, Goded, Franco, Saliquet,

Fanjul, Ponte and Orgáz. Sanjurjo was designated chief of the movement and General Rodríguez del Barrio was charged with coordinating the activities of the conspirators.'[42]

When the Left returned to power after the February 1936 election, the new government took certain steps supposedly designed to weaken those within the military who might conspire against the regime. However, these moves were exceedingly mild, and quite ineffective.

Principally, the Left Republican government juggled commands, hoping to get potentially rebellious generals in posts where they could do relatively little damage in the Republic. General Francisco Franco was 'exiled' to command the garrison in the Canary Islands, off the coast of Africa – whence he had no great trouble maintaining contact with troops in Spanish Morocco, where he had considerable following. General Emilio Mola was put in command in the Navarre region in northern Spain, where he promptly recruited the Carlists, who were very influential in that region and had significant para-military forces, to the conspiracy. General Manuel Goded, about whom there were also suspicions, was set to command the garrisons in the Balearic Islands, from which he maintained close contact with the much more important body of troops in Catalonia.

José Bullejos claimed: 'For some time military officers and generals loyal to the Republic informed the head of the government of the preparations for a *coup d'etat* and of the people, civilian and military who were involved. Cásares Quiroga never paid attention to these reiterated warnings, or took indispensable precautions.'[43]

One significant Left Republican politician of the time has suggested two reasons why the government of February–July 1936 did not carry out a more thorough purge of the armed forces. One was that anti-Republican sentiment was widespread in the officer caste, and a thorough purge of hostile elements would virtually have meant the dissolution of the armed forces, because of the depth and width of the dissident elements in the officer corps.

The other reason why the government did not thoroughly purge the army, according to this Left Republican politician was that to have done so would have been to alter the balance of power at that moment. The Republican parties were caught between the Socialists on the Left and the various conservative parties on the Right. If the government had really purged the army, the Republican parties in the government would have had to rely on the Socialists' paramilitary militia to maintain order, and thus felt that they would have been completely at the mercy of the Socialist Party.[44]

Before the uprising began, General José Sanjurjo was the principal leader of the conspiracy. He was a Civil Guard general who had led an uprising in Seville against the Republic in August 1932 which failed, after which he was arrested and sentenced to a long jail term. However, the Rightist regime had released him after it came to power. Sanjurjo died in a plane crash in Portugal just as the insurrection was getting under way.

The more or less official Communist account of the Civil War has stressed the importance of officers who had spent much of their careers in Spanish Morocco, first in fighting the almost endless war there, and then in pacifying the colony, in leading the Rebellion of 1936. This source wrote: 'In the colonial war against the Moroccan people there was being formed of a group of military men called 'Africanists', chiefs and officers of monarchic and extremely reactionary sentiments, the majority in Moroccan hired units ... or in mercenary troops of the Foreign Legion. Such were Sanjurjo, Manuel Goded, Franco, Yague, Millan Astray ... García Valino ... Muñoz Grandes ... and others.'[45] In addition, during the period in 1935 in which José María Gil Robles was minister of war, he placed these people in key posts within the military hierarchy.[46]

The generals and other officers participating in the conspiracy did so almost openly. In spite of frequent public warnings from anarchists, Communists, POUMists and left-wing Socialists about what was transpiring, the government did virtually nothing to interfere with the conspirators. Indeed, on May 18, it officially published a note which said, 'All the Chiefs and Officers of the Army are loyal to the Republic and it is calumny to say anything to the contrary.'[47]

The accepted wisdom is that the vast majority of the officer corps of the Spanish armed forces was involved in the uprising of July 1936. Thus, Salvador de Madariaga has written: 'With few exceptions, it may be said that every army officer who was free to do so joined the rebels. Of the officers who sided with the Government, only a minority did so out of personal conviction. The majority would have joined their comrades had they been in a position to do so; they often tried and at times succeeded in crossing the Line.'[48]

Although the Rebels also pictured their movement as one of the army as an institution, this was clearly not the case. Most of the top officers of the armed forces were not involved in the conspiracy, and in many cases it was their second-in-commands who revolted, seizing control from the superior officers.

However, José Costa Font and Ramón Martínez González have noted that only one of the eight chiefs of military regions revolted; 17 of 21 generals remained loyal; all six generals of the Civil Guard remained loyal, as did the general in chief of aviation. Of the 59 brigadier-generals only 17 revolted.

Sixteen generals who could not escape from areas where the Rebels were successful were shot. Costa Font and Martínez commented: 'Never was so much blood of military chiefs of high rank spilt as in this combat for the defense of the Republic.'

Among those high officers who were executed by the Rebels were the captain-general of the Second Region (based in Seville) and the commander of the Eighth Military Region (Galicia). In addition, the generals who were military governors of Granada, Zaragoza, La Coruña, Seville, Burgos, Salamanca, and the three Moroccan cities of Tetuan, Melilla and Ceuta were executed by the Rebels. Costa Font and Martínez observed: 'The first victims of the uprising of July 1936 were not civil governors, mayors, deputies in the Cortes, members of the left political parties and the workers unions, but generals, military chiefs who shed their blood in defense of legitimacy.'[49]

Stanley Payne has stressed the number of regular army officers who remained loyal: 'At least 70 percent of the officers on active duty were to be found in the leftist zone, and of these no more than one-third had actively participated in the rebellion. Altogether, a pool of approximately 10,000 Professional officers who were not committed to the rebels was available to the leftist zone. Had there been intelligent and imaginative leadership politically these men might have been used militarily to decisive effect. The revolutionary onslaught that erupted after July 19 largely precluded this possibility.'[50]

Outbreak of the Civil War

The signal for the beginning of the Rebellion was the flight of General Francisco Franco from the Canary Islands on July 17 1936, first to French Morocco and then to the Spanish colony on the next day. Before the arrival of Franco in Spanish Morocco, his co-conspirators there had moved to seize total control in the colony. Almost, immediately, steps were taken to move troops from there (principally Moroccans and Foreign Legionnaires) to the Spanish mainland.

The Republican government's reaction to the events of July 17 was torpid, to put it mildly, Prime Minister Santiago Cásares Quiroga on July 18 announced that the uprising had been contained, at a moment when it had already spread to Seville and Málaga. But on July 19, Cásares Quiroga resigned and President Manuel Azaña appointed Diego Martínez Barrio to form a new cabinet. Martínez Barrio sought to compromise with the Rebels, reportedly even going so far as to offer General Mola the position of minister of defense. His cabinet lasted less than 24 hours.

Finally, President Azaña named the Left Republican leader José Giral as prime minister, and Giral finally conceded to the demand of the labor movement and loyal parties to arm the workers and others who wanted to defend the Republic. This was a particularly important decision in so far as Madrid was concerned.[51]

Stanley Payne has noted the catastrophic effect of the indecisiveness of the Left Republican leaders in the face of the military rebellion:

[They] sank into almost absolute paralysis ... During the days of July 17 to 19 scarcely half the Spanish Army followed the conspirators into rebellion, while most of the Navy, Air Force, and police remained loyal. If Azaña ... and his colleagues had made a determined, all-out effort to preserve the integrity of the state after July 17, it need not be assumed that such an attempt would have been doomed to failure ... Only two regiments in the capital joined the military rebellion, and it is not impossible that the situation might have been controlled without turning the revolutionaries loose. In his last conversation with Azaña on the night of July 18–19, Miguel Maura had called for absolute concentration of authority in the hands of the Republican government, but that required a courage and audacity that Azaña altogether lacked. Azaña believed that in a crisis the revolutionaries would not obey the orders of the government without being granted duality of power. Large-scale, violent street demonstrations against the Martínez Barrio cabinet in Madrid on July 19 reinforced this impression. Very possible Azaña's belief was correct, but the fact remains that he refused to test it.[52]

The CNT National Committee and the Beginning of the Rebellion

In the face of the indecisiveness of the government towards the outbreak of the rebellion of Franco and the other generals, the national leaders of the CNT, like other groups which were willing to confront the uprising, felt growing frustration. Many years later, F. Crespo, writing in the exile anarchist publication *Espoir*, described the activities of the national committee of the CNT, which was then located in Madrid:

From the afternoon of the 17th until the morning of the 19th, the telephone of the National Committee of the CNT dispatched some 80 messages, and various others in answer to the Regional, Provincial, and *comarcal* organizations of the Libertarian Movement. All opinions coincided, and the initiative, the resolution and the reply to the fascism imported from Berlin, Rome and Lisbon was taken by anarcho-syndicalism ... Convinced that the 900,000 workers belonging to the CNT ... were ready for the struggle, at three o'clock in the afternoon, the communique was written for the revolutionary undertaking which would be undertaken a few hours later. The National Committee of the three branches of the Libertarian Movement, CNT, FAI and JJLL, with the same common vision, resolved to force the suicidal indecision of official antifascism...

As a result of this decision Crespo wrote:

At seven in the evening, the National Committee of the CNT, ready to overcome whatever resistance or inconveniences it might confront, entered the building of Radio Emisora Nacional, asking to broadcast over it for not more than six minutes. Somewhat surprised, and wanting to know what the CNT wished to broadcast, but without concretely prohibiting it, because the National Committee made clear their resolution to do so; the broadcasting apparatus transmitted the decisive accord, that anarcho-syndicalism launched without delay the revolutionary combat, confronting fascism wherever it manifested itself and wherever without having done so, it was known to be entrenched.

The CNT national committee members then left the radio building. At 10 p.m. that same evening of July 19, the UGT broadcast a similar announcement over the same station.[53]

The Rebellion in Catalonia

The anarchists for several years had had defense groups in various parts of Barcelona. They had developed strategy and tactics to be used when they sought to seize control of the city. However, after the February 1936 election, when the possibility of a military coup against the Republic became increasing possible, they altered their plans to permit then to deal with such a movement of the armed forces.

As it became increasingly clear that a military *coup* was almost certain, the anarchists entered into contact with Catalan President

Luis Companys, with a view to thwarting that eventuality. A contact committee was established between the Catalan government and the anarchists, to keep track of the developing military conspiracy. On July 16 a CNT regional plenum asked the government to provide a thousand rifles.[54]

However, President Companys and his government continued to reject the demands of the anarchists to arm the workers, so that they could confront any military uprising. As a consequence, in the days preceding the military uprising, the anarchists undertook raids on gunshops, where they mainly acquired shotguns but not rifles and other heavier equipment.

The anarchist port workers undertook to raid the ships which were then in the harbor of Barcelona, and to take over the weapons which they knew that all vessels kept 'just in case'. However, the Catalan government reacted against that and sent Assault Guards to recover the weapons, A compromise was reached, whereby the anarchists gave up a part of what they had seized, but kept most of them. The anarchists also disarmed the *serenos*, or private guards in much of the city, and secreted their weapons.

In other ways, too, the Catalan government refused cooperation with the anarchists. Censors refused publication in *Solidaridad Obrera* of FAI instructions to workers for action in case of military insurrection. The FAI immediately published the instructions as a leaflet. The July 18 issue of *Solidaridad Obrera* was also censored because it reported the military uprising in Morocco the day before, as was *La Vanguardia*.

However, anarchist infiltrators in the local barracks informed the CNT that the uprising was to begin in the early hours of July 19. So the CNT informed the Generalidad that it would requisition vehicles to maintain contacts among the anarchist defense committees in various parts of Barcelona. Cars with CNT–FAI signs on them began to circulate throughout the city.[55]

The July 19 issue of *La Vanguardia* carried a front-page lead article headed 'Order Was Complete', and cited the Catalan councillor of government to that effect. However, at the bottom of the same page, under the subheading 'Arrests and Arms Seized', was a note: 'In the early hours of last night there were in the cells of the General

Commissariat of Public Order a large number of arrested people, in their majority of fascist affiliation, and in various police posts there are large quantities of arms and sidearms of various kinds and calibers taken in numerous searches during the early morning and the day by the police in different political centers, particularly those of the extreme-right.'

In the early hours of July 19, the army forces began to move out of the various barracks of Barcelona to try to take over the city. As a result, the sirens of all factories and of ships in the harbor were sounded as the anarchists had planned.

The anarchists had gathered their defense forces in various union offices in the city, with their principal headquarters in the Construction Workers Union. (Frank Jellinek was wrong when he stated that there were 'no militia' in Catalonia, since the anarchists had for several years been organizing defense committees.)[56] They had agreed to allow the military to leave their barracks so that they could be confronted in the streets of the city, rather than trying to make frontal assaults on the various army posts. The rebellious army forces were thus able to move into the center of the city, where they seized the principal buildings in the Plaza de Catalunya, including the Hotel Colón and the telephone building.

However, in the working-class wards of the city, anarchist defense committees were able to overcome the military units. As they defeated the soldiers in various barracks, they acquired increasing amounts of weapons, including machine guns and even cannon. They were aided by the Assault Guards who remained loyal.

There was considerable doubt about whether the Civil Guards were also loyal. Apparently there was good reason for this doubt, since most of the principal officers of the Civil Guard units in Barcelona were pledged to the conspiracy.[57] However, they finally threw in their lot with the Republic, and were of major importance in recapturing the Rebels' strongholds in the Plaza de Catalunya, in the center of the city.

By the morning of July 20, the rebellion had been defeated in virtually all of Barcelona, except the Ataranzanas barracks. During a massive attack on that Rebel stronghold which was successful, the anarchist leader Francisco Ascaso was killed. By noon of July 20, the military rebels had been defeated, not only in Barcelona, but also throughout Catalonia.[58]

Scattered shooting continued in Barcelona several days after the general end of hostilities. The Barcelona newspaper *La Vanguardia* on July 24 carried instructions from 'the delegate of the CNT, Torhyo', which had been broadcast the night before, concerning these random firings: 'In the first place, the militiamen are instructed on the tactics which they should follow when they are confronted with people shooting from rooftops. In those instructions it is said that they must not use munitions, as they have been doing until now, in excess without obtaining any positive results. Instead of that, what must be done is to localize the place from which the shots are coming, and if they cannot find immediately the person who is shooting, as soon as the house from which the shots come has been located, the edifice should be searched until the authors of the shots are found...'[59]

However, that same issue of *La Vanguardia* carried notices of orders to return to work by the Barcelona and Catalan regional federations of the CNT, as well as similar notes from several individual unions.

The Rebellion in the Balearic Islands

General Goded, one of the principal military conspirators, was in command of the military district of the Balearic Islands. On July 18 and 19, the CNT held a regional congress in Palma de Mallorca. On the 18th, when news came of the uprising in Morocco, CNT leaders and other forces loyal to the Republic asked the civil governor of the islands to distribute arms to the people to defend the regime against possible rebellion in Mallorca. He refused, saying that General Goded had visited him to say that he was totally in support of the Republic.

Early the next morning, July 19, however, arms were being distributed to elements of the Falange, the point of distribution being the cathedral of PaLma de Mallorca. The majority of the unionists on that island were members of the UGT, which apparently did not take any initiative to deal with the situation. However, General Goded moved swiftly to declare a state of war in the region, thus joining the Rebellion. Many of the CNTers who had gathered for the regional congress were arrested and shot, including some who had come from other parts of Spain. It is estimated that 75 anarchists were executed.

However, things turned out differently in the island of Menorca. There, the majority of the unionists belonged to the CNT, and they took energetic measures to get control of the island as soon as they received news of the beginning of the Rebellion in Morocco.'[60]

The Rebellion in Madrid

In Madrid, the Rebels hesitated. One important Left Republican politician has suggested that this was because the military commander there, General Joaquín Fanjul, was really more a politician than a general. He had been a deputy, and he hesitated at the crucial moment.[61]

Although General Fanjul confined the army troops to their barracks, had arms transferred to the Montaña barracks, and a number of loyal officers were killed, the troops did not move on July 18 or July 19. Meanwhile, CNT leaders who had recently been jailed were released, and they reopened their headquarters which the government had closed down. Both the CNT and UGT declared a general strike, and the Socialists, led by Carlos de Baraíbar, set up a communications center in UGT headquarters where, with the help of post office and railroad workers, they could keep in touch with developments in various parts of the Republic. On July 19, some 5,000 rifles were distributed to the workers from the Artillery Park, where troops remained loyal.[62]

On July 18, the Madrid CNT formed a local defense committee. Soon afterwards, the anarchists seized arms from a truck at the Cuatro Caminos square. They also threatened to assault the local prisons to free CNT prisoners there, whereupon Prime Minister Giral released them.[63]

Fighting broke out on the morning of July 20. In Getafe, on the outskirts of Madrid, the garrison of the First Squadron of Aviation remained loyal, and when the rebellious First Regiment of Light Artillery began to fire on the town at 6 a.m. on July 20, CNT workers dispatched from Madrid joined with soldiers from the airbase to attack and overrun the artillery barracks. Weapons seized there were of great use later in the day in reducing the garrisons in Madrid itself.[64]

Meanwhile, the Montaña barracks was besieged by armed workers, supported by Assault Guards. The besiegers had three cannon to aid them, and were supported by planes from the military airport where the revolt had already been crushed. Meanwhile a struggle was taking place within the barracks, which apparently explained why on two occasions a white flag was raised, but when the assailants surged forward they were met with machine-gun fire.

Finally, a mass attack was made on the barracks which, although bloody, was successful. Most of those inside the barracks were killed. By the end of July 21 pro-Rebel civilian snipers had been hunted out. The militia then sent out columns from Madrid to recapture Guadalajara, Toledo, Cuenca and Alcalá de Henares, which Rebel troops had first seized.[65] Even the official Communist account of these early battles, although stressing the role of Communist militiamen, recognized the significant participation of anarchist units in these conflicts.[66]

Many years later, the POUMist leader Juan Andrade, who was in Madrid during the uprising there, paid special tribute to the role of the Assault Guards in putting down the revolt in the capital: 'It must be said that the assault guards played an absolutely crucial role, which was almost always overlooked. The guards were the only efficient police corps created by the republic, and in Madrid they were a revolutionary force made up almost exclusively of socialist youth or other left wingers. Their importance in the fighting that was about to come was equally decisive; it was they who, in the first couple of months, virtually saved Madrid.'[67]

The Rebellion in the North

In the northern region of Navarre, General Mola's army units were quickly joined by paramilitary units of the Carlists, and the whole area was rapidly overrun. But the situation in the neighboring Basque region was quite different. Although Mola's forces were able to seize control of the province of Alava, bordering on Navarre, this did not occur in the provinces of Vizcaya (centering on Bilbao) and Guipuzcoa. In those two provinces, the Basque Nationalist Party, the largest political group in the region, called upon the people to be loyal to the Republic. The army garrison in Bilbao did not move.

Many years later, Juan Ajuriaguerra, president in 1936 of the Basque Nationalist Party in Vizcaya, recounted the result of a night-long meeting of his executive committee, after hearing of the uprising in Morocco: 'As the night wore on, one thing became clear: the military rising was the work of the right-wing oligarchy whose slogan was unity – an aggressive Spanish unity which was aimed at us. The right was ferociously hostile to any autonomy statute for the Basque country. The legal government on the other hand, had promised it to us and we knew we would receive it in the end. At 6 a.m., after a sleepless night, we reached a unanimous decision. We issued a statement declaring our support of the republican government.'[68]

In San Sebastian the troops in one army barracks, and the Civil Guards, did revolt, but not until the workers had had time to mobilize, and the Rebels were overcome. Many years later, Miguel González Inestal, the leader of the San Sebastian CNT fishermen's union told what had occurred. According to him, when he went to talk with Civil Governor Artola, a Left Republican, about calling off a fishermen's strike in view of the uprising in Morocco, he found that the governor was unaware of what had happened, and when informed, was very hesitant about doing anything about it. Thereupon, González Inestal said, 'I went to the phone and rang up my union headquarters. I told the lads there to prepare for the trouble that was about to hit us. At the other end of the line, the voices sounded pleased.'[69]

In Santander, immediately to the west of the Basque region, the garrison was quickly surrounded by armed workers, and surrendered.[70]

Further to the west, in Asturias, the situation remained confused for several days. Although the workers were mobilized in the regional capital, Oviedo, on the afternoon of July 18, Colonel Aranda, the local military commander, assured the union leaders of his loyalty to the Republic. When the Socialist and anarchist leaders decided to answer a call for reinforcements from Madrid, Aranda helped them to organize a column of 3,000 men, including miners with dynamite, to head south. Later the Communists claimed that they had opposed this denuding of Oviedo of militia force.[71]

Once the workers' militia had left Oviedo, Aranda made his real intentions clear. He had ordered the army troops to stay in their barracks and had summoned Civil Guards from throughout the region to hasten to Oviedo. Although the anarchists and Largo Caballero Socialists withdrew from negotiations with the colonel, the right-wing Socialists and Republicans continued parleying with him. Aranda used an excuse to leave the meeting, joined his troops and proceeded to seize control of the city, in support of the Rebellion. Oviedo was not captured for the Republic during the rest of the Civil War, and extensive resources were diverted to fruitless attempts to capture the Asturian capital.[72]

Meanwhile, the anarchists and Socialists succeeded in gaining control of the rest of Asturias. In Gijón, the second city of the region, the Rebel officers in the two barrack's, hesitated two days before declaring their support of the uprising, by which time forces loyal to the Republic had seized control of the rest of the city, and organized militia groups to attack the barracks. However, more than two weeks passed before the Simancas barracks was stormed, a period in which three Rebel warships had sought to aid the besieged army Rebels by bombarding the city.[73]

In the north-western part of the country, Galicia, the Rebels finally won out, although there was some severe fighting. Sailors of the units of the fleet in the Galician ports seized control of their ships, killing many of the Rebel officers. For a short while, they were able to seize control of the ports as well, but the Rebels were able to recapture them, although fighting in Galicia continued for several weeks.[74]

Rebel Success in Zaragoza

Zaragoza was one of the major strongholds of the anarchists, and the reunification of the CNT had come about in a congress there just two months before the Civil War began. However, the city fell to the Rebels during the first days of the Civil War.

The local military commander, General Miguel Cabanellas, although having a reputation as a Republican, was one of the leaders of the military conspiracy. When news of the revolt in Morocco reached Zaragoza, he proclaimed his loyalty to the government, but declared a state of siege and admitted Falangistas and other civilian sympathizers with the Rebels into the barracks to join his troops.[75]

The labor organizations had suspected a revolt, and before the War started had come to the civil governor and told him that the military governor was not to be counted upon, and that he should petition Madrid for his removal. However, the civil governor refused. Once the Civil War broke out, the troops in Zaragoza did not indicate right away what their intentions were. There were long conferences with the top officers. Meanwhile, the labor people, who had members in the barracks and knew what was going on there, urged the civil governor to turn over arms from arsenals held by loyal troops to the workers. However, this he refused to do. The workers groups only had pistols. The civil governor finally issued an order that no civilians were to have arms, and that a policeman could shoot on sight anyone found to be armed. This was the excuse, finally, for a general massacre of the left-wing groups which were shot down in cold blood in the streets and in their homes. One Socialist Youth witness to these events subsequently testified that only two of the more than 500 members of his organization survived these murders.[76]

On July 19, by the time the Army and Civil Guards began rounding up CNT leaders, it was too late for an effective reaction. A general strike was declared, but the army soon had the city totally under its control, and Rebel troops moved out to seize virtually all of the Aragón region, of which Zaragoza was the capital.[77]

The Rebellion in Andalusia

The southern region Andalusia had for 75 years been the most important center of anarchist strength among the rural workers. The CNT also had strong support among the workers of Seville, Cadiz and other cities of the region. The Socialists also had wide backing among the urban workers of Andalusia. However, in most of the cities the Rebels were quickly successful, in large degree because the workers and their leaders were outwitted by the rebellious army leaders, and because the civil governors refused to arm the workers and peasants.

Algeciras, near Gibraltar, fell to the Rebels easily. In Cadiz, the Assault Guards distributed arms to the unions, which declared a general strike on July 19. But the civil governor vouched for the loyalty of the army garrison, apparently putting the workers off their guard. When the army revolted in Cádiz on July 20, supported by a Rebel warship, it was able to get full control within 24 hours.

In Seville there occurred perhaps the most bizarre victory of the Rebels in the first days of the War. Only the commander of the Civil Guard was committed to the uprising. He brought Falangistas and other civilian sympathizers into the Civil Guard barracks. The barracks of the Assault Guards were then stormed by the Rebels, and all of the Assault Guards were killed.

Meanwhile, Army General Queipo de Llano, who had just arrived in Seville, joined a small group of Rebels who seized Radio Seville, and announced over it that he was now in charge of the city, after having the Republican anthem played to introduce his speech. The Socialists and anarchists were apparently misled by this proclamation. By the time they became aware that Queipo de Llano was ordering the arrest of their leaders, it was too late for them to mobilize effectively to confront the Rebels. Troops from Morocco were already arriving in Seville to back up the Rebel general.

Queipo de Llano apparently liked his first broadcasting experience. Thereafter, he became famous, as the Radio General, for his frequent and sometimes bizarre radio addresses.

Most other Andalusian cities were captured by the Rebels, including Córdoba, Granada and Huelva.

The one important city in the region which the Rebels did not win was Málaga. At the beginning, the local military and Civil Guard leaders were committed to the conspiracy, only the Assault Guards being loyal. The workers' organizations had few arms.

The local army commander ordered his troops out of their barracks on July 17, and seized the center of the city. However, the Civil Guards garrison mutinied and arrested their commander, so they did not enter into action to support the uprising. On July 18, the army chief ordered his troops back to the barracks, for reasons which are not clear. Thereafter, large numbers of civilians gathered around the barracks. With few arms, they set fire to houses around the barracks, and shot dynamite into the barracks. In the face of that situation, the soldiers surrendered to Assault Guards.[78]

Pedro Vallina, a medical doctor and the most outstanding anarchist leader in Andalusia at the time of the outbreak of the Civil War, has described what happened in the villages and rural areas of that region and nearby parts of Badajóz Province and New Castille:

> At the first notice of the fascist uprising all the villages and rural areas rose at the same time, without previous agreement as if impelled by a spring, arming themselves however they could with from stones and shovels to hunting guns and pistols. They emerged with the most antiquated arms, inservicable, with the desire to arm the people... The municipalities were dissolved and substituted by Revolutionary Committees named by the people; money became inservicable, private property was abolished, particularly in the countryside; the churches burned; the barracks of the civil guard taken by assault, the recognized fascists jailed or shot. From the first moment there was manifested in the masses, as if it were a natural tendency, the aspiration to libertarian communism, without previously having knowledge of these ideas.[79]

In the mining town of Almadén a revolutionary committee was established, headed by Dr Vallina. Within a short while, conditions returned more or less to normal, with the workers, including the miners returning to work.[80]

However, in subsequent weeks the larger part of Andalusia was overrun by Rebel troops.

The Uprising in Valencia

For nearly two weeks, there was a deadlock in Valencia, in spite of the fact that leading elements in the garrison there were committed to the revolt, and *a priori* there seemed to be considerable civilian backing for it as well. The Valencia element of the CEDA Right-wing coalition was the Derecha Regional Valenciana (DRV), led by Lluis Lucia, who had been part of the conspiracy of the disloyal military. He was reported to have offered 50,000 Right-wing militia within three days of the beginning of the planned revolt, to support the Rebels.[81]

On the other hand, the Valencia affiliate of the Falange was reportedly 'nervous', fearful of being involved in a movement which was opposed to its ideals. It offered only 60 militiamen to the rebellious military.[82]

Another important political group in the area before the Civil War was the Partido D'Unión Republicana Aatonomista, which had been founded by the famous writer Vicente Blasco Ibáñez, and in 1936 was headed by his son, Sigfrid Blasco. It had been the largest party in the area, but by 1936 had lost a lot of ground to the Republican parties. During the Civil War it was outlawed by the Republican authorities, although it took a neutral position on the conflict.[83]

The garrison in Valencia did not join either side. The soldiers were ordered to remain in their barracks. At midnight July 18–19, the CNT and UGT declared a general strike, and the CNT Strike Committee ordered its followers to surround the barracks. However, the civil governor resisted for several days the demand that he provide arms for the workers' militia. After the CNT victory in Barcelona, the militia there dispatched substantial arms to their comrades in Valencia.[84] The Guardia de Asalto remained loyal and the 50,000 militiamen promised by the DRV failed to materialize.[85]

The person who was originally scheduled to lead the uprising in

Valencia was General Goded, the army commander in the Balearic Islands. However, he was sure that in Valencia 'everything is in hand and his presence was not indispensable', and he chose to head the revolt in Catalonia, instead.[86]

The commanding general in the area, General Martínez Monje, proclaimed his loyalty to the Republic. However, he strongly rejected demands that he distribute arms to the workers, and demanded an end to the general strike, as being 'unnecessary'.

Meanwhile, the anarchists, Socialists, Republicans and others seized control of all public buildings. The CNT and UGT declared a general strike, seized arms in the port and in ships in the harbor, and began issuing a paper, *UGT–CNT*. They established a new *de facto* civil administration for the region, and began to mobilize militia units. It was not until ten days later that a relatively bloodless general assault was made on the barracks, after the enlisted men challenged their 'neutral' officers, finally assuring that Valencia and the whole of the Levante region would remain loyal to the Republic.[87]

Resistance in the Canary Islands

Even in the Canary Islands, General Franco's base, there was substantial resistance to the Rebels. Although in the early hours of the morning of July 18, insurrectionary troops seized the center of the city of Las Palmas, fighting went on in and around the city most of that day, with Civil Guards and Assault Guards joining with workers in the resistance.

Elsewhere, on the island of Santa Cruz, Assault Guards fought to defend the Republic. Joined by workers, they were able to hold out for ten days. However, by the end of July the Rebels had full control of this Atlantic outpost of Spain.[88]

From Coup to Civil War

A few days after the beginning of the rebellion in Spanish Morocco on July 17 1936, what its fomenters had thought would be a mere *coup d'état* was converted into a civil war. The rebellion had failed in Catalonia, the Levante region, New Castille, the Basque region, Santander, Asturias and half of Extremadura. It had not succeeded in most of the country's major cities; it had failed in the two principal industrial areas, Catalonia and the Basque region.

The main regions which the Rebels had been successful were the predominantly agricultural regions in the south (Andalusia and Extremadura), in the center (Old Castile and Leon), north (Navarre and province of Alava and north-west (Galicia). The main mining area captured by the Rebels was that of the Rio Tinto tin mines, in Andalusia.

Both the Republican and Rebel areas were split into two segments. In the south, the Rebel segment included much of Andalusia and southern Extremadura, and it was cut off from Rebel-controlled regions in Old Castille, Leon, Galicia, Navarre and Aragón by Republican-held regions in northern Extremadura and New Castille. For its part, the Republic was also split – with the larger segment in central and Mediterranean Spain being separated from the Basque, Santander and Asturias regions in the north by the Rebel-held areas of Aragón, Old Castille and Leon.

The country was sharply split in other ways. The urban wage workers and wage earners in agriculture were overwhelmingly on the side of the Republic. Landowning and tenant peasants, small businessmen and professional people were sharply divided in their loyalties between the Republic and the Rebels. Large landholders, industrialists, bankers were all but unanimous in their support of the Rebels.

There was also division along religious lines. Most of the Roman Catholic hierarchy and priesthood supported the Rebels. However, there was one major exception to this, in the Basque provinces, where the hierarchy, the priests and the laity, generally supported the Republic. There were also scattered more liberally minded Catholics in other areas who also backed the Republican cause.

Finally, the armed forces themselves were by no means unanimous in their support of the Rebels. As we have noted earlier in this chapter, a substantial part of the officer corps remained loyal to the Republic, and no small number paid with their lives for this loyalty in the first days of the uprising. However, the loyal officers would continue throughout the Civil War to be subject to suspicion on the part of Loyalist civilians, particularly among the anarchists.

Part Two

The Role of the Anarchists in the Republican Military

5

The Overall Role of the Anarchists in the Spanish Republican Military

One aspect of anarchist participation in the Spanish Civil War that has received inadequate attention, both from those who were chronicling the War when it was in progress, and those who have written its history subsequently, has been the anarchists' role in the military forces that fought for the Republic. Both the chroniclers and the historians tended to treat the subject in one of two ways: to ignore it, or to emphasize the 'indiscipline' of the anarchist forces.

Hugh Thomas, in his long history of the Civil War, largely ignores the important part played in the military by the anarchists, giving them virtually no credit, for example, in the victory of the battle of Guadalajara, where they were a crucial factor, and concentrating instead in that battle, and many of the others, on the supposedly key role of the International Brigades. For their part, of course, the Communist commentators and historians have had little to say about the anarchist troops except about their alleged lack of discipline. Typical of the observations of the Stalinists and their fellow-travellers were those of Louis Fischer: 'The Anarchists usually fought badly'. Elaborating on this in connection with the battle of Madrid, he said, '... Many anarchists were interested first of all in establishing a libertarian republic in Spain and did not see eye to eye with the Socialists and Communists or the bourgeois Republicans, and were none too enthusiastic about dying for the Caballero government. It was not "important".'[1] He also claimed that the anarchists 'kept their arms and their men for the Revolution while Franco won victories which would wipe out all social gains'.[2]

Even the anarchists themselves have tended to give very little emphasis to their military participation in the conflict. Rather, in their accounts during and after the War they preferred to write about their role in reorganizing the rural and urban economy of Loyalist Spain, and about their participation in the Catalan and Republican governments; dealing with military matters, if at all, only in passing.

There have been a few exceptions among the anarchists. Eduardo de Guzmán recounted something of their part in the battle of Madrid, Ricardo Sanz wrote memoirs of his experiences as successor to Durruti as commander of the Durruti Column (later the 26th Division), and Cipriano Mera similarly wrote his memoirs, which included an account of his role as a major military leader on the Madrid front during most of the War. Diego Abad de Santillán, Juan García Oliver and César Lorenzo, in their accounts of the Civil War, dealt with some limited aspects, as did José Peirats in his study of the CNT in the Civil War, while Abel Paz wrote a study of the Iron Column. However, no anarchist writer has drawn an overall picture of the role of the anarchists in the Spanish Republican army.

General Development of the Military Phases of the Civil War

Following the fighting of the first few days after July 17 1936, it became clear that what was underway was a civil war, not a traditional military *coup* or *pronunciamiento*. The country was clearly divided between those regions which had remained loyal to the Republic, and those which had been seized by the rebellious military conspirators and their civilian allies. The Civil War, which divided Spain after the failure of the insurgents to be immediately successful throughout the peninsula, lasted for 32 months.

During the first phase of the conflict, the Rebels conducted campaigns in both northern and southern sectors. In the south, General Franco's forces first drove north in Extremadura to take Mérida and

Badajóz, near the Portuguese frontier, where they conducted one of the war's most atrocious mass murders of Republicans and their sympathizers in the city's bullring. They then drove north into New Castille, seizing Talavera de la Reina, and relieving the Loyalist siege of the Alcazar of Toledo, ending up in the outer fringes of Madrid. In the process of this campaign, the northern and southern Rebel armies were joined, and the Republican Basque country, Santander and Asturias were definitively isolated from the rest of Loyalist Spain.

In the north, General Mola's troops drove from Alava into the Basque province of Guipuzcoa, first seizing Irun, on the French frontier, and then driving further south to take the city of San Sebastian. Further west, Rebel troops drove from Galicia into the western segments of Asturias, and ended up by relieving the besieged Rebel garrison in the Asturian capital of Oviedo, succeeding in maintaining a thin line of contact between that city and the westernmost Rebel forces.

In this same early period of the Civil War, Loyalist forces, consisting principally of anarchist militiamen from Catalonia, moved rapidly into the Aragón region, reconquering about half of it for the Republic. Catalan forces also mounted an attack on Mallorca, the largest of the Balearic Islands, which the Rebels had been able to seize, but this assault failed.

The second phase of the Civil War, lasting from early November 1936 until March 1937, centered on Madrid. Although the forces of Franco and Mola had expected that the national capital would easily fall into their hands, after the unbroken series of defeats which the Republicans had suffered to the south of Madrid, Loyalist forces put up an amazing defense, which finally brought Franco to give up, temporarily, efforts to capture the city, and shift to other fronts.

Before the mounting of the Rebel attack on the isolated northern Republican areas, two unsuccessful Loyalist offenses took place. The government of Prime Minister Francisco Largo Caballero had planned a major attack on Rebel forces in Extremadura, designed to split the Rebel armies into two separated sectors by driving to the Portuguese border, as well as to mobilize the resistance of the strongly pro-Loyalist population of northern Extremadura. However, for political reasons which we shall note in a subsequent chapter, this offensive never took place.

Subsequently, the new Republican government of Prime Minister Juan Negrín launched an offensive against Brihuega, in the Madrid area, which after an initial success, was turned back, with the help of Rebel troops brought down from the north. Shortly afterwards, another Loyalist offensive was undertaken against Belchite, on the Aragón front, with the objective of possibly breaking through to make contact with the Republican forces in the Basque country. As in the case of the Brihuega offensive, that against Belchite also failed.

The next phase of the Civil War centered on the north. One of the major handicaps which faced the Republican forces in the north was what came to be known as the 'cantonalism' of the area. The northern front consisted of three distinct regions, the Basque Republic, Santander, and Asturias. Each had its ruling body, and all efforts effectively to coordinate the Republican military effort in the region tended to be thwarted by the autonomy of each of these bodies.

The Communist history of the Civil War quite correctly noted the effects of this cantonalism: 'Each of these organs dedicated itself to issuing its own money ... each one had its own militia and military leadership; each one had its commercial apparatus and its own supply services; each one put artificial obstacles in the way of reciprocal cooperation which the war clearly required.'[3]

Beginning on March 31 1937, the forces of General Mola began the effort to eliminate the northern sector of Republican Spain, by opening an offensive against the Basque province of Vizcaya. After several weeks of combat, the supposedly impregnable fortifications protecting Bilbao were overcome, the city was captured on May 19, and most of the rest of Vizcaya soon fell to the Rebels. After a short period of regrouping, the Mola forces then attacked Santander, to the west of the Basque provinces, and overran it with relative ease.

However, the final struggle in the north, for the Asturias region, was a much more hard-fought campaign. It lasted for two and a half months, with the Asturian militiamen and other troops fighting for nearly every inch of ground, and was not over until October 21 1937.

The liquidation of the northern front had more than military significance. It put under Rebel control the substantial economic resources of the iron and coal mines of the region, as well as the principal center of iron and steel production, which were not only useful for the provision of material for the insurgent forces, but also made it possible for the Rebel regions to acquire extensive foreign exchange through sale of minerals abroad, particularly to Great Britain.

The next campaign was an offensive by the Loyalists. This was an attack on the Teruel sector in southern Aragón, and was launched on December 15 1937, and lasted for more than two months before the Republican forces were decisively thrown back across the Ebro river on February 11 1938.

Only a few weeks later, on March 9 1938, the Rebels launched their attack on the Aragón region. In spite of strong resistance by the Republican forces there, the Franco army overran the region, and even conquered the Lerida section of south-western Catalonia. Following this victory, the Rebels were able to drive to the Mediterranean coast, splitting Loyalist Spain once again into two separated sectors, Catalonia to the north, and the rest of the Republican area to the south. Efforts by General Franco's forces to drive south and take Valencia were finally stopped by determined Loyalist resistance.

On July 25 1938, the Loyalists launched their last major offensive of the Civil War. This was the so-called Ebro campaign, in which the Republican forces crossed that river, taking the Franco forces by surprise. Again, after initial success, the Republican forces, drawn largely from those based in Catalonia, were decisively defeated by the Rebels, but only after three months' bitter fighting. This Loyalist defeat opened the way for the final phase of the conflict. The Ebro battle ended on November 15.

During this last phase of the war, the economic situation in Republican Spain approached the desperate. Adolfo Bueso, a POUMist trade union leader who lived through the experience, described the food situation in Barcelona in the months before Franco troops overran Catalonia:

...Rationing of food was rigorous and there was real hunger. The *rabassaires*, who now had 'their' land once again, proved the most egoistic people in the world, and what they produced was carefully hidden to 'exchange' for other goods, not for money, which was virtually worthless. This situation brought about a great movement towards the countryside, periodically, of those who had something of value to exchange for agricultural products. The trains – scarce – and the buses left, daily, full of women and some men, with baskets containing objectives of value, or tobacco, acquired who knows how, and in the towns they dedicated their efforts to look for 'whatever' to be able to feed the family, since in Barcelona, in the markets and shops, nothing was to be found...

What the government succeeded in importing 'with the gold which remained', went, naturally, in part to the army, other parts to the armed police, another to the immense bureaucracy which had its cooperatives, and for the workers nothing was left except the famous lentils of Doctor Negro, which were not really such, but a kind of carob bean seed. Bread, rationed, was for the undistinguished people, of terrible quality, almost black and enormously heavy. The distinguished ones enjoyed another kind of bread, which, although not completely white was very superior to that distributed in the rations. This first class bread was made, officially, for hospitals, sanataria and other such centers, but also found its way to the table of the ministers, councillors and the whole bureaucracy which surrounded them.[4]

In the last days of December 1938, the Franco forces began their campaign to liquidate Republican Catalonia. They had completed it by the first week of February 1939, when the last Republican forces of the Catalonia region, together with hundreds of thousands of civilians crossed the French border, and the Franco forces reached the same frontier.

After the collapse of Republican Catalonia, there was a hiatus in the military conflict. The Franco forces apparently awaited the disintegration of the Loyalist forces in the remaining Republican area. It was not long in coming.

Although Prime Minister Juan Negrín returned to the area still held by the Republic, his decision to turn definitive control of what remained of the Loyalist military over to the Communist Party provoked a violent reaction. Led by Colonel Segismundo Casado, and supported by anarchists, Socialists and most Republicans, and troops under their control, an insurrection in Madrid declared the end of the Negrín regime and establishment of a National Defense Council on March 5 1939. It had to face a counter-insurrection by Communist-led troops, who were ultimately defeated.

The National Defense Council sought an 'honorable' peace with the Franco forces. However, Generalissimo Francisco Franco was unreceptive to that idea and, when it became clear that no accommodation would be possible, the remaining Loyalist forces disintegrated. By the end of March 1939, the Republic had ceased to exist and, on March 28 1939, Franco's forces finally entered Madrid, symbolizing the end of the Spanish Civil War.

Significance of Anarchist Participation in the Military Struggle

The anarchists were a major force in the military defense of Republican Spain. In the first place, they were largely responsible for the original failure of the Rebels in Catalonia, the Levante and much of Andalusia, as well as in Santander and much of Asturias. It was principally anarchist militiamen who reconquered half of Aragón during the first weeks of the War, although they were not successful in capturing either Zaragoza or Huesca. Similarly, it was anarchist militiamen who formed the core of the last-ditch but unsuccessful defense of Irun and San Sebastian during that same period.

Anarchist militiamen played a very significant role in the defense of Madrid, and other anarchists were largely responsible for constructing defense works in and around the capital, although one would hardly know either of these facts from most accounts of the conflict. Similarly, they made up most of the troops in the ill-fated defense of Málaga, and together with Socialist troops were the major defenders of both Santander and Asturias.

During the first year at least of the Civil War, anarchists made up the considerable majority of the rank and file soldiers in the

Republican military. When, in time, the Loyalist Army became increasingly a conscript force, their numerical importance undoubtedly considerably declined, but they continued until the end of the war to constitute a very large part of the Republican soldiery.

The Major Difficulties of the Anarchists in the Military

However, in the military struggle, and in the constant political maneuvering in and around the armed forces which continued throughout the War, the anarchists had two severe handicaps. These were their own ingrained anti-militarist prejudices, and the rapid growth of Communist influence within the Republican military hierarchy at all levels, virtually from the onset of the War.

As principled enemies of authority of all kinds, the Spanish anarchists were particularly opposed at the beginning of the Civil War to military authority, the chain of command, and the very idea of command itself. It took time for the anarchists to compromise these principles in the face of the exigencies of organized modern warfare, and (being the decentralized kind of movement they were) it took some anarchist groups and individuals longer than others to adapt to the needs of the military conflict.

In the beginning, the anarchist armed forces were militia groups of more or less lightly armed civilians. They at first tried to run their militia organizations like units of the CNT, with abhorrence of hierarchical ranks, and plenums to decide on tactics and strategy.

However, the anarchists more or less quickly came to realize the inadequacy of this kind of organization and behavior for fighting a modern war. They were faced on the other side of the fighting front with a highly disciplined regular army, and very soon with Italian and German regular forces (despite their disguise as volunteers) as well. Even the Falangista and Tradicionalista militiamen on the Franco side readily accepted military discipline.

So the anarchists more or less quickly had to face the fateful conflict between their traditional beliefs and principles, and the requirements of fighting a civil war. They had to accept 'militarization' of their militia. What was probably most surprising about this

150

acceptance of a very considerable degree of hierarchization and centralized command by the anarchists was the rapidity with which it came about.

However, one long-lasting effect of their initial reluctance was that the officer corps of the Republican army did not reflect the proportion of anarchist troops in the rank and file. Ideological inhibitions prevented many anarchist militiamen who might have become officers from applying to officers' training schools, even though one of their own, Juan García Oliver, was in charge of organizing and directing them during the early months of the War. This numerical deficiency of anarchist officers persisted throughout the conflict, in part at least because of the late start in recruiting CNT–FAI personnel for posts of command.

Communist Gains in the Military

The military reticence of the anarchists was undoubtedly an important factor in the rapid rise of Communist influence within the Republican armed forces. From the very beginning of the conflict, the Communists were perfectly willing to accept the full extent of military hierarchy and discipline. After all, their own party was organized along hierarchical and highly disciplined lines, and their famous Fifth Regiment, originally established in Madrid during the first weeks of the War, became a model for the new Popular Army which the government of Prime Minister Francisco Largo Caballero began to organize. Officers and men from it quickly rose to positions of command in the units of that new army in various parts of the Republican territory.

Burnett Bolloten cites the explanation of Fernando Claudín, a long-time member of the Communist Party, for the rapid rise of influence of the Communists in the Republican military:

The Communist International and the Communist party of Spain understood from the first moment the decisive nature of the military problem. With the help of Soviet technicians and Communist cadres from other countries, the Spanish Communist

151

party concentrated all its energies on the solution of this problem. Its structure, its method of functioning, the training of its cadres, made it particularly adept for this task... The semimilitary features of the Bolshevik model after which it had fashioned itself enabled the Communist party of Spain to convert itself rapidly into the *military party* of the Republic, into the organizational nucleus of the army, that had to be created quickly and without which everything was condemned to death...[5]

David Cattell has suggested: 'It would be quite true to say that without the Communists as the unifying and driving factor, the Loyalist forces would have been defeated long before 1939.'[6] Although this may be something of an exaggeration, it is undoubtedly true that the Stalinists' immediate acceptance of the need for a regular army to confront that of Franco paid them very extensive political dividends throughout the war.

The Communists' attitude towards things military gave them several advantages from the outset. On the one hand, it provided them with more efficient troops in the early months of the War than the rather loosely organized and commanded militia units which were under the leadership of the anarchists and other political and trade union forces. On the other hand, the Communists' willingness to accept fully the rigors of military discipline attracted many of the regular officers who remained loyal to the Republic, many of whom were appalled by what they conceived (by no means entirely correctly) as indiscipline bordering on chaos in many of the militia units. Many of the most famous of these regular officers, such as Generals José Miaja, Sebastian Pozas and air-force commander Ignacio Hidalgo de Cisneros, probably joined the Communist Party and belonged to it for a longer or shorter period during the conflict.

One ranking professional officer who was widely presumed at the time to have joined the Communist Party, Vicente Rojo, apparently never did. He was in fact a man of conservative inclinations and a practicing Catholic. However, after his key role in the defense of Madrid, he was the beneficiary of widespread praise from the Stalinist propaganda machine, and worked closely with them for a considerable period of time.

Concerning the politics of Rojo, Palmiro Togliatti reported to his Moscow superiors: 'It is at least strange to observe that each time a military disaster was about to be produced, he took a step towards the CP. In 1937–1938, before the second phase of the operations of Teruel, he declared that the only party in which he could enter was the CP. In 1938, on the eve of the fascist offensive, his son asked for a party card and Rojo himself asked Negrín to authorize him to enter the Communist Party (Negrín refused the authorization).' However, Togliatti concluded that, in the light of Rojo's friendship with certain other military leaders, including General Miaja, 'his philocommunist declarations are at least strange.'[7]

In retrospect, Togliatti was critical of how the Communist Party had handled the professional military men it recruited. He noted, in reporting to the Comintern: '...The party accepted many elements (career men) without control and without making efforts to educate them as Communists or insisting that they always respond to the party for their actions (no known military man was publicly castigated for his weaknesses or errors)... That is one of the reasons why so many Communist military men betrayed us at the last moment.'[8]

With the advent of substantial Soviet military aid and the arrival of Soviet military advisers, starting at least as early as October 1936, the Communists' hand in the control and direction of the military was greatly strengthened, to the detriment particularly of the anarchists. Throughout the War, the anarchists complained bitterly about the refusal of the Russians to allow the provision of sufficient arms to their troops, and there is enough evidence to indicate this complaint had considerable justification.

Burnett Bolloten has drawn on several sources to describe the extent of the influence of Soviet military men in the higher reaches of the Republican military establishment:

'As time went on,' writes Colonel Segismundo Casado, operations chief on the general staff is the early months of the war, 'Russian influence was increased at the War Ministry. [The Russian military advisers] looked over the plans of the General Staff and through the minister they rejected many technical proposals and imposed others.' In a later passage he says: 'These "friendly advisers" exercised authority just as much in the Air Force and in the Tank Corps.' Of Russian influence in high places, Luis Araquistáin writes: 'The Air Force directed by the Russians, operated when and where they pleased, without any coordination with the land and sea forces. The navy and air minister, Indalecio Prieto, meek and cynical, made fun of his office to anyone who visited him, declaring that he was neither a minister nor anything else because he received absolutely no obedience from the Air Force. The real air minister was the Russian General Douglas [Yakov Smuchkevich].' Later on, he adds: 'Behind the [Russian officers] were innumerable political agents who were disguised as commercial agents and were in real control of Spanish politics. They directed the Russian officers, the Communist party and Rosenberg himself, the Soviet ambassador, who in reality was only an ambassador of straw. The real ambassadors were those mysterious men who entered Spain under false names and were working under direct orders from the Kremlin and the Russian police.[9]

However, Soviet influence in the Republican military establishment had other effects which also favored both Soviet objectives and those of the Spanish Communists. The Russians had virtually complete control of the Republican air force, and could provide or deny air support to Republican land operations as they saw fit. The most notorious case of their refusal of such support was Largo Caballero's proposed offensive into Extremadura in May 1937. In addition, the anarchists frequently claimed that Soviet and Spanish Communist influence within the land forces was frequently exercised to send Communist-controlled troops into action where success and consequent glory was most likely, reserving for anarchist troops the most difficult and more or less hopeless assignments, with the disadvantage for the anarchists that their casualties were particularly high and that their 'inefficiency' could be blamed for failure.

The early approach to hegemony which the Communists obtained within the Republican armed forces gave them the opportunity to use another weapon against not only the anarchists but also against other elements, such as the Largo Caballero Socialists, who sought to block their rise to total control of the military. This was the instrument of coercion and intimidation, used to recruit unwilling officers and soldiers into the Communist Party, to eliminate, sometimes physically, those who were unwilling to do so, and to attempt to put Communist officers in command of predominantly anarchist or Socialist military units, from which positions they could work to get the troops under them to follow the Communist line.

Finally, the Communists had another advantage in their struggle with the anarchists within the armed forces. This was their propaganda apparatus both within Spain itself and in the rest of the world. The anarchists could not match that apparatus within the Republic, particularly after a generally Communist-controlled censorship was imposed following the May 1937 events in Catalonia. Nor could they even approach the efficiency and extent of Communist propaganda in the rest of the world; outside of Spain, the anarchist movement was exceedingly weak, had few propaganda resources of its own, and had little access to the capitalist press, while the Communists had a world-wide, highly disciplined and amply funded propaganda apparatus.

The upshot of this was that the Communists had an extensive ability to create myths about their 'heroes' or about others they wanted to make heroes (whether the Communists Lister and El Campesino or regular officers such as Generals Miaja and Rojo). At the same time, they were able to ignore the feats of such anarchist military leaders as Cipriano Mera and Ricardo Sanz, and could totally destroy the reputations of those regular army officers who would not join their ranks or submit to their domination. A notorious case of this was that of General José Asensio.

The Significance of Anarchist–Communist Rivalry in the Military

Throughout the Civil War, the most significant political struggle behind the Republican lines was that between the anarchists and the Communists. At the beginning of the War, anarchist influence was predominant in Catalonia, Aragón, the Málaga region, while in the Levante and Santander and Asturias, they shared the leadership of the Loyalist regime with the Socialists. The Communists clearly knew that, if they were to be able to get complete control of the Spanish Republic, and direct it in conformity with the international strategy and tactics of the Stalinist regime, they would have to destroy the anarchist movement.

Nowhere was this more the case than within the Republican armed forces. So long as the anarchists continued to have a substantial part of the Republican army under their command, Communist control of the regime could not be assured. This was clearly demonstrated at the time of the uprising led by Colonel Segismundo Casado in the last weeks of the War.

From the point of view of the anarchists themselves, their participation in the armed struggle against the Franco forces presented them with grave ideological and political problems. Although the anarchists were forced by the circumstances of the War to make basic ideological compromises in the economic sphere, in social and cultural matters, and in politics, they had to make the greatest concessions of all in the military arena. It was not easy for them to do so, but the degree to which they did was probably most amply demonstrated by the fact that at the end of the War they were in a position, through their control of key army units, to offer a successful armed challenge to the Communists' final drive to get control of what remained of the Republican Army, Unfortunately for the anarchists (as well as for the rest of the supporters of the Republic), it was none the less too late at that point to prevent the overwhelming and conclusive victory of the Rebel forces, ushering in the long night of the Franco regime.

Conclusion

In the chapters which follow in this section we hope to make up to at least a modest degree for the failure of historians of the Spanish Civil War to give sufficient attention to the participation of the anarchists in the military struggle. We shall trace the role of the anarchist-led troops on the Aragón–Catalan front, in the defense of Madrid, and in the Republican military in other parts of Spain. We shall then trace the struggle over the question of 'militarization' of the anarchist militia, and the results of the anarchists' (tardy) acceptance of that requirement. I hope that these chapters will present a more correct and adequate view of the anarchists' role in the armed defense of the Spanish Republic than that offered by 'the accepted wisdom'.

Anarchists played a significant role in all phases of the military struggle of the Spanish Civil War. In a few instances, they had important positions of leadership, although, for the reasons we have already noted, except on the Aragón front in the first year, and in Santander and Asturias, they were always overshadowed by other political elements, particularly the Communists. In subsequent chapters, I will sketch more exactly the role the anarchists did play in the military phases of the Spanish Civil War.

6

Anarchists in the Army in Aragón and Catalonia

Once victory over the rebellious military men and their allies had been achieved in Catalonia, one of the major tasks facing the anarchists and their allies was that of dealing with the fact that the military rebels had won control of the capital city of the neighboring region of Aragón, Zaragoza, and most of the rest of that province. The mobilization of a military force to reverse this situation was of greatest urgency.

This task was undertaken by the new General Council of Antifascist Militia, in which the anarchists were the overwhelmingly dominant element. The militia units which were recruited in the days and weeks following the defeat of the military rebellion in Catalonia became the core of the Republican Army units which confronted General Franco's forces in the neighboring region of Aragón, and ultimately in Catalonia itself for more than two years.

The Aragón–Catalonia region was the part of Spain in which the anarchist role in the Republican Army was most pronounced, both in terms of the rank and file soldiers and the commanders of key military units. However, it was also the area in which anarchist-controlled military units suffered most clearly from the determination of the Republican government to deprive the anarchist military of the financial support, arms and equipment, which they needed to play what might have been the decisive role in the victory of the Loyalist cause in the Civil War.

First Recruiting of Militia Units

Soon after they had triumphed in Catalonia, the anarchists realized that the Rebels had succeeded in occupying Zaragoza and most of Aragón. It was clear to them that it was urgently necessary to send armed units into Aragón, not only to recapture what they thought of as the most anarchist city in Spain, but also to prevent Zaragoza from being used as a base for an attack on Catalonia. Furthermore, the capture of Zaragoza would pave the way for a drive to link up the Catalonia–Aragón Republican area with the Loyalist forces in the Basque region, Santander and Asturias.

It was thus decided to organize 'militia' units to battle the Rebel troops in Aragón. On July 22, Juan García Oliver made a speech on the Barcelona radio in which he announced the forthcoming formation of Militia columns. According to the account of the speech in *Solidaridad Obrera* the following day, he announced the reason for the columns as being 'the domination of Zaragoza by the military, and the possibility of an advance of the fascist columns of the Aragónese region into Catalan land....'[1]

The General Militia Committee decided that the first militia column should mobilize at the Paseo de Gracia in Barcelona at 10 a.m. on July 24.[2] At eight o'clock that morning, Buenaventura Durruti went on the radio and called on the workers of the city to bring food and other requirements for the new militia column to the assembly area.[3]

The Consejo de Milicias had at first calculated that they needed 12,000 armed men to carry the campaign to Zaragoza.[4] However, the first column, commanded by Buenaventura Durruti and Lieutenant-Colonel Enrique Pérez Farras, as political leader and military adviser respectively, was by no means of that size. The major biographer of Durruti estimated the number at 2,000;[5] Diego Abad de Santillán put the figure at 3,000, whereas García Oliver said that it was 5,000.[6]

Louis Mercier, a Chilean Frenchman who fought in the Durruti Column during the first six months of the War, has noted that at its inception, the column, like most of the militia units, was made up mainly of people with no military experience. The leaders were people who had perhaps done their two years' conscription, had fought in some other war, in Africa or somewhere else, even in the Great War, but who had not shot a rifle in years. There was a sizeable group of foreigners in the Durruti Column, who were the main technicians of the group. There were ultimately as many as 500 of them, and Germans were particularly heavily represented.[7]

Apparently, Durruti at first thought of recruiting some of the soldiers from the Barcelona garrison for the expedition to Aragón. Durruti and infantry Major Salavera visited the barracks of the Alcantará and Badajóz infantry regiments soliciting volunteers for the Durruti Column, and reportedly met enthusiastic response from the soldiers and noncoms.[8] However, for whatever reasons, these soldiers were not used in the Column.

After the departure of the Durruti Column, the militia recruiting campaign continued. Abad de Santillán commented: 'Within a few days, more than one hundred fifty thousand volunteers enlisted to fight where necessary against the military rebellion.' He added: 'To half-way organize this huge mass, we did not have any vestige of the old army.'[9] As one part of the recruiting campaign, a special committee was set up 'to bring together and channel soldiers who had abandoned their units and wanted to go voluntarily into combat.'[10]

Several other militia columns were soon organized. The second was commanded by Antonio Ortíz, like Durruti, a member of the anarchist group Nosotros. In addition, the anarchists organized a column commanded by Domingo Ascaso and Cristobal Aldabaldet-reco, and the Tierra y Libertad Column commanded by *companero* Maeztú. The Catalan Communist Party, the Partido Socialista Unificado de Catalonia (PSUC), also organized the Karl Marx Column, led by Manuel Trueba and José Del Barrio, and the dissident Communist Party, the Partido Obrero de Unificación Marxista (POUM) sent the Lenin Column, commanded by José Rovira. The Catalan Left Party organized the Macía–Companys

Column. Finally, 'there was sent to the front of Huesca a small unit of *carabineros* and Assault Guards, which fought well when they had to operate in support of the militia,' according to Juan García Oliver.[11]

García Oliver summed up this early mobilization of Catalan militia: 'To cover what came to be the front of Aragón, some 300 kilometers from the French frontier to Belchite, there were sent forces consisting of 30,000 militiamen, of whom four-fifths were anarcho-syndicalists.'[12]

The Early Victories of Catalan Troops

The various militia columns organized in Catalonia completely freed their region of Rebel troops. They then moved into Aragón. On July 26, the Barcelona daily *La Vanguardia* announced that the Aragónese city of Caspe had been occupied by loyalist troops, 'after a small bombardment'.[13] From there, the Durruti Column continued to move north-east, taking a number of towns including, on July 27, Bujaraloz, where the column was ultimately to establish its general headquarters.[14]

However, the avowed objective of the Durruti Column from the time it left Barcelona had been to recapture Zaragoza. Thus, Franz Borkenau, who visited Catalonia early in August 1936, found that the issue seemed to be not whether Zaragoza would be reconquered by the Loyalist forces, but rather when this would take place.[15]

Abel Paz (Diego Camacho), the biographer of Buenaventura Durruti, has explained the circumstances of the failure to take Zaragoza. First, he noted that the day after the capture of Bujaraloz, as the militia column headed towards the Aragón capital, it 'came into contact with the reality of war. The fascist airforce bombarded it, which demoralised not a few of the militiamen who, panic-stricken, began to run... The bombardment, to their surprise, had been deadly, costing a dozen deaths and more than twenty wounded... In the face of that blow, Durruti felt that it was preferable to withdraw and become better informed about the enemy's positions, so as to avoid an ambush...'[16]

Subsequently, according to Abel Paz, the Durruti Column continued its advance, coming within 20 kilometers of Zaragoza, 'but was detained by the river and the resistance offered by the troops of the Aragónese capital. As a consequence, the Durruti Column established a good and useful network of trenches and machinegun nests in their forward positions.' The Central Militia Committee of Catalonia then ordered them to await reinforcements from militia units operating on the other (Zaragoza) side of the Ebro river.[17]

The Communists frequently attacked the initial failure of the anarchist militia to take Zaragoza. They went so far as to blame it on the CNT troops' insisting on working only an eight-hour day, when a few more hours might have taken them to the Aragónese capital.[18] Given the initial enthusiasm of the anarchist troops, and the importance of Zaragoza as one of the principal centers of anarchist strength before the War, this seems rather unlikely. More probable explanations would seem to be the utter inexperience of Buenaventura Durruti with military strategy and tactics (even though he was advised by a professional officer) and the fact that, in the ten days that transpired between the Rebel uprising and the arrival of Catalan militiamen in the vicinity of Zaragoza, there was sufficient time for the military leaders there to organize an adequate defense against a force of untrained and lightly armed civilians.

In the meantime, other Catalan militia columns, which recruited more members from the various parts of Aragón into which they entered, were occupying most of Aragón east of the Ebro river, and small areas on the other side of the river. Although most of these units were composed of and led by anarchists, other political groups were also represented in the spontaneous army which appeared after July 19. Franz Borkenau reported at the time that these early columns also received an appreciable number of recruits among deserters from the Rebel Army, many of whom had been Socialists or Anarchists before being drafted.[19] However, he also commented on the failure of revolutionary villages to send their young men into the militia.[20]

These early militia columns had only the most rudimentary training before going off to battle. Franz Borkenau commented on this early in August; 'I had dinner with a group of militia, who talked about their military training, and I was horrified to learn that all they were taught, before going to the front, was the use of their rifles; no training in the terrain, in digging trenches, etc.'[21]

Once the front had stabilized in Aragón, the political alignment of the various forces which were to man the Aragón front for the first year of the War became clear. At the far north, on the French border, was a small Catalan Left Party column. Just south of it, facing the Rebel-held city of Huesca, was the Lenin Column of the anti-Stalinist Partido Obrero de Unificación Marxista. Abutting it to the south was the anarcho-syndicalist Ascaso Column, led by Nosotros member Gregorio Jover, which had on its left the Aguiluchos Column, composed of Juventudes Libertarias, and for a short while commanded by Juan García Oliver, but then by Miguel García Vivencos.

Just south of the Aguiluchos Column was the Carlos Marx Column, organized by the Catalan Stalinists, the Partido Socialista Unificado de Catalonia, and led by José del Barrio. It was flanked to the south by another POUM militia group, the Maurín Column, led by José Rovira, which had on its left the Durruti Column.

In the far south of the Aragón front, to the south of the Ebro river, were the sizeable anarcho-syndicalist Ortíz Column, led by Antonio Ortíz, and two smaller groups, the Peñalver and Mena Columns, both of which had been organized in the Catalan city of Tarragona,[22] and the Macía–Companys Column of the Catalan Left Party, which connected on its left with the Iron Column from the Valencia region.[23]

A small number of regular army officers and rank and file were also found in the Republican troops on the Aragón front. Centered on Barbastro, and led by Colonel José Villalba, these elements remained loyal to the Republic and began operations against Huesca and Jaca, which unfortunately bore no fruit.[24]

Defeat in the Balearic Islands

One early defeat of the Catalan troops, including both anarchists and units of other political coloration, was the unsuccessful expedition in the Balearic Islands in August 1936. In the two smaller islands of

Menorca and Ibiza, the rebellion of July 19 had been put down, but in Mallorca it had succeeded. The islands had considerable interest for the Catalans, both because of their strategic importance and because the people of the area spoke Catalan.

However, at the beginning of the war, the Catalan Central Militia Committee had made the decision to concentrate its efforts on the campaign to retake Aragón, and quite deliberately did not plan for an attack on Mallorca. Nevertheless, Captain Alberto Bayó, an aviation officer who had remained loyal, decided to undertake on his own, without consulting the Central Militia Committee, an expedition to recapture Mallorca. Juan García Oliver subsequently suspected that Bayó had the support of Catalan President Luis Companys in this effort.

More important than the backing of Companys, however, was the fact that Bayó won the support of the maritime section of the CNT's Transport Workers Union of Barcelona. Claiming to speak not only for Companys but also for the Militia Committee, Bayó asked the help of that union to obtain the fleet and men necessary for the expedition. The maritime unit was a particularly independent part of the CNT, and had at his disposal not only two destroyers, a gunboat, a torpedo boat, three submarines and various other units, but also about 5,000 men, A small group commanded by a Civil Guards captain also joined the expedition from Valencia, but most of the Valencians returned home before landing on Mallorca, as the result of a controversy between Captain Bayó and Civil Guard Captain Uribarry over who should be in command.

Instead of making a frontal attack on Palma de Mallorca, which was defended by less than 600 soldiers, and where the people were strongly republican and anarchist in sympathies, Bayó landed his forces on isolated beaches a long distance from the city. There his forces were subjected to attacks by small enemy units, and were finally pinned down to a small area on the coast.

At that point, Bayó sought help from the Central Militia Committee of Catalonia. After sending two observers to the island, the committee decided to Provide him the cannon and other equipment which he had requested. However, even with that reinforcement, Captain Bayó was unable to make any headway. Large numbers of

Italian troops landed to back the Rebels. After about two weeks, Bayó executed a disastrous retreat during which he lost many prisoners and a large part of the equipment which he had taken on the expedition. This incident resulted in putting the Italians in firm control of the largest of the Balearic Islands.

Upon his return to Barcelona, Captain Bayó was arrested. Although most members of the Militia Committee, of all political colors, thought that he ought really to be court martialed and executed, they decided, for political rather than military reasons, merely to separate him from the Republican armed forces.[25]

Many years later, this same Captain Alberto Bayó won himself another footnote in history by being the person who gave guerrilla training to the small force of Fidel Castro's 26th of July Movement before it took off from Mexico to invade Cuba late in 1956.

Organization of Catalan Forces on the Aragón Front

So long as the General Committee of Antifascist Militia existed as the *de facto* government of Catalonia, the militia columns in Aragón were under its command. Once the anarchists had entered the Catalan government and the Antifascist Committee was ended, the Catalan troops were under the overall command of the Consejería de Defensa of the government of Catalonia, headed by Colonel Felipe Díaz Sandino, but in which the CNT was effectively in control, one of its leaders being secretary-general of that ministry. Until he entered the Republican government early in November 1936, Juan García Oliver held that post – similar to the position he had held in the General Militia Committee.[26] Thereafter, until after the events of May 1937, Juan Manuel Molina of the CNT, was secretary-general of the Consejería de Defensa of the Catalan Generalidad.[27]

After the armed conflict in Barcelona and some other Catalan cities early in May 1937, the Catalan government lost its control of the armed forces on the Aragón front. At the same time, the situation of the anarcho-syndicalist commanders, officers and troops became increasingly difficult in the face of pressures and persecutions from the Communists.

At the beginning of the Civil War all of the militia units which fought on the Aragón front were led by politicians or trade union leaders. With very few exceptions, these men were without any military experience, and in a great number of cases had been lifelong anti-militarists.

The anarchist leaders, both those who led units to the front and those who remained in the rear echelon to participate in the organization and conduct of the government, the economy and other aspects of civil society, realized the need for people with military training and experience (and more or less skill). So, from the outset, the leaders of the various columns were accompanied and assisted by military advisers, who were career military men. Of course, the great majority of the military officers in Catalonia, as elsewhere in Spain, had joined in the Rebellion of the armed forces on July 19–19 1936. However, there were enough loyal officers to provide at least some strategic and tactical advice to the leaders of the militia columns, and to help organize them into units which could conduct a more or less modern war.

In spite of the supposed subordination of the various militia columns to the Central Militia Committee in Barcelona, the fact was that for many months, each militia group was more or less sovereign within the area where it was located and which it was protecting. As a result of each unit being of a particular political coloration, there was considerable tension, and sometimes even conflict, between units of different ideological persuasions.

The Militia Committee, and subsequently the Consejería de Defensa of the Catalan government, tried from time to time to establish a unified command, and to tighten its control over the various units. As early as September, the Committee named a regular army officer, Lieutenant-Colonel Reyes, as head of a unified command. However, a meeting of the principal officials of the military sector of the Militia Committee and the commanders of the various militia units seems to have concluded without ratifying that decision.[28]

With the passage of time and the attempts of both the Catalan and Spanish Republican governments to militarize the various militia units, some of these peculiarities of the early Loyalist armed forces of the Aragón–Catalan region were more or less overcome. However, the political rivalries within the armed forces, there and elsewhere in Loyalist Spain, were never dealt with. Rather, with the beginning of the shipment of arms to the Republic by the Soviet Union, the Spanish Communists received a very powerful tool to use in their drive for complete power within the Republican army, and the Republican regime in general, and political dissension intensified.

The Issue of Discipline Among the Anarchist Troops

Both during and after the Spanish Civil War a great deal was said about the lack of discipline in the anarchist troops, on the Aragón front and elsewhere. César Lorenzo, the son of CNT leader Horacio Prieto, born and brought up in France, who wrote a study of Spanish anarchism, claimed: 'the weaknesses of the confederal columns were evident to the eyes of everyone ... The men, without discipline, without arms, fell by the thousands. There was no single and undisputed command. Worse, it was impossible to give orders. The militiamen were all equal, they conferred on what to do, they discussed everything proposed by the more serious and lucid militants, they elected their chiefs every day...'[29]

There is reason to believe that César Lorenzo's statement of the discipline issue is an exaggerated one. First, there is the evidence that throughout the War, the troops on the Aragón–Catalan front were in their large majority drawn from anarchist ranks, and in many cases were under leadersilip of anarchist commanders. These troops gave a very good account of themselves, not only in the first push into Aragón, which saved half of that province for the Republic, but in subsequent crucial battles including the attack on Teruel late in 1937, and the subsequent campaigns when Franco troops attacked in Aragón, and then in the final battles in Catalonia itself. Anarchist troops were able to conduct orderly retreats when non-anarchist forces on their flanks were fleeing in disorder. There is no recorded case of which we are aware of a Loyalist defeat in the north-east – or anywhere else in Spain – being due to insubordination of anarchist troops.

It is true that many of the anarchists had a different concept of discipline than that of the Communists or professional military officers. Diego Abad de Santillán stated this concept late in 1937, when he wrote:

> We have conducted much propaganda in favor of discipline at the front and behind the lines, but we refer to a discipline which signifies a sense of responsibility, from which is not excluded the man, his conscience, his personality ... We coincide with members of other tendencies in advocating discipline, but we coincide in words, not in the spirit ... In the face of a Prussian discipline, a discipline which kills, we prefer always systematic indiscipline, the spirit of permanent rebellion and the chaos of external appearances ... we prefer the troops of warriors who went happily to death or to victory, animated by a faith and by the consciousness that they were defending a grand and noble cause.[30]

Testimony from those who actually participated in the anarchist troops in the Aragón-Catalan area indicates that although to a considerable degree there was lacking in them what is known in the US armed forces as 'military courtesy' – that is, the saluting of officers, the wearing of proper uniforms and always addressing officers as 'sir' – more essential elements of discipline were present. For instance, José Peirats, who later became a historian of the CNT's role in the War, claimed that his experience in the Durruti Column was that the soldiers of that group were always willing to attack and to do generally what was required of them; there was never a lack of volunteers to go on dangerous patrols and they had a spirit of self discipline and abnegation which 'was marvelous to watch'.[31]

A pamphlet published by the CNT–FAI after Durruti's death described the nature of Durruti's military discipline: 'Durruti's greatness was due to the fact that he hardly ever commanded but always educated. The comrades used to go to his tent – after his return from the front lines. He explained and discussed the reasons for his operations to them. Durruti never commanded, he convinced. Only by conviction, a clear and precise action is guaranteed. Everyone of us knows the reason for his action and is convinced of its necessity. Thus everyone wants to obtain the best results of his action, at any price. Comrade Durruti gave the example.'[32]

Ricardo Sanz, who commanded the Durruti Column (26th Division) from the death of Durruti until the final retreat into France, bore similar witness. He said that if by discipline is meant a willingness to go into battle when told to do so, or when volunteers were asked for, the anarchist troops had discipline as good as or better than that of any other elements in the Republican army.[33]

Diego Camacho, the biographer of Durruti, who also was in the Durruti Column, observed that in the early months of the War many decisions were made in assemblies of men of the division, which existed parallel to the orthodox military hierarchy. The assemblies would pass judgment on the behavior of the officers, conditions of the troops, sometimes even on strategy. However, he added that when they went into battle, the hierarchical officers gave the orders and there was no questioning of them.[34]

The existence of soldiers' assemblies, at least in the early months of the War, was also attested to be Mariano Casasus Lacasta, who served as a captain in the Ortíz Column, which became the 25th Division. However, he claimed that with the militarization of the militia late in 1936, the assemblies no longer functioned.[35]

Sr Ballesta, who served in the Rojo y Negro Division headed by Domingo Ascaso throughout the War, claimed never to have known of a case of refusal to carry out an attack by elements of that division. He added that officers had to talk 'like comrades' and not arbitrarily issue orders, but that their orders were none the less obeyed.[36]

On the other hand, there were undoubtedly some cases of indiscipline among the anarchist troops. Miguel Celma, who was in the Durruti Column, remembered two such instances, in which troops refused to advance when they were convinced they were being ordered on a suicide mission which was purposeless.[37]

Also, José Torrente, a Catalan Socialist, who throughout the War was with the troops in the Aragón–Catalonia area, many years later attested to an incident he had witnessed in the vicinity of Huesca. There, late in 1936, anarchist units which had been ordered to launch an attack on Huesca refused to do so, and many of them instead went to Barbasto some 30 kilometers away, where their unit had its headquarters, and held an assembly to discuss the question.

Interestingly enough, Torrente, who generally regarded the anarchist troops on the Aragón front to have been indisciplined, felt that the Durruti Column was an exception. He commented that from the beginning of the conflict, the leadership of that column made decisions 'from a military point of view, not from an anarchist one'.[38]

In another instance, Mariano Casasus Lacasta of the 25th Division, recalled an incident in the battle of Teruel, in which his unit was ordered to go up a sharp incline and take the city cemetery. They were accompanied by three small tanks, driven by Soviet soldiers. Following what they claimed to be their orders, the Soviet tankmen refused to move beyond a certain point, whereupon the 25th Division soldiers got them out of the tanks, recruited their own Spanish tank drivers, and completed the push up the hill and took the cemetery.[39] This incident might or might not be considered insubordination, depending on how one looks at it.

The final evidence one can offer on the 'lack of discipline' of the anarchist troops is that in the face of very great provocation by the Communists on at least two occasions, they did not abandon their military duties at the front. These occasions were the May 1937 conflict in Barcelona, and the sweep of Communist commander Lister's Column like conquerors three months later to take the region from the control of the anarchists.

In May, although they knew very well what was transpiring in the Catalan capital, the great majority of the anarchist troops on the Aragón front stayed at their posts. A scattering of troops from the Durruti Column, together with some peasants from the nearby Aragón collectives, did start to head for Barcelona. However, when they got to Lerida and were ordered to return to the front, they did so.[40] In the case of the Ortíz Column (25th Division), several companies were ordered by the local commanders to head for Barcelona, but they too returned to the front after reaching Lerida and receiving orders to go back.[41]

At the time of the attacks of the Lister Brigade on the Council of Aragón and the peasant collectives, the soldiers of the anarchist divisions in Aragón 'ardently desired' to resist Lister, according to César Lorenzo. However, he adds, 'the C.N. of the CNT and the CP

of the FAI intervened to prevent the outbreak of a new civil war ...
the anarchist troops did not move.'[42]

On balance, although it is clear that, particularly in the early stages
of the War, the anarchist troops for the most part had little use for
the niceties of military courtesy, they were far from being an undisciplined mob. Although they found it hard to give up the anarchist
custom of having assemblies to make any decisions which seemed to
the rank and file to be of importance, they ultimately did so. When,
after more than a year of relative inaction, with its accompanying
boredom and inducement to slothfulness, the anarchist troops in
Aragón had to face up to the overwhelming numerical and armament
superiority of the Franco forces in the campaigns of Aragón and
Catalonia, they proved to be dedicated and capable soldiers.

Although there were isolated cases of refusal to obey orders, it is
doubtful whether these were more prevalent among the anarchist
troops on the Aragón–Catalan front than among other units of the
Republican Army, or than happens from time to time in any army.
Perhaps the surprising thing was that the morale of the anarchist
troops remained as high as it did, in the face of intensified attempts
by the ministry of war, and Republican government in general, both
under increasingly tight control of the Communist Party, to undermine the anarchists in the armed forces through proselytization,
intimidation and outright murder, particularly after May 1937.

The Question of Lack of Arms for the Aragón Front

In their growing campaign against the anarchists between July 1936
and May 1937, the Communists made a particular point of the fact
that after the first rush into Aragón by the largely anarchist Catalan
militia, which saved for the Republic more than half of the territory
of that region, nothing more of military consequence seemed to
happen there. This same criticism was sometimes made by non-
Communists as well.

The Communist ex-minister Jesús Hernández himself noted this
Communist campaign about the 'silence' of the Aragón front: 'The
Communist ministers, the Communist periodicals, the Communist

leaders asked the Government why the Aragón front was immobilized, why that arsenal of munitions and arms remained passive, without more shots than there were when innocent men are trying to avoid being robbed. But Señor Largo Caballero shrugged his shoulders in complicity...'[43]

Of course, the anarchists replied to this campaign of the Communists and their allies to discredit the anarchist troops on the Aragón front. As their periodicals pointed out, it 'is the only front where ground has been gained and a position has never been lost'.[44] However, these protests were no more successful than their appeals to the central Republican authorities in getting the arms, equipment and munitions needed to launch a real offensive on the Aragón front.

All anarchist authorities agreed, then and after the War, that the main cause of the quietness on the Aragón front was a lack of sufficient arms and equipment to push the much longed-for attacks on Zaragoza and Huesca. Thus, in its report to the conference of the International Workingmen's Association in Paris in December 1937, the CNT wrote, after noting the insufficiency of the converted war industries of Catalonia to provide all the arms and equipment needed in Aragón: 'To ask aid of the Government of Madrid was useless for two reasons: because Catalonia was in the power of the Anarchists and because Madrid and the fronts of the Center and South were in much worse situation than that of Aragón. From Catalonia we had to send to the Central and Southern fronts armed militiamen, artillery and projectiles made by us...'[45]

Juan P. Fabregas, CNT member of the Catalan Consejo de Economía, reported to a Catalan regional plenum of the *confederación* on September 24 1936: 'I must inform you of the difficulties imposed by the Government of Madrid, which has denied as all economic and financial support, because certainly it hasn't much sympathy with the work of a practical nature being carried out in Catalonia ... We sent a Commission to Madrid and asked the Government for a credit of 800 million pesetas, another of 30 million to acquire war material and another of 150 million francs for the acquisition of raw materials ... Everything was denied us. We don't know why, particularly since the financial conditions of Spain are the best in the world...'[46]

Diego Abad de Santillán, in his book *Por qué Perdímos la Guerra*, written a year after the end of the Civil War, commented on this same problem of lack of arms: 'All the chiefs of the Aragón front drove us crazy with their continuous demands for arms and munitions. With more insistence and tenacity than anyone was Durruti ... We couldn't give him or anyone anything, because we didn't have anything...'[47]

Santillán added: 'Some material bought through the intermediary of the Russians had begun to reach Spain, and through a purchasing commission of the Government. Orders had been given that none of these shipments should touch at Catalan ports. This attitude made us greatly indignant. Particularly when it was promised that such and such a load would be for us, and nothing arrived.'[48]

Perhaps unwitting evidence that there was a ban on the sending of Russian arms to the Aragón front was provided by the Stalinist Party in Catalonia, the PSUC. In a document labelled 'Plan for Victory', issued in April 1937, long after Soviet arms had begun to arrive in Spain in substantial quantities, the PSUC said: 'Catalonia has been unable to send all that was wanted to the Aragón Front because of misunderstandings and attempts at private profit which naturally cause disagreement among antifascist forces and divert attention from the real problem of the war.'[49] This would seem to indicate that Catalonia was to be the only source of providing arms in Aragón, and totally ignores the possibility that Soviet arms might be sent there. It seems unlikely that this was an oversight by the Catalan Stalinist leaders.

Juan Manuel Molina, who was sub-secretary of defense of the Catalan governmeant from November 1936 until May 1937, and was a leader of the CNT, has provided some details of this Republican government boycott of provision of armament for the troops in Aragón. He recounted a shipload of machine guns from Czechoslovakia, perhaps 8–10,000 of them, of which he requested 5,000 for the Aragón front, but was completely turned down by the Republican government. In another instance, a ship loaded with arms came down the Catalan coast from France, with two minesweepers of the Catalan navy accompanying them. When Molina suggested to the Republican government in Valencia that the snip put in at Barcelona, and the arms be shipped from there by train, he got peremptory orders that it should proceed to Valencia – the ship was sunk between the Catalan border and Valencia.[50]

However, it was not only the anarchists who protested the lack of arms for the Aragón front. An American who visited the front early in 1937 quoted one of the professional artillerymen in Aragón as saying,

> If we had the necessary armaments and if the Madrid govern-
> ment were willing to spend a part of its gold supplies for the
> purchase of such arms, I can assure you that by March we would
> already establish contact with the forces operating in the Bilbao
> sector and we would be in a position seriously to threaten the
> Fascist forces north of Madrid.
>
> I went to Madrid several times and each time I asked some-
> thing for the campaign in Aragón, I was told that it is necessary
> to reserve the gold supply for the reconstruction of Spain after
> the war, as though this were now more important than the
> crushing of the Fascist forces.[51]

Soon after Francisco Largo Caballero became prime minister, in September 1936, Buenaventura Durruti was sent to Madrid to request financing of an offer of arms to be shipped from France, which had tentatively been arranged by the French anarchist Pierre Besnard. At first, Pierre Besnard later reported, Largo Caballero and the cabinet agreed to allocate 1,600,000,000 pesetas to this arms purchase, with it being agreed that one-third of the material would be for the Aragón–Catalan front.[52] However, this decision was subsequently reversed, Besnard being convinced that the change was due to the urging of the recently arrived Soviet ambassador, Marcel Rosenberg.[53]

The Catalans sometimes resorted to extraordinary measures to try to get the arms they needed or the money to finance purchases of arms. At one point, an anarchist unit on the central front succeeded in diverting to Catalonia a convoy containing 70–80,000 cartridges. On another occasion, when the Catalan government got an urgent request for gasoline from the Loyalist regime on the island of

Menorca, they sent a ship with the gasoline, but refused to allow it to be unloaded until there was sent in return some two million cartridge shells store in the castle of Mahon, which were of no use on Menorca, and had been many times requested from the Republican government by the Catalans.[54]

However, the most dramatic *coup* to get funds for arming the Catalan front, which was planned but in the end not executed, was a proposal to rob part of the Spanish government's gold supply from Madrid. The leader of the plot was Diego Abad de Santillán, and he planned to use some of the anarchist Tierra y Libertad militia column which was stationed in the Madrid area for this effort. Just before Santillán and others were ready to put the plot into effect, they decided to inform the CNT national committee of the project. Santillán reported that that news caused 'chills of fear in the friends'. So he and the others called it off, not wanting to carry it out in the face of opposition of the CNT leadership.[55] Of course, a few weeks later, nearly all of the Spanish gold supply was shipped to the Soviet Union, in advance payment for the arms which Stalin was going to deign to send to the Spanish Republic.

Gaston Leval, the French anarchist who spent almost all the Civil War in Spain, was convinced that the failure of the Republican government to provide sufficient arms and equipment for the troops on the Aragón front contributed substantially to the ultimate defeat of the Republican forces. After noting that the Republican government left the Aragón front 'without artillery, without aviation, without antiair defense', Leval wrote: 'During the first year of the war it was possible to break up the Fascist front; the enemy military forces were composed of some thousands of men with trucks who were rushed to points of danger. With fifty thousand militiamen adequately armed, we could have conquered Zaragoza...'[56]

George Orwell, who spent several months during this period with a POUM unit on the Aragón front, has graphically described the lack of arms and other equipment: There was a 'complete lack of war materials of every description. It needs an effort to realize how badly the militias were armed at this time. Any public school O.T.C. in England is far more like a modern army than we were. The badness of our weapons was so astonishing that it is worth recording in detail.' Orwell then went on:

> For this sector of the front the entire artillery consisted of four trench-mortars with *fifteen rounds* for each gun. Of course they were far too precious to be fired and the mortars were kept in Alcubierre. There were machine-guns at the rate of approximately one to fifty men; they were oldish guns, but fairly accurate up to three or four hundred yards. Beyond this we had only rifles, and the majority of the rifles were scrap iron. There were three types of rifles in use. The first was the long Mauser. These were seldom less than twenty years old, their sights were about as much use as a broken speedometer, and in most of them the rifling was hopelessly eroded; about one rifle in ten was not bad, however. Then there was the short Mauser, or *mousqueton*, really a cavalry weapon... Actually they were almost useless. They were made out of reassembled parts, no bolt belonged to its rifle, and three-quarters of them could be counted on to jam after five shots. There were also a few Winchester rifles. These were nice to shoot with, but they were wildly inaccurate, and as their cartridges had no clips they could only be fired one shot at a time, Ammunition was so scarce that each man entering the line was only issued with fifty rounds, and most of it was exceedingly bad...
>
> We had no tin hats, no bayonets, hardly any revolvers or pistols, and not more than one bomb between five or ten men... And apart from weapons there was a shortage of all the minor necessities of war. We had no maps or charts, for instance... We had no range-finders, no telescopes, no periscopes, no field-glasses except a few privately-owned pairs, no flares or Very lights, no wire-cutters, no armourers' tools, hardly even any cleaning materials.[57]

This situation continued, according to Orwell, even after Russian arms and supplies had begun to come into Spain: 'The Russian arms were supplied via the Communist Party and the parties allied to them, who saw to it that as few as possible got to their political opponents... This was why there were so few Russian arms on the Aragón front, where the troops were predominantly Anarchist. Until April 1937 the only Russian weapon I saw – with the exception of some airplanes which may or may not have been Russian – was a solitary sub-machinegun.'[58]

As we have seen, the anarchists themselves admitted that the paucity of arms on the Aragón front, and the lack of central government interest in that part of the conflict could be explained between November 1936 and March 1937 by the preoccupation with the defense of Madrid. However, once the battle of Madrid had been won, and Franco had turned his attention to the reduction of the Loyalist strongholds in the Basque country, Santander and Asturias, that reason no longer existed.

Given the isolation of the northern front from the rest of Loyalist Spain, the only possibly effective way of meeting Franco's offensive there was a Republican attack launched from Aragón which would divert the attention and resources of the Rebel forces, and if successful might well have linked up the two parts of Loyalist Spain. However, George Orwell was probably right when he argued: 'There is very little doubt that arms were deliberately withheld lest too many of them should get into the hands of the Anarchists, who would afterwards use them for a revolutionary purpose; consequently the big Aragón offensive which would have made Franco draw back from Bilbao, and possibly from Madrid, never happened...'[59]

The Activities of the Aragónese Military During First Year

For more than a year the Aragón front was relatively calm. George Orwell has borne eloquent witness to the frustrations of boredom for the troops in Aragón during that period.[60]

The stabilization of the Aragón front took place at the height of the 1936 harvest season. At the suggestion of Buenaventura Durruti, the council of war of his column decided 'to let the militiamen know the work which was being done, and suggest that instead of remaining idle, they should collaborate with the peasants in this period of wheat harvest. Furthermore, those who were better informed could discuss with the peasants the libertarian society and its economic organisms.' Durruti's biographer noted: 'The results of that initiative were highly positive. Groups of young libertarians were the first to present themselves as volunteers to fulfill the role of combat-producers...[61]

Elements in each of the anarchist military units put out publications for their organizations, as did those of other political orientation. For instance, the Ortíz Column (25th Division) put out what began as a weekly newspaper – *25th Division*. It was first printed on a moving truck, with a rather primitive press. Then they got a regular printing press in Barcelona, and began putting out a daily. They also published a magazine, *Cultura y Acción*.[62]

Other anarchist military publications included *Mas Alla*, put out by the Francisco Ascaso column and *El Frente*, issued by the Durruti column (26th Division). These periodicals dealt both with issues directly confronting their military units, and with broader questions.

El Frente in its issue of October 11 1937 had a front-page article by A. Flores, the 'Assistant Commissar of the Division' entitled 'Victory' and on the third page carried a notice headlined 'Of Interest' and signed by 'The commissar of the division', asking all teachers in the division who were engaged in any cultural activity, or who wanted to be, to submit within a week a report on what they were doing, on their background and their location.[63]

The November 20 1937 issue of *El Frente* was devoted to the first anniversary of the death of Durruti. There were various articles on him, and one on the current commanders of the division: Ricardo Sanz, 'our chief', his aide Francisco Ed, Political Commissar Ricardo Rionda and his aide, Angel Flores.[64]

Mas Alla's issue of May 10 1937 had an article on 'Discipline'. 'We repeat our request for discipline, especially from our comrades. Discipline to win the war, discipline to make the revolution; discipline in all and for all comrades.' This same issue had articles on anarchist history, and on 'the cowardice of the democracies'.[65]

A later issue of *Mas Alla*, that of August 11 1937, had a polemical article entitled: 'What do the Authorities of the PSUC Propose in the

Rearguard?' It contained extensive information on persecution of libertarians by elements of the PSUC. It ended: 'What do the men of PSUC propose? Do they want to do to the Confederation what they have done to the comrades of the POUM? If so, we say serenely: you are mistaken, completely mistaken. The Confederation is a power and whoever wishes to attack it, will get to know the iron of its men.' On the last page there was an article on a 'victorious advance' of 30 kilometers of the 25th Division.[66]

There was also some attention paid to educating the members of the anarchist columns. This was undoubtedly designed not only to teach the soldiers basic cultural subjects but also to instil them with the ideas of libertarian communism.

Loss of Anarchist Control on the Aragón Front

From July 1936 to May 1937, control of the Aragón front and of the Catalan troop's who largely manned it was in the hands of the Catalan regime, at first the Central Militia Committee of Catalonia, and then of the councillor of defense of the Generalidad of Catalonia. During all of that period, the influence of the anarchists in the Republican armed forces in Catalonia and Aragón was predominant. From September to December 1936, the councillor of defense was Colonel Felipe Díaz Sandino, a regular army officer who was on quite friendly terms with the CNT–FAI.

After the reorganization of the Catalan Generalidad in December 1936, the CNT took over formally the councillorship of defense, in the person of Francisco Isgleas, with Juan Manuel Molina, also of the CNT, as his second-in-command as sub-secretary of defense. This situation persisted until the May Days of 1937, when the 'civil war within the civil war' took place in Barcelona and other Catalan cities.

The Republican government took advantage of the May Days' events to order the official dissolution of the councillorship of defense of the Generalidad, and to place the troops of the Catalan–Aragón region under control of the national ministry of defense. That ministry named General Sebastian Pozas, by then a member of the Communist Party, as commander of the army of the east, covering Catalonia and Aragón.

Juan Manuel Molina has recounted how this process of displacement of anarchists from control of the Republican armed forces on the Catalan–Aragón front took place. At the time of the May Days, Defense Councillor Isgleas had disappeared, and Molina had taken over control of the councillorship. Molina was thus the one with whom Pozas had to deal when he sought to take over his new command.

Molina has recounted that Pozas came into Barcelona more or less incognito, and called up Molina to inquire whether it would be safe for him to come to the office of the councillorship of defense to assume command. Molina replied that he had no intention of giving up his position without direct orders from Catalan President Luis Companys, and suggested that Pozas first go to see Companys. This Pozas did, and Companys called Molina by phone, indicating that he was acquiescing in the Republican government's assumption of control of the Republican military forces theretofore controlled by the Generalidad and Molina demanded a statement to that effect in writing.

However, when Pozas finally came to his office with the document from Companys, Molina indicated to him that he was still not willing to turn over his post without express orders from the CNT, which had chosen him for the position. Valerio Mas, then regional secretary of the CNT, assured Molina by phone that the anarchists had agreed to the control of the military being turned over to Pozas. Again, Molina demanded that statement in writing, signed by not only Mas, but also by the regional secretaries of the FAI and the Juventud Libertaria.

Only with these two documents in hand did Molina finally formally turn over control of the Catalan–Aragónese military forces to General Pozas. The latter insisted that Molina continue on as chief political commissar of the Army of the East, which Molina only agreed to do after a meeting of CNT–FAI–JL leaders, and a passionate speech by Federica Montseny had urged him to assume the new post.

At a meeting of General Pozas with 'representatives of all the antifascist organizations', it was agreed to distribute the various sub-commands of the Army of the East proportionately, and Molina was confirmed as commissar general of the Army of the East. However, as Molina has noted this was: 'Not for long. The puppets of Moscow would not be satisfied with a partial victory. They wanted a complete, absolute one. So, within a few days, without consulting Catalonia, or anything else, there was named by Decree as Commissar of War in Catalonia the ex-comic actor and fanatical Communist Virgilio Llanos, and as the other commissar positions had already been apportioned, the CNT was once again deceived and ousted from its last military positions and, with 80 per cent of the combatants in Catalonia and Aragón, lost all influence in the military apparatus, which passed completely into the hands of the Communists, with the disastrous results which followed.'[67]

José Peirats has noted that the turning over of command to General Pozas not only meant the end of anarchist control of Republican armed forces of Catalonia and Aragón, but also surrender of that control by the Catalan government to the Republican ministry of defense, and that the Catalan councillorship of defense 'automatically ceased to exist'.[68]

However, although the anarchists thus lost all control and virtually all influence in the central direction of the military forces in Catalonia and Aragón, CNT–FAI officers continued to control major units in the field. Also, to a greater or less degree, the original anarchist recruited and organized columns (by then divisions) remained more or less homogeneous.

Anarchists in the Battle of Teruel

Anarchist troops played a significant role in the battle of Teruel, from December 15 1937 until February 22 1938. Teruel, in the southern part of Aragón, had been in the hands of the Rebels since the beginning of the War. After the fall of the northern front to Franco's troops, there was strong reason to believe that the Rebel high command was planning another 'final offensive' against Madrid.

It was at least in part in order to avert this that the Republican general staff decided to launch a diversionary attack on Teruel which, if successful, might well have made it possible for advancing Republican troops to join forces with those coming from the central front.

During the first few days, the Republican attack was successful. Teruel was surrounded, and in part occupied, and a few days later the surviving Rebel holdouts in the city surrendered. However, Franco rushed in reinforcements both from the north and the Madrid region, and the Loyalist attack was stopped. A massive counter-offensive by the Rebel forces was strongly resisted but, by February 22, it had triumphed and the last Republican troops were withdrawn from Teruel.[69]

Ricardo Sanz, part of whose 26th Division provided some of the Loyalist troops involved, concluded: 'If we draw a balance of the battle of Teruel, we can affirm that, if the Republican forces could have counted on sufficient war material to continue its attack in that sector, the Rebel army would have confronted, in facing us, a most difficult situation, which sooner or later would have produced catastrophic results and a magnificent victory for Republican arms.'[70] Broue and Temime agree with Sanz that the basic cause of the failure of the Republicans' Teruel offensive was lack of sufficient resources.[71]

Anarchist troops were heavily involved in the Teruel battle. According to José Peirats, 'Among the attacking forces was, playing an important role, the 25th Division. Shortly before the town was again lost, there were transferred to that front the 125th and 126th brigades of the 28th Division, also CNTista...'[72]

Valentín González, famous as the Communist military commander El Campesino, wrote many years later, after he had ceased being a Communist, about what he claimed was the purposeful sacrifice of anarchist troops in the last days of the battle of Teruel, both as a means of discrediting them and of helping to oust Minister of Defense Indalecio Prieto. González wrote that the capture of Teruel 'gave the people new faith and new courage. It also gave renewed prestige to the Socialist leader Indalecio Prieto, under whose orders as Minister of Defence the action had been carried through. The Communists did not like this. Prieto was no pawn of theirs and stood in their way. While he remained at the head of the defense ministry, with his influence undiminished, they could not hope to gain complete control of military affairs. Thus they set out to torpedo Prieto, at the cost of losing Teruel.'

González said that the first step in the Communists' plan was the removal from command of the Teruel front of General Sarabia, 'a faithful friend of Prieto', and his replacement by the Communist commander Juan Modesto. He went on, 'Then they began to put their plot into practice. The advanced defense positions of Teruel were held by Anarcho-Syndicalist divisions. These units were denuded of artillery. Without heavy guns, they could not possibly hold out; they were sure to be driven back from their positions. Teruel would be lost. But the Anarcho-Syndicalists as the troops immediately responsible, and the Socialist Prieto as the minister of defense, would be discredited – at a price.'[73]

The Anarchists in the Battle of Aragón

Catalan anarchist troops played a secondary part in the battles of Belchite and Teruel in the latter months of 1937 and beginning of 1938, and military forces of other political orientation probably made up the majority of the attacking troops. However, the anarchist units had a major role in trying to defend Aragón from the massive attacks by the Franco forces which began in March 1938 and resulted finally in the Rebels breaking through to the Mediterranean Sea and splitting the Loyalist territory into two separate segments.

Marshal R. Malinovski, one of the principal Soviet military advisers to Republican forces during the Spanish Civil War, writing a quarter of a century later, presented an uncomplimentary picture of the anarchist troops' behavior during the battle of Aragón: 'The anarchist units ... retired like their souls were taken by the Devil, without offering combat.' He particularly mentioned that what was left of the 153rd Brigade refused orders to stand and fight.[74] He claimed that only Communist and PSUC troops fought well in the campaign.[75]

However, Ricardo Sanz has told at length the story of the participation of his unit, the former Durruti Column, reorganized as the 26th Division of the Republic's Popular Army, in this campaign. His account differs drastically from that of the Soviet marshal.

The 26th Division had from the early weeks of the War held a large area of the Aragón front, extending north and south of Zaragoza, and coming within a few miles of that Rebel-held city. Sanz and other leaders of the 26th Division became aware of the Franco build-up preceding the Rebel offensive, and warned the Republic's top military authorities of what was occurring.

Soon after the Franco offensive began, the 44th Division and the XI International Brigade, just to the south of the position of the 26th Division, were quickly overrun with relatively little resistance. The 26th Division was as a result forced to undertake the defense of positions abandoned by the 44th, and to try to rally as many of the demoralized troops of that unit as possible. At one point, it was holding a front of 170 kilometers, although the normal area covered by a division was considered to be about one tenth of that. Somewhat later, there were also breakthroughs on the front to the north of the positions held by the 26th.

Finally, after a few days of fighting in which large portions of the 26th Division had had little respite from combat, Sanz came to fear that his unit faced complete encirclement and annihilation. In spite of continued explanations by Sanz to the overall Republican command of the seriousness of the 26th's situation, he was unable to get any explicit orders from them as to what to do. At one point, he even had a confrontation with General Pozas, in command of the Aragón front and General Rojo, chief of staff of all the Republican forces, but was unable to get explicit orders from them.

Ricardo Sanz finally undertook on his own authority to command an orderly retreat of the 26th Division from its exposed position.[76] At one point during their retreat, there occurred what Sanz called 'the incomprehensible'. He explained: 'There came in the direction of the front, forces of Carabineros, coming from the rear echelon. They are fresh forces, which have not been in combat. They come in magnificent trucks. And long before arriving at the front, without descending, they turned around, saying that they were going to reorganize. We don't know where they would go to reorganize, these forces which had not established any contact with the enemy. Cowards!'[77]

The 26th Division finally succeeded in helping stabilize the Catalan front along the river Segre. On their flanks in their new position was the division headed by the Communist general, Valentín González.[78]

The Political Situation in the Military in Catalonia after the Fall of Aragón

After the Loyalist forces were driven out of Aragón, the remaining Republican forces in Catalonia were divided into two units, the so-called Army of the Ebro, largely guarding the southern front, and the Army of the East, in the center and north of Catalonia. The former of these was largely officered and controlled by the Communists; the Army of the East was, in turn, largely free of Communist control, and contained most of the anarchist military units, including the Durruti Column, the 26th Division.

In the months that followed the Aragón defeat, the Communist Party, the government of Juan Negrín, and the government-controlled mass media went out of their way to laud and praise the supposed valor and fighting qualities of the Army of the Ebro, while saying little in the same vein about the Army of the East. At the same time, there were massive promotions of officers in the Communist-controlled units, and few such advances for those commanding the Army of the East.[79]

Furthermore, according to Ricardo Sanz, the heads of the Army of the Ebro 'did not follow regulations. They dealt directly with the Subsecretary, with the Central General Staff or with the Premier and Minister of National Defense, Negrín, bypassing the fundamental norms of the Army, with their normal hierarchical steps.'[80]

During the ensuing months, the Communists made determined efforts to try to gain control of the units in the Army of the East. However, they ran into the strong opposition of that unit's commander, Colonel Perea. Ricardo Sanz wrote:

Perea tolerated nothing of the sort, in spite of a series of attempts which were made which, if they did no damage to the organization and development of this Army, nonetheless at various times made some of the military chiefs of the Large Units suffer the impertinence, first of courting and promises and then in one way or another, the actions of high ranking officers who tried to place upon us the stamp of a politics with which we disagreed absolutely ... if it had not been for the brake represented by the chief of the Army of the East we certainly would have suffered internecine struggles resulting as had always occurred, in prestigious chiefs of the Army who did not wish to submit to the wishes of certain 'señores' being relegated to an anonymous status in spite of being good military men and excellent anti-fascists.[81]

It was during this period, too, that there was a great proliferation, in the Catalan part of the Republican army at least, of Russian advisers. Ricardo Sanz argued that 'their counsels were of absolutely no use in a practical sense', adding, 'they multiplied everywhere, to the extreme that they were disseminated in the General Headquarters of Divisions, Army Groups, and even in some cases of those of Brigades.'[82]

It was also after the battle of Aragón that a major effort was launched to mobilize the civilian population to build fortifications to defend Catalonia. On March 31 1938, an appeal signed by representatives of the CNT, FAI, UGT and all of the Catalan parties, was issued to rally 100,000 volunteers 'for the construction of 50,000 fortifications. That effort was under the direction of a Commission of Control of Mobilization, composed of a president named by the Councillors of Finance, Economy and Labor, and Public Works and the UGT and CNT respectively.'[83]

The fall of Aragón also intensified the problem of refugees in Catalonia, fleeing the Franco armies. As early as the end of 1936 it was estimated that there were 300,000 refugees, equivalent to 10 percent of the total population of Catalonia.[84] By March 1938 this number had risen to 700,000.[85]

It was the Army of the Ebro in the name of which the last major

Republican counter-offensive of the War, the so-called battle of the Ebro, was made. Starting in July 1938, this struggle lasted three months, and after initial Loyalist successes, it resulted in a disaster for the Republic. Large segments of the units of the Army of the East were sent in to reinforce the Army of the Ebro. Ricardo Sanz has argued that in many cases those units were forced to remain on the fighting front for many days without any relief, while units of the Army of the Ebro were being rested. Of some such detached units from his own 26th Division, Sanz noted that 'upon return to their respective Brigades, they had more than 75 percent casualties, among them the death of one Political Commissar, and with loss of 95 percent of their material.'[86]

Other anarchist units, in addition to the 26th Division, were also involved in the battle of the Ebro. Enrique Castro Delgado noted an important role played by the 60th Division, 'commanded by the anarchist Mora' in confronting the Rebel army's third counter-offensive during the battle.[87] There were undoubtedly other units under anarchist command which also participated in the battle.

One other factor which angered the anarchists and other non-Communists in the Republican armies in Catalonia between the fall of Aragón and the final attack on Catalonia, was that 'we saw growing each day the number of *carabineros*, who constituted the Praetorian Guard of Negrín. The same thing happened with the Assault Guards.' Ricardo Sanz noticed that while clothing and even food were in increasingly short supply for the troops in the field, and there was growing hunger among the civilian population, 'the "war-like" and "valorous" *carabineros* and Assault Guards ... dressed well, had magnificent equipment, ate abundantly and as if that were not enough, could provide food for their families.'[88] The *carabineros* and Assault Guards were not sent to the front until the beginning of the Franco forces' final onslaught on Catalonia – and there they did not cover themselves with glory.[89]

The Final Battle for Catalonia

When the final attack by the Franco forces on Catalonia was about to begin, the leaders and soldiers of the 26th Division were very much aware of the preparations being made on the other side of the lines. And it was they who felt the first brunt of the Rebels' attack. However, along the line defended by the former Durruti Column, the first attacks were largely turned back in the first days.[90] This fact refutes the claim of Gabriel Jackson that 'only the Communist-led units of Lister, Galan and Taguena opposed serious resistance 'to the Franco drive into Catalonia.[91]

The Franco forces then switched the main force of their attack to the southern part of the front, held by the Army of the Ebro. There, the resistance was minimal. Whether the Army of the Ebro had not recovered from the disaster of the battle of the Ebro, or whether the morale of its officers and men had been undermined by the relentless drive of the Communists to submit all elements within it to their iron control, it was unable to stand up effectively to the Franco forces, in which Italian units made up a considerable part, in that area. Republican army units disintegrated, and on some days the Rebels were able to advance as much as ten kilometers a day.

One Catalan city after another fell to the southern arm of the invading forces. Valls, Reus, Tarragona, and then the way was open for the Franco forces to take Barcelona itself.

No serious effort was made to defend Barcelona. Ricardo Sanz argued that one reason for this was that the people of the city did not believe until it was too late that their city was in serious danger. They had taken fright after the fall of Aragón the previous year, but had then been saved by a 'miracle' when a solid line of resistance had finally been re-established in the southern part of Catalonia. According to Sanz, they expected another 'miracle' in January 1939.[92]

The government seemed paralyzed. It took no measures to fortify the city. Finally troops from the Army of the Ebro fled through the metropolis on their way farther north towards the French border. In spite of proclamations of its intention to stay in the Catalan capital, the Spanish Republican government fled to Gerona. That of Catalonia retreated to Figueras.

Elements of the Federación Anarquista Iberica, including Diego Abad de Santillán, during the last few days before the fall of Barcelona, discussed the possibility of attempting to organize a last ditch defense of the city. They rejected a scorched-earth policy. Santillán commented, 'We could destroy factories, set half the city afire. For what? We refused a vengeance of impotence, the consequences of which would have been the impoverishment of the situation of those who remained.'

However, at midnight of January 24–25 1939, the FAIistas were telephoned by General José Asensio, who still remained in Barcelona, and who offered to try to lead in establishing a resistance effort, if he could get the fugitive government to name him commander of the city. They agreed to work with him. However, throughout the 25th they heard no further from him and concluded that he had been unable to get the appointment.[93] Meanwhile word was received that a shipment of arms and munitions which had been on the way from France had been derailed on the French side of the border.[94]

Finally, nothing came of all of this. Santillán observed: 'Still on January 25 one could have organized the defense of the city. By the 26th indifference, including our own, would have made any attempt impossible. The enemy didn't enter Barcelona that day, because he must have considered evacuation preferable.'[95]

Martin Gudell, secretary of foreign propaganda of the CNT–FAI claimed after the end of the War that one of the few places in Barcelona where the Franco troops met resistance was the CNT/FAI headquarters on Via Durruti.[96] We have no confirmation of that from other sources.

The remnants of the Army of the East in the central and northern parts of Catalonia continued the struggle after the fall of Barcelona. Ricardo Sanz wrote: 'It is enough to say what happened in the Northern sector. The 26th Division, which had been fighting during sixteen days without truce or rest, had crossed the Segre River, arriving at Artesa de Segre. A most orderly retreat, in which not a single man nor a single gun was lost. After sixteen days of struggle, the enemy had only succeeded in advancing an average of a kilometer a day. The 31st Division relieved the 26th in its post of honor.'

By this time, the central general staff of the Republican Army had disappeared. The governments of both Spain and Catalonia had fled to France, and set up their headquarters in Paris.

Finally, with hundreds of thousands of civilians and fugitive military men from the Army of the Ebro fleeing across the border into France, the Tenth Army Group, to which the 26th Division belonged, attempted to set up a final line of defense to permit as many people as possible to escape. However, they were running out of ammunition and could hold out only a few days. The commanders of the Tenth Army Group finally gave orders for the troops still remaining under arms to seek refuge in France.

Ricardo Sanz wrote of this denouement: 'Thus it was that on February 10, 1939, the forces of the X Army Group, all that remained in the Northern sector of Catalonia, abandoned the soil of the Mother Country. Among them went those of my beloved Division, the 26th. They marched in full order, by companies and by battalions, with their officers.'[97]

7

Who Saved Madrid?

One of the most controversial aspects of the anarchists' participation in the military during the Spanish Civil War concerns their role in the defense of Madrid. Many, if not most, commentators on that struggle tend to discount the role the anarchists played, or even to picture it as damaging to the defense of the city. Some anarchists, on the other hand, are inclined to picture the role of the CNT forces as decisive in saving the city from the forces of General Franco.

Neither of these versions gives an accurate picture of the defense of that city and the part which the anarchists played in it. The first drive of the Franco forces from the suburbs of the Spanish capital to the outer fringes of the city itself was halted by the extreme efforts of the hitherto demoralized militiamen – anarchists as well as those of other political persuasions – and of the people of the city. Subsequently, the defense of Madrid was aided by troops from other parts of Spain, including, among others, anarchist contingents and elements of the new International Brigades, as well as by the arrival of the first shipments of arms, including fighter planes, from the Soviet Union.

Three of the principal anarchist military leaders to emerge during the War – Buenaventura Durruti, Ricardo Sanz and Cipriano Mera – played important roles in the defense of Madrid, and Durruti died there early in the conflict. Anarchists also played an important part in the 'civilian' side of the Madrid battle, in constructing hastily built defenses for the city, in the Junta de Defensa, which was established at the beginning of the conflict to be in charge of the organization and maintenance of the rearguard and in helping keep up the morale of the people of the city who were, in effect, on the front lines.

On balance, as we shall see, the role of the anarchists in the defense of Madrid was an honorable and significant one. Neither they, nor the International Brigades nor any other single element, was 'decisive' in the defense of Madrid. That was an effort which was successful because of the contributions on the front lines and in the maintenance of the life of a city of a million people just beyond the front line of the militiamen of all political colors, of the small number of loyal professional soldiers, and the great mass of the civilians who bore bravely week after week of bombardment, scarcities and all manner of danger and inconvenience without giving up hope of victory or determination to achieve it.

General Characteristics of the Battle of Madrid

The battle of Madrid began on November 6 1936. It went on, with only slight interruptions to regroup and maneuver, until March 21 1937, when the Italian Fascist volunteer divisions were finally routed near Guadalajara, and General Franco gave up his attempt to take the Spanish capital, turning instead to other theaters of operations.

The objectives and stake in that battle were clear. Generals Franco and Mola felt that when they captured Madrid – as they confidently expected to do when the battle began – that would be the beginning of the end of the Civil War. They felt that the Republican forces would be so disorganized and demoralized by the loss of the capital city, that effective resistance in the remainder of Loyalist Spain would become almost impossible. Furthermore, with the Spanish capital in their hands, the Nationalists would be in a position to demand formal recognition of their regime by virtually all foreign powers.

On the other hand, the defenders of the city were equally aware of the singular importance of the battle. For the people of the city, they were defending their homes, their freedom and their lives. The soldiers at the front, faced as they were at first with largely Moorish troops and those of the Foreign Legion, and subsequently German and Italian forces, in many cases saw themselves as defending their country from foreign invasion. The anarchists among them undoubtédly saw themselves also as defending their Revolution which was for them inseparable from the War. All of the defenders realized that their success would be a major victory against the Franco forces and would keep alive the possibility of ultimate triumph in the Civil War.

The battle of Madrid fell into four separate series of operations. The first, beginning on November 6 and lasting throughout the rest of the month was a frontal attack by the Franco forces, attempting to overrun the city by main force.

Ramón Sender indicated the areas within which this phase of the battle was fought: '...we had the following centres of battle: a working-class suburb of small houses of one or two stories (Carabanchel), in whose irregular streets the machine guns sang; a very large enclosed park (the Casa de Campo) with a lake in its centre, which lay between the opposing lines; and lastly, the University City, a great limestone plain with wide asphalted avenues and massive buildings with rows of windows: the Faculty of Pharmacy, of Philosophy and Literature, of Medicine, the Clinical Hospital; a small city separated from Madrid, laid out on a definite plan...'[1] The onslaught of the Rebel forces was halted at the University City without reaching the heart of the metropolis.

In the following month, extending into the first days of the New Year, there was an attempt by the Franco forces to attack north and west of the city, by taking the nearby royal palace of El Pardo in the hope of surrounding the city from the rear. This effort netted only a few miles of advance and was turned back far short of its objectives.

The third phase of the battle of Madrid, which is often referred to as the battle of the Jarama, was an effort by the Franco forces, with help of the new German Condor Division of artillery, aircraft and some troops, to outflank Madrid from the south-east. As exceptionally bloody conflict, it also left the Franco forces far short of their objectives and maintained intact the contacts of the city with the rest of the Republic, which the offensive had been designed to cut.

Finally, following shortly on the heels of the battle of the Jarama there came the battle of Guadalajara, an effort by a force made up in large part of Italian Fascist divisions, to sweep down on Madrid from the north-east, and to surround the city by joining forces with Franco troops in the Jarama region. That conflict ended in total disaster for the much-vaunted legions of Il Duce.

Antecedents to the Battle of Madrid

The Republican militiamen and scattering of regular troops which early in November were called upon to try to defend the Spanish capital had for two months suffered an uninterrupted series of defeats. As a consequence, when they had to face the Franco troops in the suburbs of Madrid, they were a seriously demoralized and disorganized force and seemed to justify General Franco's prediction that 'We shall enter Madrid without firing a shot...'[2]

One of the major Republican defeats preceding the battle of Madrid was the loss of Toledo. Although the city had been taken, largely by anarchist militiamen and Loyalist Civil Guards late in July, the fortress of the Toledo Alcazar held out against the Republicans. Only 100 Civil Guards and 300 militiamen were left to maintain a siege of the Alcazar, the rest of those who had captured the city returning to Madrid, whence they had come.[3]

Throughout August, little was done by the Republican forces to reduce the fortress. Although the Franco forces – and much of the foreign press – portrayed the siege of the Alcazar as a heroic gesture by the Rebel forces in the face of overwhelming odds, this was more a legend than the truth. Those in the fortress included 2,500 troops, including military cadets, regular soldiers, and armed Falangistas, who were infinitely better supplied with all kinds of arms than those besieging them. The CNT journalist Eduardo de Guzmán suggested not long after the siege that if those in the Alcazar had had the valor attributed to them by the Franco propaganda, they could at almost any time during August have swept out of the fortress and recaptured the city.

The Communist ex-minister Jesús Hernández claimed a few years after the Civil War that the Communist' Fifth Regiment had volunteered to take the Alcazar 'in 48 hours'.[4] Whether they could have done so remained an open question, because it was clear that until shortly before the arrival of Rebel troops on the outskirts of the city, the battle for Toledo's Alcazar was not high on the government's list of preoccupations.

Late in September the Franco troops swept up to the environs of Toledo from the south. Reinforcements were rushed to the Republican forces from Madrid, and three efforts were made to set off mines under the Alcazar and to storm the fortress, but they failed. With the final arrival of Moorish and Foreign Legion troops of the Rebels, the besieged troops finally joining in battle, most of the Republican troops were routed on September 27. The few anarchist militiamen who put up disastrous resistance in a few reinforced buildings in the city were wiped out.[5]

Another serious defeat of the Republicans took place in Siguenza to the north-east of Madrid almost a month after the fall of Toledo. After the city was liberated by Loyalist forces in late July, it was garrisoned by about 700 CNT militiamen, a battalion of UGT railroad workers and some POUM militiamen. For some time, also, guerrillas based there made incursions into nearby areas held by the Rebels. In charge was Feliciano Benito, a CNT militiaman.

In mid-September, the Rebels began a drive on Siguenza with regular army and Foreign Legion troops, backed by bombardment of the city from the air. By the end of September, the Loyalist forces in Siguenza were surrounded, but the city's defenders succeeded in recapturing Peregrina and temporarily breaking the encirclement. On October 8, the Communist Pasionaria Battalion was sent as reinforcement, but reportedly retreated again after heavy air bombardment. That day, the city was again surrounded. Thereafter, in spite of urgent appeals by Benito and the CNT Defense Committee in Madrid for help for Siguenza, it was October 17 before a relief column was sent. It was quickly forced to retreat without getting to Siguenza. The situation in the city became desperate, and finally the 300 remaining militiamen fortified themselves in the cathedral, as the Franco forces swept into the rest of the town. They held out there for another week, after which the survivors ran out of the building, shooting at their besiegers as they left, and were all killed.[6]

Numerous other less dramatic defeats were suffered by the Republican militiamen. The survivors from these events, as well as from the fall of Toledo and Siguenza, were among those who early in November were called upon to try to defend Madrid. Robert Colodny has noted that just before the battle of Madrid began, an anarchist unit mutinied on November 6, killed its officers and fled.[7] However, Colodny has also said that during the Loyalist retreat towards Madrid, Rebel General Varela's column 'was harassed South of the Tagus by anarchist del Bayo and Uribarri columns'.[8]

The Confusion of the First Days of Battle

Thus, most of the Loyalist troops in and near Madrid by November 6 were remnants of militia columns which had been retreating for many weeks, Colonel Vicente Rojo wrote: 'In human terms there existed a veritable dustcloud of men and combat units, grouped in an arbitrary manner, irregular ... some were commanded by professionals of modest rank and most by militia chiefs designated by the political parties or by the General Inspection of Militias.'[9]

Enrique Castro Delgado, the organizer of the Communist Fifth Regiment, claimed: 'The fundamental forces which had to defend Madrid were in the hands of the Communist Party, through the Fifth Regiment.[10] Similarly, Jesús Hernández said: 'What saved it was the example of tens of thousands of Communists, willing to die and who knew that with their action, they would arouse, direct and carry to the heights of the sublime that heroism and that willingness.'[11] However, in fact, the situation was more complex than that.

Colonel Vicente Rojo noted that the largest coherent unit in the vicinity, commanded by Lieutenant-Colonel Barceló, had about 4,000 men. But these consisted of 'the remains of many small units with from 40 to 600 men. Of these, seven were the remains of units of regular troops ... the rest were militia units ... which, although some were called Battalions, were mere groups of 200 to 300 men, some without officers; of these so-called Battalions, only one had 600 men and another 400.' He added: 'Of the other Columns ... one can say the same: there existed among them some small "autonomous" units, with less than 50 men. The difficulties of a tactical nature which had to be overcome by the Column Committees don't need to be underscored.'[12]

The confusion in the Loyalist camp was intensified by the fact that the government had left Madrid for Valencia the night of November 6, turning over the defense of Madrid to General José Miaja, whom Soviet journalist Mikhail Koltsov called 'an old man whom no one knows',[13] with Lieutenant-Colonel Vicente Rojo as his chief of staff. On the spot, Colonel Rojo had to choose the members of the General Staff of Defense of Madrid. Of this selection, he commented that 'the comrades whom I asked to form the General Staff of Defense answered resolutely and without hesitation...' All but two of these were officers who outranked Rojo himself in terms of length of military service.[14]

In spite of the natural confusion caused by the departure of the government from the capital city, Colonel Rojo, whom Koltsov called 'the man who in fact directs all of the defenses of Madrid',[15] has indicated that there were advantages to this move from the point of view of the defense of Madrid: 'With the departure of the government towards the Levante ... there left with it the pessimism, jealousy, discord, defeatism of some egotistic elites, and why not say it also, the panic, the panic which hundreds of people were not able to overcome... The long and painful night of defeat seemed to leave with those who left, and the light of a morning began to shine for those who deserved the triumph.'[16]

The local federation of unions of the CNT, in a statement it issued at the time of the departure of the ministers for Valencia, expressed the same basic idea as Rojo, if in somewhat more strident terms: 'Madrid, free of ministers, of commissars, and of "tourists" feels more secure in its struggle... The people, the Madrid working class, has no heed of all these tourists who have left for Valencia and Catalonia. Madrid free of ministers, will be the tomb of fascism. Forward, militiamen! Long live Madrid without Government. Long live the social Revolution.'[17]

The new general staff had virtually to start its work from scratch.

Rojo noted: 'We began our task without dossiers or organized dispatches; a little information, some plans, a bulk of papers, many indecipherable, and some personal notes with data which each had on his action hitherto.'[18]

General Miaja called in the city's trade union leaders on November 6. According to Robert Colodny:

> The General explained the gravity of the situation on the front, concealing nothing and demanding that 50,000 men be mobilized for the next day's battle... To the question concerning the arms for the mobilized workers, Miaja replied with the demand that all the stores of arms and dynamite known to be hidden in the city be made available to the Junta of Defense, and he gave the workers authority to utilize the radio to mobilize their forces.
>
> [By the early morning of November 7] Madrid workers in leather jackets and peaked caps were moving up to the front. These were the men selected by the trade union and political party leaders, men picked for reliability and sent to the sectors considered the most vital for the defense of the city. Many moved, without arms, up to the barricades facing the Manzanares. They obeyed General Miaja's orders, transmitted through the trade union headquarters, that they should take the arms from the dead; that no time should be lost when a man fell – only the moment necessary to push the corpse out of the way and shove in a new clip.'[19]

The work of the general staff was far from normal military routine in the first days of the battle, according to Rojo: 'In the first week of the defense, we met the problems of each moment and each day as they arose... There were no working shifts; only for meals; and one slept – or rather, napped – when one could. During the first four days of work I think that I remember that no one napped...'[20]

In spite of the confusion and improvisation of the first days of the battle, Franco's troops were largely halted on the edge of the city. One factor which favored the defense was the capture on a prisoner of the enemy's Order of the Day, outlining his tactics for taking Madrid, and letting General Miaja and his colleagues know where the major offensive was going to fall.

However, Colonel Rojo wrote of this: 'If in reality knowledge of the adversary's Order of Operations and the command dispositions which were possible as a result contributed decisively to the failure of the attack ... the true root of the success of the defense was in the change which had taken place during the first 24 hours in the morale both of the fighting forces and in their immediate collaborators in the rear guard. This was made clear precisely in the combats of the 7th, in which our combatants fought with an indomitable will and with the highest spirit of sacrifice ... The lack of arms, of organization, of technique, of fortifications was overcome with a really superabundance of spiritual force, of exalted morale, of small and valorous leaders and the mass of citizens ...'[21]

Some commentators on the battle of Madrid, particularly these early phases of the conflict, have given major credit to the Russian adviser General Goriev (ostensibly the military attaché of the Soviet Union) for being principally responsible for establishing the city's defense. For instance, Burnett Bolloten claimed that Goriev was 'the real organizer of Madrid's defence.'[22] Louis Fischer used much the same phrase, calling Goriev 'the savior of Madrid'.[23]

However, Colonel Vicente Rojo strongly denied this: 'As Chief of the EM General Staff I affirm roundly that that is false, as it is rigorously certain that ... Goriev cooperated efficaciously with the Committee of Defense, which did not cease to exercise its authority for a single moment ...'[24]

The Role of the International Brigades

The first serious reinforcements for the Madrid front did not begin to arrive until November 10, four days after the beginning of the battle. Among those to arrive was the first of the International Brigades.

The accepted wisdom of many who have written about the battle of Madrid is that the International Brigades played the most crucial role in that conflict. Thus, Pietro Nenni, who was a captain in the Garibaldi Battalion, has written: 'As to the contribution of the International Brigades, one can say without exaggeration that in November 1936, it was decisive. In the Casa del Campo, on the banks of the Manzanares, in the University City, the International Brigades and the Garibaldi Battalion of the Italian anti-fascists sustained with admirable courage the shock of the Franco troops...'[25]

Similarly, Louis Fischer, who at the time was a Communist fellow-traveller although later he became a bitter opponent of the Stalinists, wrote in 1937: 'Just as Madrid was about to fall into Franco's lap, the International Brigade's first unit, 1,900 strong, marched into the fray. For the first time, the Moors were stopped. For the first time, the militiamen saw the heels and back of Franco's soldiers.'[26] Similarly, Soviet Admiral N. Kuznetsov claimed that Madrid was saved by 'Soviet aid and the International Brigades.[27]

Hugh Thomas makes a somewhat different argument. First of all, he incorrectly reports that the first International Brigade arrived in Madrid on November 8, and 'marched in perfect order along the Gran Via towards the front'.[28] He concedes that the two International Brigades involved in the battle within Madrid were a force 'too small to have turned the day by numbers alone. Furthermore, the militia and workers had checked Varela on November 7, before the arrival of the Brigades. The victory was that of the populace of Madrid.' But, he adds, 'The example of the International Brigades fired the militiamen to continue to resist, while giving to the Madrileños the feeling that they were not alone...'[29]

A further reading of Thomas's account of the four phases of the battle of Madrid tends, however, to emphasize the accepted wisdom which we described. It concentrated almost exclusively on the role that the International Brigades played in those segments of the battle, apparently because the author thought that the heart of the resistance lay in the foreign troops engaged in it on the Republican side.

Even George Orwell, who certainly was no friend of the Stalinists, has contributed to this view: 'The Russian arms and the magnificent defense of Madrid by troops mainly under Communist control had made the Communists the heroes of Spain.'[30]

Colonel Vicente Rojo, chief of staff of the defending forces throughout the battle of Madrid, provided a rather different version of the role of the International Brigades in the conflict. He made five points concerning them. First, 'At the beginning of the battle there was not on our front of Madrid a single International Brigade, nor even scattered Battalions.' Second, 'The first of these units which was put at the disposition of the Defense Command, entered in the line on the 10th, and precisely in the sector in which it was engaged, in spite of its energetic action, on the 13th, the enemy's Column 1 would reach the Manzanares and two days later would break through the front to penetrate the University City.'[31] (This contradicts the claim of Gabriel Jackson and Mikhail Koltsov, the Soviet journalist, that the International Brigade entered the conflict on November 8.)[32]

Colonel Rojo's third point was: 'During the battle in the Madrid front proper, the largest forces were normally those of one Brigade; exceptionally two, and two others were only used on the Jarama and in Guadalajara. In Madrid the XI and XII were located in sectors on the right wing, from University City towards Boadilla, where they were grouped with other Spanish Brigades...' Fourth, Rojo noted: 'In no case or situation did they operate with autonomy, separate from the Spanish officers, who hierarchically directed the operations. Nor did they form by themselves a Large Unit, such as Division or Army Corps, although in some cases and for certain operations two were grouped under a single command.'

Finally, Colonel Rojo concluded: 'Their officers, like those of whatever other unit, when by their irregular conduct they deserved it, were punished. This happened to General Kleber, commander of the International Brigade on the University City front, for giving his activities more a political than a military significance.' General Kleber was removed from command for six months, not resuming it until his successor as head of the XI Brigade was killed in battle.[33]

Colonel Rojo summed up the advantages of the International Brigades thus: 'Their organization was similar to that of the Spanish mixed Brigades, from which they differed in: greater amounts of armaments, material and transport, as well as field artillery (eventually); better officers (some, excombatants in the First World War);

better training of many of their soldiers, and their political conviction which to a great degree was the basis of their high morale as combatants.'[34]

The CNT journalist Eduardo de Guzmán, in his account of the defense of Madrid, also assessed the positive aspects of the International Brigades, and what the CNT militia learned from them: 'They knew how to take advantage of accidents of terrain, manipulate bombs, place machine guns, distribute their men. They have, furthermore, magnificent equipment, such as none of our columns has so far had ... Our men see them fight with ability and unlimited audacity. They see how they have munitions, how one constructs a foxhole, how to confront tanks and make them flee through the use of hand grenades. They see this, and with that power of marvelous adaptation of the Spanish people, they imitate them without loss of time.'[35]

The Anarchists in the Defense of Madrid

Militiamen organized by the CNT–FAI played a significant role in the defense of Madrid. They helped turn back the first frontal attack on the city by the Franco forces in November 1936, and were also prominent in the later three phases of the battle.

At the time and subsequently, the role of the anarchist soldiers was underestimated. Both those who wrote about the battle as it was in progress, and historians who recounted it in the decades that followed, tended to play down the role of the anarchists and to exaggerate the part played by troops under Communist command, both Spanish groups like the famed Fifth Regiment, and the International Brigades.

There were two principal anarchist groups involved in the defense of Madrid. One was the units sent from Catalonia, at first commanded by Buenaventura Durruti, and after his death by Ricardo Sanz, and which returned to the Aragón front at the end of the battle of Madrid. The other consisted of militiamen raised principally in the Madrid areas itself and commanded throughout its existence by Cipriano Mera, which continued throughout the War to be one of the principal military units in the Madrid area. Many of these militiamen were there when the battle began, Mera arrived with some of the troops he had led in capturing the province of Cuenca, on November 10, and assumed command of the anarchist troops at Madrid.

The Role of the Defense Committee of the CNT

During the battle of Madrid (and the rest of the War), a major role in the functioning of the anarchist units on the Madrid front was played by the Defense Committee of the Center of the CNT (Comité de Defensa del Centro de la CNT). It directed the struggle of the anarchists at the time of the suppression of the Rebellion in Madrid in July, and immediately after the defeat of the Rebels in the capital was assured, the defense committee undertook to defend towns and cities which the quickly recruited militia might reinforce, or might recapture where they had fallen to the Rebels.

On July 21, the Comité de Defensa met, to deal with 'breaking the circle around Madrid'. Eduardo Val, the head of the *comité*, reported on the seizure by the Rebels of virtually all of Old Castille: 'In contrast, all of Levante and Catalonia are in the hands of the workers. Cutting our communications are Alcalá, Guadalajara and Toledo. Once these three cities are taken, Madrid will have communications with the South and East ... Taking them, we make sure all of the provinces of Cuenca, Guadalajara, Toledo and Ciudad Real, Albacete, isolated, will fall of its own weight. Beyond that, we shall open for ourselves, with the seizure of Guadalajara, the road to Zaragoza ...'[36]

The Defense Committee then rapidly organized improvised militia columns and dispatched them to Guadalajara, Alcalá de Henares and Toledo. Within a few days they had been successful – except for the fact that the Alcazar of Toledo remained in Rebel hands.[37]

With the victories in Madrid, Alcalá, Guadalajara and Toledo, the CNT Defense Committee had only begun the work of organizing and directing the anarchist participation in the military struggle in Madrid and neighboring areas. At the beginning of the War, the

Defense Committee consisted of Eduardo Val as secretary, Mariano Valle and Barcia. However, the heart and soul of the committee was Val. Of him, Ricardo Sanz said: 'Everything is concentrated in him. Nothing, not the smallest detail escaped his powerful imagination, and every problem presented to him received an immediate solution. His was a capacity which was not exhausted.'

Sanz assessed the overall role of the Defense Committee in somewhat exaggerated terms: 'The defenders of Madrid, those who were in the trenches, when they have to consult on something, don't go to the official offices. They know that there nothing was resolved. Everything is completely dead in Madrid. Only in one place in the capital, the war was felt and lived ... Cars are seen coming and leaving rapidly. Trucks approach and disappear soon.'[38]

Most of the anarchists who have written about the battle of Madrid have stressed the importance of the Defense Committee of the CNT, for consultation among the anarchist militia leaders, and as a means of getting their problems and views placed before the top officers in the general staff of the Madrid command. It also exercised leadership and in so far as anarchist ideology permitted, command over the CNT troops. Eduardo de Guzmán noted that Eduardo Val 'is a cool fighter who thinks and orders with few words. The comrades completely accept his directions...'[39]

By early September, the Defense Committee had drawn up 'Regulations of CNT Militia'. They were brief, consisting of six articles. Article One said that 'Every militiaman is obliged to comply with the norms of the Battalion Committee, and Centuria and Group Delegates.' Article Two provided that 'He cannot operate for his own account in military affairs and will accept without discussion the posts and places which are assigned him, both at the front and in the rearguard.' Article Three stated that 'Every militiaman who doesn't obey the norms of the Battalion Committee, Delegate of the Century or of the Group will be sanctioned by the Group, if the offense is light, and by the Battalion Committee if the offense is grave.' According to Article Four, 'Considered as grave will be: desertion, abandoning one's post, sabotage, pillage, and utterances which bring generalization.'

Article Five specified: 'Every militiaman must know: that he has voluntarily entered the Militia, but once a part of it, as a soldier of the Revolution, his conduct has to be to OBEY AND COMPLY...' Finally, Article Six said: 'Anyone who acts apart from the Militia will be considered a rebel and will suffer the punishment which the Battalion Committee to which he belongs determines.'

The regulation ended with an exhortation: 'Militiamen! These norms of action and contact are not barracks discipline. It is the effort of everyone, in community, united and disciplined. Without this cohesion of energy no triumph is possible. Militiamen, obey, comply and you will win!'[40]

It was the Comité de Defensa which was in charge of recruiting the CNT militia units. According to Eduardo de Guzmán, it operated through the unions and *ateneos* of the CNT in Madrid and vicinity, sending out notice to them of how many volunteers it could supply with arms at any given moment. The *comité* also exercised certain selectivity in recruiting. According to de Guzmán, 'Men would not go to the front who shouldn't because of their physical condition. Nor would those go whose antifascism was not worthy of complete confidence.'[41] The *comité* kept a card file on all those it recruited.[42]

Finally, the Comité de Defensa named the commanders of the early CNT columns organized in the center. Its first nominee was Lieutenant-Colonel del Rosal, a man 'of absolute confidence'.[41]

The committee also organized the supplementary services needed by armed forces. These included a medical service – for which several buildings in Madrid were taken over – and a supply service, to provide food, clothing and other requirements of the militia units. At the beginning of the War, if the CNT's defense committee had not organized these for the anarchist troops, it is unlikely that anyone else would have, since the central military organization of the ministry of defense was virtually non-existent.[44]

One other somewhat curious function of the defense committee might be noted. Burnett Bolloten, citing a letter from García Pradas, wartime editor of *CNT* of Madrid as his source, said that after militarization of the CNT militia there, 'the officers in the Anarcho-syndicalist units on the central front handed the greater part of their pay to the CNT Defense Committee of Madrid, which used the money for the benefit of the agricultural collectives.'[45]

Durruti and García Oliver in Madrid

As the Franco troops approached Madrid, the political and military leaders of Catalonia, particularly the anarchists, felt increasingly the need to provide what help they could for the capital city. On November 4, there was a meeting of all of the Catalan military commanders with the Council of Defense of the Catalan government where the problem was discussed.[46]

Then, on November 7, after the battle of Madrid had begun, Juan García Oliver, who had returned to the capital and had just become minister of justice, made a personal telephone call to Eugenio Vallejo, CNT leader of the old Hispano Suiza plant in Barcelona, asking for the immediate dispatch of 20,000 hand grenades. After this conversation, arrangements were made to that end, and several days later, when he was back in Madrid, García Oliver was informed by Colonel Rojo that the weapons had arrived.[47]

This conversation of García Oliver arose from a discussion which he had had with Colonel Rojo and the Russian ambassador, Marcel Rosenberg. According to García Oliver, they had consulted him – because of his presumed knowledge about how to seize a city as a result of his leadership in July 19 in Barcelona – about how he thought the Franco forces would be most likely to try to penetrate the city. García Oliver had first pointed out that the sewer system of Madrid, the exit from which was in hands of the Franco forces, would be a easy means of penetration. He urged the setting up of machine gun and hand grenade nests at key junctures of the sewer system. This was done, and Colonel Rojo later reported to him that when, as García Oliver had predicted, the enemy did seek to penetrate the sewer system, 'it was an enormous slaughter for them', and they were turned back.[48]

García Oliver had also suggested to Colonel Rojo and the ambassador the utility of evacuating the buildings at the beginnings of the main streets going from the then battlefield into the center of the city, and placing on their roofs and top floors squads with large numbers of hand grenades and Molotov cocktails, to throw upon the advancing troops. Rojo later reported that these steps had been taken, but fortunately the Franco troops had not gotten as far as where these buildings were located.[49]

On November 10, García Oliver had returned to Madrid and was in his Madrid office early that morning, when Buenaventura Durruti soon appeared, to García Oliver's surprise. Durruti announced that he was there to help save Madrid. After some discussion of what Durruti's role might be, the two men went to see Francisco Largo Caballero, who had also just returned to the capital, in his capacity as minister of defense, concerning what role Durruti might have in the defense of Madrid. It was finally agreed that, when two weeks later, as was expected, three new 'mixed divisions' would arrive in the city, Durruti would be put in command of them, with the rank of major, which was the highest military grade then being given officers from the militia.[50]

However, this agreement was not to be fulfilled, largely due to the civil and military authorities, particularly the anarchists, of Catalonia. On the evening of November 11, a new meeting of all of the Catalan militia column commanders and the Council of Defense was held in Barcelona. There it was decided, with particular insistence of Diego Abad de Santillán and Federica Montseny, who attended the meeting, that a militia column, commanded by Durruti, should immediately be recruited from the Catalan troops of Aragón and dispatched to the Madrid front.[51]

On the morning of November 12, Durruti telephoned his aides at Bujaralóz, telling them which units from his column should be sent post-haste to Barcelona, for rapid transfer to the Madrid front. Durruti himself went immediately to Valencia, and from there he and Juan García Oliver went to Madrid, where they arrived on the afternoon of November 14.[52]

Meanwhile, apparently on the 14th, before García Oliver and Durruti left for Madrid, what might have been a major decision in so far as anarchist participation in the defense of Madrid was concerned, was taken at the first meeting of the newly formed Superior War Council, to which García Oliver belonged. Francisco Largo Caballero brought up in the council what he considered to be the insubordinate behavior of General José Miaja who 'was not conducting himself as chief of a Junta with delegated functions, created by the government to represent it, but ... with much demagoguery was getting the members of the Junta de Defensa to consider themselves the government, not only of Madrid, but of all Spain.

Largo Caballero asked for suggestions for a replacement for Miaja, and García Oliver suggested the name of Buenaventura Durruti. García Oliver reported that Largo Caballero replied, 'I'm inclined to accept Durruti. Only I must ask for the greatest secrecy, since I need eight days, to give more time for Durruti to become known in Madrid, and so that I can go there, both to talk with him, and turn over his position to him.' Again according to García Oliver, no one, not even the Communist minister of agriculture, Vicente Uribe, dissented from this decision.[53]

Of course, nothing came of this proposal. Within eight days, Durruti was dead, and Miaja remained in command of the Madrid front for most of the rest of the War. In any case, García Oliver, at least, had a good impression of Miaja in the role assigned to him: 'I became aware of the wisdom of Largo Caballero in choosing Miaja as president of the Junta de Defensa of Madrid. Miaja was an inexhaustible source of optimism. Perhaps he didn't know much about operations, but to raise the fallen morale of everyone with whom he entered into contact, he was insuperable.'[54]

Durruti spent an unhappy day in Madrid, November 14–15. His own militiamen had not yet arrived in the city, and his efforts to assume command of a column which the Catalan Communists had rushed to the scene (about which I shall say more later) were unavailing. Although he asserted that he had orders from the Council of Defense of Catalonia to assume control of all Catalan troops on the Madrid front, he had no such written orders in his possession, and so the Communist troops refused to accept his word on the subject.[55]

García Oliver and Durruti conferred with General Miaja and Colonel Rojo and, at Durruti's request, he was assigned a Soviet military adviser. They then sallied forth to 'the front', near the Frenchmen's Bridge, where the Catalan Communist unit was fighting. Durruti, García Oliver and the commander of the unit, Captain López Tienda sought fruitlessly to rally troops which were fleeing from the scene. All of these men and others accompanying them themselves took an active part for a while in the defense of that bridge. However, in a lull in the fighting, García Oliver approached Durruti and told him: 'This is not a command post, Durruti. This is not your post.' The CNT leaders apparently soon left the area.[56]

Finally, the 1,400 or so men of Durruti's column arrived in Madrid about nine in the morning of November 15. They had left Barcelona in freight cars the night of November 13, had been met at the city of Turia by Durruti and García Oliver at about noon on the 14th, after which the two anarchist leaders went on by police car to Madrid, while the troops made the rest of the way to the capital in trucks and cars, because the rail lines had been partly disrupted by bombing by the Franco airplanes.[57]

The evening of the arrival of the Durruti Column in Madrid – November 15 – there was a meeting of the Committee of Defense of the CNT, attended among others by Eduardo Val, Durruti and Cipriano Mera. It was explained to Durruti why it would not be possible to merge the forces he had brought with those of Mera, since they were assigned by the high command to different sectors. Durruti finally agreed to place his forces in the part of the University City line which had been indicated to him. A few hours later the Durruti Column entered into battle for the first time on the Madrid front.[58]

The Alleged Flight of the Durruti Column Under Fire

The accepted wisdom of many historians of the Spanish Civil War has been that the militiamen of the Durruti Column broke and ran the first time they were thrown into battle on the Madrid front. Robert Colodny has claimed that this happened on November 15.[59]

Hugh Thomas has described the supposed event thus: 'At the same time as the XIIth International Brigade arrived, Durruti also came to Madrid, with a column of 3,000 Anarchists ... He demanded an independent sector of the front, so that his men could show their prowess. Miaja unwisely agreed to allot to the Anarchists the Casa de Campo ... Durruti received orders to attack on November 15, with all the Republican artillery and aircraft in support. However, when the hour came, the machine guns of the Moroccans so terrified the Anarchists that they refused to fight. Durruti, furious, promised a new attack the next day.'[60]

Hugh Thomas's account would seem to be in error on at least four counts. First, he doubles the number of men that Durruti actually had in the column which followed him to Madrid. Second, the Durruti Column did not first enter into combat in the Casa de Campo but in the University City. Third, and most serious, the Durruti Column was not in battle at all on November 15, and did not start to participate until the early morning of the 16th. Finally, the evidence would seem to indicate that Hugh Thomas confused the anarchists' Durruti Column with another Catalan unit which had arrived in Madrid at least a day before the Durruti Column did.

After the first meeting of the Catalan Council of Defense on November 4 with the commanders of the various militia columns concerning the provision of aid to the Madrid front, the Partido Socialista Unificado de Catalaunya (the Catalan Communist Party) decided to organize on its own a column for this purpose to abort the political effects of the possible arrival of a column led by Durruti 'to save Madrid'. According to Francisco Hidalgo, one of the officers of this group, which became known as the Libertad-López Tienda Column, it was made up of UGT and PSUC members recruited in Barcelona, some people from the PSUC columns in Aragón who had returned to Barcelona, and some 1,935 draftees who had not been able to return home after the official dissolution of the old army. It was largely led by regular officers who, to gain protective coloring (due to unpopularity of regular soldiers immediately following July 19), had joined the UGT.

This unit, which consisted of about 2,500 men, was given absolutely no training, according to Hidalgo. It was dispatched from Barcelona on November 9, received some arms on the way to Madrid, and arrived in the capital on the morning of November 13. That afternoon the Libertad-López Tienda Column took positions in the Parque del Oeste sector.

The column saw no action on the 14th. However, the next day it was ordered to the Frenchmen's Bridge, to try to prevent the Franco forces from crossing the Manzanares river there. Having had no previous training, the column, according to Francisco Hidalgo, 'crossed the Parque del Oeste in a manner, militarily speaking laughable for its absurdity', and as a result suffered its first casualties getting into position.[61]

It was certainly the Libertad-López Tienda Column, not that of Durruti, to which Colonel Vicente Rojo referred when he wrote that '...the attacker had applied maximum power on a very narrow front, and furthermore had had the good fortune to provoke panic in one of our improvised units which, having come from other fronts and not having lived through the crisis of moral reaction of the 7th, had not yet caught the spirit of the fighting in Madrid. That unit retreated in disorder, infecting other units, and the enemy could roll them back, penetrate the University City and occupy several buildings, getting to the Clinic as their most advanced positions.'[62] I have already referred to the role of Durruti and García Oliver in seeking to halt the flight of these militiamen.

However, the more or less official Stalinist history of the Civil War repeats the story of the collapse of the Durruti column under fire. It adds, for good measure: 'The Durruti Column had to be relieved, in large part disarmed, and sent to the Levante.'[63] In fact, what remained of the Durruti Column remained at the Madrid front, was reinforced by other CNT troops after the death of Durruti, and when it was finally withdrawn in April 1937, went to the Aragón front, not Levante, and joined forces with those elements of the original Durruti Column who had remained in Aragón. It participated in the battles of Aragón and Catalonia, and was one of the last Republican forces to withdraw into France upon the fall of Catalonia.

The Actual First Participation of the Durruti Column

Abel Paz (Diego Camacho) has described the actual participation of the Durruti Column in its first few days at the Madrid front. He has based his narrative on written accounts by two important participants in the column at that time.

211

The Durruti Column was in position in a part of the university city front assigned to them by 2 a.m. on November 16. They entered into battle soon after daybreak. By seven in the morning they had retaken the Clinical Hospital, but that post was taken over four hours later on the written orders of the general staff, by an element on the Communists' Fifth Regiment. The anarchist forces there after concentrated on attacks designed to capture the Casa de Velázquez and the Faculty of Philosophy and Letters buildings of the university city. Fighting continued through most of the night of November 16–17 and, 24 hours after beginning their attack, the Durruti Column had had little respite and virtually nothing to eat.

Later in the day of the 17th, the efforts of the Durruti Column centered on defense of the Santa Cristina Asylum where the fighting was 'most violent'. At one point, troops that the Fifth Regiment had left in the Clinical Hospital fled, and were stopped at the Plaza de la Moncloa by a group led by one of the leaders of the Durruti Column, Miguel Yoldi, who reorganized them and brought them back into battle alongside the Durruti Column militiamen.[64] This may be the incident to which Robert Colodny refers when he says that the Durruti Column fled on November 17.[65]

The Durruti Column was in the front lines for three days or more without being relieved, although at least some of the units around it were replaced during that period. Apparently, shortly before his death, Durruti had arranged with General Miaja and Colonel Rojo for the relief of the CNT militiamen.[66] By that time, casualties of the Durruti Column were more than 50 percent.[67]

The Death of Durruti

Buenaventura Durruti was shot at about 2 p.m. on November 19 1936. He was taken to a hospital run by the CNT in the Hotel Ritz and died there at 4 a.m. on November 20. That is all that one can say for sure about the death of the leader of the Durruti Column.

Almost before Durruti died, controversy began to arise over how he had come to be fatally wounded. The official version was that he had been the victim of enemy fire from the general direction of the Clinical Hospital of university city, which was occupied by Franco forces. However, there were those among the anarchists who were convinced that he had been killed by Communists, because the Stalinists feared the growth of a legend of Durruti as 'the savior of Madrid'.[68]

On the other hand, the Communists themselves spread the story that Durruti was on the point of becoming a Communist, and was shot by the anarchists themselves as a result. A somewhat modified version of this claim was presented by Louis Fischer; who wrote that Durruti 'Was shot in the rear, and it was generally assumed that his own men assassinated him because he favored active Anarchist participation in the war and cooperation with Caballero...'[69]

Finally, there was the version that he had been shot accidentally by a gun which he was carrying.

Abel Paz, who has probably done as thorough a job as anyone in investigating the circumstances of Durruti's death, could come to no final conclusion: 'The polemic surrounding the death of Durruti will continue because it is now an historic enigma. Unfortunately, men are more attracted by enigmas, because of their mysterious nature, than by a profound reflection on the events of a life...'[70]

Whatever the cause of Durruti's death, his funeral in Barcelona was the occasion for an outpouring of tribute and admiration for the fallen anarchist leader. A six-man British parliamentary delegation happened to be in Barcelona that day. They reported that '...on our arrival in that city we witnessed an immense demonstration of perhaps 500,000 people. A procession of military, political and industrial units marched through the main streets of the city. It marched for five hours, amidst scenes of great enthusiasm...'[71]

A pamphlet on Durruti published by the CNT-FAI after his death noted that the funeral procession of the fallen anarchist leader was headed by President Luis Companys, the Soviet and Mexican consuls, and García Oliver. It added: 'They were followed by the whole people, the entire populace of Barcelona. All organizations had invited their members to participate in the funeral procession. Banners of all antifascist organizations waved, all the militiamen staying in the city followed the first militiaman of Catalonia.

Hundreds of thousands walked in the procession, and more hundreds of thousands covered the sidewalks and the streets and held up their fists in a last salute.'[72]

The Durruti Column in Madrid After Durruti's Death

The CNT leaders in Catalonia, almost as soon as they heard of Durruti's death decided to send Ricardo Sanz, a fellow-member of the Nosotros group, to take command of the remains of his column in Madrid. He arrived in Madrid on the morning of November 21.

Sanz found the survivors of the Durruti Column considerably demoralized as a result of the death of their leader. Most of them wanted to return immediately to the Aragón front. However, as Ricardo Sanz has written, 'In spite of this confused situation, aided by the support of Minister Federica Montseny and other good friends, who were in Madrid and had made the promise of not abandoning it until it was completely saved, only a very small number of combatants returned to Aragón, and the majority remained in Madrid, disposed to defend it above all else.'[73]

A few days later reinforcements for the Durruti Column were sent by the Defense Council of Catalonia. Sanz commented: 'Thus the Durruti Column of Madrid was replenished and in a position to take a place of honor at the front, which it did immediately, relieving one of the International Columns which occupied positions from the Casa de Campo to the vicinity of Aravaca.'[74]

Ricardo Sanz, like Durruti before him, had had no military experience until the outbreak of the Civil War. He had been a major leader of the CNT construction workers' union of Barcelona and virtually the only member of the Nosotros group who remained in Catalonia during the Primo de Rivera dictatorship.[75] Right after the suppression of the July 19 rebellion in Catalonia, he had been a member of the four-man committee set up by the Central Militia Committee of Catalonia to organize military units to be sent to the various fronts.[76] At the time of Durruti's death, he was inspecting the coastal defenses of Catalonia, when he was suddenly told of his appointment as Durruti's successor.[77]

According to Joaquín Morlanes Jaulín, a professional army officer who was one of Ricardo Sanz's principal lieutenants in the Durruti Column (later 26th Division), 'Sanz – one hundred percent anti-militarist – adapted to the necessities of the moment, and accepting the militarization of his own rank, assimilated military techniques and was converted into an acceptable military man and an excellent chief to a Large Unit.'[78]

The last major participation of the Durruti Column in the battle of Madrid was in December 1936–January 1937, when the Franco forces tried to seize El Pardo and outflank Madrid from the north and west. It was during this battle that, according to Morlanes Jaulín, Ricardo Sanz was converted from a militia leader into a military man.

At one point in this battle, on January 6, less than 200 men of the Durruti Column were holding a position near Casa Quemada, almost in the center of the battlefront. Elements on each side of them had fled, leaving arms and equipment behind them. Morlanes Jaulín, who was in charge of that segment of the column, put in a call to Sanz at column headquarters, asking for men to back up his unit, and particularly to gather up the arms which had been thrown away by those who had fled.

Instead of sending such a unit, Ricardo Sanz himself arrived with a handful of men, and Sanz began firing at the enemy from a machine-gun nest. When Morlanes Jaulín insisted that this was not the appropriate role for the commander of the Durruti Column, that he should be organizing a further defense line behind where they now were, to which the unit of Mornales Jaulín could retire if necessary, Sanz was furious. But he finally did return to the rear, with the results which Mornales Jaulín described: 'Ricardo Sanz, who still thought as a 'militiaman', went to the rear, less than a kilometer from that place, and, together with Cipriano Mera, Lieutenant-Colonel Palacios (a professional) and other political and trade union leaders converted into accidental military men, organized as if by magic a principal line of resistance ... against which the fascists broke their horns, if they had any.'[79]

Incidentally, this was also probably one of the last times that the Durruti Column as a whole behaved as a militia group instead of a military unit. Ricardo Sanz explained to Mornales Jaulín that he had not sent the unit which had been requested because, according to Sanz, 'The Reserve Battalion refused to come. They are having an Assembly to decide what they are going to do.'[80]

Elements of the Durruti Column, by then the 26th Division of the new Republican army stayed in the Madrid area until April 1937. By that time, the Madrid front had been stabilized, and the government of Catalonia ordered the elements under Ricardo Sanz to return to the Aragón front where they rejoined the elements of the old Durruti Column which had remained there. Ricardo Sanz became the commander of all of the reunited 26th Division. He became a lieutenant-colonel, although normally the command which he had would have called for him to be a major-general.[81]

The Beginnings of the Cipriano Mera Column

The second important anarchist military element in the defense of Madrid was the column of Cipriano Mera, which became the 14th Division of the Republican army, and remained in the Madrid region throughout the War. Mera was a young leader of the CNT construction workers' union in Madrid, and shortly before the outbreak of the War had been a leader of a building strike which had become a conflict between the CNT and UGT, and had resulted in Mera's being jailed. He was not released until the beginning of the military uprising.[82]

Immediately upon his release, Cipriano Mera organized his first column of militiamen, presumably principally from among the Madrid construction workers. At the head of '800 men and a machine gun', Mera recaptured the city of Cuenca from the Rebels.[83] His column was also credited with capturing Guadalajara, which the Rebels had first seized.[84] After the beginning of the battle of Madrid, Cipriano Mera was, according to García Oliver, 'recognized in the Operation Room of the Ministry of War, as the military chief of the anarchosyndicalists,' in the Madrid region.[85]

Ramón Sender, writing at a time when he was still a Communist, paid tribute to Mera's role in the defense of Madrid: 'A few weeks after the beginning of the attack on Madrid, we saw that alongside an heroic Communist leader like Lister, or the 'Campesino', Modesto or Galan, we had such an anarchist hero, with special talent for leadership as Cipriano Mera, who, at the head of his legions of masons, perfectly disciplined, fought just as Durruti before him had fought, and as well as a young professional soldier.'[86]

The Terancon Incident of November 6–7

A curious incident involving militia troops under the general control of Cipriano Mera occurred late on November 6 at Terancon, 40 kilometers from Madrid, on the road to Valencia. These militiamen, under the direct leadership of José Villanueva, had fought in the unsuccessful attempt to hold Siguenza. Now, on the evening of November 6, they had received orders from Eduardo Val to turn back anyone fleeing from Madrid to Valencia.

In compliance with those orders, Villanueva's forces held up a group of cars, taking government ministers and other people, including the mayor of Madrid, Pedro Rico, to the new seat of the government in Valencia. Among those forced to leave their cars by the militiamen were the Communist ministers Jesús Hernández and Vicente Uribe, and the CNT ministers Juan López and Juan Peiró, as well as Julio Alvarez del Vayo, Socialist minister of foreign affairs. Those stopped also included General José Asensio, vice-minister of War, and General Sebastian Pozas, newly appointed commander of the army of the center.

While this was going on, Cipriano Mera arrived on the scene. After finding what had happened, he called Eduardo Val, informing him of the incident. Val immediately left Madrid for Terancon, arriving there at 2 a.m. on November 7. After conferring, Val and Mera decided to let the ministers proceed to Valencia. However, Mayor Rico was forced to return to Madrid, where he sought refuge in an embassy.

One curious, and fortunate, result of this incident was that through Val, General Miaja was informed that General Pozas was in Terancon Miaja had decided to open sealed orders from Largo

Caballero, which he was not supposed to look at until 6 a.m., and had discovered that he had received General Poza's orders. Put in contact with Pozas in Terancon, he was able to find out just what in fact his orders had been, since General Pozas had received them, also by mistake.[87]

Hugh Thomas mistakenly attributes this incident in Terancon to the 'Iron Column', of Valencia, whom he refers to as 'the *cagoulards* of the Spanish Revolution'.[88] Julio Alvarez del Vayo makes the same mistake, compounding it with a somewhat theatrical description of what occurred: 'They were a band of undesirables who labelled themselves "Anarchiststs" and were very brave when it came to pillaging the countryside, but they were not quite as heroic on the battlefront. They numbered several hundred men, we few, armed with revolvers, stood them off. After an hour of parley with the leaders, alternating threats and arguments, we forced them to let us continue our journey.'[89] Robert Colodny makes the same error, in associating the 'Iron Column' with the events in Terancon[90]

The Cipriano Mera Column in the Defense of Madrid

The Mera Column, which became the 14th Division of the new Spanish Republican army, played a significant role in all phases of the battle of Madrid. They were in the front lines through virtually all of the first phase of the battle in November. Eduardo de Guzmán has noted that next to what remained of the Durruti Column during this period were 'the men of Mera and Palacios. Beyond them was the España Libre which after the defense of Carabanchel had come to substitute for one of the battalions of the International Brigades.'[91]

All of these units soon came under Mera's command, except the Durruti Column which ultimately returned to Aragón. Both the ex-Durruti and Mera units played a key role in defending the Loyalist lines during the December–January effort of the Franco forces to cut off Madrid by taking El Pardo.[92]

There is relatively little information available concerning the participation of anarchist led troops in the Jarama phase of the battle of Madrid. Marshal R. Malinovski, who participated in it as a Soviet adviser, did note that the 70th Anarchist Brigade fought well during the battle, but gave major credit for that to the brigade's Soviet adviser, 'Comrade Petrov'.[93]

Troops under Mera's command played a particularly important role in the so-called battle of Guadalajara, the last phase of the battle of Madrid. In the Guadalajara conflict the bulk of the Franco forces were made up of Italian troops – Colonel Rojo estimated that 60,000 of the 75,000 soldiers on the Franco side in this conflict were Italians.[94]

Fighting along the Brihuega–Torija road, Mera's forces of the 14th Division had attached to them the XIIth International Brigade, which included the famous Garibaldi Battalion, made up of antifascist Italians.[95] The position of the 14th Division constituted the right flank of the Republican forces in the Guadalajara conflict.

Colonel Rojo has described the role played by Mera's troops in the Loyalist counter-offensive, which utterly defeated Mussolini's legions. He wrote: 'On the right wing of the forces which moved on Brihuega, in an audacious maneuver, the 14th Division had cut off most of the Coppi Division, although on the high ground some groups resisted; those that had been able to escape encirclement fled in disorder, abandoning their Artillery and the headquarters of the division's general staff, being pursued by our soldiers. On that wing began the crisis of the Italian fascist forces.'[96]

The battle of Guadalajara provides a prime example of how the role of anarchist forces involved in the defense of Madrid was overlooked or ignored. Although Hugh Thomas mentioned that 'along the Brihuega–Torija road, the Anarchist Cipriano Mera had established himself with a division,' he goes on to attribute the Republican victory largely to the Garibaldi Brigade and Soviet tanks.[97] For his part, Franz Borkenau, in his account of the battle, did not even mention the presence of Mera and the anarchist troops, attributing the Republican victory to two International Brigades, one Basque one, and two elements of the Communists' Fifth Regiment.[98] Castro Delgado also emphasizes the part played by Lister and El Campesino, and the International Brigades.[99]

After the end of the battle of Madrid, Cipriano Mera's Division remained on the Madrid front for the rest of the War. Even Hugh

Thomas, who was not prone to lavish praise on the role of the anarchist troops during the Civil War, referred to Mera as 'the leading Anarchist general produced by the war',[100] and 'the best commander the CNT produced in the war'.[101] By the end of the conflict Cipriano Mera was in command of the 4th Army Corps.[102] He and his troops played the most crucial role in the uprising which overthrew the government of Prime Minister Juan Negrín shortly before the end of the War – a role which we shall look at in due time.

The Role of the CNT Construction Workers

In the weeks before the siege of Madrid little was done to fortify the capital and its environs. The issue was even presented to Prime Minister Largo Caballero, who found reasons not to carry out such an effort.[103]

However, as the Franco forces moved into the suburbs of Madrid, a massive effort was finally made to construct fortifications, trenches and other defenses. Many thousands of CNT members who were not principally fighting in the militia were involved in these efforts. Although Jesús Hernández has claimed that the Communists mainly inspired this effort, the truth seems to lay elsewhere.[104]

As Franco's armies approached the capital, there were virtually no physical defenses, except for the buildings of the city itself and of the university city. But at the same time the construction workers of Madrid were virtually without work, since no construction was underway, particularly after the Franco forces began to bomb the city. Although many of them, under Cipriano Mera's leadership, had joined the first militia columns, there were still thousands of construction workers available in the city and they were mobilized by the CNT.

Eduardo de Guzmán has explained that 'there was only one preoccupation, one aspiration, one duty: to build fortifications. And the men rushed to build fortifications. They had no technicians, they lacked material, sometimes they didn't have the picks and shovels they needed. But the moment required that they overcome all obstacles. And they did. Later, when the danger relaxed, the engineers, administrators, technicians appeared to explain that the trenches and parapets were made according to one plan or another... The truth is that it was only the construction workers who were in their posts in those critical hours.'

'Trenches were dug, underground shelters grew, barbed wire was strung.' Also the construction workers suffered extensive casualties. After the crisis was over, the CNT announced that 5,000 members of their United Construction Workers Union had died in the process of building fortifications.[105]

Anarchists in the Junta de Defensa de Madrid

The civilian counterpart of the military general staff, organized when the Republican government left Madrid with the Junta de Defensa de Madrid. General José Miaja presided over both of these organizations. According to the instructions which Prime Minister Francisco Largo Caballero left with Miaja this *junta* 'will have delegated faculties of the government for the coordination of all means necessary for the defense of Madrid...'[106]

The CNT and the Juventudes Libertarias were represented in the Junta de Defensa. I will consider elsewhere some of the political problems which the anarchists encountered in their work on the *junta*, and their role in organizing and controlling the city's war industries.

Conclusions

It is a fair conclusion to say that no one 'saved Madrid'. It was saved from being overrun by the Franco forces between November 1936 and March 1937 by the combined efforts of the people of Madrid, the militiamen from various parts of Spain, who were there when the battle began and who were sent in during the months the battle of Madrid was in progress, with important help from the foreign soldiers of the International Brigades, all of whom used the Soviet-supplied arms which saw their first service in the battle of Madrid.

What clearly blunted the first drive of the Franco forces to enter the Spanish capital was the transformation of the psychology of the people of the city and the militiamen who were trying to defend it which occurred in the hours after the government of the republic abandoned the city. Rather than spreading panic, that action by the government convinced the people of the city and the militiamen that they were going to have to defend the city themselves, and generated a conviction that they could and would do so. Thereafter, as new soldiers were thrown into the battle, and as Soviet and other arms became available to the city's defenders, this conviction was reinforced and confirmed.

The lines of siege on the western and southern edges of Madrid were largely established in the first half of November 1936. The subsequent drives of the Franco forces to the north-west, in the Jarama river area to the south-east of the capital, and towards Guadalajara to the north-east were all part of the battle of Madrid. However, Gabriel Jackson was correct in saying that in the area of the first Rebel onslaught on the capital, 'from late November 1936 until the end of the Civil War, the lines never varied more than one hundred yards in any sector.'[107]

Within this broader context of the defense of Madrid, the anarchists played a role of some consequence. The claim of some anarchists that the arrival of the Durruti Column saved Madrid is no more true than the claim of the Communists and their sympathizers that the International Brigades saved Madrid. But it is true that anarchist troops of both the Durruti Column (later 26th Division), and the Mera Column (later 14th Division) fought long and bravely, and in some parts of the battle of Madrid their role in the conflict was crucial to the success of the defense of the Spanish capital. At the same time, the work of the CNTers of Madrid in building trenches and other military installations and in organizing a modest defense industry in the city during the worst phase of the fighting also was a significant contribution to the victory of the Republican forces in the battle.

If it can correctly be stated that the anarchists did not save Madrid, it can also be said that their contribution to the defense of the city, in both military and other terms, has generally not received the recognition, either then or in subsequent history books, which it deserves.

8

The Anarchists' Military Role on Fronts Other Than Catalonia– Aragón and Madrid

We have seen that anarchist military units made up the largest part of the Republican forces on the Aragón–Catalonia front, and played a significant role in the defense of Madrid. However, they were also of consequence in all of the other sectors in which the Civil War was being fought.

The accepted wisdom on the Spanish Civil War, as we have noted, tends to overlook or dismiss the importance of the part played in the War by the CNT–FAI military units. When some notice is taken of this role, it usually is to comment on the supposed 'irresponsible' behavior and 'lack of discipline' of anarchist armed forces units. Although there certainly were such examples, much more common was the dedication and sacrifices made by the anarchist troops. They differed from military units of other political orientations principally because the anarchists, unlike the Communists, Republicans, Basque and Catalan Nationalists and even many of the Socialists, saw themselves as fighting not only for the preservation of the Republic, but for the maintenance of the Revolution that had occurred in Loyalist regions at the outbreak of the Civil War.

The Iron Column

The anarchist military unit which was to a large degree most responsible for the reputation of CNT–FAI units for being 'uncontrollable' and 'undisciplined' was the Iron Column, organized by the anarchist elements of Valencia and its surrounding area. It was one of the principal units of the Republican forces operating on the Teruel front during the early part of the War.

Elsewhere in this volume we have seen the confusion that reigned in the Valencia region in the early days of the Civil War, with the army garrison remaining 'neutral' for more than a week, and extensive political maneuvering taking place among the political groups remaining loyal to the Republic. Once the army units had been forced to surrender and the regional Popular Executive Committee, representing all of the elements supporting the Republican cause, had been confirmed in power in the region, it became necessary to begin to recruit militiamen to go to the front, particularly in the vicinity of Teruel in southernmost Aragón. The seizure of Teruel by the rebellious army had been an important setback for the Republican cause, since it was a major railway center, with connections with Zaragoza, Catalonia, Madrid and Valencia. The task of trying to recapture the city for the Republic fell principally to militia forces raised in Valencia and the Levante in general.

The first effort to send troops to the Teruel front ended in disaster. A column, recruited principally in Castellón, consisting of about 1,000 militiamen and more than 400 Civil Guards and *carabineros* was dispatched about a week after the outbreak of the War. One part of the column got as far as Mora de Rubielos, and another segment of it captured La Puebla de Valverde on July 29. However, on the night of July 30, the Civil Guards mutinied, seized the leaders of the column and most of the militiamen (a number of whom they executed), as well as all of the armament of the expedition. They then went over to the Rebels.[1]

The American newspaper correspondent Lawrence Fernsworth, who visited the part of the Teruel front manned by the Iron Column early in 1937, described this incident, which very much influenced

the column's attitude towards the Civil Guards and other elements of
the old regime:

> It was in this town that the Socialist deputy, Francisco Casas
> Sala, a colonel of *carabineros*, and 63 militiamen were murdered
> by the civil guard acting in treacherous combination with the
> rebels... The Civil Guard, feigning themselves to be loyal, had
> come up here with an unarmed militia column which they
> promised to arm upon arrival at the front. Instead they turned
> and fired point blank upon the militiamen while they were
> peacefully resting and lunching in the plaza. Those who were
> captured were taken next day to the cemetery and there
> executed *en masse*...
>
> As the story had been widely published by the Spanish press I
> was anxious to check on it, as providing a clue to the probable
> veracity of similar stories. I found it not only true in its main
> reported details but in some respects understated. Witnesses and
> participants of the tragedy told me their stories and showed me
> the place wherein it transpired, the blood still caked in the
> ground.[2]

Meanwhile, the anarchists in the Levante area had begun the task of
raising militia to go to the Teruel front. This job was in the hands of
the CNT's revolutionary military council. It put advertisements in
the papers for volunteers, formed those who came forward into
militia units, and organized their dispatch to the Teruel front. The
committee also set up the equivalent of a non-commissioned officers'
school for its militiamen. There they were taught much the same kind
of things that might have been in the curriculum of a regular army
school, such as geography, topography, weapons, except that there
was no indoctrination in military hierarchy.[3]

By early August, two militia columns had been organized. One was
the Iron Column which, according to one of its participants, Roque
Santamaria, was made up of 'the most extremist elements of the
CNT and the FAI'. The other was the Torres Benedicto Column,
which was organized principally by CNT elements who had been
associated with the Treintistas.[4]

In the beginning, enthusiasm for the Iron Column ran high. According to Roque Santamaria, 12,000 people volunteered for it in the first month, although there were only arms enough for 3,000. The column was made up of peasants and industrial workers, and subordinate units were homogeneous, with groups of peasants of industrial workers electing delegates to lead the various *centurias* which made up the column.[5] There were apparently at least some professional officers associated with the column.[6]

Among the recruits were a number of ex-prisoners from the San Miguel de los Reyes penitentiary, who had been freed by the anarchists at the outbreak of the War. Of them, Roque Santamaria said that 'they behaved and fought in an extraordinary manner, valiant and dedicated',[7] However, Burnett Bolloten has argued that 'these former convicts soon brought opprobrium upon the Iron Column; for, although some of them had been moved to embrace anarchist ideals in the course of their internment, the immense majority were hardened criminals, who had suffered no change of heart and had entered the column for what they could get out of it, adopting the anarchist label as a camouflage.'[8] Their presence in the Iron Column opened it up to strong attacks, particularly from the Communists.[9]

The Iron Column left Valencia on August 8, heading first for Sagunto, from where they took the road to Teruel.[10] On August 12, the militiamen had their first contact with the enemy at Sarrión. There they defeated the troops which had come from Teruel to confront them. Subsequently, the column proceeded to La Puebla de Valverde, which they occupied without resistance, and advanced as far Puerto Escandón, only a few kilometers from Teruel.[11]

Lawrence Fernsworth described the Iron Column militiamen as he saw them at the Teruel front early in 1937:

> The militiamen dressed in varied uniforms to suit their fancies. They wore blue overalls and jackets; the whole or the half of regulation army uniforms; working clothes with belts and straps to give them a martial appearance; many red kerchiefs about the necks; natty militia caps ending in a slight peak fore and aft, which were now much the vogue or, if they chose, broad-brimmed straw or felt hats and other most un-uniform headgear.

They were a well fed, bright-eyed, amiable lot. Many of them had grown black chinbeards and sideburns which had now become quite *la moda*. A group of them invited me into their dugout and there we held forth in discourse about many things. Through the sight-holes we could see the rebel dugouts in the opposite hill, across a gully.[12]

By the end of August the Teruel front had been stabilized. The anarchist troops there were in a situation similar to that of the Durruti Column to the north. They could virtually see Teruel, but could advance no further towards it since the garrison there had been strongly reinforced, and fortified defenses had been constructed – just as the Durruti Column was on the outskirts of Zaragoza but was unable to take that city.[13]

The Iron Column organized a number of subsidiary activities. Once the front had stabilized, all of the militiamen were not in the front lines as the same time. Some of them helped the work of the peasants in the libertarian communes which had been organized in the wake of the arrival of the Iron Column in the area between Sarrión and Teruel.[14]

Elements of the Graphic Arts Union in the Iron Column established a newspaper, *Linea de Fuego*, early in September and it was distributed to all of the members of the column. The Torres Benedicto Column also began to publish its own newspaper, *Victoria*.[15] Then, early in November 1936, the Iron Column established its own radio station, Radio EA5 Columna de Hierro.[16]

In this early period, the column suffered from shortages of almost everything. The Popular Executive Committee of Valencia reported in January 1937 that the provisioning of the militia 'presented one of the most arduous and difficult tasks that one could undertake, because, in those first moments, the columns of combatants inspired by popular enthusiasm lacked the most indispensable goods and provisions. They didn't have clothing, or equipment or shoes.'[17] In November 1936, the Iron Column itself reported that it had received only 1,000 rifles from the government, 20 per cent of its total. The rest had been taken from the enemy.[18]

The Iron Column participated in various military operations that occurred on the Teruel front. In November it began constructing fortifications with local labor. It also recalled all of its members who were on sick leave in Valencia and its vicinity on the grounds that there were now enough hospitals near the front. Terence M. Smyth has noted: 'This was a step taken to control the militiamen.'[19]

One offensive of the column took place in late December 1936–early January 1937, in which the column was reported to have 'taken from the enemy ten trenches with two machine guns and have caused a great number of casualties, with 60 soldiers defecting to us with armament and munitions.'[20] At the same time, the Torres–Benedicto Column took a small town and cut the enemy's railway communications.[21]

In the early months of 1937 the column was sent to the rear for regroupment. It returned to the front lines in May, to relieve the España Libre Column (63rd Brigade), although being provided with very inadequate armament. Near the end of July 1937, the column (by then the 83rd Brigade) was badly mauled by Moorish troops in a battle at Moscardó, and again had to be withdrawn from the front.[22]

However, the Iron Column was back at the front in time for the major Republican offensive against Teruel at Christmas time 1937. It took the towns of Gea and San Blas during that offensive.

Of course, the Republican victory in Teruel was shortlived. Manuel Velasco Guardiola, a member of the Iron Column, many years later described one of the final military actions of the column after Franco's forces recaptured the city: 'Then commenced the offensive of the nationalists against Levante, in which the 83 Brigade always responded and gave the maximum it could, including the maintenance of the front near Morelia, after which it had to break through encirclement by the Nationalists and march on Castellón, but ten or twelve miles from that capital, the Nationalists cut the highway, and we had to escape as best we could.'[23]

We have little information about the functioning of the Iron Column in the latter part of the War. However, one of the more asinine accounts of its supposed disbandonment is that given by Julio Alvarez del Varyo, the Stalin Socialist foreign minister who, writing about something which he says happened in November 1936, says that Largo Caballero, as minister of war, 'sent some lorryloads of trusted militia to where the "Iron Column" was encamped; it dissolved without a shot being fired.'[24]

The Black Legend of the Iron Column

However, it was not the behavior of the Iron Column in the front lines that was responsible for the black legend that developed around it. Rather, it was the unit's behavior behind the lines that won it ill fame. There were at least five major incidents and various less significant ones involved.

The first major incursion of the members of the Iron Column into the affairs of civilian society took place on September 28 1936. The column had serious complaints about receiving insufficient armament at the front, while at the same time there were substantial numbers of Civil Guards in the rear guard in the Valencia area who were relatively well equipped. The militiamen's unhappiness was intensified by their innate distrust of the Civil Guards, particularly in view of the disaster which had occurred at La Puebla de Valverde less than two months before.

The decision was made, therefore, to dispatch some elements of the column to disarm Civil Guards units in Valencia, and bring their arms back to the front. Without any armed clashes, they succeeded in relieving guardsmen of four posts in the city of their rifles. But then they attacked the Palace of Justice and police stations, carrying out all property registers, and also seizing criminal records, putting all of these documents to the torch in the main square of the city.[25] Broué and Temime maintain that these members of the Iron Column then 'moved on to the nightclubs and cabarets, relieving customers of their jewelry and their wallets'.[26]

These incidents provoked a strong negative reaction on the part of the regional committee of the CNT, in a meeting with representatives of the Iron Column. At the end of this meeting, the column representatives said that they would now return to the front, but that 'If the Organization has not decidedly applied a revolutionary program, the Iron Column will return to Valencia and do what it considers will best serve the revolution.'[27]

Shortly after these events, elements of the Iron Column went to the city of Castellón de la Plana, where they seized and burned all criminal and property records. They also took from the local jail a number of prisoners, perhaps as many as 65, whom they regarded as fascists, and killed them.[28]

The Iron Column's attack in Castellón subsequently brought a response from the second major Valencian anarchist military unit on the Teruel front, the Torres–Benedicto Column. It sent elements to the city 'to protect the revolutionary order' there, which Terence M. Smyth interprets as meaning trying 'to avoid a repetition of the massacre of the Iron Column...'.[29]

The other three major incidents involving the Iron Column were more clearly responses to efforts of the Communists and their allies to undermine the Revolution which had occurred at the outbreak of the War. Late in October 1936, a delegate of the column in Valencia, Tiburcio Ariza González, was assassinated in the streets of Valencia. Both the Iron Column and the Torres–Benedicto Column decided to send strong delegations to their comrade's funeral. As the cortège was marching through the Plaza de Tetuan, it was fired upon from the old headquarters of the captain-general and the headquarters of the Communist Party on opposite sides of the Plaza. In a statement issued after the event the Iron Column claimed that 30 of its members had been killed and more than 60 wounded, while 38 members of the Torres–Benedicto Column had also been casualties of the shooting.

In that same statement, the column noted: 'Although we now return to the front, until the fascists are eliminated, the day will come in which examining and remembering these facts, things and people will be put in the place that they deserve.'[30]

Two other incidents took place in March 1937. Vicente Uribe, the Communist minister of agriculture, had mounted a strong campaign against the CNT–UGT rural collectives in the Levante region, not only depriving them of credit, but also seeking to use the police to destroy not only them, but some of the urban collectives as well. It was against this campaign that the Iron Column reacted.

Assault Guards were sent into rural areas to arrest hundreds of peasants from the collectives. Elements of the Iron Column supported the peasants and clashed with the Assault Guards. Only after the intervention of the CNT minister of justice, Juan García Oliver, and Socialist minister of government Angel Galarza (a supporter of Largo Caballero) was the status quo ante more or less restored, and most but not all of the peasant leaders released.

At the same time, Assault Guards seized the metallurgical plant at Borriana, controlled by the CNT, and very important for the anarchist soldiers, since it was one of their few sources of supply of war material. Again, elements of the Iron Column got involved, and only the intervention of García Oliver prevented what might have been a bloody conflict. The factory was returned to CNT control.[31]

All of these incidents created great tensions between the Iron Column and the leadership of the CNT. So did the column's opposition to militiarization of the militia (which I will discuss more fully in a subsequent chapter), and to the entry of the CNT into the government of Prime Minister Largo Caballero.

Terence M. Smyth has noted that in a regional meeting of CNT unions in November 1936, 'throughout the congress there were clear signals of disillusion with the column, for one reason or another,'[32] although in the final session of a meeting which lasted six days, and where there were 'very few delegates' a motion was passed in which 'the structure and activities . . . of the Iron Column were going to be approved . . .'[33]

In December, the anarchist daily *Fragua Social* openly attacked the Iron Column. It denounced Century No. 30 of the column for having deserted the front.[34]

Anarchists and the Fall of Málaga

One of the most serious early defeats of the Loyalists in the Civil War was the overrunning of the city of Málaga, the most southerly city along the Mediterranean coast which had originally stayed with the Republic. It was significant not only because of the first appearance in that campaign of organized Italian units on the side of the Rebels, but because it provided the first serious opportunity for the Communists and other opponents of Prime Minister Francisco Largo Caballero to attempt to undermine his leadership of the government.

Anarchist troops made up a large part of the militia organized in Málaga after the outbreak of the War. In the beginning, five of the ten military units organized in the area were controlled by the CNT. With the militarization of the militia, the CNT had four battalions, compared with the one which the Communists controlled.[35]

Although Málaga was in a particularly exposed situation, as the center of a relatively narrow coastal sector held by the Loyalists, the Republican government refused to send it any aid until the city almost fell. Near the end of November 1936 the local military authorities received, in a reply to a request for arms and munitions, a telegram from Minister of War Largo Caballero which said, 'Not a rifle, not a cartridge from Málaga'. Although in sending this message, Largo Caballero may have mainly had in mind the perilous situation of Madrid at that time, and its need for what arms were available, the attitude of at least part of the Republican government may have been better reflected in the reply of Naval and Air Minister Indalecio Prieto to a request by a group of Socialists, Republicans and Communists for aid for Málaga: 'For Málaga, the FAI will have to suffice!'[36]

Only shortly before the final attack on Málaga by the Rebels did the government send in Colonel José Villalba to attempt to organize its defense. However, by that time, according to Burnett Bolloten, 'everything was fusing into disaster'. In any case, the Republican government was no more willing to respond to his requests for reinforcements and equipment than to those of the local military and political authorities.[37]

On February 3 1937, the attack on Málaga began, by Spanish troops and Italian units led by General Mario Roatta. By February 8, the city was occupied by the Franco forces, while thousands of refugees fled north towards Almería.[38]

There were a number of reasons for the fall of Málaga. A major one, as we have seen, was the lack of adequate arms and equipment to defend that sector of the front. However, Burnett Bolloten has described number of other factors: 'The absence of military discipline and organization on the Málaga sector, the muddle and disorder in the rear, the irresponsibility of professional officers and militia leaders, the struggle between the different factions to the prejudice of military operations, the proselytizing efforts of the Communist party, the appointment of an excessive number of Communist political commissars by Cayetano Bolivar, chief political commissar of the Málaga sector, the wanton neglect of defensive works, the treachery of the two commanders in charge of fortifications, Romero and Canejo, who deserted to the enemy...'[39]

Franz Borkenau, writing shortly after the fall of Málaga, similarly stressed the importance of political factors in the fall of Málaga: 'The wild excitement was present which might have been made the basis of a fight of despair. But the disintegration of the political forces was too deep to make use of it. In July and August the anarchists might have led such a fight and still later the political committee. Now the anarchists had been pushed back, and had been compromised by the memory of their sanguinary excesses; the political committee had been weakened from without and within. The civil administration carried no authority whatsoever...'[40]

Once Málaga had fallen, various people were charged with being those 'responsible' for the fall of the city. One of these was an anarchist militia leader, the other two were prominent regular army officers.

The anarchist leader involved was Francisco Maroto, leader of a militia column in the Málaga area, not far from Granada. He was arrested and charged with 'complicity with the enemy.'[41] The Communists went so far as to accuse Maroto during the retreat from Málaga of 'trying to take for Franco the stronghold of Almería'.[42]

Maroto was kept under arrest for more than a year, but some months after the fall of the Largo Caballero government, when CNT ex-minister Juan García Oliver was laying plans for organizing a guerrilla campaign in the region of Granada against the Franco forces, he was able to talk at length about his plans with Maroto, who promised to collaborate with him if the plans came to fruition.

However, in the end, nothing came of these plans.[43] Maroto was finally exonerated of any charge of treason.[44]

The second person charged with treacherous behavior in connection with the fall of Málaga was Colonel José Villalba. Burnett Bolloten has suggested that he was 'selected by the war ministry as a scapegoat'. He was jailed for more than a year and then was 'exculpated from any blame for the disaster and rehabilitated'.[45]

Juan García Oliver observed that when he crossed the border into France at the time of the collapse of Catalonia, 'The military commander of that part of the frontier was my old acquaintance and good friend, Colonel José Villalba, whom the Communists had wanted – and succeeded – to humiliate, submitting him to a trial for supposed betrayal for the loss of Málaga. Afterwards, they had to revindicate him and even give him a post of command to guard the frontier. As we said goodbye, we embraced.'[46]

The assessment of Villalba's role by Franz Borkenau, who was in Málaga only a week before its fall, is worth considering:

> As to the local command, it has certainly not proved up to its task. The root of its inefficiency, in my opinion, lay in its incomprehension of the type of war it was directing... In a military sense, Villalba's judgment of the situation may have been sound. Málaga would be encircled and taken from land and sea; better to evacuate it at top speed. But he had left out the political factor. The insurgents, who were little afraid of his troops, were afraid of one thing only: of a fight of desperation. That's why they left the main road open. The assumption on which was based Villalba's whole appreciation of the situation did not take effect...
>
> The military command ... did not only not understand what such a fight would mean, it disliked heartily the popular elements on which it needed to rely at such a moment. The case of the Basque country in mid-September, the case of Madrid on 8 November, both show that in situations apparently hopeless in a military sense, a fight to the finish backed by popular enthusiasms, has always a chance in this civil war, where popular forces are at least as important as military ones...[47]

The most important target of the Communists and others, who were seeking someone to blame for the fall of Málaga, was General José Asensio. He had been predecessor of Villalba as overall commander of the Málaga front. César Lorenzo has noted that the Communist Party, 'in its efforts to seize control of military commands had at first obtained the separation from Málaga of General Asensio, who got along too well with the libertarians ... but his replacement, Colonel Villalba, was not any better disposed towards the Communists.'[48]

Largo Caballero, as minister of war, had then made General Asensio his under-secretary. The Communists certainly regarded the general as a major stumbling block in their efforts to get full control of the Republican military. They therefore sought to use the fall of Málaga as an excuse to remove him as Largo Caballero's principal assistant in the war ministry. Hugh Thomas has described Asensio as Largo Caballero's 'favorite general'.[49]

Some years later, Largo Caballero described the Communists' campaign against General Asensio following the fall of Málaga: 'The campaign launched by the Communist Party against General Asensio has no name... They insisted on my removing him from the ministry. "Why?" I asked them. "Because he is a traitor." Proofs! Evidence! "We have much," they answered, "We shall bring it!" This scene was repeated constantly with the Committee of the Communist Party, with their ministers, with their ambassador ... but they never brought it...'[50]

However, Largo Caballero finally had to concede to the Communists' pressure. General Asensio handed in his resignation on February 21.[51] Subsequent to the fall of the Largo Caballero government, Asensio was brought to trial 'for neglecting to supply the Málaga front with the necessary arms and munitions...'[52] One of those testifying on his behalf was Largo Caballero himself, who argued that if charges were to be levelled, they should be brought against Largo Caballero himself as Asensio's superior. Asensio was finally exonerated.[53]

It is clear that the Communists mounted a major propaganda campaign against both Villalba and Asensio. They were joined in this by Right-wing Socialists led by Indalecio Prieto and by the Republicans.[54]

One of the most surprising aspects of this campaign was that the CNT press also joined in the attacks on the two military leaders. This is difficult to understand, at least in retrospect. By that time, the alliance of Largo Caballero with the anarchist members of the government, against the Communists and their allies, was a reality. The anarchist ministers, at least, certainly must have understood that the Communist campaign against General José Asensio was really aimed more against prime minister and minister of war Francisco Largo Caballero than it was against the unfortunate general.

One result of the Communist propaganda campaign was that 'due to the weakness of Largo Caballero', according to Juan García Oliver, an inter-ministerial committee, composed of García Oliver, Communist minister of agriculture Vicente Uribe and Left Republican minister Julio Justo, was sent to Almería to try to ascertain the causes of the fall of Málaga. Each of these ministers made his own report. García Oliver said: 'I limited myself to explaining that one could not talk of deficiencies and treason of military commanders if, in a reality, there existed no established front in Málaga, where a disorganized and badly armed force of some fifteen thousand men had to cover a front of two hundred kilometers, against fifty thousand enemy combatants with the support of airplanes, artillery and Italian tanks.'[55] García Oliver, at least, refused to join the hue and cry against General Asensio and Colonel Villalba.

One thing that, understandably, the Communists did not talk about, in their effort to use the fall of Málaga to undermine the government of Largo Caballero, was the gross misbehavior of some of their own Málaga comrades. Six months later, Mariano Vázquez, secretary of the national committee of the CNT did point out one outstanding case: 'Anyway, we will give one notice, so that the Central Committee may take it into account when they speculate about the fall of Málaga: that Antonio Guerra, delegate of the Communist Party in the Military Command of Málaga, stayed there with the rebels. We want to say that in speaking of the responsibility for the fall of Málaga, we must start by examining that part which each of us has.'[56]

Anarchists in the Republican Forces in Andalusia

The anarchists played a significant role in the Republican armed forces in the Andalusia region, much of which came into the hands of the Franco forces very early in the War. One unit under anarchist leadership was a column originally organized by workers who had first fought to keep Granada in the Loyalist camp but, when defeated, fled to Republican territory. It became the 89th Division of the Popular Army, and ultimately received Russian arms, which one of its anarchist officers claimed consisted largely of material of First World War vintage. They also had some Russian 'technicians' associated with them, as well as a handful of French officers, who in contrast to their Russian counterparts were said to be very knowledgeable and capable.[57]

Another important anarchist military unit in the Andalusian area was the Maroto Column, which had originally operated in the area between Granada and Málaga, and which remained under anarchist control as the 147th Brigade even after the deposition and house arrest of Francisco Maroto.

Franz Borkenau bore witness to the rather chaotic military situation on much of the Andalusian front during the early weeks of the Civil War. He recounted seeing a battle at Cerro Muriano, not far from Cordoba, where:

> There were ... differences between the various small units of militia. While the troops from Maen and Valencia ran away before our eyes, a small group of militia from Alcoy, an old revolutionary center in the province of Murcia, arrived. They stood the bombardment – which, I must repeat, did no real damage – with the proudest gallantry and unconcernedness... Discipline, however, was lacking to an almost incredible extent... [The militiamen from Alcoy were undoubtedly anarchists.]
>
> It is difficult to find appropriate words to characterize the conduct of the staff. The officers in the front line lacked even ordinary courage... There remain certain disastrous peculiarities of the militia itself. It cannot stand the impact of modern arms, air-raids, and shelling, even from small guns. And it has

no conception that a position must never be left without express orders from the command...

Thorough training would certainly help to make the militia fit for fighting, but discipline is still more important...[58]

In Andalusia as elsewhere, the CNT and other militia units were converted into elements of the Popular Army. Also, as was true in various other areas, although they supplied a substantial proportion of the manpower in the Army of Andalusia, the anarchists were no match for the Communists and their allies when it came to obtaining positions of command.

The FAI in September 1938 reported that the Army of Andalusia was 'a real fiefdom of "the Party"'. At that time, anarchists commanded only one brigade, the old Maroto Column rechristened the 147th Brigade, out of ten; and one division, the 20th, out of four.[59]

The Anarchists in the War in the Basque Country

Of the three Basque provinces of Alava, Guipuzcoa and Vizcaya, the first fell to General Mola's Rebels immediately at the outbreak of War. A month to six weeks after the beginning of the conflict, Guipuzcoa and its major cities of Irun and San Sebastian, were largely overrun by Mola's troops. Only in Vizcaya did the conflict continue through most of the first year of the Civil War.

Elsewhere in this volume I consider the role played by the CNT in the political leadership of Guipuzcoa and Vizcaya in the first weeks of the War. The anarchists were also of major significance in the short-lived military struggles for Irun and San Sebastian, and of considerable significance in the war in Vizcaya, which early in October 1936 became the Basque Republic.

At the outbreak of the War, the CNT organized five militia battalions in the Basque area: Batallon Malatesta, Batallon Sacco y Vanzetti, Batallon Isaac Puente, Batallon Bakunin and Batallon El Celta. In October 1936 the Batallon Malatesta, with about 1,000 members, was sent to the Asturias region to participate in the siege of

Oviedo, which had fallen to the Rebel forces in the first week of the War.[60]

Before the offensive against Irun and San Sebastian by the Rebels began, the anarchists, who constituted a major part of the militia force there, sent an appeal to the Central Militia Council of Catalonia for arms. The Catalans loaded 'several hundred rifles and some machine guns' on to trucks and sent them through France towards Irun.[61] There are different accounts of what happened to those arms. César Lorenzo claimed that 'the French authorities blockaded them at Hendaye...'[62] However, Diego Abad de Santillán insisted: 'The vehicles had problems on the way, but still got on time into the hands of the Local Federation of Unions of Irun, which sent us a receipt.'[63]

What is clear is that a shipment of 30,000 cartridges, which the Catalan Militia Committee also set aside for the defenders of Irun, never reached their destination. The committee requested an airplane from the ministry of navy and air in Madrid for the transport of this cargo. Diego Abad de Santillán wrote: 'We had prepared everything, the popular forces of Irun still controlled the airdrome, waiting anxiously the arrival of the munitions. The Ministry ... promised to send a Douglas airplane and we deposited the cargo in the Prat field, so as not to lose a moment.' However, the plane from Madrid never arrived.[64]

The final battle for Irun, the border town with France, was a bitter one. After days of bombardment both from Rebel warships and Mola's forces, the Rebels attacked on September 3. The brunt of the assault was borne by CNTers who included, according to Hugh Thomas, 'some ... from Barcelona', and by Communists, including some French and Belgian 'technicians' sent by the French Communist Party.[65] Broué and Temime noted: '...The war commissar crossed the French frontier three days before the fall of Irun. Then the Communists and the men of the CNT, along with a handful of international volunteers fought to the last round...'[66] Thomas noted that the Rebels occupied a 'burned and ruined town'.[67]

The fate of San Sebastian, which fell to the Rebels a little more than a week after Irun, was different. According to César Lorenzo, although the CNTers among its defenders felt that the city could be defended, because the enemy's lines of communication were greatly extended, and the Loyalist militia could get additional needed supplies easily from Bilbao, the Basque Nationalists among the Republican troops were fearful of the destruction of the city and, because of hostility towards the anarchists, 'vehemently refused to resist and convinced the Communists and Socialists to support them'.

Lorenzo describes the denouement of this situation: 'Completely abandoned by the other organizations, the CNT could not by itself confront the rebel army. San Sebastian fell without combat on September 31, 1936; by one blow the front was rolled back by thirty kilometers to the West...'[68]

In Vizcaya the anarchists constituted a substantial part of the Loyalist forces. They controlled six battalions, and a seventh was composed half of CNTers and half of mixed elements of other political orientation. This compared with 22 battalions led by the Basque Nationalist Party (PNV), 14 by the Socialists and their union, the UGT; seven by the Communist Party, two by the Basque Nationalist Action, and one by the Republicans. Unlike the CNT units elsewhere in Republican Spain, those in the Basque country did not resist militarization of the militia.

However, the CNT military units became involved in a running controversy between their unions and President José Antonio Aguirre of the Basque Republic. Although the CNT had been represented in the regional government which had preceded the establishment of the Basque Republic in early October 1936, Aguirre refused to admit the anarchist trade union group to his government until the penultimate moment. He kept insisting that his government was one of parties, not union groups, and that the anarchists should be represented through the Federación Anarquista Ibérica, their 'political' group, a proposal the anarchists refused.

Shortly before the final battle for Vizcaya began, according to César Lorenzo, 'The CNT battalions began to waver and even to abandon the positions they had at the front.' At that point, in May 1937, Aguirre invited the CNT to enter his government, but Rivera, commander of the Sacco and Vanzetti Battalion of the CNT, suddenly rejected the idea, claiming that anarchists had no place in a government. Aguirre thereupon postponed his invitation to the CNT, but shortly afterward the final battle for the Basque country was under way and time had run out.[69]

When the final battle for Bilbao began, the CNTers again favored last-ditch resistance, as they had at San Sebastian. However, the Basque governmeant and most of the garrison left the city. Both Hugh Thomas and Broué and Temime have described the efforts by anarchist troops to initiate a kind of scorched-earth defense of the city, in which they were largely thwarted by the sudden defection to the Rebel side of the remaining Civil Guards, Assault Guards and regular army people in the Bilbao garrison.[70]

The Anarchists in the Military in the Santander Region

Santander, the region between the Basque provinces and Asturias, was not a stronghold of the CNT. In fact, a number of anarchist-controlled unions in the area were affiliated with the Unión General de Trabajadores. However, the anarchists played a very significant role, not only in the political structure which evolved after the beginning of the Civil War, but also in the military forces organized to hold the region for the Republican cause.

In the first months of the War, the militia units raised to defend the Santander region were not differentiated according to political party or trade union affiliation. Anarchists, Socialists, Communists and Republicans all belonged to mixed units. However, when the decision was made to have politically homogeneous military groups, the anarchists organized two new battalions, Libertad and CNT-FAI. Even then, the politically mixed units were not broken up. After the transfer of the Socialist Bruno Alonso to Cartagena to be commissar general of the Republican Navy, the anarchist leader of the port workers of Santander, José González Malo, the region's most important libertarian leader (although his union was affiliated with the UGT) was named general commissar of Militia for the Santander region.[71]

The Rebel attack on the Santander region came in August 1937, after the fall of the Basque province of Vizcaya. Although the forces defending Santander were ordered from Valencia to retreat to the

Asturias region to the west, this proved all but impossible, and those defenders who could do so escaped by sea to France.[72]

The Anarchists in the Military Struggle in Asturias

As referred to earlier, the capital of the Asturias region, Oviedo, was seized by the Rebels under Colonel Antonio Aranda. However, after the collapse of tenacious resistance by Rebel troops in Gijón in the middle of August 1936, that city, the second largest, was firmly in the hands of the anarchists. Much of the rest of the region was dominated by the Socialists. Cooperation between the CNT and the Socialists continued to be close, as it had been since the Asturias revolution of October 1934.

The armed resistance of the workers of Asturias in July 1936 was, to a large degree, a renewal of the struggle by many of the same people who had undertaken the Asturias revolution of October 1934. Juan Antonio de Blas and Paco Ignacio Taibo have noted: 'The same experience of the Revolution of October has brought about a selection of the natural leaders of the workers, and because of this there arose from the fighting base of October a great number of militants little known outside of the local ambience ... They are in their great majority, manual workers. Far above all other groups, the miners and metal workers.'

De Blas and Taibo offer a 'preliminary list of first commanders of the future Republican army' in the Asturias region, consisting of 25 names. These include four anarchists: 'Onofre García Tirado, leader of the metal workers union, Cenetista of the Duro plant in Felguera; Higinio Carrocera, metal worker of the CNT; Celestino Fernández, "El Topu", Cenetista metal worker of Duro ... Víctor Alvarez, Cenetista of Gijón.'[73] Diego Abad de Santillán referred to Carrocera as 'an authentic hero'.[74]

Javier R. Muñóz noted that aside from three battalions organized under the leadership of loyal Republican military men:

All the other battalions will be formed on the basis of political and trade union organizations. Thus, the CNT organizes, by transformation and amplification of its previous groups, CNT Battalion No. 1 of Onofre García Tirado, and CNT Battalion No. 2 of Víctor Alvarez. Also, the battalions of Celestino Fernández, Higinio Carrocera and the Galician one, made up mainly of Gallicians of anarchist ideology commanded by José Penido. Another battalion of the CNT, which included the Cubedos Company formed by the Partido Sindicalista was commanded by José Perida. There existed in addition, some groups which did not constitute a battalion, such as the FAI Group (150 men) of Leonardo Pevida.[75]

According to César Lorenzo, the anarchists were not represented in the leadership of the military units raised to defend the Asturias region once the Civil War had begun in proportion to their numbers in the armed forces. This was largely due to their own attitudes.

Lorenzo noted that generally 'in Asturias, the centuries and columns were not rigorously separated according to ideological differences; the anarchists and socialists, the Communists (very few in number) and some republicans were amalgamated in the same units.'[76] However, later, he noted: 'The number of battalions of the CNT (Fifteen out of a total of sixty battalions) did not correspond to its real force. In fact, the repugnance of the Asturian libertarians towards militarization, although less marked than in other regions of Spain, made them lose numerous command positions which the political parties hastened to assume. Thus, members of the CNT were brigaded en masse in military formations under orders of Republicans or Communists, for example, although before the decree of October 14 the confederation's columns provided nearly half of the total effectives of the Asturian militia.'[77] According to one of the Asturian CNT leaders, Solano Palacio, 'What revolted the militiamen more than anything else was the fact that they were compelled to salute their officers, whom they had hitherto regarded as comrades.'[78]

This traditional anti-militarism of the anarchists was reflected in the relative paucity of CNT–FAI commanders in the Asturian armed forces. Juan Antonio de Blas has cited data that indicated that in 1937 there were 40 ranking Socialist officers, 37 Communists, and only 19 anarchists.[79] However, among the outstanding anarchist military leaders were Víctor Alvarez, who came to command a division, and Higinio Carrocera, Celestino Fernandez, José Penido, and Manuel Sánchez, who became brigade commanders. In addition, 11 anarchists became brigade or division political commissars in the Asturias region.[80]

According to Javier Rodríguez Muñóz, 'If we examine the political affiliations of the Asturian army, we can see that the PSOE [Socialist Party] had the largest number of superior commands, and in addition, between the PSOE and the CNT they dominated two-thirds of the total.' His figures show that the CNT had one division commander, four brigade commanders, and 13 battalion chiefs, for a total of 18. This compared with three Socialist division commanders, eight in charge of brigades, and 26 commanding battalions, for a total of 37; and three Communist division chiefs, five in charge of brigades and 25 commanding battalions, for a total of 33.

However, Rodríguez Muñóz said: 'In spite of that, the power of the Communist Party within the Asturian army was very important, and certainly much superior to their real membership.'[81] He added: 'The PCE had been successful in getting many commands due to the positions it quickly took in the war apparatus, independent of the quality of its members. Ambou was the first organizer of the army from the post of Councillor of War, and Horacio Arguelles was in charge of recruiting during the first months.'[82] (Ambou and Arguelles were two of the principal Communist leaders in Asturias.)

Anarchist troops fought in all phases of the Civil War in Asturias. These included the two attempts to capture Oviedo in October 1936 and February 1937, and the final struggle in the Asturias area from August to October 1937. In this last phase of the conflict, CNT commander Higinio Carrocera was awarded the Republic's Medal of Liberty for his leadership of the troops resisting the Nationalist drive along the coast from Santander.[83] The anarchist soldiers and commanders were also prominent among Asturian troops sent to the defense of the Basque province of Vizcaya, as well as the Santander region, after the fall of Vizcaya.[84]

The improvised authorities of the Asturias region sought to centralize military commands and to strengthen discipline. However,

César Lorenzo has noted concerning the Asturian militia units: 'As almost everywhere in Spain the militia were badly organized, badly armed, and led into combat by chiefs of extraordinary courage but without the least notion of the art of war, since they were working-class militants who from one day to the next were converted into officers.'[85]

Much of the Asturias region continued under anarchist–Socialist control for 15 months after the outbreak of the War. However, following the fall of Vizcaya and Santander, the Rebels finally launched their attack on Asturias on September 1 1937. For six weeks, the resistance of the Republican forces was exceedingly strong. However, after the middle of October, when two invading Rebel columns were able to join forces, the resistance crumbled. Gijón, the last major strongpoint of the Republican forces, was overrun by the Rebels on October 21.

Nevertheless, according to Hugh Thomas, even the conquest of Gijón did not completely end the War in the Asturias region: 'Though the whole northern front had now disappeared, 18,000 men maintained themselves as guerrilla forces in the Leonese mountains until March ... and until the end of the war Asturias was closely patrolled.'[86]

The Anarchist Role in the Navy and Air Force

Finally, a few words should be said about the anarchist role in two other parts of the Republican military, which were not fronts in a geographical sense, but were important parts of the Loyalist armed forces. These were the navy and the air force.

As mentioned earlier in this volume, the majority of the ships in the Spanish navy were seized at the outbreak of the War by their crews and a scattering of junior officers who were loyal to the Republic. According to Diego Abad de Santillán, 'the libertarian movement had majority representation in the Navy'.[87] This judgment was confirmed to me by an anarchist sailor who took part in the seizure of the fleet by anti-Franco forces, and who argued that the fleet was virtually completely in CNT hands, since the great majority of the

245

sailors either belonged to or sympathized with the CNT.[88] It is also borne out by Admiral N. Kuznetsov, one of the principal Soviet advisers to the navy in the early part of the Civil War, who conceded that 'in some ships anarchists were the majority', and that at the beginning of the War there were few Communists in the navy.[89]

However, this situation did not last for long. As Abad de Santillán noted, 'Immediately a campaign was started against those who had saved from the enemy the units with which we could count. They were being replaced, little by little, and from the middle of 1937 they were openly disembarked, remaining aboard almost exclusively Communists and Communist fellow-travellers, in spite of the fact that Prieto had a commissar of the fleet who had his fullest confidence.'[90]

One informant said that the minority of officers of his ship who had stayed loyal were worried by their prerogatives being cut by the men who had taken over. Most of them, he said, therefore joined the Communist Party, as a way of strengthening their positions *vis-á-vis* the crews. On his ship, the situation had gotten so bad from the point of view of a CNT member that he left in February 1937 and joined the Marines, as a member of which he was during the rest of the War, stationed on the Madrid front.[91]

As in other parts of the Republican armed forces, the Communists succeeded in getting the top echelons of the navy dominated by their party members. Although Admiral Kuznetsov claimed that while he was minister of marine, Indalecio Prieto tried to keep Communists out of top places in the navy, that situation did not last.[92] Santillán claimed that on December 15 1938, the general staff of the navy consisted with one exception entirely of Communist Party card holders.

Although Santillán said that from the beginning the Russian advisers, headed by one who went under the pseudonym 'Nicolas',[93] Russian and Communist control did not serve to heighten the efficiency of the Republican navy: 'Numerous were the suggestions to have the naval initiative return to our hands, to improve the situation of the fleet and give it more efficiency. The Russians did the same in this field as in the aviation and the army: a good job of political conquest for their policy of party hegemony, but not one insofar as victoriously confronting the enemy was concerned.'[94] As a matter of fact, during most of the War, the fleet rarely ventured out from its base in Cartagena.

The principal task of the Loyalist navy during most of the Civil War was convoy duty guarding ships going to and from the Soviet Union. After the first few months there were few direct encounters between the Loyalist fleet and the Rebel navy and the Italian and German ships collaborating with it.[95]

The role of the anarchists in the Republican air force was even less than in the navy. At the beginning of the War, the air force consisted of a relatively small group of regular officers and men who had stayed loyal to the Republic. With the arrival of Russian machines and aviators, control of the air force passed almost totally to them.

Segismundo Casado, who for part of the War was chief of operations on the general staff of the war ministry, described the situation thus: 'I can state clearly that during the whole war neither the air force nor the tank corps was controlled by the minister of national defense, nor in consequence by the general staff. The minister and his staff were not even aware of the quantity and types of their machines and only knew the situation of those which were used in actual operations. In the same way the minister and his staff were not aware of the situation, and even of the existence of a great number of unknown (airfields) maintained in secret by the "friendly advisers" and certain of the aviation chiefs who were entirely in their confidence.'[96]

Under such circumstances, clearly, there was no chance for the anarchists to get even a foothold in the Republican air force.

Conclusion

It is clear that on all of the fronts of the Spanish Civil War, anarchist troops made up a substantial proportion of those fighting in the Republican forces. On the Catalan–Aragónese, Levante–Teruel, and Asturias areas they constituted the majority of the soldiers fighting against the Rebels; elsewhere they were not numerically as significant but none the less constituted an important part of the Republican forces. As a general rule, they fought tenaciously and well and, on some fronts, held out when most other elements were ready to give up. In some areas, CNT leaders such as Ricardo Sanz, Cipriano Mera, and José González Malo played key roles in organizing and leading important elements of the Republican army.

It is true that there were instances in which anarchist elements behaved in an unruly manner, as I have indicated. However, in their campaign to discredit the overall role of the anarchists in the Civil War and to gain complete power in the Republic, the Communist propagandists and their allies grossly exaggerated and generalized these incidents.

One of the issues in relation to the anarchist participation in the Loyalist armed forces which the Communists most exploited was the supposed resistance of the CNT–FAI elements to the so-called 'militarization' of the militia columns. It is to that subject that we turn our attention in the next chapter.

9

The Militarization of the Militia

One of the most bitterly debated issues in Republican Spain, and particularly among the anarchists, was that of the 'militarization' of the militia in the Republican armed forces. This question had not only major military implications but deep political ones as well.

The issue of militarization involved the conversion of the quickly recruited, loosely organized and egalitarian militia units which had first been organized to fight for the Republican cause into a more or less regular army. This process required the reorganization of the militia centuries and columns into companies, regiments, brigades, divisions and larger regular military units; and the institution of standard military ranks, uniforms and insignia. It also meant the establishment of regular discipline and military law in the armed forces. Finally, in the special case of the Spanish Republican army, it meant generalization of the system of 'political commissars' which the ministry of defense early began to establish.

The first step towards trying to reorganize a regular army had been taken by the Giral government on July 28, when it called into service the 1933 and 1934 draft levies. This was strongly opposed by not only the anarchists but also the Socialists, with only the Communists supporting it. In Catalonia, the CNT instructed its militiamen who received conscription notices to stay in their militia units.[1]

According to Stanley Payne, 'One of the two principal objectives of the Largo Caballero government was the formation of a regular organized People's Army to defend the revolution. The creation of the People's Army may thus be dated from the month of September 1936, and the initial leaders were Largo's own chief military advisers, Col. José Asensio and Gen. Martínez Cabrera.' He also noted that Largo Caballero, almost immediately upon taking office, 'appointed an official military commander-in-chief, together with a regular General Staff section, for each main theater of operations.[2]

The militarization of the militia presented particularly dramatic problems for the anarchists. These difficulties were ideological, political and military.

Of course, the ideology of the anarchists was fundamentally opposed to the military and most particularly to militarism, that is, the hierarchy, strict discipline and general regimentation involved in the armed forces. As I have reported earlier, the only concession to the need for a military organization, even after a successful Revolution which the anarchists made before the Civil War was the maintenance of a locally based military which could be called together to confront any attempt to invade the country to destroy the Revolution.

With the outbreak of the Civil War, of course, the CNT–FAI had organized their own military units. However, to the greatest degree possible they had established them on the basis of the outlines that the CNT had adopted at the May 1936 congress of Zaragoza. For them to accept the substitution of a regular army for this militia structure meant a fundamental break with a basic element in their beliefs.

However, there were also questions of practical politics which increased the scepticism of the CNT–FAI about the issue. By the time the drive to form a regular Loyalist Army got well under way, the influence of the Communist Party and their Right-wing Socialist allies in the Republican military establishment had begun to rise rapidly. As a result, some of the more knowledgeable and sophisticated anarchist leaders had grave reservations about militarization because they saw it as a means of increasing the efforts of the Communists and their allies to seize control not only of the military but of the entire Republican regime.

On the other hand, many of the leaders of the CNT militia, as well as the majority of the other anarchist leaders, came to realize that the Franco forces could not be defeated by a militia army organized as it was during the first months of the Civil War. Increasingly they came to accept the idea that to defeat a regular army such as that which Franco controlled, backed as it was by foreign troops from Italy and Germany, it was necessary to have another army organized to a greater or lesser degree on the principles of modern military science.

Therefore, as a consequence of the realities of the Civil War, the anarchists were forced to accept the idea of the establishment of a regular army to defend the Republic. This decision – and even more, their tardiness in accepting it – not only reduced their influence in the Loyalist armed forces, but also weakened the general political position of the CNT–FAI within the Spanish Republic.

Nature of Militia Columns

Once the army uprising of July 17–20 1936 had been suppressed in a large part of Spain, one of the first tasks of the new authorities, which appeared in various parts of the Republic, was to organize military forces to confront the regular army in those areas where it had been successful in its *coup*, and to prevent its incursion into areas still loyal to the Republic. Various military fronts appeared within the first days of the outbreak of the Civil War. These included Aragón, where the bulk of the weight of defense fell on forces recruited in Catalonia; the Teruel front in southern Aragón and nearby areas, where the task fell to troops recruited in the Levante; the Málaga front, drawing in the first instance on locally recruited militiamen. There was also the Andalusia–Extremadura front in the south-western part of the country, where the Republicans suffered some of their first serious defeats; and within a few months the Madrid front, protected by forces retreating from farther south and by others from Catalonia and other parts of the country. Finally, there were the three fronts in the north, in the Basque provinces, Santander and Asturias, where separate locally recruited units were soon established.

The task of putting an armed force in the field right at the beginning of the War fell to the various political parties and trade union groups that had taken up arms in defense of the Republic. José González Malo, principal CNT leader in the Santander region, has described how these quickly recruited forces were formed into groups of 100 men each, the famous *centurias*. Each such unit elected offices, including one captain, two lieutenants, and a number of sergeants – although those individuals had the title of *delegado* rather than an orthodox military rank. Once recruited, and armed with whatever was available, these units were rushed off to the nearest front.[3]

This pattern was repeated throughout Loyalist Spain. For instance, on the Aragón front, there were soon three columns (roughly comparable in size and importance to brigades) under anarchist leadership (Durruti, Red and Black, and Ortíz); the Lenin Column organized by the Partido Obrero de Unificación Marxista (POUM); one led by elements of the Partido Socialista Unificado de Catalunya, the Catalan branch of Stalinism; and one organized and led by the Left Catalan Nationalists. There was also one unit, commanded by Colonel José Villalba, composed of regular soldiers.[4]

Perhaps as typical as any of these early militia units, in terms of organization was the most famous of them all, the Durruti Column. After the first few weeks, it had as its highest authority a five-man war committee (Comité de Guerra).

Abel Paz has noted that under the Comité de Guerra the 'largest unit, the *Agrupación*, was composed of five *centurias* of one hundred men, divided into four groups of twenty-five. Each of these units had at its head a delegate named by the rank and file, and recallable at any moment. Representative responsibility did not confer privilege or hierarchy of command.'

Also under the Comité de Guerra was a Technical-Military Council (Consejo Tecnico-Militar). It was made up of professional officers, 'and the mission of this council was to advise the Comité de Guerra. It did not have any privilege or hierarchy of command.'

In addition to these elements there was an 'autonomous' International Group, with some 400 men, including Frenchmen, Germans, Italians, Moroccans, British and Americans. The difference between this group and the International Brigades, organized subsequently, should be stressed. Although autonomous, the Durruti Column's International Group was an integral part of the Column.

Finally, there were guerrilla units of the Durruti Column. According to Abel Paz, their job was to work behind the enemy lines.[5]

Under the general supervision of the Comité de Guerra, there were specialized departments of artillery, supply, health and medicine, transport, and armaments. On another level, there were units dealing with propaganda – including the column's newspaper and radio station – with education and with general cultural activities.[6]

Strengths and Weaknesses of the Militia

The militia as a fighting force undoubtedly had both its strong points and its weaknesses. Unquestionably, the great advantage of the militias was that they were volunteers, who were fighting for a cause – particularly in the early phases of the War – in which they strongly believed.

General Vicente Rojo, chief of staff of the defense of Madrid, has perhaps penned the most eloquent tribute to this strength of the militia, during the first phase of the defense of the capital: 'The militiaman had triumphed again ... He was less political and more a soldier; he knew why and for what he fought, measured with more pride and greater conscientiousness his quality as a Spaniard, facing the adversary in front of him, whatever he was, Moor, legionnaire or Spaniard; he recognized having less technique, being more poorly trained, but for that same reason understood that to win he had to be more valiant, and he notably was. Their chiefs gave the best example of this. For that reason they could continue the struggle without attenuating the vigor of their resistance ...[7]

George Orwell, who fought in a POUM unit on the Aragón front, also eulogized the militiamen of the first months of the War:

In the circumstances the militias could not have been much better than they were. A modern mechanized army does not spring out of the ground, and if the Government had waited until it had trained troops at its disposal, Franco would never have been resisted. Later it became the fashion to decry the militias, and therefore to pretend that the faults which were due to lack of training and weapons were the result of the equalitarian system. Actually, a newly raised draft of militia was an undisciplined mob not because the officers called the privates 'Comrade' but because raw troops are always an undisciplined mob. In practice, the democratic 'revolutionary' type of discipline is more reliable than might be expected... In the militias the bullying and abuse that go on in an ordinary army would never have been tolerated for a moment. The normal military punishments existed, but they were only invoked for very serious offences. When a man refused to obey an order you did not immediately get him punished; you first appealed to him in the name of comradeship. Cynical people with no experience of handling men will say instantly that this would never 'work', but as a matter of fact it does 'work' in the long run. The discipline of even the worst drafts of militia visibly improved as time went on...

The journalists who sneered at the militia-system seldom remembered that the militias had to hold the line while the Popular Army was training in the rear. And it is a tribute to the strength of 'revolutionary' discipline that the militias stayed in the field at all. For until about 1937 there was nothing to keep them there, except class loyalty. Individual deserters could be shot – were shot, occasionally – but if a thousand men had decided to walk out of the line together there was no force to stop then. A conscript army in the same circumstances – with its battle-police removed – would have melted away...[8]

Orwell claimed: 'As usual, the breaking up of the militias was done in the name of military efficiency; and no one denied that a thorough military reorganization was needed,' but some concluded that 'It would, however, have been quite possible to reorganize the militias and make them more efficient while keeping them under direct control of the trade unions; the main purpose of the change was to make sure that the Anarchists did not possess an army of their own.

Moreover, the democratic spirit of the militias made them breeding-grounds for revolutionary ideas.'[9]

The great weaknesses of the militia-type army in the first months of the War were the lack of formal military discipline, and failure to establish an effective overall direction of the Republic's military forces. Each of these questions was hotly debated within the anarchist ranks.

Burnett Bolloten has presented a considerable number of 'horror stories' from witnesses on both sides of the fighting line about the deficiencies of the militia in the early months of the War. These deficiencies included the inability of supposedly superior officers on a front to give orders for coordinated tactical advances because of the necessity for first getting all column leaders involved to agree; failure of units to move when and where it had been agreed that they would; jealousies among columns of different parties and unions, sometimes going so far as one column rejoicing at the defeat of a neighboring one led by a different party or union group; refusal of particular columns which had area and equipment necessary for a given operation to share them with another column. In addition, of course, there was just the plain lack of military experience and technical military know-how of both leaders and rank and file of the militia columns.[10]

According to Abel Paz, 'Discipline was based on the characteristics of the voluntary forces: freely agreed to, based on class solidarity. Orders were given from comrade to comrade. Being a delegate did not confer any kind of privilege. The principal was equality of rights and duties. Moral coercion of the social situation took the place of the punitive character of military regulations.'[11]

In practice, however, this extreme egalitarianism, particularly in the CNT militia, not infrequently meant that tactical military decisions were submitted to a vote of the soldiers who were to be affected by them. Joaquín Morlanes Jaulín, the regular army officer who was a principal aide of Ricardo Sanz in the former Durruti Column throughout most of the War, recounts an instance of the kind of exaggerated 'democracy' that existed in the militia columns in the early months of the War.

During the second phase of the battle of Madrid, in January 1937,

Morlanes Jaulín was in charge of a unit of the Durruti Brigade which was successfully resisting an advance of the Rebels, which had routed other Republican units on both sides of it. He sent word back to Ricardo Sanz, urging him to use the brigade's reserves to gather up arms and munitions which had been discarded by fleeing militiamen, and organize a second line of defense behind the position Morlanes Jaulín's unit was holding.

Sanz appeared at the front shortly after Morlanes Jaulín's phone call. The latter has recorded what happened then:

'"Did you bring the men I asked for?" I asked. "It is essential to recover the abandoned arms..."

'"Those in the reserve battalion have refused to come," answered Ricardo. "They are having an Assembly to decide what they are going to do."

'"An Assembly?" I exclaimed, surprised. "In the present circumstances they shouldn't be permitted to hold Assemblies. That is all right for normal times, but not for a war period..."' [12]

Cipriano Mera also commented on the insufficiency of the self-discipline which the anarchists had always supported: 'I had witnessed painful scenes. There were moments when Major Palacios and I, together with our aides, confronted groups in full retreat to tell them that they were committing acts of cowardice, that it was necessary to stop running, to defend Madrid. For the moment, the greater part of them paid heed to us, but when we had departed and the enemy aviation or artillery opened up, the majority again fled. I didn't cease asking myself, Why do these people, when they see you at their side, express their enthusiasm, and then, at the moment of difficulty, abandon you? Could we win this way? Clearly not.' [13]

Subsequently, an official statement of the FAI itself pointed out the inadequacies of the militia in fighting the War against a modern army. In the document defending the Spanish anarchists' behavior presented to a meeting of the IWMA in September 1937, and signed by Federica Montseny, Pedro Herrera and Diego Abad de Santillán, the argument was presented in strong terms: 'We paid dearly for the loyalty to our ideas which we maintained for so long. Would the rebellious forces have been able to go from Sevilla to Badajóz and from Badajóz to the doors of Madrid, if we had not opposed for so long, so bitterly, the organization of the army which we needed to fight the enemy? Our militias, without firing practice, without military training, disordered, which held plenums and assemblies before going into action, which discussed all orders, and often refused to comply with them, could not confront the formidable military apparatus which Germany and Italy provided the Rebels...'[14]

Equally serious in the first months of the conflict was the lack of central direction of the Republican war effort. Until the government abandoned Madrid early in November 1936, the Madrid front and areas to the south of it were perhaps the only theater of war which were more or less directly controlled by the central government. Elsewhere, the local or regional authorities, which had appeared right at the beginning of the war, assumed and asserted authority over the front nearest to them. This was the case with the General Council of the Militias and subsequently the Defense Ministry of the government of Catalonia, on the Aragón front; the Popular Executive Committee of Levante on the Teruel front; the Basque Republican government in Vizcaya in facing General Mola's forces in Navarre, and completely separate regional authorities in the Santander and Asturias regions further west, which had amazingly little contact between themselves and with the Basque Republican government. Similar situations prevailed in other parts of Republican Spain.

The problem was still further complicated by the fact that on nearly all the fronts, the political parties and trade union groups which had recruited particular units continued to have a considerable degree of control over those units. The CNT and all of the other groups involved had their military committees, which looked after the welfare of their troops at the front, in some cases arranged for paying their meager salaries, and were consulted by the commanders of their respective columns.

After Francisco Largo Caballero became prime minister and minister of defense on September 4 1936, he set about the work of trying to establish a centralized military command. To this end, he sought to mount a Popular Army, which would have a central leadership to plan the strategy and tactics of the Loyalist forces. This was the heart of the issue of 'militarization of the militia'.

Militarization of the Militia in Asturias

The first part of Republican Spain where the anarchists clearly accepted the idea of militarization of the militia was in Asturias along the Cantabrian coast. Javier R. Muñóz has recorded: 'The first accord for militarization and a unified command for the militia of which we have record appears to be signed in Cornellana on September 4.'[16]

Less than a week later, a meeting in Grado of the region's Republican political and military leaders debated the issue of militarization. According to Juan Antonio de Blas, '...the positions of the Socialists and Communists coincided in the need for militarization, the opposition coming from the representatives of the FAI. Defense of the anarchist position was obstinately supported by Eladio Fanjul, but it was defeated. The military chiefs of the CNT, Higinio Carrocera, Víctor Alvarez, Celesto "el Tup" and Onofre García, who had been combating the rebellious military men from the first day, agreed with the positions of Ambou [the Communist chief in Asturias]...'[17]

Support of militarization appears to have had the general backing of the Asturian anarchist leadership. This was indicated in the anarchist-controlled press of Gijón, the editorials of which were generally written in that period by Acracio Bartolomé, the most outstanding anarchist journalist in the region.

An editorial in *La Prensa* of Gijón on September 6 1936 entitled 'Unity of action and discipline', noted: 'An hour, a minute lost in sterile arguments of doctrine can endanger us to the highest degree. The hour has come to act. With a firm hand and serene pulse. We unify command and action and discipline ourselves. This will be the base of the triumph, of the victory, of economizing powder and blood. We must act... War has to be conducted by soldiers... With uniform or without it. With insignia on the collar or cap; but in any case a militaryman. Recruit or militiaman must signify the same things: discipline, obedience to the one in command...'

The same issue of *La Prensa* published a document, 'Instructions for the Heads of Columns', issued by the anarchist-controlled Council of War of Gijón, which also emphasized the need for militiamen to 'obey the unitary command, fulfilling exactly the orders of the Chief of this group, the group chief fulfilling that which comes from the column and those which come from the general command...' Among the signatories of this document was Onofre G. Tirador, one of the outstanding CNT-FAI militia leaders.[18]

Avelino G. Mallada, a major Asturian anarchist leader soon to become mayor of Gijón, who was then regional war commissar, commented early in September 1936: 'Cursed forever by the war which obliged us to reject, although momentaneously, the purest of our condition as idealists! But precisely in defense of those cherished ideas, we had war imposed upon us by fascism and we must accept discipline like another weapon.'[19]

The acceptance of the organization of the anarchist militia groups into more or less regularized army units does not seem to have been challenged in Asturias after the first week of September 1936.

Other Early Anarchist Supporters of Militarization

Major anarchist military figures were among those who became most firmly convinced of the need for militarization of the militia. The more or less official Stalinist history of the Civil War has said that Durruti understood – the first among the anarchist leaders – the necessity for a disciplined army. But he could not introduce in his column the necessary changes to convert it into an effective military unit. That came to pass later, when that column got to the Madrid front.[20] However, there is no indication from anarchist sources that Durruti really supported what came to be known as the militarization of the militia.

One of its most outspoken early anarchist supporters was Cipriano Mera. Many years later, he wrote:

Everything which had happened convinced me that it was not possible to confront the enemy army if we did not have another army equally organized and in which there was iron discipline. It no longer was a matter of street fighting in which enthusiasm could make up for the lack of preparation; nor was it a matter of simple skirmishes in which everyone could do what he thought best. This was a war, a real War, and therefore it was essential to organize adequately, with militarized units, with commands capable of planning the operations or of facing the enemy with the least possible loss of men and material. Above all, it was necessary that we all be disciplined. There was no other way we could win the war which had been imposed upon us.[21]

Mera added that although he had always defended the concept of self-discipline, 'It is sad to recognize it after one has defended an ideal all one's life, that if we really proposed to win the war, we had to accept the formation of an army with its consequent discipline... It was horrible for me to have to dress as a military man, but I saw no other way, and I said to myself: my conduct will be in the future be testimony to my honor, as it was in other ways and in other circumstances in the past.'[22]

General Vicente Rojo recounted the dramatic 'conversion' of Mera to the need for militarization of the militia. He said that at two o'clock in the morning after a particularly bitter struggle for the San Fernando Bridge on the Madrid outskirts, Cipriano Mera (whom Rojo identifies only as M) turned up in Rojo's office. Obviously exceedingly tired, and at first reticent to speak, Mera finally said: 'I had to see you immediately. There, nothing is happening, or will happen... I come to be made something, to get some rank. Make me a Sergeant... I am no longer "responsible one" M; I want to be Sergeant M, or whatever you wish.'

Although Rojo sought to encourage Mera, saying, 'What happened today has been a success for you and a triumph for your unit,' Mera continued to insist that he should have some formal military rank. Rojo continued: 'The psychological resolution of the incident could not be postponed. I took him to the General, who had just retired to rest. And "the responsible one" M left the General Headquarters that morning with the rank of Major. The politicians had made gifts of many ranks, but this was not a gift!'[23]

Cipriano Mera made clear to his anarchist comrades his acceptance of the militarization of the militia. Thus, he wrote in *Tierra y Libertad*, organ of the Federación Anarquista Ibérica: 'I am convinced, every day more firmly, that to carry on and win the war, it is necessary to do it in an organized manner, and I consider that the most efficacious organization so far is that of the military; for that reason, I accept it; but with all of the consequences. Be sure of that.'[24]

Similarly, Ricardo Sanz, who together with Cipriano Mera, was one of the most important anarchist military leaders to emerge from the war, as Buenaventura Durruti's successor in command of the Durruti Column, also accepted militarization. Retrospectively, he wrote: 'In this atmosphere of sacrifice and abnegation, honoring the magnificent phrase of the idol of the people, of Durruti: "we renounce all except victory", an infinity of men who had always been antimilitarists, who had propagated during more than a quarter of a century in all corners of the world their antimilitarist feelings, contrary to war and all destructive action, didn't have the least inconvenience in becoming militarized, disciplined, accepting military positions of great responsibility, and fulfilling with abnegation, with enthusiasm, the mission with which each one was charged.'[25]

For its part, the Defense Committee of the Center of the CNT also saw the need for a more military organization of the militia. Eduardo de Guzmán recounted that Eduardo Val, speaking to the heads of all of the CNT units in the Madrid area, said, while the first phase of the battle of Madrid was still in progress: 'We cannot continue as we have until now. A single command is not only a slogan with us. From today, all of the CNT Militia of the Center will be united, with a General Staff which coordinates and directs its operations.' Such a unitary command was established at that time.[26]

The Case of García Oliver

Juan García Oliver was another anarchist leader who quickly came around to accepting the need for a regular army. In a speech in Barcelona in January 1937, he argued: 'The people, if it has arms, can never lose the revolution; but the people which doesn't lose a revolution can lose a war, if it doesn't have the adequate instrument for war, that is, military technique, and the army in the service of the revolution.'[27]

However, long before he gave that speech, García Oliver had been working for the conversion of the militia into a more orthodox military force. He was secretary of the military department of the Council of Militia of Catalonia when, on October 24 1936, it 'imposed militarization of the militia' of Catalonia, a move which 'was going to provoke strong reactions among the combatants and among the youth, hostile in their great majority to the renaissance of an institution which had only brought the country evil and oppression...'[28] He had also been actively working to create a new corps of officers for the new Republican armed forces, on both the Catalan and Spanish Republican level.

A few weeks after the outbreak of the Civil War, García Oliver, in his capacity as head of military affairs for the Comité Central de Milicias, was told by Lieutenant Colonel Escobar, in charge of the military personnel department under him, that they would soon run out of regular officers on whose loyalty they could count, in view of the casualties among them. García Oliver then suggested the establishment of an Escuela Popular de Guerra (Popular War School) to give 90-day training to prospective officers chosen from the militia ranks. Escobar and Major Vicente Guarner quickly accepted the idea, although expressing some scepticism about the possibility of training new lieutenants in such a short time period.

Guarner suggested Major Lara de Rosal to organize the new school. That officer quickly located a headquarters, a former Jesuit school occupied by a local CNT group. García Oliver also commissioned Lara de Rosal to choose a list of professional officers to serve as faculty, stressing that they should be officers about whose loyalty to the Republican cause he had some doubt. Explaining this, García

Oliver told the major, 'The loyal officers we want at the front, the doubtful ones I prefer in the rear guard, where they can be watched and we can avoid having to shoot them.'[29]

In spite of the somewhat unorthodox basis used for choosing the instructors in the Escuela Popular de Guerra, García Oliver commented: 'I must say, for their satisfaction and that of their descendants that the behavior of the teachers was so scrupulous and their efficiency so great that the School was soon very much admired.'[30]

The students were chosen from people recommended by the various parties and trade union groups represented in the Consejo de Milicias. In so far as possible, they were assigned for the various branches of the service in conformity with their educational backgrounds; for instance, those with some mathematics training were assigned to artillery, those with architectural and engineering backgrounds to the engineers.

In a talk with the students, García Oliver outlined the objectives and attitudes of the Escuela Popular de Guerra: 'The disciplinary principle that is observed with you is congruent with that which you must observe once promoted to lieutenants and incorporated in your respective military units, where you must succeed in transmitting the spirit of discipline learned here, with respect and tolerance for your subordinates when they are not on active duty, but with rigidity when fulfilling orders received when facing the enemy. You must not behave with egotism when considering the small difference in rank which will exist between you and your subordinates; on the contrary, there must exist in you a total absence of any sense of superiority, without forgetting that in the field the lives of the commands confided in you will depend upon your competence and sense of responsibility.'[31]

Once he had entered the Republican cabinet of Francisco Largo Caballero in November 1936, García Oliver was asked by the prime minister/minister of war to organize on a national basis the kind of officers' training schools that he had earlier established in Catalonia. García Oliver explained the thinking of Largo Caballero and the CNT ministers in establishing these schools on a national basis.

'It was designed to create an organism parallel in influence within the Army to what the Communists had with the Commissariat, with the creation of Escuelas Populares de Guerra, which the anarchosyndicalists and Socialists could have, with the possibility of suppressing in time the Commissariat, as an emergency organism, antipathetic to the professional and militia commanders, and almost intolerable for the soldiers and militiamen, for the inquisitorial practices employed by the Communist commissars.'[32]

To organize the Spanish Republic's Popular War Schools García Oliver summoned Major Lara del Rosal, who had organized the school in Barcelona, and named him inspector general of Popular War Schools. They then set about to organize four schools: one for infantry, cavalry and supply; a second for artillery, a third for engineers, and a final one for communications.[33] Locations for these four installations were soon found, an assignment of necessary arms for training was made by the ministry of war as well as 2,000 Remington rifles by the Catalan Defence Council. Regular officers were named as instructors, and students for the three-month courses were chosen from lists submitted by all the parties and labor organizations backing the Republic as well as by the Federal Union of Spanish Students.[34]

The four schools turned out their new officers on regular three-month schedules during García Oliver's tenure as their general supervisor. Only relatively minor incidents occurred to interfere with the smooth running of the institutions. Two students had to be dropped for indiscipline, one a CNTer and the other the son of a regular army officer who had stayed loyal to the Republic.[35] More serious was an effort by General Miaja to prevent the return to the artillery-school of cadets who had been sent to the Madrid front for practical training in directing artillery fire, as part of their regular course. However, García Oliver was finally able to get General Miaja to back down and to allow the cadets to finish their course in Valencia.[36]

During those first months of the Popular War Schools, García Oliver kept close track of their progress. There were also occasional visits by distinguished figures. These included Generals Orlov and Petrov, chiefs of the Soviet GPU in Spain,[37] and by prime minister/minister of war, Francisco Largo Caballero. Of that latter visit, García Oliver noted: 'The visit was exceedingly thorough. The inspection, most rigorous. Everything was seen, inspected and sensed: the study halls, dormitories, dining rooms, kitchen, toilets and showers.' The prime minister was very much impressed, and when he left, he told García Oliver: 'You and all your collaborators must accept my most emotional congratulations. Furthermore, receive the thanks of this minister of war, who hoped for much, but not for so much in so short a time. I think I have understood the key of your success: you believe in the creative capacity of the workers. So do I.'[38]

Other people than García Oliver himself bore witness to the efficacy of his efforts in organizing the Popular War Schools. A professional officer, Colonel Martín Blazquez commented: 'Cordon and I entered into contact with him, but all that he allowed us to do was to do was carry out instructions. Barracks, instructors, equipment, all that we could ask, was conceded immediately. Oliver was indefatigable. He decided all and supervised everything personally. He occupied himself with the most minimal details, and sought the perfect execution of his decisions. He was interested in the hours of the students and their meals. But, above all, he insisted that the new officers were trained in the strictest discipline.'[39]

Largo Caballero also assigned García Oliver the task of organizing the first 'mixed brigades', which were to become the basic units of the new Republican army. According to García Oliver, Largo Caballero asked him 'in pushing forward the development of the Mixed Brigades . . . not to wound the sensitivities of Martínez Barrio, who was in Albacete with a similar task which he was carrying out in an amply decorative manner.'[40]

However, García Oliver commented later: 'I was not much involved in the preparation of the Mixed brigades and the international brigades. The former, because they were already being taken care of by Martínez Barrio, and the latter because they didn't admit interference by the Spaniards. They tended to constitute a State within another State. I dedicated all my free time to the organization of the Popular War Schools, from which must come the force which will free us, at the opportune torment, from the two layers of the Communist Party: the Commissariat and the International brigades.'[41]

Anarchist Opposition to Militarization of the Militia

In spite of strong support for conversion of the militia into a regular military force by key figures in the anarchist movement, there did continue to be substantial opposition to this move within anarchist ranks. This attitude was widespread throughout the CNT–FAI, and was particularly strong in some of the anarchist militia columns.

The CNT had early expressed the traditional anti-militarist stand of the anarchists. It issued a manifesto saying: 'We cannot defend the existence of a regular army, uniformed, obligatory. This army must be substituted by popular militias, by the people in arms, only guarantee that freedom will be defended with enthusiasm, and that in the shade new conspiracies won't be incubated.' The FAI made similar arguments in August 1936.[42]

Early in September a national plenum of regional groups of the CNT, a resolution was adopted proposing: 'Creation on a militia of war which is obligatory, and control of the militias by Councils of Workers and Militiamen, made up of mixed commissions formed by the CNT and the UGT. Simplification of commands, circumscribing them to ... military techniques. Creation of a single military leadership, consisting of a war commissariat named by the National Council of Defense and with representatives of the three sectors which are fighting against fascism.' Peirats noted that these three sectors were the Republicans, Marxists and anarchists.[43]

García Oliver himself recognized that there was strong reticence on the part of anarchist organizations and militia units about sending candidates to the Popular War Schools which he organized while in the Largo Caballero government. 'This resulted in my bringing the matter up seriously before the national committee of the CNT, and in an agreement being reached and carried into practice whereby all the Regional Committees of Defense were to pay special attention to the recruiting of students for the training schools.'[44]

Certainly, Diego Abad de Santillán was one of the anarchist leaders who most strongly opposed militarization of the militias. Although he does not provide any details about his opposition, he

certainly well stated the attitudes of those in the CNT–FAI ranks
who were against the establishment of a regular Republican army:

> In the face of a Prussian-like discipline, of a discipline that kills
> the spirit, we would have preferred the systematic indiscipline,
> the spirit of permanent rebellion and the chaos in external
> appearance. In the face of the armies created by imposition of
> the Central Government, which in their turn were nothing more
> than an instrument in the hands of the invaders of Finland,
> armies in which the soldier had ceased to be a man of free
> sentiments and thoughts, we would have preferred the troops of
> warriors who went happily to death or to victory animated by
> an indestructible faith and in a consciousness of defending a
> noble and great cause...[45]
>
> It appears inconceivable that a few months from the events of
> July ... we had forgotten to whom we owed the triumph of July,
> and we had destroyed them on the pretext of making more
> efficacious their work in defense of liberty. The militarization of
> the militias was a double error:
> 1. A military error, because no improvised army, without
> commanders, no matter how strong in imposed discipline it was,
> could compete in combative qualities with that of enthusiastic
> volunteers of the first hour and subsequent hours.
> 2. A political error, because it deprived the war of popular
> initiative and warmth, converting it into a monopoly and an
> exclusive attribute of the State, with little by little the cooling of
> the enthusiasm and the understanding of the objectives of the
> bloody struggle.[46]

The Italian anarchist Camillo Berneri, who was then living in
Barcelona and working for the CNT and FAI, was also critical of the
militarization of the militia. He wrote in his Italian language weekly
newspaper on November 15 1936: 'The militarization of the militias
is not the only solution of a technical kind. It is a political mistake to
have accepted it pacifically, without clarifying the intentions, or
making clear the obscure points, or having discussed the general
lines.'[47]

Resistance to Militarization by the Iron Column

The strongest resistance of all to militarization came from the Columna de Hierro (Iron Column), the orthodox anarchist unit from Valencia on the Teruel front, which resisted militarization until late in March 1937.

From its inception, the Iron Column had been peculiarly recalcitrant to any kind of traditional military routine or formality. It was reported that it went so far as drawing lots to determine who should go on guard duty, so as to avoid anyone's being assigned to do so.[48]

In an evident move to head off pressure for militarization, the Iron Column had 'reorganized' its structure early in December 1936. It sought to establish a uniform structure for each *centuria*, and announced the creation of 'divisions' within the column, each of which would consist of ten centuries, The reorganization also strengthened the position of the *delegados*, or officers, within the column. Abel Paz noted: 'Coincident with this restructuring, all comrades are advised that they cannot abandon their parapet or the revolutionary mission which has been assigned to them without express authorization of the *delegado* of the *Centuria* or the comrade at the head of the Department. Every comrade who contravenes this accord taken by the delegates of the *Centurias* and the Committee of War will be expelled from the Column and his name will be advertised in the antifascist press as an undesirable person.'[49]

However, government pressure grew on the Columna de Hierro to accept militarization. At the end of December 1936, two decisive steps were taken. As minister of war, Largo Caballero announced that henceforward the Teruel front would be put directly under the supervision of the ministry of war, and José Benedito, the commander of the other major CNT unit on that front, would be put in overall command. At the same time, payment of the salaries of all members of the Republican armed forces would be centralized under a new payroll department.[50]

By the end of 1936, the Committee of War of the Iron Column recognized that the struggle against militarization had virtually been lost. In a long statement addressed to the members of the column, that committee commented: 'We know the inconveniences of militarization. It doesn't conform to out temperament, since it doesn't conform to those of us who have had a good concept of liberty. But also we know the inconveniences of trying to continue outside the orbit of the Ministry of War. It is sad to admit, but there are only two possible paths: dissolution of the Column or militarization. Everything else will be useless...'[51]

However, almost three months more passed before militarization was formally accepted by the Iron Column. Pressure was brought by the CNT national leadership to have the column conform. In this connection, the Iron Column periodical *Nosotros* published an interview with Mariano Vázquez, the national secretary of the CNT, in which he explained that militarization would not mean conversion of soldiers into robots, nor would it mean that the homogeneity of anarchist-controlled units would be ended.[52]

Finally, on March 21 1937, a general assembly of the Iron Column met in the Teatro Libertad in Valencia at which the fateful decision to accept militarization was taken. The minutes of that meeting recorded: 'The assembly was asked if it was in agreement with militarization, and it was agreed to unanimously.'[53]

The Conditions of Anarchist Acceptance of Militarization

Sometime after the entry of the CNT ministers into Francisco Largo Caballero's cabinet on November 4 1936, the top anarchist leadership formally accepted the need for militarization of the CNT militia units.[54] However, in agreement with Largo Caballero, there were certain conditions set to this acceptance, the most important of which was that the existing anarchist military units would continue under anarchist control, and that the CNT would be allowed to organize additional ones.

In his interview with *Nosotros*, Mariano Vázquez had elaborated on that point. When asked whether militarization would mean the disappearance of 'our columns', he replied:

Yes, they will disappear. It is necessary that they disappear. When we came to the National Committee, the agreement had already been made that our columns, like all of the others, would be transformed into brigades – the name doesn't create the fact – providing them everything necessary to make their work efficacious. However, this transformation does not imply, if one looks carefully, a fundamental change, because, when being transformed, there will remain in the brigades the same commanders as in the columns; it can be said that the comrades who are fond of those who have operational responsibility can be sure that they will not be obliged, due to capricious changes, to accept those whose ideology, and consequently personal treatment, would not please them. Furthermore, the Political Commissars, who are the real chiefs – don't be afraid of the word – of the brigades, will be named by the confederal organization, to which they will always be responsible.[55]

Burnett Bolloten has said that the maintenance of clearly anarchist brigades within the new Popular Army was agreed to by Largo Caballero:

Although Largo Caballero, for political and technical reasons, had approved the militarization of the militia on the basis of mixed of brigades, his present desire for easy relations with the CNT, stemming from his growing antipathy to the Communists, inhibited him from attempting seriously to enforce the measure. As a result, the anarcho-syndicalist units, while submitting to the general staff for the purpose of military operations, remained under the exclusive control of the CNT and were composed of men and officers belonging to that organization...[56]

That Largo Caballero had assented to and had not simply connived at the evasion of the rigorous form at militarization agreed upon with the Russians is proved by the fact that General Martínez Cabrera, the chief of the war ministry general staff, who enjoyed his entire confidence, authorized the committee of war of the anarchist Maroto Column in February 1937 to organize a brigade composed entirely of that column's members. That this was done either without the knowledge or in defiance of Meretzkov, Martínez Cabrera's Russian adviser, a future marshal of the Soviet Union and Red Army chief of staff, can be open to little doubt.[57]

Certainly, this CNT insistence on the maintenance within the new Popular Army of units which were recognizably under anarchist control was a matter of self-preservation. Franz Borkenau, writing in February 1937, commented with regard to the anarchists, that 'sooner or later they will be destroyed unless they keep an army of their own.'[58]

Although most anarchist militia units converted into elements of the Popular Army remained principally under anarchist command throughout the war, this was not true in all cases. Thus, Francisco Romero, who served in the last eight months of the War as a major in the 73rd Division of the Army of Maneuver (the main source of reserves), has noted that although that unit began the War under general anarchist control, by the end of the conflict its officers included men of virtually all of the different political elements in the Republic.[59]

Of course, the militarization of the militia columns not only involved the changing of their names. It included the substitution of military uniforms for the workers' overalls which had been the hallmark of the militiaman; the use of military ranks, from private to lieutenant-colonel (and ultimately even general); and (usually, although certainly not always) the military courtesy of saluting.

These outward changes struck foreign observers. Thus, Franz Borkenau, returning to Spain in late January 1937, after having first been there in August 1936, observed: 'The troops were entirely different from the militia I had known in August. There was a clear distinction between officers and men, the former wearing better uniforms and stripes ... The uniform of the privates was not yet quite unified, but the multicolored Robin Hood style of the militia-men had entirely disappeared, and there was a definite attempt towards a uniformity of clothes...'[60]

How far this adoption of the regimen of a regular army was accepted by at least some of the CNT military leaders was shown in the case of Cipriano Mera. He was quoted by *Solidaridad Obrera*, in its issue of March 23 1937, as saying: 'At my side I only want combatants. In my Division I don't know who is of the UGT or of the CNT, of a republican party or a Marxist party. It is necessary, and I have to insist from now on, to have iron discipline, discipline which has the value of being offered voluntarily. From today, I will only talk with captains and sergeants.'[61]

Eduardo de Guzmán has described the process of militarization which took place in the anarchist militia: 'At first the change was no more than nominal. The old columns changed their name and structure to be converted into mixed brigades. Little by little, the change is more profound ... In our Militia, there appeared military command structures in accord with the orders of the Ministry of War. The chiefs of battalion were transformed into majors, the *responsables* of centuries into captains; there appeared the first corporals and sergeants.'[62]

The Spartacus Column became the 70th Brigade; the España Libre Column the 77th. They were joined into the 14th Division, headed by Cipriano Mera. At the same time, the anarchist Mora, Juvenil Libertaria and Orobón Fernández Columns in Cuenca became the 59th, 60th and 61st Brigades, and were joined to form the 42nd Division, headed by an army officer, Major Barcelo, with José Villanueva of the CNT as political commissar. Similarly, the Durruti Column became the 26th Division, the Catalan Ascaso Column became the 149th Brigade.[63] Elsewhere other anarchist columns also became brigades of the Popular Army.

The Question of Political Commissars

In the process of establishing the republic's Popular Army, one issue on which the anarchists were clearly defeated was that of the establishment of political commissars, on virtually every level of the new army. The idea was adopted in spite of strong opposition by the CNT–FAI leaders.

The concept of a political commissar had its roots at least as far back as the French revolutionary armies of the 1790s. Faced with the need to use professional officers of whose political loyalty they were dubious, the French revolutionary leaders had devised the procedure of having alongside them civilians whose politics were trustworthy, with the power to keep watch on the officers and if necessary countermand their orders.

When Leon Trotsky had set about organizing the Red Army in 1918, he was faced with a similar problem, and resolved it as the French had done more than a century before. Trusted political commissars were placed alongside the professional officers inherited from the Czarist army, to keep track of their loyalty, and to intervene militarily if that seemed justified on political grounds. Even after the Russian Civil War had been won, the political commissar remained a permanent fixture in the Soviet Army. Not a few post Second World War Soviet political leaders had had careers during that conflict as political commissars.

Understandably, the Spanish Communists and their Russian and Comintern advisers strongly supported the establishment of political commissars as an integral part of the new Popular Army. They saw a crucial role for the political commissars not only in organizing the new army, but also in ensuring that it would come under Communist control.

'Carlos Contreras' (the Italian Communist Vittorio Vidali) argued: 'The commissar is the soul of the combat unit, its educator, its agitator, its propagandist. He is always, or should be always, the best, the most intelligent, the most capable. He should occupy himself with everything and know about everything. He should interest himself in the stomach, in the heart, and in the brain of the soldier of the people ... He must see that his political, economic, cultural and artistic needs are satisfied.'[64]

Antonio Mije, a member of the Spanish Communist Politburo, outlined the role of the commissar in pushing the interests of the party. He said that the Communist commissar should be 'the organizer of the party in his unit, boldly and systematically recruiting the best elements from among the best fighters and recommending them for positions of responsibility ... Teams of agitators must be created to inform the militiamen of the attitude of the party with regard to all problems ... The Communists should take upon themselves the task of recruiting for the party the best fighters at the front.'[65]

The party role of Communist political commissars was well understood by them. This is shown by the comment of an American Communist political commissar in the International Brigades, Joe Dallet who, in listing the duties of his post noted that 'It is not only the morale, the political line, etc., that a commissar is responsible for.'[66]

The anarchists were opposed to the idea of political commissars. They had not instituted such posts in the militia of Catalonia and Aragón. Rather, party or trade union leaders were the commanders of the various militia columns there and had attached to them as advisers professional officers who had proclaimed their loyalty to the Republic. Even in the center, where Cipriano Mera was at first a kind of political commissar to a professional officer who was at first the titular commander of the militia column which Mera largely organized, Mera soon emerged as the actual commander of that military unit.

Juan García Oliver explained the anarchists' opposition to the political commissars: 'I considered that the Commissariat which functioned in the rest of Republican Spain was one of the many traps suggested by the Soviet counsellors of the unprepared leaders of the Spanish Communist Party. Each of them had no other objective than to create iron belts which in time would permit to occur in Spain the experience of strangling the revolution, eliminating workers' democracy and annihilating politically anyone who didn't have a party card.'[67]

García Oliver sought to keep the officers' training schools which he organized free of political commissars. Although the General Commissariat had named four people to such posts, he refused to allow those men to set foot in the schools. Understandably, General Commissar Julio Alvarez del Vayo objected, and suggested a meeting of himself, Largo Caballero and García Oliver to resolve the situation. This, Largo Caballero refused to go along with; nor would he, on the other hand, present the problem to the Superior War Council where both Largo Caballero and García Oliver agreed that Alvarez del Vayo would lose on the issue, and be humiliated as a result.

Finally, Largo Caballero suggested a compromise to García Oliver: that García Oliver choose two CNTers he trusted, and Largo Caballero select two UGT members whom he trusted, and have them be the political commissars in the training schools. After consulting with the CNT National Committee, García Oliver accepted this compromise.[68]

Since the establishment of political commissars on all levels of the armed forces had been decided upon before the CNT joined the Largo Caballero government early in November 1936, it was not possible to get a reversal of that decision. Ultimately, the anarchists had to content themselves with trying to make sure that in military units under their command there also would be political commissars of anarchist persuasion or sympathies.

The Guerrilla Issue

Even after they had accepted the basic idea of establishing a regular Popular Army, the anarchists continued, right down to the end of the War, to put forward the idea that there also be organized guerrilla forces to operate behind the enemy Lines. They had at best very limited success in getting acceptance for this motion, and the Republican government never enthusiastically endorsed it.

One of the most serious proposals to try to open a guerrilla front in the rear of the Franco forces was put forward by Juan García Oliver, early in 1938. His idea was to organize a guerrilla campaign in Andalusia and Extremadura, based at first in the mountains of the Sierra Nevada not far from Granada. There were at the time, he calculated, at least 20,000 refugees in that area, who had escaped from Rebel-held territory in Andalusia, who might in time be incorporated into the guerrilla operation, together with some of the local peasantry, and even some people who might be attracted from the ranks of Franco's army.

García Oliver worked out his plans in considerable detail, with the help of some other anarchist leaders, including former militia commander Antonio Ortíz and Joaquín Ascaso, ex-head of the Council of Aragón. Their original plan was to commence with the formation of a nucleus of 200 men, who would be given one month's intensive training in the use of a wide range of weapons from knives to small cannon, as well as instruction in first aid, the preparation of meals under primitive conditions, and engaging in long marches and learning how to stand guard as sentinels.

The plan was for these 200 members of the first guerrilla class to be given equipment sufficient for 600 people, as well as portable radios, with which to recruit at least three times their number, and set up the first guerrilla bases in the area. They would be trained now to attack isolated military and police units and would, it was hoped, become a base for a campaign which could be extended widely in Andalusia and Extremadura, behind the enemy lines.

García Oliver, Ortíz and Ascaso then visited the area where they hoped to set up the school, and from which they hoped the first guerrillas could penetrate enemy territory. They got pledges of support from Colonel Adolfo Prada, in spite of his being a Communist, and also visited Francisco Maroto, the local anarchist militia leader who was being kept under somewhat decorous house arrest since the fall of Málaga. Maroto promised to help recruit worthy students for the first guerrilla class, as well as to get some equipment for their incursion into Franco-held territory.

Finally, García Oliver presented an extensive outline of his plan to Indalecio Prieto, who was then minister of defense, since his help would be necessary to establish the proposed training school and to provide equipment for the guerrillas. Prieto expressed interest in the proposal, and asked time to study it.

Some days later, when Prieto again received García Oliver, the minister told him that he had submitted copies of García Oliver's document to the French military attaché, who was enthusiastic about its possibilities, and to the Soviet military attaché. The latter, according to Prieto, 'told me that it should be formally rejected as inoperative'. Prieto added: 'My personal opinion coincides with that of the French military attaché, but not even as Minister of Defense can I oppose a decision to the Soviet General Staff.'[69]

A few days later, Prieto was forced to resign as minister of defense and that ended all further possibility of executing García Oliver's 'Plan de Comboríos', as he called it.

Diego Abad de Santillán was another anarchist leader who seriously sought to organize guerrilla activities behind the Franco lines to supplement the war efforts of the more or less regular Popular

Army. At one point, he presented a plan for organizing guerrilla operations behind the Franco forces in Aragón, and requested of Soviet Consul General Antonov-Ovsenko in Barcelona arms to equip a small force. Antonov-Ovsenko, himself an ex-guerrilla leader during the Russian Civil war, was at first enthusiastic about the idea. However, a few days later, he informed Abad de Santillán that his request for arms had been turned down: 'He told us that we were considered good comrades, but that one day we could become dangerous. And because one day we could become dangerous for Muscovite plans, we were refused a tiny quantity of arms.'[70]

On another occasion, with the support of Abad de Santillán, the CNT's Confederation of Aragón, Rioja and Navarre undertook to organize a guerrilla attack on Zaragoza from the rear. Some 1,500 men were involved in these plans and among other equipment they had eight machine guns and a number of mortars at their disposal. The attack was to be coordinated with efforts by loyal CNTers still in Zaragoza. This plan was taken seriously enough that the general staff of the Republican forces sent two Russian officers to look into the preparations for the proposed attack. In the end, however, the general staff ordered cancellation of that guerrilla effort.[71].

One final suggestion for resort to guerrilla warfare was male shortly before the end of the War. After the fall of Catalonia, Cipriano Mera suggested that one alternative for continuing the War was for at least part of the still existing armies of the center to be split up into guerrilla groups to conduct irregular warfare in the rear of the Franco forces, particularly in the southern part of the country. His suggestion was turned down.[72]

Interestingly enough, in retrospect, Palmiro Togliatti, the principal Comintern agent in Spain during the War, was also critical of the failure of the Republican government to carry on guerrilla activities behind the Franco lines:

> ...All the organizations of the Popular Front (including the Communist Party) and the government of the Republic paid no attention to work in the zone occupied by Franco and the invading army. It was forgotten that in that zone, and above all in the army of Franco, there was a mass of peasants and workers

who constituted a formidable reserve for the Popular Front and which if work had been done among them, would have been able to play a decisive role in weakening the fascist regime and would have constituted the base for a guerrilla movement in the countryside. It must be considered very grave that during the whole war, and in spite of the efforts carried out in 1938, the Communist Party, in particular, did not succeed in carrying out any serious work in the zone of Franco.[73]

10

The Political Struggle in the Popular Army

There is little doubt about the fact that within the Popular Army, which had been firmly established by the early months of 1937, the anarchists fought a losing battle against the Communists' drive to dominate the Republican armed forces. Although it had been the anarchists who had been largely responsible for suppressing the Rebels in most of the Mediterranean area of Spain and, in the early months, it was CNTers who made up the bulk of the forces which rushed to the colors to defend the Republic, they were no match for the Communists in the unceasing struggle for control of the Loyalist armies, until the penultimate moment of the struggle, when it was too late to matter.

The Communists' Advantage in their Struggle for Control of the Military

The Communists had many advantages on their side in the struggle to get control of the Republican armed forces. Even before the Civil War began, the Stalinists had a certain foothold in the military. The more or less official Communist account of the Civil War noted: 'In 1934; to oppose the propaganda discrediting the Republic which the UME carried on in the army, the Communist Party had constituted the Unión Militar Antifascista (UMA), which brought together military men of various ranks and ideologies, united in their adhesion to the cause of democracy. This organization was later amplified with the incorporation of other republican officers, taking the name Unión Militar Republicana Antifascista (UMRA).'[1]

This same source noted that starting in 1933 the Communist Party 'had undertaken the creation of Milicias Antifascistas Obreras y Campesinas; and although they were armed only with pistols ... they played an important role in the days of the rebellion. The MAOC were not only the first organized and disciplined shock forces against the rebels, but also the framework for organizing in combat units thousands of antifascists whom the people called, not accidentally, "militiamen".'[2]

Stanley Payne has provided more extensive information on the conspiratorial and paramilitary work of the Communists preceding the outbreak of the Civil War:

> By June the militia organization (MAOC) had 2,000 organized members in the Madrid district, and was given the goal of expanding into 'a mass organization of semimilitary character' as 'the organizational basis for the future worker-peasant Red Army'. Parallel to the MAOC was the 'Antimilitarist section' of the party, led by the Russian-trained Galician Communist, Enrique Lister, who had undergone a year or more of preparation at the Frunze Academy. Simply put, the task of Lister's bureau was the subversion of the Spanish Army. It set up Communist cells in as many military detachments as possible, and was particularly successful among noncommissioned officers in the Madrid garrison. Another semisecret military organization manipulated by the party was the Republican Antifascist Military Union (UMRA), first organized by leftist army officers in 1934 to combat the union of conservative nationalists within the Army (the UME). The UMRA's chief organizer was a Communist officer on the General Staff, Capt. Eleuterio Díaz Tendero. Such groups were further complemented by Communist infiltration into the security forces in Madrid and certain other cities where conditions were propitious ... After the Comintern

agent Vittorio Vidali (Carlos Contreras) arrived in Spain in May to assume supervision of paramilitary activities, Communist terrorist squads were separated from the regular MAOC groups in order not to compromise the latter...[3]

From the early months of the War, the Communists held key posts in the top ranks of the ministry of defense, and as the ministry came increasingly to control the Republican military, they were able to use that influence to extend their control throughout much of the armed forces. In the second place, the Communists' emphasis from the beginning on the re-establishment of regular military order within the Republican armed forces was a powerful attraction for the professional officers in those forces. Third, without any doubt, the fact that the Soviet Union was virtually the only foreign country supplying arms and equipment, which remained in notably short supply throughout the conflict, gave both the Soviet and Spanish Communists the most powerful bargaining chip of all.

The Soviet historian Roy Medvedev has given some indication of the quantity of military equipment and supplies provided by the USSR to the Spanish Republic: 'By the end of 1936 the Soviet Union had supplied Spain with 106 tanks, 60 armored cars, 136 airplanes, more than 60,000 rifles, 174 field guns, 3,727 machine guns, and an unspecified amount of ammunition. This was not very much aid considering the scale of the fighting in Spain.' Medvedev added: 'In 1937 the Soviet Union's military aid to the Spanish Republic began to decrease markedly, and in 1938, a year before the collapse of the republic, it dwindled to nearly nothing.'[4]

Although the military supplies and equipment provided by Stalin was insufficient to make it possible for the Loyalists to win the War it was overwhelmingly the largest amount of aid given from abroad. It gave particular force to the 'suggestions' of Soviet military advisers. Also, the threat, implied or explicit, to cut off aid was a powerful blackmail tool both for determining military strategy and providing pressure for political changes wanted by the Soviet and Spanish Stalinists.

Burnett Bolloten has documented the early penetration of Communists and their sympathizers in the top echelons of the defense ministry:

Indeed, during the early weeks of Largo Caballero's tenure of the war ministry, they had already secured a promising foothold. This they were able to do partly because their relations with the war minister, notwithstanding his many grievances, were still of a tolerable nature (as a result, two of their adherents, Antonio Gord and Alejandro García Val, were appointed to the operations section of the general staff), but mainly because in key positions in the war ministry they possessed men of supposedly unquestioned loyalty to Largo Caballero. These included such professional officers as Lieutenant-Colonel Manuel Arredondo, his aide-de-camp, Captain Eleuterio Díaz Tendero, the head of the vital information and control department ... and Major Manuel Estrada, the chief of the war ministry general staff, who, unknown to Largo Caballero, were being drawn or had already been drawn into the Communist orbit.[5]

From the beginning the Communists had a commanding presence in the political commissariat. According to Bolloten:

It was assured of this predominance to some extent because Mije occupied the subcommissariat of organization – the most important of the four subcommissariats created – but principally because Felipe Pretel, the secretary general, and Julio Alvarez del Vayo, the commissar general, both of whom Largo Caballero had nominated because they possessed his unstinted confidence, secretly promoted the interests of the Communist Party. Before long, the party increased its influence still further owing to the appointment of José Laín, a JSU leader and recent Communist convert, as director of the school of commissars and to the illness of Angel Pestaña, the leader of the Syndicalist party, who had occupied one of the four subcommissariats and who was replaced by Gabriel García Maroto, a friend of Alvarez del Vayo's and a left-wing socialist with pronounced Communist leanings, although critical of some of the party's methods.[6]

The Communists' Fifth Regiment

From the beginning of the War, the Communists urged the establishment of a regular Republican military force. Franz Borkenau reported as early as August 6 being told that the Partido Socialista Unificado de Catalonia, the Catalan branch of the Stalinists, favored 'the Army system'.[7]

In Madrid, the Communists themselves organized what they called the Fifth Regiment. It had been organized largely under the leadership of Enrique Castro Delgado, a Madrid Communist leader who had helped lead the struggle to seize the Montana barracks. Almost immediately after those barracks were overrun, he and his followers seized the Convent of Franco Rodríguez, where they established their headquarters and began organization, with the help of some regular army people, of a proper military unit.[8] A few weeks later, the Fifth Regiment had its first formal military parade in the Puerta del Sol, where it passed in review before President Manuel Azaña and the minister of war.[9]

Gabriel Jackson has claimed that although the Fifth Regiment was organized and led by the Communist Party, it incorporated also 'many nonpolitical youths, who were attracted by its superior spirit, and not a few anarchists, who had recognized the weakness of their own undisciplined units.'[10]

Elements of the Fifth Regiment soon moved into action. Only a little more than a month after the beginning of the Civil War, Franz Borkenau observed: 'The Communists' critics do not deny, however, that the Communists have organized good military troops, especially the famous Fifth Regiment, which has more than once saved the Government position in the Guadarrama.'[11]

According to Burnett Bolloten, preference was given by the Russians to the Fifth Regiment in the distribution of arms. Basing his comments largely on personal testimony to him by Vittorio Vidali (Carlos Contreras), Bolloten noted:

An advantage no less important than the collaboration of those professional officers, to say nothing of the foreign Communists with military experience, who were associated with the regiment for varying periods ... was the preferential treatment the regiment received, as compared with other units in the distribution of the arms that reached Spain from the Soviet Union. Indeed, it was because of this preferential treatment, because of the opportunity given to a large number of men of the regiment to train in Russia as tank operator, no less than because of the pull of the Communists' efficiency, that the regime was able to recruit heavily from non-Communist sources.

Bolloten also noted the claim of the commander of the regiment in January 1937 that it had 'thousands of machine guns and hundreds of pieces of artillery – a wealth of material certainly unequalled by any other force in the anti-Franco zone at that stage of the war...[12]

Valentín González, the wartime Communist commander who won fame as El Campesino, writing after he had become disillusioned in Stalinism, confirmed this judgment of Bolloten and Vidali: 'The Russians sought to establish the supremacy of reliable Communist detachments over all the military forces on the Spanish Republican side, through the Fifth Regiment... They saw to it that the Fifth was the best equipped regiment, and had ample funds, and that it enjoyed the advice and instruction of Russian technicians as well as of other foreign specialists operating under the close control of Russian agents.' González added: 'The Fifth Regiment was practically independent of the Defense Ministry. For that matter, it was practically independent of the Spanish Republican Government.'[13]

According to Broué and Temime, 'With Russian aid, the Fifth Regiment grew with amazing rapidity. It was equipped, trained and officered. The government smiled on it because it was a model of discipline: it reintroduced all the practices of the regular units, salutes, insignia, and ranks. Regular officers serving in other columns asked to transfer to this unit, where they found service conditions that were to them normal.'[14]

Once the process of transforming the militia into a regular army had begun, the Communists' early insistence on the necessity for this development stood them in very good stead. Five of the first six brigades of the new Popular Army were under the control of the

Communist Party, their leadership being drawn largely from the Fifth Regiment.[15]

The Communists had clearly foreseen the importance of their Fifth Regiment in helping them to get leading posts in the new Popular Army. Enrique Castro Delgado wrote:

> The Fifth Regiment ... was preparing itself for the moment in which the Decree of the Minister of War creating the Popular Army would appear, to transform its units into units of the next army, keeping its chiefs, its commissars, maintaining in the units its political hegemony... But, of this operation, the most secret and subtle carried out during the whole war, only the Communists were informed...
>
> This was the reason, the great reason why the Party pardoned its heroes their drunken spells and stupidities, their pillage and their narcissism. It was necessary to conserve their prestige so that no one would veto them at the moment of their integration into the popular army.[16]

The Attraction of the Communist Party for Regular Officers

There is no doubt about the fact that regular army officers were attracted to the Communist Party because of its emphasis on rigid military discipline. Hugh Thomas noted the case of 'Major Barceló, a Republican army officer who, like many other regular soldiers had joined the Communist party since he was attracted by its discipline.'[17] Burnett Bolloten maintained that Barceló had been a Communist since 1935.[18]

Broué and Temime referred to 'The majority of regular officers, some of whom were only Republicans before the war, if they were not of the Right, belonged to the Communist party. Take, for instance, Miaja and Pozas, and younger men such as Hidalgo de Cisneros, Galán, Ciutat, Gordon and Barceló.'[19] Burnett Bolloten noted that many regular officers 'though far removed from Communist ideology, were attracted to the party because of its moderate propaganda, superior discipline, and organization and because it alone seemed capable of building an army that could carry the war through to victory.'[20] Dolores Ibarruri and her colleagues, in their account of the Civil War, confirms the party's attractiveness for the professional officers.[21]

Juan Antonio de Blas, writing in *La Guerra Civil en Asturias* noted the same phenomenon among officers on that northern front: 'The attitude of the Communists, with their exaltation of organization and of discipline agreeably surprised the professional military men and this resulted in many commanders soliciting a membership card of the Communist Party (the most important example is that of Carabinero lieutenant Claudio Marín Barco, who would have the best military career of the professional officers assigned to Asturias before the war, coming to command a division).'[22] Another important Communist recruit was Lieutenant Francisco Ciutat de Miguel, who was sent from Madrid to be chief of staff of the Republican forces in Asturias shortly after joining the Communist Party.[23]

There was undoubtedly another factor that brought professional military men under the influence of the Communist Party: the ability of its propaganda apparatus both to create and destroy 'heroes'. Castro Delgado, referred to this: 'To convert them into slaves of the Party was easy. They knew more or less that the Party could both take a man from his bed to make him a national hero, and grab a hero from the front to shoot him as "incapable" or "traitor to the Spanish people".'[24]

In admitting professional soldiers to their ranks, the Communists were not particularly concerned about their prewar affiliations. Thus, José Peirats noted that General Miaja had been a member of the Unión Militar Española, the group out of which the plot against the Republic originated.[25]

Of course, not all of these regular officers stayed with the Communists throughout the War. However, their influence was a key element in gaining the Communists a preponderant position within the Republican armed forces.

The Political Influence of Russian Military Advisers

Certainly the presence of substantial number of Soviet military advisers also served the interest of gaining Communist control over the Republican armed forces. Largo Caballero has been quoted as saying:

> The Spanish government, and in particular the minister responsible for the conduct of operations, as well as the commanding officers, especially at headquarters, were not able to act with absolute independence because they were obliged to submit, against their will, to irresponsible foreign interference, without being able to free themselves from it under pain of endangering the assistance that we were receiving from Russia through the sale of war material. Sometimes on the pretext that their orders were not being carried out as punctually as they desired, the Russian embassy and the Russian generals took the liberty of expressing to me their displeasure, stating that if we did not consider their cooperation necessary and fitting, we should tell them so plainly so that they could inform their government and take their departure.[26]

Russian officers operated on virtually all levels, with both Spanish troops and the International Brigades. Thus, one member of the Abraham Lincoln Battalion had recounted how his unit, which had suffered heavy casualties in an attack, and then had been given permission by Lazo Rajk, one of the International Brigade commanders (and later head of the Hungarian Communist Party), to rest behind the lines, but was then charged with 'desertion'. A Soviet general attended the resulting court martial, and after hearing the Americans' case, ordered the dismissal of all charges.[27]

Finally, the Communists used massive coercion to try to curb the influence of other political elements within the Republican armed forces. I will deal with this at some length later.

There can be little doubt that their influence in the military was a key factor in the growth of Communist general strength within the Republic, and a major element in their drive to win total domination of it. As early as February 1937, after commenting on the Communists' failure to win influence among the workers during the first months of the War, Franz Borkenau reported: 'It is military and organizing, not political influence which gives the communists their strength, and indirectly makes them the politically dominant factor.'[28]

Anarchist Resistance to Communist Drive for Control of the Armed forces

The anarchists undoubtedly had many handicaps in trying to preserve their own influence within the Republican military, and to block the Communists' drive to dominate the Popular Army. One handicap certainly arose from the hesitancy to accept, and even resistance of the CNTers to, militarization of the militia. As a consequence of those attitudes, the anarchists did not in the early months take advantage to a sufficient degree of the fact that one of their leaders, Juan García Oliver, was directing the Popular Army's new officers' training schools. The upshot was that even during the Largo Caballero government the ratio of anarchist officers was in no proportion to rank and file troops coming from the CNT. This disproportion undoubtedly was a severe handicap for the anarchists, and it grew throughout the rest of the War.

Once the Largo Caballero government had been forced out and succeeded by that of Juan Negrín, the anarchist situation within the armed forces undoubtedly got worse. One of the first measures of the new minister of war Indalecio Prieto was to dissolve the military training schools set up by García Oliver. Of this, García Oliver himself wrote:

'...the War Schools were dissolved when the CNT ministers left the government... The Communist Party demanded the dissolution of the Popular War Schools, because they had no interest in entry into them being democratically distributed among all the antifascist sectors, because, with that, the Communists could never get control of all the military commands in the army... The War Schools were replaced by so-called training courses of the military units of the fronts. In that way, in view of the fact that the majority of the military units had Communist or crypto-Communist commanders, the only people attending such training courses who would become officers were those who carried a Communist Party card.[29]

The Communists also sought to monopolize the more specialized branches of the armed forces, which was facilitated by their control of key posts in the military hierarchy. According to José Peirats, 'The combatants from the fronts had priority to enter certain specialties (aviation, tanks, etc.) and to attend the war schools. The calls for volunteers were published in the *Diario Oficial del Ejercito*. But before this publication, the Communist brigades were alerted by the "Party" to prepare their aspirants. Normally, the *Diario Oficial* arrived late at the front, so that the non-Communist combatants always presented their applications late. This maneuver was carried out by Antonio Cordón, the subsecretary of the Land Army.'

Another tactic used by the Stalinists was rapid promotion of party members within the ranks. Peirats noted:

> One can easily understand that the Communist combatants had rapid military careers. During the month of May 1938 in the 27th Division (formerly Carlos Marx), for example, there were 1,280 promotions (corporals, sergeants, lieutenants, captains, majors and commissars of all ranks). Those newly promoted were destined to cover vacancies in other Divisions, Brigades and Battalions, where because of the political inclinations of their members those members couldn't rise so easily. The Communists thus conquered new positions in the anarchist, Socialist, republican or neutral units. [The FAI had reported] We can affirm without fear of equivocation that if since May there have been promotions, on various levels, of 7,000 combatants, 5,500 belonged to the Communist Party.[30]

The Communists made strenuous efforts to infiltrate their members or sympathizers into commands or political commissariats of predominantly anarchist units. Although the more important anarchist-controlled formations were largely able to thwart these efforts, there were undoubtedly instances in which the Communists succeeded.

Ricardo Sanz recounted how he prevented Communist infiltration in the 26th Division (old Durruti Column) which he commanded, after it was reunited on the Aragón front. A 'fanatical Communist', Colonel Francisco Galán was in charge of the army group of which the 26th Division was part, and he sought to undermine CNT control of the 26th. He tried to siphon off new officers whom Sanz trained in a training school. These were put in Communist divisions where they could be controlled, and they were often abused. Also, Galán several times disciplined Sanz's junior officers for minor infractions, sometimes fictitious, over Sanz's head. Finally, Sanz went to Galán's headquarters, armed with his pistol, when no one was around, and complained strongly to Galán, threatening him that if he didn't quit harassing the 26th Division, Sanz would send a group of dynamiters from the division and blow up Galán's headquarters. Sanz maintained that from that time on Galán left the 26th Division alone.[31]

The anarchists were not so lucky in the Tierra y Libertad Column, which became the 153rd Brigade. The same Colonel Galán was involved in its fate. After the battle of Aragón in March 1938, Galán, in command of the XI Army Corps, began removing anarchist officers from the brigade. José Peirats commented: 'The XI Army Corps named constantly to the Brigade Communist personnel on all levels, including certain kinds of enlisted men. They came without specific assignments and were relieved of all military duties. Then in October 1938 the whole general staff of the Brigade was arrested.'

José Peirats himself was witness to what was happening in the 153rd Brigade. As a lieutenant in the 119th Brigade, he listened to several officers of the 153rd, who came to the headquarters of the 119th, 'who told of the terrible situation of their unit and the persecutions to which they were subjected'.

A report of the Executive Committee of the Libertarian Movement of Catalonia of November 24 1938 reported on the denouement of the situation of the 153rd Brigade. 'Of all of the officers there were in it, only two remain; all the rest have been transferred to other brigades and divisions, and there have been brought to take their place, commanders, officers and commissars of the "Party".'[32]

Extent of Communist Control of the Army

Relatively early in the War, in November 1937, Palmiro Togliatti reported to his bosses in the Comintern about the extent of Communist control of the Republican army. He noted that of the 21 army corps, seven were commanded by Communists, five by sympathizers, two by CNTers, five by Republicans and two by non-arty people. Of the 52 divisions, the Communist's commanded 27, one was led by a sympathizer, two by members of the Catalan PSUC, two by Socialists, eight by CNTers, seven by Republicans, three by non-partisans and two by 'undefined'.[33]

On September 30 1938, after the disaster in Aragón, but several months before the final push of the Franco forces into Catalonia, the military secretariat of the Federación Anarquista Ibérica presented a report on the number of major commands which were at that time in the hands of the libertarians, as compared to other political elements, particularly the Communists. It began by insisting that '...all the top controls of the army are in the hands of the Communists.' The central general staff was headed by General Vicent Rojo, whom the FAI considered to have 'submitted completely to the directives of "the Party".' The Communists also controlled the information and personnel branches of the central general staff. Similarly, although the general inspectorates were in the hands of Socialists and Republicans, 'the immense majority of the subalternate commands are in the hands of the Communists'. Furthermore, the FAI insisted that 'the Aviation, Tanks and other armored units, are closed to all elements outside of the "Party".' The anarchists had no responsibility in the new military police, the (SIM).[34]

At that time, there were two army groups in the Republican armed forces, one in Catalonia, the other in the center, and there were six armies, four in the center and two in Catalonia. The FAI gave a summary of the command situation of the anarchists and their friends in these formations and their subordinate army corps, divisions and brigades.

The CNTers did not have command of either of the army groups. The FAI considered that General Hernández Sarabia, in charge in Catalonia was 'a loyal instrument in the hands of the Communists', and his counterpart in the center, 'General Miaja was 'an element without character, alongside of whom the Communists have taken care to place an element of their confidence'.[35]

The FAI's overall accounting of the command positions within the Loyalist armed forces unfortunately mentioned only two categories, Libertarios and Communists and Others, with no numerical differentiation between the Communists and non-Communists in the latter category. However, the FAI's figures do show the relative paucity of anarchist commanders.

Below the level of army groups, the FAI report said that of the six armies then in existence, two were commanded by libertarian sympathizers, and one by a neutral, the other three by Communists and others. Of the 21 army corps, only two were commanded by anarchists, four by anarchist sympathizers, and 15 by Communists and others. Of the 70 divisions, only nine were commanded by CNTers, and of the 193 brigades, only 33 had anarchist commanders.

The CNT report added: 'Undoubtedly, our Organization has an immense number of inferior commands distributed in almost all the units, but we must not forget that the Communists have a much larger number than we.'[36]

A similar situation existed in so far as various levels of political commissars was concerned. 'The FAI report noted:

Our representation in the Commissariat ... isn't much different from the distribution of military commands ... that is to say, we have as few commissars as military commands. At the present time, our Organization has one commissar of an Army Group, the Communists have the other (Central Zone), we have one Army commissar (Andalusia), the Communists have that of the Ebro, and the Socialists the rest. Of the 21 Army Corps, our Organization has the Commissar of four of the... As for

Divisions and Brigades there is little difference from military commands as we have previously indicate... We have many commissars in the Services and others scattered in different specialties...[37]

Demoralization Within the Republican Army

There can be little question but that there was growing demoralization within the armed forces of the Republic during the last year of the Civil War. Certainly this was due in part to the almost unending defeats of the Loyalists during that period, and the growing conviction that the War was lost.

However, equally certain is the fact that there were other causes that either contributed to, or were perhaps the more important reasons for, the spread of demoralization. José Peirats has indicated some of these:

Demoralization had also affected even the volunteer combatants, who had been at the front from the first days of the War. On August 25, 1938, the commissar of the Group of Armies of Catalonia, Gil Roldán, informed his organization (the CNT) of the numerous desertions that were taking place at the fronts. Many of these soldiers who deserted were veterans who had fought valiantly on all occasions. The desertions were not to the enemy zone, but towards the rear, and were principally occasioned by discontent. There was: scarcity of food, lack of clothing and especially of shoes (many soldiers protected their feet with bits of sacking), tardiness of pay, news that their families were in want in the rearguard, irregularity of the postal service (because of the censorship, slow and stupid).

There was another kind of deserters: those who could not endure the discipline established in the Communist brigades, stupid as well as sanguinary. These deserters, for the most part, limited themselves to changing brigades. If they were libertarians, their desertion consisted of taking refuge in a CNT brigade.

293

Peirats gives an example of this kind of discipline. At one point in the summer of 1938 on the Levante front, a group of artillerymen were ordered by their officer to destroy their guns in the face of enemy advances. But they, noting that the enemy were no longer moving forward, decided instead to take their guns back to their own lines, thus saving them. However, 'the officer, who had committed the error of not knowing the situation of the enemy, was about to order the execution of those devoted soldiers, so well endowed with initiative and ignorant of the absurdities of discipline.'[38] Peirats does not indicate whether the men were in fact executed. He continued:

> The difficulties were not borne stoically now as in the first months of the War. In those first months, the struggle had a pure and romantic character. The military bureaucracy had not yet appeared. There were not seen then the new uniforms of the armies of the rearguard: *policia de asalto* and *carabineros* (Negrín had an army for his personal use, the *carabineros*, the 'hundred thousand sons of Negrín', as the people baptized them). The new military caste was in the process of generating all the defects of the old army. Its concept of discipline surpassed the limits of the grotesque. The war schools for training of officers, as well as the schools for commissars, were it monopoly of the Communist Party.
>
> However, among the combatants, the major source of demoralization came from the political proselytizing which was carried out in the army. Orders and decrees were issued repeatedly to end this, but they were always inefficacious. Many of the military operations were conceived of with political objectives and had catastrophic results. The anarchist combatants protested with alarm that they were being used as cannon fodder...[39]

Conclusion

Clearly, the anarchists did not have positions in command levels of the Republican armed forces anywhere near consonant with their proportion of the rank and file of the Loyalist military. The FAI estimated that even in September 1938, 60 per cent of the troops on the Catalan front were from the ranks of the CNT. This was due to a variety of causes.

First of all, the anarchists themselves were partly to blame for this situation. Because of their deeply ingrained anti-militarism, they refused to take advantage to the degree that they might have done of chances they had to become officers of the emerging popular army. This same factor undoubtedly largely explained the fact that the majority of the professional officers who stayed with the Republic tended to have much more sympathy for the Communists than they did for the anarchists.

Second, the Communists were successful in getting key positions at the top of the Republican military hierarchy early in the War, positions which they used effectively to spread the Party's influence on all levels of the armed forces. Particularly after the fall of the Largo Caballero government, they had widespread cooperation in these efforts by the two last ministers of war, first Indalecio Prieto, and then Juan Negrín.

Third, the Communists (and most other political groups supporting the Republic) accepted from the beginning the establishment of a regular army, and set about organizing units – notably the Fifth Regiment – which could be and were the seedbeds of the units of that army.

Finally, the Communists were willing to use all conceivable methods to inveigle, entice and coerce both officers and men of the Republican armed forces to join the Party's ranks. These methods included not only virtual 'blackmail' by the Soviet military advisers, but also widespread political discrimination, terror and even murder against those who tried to resist – a theme to which we shall return in a later chapter of this book.

Part Three
Anarchist Agrarian Collectives

11

Overall View of Anarchist Rural Collectives

The Spanish anarchists came nearest to carrying out their ideals and putting their program into practical execution in the many hundreds of rural collectives which they established in various parts of Republican Spain during the Civil War. There had been sporadic efforts on the part of the anarchists to establish libertarian communism in the countryside dating back to the nineteenth century, But these had usually been quickly suppressed by the agents of law and order. However, during the 1936–9 Civil War, they had their first real opportunity to put into practice on a large scale their ideas for reorganizing the economy, society and polity in substantial parts of rural Spain.

Of course, the path of the agrarian members and supporters of CNT–FAI was not a smooth one. They had no clear blueprint of exactly what it was that they wanted to do, and there was very considerable variety in the patterns they adopted. The exigencies of war and politics made them make many compromises which they would have preferred not to have had to make. They were confronted with bitter and violent opposition from the Communists and their allies, not only in the form of virulent propaganda against the 'Utopian', 'corrupt', and even 'subversive' nature of what they were trying to do, but also in the form of widespread armed assault on the rural collectives.

Finally, the anarchists' rural bulwarks, like the rest of Republican Spain, were (where they had survived Communist attack) overrun by the conquering Franco armies, and their organization of the countryside was completely destroyed. None the less, their agrarian experiments remain one of the most notable aspects of the Spanish anarchists' experience of having – and sharing – power.

Spanish Landholding Patterns in 1936

The agrarian problem had remained one of the great unresolved dilemmas facing Spain during the nineteenth and early twentieth centuries. Landholding patterns varied greatly from one part of the country to another, ranging from widespread small proprietorship and fixed-term tenancy in Galicia and the Basque provinces; to fairly secure sharecropping arrangements in much of Catalonia; to a mixture of large holdings, sharecropping, cash rental and small proprietorships in Aragón; to fairly prosperous small and medium proprietorships and sharecropping arrangements in the Levante; to vast semi-feudal types of large landholdings in the regions south and west of Madrid.[1] Overall, Spanish agriculture, with some notable exceptions, remained technologically backward and relatively un-productive. Gaston Leval also emphazises the topography, poverty of the soil and climatic conditions as well as landholding patterns, as explanations for the country's relatively backward agriculture in 1936.[2]

Walther Bernecker has sketched the general distribution of land-holdings in pre-1936 Spain.

[The landholding pattern] was characterized on the one hand by a predominance of extreme inequalities and, on the other, great regional differences. Whereas the large holdings cultivated by day laborers or renters were concentrated (and are concentrated) basically in New Castille, Andalusia and Extremadura, in parts of Old Castille, Galicia and León there was dominant (and are concentrated) small agricultural properties, the cultivation of which barely assured (and assures) the survival of a family, forcing the proprietor (or renter) in most cases to look for additional income. The middle-sized holdings, with from 10 to 100 hectares, were fundamentally located in Catalonia, the Basque Country and the Levante. Almost all the South and particularly the Southeast was subject to a latifundist economy.

Bernecker also noted that in 1930, holdings in the south and south-east of more than 100 hectares (approximately 250 acres) contained twice as much land as those of less than 10 hectares:

> The landlords there had more than 66.5 percent of the land. The properties of more than 500 hectares included in the South 53 percent of the total land area.
>
> [In contrast] in the center of the country the land occupied by the latifundists was less than half of that of small proprietors; in the North, the large holdings didn't contain 25 percent of the soil. In 1930, the latifundias, which we were only 0.1 percent of all holdings, occupied 33.28 percent of the total area, while the tiny landholders (mini-fundios) which were 96 percent of all units, only had 29.57 percent of the land...
>
> A global characterization of the property relations presents a clear dichotomy: in the southern third of the country dominated (and still dominates) latifundia, exploited on grand holdings mainly by agricultural laborers; in the Center and the North of the country the traditional structure of agriculture is characterized in general by the coexistence of peasant proprietors with very little land, and large proprietors whose land was worked as much by agricultural laborers dependent on a wage as by small renters with small holdings.[3]

Spread of Anarchist Influence in Rural Regions

In a previous chapter I considered the influence of the early anarchists in rural Spain in the periods just before, during and after the First Spanish Republic, in the 1860s and 1870s. Anarchist influence in the agricultural regions of Spain spread even further during the early decades of the twentieth century.

Gerald Brenan has described anarchist proselytism in rural Spain as he himself observed it:

> An extraordinary ferment, as suddenly and apparently as cause-less as a religious revival, swept over the country districts. In the fields, in the farms and wayside inns only one subject was discussed and always with intense seriousness and fervor. In the midday rests and at night, after supper, groups were formed to listen to a laborer reading aloud from one of the Anarchist papers. Then came speeches and comments. It was known and felt all their lives...
>
> An immense desire sprang up to read and learn, so as to have access to this store of knowledge and wisdom provided by the Anarchist press. One met peasants reading everywhere, on mule back, at meal time under the olive trees. Those who could not read, by force of hearing others spell out aloud their favorite passages, would learn whole newspaper articles by heart.

He noted with regard to the individual participant in this process:

> The scales would fall from his eyes and everything seem clear to him. He then became an *obrero consciente*. He gave up smok-ing, drinking and gambling. He no longer frequented brothels. He took care never to pronounce the word God. He did not marry but lived with his *companera*, to whom he was strictly faithful, and refused to baptize his children. He subscribed to at least one Anarchist paper, read the little books on history, geography and botany brought out by Ferrer's press and held forth on these subjects whenever possible. Like other unedu-cated people who have suddenly had their eyes opened to the possibilities of knowledge, he spoke in an inflated style, using long incomprehensible words.[4]

Later in his study, Gerald Brenan had observations which are peculiarly relevant to the rural collectivism of the anarchists during the Civil War:

> When one seeks to penetrate into the real meaning of the Spanish Anarchist movement, one is struck, I think, by two main aspects that in practice fuse into one. There is first of all its strongly idealistic and moral-religious character. These anarchists are a set of men who are attempting to put into practice their utopia (which is severe and almost ascetic like the old Jewish-Christian utopia) at once, and, what is significant, by force. Secondly, they are Spanish villagers and workmen who are trying, though without being consciously aware of it, to reconstruct the primitive agrarian conditions (in this case the collectivist commune) that once prevailed in many parts of Spain so to recover the equality and leisure, and above all the dignity, that to a greater or lesser extent, they enjoyed in previous centuries.[5]

Brenan elaborated on each of these points:

> The Anarchists stand then above everything else for liberty. But here the dilemma comes. These stern moralists, these children of the categorical imperative, disapprove of the present organization of society. But what is it they demand? They demand that everyone shall be free. Free to do what? Why free to lead the natural life, to live on fruit and vegetables, to work at the collective farm, to conduct himself in the way that anarchists consider proper. But if he does not want to do these things, if he wants to drink wine, to go to Mass, to dig in his own field and refuse the benefits brought into the world by *comunismo libertario*, what then? Why then he is one of *los malos, los perversos*, possibly curable but, if he does not come from a working-class family, more likely corrupt and vicious out of upbringing and heredity, and therefore unfit to partake of the Anarchist paradise...[6]

Brenan argued that the Spanish rural village was peculiarly appropriate for the kind of experiments that the anarchists sought to carry out during the Civil War:

> It argues a great deal of simplicity to believe that out of the welter of violent revolution in a modern country such a stateless form of society could appear. Only in small towns or in villages where the immense majority were laborers or poor peasants, prepared to work their land in common, would anything of the kind be possible. But what in the mind of Bakunin was a mere revolutionary's day-dream has appealed to Spaniards precisely because they are accustomed to think so much in terms of their own village. A change, that in a highly organized community would be quite utopian, might be feasible here ... By getting rid of a dozen landowners and a priest, the rest can divide up the land and live happily. And there is nothing illusory in such a belief. Anyone who has known the Spanish poor will agree that by their kindly and generous feelings for one another and by the talent they have so often shown for co-operation they are perfectly fitted for playing their part in an 'anarchist commune'.

Finally, Brenan noted what he called the 'atavistic' aspect of what the Spanish rural anarchists were trying to do:

> If anarchism is, in one sense, a utopian conception of life that opens out its arms to the future, it is also true that the Anarchists have, like the Carlists, their inner eye upon the past. Rural anarchism is quite simply the attempt to recreate the primitive Spanish communes that existed in many parts of Spain in the sixteenth and seventeenth centuries. Today they call them collectives, but till the Russians invented this word and modern machinery gave them a new scope, it was the old commune where the land was divided every few years by lot that they hankered for.[7]

Burnett Bolloten made somewhat the same point as Brenan. He said that, for the anarchists, rural collectivization, 'was one of their prime objectives and held their minds with a powerful fascination. They believed not merely that it would result in an improvement in the standard of living of the peasant by the introduction of scientific agronomy and mechanical equipment, not merely that it would protect him from the hazards of nature and from the abuses of intermediaries and usurers, but that it would uplift him morally.'[8]

The reunification congress of the CNT in Zaragoza in May 1936 passed a resolution which set forth what the anarchists proposed for the rural economy and society just before the outbreak of the Civil War. After denouncing the official agrarian reform law as 'a vain illusion', that resolution called for:

1.) Expropriation without indemnization of properties of more than 50 hectares of land. 2.) Confiscation of cattle, working tools, machinery and seeds that are in the control of the expropriated landlords. 3.) Review of communal goods and transfer of them to the peasant *sindicatos* for cultivation and exploitation in collective form. 4.) Proportional and free transfer of use rights of these lands and goods to the peasant *sindicatos* for direct and collective exploitation of the same. 5.) Abolition of contributions, land taxes, debts and mortgage charges on properties, working tools and machinery which constitute the means of livelihood of their owners who cultivate their land directly by themselves, without ... exploitation of other workers. 6.) Suppression of rent in money or kind which small renters, *rabassaires*, forest renters etc. are presently obliged to pay the large landowners. 7.) Development of hydraulic works, means of communication, cattle, chicken farms, reforestation, and creating of agricultural schools and experiment stations. 8.) Immediate solution of unemployment, reduction of the working day and equalization of wages to the cost of living. 9.) Direct acquisition by the peasant *sindicatos* of lands which because of insufficient cultivation constitute sabotage of the national economy.[9]

José Peirats has pointed out that long before the Civil War there had existed isolated experiment by groups of peasants, who had establishe d libertarian communism in their communities. After noting such experiments during anarchist insurrections, he wrote:

> Experiments with libertarian communism were made, also, peacefully, by mutual and free accord of some nuclei of small peasant proprietors. *La Revista Blanca* of May 1, 1933 pointed out several of these examples of free communities which had occurred in the province of Burgos, in that of Santander, in the lowland of Lerida, in the countryside of Siria, Asturias, Andalusia and Extremadura ... In a silent, slow and gradual way libertarian communism was being proclaimed in Spanish agrarian communities. Even the bourgeois press, surprised, could not do anything but recognize the fact, commenting with admiration on the spontaneity of this movement.[10]

Peasants' and Rural Workers' Organizations Before July 19

The anarchists were by no means the only element that had organized the peasants, tenants, sharecroppers and agricultural laborers before the outbreak of the Civil War. Most notably, the Socialists, through the Unión General de Trabajadores, had a substantial rural organization.

Several of the political groups which supported the Franco uprising had a peasant following. The Carlists, for instance, had a substantial rural constituency in Navarre. Also, Richard Robinson has noted in relation to the largest Right-wing party, the CEDA, led by José María Gil Robles, that 'Most of the CEDA's mass following came from the peasantry of Castille and León, where Catholic agrarian organizations were strongest.'[11] The largest of these Catholic groups, the Confederación Nacional de Campesinos (CNCA) had been founded in the Castille–León area in 1917, claimed a membership of 600,000 by 1920,[12] and, according to Robinson, had within it by the end of 1935 some 200,000 families, or about a million people all told in 39 different provinces. There were, in addition, at least two smaller Catholic peasant groups.[13]

In Catalonia, the Catalan Left Party was particularly strong in the rural areas, through its alliance with the Unión de Rabassaires. In the three Basque provinces, the rural population tended generally to be aligned with the Basque Nationalist Party. In Asturias, they supported the Republican parties.

At the time of the outbreak of the War, the Communists had little or no organized following in rural Spain. However, during the War, the Stalinists recruited extensively among the peasants, notably among those who had formerly been aligned with the Right, and within a few months of the outbreak to the War, they constituted a major opponent of the anarchists among the rural population.

There were four regions of Spain in which the CNT's rural following was probably most extensive before the outbreak of the War: Aragón, the Levante, Andalusia and Galicia. Unfortunately for the anarchists, the Franco troops overran virtually all of Galicia and much of Andalusia during the first weeks of the War, resulting in the death, imprisonment or flight of virtually all of the active anarchists in those parts of the country.

In Aragón, the anarchists were able, during the first year of the War, to carry out their most extensive rural experiments with the establishment of libertarian communism. Many of these collectives were crushed in August 1937 by Communist-controlled troops sent in to liquidate them, and those which had survived the Communist assault were destroyed when Franco's troops conquered the region in March 1938.

In the Levante, the rural organization of the CNT was perhaps more highly developed than in any other part of Loyalist Spain during the War, and the anarchists themselves regarded it as the most successful experience with rural collectivization that they had anywhere in the country. Most of the collectives there, as well as their regional federation, continued to exist until the final collapse of the Republic in March 1939.

In two regions, which remained under Republican control during most of the War, the anarchists' rural strength had been relatively limited when the conflict began. In Catalonia, in spite of the CNT's strength in the cities, the anarchists continued to be a minority element in the rural areas, although they were able to establish a substantial number of agrarian collectives in the region during the

War. In contrast to Catalonia, in rural New Castille, where the CNT had been almost non-existent before the outbreak of the War, it grew rapidly during the first months, and a relatively large number of rural collectives were established in the region, where many of the Socialist rural unions were also involved in the collectivist movement.

The Socialist-controlled Unión General de Trabajadores had long had extensive organization among the country's rural wage earners and even among small proprietors. According to Walther Bernecker, as early as 1919 about a third of the members of the UGT were agricultural workers, and he has claimed: 'From 1932 – until the civil war – the UGT was the strongest union of Spain, the mass of its members since 1919 having been fundamentally agricultural workers, while the CNT was converting itself increasingly into the representative of the interests of the industrial workers, basically in Catalonia.'

In 1930 the UGT had organized the Federación Nacional de Trabajadores de la Tierra (sometimes also referred to as Federación Española de Trabajadores de la Tierra) which, according to Bernecker, had 400,000 members by 1932.[14] It was particularly strong in New Castille, Extremadura and western Andalusia.[15]

During the Civil War, the Federación Nacional de Trabajadores de la Tierra continued to be controlled largely by the Left-wing Socialist followers of Francisco Largo Caballero. Like the CNT, they were interested in organizing agrarian collectives, although they perhaps put more emphasis on their being voluntary than did the CNT.[16] As a consequence, in most of Republican Spain, particularly in the areas of New Castille an the Levante, the UGT agricultural workers' organizations generally worked more or less closely with those of the CNT. In quite a few cases, joint collectives were formed by members of the two organizations. The one exception to this was in Catalonia where, throughout the War, the UGT was dominated by the Communists of the Partido Socialista Unificado de Catalanya, and became the haven for those opponents of agrarian collectivization who were not already in the Unión de Rabassaires.

In so far as the peasant group which, before the War, had been aligned with the Right, was concerned, their wartime trajectory in various parts of the country depended on which side was victorious in a given area at the onset of the conflict. In Navarre, it would seem that the influence of the Carlists among the peasantry was not diminished, and they contributed many recruits to the Carlist militia of General Mola's army, which controlled the region from the beginning. On the other hand, the Basque peasants continued to support the Basque Nationalist Party, which led the Republican forces in that region. Finally, in the Levante region, the peasant groups formerly associated with the Right-wing Autonomist Party of that area were quickly taken under the wing of the Communist Party, and formed the bulk of the membership of the peasant federations established there by the Stalinists.

The Communists, who had no peasant groups under their control at the beginning of the War, were able within a few months to establish peasant federations in the provinces of Valencia, Alicante, Castellón, Almería, Teruel and Madrid. By all odds, that in Valencia was the largest of these groups, having absorbed more or less entirely the Catholic-influenced agrarian *sindicatos* hitherto associated with the Partido Autonomista. At the beginning of 1938, agreements were made to merge the Communist-controlled federations in Valencia, Alicante and Madrid with their counterparts of the Federación Nacional de Trabajadores de la Tirre of the UGT.[17] However, it is not clear to what degree such mergers in fact were achieved.

The Federación Nacional Campesina

At the start of the Civil War, the CNT had few peasant organizations above the local level. Very quickly, after the beginning of the War/Revolution, federations of local collectives and agrarian *sindicatos* were established on the *comarcal* (equivalent to a US county) level. During the first few months of the War, regional federations were also established in Catalonia, Aragón, the center (New Castille), and Andalusia and Extremadura (in a single organization).

However, it was June 1937 before a national organization to bring together all of the CNT rural groups was established. Between June 12–14 there met, at the CNT headquarters in Valencia, the National Plenum of Regional Peasant Organizations, with representation of all of the by then existing CNT regional peasant organizations. The meeting, which was attended by Mariano Vázquez, the secretary of the CNT National Committee, 'dealt with the important matters which affect the peasant collectives which are increasing every day; there were given reports of exceptional interest, and there were approved the Statutes of the Federación Nacional Campesina (CNT), which were proposed by a committee composed of Comrade Cardona Rosell, representing the NC of the CNT, and a delegate of each of the regional organizations attending the Plenum.'[18]

This lengthy 35-article resolution establishing the FNC falls logically into two sections. One deals with what might be called the 'bureaucratic structure' of the new organization, the other with the way in which it foresaw the reorganization of all of that part of the rural economy of Loyalist Spain which was under the control of elements of the CNT. Both sections represent substantial innovations in traditional Spanish anarchist philosophy and procedure.

The bureaucratic part of the statutes provided that a plenum or congress of the organization would be held regularly each year, or extraordinarily on the initiative of the FNC National Secretariat, two of the regional federations, or the National Committee of the CNT. Article 14 provided that the decisions of plenums and congresses were 'obligatory for all its components'.

In between such meetings, the organization was to be led by the National Secretariat, consisting of a secretary chosen by a plenum or congress and representatives from each of the regional federations. Various specialized committees to deal with particular agricultural and related problems were to be established by, and be subordinate to, the National Secretariat. The regional federations were to establish similar bodies, and if they or the National Secretariat decided, counterparts were to be set up on a *comarcal* or local level as well.

The statutes sketched the subordination of the FNC to the CNT and of constituent parts of the FNC to its leading body. Article 3 provided: 'The Federación Nacional Campesina is part of the Confederación Nacional del Trabajo, of which it is the trade union and economic organ of the peasants affiliated with it, and is therefore obliged to fulfill the accords of the CNT,' while Article 35 stated that the FNC could not be dissolved without the approval of a national congress of the CNT. To complement this, Article 9 said: 'The official representation of the Federación Nacional Campesina and the execution of its national accords and the application of the present Statutes, correspond to its National Secretariat, which has the functions appropriate to any Committee or National Council of a National Federation of Industry.'

The FNC was to be financed, according to Articles 22 and 23 from '1.) Proceeds from the participation of the Federation in the trade union dues collected from members by the *sindicatos* which make up the regional federations. 2.) Proceeds from the agrarian economy associated with the organisms adhering to the Federación Nacional Campesina.' The dues share going to the FNC 'will be freely determined by the National Secretariat of the Federación Nacional Campesina, based on proposals of the Regional Federations ... but never can exceed one-third of the dues paid by their members to the respective unions.'

Under the heading General Dispositions, Article 33 provided, 'The interpretation of doubts that might arise concerning the application of the present Statutes shall fall to the National Secretariat,' while Article 34, 'cases unforeseen in these Statutes' would be resolved either by a Plenum or congress of the FNC or 'by agreement of the National Secretariat' of the federation, 'submitted for amendment and approval of the National Committee' of the CNT. It added that 'only when this approval has been formally contained can the case be considered resolved.'

The more purely economic parts of the statutes indicated the intention of the founders of the FNC to bring under its supervision and control virtually all aspects of the activities of the collectives affiliated with it as well as those of the small proprietors who belonged to the CNT. It established a framework for FNC control of the land use, disposal of surpluses, purchases of inputs and consumers goods, and provision of insurance for that segment of national agriculture controlled by CNT-affiliated peasants.

Thus, Article 26 provided:

Both the peasant collective and the small peasant proprietor or individual cultivator belonging to the Federación Nacional

Campesina shall have complete freedom of initiative and execution for agricultural development of the terrain they occupy; but they will be subordinated to the national agreements of the Federación Nacional Campesina and its National Secretariat, insofar as obtaining a better return from cultivation, propagation and appearance of pests in the countryside, and transformation or substitution of those crops which it is not convenient to continue because of insufficient value, for the purpose of guaranteeing the peasant workers a better level of living.

In conformity with this, the same groups and individuals 'will be obligated to provide the Federación Nacional Campesina whatever data is asked for with regard to existing and predictable production, as well as those of any other type that are necessary for the Federation, with regard to the progress of individual and collective cultivation.'

On the other hand, this same article provided that 'the collective entities of individuals ... will recognize the Federación Nacional Campesina as the only organ of distribution of output, and exportation in such cases as export is necessary.'

Although recognizing the right of collectives and CNT individual cultivators 'to separate from their own production the amount they esteem necessary for their own consumption', there is none the less recognition of the objective of obtaining 'an equitable distribution of the products obtained by the agrarian economy so as to assure an equal right to all consumers in the social body, in the widest sense of the word.' In view of this, the FNC members 'accept restrictions which at any moment are necessary to assure the peasant his equal right of consumption'. Such restrictions will only be obligatory on the peasants when 'expressly agreed to by the Secretariat of the Federación Nacional Campesina'.

All excess production will be turned over to the FNC, through the regional federations, and the FNC 'will pay the corresponding value, this value being that prevalent in the producing locality or which will be determined by a single national organism which regulates prices, constituted totally by the Federación Nacional Campesina or with strong representation on it and accepted by its National Secretatiat.'

On the other hand, the FNC affiliates will get from the national federation through the regional ones, 'articles of all kinds needed for developing their agricultural activities and also for the provisioning of consumer cooperatives, communal distribution warehouses...' The FNC will provide these 'at the same prices for which they were obtained, with only addition of costs of transport and administration...'

It was also provided that the FNC would organize *cajas de compensación* to act 'as offices of collection, payment and exchange'. It would also, in conjunction with its regional affiliates, 'provide compensation for disasters and losses from accidents, fires, insect invasions, etc. and also to establish solidarity and mutual support to cover risks of illness, old age, orphanhood of the peasant workers and their family members who do not belong to the collectives, since in these things it is unnecessary that they remain unprotected.'[19]

According to Walther Bernecker:

> The principles of the FNC were in open contradiction with some basic anarchist postulates. The obligatory character of the accords of the federation for its individual affiliates, *sindicatos* or collectives was difficult to see as compatible with the model of taking decisions from the bottom up which had always been advocated by the CNT...[20]
>
> The CNT had to recognize that its idealistic notions of a self-regulated economy capable of satisfying the needs of all individuals had not achieved real existence in the conditions of civil war. The change of concepts between the Congress of Zaragoza ... and the assembly of Valencia ... signalled a continuous evolution from the utopia of an economic and social order based on workers' councils and free from domination, to the reality of an economy subject to state intervention and a hierarchically structured society.[21]

The FNC made only modest progress towards establishing the kind of restructured agricultural economy foreseen in its statutes. For one thing, within two months, its regional affiliate in Aragón was largely dismantled by Communist soldiers, as were many of the collectives and *sindicatos* there. Although there is some indication that the FNC may have had some role in facilitating exchanges of products between its regional federations in the Levante and the center, it certainly never achieved the kind of integrated structure orienting production and handling exchange, credit and insurance for at least the CNT-dominated part of agriculture, which had been aspired to by its founders.

One of the projects it undertook was the establishment of a number of agricultural schools which, in addition to giving basic general education, would give extensive specific training in the widest range of agricultural subjects. Included in the plans was the ultimate establishment of an agricultural university. Little information is available on the degree to which the FNC was able to begin to put this programme into effect, which was only developed at the end of 1937.[22]

Another National Plenum of Peasant Regional Organizations of the CNT met at the end of October 1937. Its major decision was to merge the Federación Nacional de Campesinos with the Federación Nacional de Alimentación (food workers), to establish the Federación Nacional de Campesinos y de las Industrias de la Alimentación. The new federation consisted of eleven subsections including those of agriculture, milling, sugar production, viniculture, food production in general, restaurants and bars, grazing, forest products, vegetable oils, trees and plants, and 'various industries'.[23]

Agrarian Reform Before the Civil War

Certainly one of the factors lying behind the massive outburst of rural collectivization, largely (although by no means exclusively) under anarchist leadership which took place during the Civil War, was a history of the peasants' long-time frustration with agrarian reform. This frustration had been particularly acute during the Second Spanish Republic (April 14 1931–July 18 1936).

When a Left Republican–Socialist government came to power soon after the overthrow of the monarchy, one of its promises was that there would be a major agrarian reform. However, during the two-year existence of the government of Prime Minister Manuel Azaña, only the most tentative steps had been taken in that direction.

There was a rather protracted debate in parliament over the nature of the proposed reform. The Left Republicans favored granting expropriated land to individual peasant proprietors, the Socialists favored granting it to groups of peasants organized in collectives.[24] The revolt of General Sanjurjo against the Republic in August 1932 served to hasten the passage of the agrarian reform bill and, as a result of the insurrection, two groups were added whose land was to be taken without compensation. These were all those who supported Sanjurjo's coup, and the grandees of Spain. The grandees consisted of a group of 70 to 80 large landholders, whose particularly privileged position may perhaps have dated from the period of the Reconquista. They were the most elite of the Spanish aristocracy.[25]

The Agrarian Statute which was finally passed in September 1932 provided for the establishment of the Institute of Agrarian Reform (IRA). It was to be assured an annual appropriation of at least 50 million pesetas, and was to establish a National Agrarian Bank to lend money at cheap interest rates to beneficiaries of the agrarian reform.[26] Gerald Brenan noted that all estates over 56 acres not worked by their owners were subject to expropriation, with compensation determined by what the landowners had declared their land to be worth for tax purposes – assuring them compensation at less than the market rate.

According to Brenan, 'One should observe that the Agrarian Statute applied only to the center and south – to that part of the country where large estates are common... Nothing was done to assist the innumerable families in the north who had too little land or to convert the variable and usually excessive rents of Castille into a fixed amount.'[27]

However, the major weakness of the Agrarian Statute during the Left Republican–Socialist period, was its limited application. Although in some areas, as in the Toledo region, a modest start was made with grandees' land for which no compensation at all had to be paid, the authorities there tended to make such grants as they carried out to individual peasants. The man who was in charge of the IRA in the Toledo area in 1932–3 said, many years later, that in dividing the land he tried always to give most of a grant to those who already had a little land, on the grounds that they had shown initiative and intelligence enough to handle land, and to intersperse with these people some who had never had any land.[28]

Nevertheless, only the modest start had been made in the agrarian reform by the time the Azaña government was ousted soon after the middle of 1933. Walther Bernecker has noted: '...the Azaña government, particularly the minister of Agriculture, Domingo, showed after ratification of the law, manifest disinterest in its execution ... Azaña and Domingo refused to adopt, in the fulfillment of a law revolutionary in its consequences, measures equally revolutionary, postponing necessary steps...'[29] According to the Institute of Agrarian Reform, by August 1934 only 9,916 families had received land under the law.[30]

The Communists' history of the Civil War put the number of peasants who had benefited from the agrarian reform during the first (Left Republican–Socialist) phase of the Republic at 12,260.[31] Whatever the correct figure, it is clear that the process of land redistribution had barely gotten started in that period.

Gerald Brenan has noted the long-term political consequences of the failure of the Azaña administration to carry out a vigorous agrarian reform. '...One may say that the Republican parties lost a great opportunity, not only of curing some of the crying abuses of the countryside, but of gaining adherence for themselves, and strengthening the regime.' He cited as confirmation of this an article in the anarchist daily *Solidaridad Obrera* to the effect that 'had the Republicans at once expropriated without indemnity all of the large estates, as happened in the French Revolution, the bourgeois republic would have lasted many years. The workers, even the Anarchists, would have tolerated it.'[32]

Needless to say, the Right-wing governments of the 1933–6 period not only went no further with agrarian reform but largely undid what had been done in the previous years. It was not until the election of the Popular Front government in February 1936 that the subject of agrarian reform would again come up for serious discussion.[33]

Perhaps even more depressing and infuriating for many of the

Spanish peasants than failure to bring about an agrarian reform during their period in power was the Left Republicans' and Socialists' seeming unwillingness or inability to bring about relaxation of the exceedingly oppressive social and political conditions which existed in much of rural Spain, particularly in the south. The Azaña government, like its predecessors, ordered out the Civil Guard to crush even a hint of resistance or revolt on the part of the peasants.

One such incident, in the Andalusian village of Casas Viejas, where the Civil Guard set fire to the house of a local CNT leader, burning him and several members of his family to death, and shooting down those people who tried to escape from their inferno, created a major scandal. It was used in parliament to widely discredit the Azaña government, and was a major reason for the anarchists abstaining from the 1933 election.[34]

After the February 1936 election which gave victory to the Popular Front, the agrarian reform process got under way once again in a much more intense fashion. This much more rapid application of the 1932 law was in considerable degree provoked by widespread seizures of land by peasants, whose actions were in many cases merely legalized by the Institute of Agrarian Reform. Such seizures were particularly widespread in New Castille, Andalusia and Extremadura.

The Republican Government's Agrarian Reform Measures During Civil War

From September 4 1936, when the first Largo Caballero government took office, until virtually the end of the Civil War, the minister of agriculture was Vicente Uribe, a member of the Politburo of the Spanish Communist Party. In administering that post, he clearly carried out the policies of the Communist Party, although these also enjoyed the backing of at least substantial elements in the middle-class Republican parties and the Right-wing Socialists.

The Stalinist position throughout the War was one of strong, and even violent, opposition to the agrarian collectives organized by the anarchists and Left-wing Socialists of the UGT. Although this stand might, *a priori*, appear paradoxical in the light of the fact that only half a decade before Stalin had forced virtually all Soviet peasants into collective farms, it is understandable in terms of the general political situation in which the Communists found themselves during the Civil War.

Starting out as a small, although tightly organized and highly disciplined, element among the forces supporting the Republic, and faced with the fact that the Spanish working class was (at least at the beginning of the War) already almost totally mobilized in the anarchist CNT or the then Left–Socialist UGT, the Communists sought to recruit rapidly among those who opposed, or were greatly disturbed by, the revolutionary changes which had taken place in most of Loyalist Spain where the Rebels had been defeated. Among those groups were a largest part of the landholding peasantry and those renters and sharecroppers who aspired to become individual landowners.

One of the major revolutionary changes which took place right after July 19 was the seizure of larger landholdings, particularly those belonging to supporters of, or sympathizers with, Franco, by small peasants, tenants, sharecroppers and agricultural laborers. This was done more or less spontaneously, without waiting for authorization from governmental authorities who, in the first days and weeks of the Civil War, virtually disappeared from the scene in any case. Along with these land seizures went the beginning of the process of setting up agrarian collectives, both by the anarchists of the CNT and a substantial proportion of Socialist-influenced peasants of the UGT.

One of the first steps taken by Vicente Uribe as minister of agriculture was to put into place his party's agrarian policy the decree of the Republican government of October 7 1936, which legalized the seizing for the State of all land, 'becoming on July 18 to natural persons or their spouses or to legal persons that have intervened directly or indirectly in the insurrectional movement against the Republic.'[35] However, José Peirats has claimed that the decree recognized the right of heirs of those from whom property was seized to eventually recover it.[36]

According to Burnett Bolloten, 'under the terms of the decree, the estates that had been cultivated directly by the owners or by their stewards or had been leased to large tenant farmers were given in perpetual usufruct to organizations of peasants and agricultural workers to be cultivated individually or collectively in accordance with the wishes of the majority of beneficiaries. Small cultivators who had leased estates were promised the permanent use of their holdings, not to exceed 30 hectares in dry sections, five in irrigated districts, and three in fruit-growing areas...'[37]

However, according to Aurora Bosch Sánchez, 'Although this decree explicitly supported the old renters, sharecroppers, and small landholders, it had an ambiguous, or even contrary, position regarding those lands which, not belonging to people involved in the military insurrection, had been seized and collectivized by the *sindicatos*. In this situation, the rural proletariat and the unions were clearly at a disadvantage with regard to the landholders and renters...'[38]

Walther Bernecker has noted: 'V. Uribe submitted the agrarian collectives to a complicated procedure for legalization, with the proviso that if this was not conformed to, the collective could be dissolved and its lands returned to their former owners.' He added: 'The decree of nationalization was designed in the first place to control the collectives and to put a brake on their further diffusion; when it was promulgated, the self-organization of the peasants was already a consummated fact in wide zones of republican territory.'[39]

However, the Communists pictured the October 7 1936 decree as the emancipation of the peasantry. Their publication *Frente Rojo* claimed: '[It] is the most profoundly revolutionary measure that has been taken since the military uprising... It has abolished more than 40 percent of private property in the countryside.'

Another Communist paper, *Mundo Obrero*, asserted: 'This decree breaks the foundation of the semifeudal power of the big landlords who, in order to maintain their brutal caste privileges and to perpetuate salaries of two pesetas a day and labor from dawn to dusk, have unleashed the bloody war that is devastating Spain.'[40]

Similarly, José Duque, head of the Communist Party in Aragón, wrote: 'The Government of the Republic had issued an important agricultural decree which, practically, represented the carrying of the

Agrarian Reform to its ultimate consequences, giving the land of the large landholders and of all who had participated in the uprising, to the peasants and agricultural workers, to work the land in usufruct and above all, in accordance with wishes and desires of the peasants themselves, insofar as which system of cultivation to employ.' Significantly, he added that this was 'a measure the political consequences of which served the Communists in their simple purpose of ending the confusion and desperation sown,' according to him, by the anarchist-controlled Consejo de Aragón.[41]

However, neither the Socialist nor anarchist peasant leaders took the Communists' view of the October 7 decree. Ricardo Zabalza, general secretary of the UGT's peasant federation, commented: 'We have read such things as this: "Thanks to the decree of 7 October, a measure of a Communist minister, the peasants have the land today." Such statements no doubt make very effective propaganda among the ignorant, but they cannot convince anyone who is half-acquainted with the facts... Before any Communist minister was in the government, the peasant organizations on instructions from our federation had already confiscated de facto all the land belonging to the rebels.'

For its part, the anarchists' daily *CNT*, commented:

The minister of agriculture has just promulgated a decree confiscating in favor of the state all rural properties whose owners intervened directly or indirectly in the fascist insurrection of 19 July. As usual, of course, the state arrives late. The peasants did not wait for such a vital problem to be settled by decree; they acted in advance of the government, and from the very beginning ... they seized the property of the landowners, making the revolution from below... They expropriated without making any distinction between owners who had intervened and owners who had not intervened in the rebel conspiracy... The expropriation, as a punishment, only of those who have intervened directly or have helped the fascists, leaves the supreme problem of the Spanish Revolution unsolved.

Finally, Rafael Morayta Núñez, who served at the beginning of the

Civil War as head of the Institute of Agrarian Reform, wrote after the War: 'I can state positively, and this everyone knows, that it was not the government that handed the land to the peasants. The latter did not wait for a government decision, but appropriated the estates and cultivable lands themselves... Hence, the much-vaunted decree of 7 October, which a certain political party practically claims to be exclusively its own creation, did not give those estates to the peasants, or to anyone else...'[42]

Whatever the differing perspectives of the Communists on the one hand, and the Socialist and anarchist peasant leaders on the other, were the legal application of the October 7 decree moved slowly. Dr Bosch Sánchez has observed that the attitude of many peasants and their *sindicatos* was, therefore, to 'remain apart from legality and governmental disposition'. As a consequence, she says, 'In the Spring of 1937, the Ministry of Agriculture had not achieved many of its objectives of 1936, since a great part of the republican agricultural wealth still remained under trade union control.'[43]

Gaston Leval has noted the violent propaganda campaign carried out by Uribe before and after the October 7 decree: 'During months he gave speeches carried by the radio, inciting the peasants not to enter the collectives, calling on the small proprietors to combat them. He always spoke as minister, so that the conservatives and reactionaries of the countryside felt support by the government in their instinctive resistance of in their conscious sabotage...'[44]

However, during the spring of 1937, Communist-controlled police, military units and other groups began many physical attacks on collectives in Catalonia, the Levante, Castille, and these were even beginning in Aragón. The confusion and disorganization which these events caused in the Loyalist countryside threatened seriously to endanger the forthcoming harvest. This fact gave rise to the second major decree issued by Minister of Agriculture Vicente Uribe, by then a member of the government of Juan Negrín.

This measure was the so-called Law of Temporary Legalization of Agricultural Collectives of June 1937, the avowed objective of which was for the collectives 'to carry out as well and as rapidly as possible, the agricultural harvests appropriate to this time'.[45] It 'temporarily' gave legal recognition to all collectives 'for the present agricultural cycle'. According to Dr Aurora Bosch Sánchez, 'In addition to trying to save the harvest, this decree implicitly recognized the economic importance of the *sindicatos* and collectives as a group in the republican economy, and so tried to ameliorate the governmental abandonment and marginalization which the decree of October 7, 1936 had imposed on collectives and landless laborers vis-à-vis the small proprietors and former renters.'[46]

Of course, the ministry of agriculture's June 1937 decree protected CNT collectives only marginally from the violent attacks on them by Communist troops, police and other groups. Indeed, only two months later, Communist-led troops of Lieutenant-Colonel Lister's 11th Division invaded Aragón, and together with the Karl Marx Division and the Left Catalan 30th Division, pillaged and broke up many of the collectives there. Also, once the crop had been taken in, anarchist and other collectives were again subject to violent Communist attacks in several other parts of the country.

In so far as the anarchists themselves were concerned, the idea of accepting legalization of their agrarian collectives by the Republican government was very much contrary to their traditional ideas and philosophy. However, after the July 1937 decree, the CNT apparently accepted the idea, and several hundred anarchist collectives were in fact legalized by the ministry of agriculture. In at least a few cases, such recognition helped some collectives to defend themselves against attempts to destroy them. Also, a significant number of collectives in addition received financial credits from the ministry's Servicio Nacional de Credito Agricola. Among others, Mariano Vázquez, national secretary of the CNT, urged them to seek such credits.[47]

Burnett Bolloten has cited a Communist source which indicated that between the October 7 1936 decree and June 1937 the Ministry of Agriculture's Agrarian Reform Institute had extended 50 million pesetas in 'credits, farm implements, seeds and fertilizers'. However, he added that 'this assistance must have gone solely to collectives that accepted the intervention of the institute; for the CNT, which rejected state intervention because it threatened the autonomy of its collectives, charged that the latter were denied all help from the minister of agriculture.' He added: 'Moreover, although, according to Cardona Rosell, it extended very substantial credits to collective farms that applied for assistance, some CNT collectives did not take advantage of it for a long time owing to their suspicion of official bodies and the fear that these might curb their independence.'[48]

The Communist Minister of Agriculture's Return of Land to Landowners

Although the ministry of agriculture under Vicente Uribe extended credit to some rural collectives, it also undertook to return land to landholders whose property had been included in collectives, whether on a voluntary basis or otherwise, Burnett Bolloten has said of the Communist Party: 'Seeking support among the propertied classes in the anti-Franco camp, it could not afford to repel the small and medium proprietors who had been hostile to the working-class movement before the Civil War, and, indeed, through the Ministry of Agriculture and the Institute of Agrarian Reform, which it controlled, it seconded, on the basis of the limitations of the decree of 7 October, many of their demands for the restitution of their land.'

Bolloten quoted a leader of the Libertarian Youth in the Castille region on the subject, who commented:

> I can tell you about the Castillian countryside because I am in daily contact with all the agricultural districts of Castille, districts to which the delegates of the Ministry of Agriculture go ... with the object of returning to the bourgeoisie, to the fascists, to the landowners, the property they once possessed. The minister of agriculture claims that these are small proprietors. Small proprietors, with a splendid number of acres! Are the political bosses of the villages and those who used to conspire against the workers small proprietors? Are those who have twenty or twenty-five workers and three or four pairs of bullocks small proprietors? I must ask where the policy of the minister of agriculture is leading and just what is the limit to the term 'small proprietor? ...'[49]

Encouraged by the support they received from the Communists, many right-wing tenant farmers and sharecroppers who had accepted collectivization in the first months of the Revolution demanded the return of their former parcels.

Bolloten cites Ricardo Zabala, head of the UGT agricultural workers' federation:

Our most fervent aim today is to guarantee the conquests of the Revolution, especially the collective farms that were organized by the different branches of our federation and against which a world of enemies is rising up, namely, the reactionaries of yesterday and those who held land on lease because they were lackeys of the political bosses, whereas our members were either denied land or evicted from their wretched holdings. Today these reactionaries protected by the famous decree of 7 October, and enjoying unheard-of official aid, are endeavoring to take by assault the collectivized estates with the object of dividing them up, distributing their livestock, their olive trees, their vineyards, and their harvests, and of putting an end to the agrarian revolution...'[50]

The Way Collectives Were Formed

Certainly there was variation in the manner in which rural collectives were formed in the first days and weeks of the Civil War/Revolution. However, Burnett Bolloten has sketched the general manner in which this took place:

A CNT–FAI committee was set up in each locality where the new regime was instituted. This committee not only exercised legislative and executive powers, but also administered justice. One of the first acts was to abolish private trade and to collectivize the soil of the rich, and often that of the poor, as well as farm buildings, machinery, livestock, and transport. Except in rare cases, barbers, bakers, carpenters, sandalmakers, doctors, dentists, teachers, blacksmiths, and tailors also came under the collective system. Stocks of food and clothing and other necessities were concentrated in a communal depot under the control of the local committee, and the church, if not rendered useless by fire, was converted into a storehouse, dining hall, café, workshop, school, garage or barracks...[51]

The Number of Agrarian Collectives

There are no definitive figures available of the number of agrarian collectives established in Republican Spain during the Civil War, or of the number of peasants and other people associated with them. Gaston Leval, who was one of those people who studied the phenomenon most extensively while it was in progress, has merely noted: 'We lack an exact figure on the number of collectives created in all of Spain. Basing myself on the incomplete statistics of the congress of February in Aragón, and data I collected during my long sojourn in the area, I can affirm that there were at least 400. There were 500 in the Levante in 1938. One must add the others in other regions.'[52]

Walther Bernecker, writing much later, and with information available to him which Leval apparently did not have, has said: 'In August 1938, according to the data of the Institute of Agrarian Reform, there were 2,213 legalized collectives, given that Aragón and Catalonia and the Levante are not reflected in these statistics, the absolute number of collectives must be supposed to have been much higher; according to current data of the Spanish anarchists, there were in Aragón, Catalonia and the Levante, 2,700 collectives, and in New Castille, 340. According to all of these data some three million people took part in these experiments with a collectivized economy in Republican Spain.'[53]

Bernecker went on to assess the significance for all of Republican agriculture of the three million people who were in collectives: 'Supposing an agrarian population of some 17 millions – which represents a probably low estimate – the 3 million who took part in collectivist experiments is the equivalent of approximately 18 percent of the total Spanish agrarian population. If one takes account of the fact that by the end of 1936 a large part of the predominantly agrarian regions of Galicia, Old Castille, Andalusia and parts of Extremadura had been occupied by the "nationalists", the percent of collec tivists rises considerable in the Republican zone...'[54]

Finally, Edward E. Malefakis estimated that about one-third of all the rural land in Republican Spain, and two-thirds of the cultivated land, was taken over by the collectives.[55] Clearly, the establishment of rural collectives was one of the major events transpiring during the Spanish Civil War and Revolution.

There were some parts of Loyalist Spain in which there were virtually no rural collectives established. This was particularly the case in the three northern regions which during the first year or more remained part of the Republic, that is, the Basque provinces, Santander and Asturias.

In the Basque regions, the anarchists had virtually no influence in the rural areas. The peasants tended to be aligned with the Basque Nationalist Party, which was strongly Catholic, and was not in favor of social revolution, whether in the urban or the rural sector. Furthermore, the landholding pattern of that area tended to be one of small and medium-sized enterprises, rather than large estates.

The land ownership system in Asturias was somewhat similar. In spite of the fact that anarchist influence in the region was quite substantial, particularly during the Civil War, rural collectives were rare. Ramón Alvarez, a CNT leader in Asturias during the conflict, has written: 'There were not peasant collectives properly speaking, during the Civil War. There were not, in our region, large cultivable extensions of land; they are all small proprietorships or farmers or grazers with rented land, which explains very well the fact that there were no great social changes in agriculture. The CNT created a Regional Peasant Federation, which initiated studies both on the property and labor situations in the countryside, as well as the adequacy of cultivation, kinds of fertilizers most advisable and a multitude of other aspects of Asturias agriculture.'[56]

The Common Problems of the Agrarian Collectives

There was wide diversity among the anarchists' agrarian collectives.

However, there were certain problems which were common to almost all of them. Some of these questions arose from the nature of anarchist philosophy, others from the practical day-to-day experience of trying to run an agricultural enterprise, still more from the question of the relationships of the agrarian collectives with the world around them, and finally, the War itself presented serious problems.

One issue which faced every collective as soon as it was established was that of deciding what kind of rule it was going to live by. In the great majority of cases, the local groups adopted statutes setting forth how they were to be structured, and how they were to function. However, there were cases such as the Ballobar collective in Aragón in which 'on principle', they would not adopt any written statutes.[57] The various regional federations sought to get their member collectives to adopt a more or less uniform set of statutes.

Another problem common to all of the collectives concerned their relationships with 'individualists', that is, those peasants, artisans and others who did not want to join the collective. There was considerable diversity on this issue. Some collectives established libertarian communism, in which all members of the community belonged to the collective; others set forth the conditions under which people could stay out, and what their relationship to the collective would be – in terms of disposition of their output, access to the cooperative store or common warehouse, even use of implements and machines belonging to the collective.

Burnett Bolloten has argued with respect to the individualist peasants and collectivization: 'There can be no doubt that an incomparably larger number doggedly opposed it or accepted it only under extreme duress. The aversion to rural collectivization on the part of smallholders and tenant farmers was on occasion conceded by the anarcho-syndicalists, although they sometimes claimed that they had overcome it.'[59] In what follows, we shall see that the situation with regard to the smallholders differed considerably from one part of the country to another, and from one collective to another.

Internal organization of the collectives also varied a good deal. However, in all of them, the general assembly of members was sovereign. It met weekly, fortnightly or monthly. Virtually all had some kind of administrative committee, but usually its members served at the pleasure of the general assembly, had little or no power to discipline the collective's members and, in most cases, the members of the administrative committee worked as regular members of the collective, conducting the committee's work after the regular work day was completed.

One thing the statutes had to spell out was the conditions for acceptance of new members, once a collective was under way. According to José Peirats, 'At first one entered the collectives without formalities. In other cases, the collectivist aspirant had to turn over to the collectives all of his goods: land, tools, working animals. Everything turned over was registered and given a value. In case of leaving the Collective the one involved was given back what he had contributed or the equivalent in pesetas.' However, these rules were far from uniform.

The conditions for being expelled from a collective also had to be spelled out: 'It would seem that there were few cases of expulsion for immorality. Those who violated collective norms were warned first; in the case of a second fault, the matter was presented to the general assembly. Only it would decide upon expulsion after hearing the accused and those accusing...'[59]

The work to be done in the collective was usually carried out by teams or gangs, often self-chosen, who did particular tasks. These units had elected delegates, who most frequently would meet in the evening – sometimes jointly with the administrative committee – to plan the next day's work.

There was wide divergence in so far as methods of distribution of the output of the collective – and other things brought in from the outside – was concerned. Almost always there was some kind of community warehouse or warehouses from which such things would be dispensed, although there were some collectives which still had some private stores in their midst. There might also be common-service establishments, such as barber shops, although in this case, too, there was no uniformity.

The great majority of the agrarian collectives undoubtedly adopted the principle of 'from each according to his ability, to each according to his need'. Each family was assigned its share in accordance with its number of members. But, again, there was great variety in the way in which this principle was applied.

Reflecting a widespread anarchist belief that money was one of the major roots of the evil of the capitalist system, a large number – probably a majority – of the collectives aboLished the circulation of legal tender money within their confines. Of course, even most of those which took this step had to make the Republic's currency available to those of their number who for one reason or another went outside of the collective.

There was much variation in what the collectives substituted for money. There were some which experimented with merely allowing the families belonging to the collective to take out of the common storehouse what they needed, without further ado. However, even in such cases, it was often necessary to establish a ration system for goods which were in short supply, particularly those coming from outside the community. In some cases, a general ration system was established, where every family was allotted a given amount of every product depending on the number of members it had – even in these cases there was sometimes provision for a family's exchanging part of its ration of one product for more of another one.

Perhaps in the largest number of cases in which the collective suppressed the circulation of regular money within their bounds, there was substitution of something else of local manufacture which served much the same purpose of money. Usually printed, such instruments were called 'bonds' or 'tokens', or were given some other name, rather than 'money'. From the anarchist point of view, they had the virtue that they were only expendable within the collective, and so discouraged saving, which might before very long have engendered differences in wealth among the members of the group.

All of the collectives had to develop some system for disposing of their surpluses and acquiring things from the outside which they needed. In the early months, the most usual system seems to have been direct exchange or barter by individual collectives with each other, with worker-controlled industries in neighboring cities, or with other institutions. Soon, however, there developed *comarcal*, provincial and regional federations of collectives which undertook this process in a more organized and centralized fashion. As we have seen earlier in this chapter, the avowed purpose of the Federación Nacional Campesina was that it became the overall agency through which such exchanges would be handled, although it had only the most minimal success in bringing that about.

These federations served other purposes. They helped to make somewhat more uniform the situation among the various collectives, in terms of accounting methods, standardized statutes and training facilities for those administering the collectives. They also sought to foster solidarity among the collectives, by getting the richer ones to contribute funds and even commodities to those collectives that were less well off; there was always a danger of the development of 'neo-capitalism', in which individual collectives would become exclusively concerned with their own welfare, to the exclusion of the interests of others.

Most of the collectives showed interest in expanding their productive capacity. This often meant not only bringing hitherto uncultivated land into use, but also extending irrigation and other installations, as well as developing stables, hog pens, chicken coops and other facilities for raising small animals. Not infre quently also, collectives installed (or expanded where they already existed) small agro industries to process the products which they grew.

Most of the collectives were deeply concerned with the establishment or augmentation of educational and social service institutions. There was a remarkable proliferation of schools, which the children of the collectives were required to attend, usually until they were 14 years of age. Much emphasis was placed on ending the exploitation of children by their parents who had customarily sent them to work at a tender age in order to contribute to the family income, something which in the collectives was unnecessary (it was argued) because every family was provided with the goods and services it needed, within the capacity of the community. At least one 'agricultural university' was established, that set up by the Regional Peasant Federation of the Levante.

Other cultural institutions were established. Libraries particularly proliferated. In conformity with anarchist tradition, *ateneos* were established, where those interested would gather to discuss some cultural, economic or political issue which interested them.

Many observers of the anarchist rural collectives were impressed by their morality. Thus, even the Soviet journalist Ilya Ehrenburg commented on the decision of the revolutionary authorities in Barbastro in Aragón to abolish prostitution in the town: ['They] issued a decree in the language of last century. There were among them disciples of Bakunin and Kropotkin. They said that prostitution stained the sun of new humanity and impeded the arrival at universal fraternity.' The authorities also exhorted the population to 'treat these women, recuperated for life, with the greatest respect'.[60]

In quite a few collectives, the local doctors became members, and provided their services to the members of the group without payment other than what they received as members. In other instances, doctors were provided with something more than what other collective members received. In quite a few cases, where local doctors were not available, arrangements were made by the collectives for treatment of their members by hospitals in nearby localities. In a few cases, collectives themselves built hospitals; in many they acquired equipment and other things needed by their local physicians.

Most collectives had a formal retirement age, after which members did not have to work. Some provided special homes for such people. In a number of cases, the old folks, becoming bored, decided to work as much as they could in spite of being formally retired.

One of the major complaints of the collectives was that they lacked requisite skilled manpower. The federations on various levels tried to ameliorate this situation, either by providing people who had the necessary skills, or helping to train local people.

The relations of the collectives with at least two other institutions also were something of concern, and sometimes conflict – these were the local *sindicato* and the municipal government.

Although most of the collectives were organized as a result of direct or indirect inspiration and help from a local CNT agrarian *sindicato*, once a collective was established, the role of the *sindicato* often became uncertain. In some cases, the personnel of the two organizations were the same so, as Gaston Leval noted in the case of the Binefar collective in Aragón, 'the *sindicato* had practically no role.'[61] In others, the *sindicato* continued to serve as a link between the collective and individualist anarchists who did not choose to join the collective. In still others, the *sindicato* assumed a kind of watch-dog role, to assure that the collective remained true to anarchist ideas and ideals.

In most of Republican Spain, with the outbreak of the Civil War, local municipal institutions were superseded by revolutionary committees of one kind or another. Then, early in 1937, the Republican government decreed that regular municipal councils should be re-established; a step which had been taken earlier in Catalonia by the Generalidad.

In many of the small municipalities in which agrarian collectives were located,the revolutionary committee was virtually indistinguishable from the administrativecommittee of the collective. In many others, political elements other than the CNT were given representation in the revolutionary committees, which did not participate in the collective's administrative committee. With the substitution of municipal councils for revolutionary committees, the tendency was for representation of various parties and trade union organizations to be in them in the same proportion as their representation in the Catalan or the Republican government. This was to the disadvantage of the CNT, particularly after it was forced out of both the Catalan regional government and the Republican one.

Gaston Leval has summarized this aspect of the rural collectives: 'The juridical principle of the Collective was completely "new". It was neither "the *sindicato*" nor "the municipality", in the traditional sense of the word, not even the municipality of the Middle Ages. However, it was nearer to the communal spirit than to the trade union spirit. The Collective, which could just as well have been called Community, as was the case in that of Binefar, constituted a whole to which professional and corporative groups, public services, exchange, municipal functions, were subordinate, dependent upon it, although enjoying autonomy in their structure, their internal functioning, and in the application of their particular capacities.[62]

Finally, there were problems facing the agrarian collectives that originated in the Civil War itself. One of these was the recruitment (and subsequently the drafting) of their younger adult male members into the armed forces of the Republic. This resulted frequently in the much more widespread participation than previously of the women of the collectives in farmwork, and the postponement of retirement by older men, even though they were formally entitled to it according to the rule of the collectives.

José Peirats has noted another wartime problem of the collectives which became increasingly serious as Franco's troops advanced: 'As the war entered its more disastrous phase, the communities invaded by the enemy were evacuated to the rear. The Collectives absorbed a large part of those evacuated, showing an admirable spirit of solidarity. In the Spring of 1938, the problem was intensified because of the collapse of the Aragón front. The Aragón collectivists evacuated en masse to Catalonia, taking with them Everything humanly possible; machines, implements, animals, cattle. The Catalan collectives which received them were recompensed many times over ... The agricultural collective of Barcelona received 600 evacuees from the invaded zones. That of Vilabol, a hundred families...'[63]

Sometimes the War presented the collectives with peculiar emergency problems. Gaston Leval has recorded, for instance, the problem facing the collectives in the *comarcal* of Binefar in Aragón in June 1937. The harvest was about to begin, but the collectives there lacked sufficient machinery, implements and gasoline, and to purchase these they needed several hundred thousand pesetas. They were faced with the dilemma of selling goods otherwise destined for the militiamen at the Aragón front to the cities to raise the necessary funds, or risk losing a good part of the harvest. An appeal was finally made for cash contributions on their behalf to the CNT militiamen by *Solidaridad Obrera* in Barcelona. Within days, sufficient money was contributed by the anarchist soldiers to make it possible for the Binefar collectives to get the inputs they needed for the harvest.[64]

Then, of course, the ultimate wartime problem imposed on the collectives was the conquest of the regions in which they were located by the troops of General Franco. Sooner or later, that was the fate of all of the agrarian collectives.

12

Agrarian Collective in Catalonia

For more than half a century before the Spanish Civil War, Catalonia had been one of the two principal centers of anarchist strength – the other being Andalusia. However, in Catalonia, it was the urban workers who were overwhelmingly led by the anarchists, in the Confederación Nacional del Trabajo The CNT had relatively little following among the rural population of the region before July 19 1936.

The basic reason for this was that the great majority of the Catalan rural population was decidedly individualist in its ideas and prejudices. The French anarchist leader Gaston Leval recognized this, claiming that the Catalan peasant was much more like a Frenchman than like an average Spaniard in his individualism.[1]

The CNT itself recognized these inclinations of the majority of the Catalan peasants. A resolution of the CNT plenary assembly of land workers of Catalonia in September 1936, two months after the beginning of the War, noted:

> The characteristics of Catalan small landownership have their origin in the spirit of independence deeply rooted in our peasants, who, influenced by their desire to free themselves from wage slavery, or of the usury to which they were subjected in sharecropping and rent, sought only one objective: LAND! The major aspiration was to come to be proprietor of it...
>
> ... Like one in love, charged with passion, mixed with ancestral

egotism, the peasant races to conquer or obtain his objective: and withholds no efforts, works day and night, continually and without rest, both he and members of his family; he doesn't eat enough, undermines his health, and one can say that he lives worse than his work animals.[2]

The Pre-Revolutionary Land Pattern in Catalonia

Starting in the late Middle Ages, the landed nobility of Catalonia had begun the process of turning over more or less permanent tenant rights to people to work their holdings. The basis of payment by the tenants varied, from sharecropping to money rent, to a mixture of the two.

In those parts of Catalonia where grape-growing dominated, for several centuries the long-term rentals were for the duration of the life of the vines, which tended to be 50 to 75 years. However, in the latter part of the nineteenth century, when the Catalan vineyards were struck by disease and the existing vines were supplanted by ones with shorter life, conflicts arose between landlords and tenants.

With the advent of the Republic in 1931 and the establishment of an autonomous regime in Catalonia, the Catalan government passed legislation guaranteeing long-term tenure for tenants. Although this law was negated by the conservative 1933–6 regime, it was reinstated after the victory of the Popular Front in February 1936.

The vineyard tenants were known as *rabassaires*. Shortly after the First World War, an organization of these peasants, the Unió de Rabassaires y Altres Conreadors del Camp de Catalunya (UdR), was established with the help of the lawyer Luis Companys. In the following, years it became the largest peasant organization in Catalonia, coming to include many tenants and sharecroppers in addition to those in the vineyards areas.

The UdR also became a major political force in the region. With the establishment of the Esquerra Catalana as the major exponent of Catalan nationalism after the proclamation of the Republic in Spain, and the succession of Luis Companys as leader of the Esquerra after the death of its founder Francisco Macía, the Unió de Rabassaires, became the most important mobilizer of support for the Esquerra.

Shortly before the outbreak of the Civil War, the UdR called for confiscation of all large landholdings, which were to become collective property of society, and the grouping of smallholdings into larger and more economic ones. However, soon after the Civil War began, the Unió de Rabassaires became the most important opponent of the establishment of rural collectives in Catalonia.[3]

The Compulsory Sindicatos Agricolas and the CNT

An early decree of the Catalan government after the outbreak of the War was to cause considerable difficulty for the rural supporters on the CNT. This measure, adopted on August 30 1936, by the Generalidad on the recommendation of the Consejo de Economía, then dominated by the CNT, and during the period when effective power in Catalonia was still in the hands of the Consejo General de Milicias, also under CNT control, called for compulsory 'syndicalization' of Catalonia's rural population. It provided that everyone in agriculture should 'carry out through the agricultural union ... of the locality the sale and processing of agricultural and grazing products, the purchase of inputs which they need, insurance ... and credit necessary for their agricultural operations.'[4]

The *sindicatos agricolas* which, according to the decree, were supposed to be set up in all municipalities of Catalonia, were to have four sections, dealing with acquisitions, including consumers cooperatives; sales, to dispose of their products; insurance and credit. The *sindicatos* were also authorized to establish a fifth section dealing with agrarian collectives, if that was appropriate in a particular community.[5] These organizations were thus much more cooperatives than traditional rural workers' groups.

In spite of the participation of CNT leaders in the elaboration of the compulsory rural syndicalization decree, it soon aroused much opposition within the ranks of the CNT's followers in the Catalan countryside. This became obvious during the Catalan CNT's regional peasant plenum in January 1937.

The minutes of the January plenum reported: 'The peasants in their great majority indicate opposition to the decree of forced sindicalization. In that connection, it is maintained that the Councillor of Agriculture, directed by the Rabassaires, carries out a proletarizing mission. Mataró claimed that in some localities on the coast, the proprietors had joined the U.G.T. and the Rabassaires. The Agricultural *sindicatos* have some regulations that impede our work. The Regional Committee intervenes to say that the "forced sindicalization" doesn't reduce the value of the collectives...'

Debate at the meeting centered on whether the CNT collectives and other rural groups should boycott the official *sindicatos agricolas* or should try to exert influence within them. A compromise resolution was adopted, suggesting that the CNTers should participate in the *sindicatos*, but under conditions in which the collectives would still be free to dispose of their products apart from the *sindicatos*, and the *sindicatos* would be controlled by elected officials which would include CNT members.[6] Although in practice, it is clear that many of the collectives did carry out their activities without reference to the official *sindicatos*, the government never formally accepted such operations.

CNT Relations with the Unió de Rabassaires and UGT

The CNT in Catalonia attempted in the early months of the Civil War to establish working, if not friendly, relations with the Unió de Rabassaires and the rural affiliates of the Unión General de Trabajadores. However, these efforts proved fruitless.

As we have noted, the Unió de Rabassaires was by all odds the majority organization in the Catalan countryside. It became strongly committed to granting land as family farms to tenants and agricultural laborers who had formerly worked on it without owning it, and was closely allied with the Esquerra Catalá, the party headed by Generalidad president Luis Companys. The UGT, which had had virtually no rural constituents before July 19, on the other hand, was firmly controlled by the Stalinist Partido Socialista Unificado de Catalonia (PSUC) and, from the onset of the War, sought to undo the Revolution which had occurred on and after July 19.

There were at first negotiations between the UdR and the CNT to work out a mutually acceptable program for the reorganization of Catalan agriculture. When they had agreed on its general outlines, they invited the UGT to join in final discussions of the suggested program. However, that first meeting among representatives of the three groups broke up because of UGT opposition to what had been agreed upon by the other two. Another meeting two weeks later produced much the same results.

The CNT and the *rabassaires* then worked out a 12-point agreement which provided that peasants who wanted to have family farms would be free to do so but, equally, that groups of peasants who decided to establish a collective should also have that right, providing they belonged to one of the organizations signing the agreement. In situations in which individualist farmers' property was in the middle of that of a group of collectivists, there should be an exchange of land, to the advantage of the individual peasant, to put his holdings physically outside those of the collective.

When CNT representatives went to a meeting where they thought that this agreement would be formally signed, they found UGT representatives there also. The UGTers absolutely refused to sign the agreement, noting: 'The UGT did not accept collectivization of land, not for reasons of principle but because of the circumstances.' Since the UdR refused to be a party to an agreement which the UGT was unwilling to sign, that ended negotiations among the three groups.[7]

Josep Maria Bricall has noted another factor which undoubtedly caused bad blood between the anarchists and the peasant proprietors. He cited Lluis Ardiaca, the director general of agriculture of the Generalidad, as saying in April 1937: 'From the beginning the municipal councils and committees submitted the peasants to rigorous control, and paid a very low price for the harvest, after which they resold it to obtain supplementary means for financing the municipality.'[8] Since, in the early months of the Civil War, many of these local *de facto* governments were to a greater or less degree in the hands of the anarchists, they undoubtedly did not generate friendship for the CNT among the independent peasants.

The Generalidad's Revolution from the Top

Walther Bernecker has pointed out that in order to limit and, if possible, reverse the Revolution from the Bottom, which had been carried out in Catalonia, the Generalidad, dominated after December 1936 by the Esquerra Catalana and the PSUC, sought to set in place their own Revolution from the Top. Nowhere was this clearer than in the government's dealing with agrarian issues, particularly that of collectivization.

Various decrees of the Generalidad during the first eight months of 1997 were part of this Revolution from the Top. One, of January 1, ratified *de jure* the *de facto* refusal of rural renters to continue to pay rent to landholders; but at the same time made the ex-renters responsible for the land taxes the landlords had formerly had to pay. (According to Carlos Semprún-Maura, in July 1936, the Catalan peasants burned property deeds of large landowners, and the share-croppers became the proprietors of the parcel – more or less large – which they cultivated.[9]

Another decree of February 20 1937, also legalized a procedure with regard to agrarian collectives which they had been following in any case – providing that any collective member should be free at any time he wanted to to withdraw, and that upon withdrawal he must receive back whatever he had contributed upon entering the collective. Before this decree, the collectives had adhered to the policy ordered in it; their action constituting a concession of anarchist principles in the face of political realities. Another decree, of July 14 1937, legalized seizure without indemnity of all properties belonging to those compromised with the rebellion; it also provided that the *sindicatos agricolas* should provide credit to agrarian collectives – but only to those whose existence had been legalized.[10]

Another significant decree, on July 19 1937, declared dissolved the executive committees of all *sindicatos agricolas* and ordered new elections. Members of the POUM were excluded from the possibility of being elected to the new executive committees.[11] This decree clearly asserted and established the right of the Catalan government to determine the internal affairs of ostensibly private rural organizations, and sought to assure their control by the Esquerra Catalana and the Stalinist PSUC.

A somewhat earlier decree, of June 16 1937, had established the Council of Agriculture, on a regional basis, 'to establish the general norms for application of the dispositions of the government', and of Municipal Agrarian Juntas to do the same thing on a local level. The original decree provided for representation on those bodies only of the three peasant organisations. However, after the removal of the CNT from the Catalan government, another decree, of August 17 1937, added representatives 'of the political organizations which form the government of the Generalidad at the moment of publication of the present decree'.[12] This reorganization, in effect, gave the Stalinists two votes (UGT and PSUC), the Esquerra Catalana two votes (the Unió de Rabassaires and the party), for every one vote of the CNT.

However, the decree most directly affecting the rural collectives was that of August 14 1937, which provided for the recognition and regulation of such organizations. It provided that, to be legally recognized, collectives had to conform to the decree in question. From the point of view of the collectives themselves such conformity meant that all collectives with more than ten members had to adopt standard statutes set forth in the decree.

The model statutes provided for free entry and exit of collective members – in the first case contributing all of their land and machinery, animals and implements. Those wanting to withdraw had to give three months' notice; would get back all land which they had contributed if it was on the border of the collective, or its equivalent if not on the border. Other articles of the model statutes provided for regular general assembly meetings, a directive council of at least three members and an accounting committee. Article 17 provided that collectives could pay their members either in proportion to the work they had done or according to their family needs. Finally, there were provisions for possible dissolution of a collective, and for the agricultural councillor of the Catalan government to decide any controversy between a collective and any of its members.[13]

Few of the provisions of the mandated statutes, except those providing for the government's involvement in their affairs, were *ipso facto* in violation of the way the CNTers were in fact running their rural collectives. However, the fundamental conflict with anarchist principles was the intromission of the State in the collectives which the anarchists conceived of as autonomous self-governing entities. In this decree, the government of Catalonia asserted its right, rather than that of the collectives' members, to establish the form and norms of the agrarian collectives. This decree was Revolution from the Top with a vengeance.

The Regional Federation of Peasants of Catalonia

As in other parts of Republican Spain, the CNT peasant organizations, and particularly the rural collectives, were brought together in a regional group, the Federación Regional de Campesinos de Catalonia. However, this Catalan group was late in being established, and never achieved the significant role which its counterparts in the Levante, Castille and Andalusia attained.

As early as September 1936, a regional peasant congress was held. It was attended by around 400 delegates, who were said to represent 200 CNT rural *sindicatos* in the region. This meeting took the preliminary step towards establishing a peasant federation by establishing a regional peasant committee, composed of four delegates of the regional secretariat of the CNT and two from each province, with its headquarters in Barcelona.

The most important resolution of this conference was one dealing with collectivization: 'In proceeding to the establishment of collectivization of the land, so that the small proprietors will not lose confidence for a single moment in our emancipating action and, as a consequence, so that they won't be converted into enemies, impediments to or sabotagers of our work, there will be respected in principle the cultivation of land which they can cultivate by their own hands, always providing that this doesn't obstruct or make difficult the due development of the nucleii which are collectivized... What we might perhaps achieve by forcing it, will be obtained by the example which the collectivization of the land itself will give in changing the structure of cultivation...'[14]

Another regional plenum of peasants of the CNT was held in January 1937. Among other things, it discussed the failure of negotiations for a common program with the Unió de Rabassaires and the UGT. It also took a position on the issue of compulsory syndicalization of the Catalan peasantry established several months before. The resolution said that the *sindicatos* 'have an essentially economic function and thus are separated from any social or political tendency and discipline...' It demanded that the *sindicatos agricolas* be controlled by the CNT, UGT and UdR. It also insisted: 'The agricultural collectives born from the revolution can form part of these *sindicatos agricolas*, with their own personality and jurisdiction, to use their economic organizations for the acquisition of fruits, seeds, fertilizers and implements necessary for their economic development, with these collectives free to dispose of the fruits for consumption, as well as for realizing exchange of products with other brother collectives.'

The meeting also recognized that the use of money generally in the Catalan economy would continue for some time to come. It also adopted a resolution calling for the establishment of more or less uniform structures in the CNT collectives in the region.[15]

Sometime during the first half of 1937, the Regional Peasant Federation was established. There is evidence that, on August 15 1937, the federation organized a large meeting in Barcelona. The announcement of this meeting said: 'The competent comrades Callol, Tuneu and Porte, secretaries of the Federación Regional de Campesinos de Cataluña, will expound in detail on the work carried out until now by the peasants who belong to the CNT, using the collectives, which have been the only manifestations of undoubted practical results, which the new social order has produced in the countryside.'[16]

The Catalan regional organization did not apparently have the success of its counterparts elsewhere in coordinating the activities of the agrarian collectives in the region, and in acting as a vehicle for exchanging products among them and disposing of their surpluses in other ways. This is indicated by the fact that a congress of the

342

organization in January 1938 was still proposing to put in place what already existed to a greater or less degree in the Levante, the center and Andalusia.

A resolution of the January 1938. meeting thus noted: 'To relate and coordinate, as well as direct and orient to the degree that that is necessary, the economic progress of the peasant collectives, the F.R. de Campesinos de Cataluña will constitute within it the necessary economic organism with *comarcal* branches, which can also in turn become local if in the same locality there are various collectives. This internal organization ... will have for its principal mission to function as *comarcal*, local and regional councils of the CNT agricultural economy...'[17] The resolution then set forth the way in which such organisms would be established. There is no indication of the degree to which it was successful, but starting that late, and in view of the increasingly difficult military and political situation in Catalonia in 1938, it is doubtful that a high degree of integration of the activities of the CNT collectives in Catalonia was achieved.

That same January 1938 congress also adopted a resolution concerning the compulsory *sindicatos agricolas*. It called for the return of control of them and of the Superior Council of Agriculture of Catalonia to the three peasant organizations 'excluding the representation assigned to non-peasant sectors, with the sole exception of a representative of the Councillor of Agriculture...' It also called for new elections in the *sindicatos agricolas* and the municipal agrarian *juntas*, and that representation within their executive councils be in conformity with the strength shown by the three peasant groups in those elections.

Finally, that resolution called for acceptance by the CNT of the decree of land redistribution only if preference given to occupiers of land be extended to 'lands occupied by the collectives', that land be returned to collectives in those municipalities where the collectives had been dispossessed for lack of legal recognition, and that there be no compensation to landlords whose lands were taken.[18]

The Number and General Characteristics of Catalan Rural Collectives

As in the rest of Republican Spain, it is difficult to discover just how many CNT-controlled agrarian collectives there were in Catalonia. Estimates vary greatly. Gaston Leval, who took a rather dim view of the Catalonian rural collectives, argued that there were only 'about sixty' in that region.[19] On the other hand, the CNT press during the Civil War claimed that there were as many as 400, almost certainly an exaggeration, A survey made by the Generalidad of Catalonia in November 1936 found 66 collectives to exist, which is clearly a small number, since many of the Catalan collectives were established after that date. On balance, Walther Bernecker seems inclined to accept the number of 200 rural collectives in Catalonia.[20] Perhaps this is as acceptable an estimate as is available.

It is clear that there was considerable variation among the Catalan collectives. Some were remarkably small, a few were among the largest in all of Republican Spain. Quite a few were geographically isolated, while a number, particularly in the vicinity of Barcelona and Lérida, were grouped in close propinquity, and in some cases, were closely associated with CNT urban workers' collectives.

There was also differentiation among the various CNT rural collectives in terms of how their business was conducted. There were those which relied largely on exchange of goods with other rural and industrial collectives, and others which largely sold their goods to the public for cash. There were also some differences in the way the members of the collectives were compensated, although the majority apparently stuck with the anarchist principle of payment in terms of family responsibilities.

There was also great variation in the degree and type of success of the Catalan rural collectives. Some were highly effective economically and socially. Others clearly had a more or less precarious existence.

Some Examples of Catalan Collectives

More or less extensive details concerning 25 CNT collectives and one sponsored and directed by the Partido Obrero de Unificación Marxista (POUM) are available, of which I shall present a few.

Probably the most successful anarchist rural collective in Catalonia and one of the most successful in all of Spain, was that of Hospitalet de Llobregat. It was part of a group of CNT collectives in a community near Barcelona which was largely dominated by the anarchists throughout most of the Civil War.

The Colectividad Agraria de Hospitalet was formed in September 1936. It was the salvation of the agriculture of the area. There was great disorganization at the beginning of the War. There were about 200 small landowners and renters in the area, with about 1,000 people employed in agriculture altogether. Before the War, agricultural wage laborers had not worked every day, had gone to a labor market daily where some had gotten work, others had not. With the establishment of the collective, however, all were considered to be members with equal rights.

There were regular membership meetings of the collective once a month. The officials of the collective were chosen for an indefinite period, but could be removed by any membership meeting. The officials reported to the membership meeting regularly. The same people served as officials throughout the War.

There were two councils in the collective. One was administrative, consisting of a president, an assistant secretary, a treasurer and five other members. It generally supervised the administration of the collective, including its finances. The second was a technical council, consisting of about 25 members, who planned what would be grown where and how. It consisted mainly of old landowning peasants, who knew the technical problems of farming.

Once the collective was established, former distinctions between land owned or rented by individual members were abolished, and the land under cultivation was dealt with as a single unit. It covered an area of 15 square kilometers, and was divided into 38 zones of 35 hectares each, with every zone worked by a 'brigade', with its elected *delegado*. The land under cultivation was increased by about a third during the War, ultimately amounting to some 1,470 hectares.

This collective produced mainly truck gardening crops. Most of its products were brought to the central market in Barcelona, where they were sold for pesetas. Some crops, such as a special kind of lettuce, were sold in France, as they had been before the War. At first, the collective sold these directly, in its own trucks. Then the Catalan government set up a central market for export crops in Mataró, and it handled the sale, keeping the foreign exchange which was earned, and paying the farmers in pesetas. The collective also engaged in a little barter with other agrarian collectives. From time to time, it directly provided truckloads of produce to the militia and army.

All members of the collective got equal pay. This was raised from time to time to keep up with the rising cost of living. The members were paid in money. However, their health needs mere all paid for by the collective. Also funds of the collective were used to buy five tractors, which could not have been used before the war because the land had been broken up into too small plots, but were practicable with the establishment of the collective. They also bought some sowing machines, which were horsedrawn. At the end of the War, the collective had 3,000,000 pesetas in the bank.[21]

José Peirats has described another agrarian collective near Barcelona, that of Vilaboi:

> The Collective was established with the land of large proprietors who fled or were expropriated: 250 mojadas of collectivized land, and 200 collectivists. The Collective was constituted in February 1937, with 12 horses and as many carts. It had then a fund of 500 to 600 pesetas, as a result of individual donations. A daily wage of 60 centimos was paid. Once the harvest of artichokes was in, a weekly wage of 70 to 85 pesetas could be assured. They dedicate the first savings of the collective to the acquisition of horses, construction of ample stables, acquisition of irrigation motors, the purchase of fertilizers and seeds.
>
> At the end of 1938 the Collective was composed of 500 members, with an income of 150 pesetas each. They incorporated a hundred evacuees with their families, with the same

rights and duties. More than 200 members fought at the fronts. Their family members were helped. The Collective had a completely free medical and pharmaceutical service. They installed a barn, acquired from the Municipality for 32,000 pesetas, in which were housed 20 milk cows, 200 hogs, 27 calves and large numbers of barnyard animals. Production: 70,000 kilos of wheat a year, 37,000 of beans, 300,000 of potatoes, 500,000 of various fruits and around three million kilos of vegetables.[22]

One of the more interesting of the CNT rural collectives in Catalonia was that of Plá de Cabra, south of Barcelona, which grew out of long experience with various kinds of cooperatives among the peasants there. As early as 1910 a local Catalan Nationalist politician had sponsored formation of cooperatives. One processed the peasants' grapes and made wine, which the cooperative sold. It installed modern wine-making methods instead of the traditional one of treading on the grapes to get out the juice, and it modernized the fermentation processes. Cooperatives also bought jointly inputs the peasants needed. There also were established rural credit unions, which accepted the peasants' savings, and made loans to them to allow them to hold their output until it could be sold at a good price.

The Collective of Plá de Cabra was established in June 1937 with 270 members, cultivating about 12,500 acres of land. All members had an equal voice and vote, regardless of whether they were ex-landowners, ex-tenants or ex-wage workers. The members worked the land in teams, and there was a general assembly of the members to make important decisions. The collective had one paid functionary – an accountant to keep the records and finances straight.

With one exception, entry into the Plá de Cabra Collective was voluntary. A number of the landowning peasants, including some CNT members who had inherited small plots, who did not want to join were permitted to continue as individual farmers.

The one exception to the voluntarism of the collective was a local *cacique* of the Lliga Catalana, who was at first forced to merge his land into the collective against his wishes. This proved to be an error on the part of the organizers, since a year later, when the changed political conditions made it possible, he insisted on withdrawing from the collective, and convinced a few other peasants to do the same thing.

The Plá de Cabra Collective produced cereals, vegetables, wine, almonds and filberts. It had a chicken coop with 500 birds, for egg production; nine cows, six heifers and one bull.

Payment to members of the collective was in terms of the number of members in their families, and they apparently were paid in official money. A warehouse was set up in the church, and collective stores for the sale of general foodstuffs, vegetables, fish and meat were established.

Reportedly, the collective paid particular attention to supplying the needs of the militia and the army. They also did a lot of bartering of products with the CNT industrial collectives, sending people to find out what those organizations needed, and telling them what they themselves required. However, a certain amount of the output – which reportedly increased 75 percent during the existence of the collective – was sold for cash.[23]

Although the Catalan rural collectives were less prone to do so than were those of Aragón, the Cervía Collective near Lérida abolished money, at least for internal use within the group. Reportedly, most of the Catalan collectives which did this were in the Lérida area.

There were 5,000 people in and around the village of Cervía. Those who formed the agrarian collective reportedly did so on a voluntary basis, those peasants who did not want to join being free not to. However, it happened in some cases that larger landowners who had originally stayed out ultimately joined, because virtually everything else in the village, including medical attention and the pharmacy, was collectivized, and only collective members could have access to them. In other cases, sons of those peasants who stayed out were attracted to the collective by the fact that usually at 5–6 p.m. work on the collective was over for the day, which was not always the case on individual peasant holdings. When the sons joined the collective, their fathers were sometimes obliged to do so also, since they were unable to cultivate the land without their offsprings' help, and in order to hold on to an individual holding, a peasant family had to cultivate it with its own family manpower.

The general assembly of the collective was sovereign within it, and it met more or less regularly each week. An administrative committee carried out the decisions of the assembly and its members worked alongside the rest during the day. The land of the collective was divided into fields which were of a rational size, regardless of old property lines. The work was done by gangs or teams, with the administrative committee assigning people to various teams each morning. Any disputes on this were supposedly within the province of the assembly, but they seldom occurred.

There were cases of peasants who, in spite of having joined their little bit of land to the collective, continued to take special interest in the piece of land which had been theirs. The same was true in some cases with animals in the collective's stock which had belonged to individual peasants. A one-time secretary of the Cervía Collective remembered many years later cases of peasants who had worked after hours to take special care of animals which had formerly been theirs.

Payment in the collective was in accordance with family size. Payment was not in money, but in goods, with each family getting its share of various foods, cloth and other things which were available. Members were free to choose, within what was available, the particular foodstuffs or other products they wanted. Although payment was not generally made to members in money, the collective did have some money available, for use by members who for some reason or other had need to spend it outside of the collective.

The Cervía Collective had a culture commission, which established a school and a library. The latter was at first formed on the basis of what books were available, but later, if a member requested the library to obtain a book, this was frequently acquired.

The Cervía Collective was relatively prosperous, producing olives and vegetables. Its surpluses were usually not sold for money, but were exchanged with other agrarian collectives and industrial ones. Some of the excess was sent to the front, and some was turned over to some of the other collectives which were less well off. According to the one-time secretary of the collective, there was little resistance to such donations, because the general spirit of the group was that they were contributing to building a kind of Utopia, a better world – a spirit which might not have survived if the War had been won, but which he insisted existed during the life of the Cervía Collective.[24]

Although the rural collectives so far discussed were relatively large, there were many which were much smaller. Contemporary anarchist descriptions of two of these may give a flavor how they were organized and functioned.

The *Boletin de Información* of the CNT–FAI described in November 1937 the community of Altona in the province of Lérida:

> In this village ... there exists an agricultural *sindicato* which belongs to the CNT. There is also a collective which has one year of existence. It was founded by fifteen families and has almost tripled since then. The collective has a consumers' cooperative, and its members, like good collectivists are putting into practice their beautiful ideals, give to others whatever they don't need, without a desire to take advantage, exploit or make a profit...
>
> They have established the family wage. The head of the family gets 4 pesetas, 3 the wife, 3 the children of 14 to 18, from 10 to 14, 2; and 1 from the date of birth. This demonstrates how great is the interest of the collectivity to take care of the maintenance of all those beings who form part of it. Vegetables and fruits are distributed without payment, and when the cooperative has a good number of goods available, they too are distributed.

The article also noted that the collective had a flour mill, and was planning to establish a school, as well as to build up a herd of cows, build a chicken coop, and 'to go ahead constructing commodious and hygienic homes for the collectivists'.[25]

The same source carried a description of another small collective, that of Villarrodona, in the province of Tarragona. The *Boletin* reported:

> The Collective of peasants of Villarrodona, constituted in the month of November 1936, consists of 21 families with a total of one hundred family members. It had 210 jornales of land, of

which only six are irrigated. The collectivists work a great deal because they have no alternative; but the collective goes ahead, and if nothing is put in its way, it will come into port triumphantly.

They are already building facilities to house a sizeable number of chickens, more than a hundred rabbits and more than twenty hogs. They also have one of the three oil mills which exist in the locality, as well as two tractors and many other machines and working tools. They have a very well organized consumers' cooperative, of great use to the families of the collectivists.

In these days they are collecting olives and according to what they tell us, they have an extraordinary harvest of cereals, with the hope of recovering this year, if the weather aids them, from the almost nonexistent last harvest. They are also expending much energy in exploiting the forest, from which they have obtained a good return ...'[26]

Finally, mention might be made of the non-CNT rural collectives which existed in Catalonia during the Civil War. With perhaps a handful of exceptions, these were not enterprises organized and influenced by the Unión General de Trabajadores, as frequently was the case in the Levante, Castille and Andalusia. This was because of the strong control of the UGT of Catalonia by the Stalinist Partido Socialista Unificado de Catalonia (PSUC), which was violently opposed to collectivization, urban or rural.

However, in Catalonia during the first year of the War another Marxist party, the Partido Obrero de Unificación Marxista (POUM), more or less aligned with the International Communist Right Opposition, did not have the PSUC's adamant opposition to collectives. Although its general position was in favour of the distribution to tenants, sharecroppers and agricultural laborers, of the lands which they had worked, on a family farm basis, it was willing to make exceptions to this position. In a few cases, it undertook the organization of rural collectives itself.

Probably the most important of these POUM-sponsored collectives was that of Raimat, near Lérida. There were extensive vineyards there, and various grains were also produced. The workers themselves decided that it did not make sense to break up that holding into individual family farms, so it was collectivized.

They used money within the Raimat Collective. They had a cooperative store, set up after collectivization, where the people of the collective bought the things they needed. They also had a farm market, where people from outside could buy the things from the collective. They did not have any swapping of goods with other rural collectives or with urban workers' collectives.

The main emphasis of Raimat was on producing things to provide for the needs of the soldiers at the front, which was not far away, in Aragón. A large part of the produce was therefore sold to the units at the front. For the rest, the government of Catalonia set maximum prices, but the fact was that much of the produce of the collective was sold in the black market, which was very active.

The collective was financially prosperous. It also succeeded in substantially increasing its output during the period of its existence.[27]

Conclusions

Anarchist agrarian collectives were not as important in Catalonia as in some other parts of Loyalist Spain. This was due in large part to the prevalence of small and middle-sized landholding patterns in the region, as well as to opposition by the Catalan government, dominated during the last two years of the War in Catalonia by the Catalan Left and PSUC parties, both of which were strongly opposed to collectivization.

To some degree, the Catalan CNT collectives differed from their counterparts in other parts of the country. Fewer of them tried the experiment of abolishing money, they were not as successful as CNT collectives in other parts of the country in organizing a structure for centralizing the sale of their products and, as a consequence, the Regional Peasants Federation was of much less significance than elsewhere.

However, there is evidence that at least a significant number of the

CNT rural collectives were successful in at least three ways. First, they substantially increased the levels of output with which they had begun. Second, they were financially prosperous. Third, they provided their members both with higher levels of living, and a feeling of great mutual accomplishment.

13

Rural Collectives in Aragón

The part of Loyalist Spain over which the anarchists had most complete control during the first year of the Civil War was Aragón. It was also the area in which anarchist experiments with rural collectives were most extensive and, both during the War and later, Spanish and foreign anarchists probably wrote more extensively about the rural collectivization there than in any other part of the country.

On the other hand, Aragón was also the part of the country where the anarchist experiments in the countryside were most bitterly denounced by the Communists. It was the region in which Communist troops most ruthlessly invaded and broke up the rural collectives, arresting their leading members, a substantial number of whom they killed, and despoiling their land, crops, implements, livestock and machinery.

Pre-war Landholding Patterns in Aragón

Gerald Brenan has described the different circumstances under which the land was cultivated in Aragón before the Civil War: 'The old province of Aragón consists of a Pyrenean belt, where conditions tend to resemble those in Navarre, the irrigated valley of the Ebro, where properties are small and the peasants relatively prosperous, and a large dry area with very low rainfall, which includes the flat steppes of the Ebro Basin and a sparsely inhabited mountainous region known as the Maestrazgo, running south to Teruel.'

As Brenan has noted, each of these parts of the region had a different kind of landholding arrangement: 'Large estates, debt-ridden peasants and impoverished agricultural labourers characterize the steppe country, which has been strongly affected by the anarcho-Syndicalist movement. The Maestrazgo, on the other hand, has Carlist traditions.' Brenan then added a curious note about the appearance and psychology of the Aragónese peasants, which is perhaps not irrelevant to what they did during the Civil War: 'It should be added that the physical appearance of the Aragónese is very different from that of either the Basques or the Catalans: they seem to be of a more primitive stock and ... they are famous for their obstinacy.'[1]

The Importance of Anarchist Militia in the Establishment of Collectives

There is no doubt about the fact that one of the most important reasons for the rapid expansion of rural collectives in Aragón during the first months of the War was the presence in that area of predominantly anarchist militia units. At the onset of the Rebellion, the insurgent army and Civil Guard forces immediately got control of most of Aragón. However, once the situation had stabilized in Catalonia, the General Council of the Militia there undertook as one of its first priorities the recruiting of militia forces to retrieve Aragón from the Rebels. Within two or three weeks, three-quarters of the land area of the region, and half of its population, were back under the control of forces loyal to the Republic.[2] Predominantly, these were forces made up of, and led by, anarchists.

Augustine Souchy, the German anarchist, writing early in 1937, described what happened in much of the region: 'Immediately after July 19 collisions occurred in various villages of Aragón between the peasants and the fascists. In many of the villages the peasant population retired en masse, fleeing the persecution organized by the rebels. When, later, the anti-fascist columns from Catalonia and the Levante entered Aragón, the villages were liberated from the Civil Guards and the fascists. The peasant population then returned. There began a process of social transformation which has no equal in Spain, in terms of complexity and depth.'[3]

Franz Borkenau, who visited an area in southern Aragón in the second week of August 1936, recorded in his diary at the time what he saw there. He visited the towns of Fraga and Serinena, among others. In the first place, he discovered that 38 people had been killed (out of a total population of about 1,000), largely on the initiative of the Durruti Column, which had passed through the village, and these included 'the priest, his most active adherents, the lawyer and his son, the squire, and a number of richer peasants'. However, although the land and other possessions of those killed had been taken over by the local revolutionary committee, 'the land of the deceased continued to be worked as it had been previously . . .'[4]

However, in Serinena, he found that a peasant collective had already been organized. It was using the four threshing machines expropriated from four large local estates to thresh the village's wheat crop.

Borkenau concluded his observations thus:

> To sum up: as in Fraga so in Serinena there was a numerous politically indifferent element, and an active anarchist nucleus, mostly of the younger generation. In Fraga this nucleus, under the influence of the Durruti militia column, had helped to kill an enormous number of people in the village, but they had achieved nothing else. In Serinena, a similar nucleus was left to its own devices, for ahead lay not an anarchist but a POUM column, and relations between the anarchist village and the POUM militia were far from good. But, in spite of this, with much less killing, the anarchist nucleus had achieved a considerable improvement for the peasants, and yet was wise enough not to try to force the conversion of the reluctant part of the village, but to wait till the example of the others should take effect.[5]

Frank Mintz tried to get some idea of the influence overall of the anarchist militia in bringing about the establishment of collectives.

He looked at what had happened in the case of 19 collectives, of which nine were in the province of Huesca, six in that of Teruel, and four in the province of Zaragoza. He found that militiamen had participated in meetings establishing three of the nine Huesca collectives, in four of those in Teruel, and in all four of those he studied in Zaragoza.[6]

Mintz summed up: 'We conclude that collectivization was imposed by force on the part of militia recruited among anarchists from outside the region, and that, in our opinion, they organized by localities more from the point of view of a war economy for their own supply than from thinking truly of social reform. On the other hand, the Aragónese anarchists, knowing the situation, profited from the moment without abusing it, and succeeded in putting their ideas in practice with the approval of the majority of the peasants...'[7]

However, the anarchist leader Félix Carresquer denied that in general the militia imposed collectivization: 'I, who lived in Aragón during the existence of the collectives, was able to ascertain that, with the exception of a few villages where the front persisted for some time, nowhere was there imposition, nor did the militiamen go to the rear to organize collectives or any other kind of social institution.'[8]

The anarchist militia leaders, notably Durruti, on the other hand, were quite frank about the mission of the anarchist militia in fomenting collectives. Burnett Bolloten cited a comment by Durruti: 'We are waging the war and making the Revolution at the same time. The revolutionary measures in the rear are not taken merely in Barcelona; they extend from there right up to the firing line. Every village we conquer begins to develop along revolutionary lines.'[9]

On August 11 1936, the Durruti Column issued a proclamation concerning its role in bringing the revolution to rural Aragón:

> The War Committee of the Durruti Column, attentive to the desires and needs of the people of Bujalaróz, proclaims: 1. Whereas the crops are sacrosanct to the interests of the laboring people and the antifascist cause, the harvest must be gathered

without the least loss of time. 2. All goods, such as fruits, animals and means of transport, belonging to Fascists become property of the People under the control of its Committee. 3. On the date of issue of this proclamation, the private ownership of the lands of the large landowners is abolished, they becoming the possession of the People in the form the Committee shall decide. 4. All tractors, reapers, ploughs, etc., belonging to Fascists are property of the People. 5. Since the armed struggle of the militias is the safeguard of the laboring people's life, and interests, the citizens of Bujalaróz shall give them their unconditional and enthusiastic support both material and moral.[10]

Abel Paz, Durruti's biographer, also noted that early in August Durruti 'fixed his attention on the peasant collectives which were springing up in all of liberated Aragón with amazing spontaneity. The relations established between the collectives in the section occupied by the Column and the Column were very fraternal. The peasants visited the Column, either to bring food or to ask Durruti to visit the collective and give them his opinion on how things were going.' Durruti, generally, 'acceded gladly ... In the course of the visits Durruti carried out to the various communities, he assessed the importance this collectivist work could have for revolutionary expansion, and also noted the dangers to which this collectivist expansion was exposed if it didn't bring about a united force ...'[11]

Durruti also proposed to the war committee of his column that, when not occupied with military duties, the militiamen should help the peasants get in their crops. 'Furthermore, those who were better informed could discuss with the peasants the libertarian society and its economic organisms.'[12]

Obviously, the relationship between the establishment of anarchist collectives and the presence of militiamen differed from place to place. Thus, in the case of most of the villages of the *comarca* of Valderrobres in the province of Teruel, most of the active anarchists temporarily left, to gather in Gandesa, across the border in Catalonia, whence, with help from CNT elements there, they then returned to overcome within a few days the Rebels who had at first seized control of most of the villages of that area.[13]

In the village of Tamarite, in the *comarca* of Monzón in the province of Huesca, there was a stalemate between a revolutionary committee and a Civil Guard unit which remained in its barracks. On July 26, the anarchists 'organized a shock column with the antifascists of neighboring villages and made them [the Civil Guard] evacuate Tamarite.' However, armed civilian supporters of the rebellion remained barricaded in a building in the towns whereupon the Iona CNT contacted their colleagues in Lérida, who arranged for the dispatch of a plane which dropped two bombs on the building, whereupon the Rebel group surrendered.[14]

In the case of Binefar, also in Monzón *comarca* Civil Guards and civilian supporters of the Rebels barricaded themselves in the Civil Guard barracks and the church of the town. When the CNTers from the town and neighboring areas were about to assault the two Rebel strongholds, they were joined by 'a Military Company loyal to the Republic', which had just arrived from Lérida. The Rebels soon surrendered.[15]

Finally, there was the case of Alcampel, also in Monzón *comarca*, where the CNT-led peasants defeated armed civilian supporters of the Rebels, after the local Civil Guard unit had been withdrawn to Tamarite. There, on July 27, the CNT's Sindicato Unico de Trabajadores called a meeting in the public square, where they announced their intention of organizing a collective, outlining the nature of what they intended to establish, and inviting debate among those present. There was some considerable opposition expressed, particularly by the local doctor, who belonged to the POUM. At the end of the meeting, the CNT leaders announced that for the next two days, those who wanted to join the proposed collective should sign a document to that effect. Finally, 250 families, about half of those in the village, joined the collective. A few days later, the doctor himself joined it.[16]

Number of Collectives in Rural Aragón

Opinions have differed – as is true with other parts of Loyalist Spain, as well – on just how many rural collectives there were in Aragón.

Gaston Leval told me that there were about 350,[17] although in print he has put the number at 400, with about half a million peasants and others involved.[18]

On the other hand, Augustine Souchy, writing at the time, claimed: 'Five hundred villages and cities of Aragón, with a total population of approximately half a million inhabitants, established collectivism...'[19] José Peirats has estimated the number of collectives at about 450, with 433,000 members.[20] This number is accepted by Walther Bernecker, who notes that they included 300,000 people, or 70 percent of the population and over 70 percent of the cultivated land.[21] Broué and Temime accepted Peirats's figure for the number of collectives, but claimed that 430,000 peasants belonged to them.[22]

Federación de Colectividades de Aragón

As early as August 1936, Buenaventura Durruti urged the peasant collectives of Aragón to establish a federation as a means of defense of their interests. However, it was February 1937 before such an organization was put in place.

Undoubtedly one of the reasons for the tardy establishment of a federation of collectives was the existence of the Council of Aragón, established in the middle of October 1936. It sought to carry out many of the tasks which were perhaps more properly those of a collectives federation, and even after that federation was established there was some confusion of roles.[23]

Another factor which impeded an early establishment of a federation of collectives of Aragón was opposition to the idea on the part of some of the *comarcal* federations which had been established by the local collectives in the early months of the War. According to Félix Carresquer, 'To go further did not seem to enter into the calculations of the majority of those peasants who, accustomed to moving in very narrow circles and influenced by the propaganda for the "free commune" which a certain part of the Libertarian Movement had always propagated, looked with scepticism on anything which seemed to them too large and too difficult for the exercise of the necessary control from the base. Thus, jealous of their autonomy, and contradicting the federal scheme which the Libertarian Movement had always preached, they did not show themselves very enthusiastic about the idea of establishing a Regional Federation of Collectives...'[24]

A preliminary regional conference of agrarian collectives was held in Caspe in November 1936. But it did not establish any continuing organization.[25] However, the Federación Regional de Colectividades de Aragón was finally established at a congress in Caspe on February 14–15 1937. The credentials committee reported that there were 275 collectives represented by 456 delegates, and that the collectives involved had 141,430 members. The membership figures were undoubtedly underestimated, since some of the collectives involved reported only heads of families, when they should have included all members of the families belonging to them. There were also in attendance official delegations from the National Committee of the CNT, the Peninsular Committee of the FAI and the Regional Committee of Anarchist Groups of Aragón, Rioja and Navarre.

Various resolutions were passed at this congress. Perhaps the most fundamental one was that which established the Federación Regional de Colectividades 'to coordinate the economic potential of the region and to give the support of solidarity to this Federation in accordance with the principles of economy and federalism which orient us.' This same resolution called for establishment of federations in each of the *comarcas* (equivalent of US counties) in the region.

Other resolutions called on each collective to draw up statistics of production and consumption, and send these to the *comarcal* federations, which would forward them to the regional committee; and for each collective to provide a sum of money 'in accordance with its wealth' to the federation for a regional fund to help out those collectives which needed special assistance. One also urged that those collectives with an excess of manpower make some of their people available to others which had a labor shortage.

The congress resolved: 'The circulation of money inside the collectives should be abolished and be replaced by a ration card, with each collective deciding the size of the rations.' This was an effort to standardize the diverse kinds of methods used by the various Aragón collectives to distribute goods and services among their members.

Another resolution of the congress stated that the federation would accept the existence of the municipality, 'because in the future it will serve to control the properties of the people'. However, it stated that 'the local boundaries which these entities administer should have no limits', and all instruments of cultivation should be used in common by the collectives throughout the *comarca*.

Finally, the meeting adopted what amounted to the statutes of the new federation. These stated that the 'attributes' of the new group would be:

1.) To propagate intensively the advantages of collectivism, based on mutual aid. 2.) To control the experimental farms which may be created in those localities in which the conditions of the terrain are favorable to obtain all types of seeds. 3.) To care for the youth who have a disposition towards preparing themselves technically, through the creation of technical schools which will deal with their specialty. 4.) To organize a group of technicians to study the way to get the best return from labor in Aragón in the various fields of agriculture. 5.) To seek the expansion of Aragón's trade with the outside, always seeking to improve the terms of trade, and 6.) To handle commercial relations with the outside, through control, by means of statistics, of the excess production of the region, and it will furthermore have charge of a resistance fund to take care of all of the needs of the federated collectives, always in harmony with the Regional Council of Defense of Aragón.

The statutes provided for the federation to have a six-person regional committee, consisting of a secretary-general, recording secretary, accountant, treasurer and two other members. It also provided that the regional committee would have its headquarters in Caspe.[26]

Félix Carresquer felt that the establishment of the federation of collectives would have been of great potential importance had the Civil War turned out differently:

It cannot be ignored that if the Congress institutionalized what the villages had begun, in the dynamic of the Congress there were implicit new accomplishments and directions such as the following: the establishment in the whole region of the fundamental bases of the economy, of education, of health and of cultural interchanges; the abolition of property as an hereditary right and of the wage system, together with the establishment of the 'Compensatory fund' which obliged the richer *comarcas* to aid the less favored ones ... the congress fusing the comarcas in a dynamic structure of rights and obligations for all, converted into a palpable fact of true solidarity which is definitively what underlies any libertarian perspective...[27]

One of the first things the new federation did was to draw up a standardized family rationing card, in pursuance of one of the resolutions of its founding congress. This form provided on its cover for a place for the name of the head of the family, and how many family members were 14 years old or over, under 14, and under five years of age. It also noted the name and address of the collective. Inside, the ration book had a page for each week of 1937, starting 'from 1 to 7 of April 1937'. Each page had columns for 'articles', 'quantity', then a place to list for each day the number of pesetas' and centesimos' worth of the various items the family had drawn. There were 24 items listed, most of them food, but also including 'hardware', 'kitchen objects', 'dry goods', and 'shoes'.[28]

Broué and Temime have said that 'the Peasant Federation made huge efforts to organize experimental farms, nurseries, and rural technical colleges.' However, the Aragón Federation of Collectives did not last long enough to establish the kind of centralization of distribution of its member groups' output, and programs of technical assistance and financial aid to its constituents similar to those established by its counterparts in the Levante and the center. With the ruthless invasion of Communist troops into Aragón in August 1937, the federation, as well as many of its constituent groups, was for all practical purposes dissolved.

However, about a month after the Communist incursion, the CNT held a plenum of its Aragón organizations in Caspe. There it was decided to 'simplify' the CNT structure in the region. In this process, it was decided that 'together with the Regional Committee of the CNT, there will function an associated commission on collectivist relations which will assume the identical functions of the present Regional Committee of Collectives.' Furthermore, 'the Regional Federation of Collectives will become an integral part of the corresponding Committees of the Organization, on a local, *comarcal* and regional basis.' ('The Organization' is the CNT itself.)[29]

The Comarcal Collective Organizations

The federations of collectives set up in the various *comarcas* of the region were much more effective than the regional federation. Most of them were established more or less immediately after the beginning of the Civil War, and at least some of them continued to function even after the Communists' invasion of the region, disappearing only with the conquest of Aragón by Franco's forces in March 1938. There were reportedly 22 *comarcal* federations in Aragón by February 1937.[30]

Considerable information is available on the function of the Aragónese *comarcal* federations. Of a typical *comarcal* federation, Gaston Leval said, 'It was natural that it would occupy itself with the means of communication (radio, post, telegraphs, telephones) and of the means of transport. Furthermore it widely interested itself with the cultural progress of the affiliated population. And since it was a period of war and of revolution, it distributed arms and suggested strategy to the Defense Councils of the villages. In the zone of Barbastro, for example, the *comarcal* Federation organized for nine months, the defence against fascism, supplying food and all products necessary for the war.'[31]

One of the *comarcal* federations about which there is considerable detailed information is that of Monzón. There were 32 collectives belonging to the Monzón federation. As soon as it was established, the federation 'proceeded to collect data on production and consumption of each of the collectives belonging to the *comarcal*

Federation. It was discovered that there were collectives with very high economic potential, whereas others scarcely could exist...'[32]

The federation established central warehouses where the collectives brought their surpluses and whence they obtained products they needed. It also 'established exchange relations with all areas and all branches of production, and in a very effective way with the comrades of the Catalan region, given our proximity to them, with metallurgy, construction, food industries, clothing, shoes, tools etc.'

Once these arrangements for exchange of the goods of the *comarca* for products which it needed were in place, 'we went to all the collectives of the *comarca*, determining what they had and what they needed. Within two months our warehouses functioned normally. In them, the collectives were provided with textiles, clothing, knitted goods, pottery and many kitchen objects in common use. We had two large trucks which left frequently, and returned laden with the wine of Priorato and other merchandise. Our *comarca* was rich in many things, but didn't provide enough wine.' From Catalonia, too, they obtained sheep which were distributed to the collectives 'which needed them'.[33]

The *comarcal* federation also took over the distribution of the products of the only significant industrial enterprise in the area, a beet sugar refinery in the village of Monzón. The workers of the enterprise took over its management with the outbreak of the War, but the *comarcal* federation handled its distribution problem. In doing so they fulfilled pre-existing contracts of the firm, and to their surprise and delight discovered that the refinery had turned over a considerable profit, 'with which everyone was equally benefited, collectives and non-collectivists'. Before the plant could handle its second year of operation under workers' control, it was destroyed by enemy aerial bombardment.[34]

On at least one occasion, the Monzón *comarcal* federation had some problems with the Consejo de Aragón, which aspired (at least before the foundation of the regional collective federation) to become the central collector and distributor of products throughout the region. After a visit by Benito Pavón, vice-secretary of the *consejo*, to Monzón to look at the sugar refinery, the *comarcal* federation sent members to interview Miguel Servet, the economic councillor of the *consejo*. When he told them that it should be the *consejo* rather than the *comarcal* federation that organized exchanges of goods and services, the two delegates said that they would agree with this, if the *consejo* would pay them in cash what the products of the *comarca* collectives were worth – 3,000,000 pesetas. Upon hearing that figure, Servet said that the *consejo* did not have such funds and that ended the discussion, the *comarcal* federation continuing with its work without any further interference from the Consejo de Aragón.[35]

The *comarcal* federation undertook a number of projects to increase output and raise the living levels of its members. A veteran of the organization recorded many years later: 'Electric current was taken to small hamlets which had always lacked it; the means of communication, the system of transport, education and support of childhood were improved... In almost all the collectives of the *comarca* the olive oil presses, which still used animals, were transformed, being attached to electric motors, and heavy labor was lightened. As gasoline was very necessary and in those moments was restricted, we attached electric motors to the threshing machines. The electrician comrades distributed various motion picture machines to several collectives...[36]

One distinctive accomplishment of the Monzón *comarcal* federation was the establishment and maintenance, in Binefar, of a hospital, the Casa de Salud Durruti. A veteran of the *comarca* described how the hospital was established: 'After refurbishing an old farmhouse, various pavilions were installed thanks to the collective effort and to two doctors who collaborated disinterestedly and indefatigably on behalf of the ill. To obtain the necessary material, a Catalan surgeon and a member of the *comarcal* Committee of Collectives went to Barcelona. They bought the best surgical material available in that time of war, for obstetrics, traumatology, an ultraviolal x-ray apparatus, as well as sufficient material for an analytic laboratory.'

By April 1937 they had 40 beds in the hospital, in sections for general medicine, prophylaxis and treatment of venereal diseases, and gynaecology. Until July 1937, the hospital sent a midwife to the homes of women about to give birth, but thereafter, such cases were brought into the hospital. About 25 outpatients per day were handled. The hospital was open to anyone in the 32 villages of the *comarca*.[37]

In the case of the *comarcal* federation of Valderrobres, in the province of Teruel, it suffered during the first year from the fact that the winter of 1936–7 was exceptionally cold in that area, considerably damaging the olive crop, the principal product of the region. The *comercal* federation, perhaps as a consequence of this, was not as comprehensive in its activities as that of Monzón.

As in Monzón, the cooperative in the village of Valderrobres was the center of the activities of the *comarcal* organization. It was established as the result of a meeting held soon after the expulsion of the Rebels from the area. Although the various collectives at first undertook direct exchanges with other collectives, rural and urban) these were soon centralized through the *comarcal* cooperative, which established regular relations with the oil firm CAMPSA and with the sugar refinery Monzón, among other organizations.

As described by a veteran of the organization, 'The products obtained from these operations were distributed among the local collectives, in accordance with their number of inhabitants, which apportioned them to the families. It was always suggested that the same ration be made available to the noncollectivists, provided that they in compensation made available excess products they had. There were localities which had greater abundance than others, but that was not reason for them to receive a large quantity of rationed products. Rather, those which didn't have any excess products received the same ration.'[38]

As in Monzón, the *comarcal* organization of collectives in Valderrobres carried out a number of projects on behalf of the community as a whole. One of these was to extend telephones to villages of the *comarca*. Also, 'there was installed in Valderrobres *comarcal* mechanic shop for repairing the few automobiles which were available for transport of passengers and merchandise, as well as for agricultural machinery...'

The collectives of the *comarca* jointly undertook the roads and highways of the region, including the ending of dangerous curves. Also, 'a good number of buildings were repaired or transformed so that no one would be lacking housing', as well as the construction of barns, corrals and other facilities for work and domestic animals.

The *comarcal* organization paid attention to education: 'In spite of the fact that a few teachers abandoned their posts, we can say that all of the children of school age, of both sexes, were taken care of. The intention was to go on constructing ample buildings, well aired and with sunlight, so that teaching could play the role which corresponded to it in the new Libertarian Society, without there being need for the children to be exploited, sometimes from the time they were ten or twelve years old.'[39]

Augustine Souchy took note of several other *comarcal* federations: 'In Azuara there resides the Comarcal Committee of twelve villages. These send delegations which provide information on what each village can provide and what it needs. The Comarcal Committee draws up statistics on the basis of these data and effects the exchange of products. So far there have been no difficulties with this new economic system, which is nothing more than organized exchange.'[40]

In the case of Granen, Souchy reported:

The *comarca* of Granen includes 27 member collectives, with an area of 96,000 hectares. It has 11,500 inhabitants. The *comarcal* Federation has in its hands the entire exchange among the twenty-seven villages. There are two principal kinds of operations: a) direct exchange among the various villages through the medium of the Federation; b) sale of excess products and purchase of articles needed by the *comarca*. The *comarcal* Federation has to authorize all exchanges between the villages and that which has to be bought. An example: 'Authorization: Federación Comarcal de Colectividades Agricolas de Granen. This Comarcal Federation authorizes the Sangarren collective to export 3,000 kilos of wheat to Lérida, for the purpose of exchange. Granen, 3 June of 1937.'[41]

Souchy noted of the Barbastro federation:

Barbastro is the seat of one of the largest Comarcal Federations. Of sixty villages of the *comarca*, forty-seven are collectivized and belong to the Federación... In some villages of the *comarca* there also exist collectives of the U.G.T.; but these have also joined the Comarcal Federation of the CNT. The member collectives provide the Comarcal Federation with exact statistics. They indicate the number of inhabitants, land area, state of highways and roads, number of existing animals, products and productive capacity. They indicate the existing machines and those needed, of raw materials, foodstuffs, clothing. The Comarcal Federation administers the economic affairs of 15,000 collectivists...

The Comarcal Federation is a kind of Department of Economics. It has sections for Transport, Agrarian Production, provision of foodstuffs, etc. The Machinery and Implements section has the job of providing machinery to the member villages. The Comarcal Federation inherited six threshing machines which before belonged to the political bosses, and it bought two more. Eight reapers were also bought. In the comarca there are thirty-seven modern ploughs, a tractor and some other agricultural machinery. The Comarcal Federation has the obligation of sending to the villages where they are needed the machines and personnel necessary for their functioning...

The collectivized villages go to the warehouses of the Comarcal Federation for what they need. From seeds to foodstuffs which the villages lack. The Comarcal Federation established cattle sheds for the whole comarca.[42]

Was Collectivization Voluntary of Forced?

One of the most bitterly argued aspects of the anarchist rural collectives of Aragón was that of whether their members joined them freely or were forced into them by the preponderant strength of the CNT–FAI in Aragón during the first phase of the Civil War. The anarchists, understandably, tended to emphasize their voluntary nature,[43] while the Communists, in particular, claimed that the overwhelming majority of the peasants in the region did not want to belong to collectives and only did so because the presence of anarchist troops, and other elements of anarchist coercion obliged them to participate.

One of the most uncompromising denunciations of the collectives as being imposed by force or intimidation by the anarchists was that of José Duque, who served as a Communist member of the Consejo de Aragón and was head of the Communist Party in the region during the War. He claimed that whenever anarchist militiamen retook a village from the Franco forces, they proceeded to summon the villagers to a public meeting, where they were addressed my the head of the military committee of the column or by a local anarchist leader:

> Once the programmatic exposition was terminated, there came the voting on the propositions formulated by the orator. The voting had to be always and in all cases according to the procedure so characteristic of the anarchists: vote by acclamation, that is to say, declaring oneself in favor or against, but publicly, rejecting the secret vote. Furthermore, the orator in intoning praise of *free man* in a *free society*, had not forgotten to menace with terrible evils those *stubborn individualists who had not succeeded in breaking yet with their miserable petty bourgeois prejudices*. After this, it is easy to understand that the simple Aragónese peasants *enthusiastically* supported the propositions formulated by the speaker, accepting fully and without discussion all of his theses.

Duque insisted: 'In the "free collective" the entry of all the peasants, all the artisans, and all the workers was forced. The large and small stores of a locality were closed. Everything was concentrated in a large communal store, depending directly on the "free collective", and controlled in turn by the "Defense Committee".'[44]

Augustine Souchy reached conclusions almost diametrically opposed to those of Duque: 'The collectivization was not ordered by the State, nor carried out by force, as in Russia. The great majority of the peasants felt the ideals of the social revolution. To produce collectively, distribute the products with justice among themselves, this was the objective. There did not exist a defined plan for the collectivizations. There was no decrees, no governmental commission intervened, no official orientation, to which the peasants must abide, was given. They acted according to their own intuition. An active minority led. Among the peasants there lived the ideal of libertarian communism.'[45]

The British observer Frank Jellinek, who overall was more sympathetic to the Stalinists in the Civil War than to the anarchists, writing in August 1937, apparently before the Lister troops had ravaged the Aragón collectives, gave a generally favorable assessment of the collectives: 'How far the Libertarian idea had penetrated Aragón was shown by the villagers' pride in the system, a pride quite certainly not inspired by increased well-being.'[46]

A majority of the studies of individual collectives which have been encountered have noted the existence of 'individualist' peasants (or artisans or merchants in the villages) who did not join the collectives. Of the 34 Aragón collectives about which I have substantial information, individualist peasants were present in 19. In a number of other cases, there may well also have been some individualists, although there is no specific mention of their presence.

In some cases, the majority of the peasants in locality apparently did not join the collective. Thus, in Monzón, only 1,000 of 5,000 people were in it, according to Augustine Souchy,[47] while José Peirats credits the collective with having in its ranks only 450 people.[48] In Alcampel, the collective had some 250 families, which Víctor Blanco, one of the members of the collective, noted were 'almost half the population'.[49] In Fraga, about 700 families were in the collective; the same number did not join.[50]

On the other hand, in Binefar, 700 of the 800 peasant families were in the collective, as were 10 per cent of those engaged in artisan industry.[51] In Barbastro, it was reported by Souchy: 'The individualists are an insignificant minority,[52] while in Torre del Campte 'everyone entered the collective'.[53]

In Azuara, a unique situation existed. According to Souchy, there were rural collectives of both the CNT and the UGT, and a liaison committee functioned to assure friendly relations between them.[54]

It was the somewhat grudging official policy of the Regional

Federation of Collectives not to force those peasants who did not want to join the collectives to do so. A resolution of the founding congress of the federation provided that smallholders should be allowed to keep as much land as they and their families could cultivate, but that no smallholder unwilling to join a collective should enjoy any of its benefits'. On the other hand, all lands confiscated from 'fascists', and all land which had been cultivated by renters or sharecroppers, should be included in a collective. Finally, 'to deprive them of the egotism which the small proprietors might feel, their small properties should not be registered in the official register.'[55]

Ex-CNT national committee member Félix Carresquer admitted to me that there were some collectives in Aragón in which peasants were coerced to join, particularly where very young anarchists were involved. However, he insisted that national CNT leaders tried to prevent such actions.[56]

Some light is cast on the relationships between the collectives and the individualists established by a resolution adopted by the collective of Oliete on April 22 1937. Among other things it stated: 'All comrades who are discontented within the collective, will be free to retire and work their properties individually, provided that no one can have more land than he can work with this own efforts, although they can work together if there is no exploitation of man by man in this collaboration. The individualist comrades will abstain from working against the collective, since if they do they will be judged to be counter-revolutionaries.'

Another provision of the resolution stated: 'The Cooperative of the Collective will open an account for each individualist to the value of the articles he provides, with which account said individualists can withdraw products which are in the Cooperative, provided the Collective doesn't need them.' It went on, 'The cattle of the individualists can be pastured throughout the municipality, respecting planted areas as is customary, and being limited to twenty-five head the number of cattle that each individualist may have as a maximum. It is their obligation to respect the pasture grounds...'[57]

There were sometimes conflicts between the collectivists and the individualists. The most serious case of this took place in the collective of Esplus in the *comarca* of Monzón. There, at the outbreak of the military uprising, a revolutionary committee had been established by the Izquierda Republicana Party and the CNT. The anarchists organized a collective early in September, but most of the Izquierda Republicana peasants and artisans did not join it. Rather, they soon withdrew from the revolutionary committee, formed a local of the UGT, and entered into contact with the Communist Party. The new UGT demanded equality with the CNT on the revolutionary committee, distribution of arms equally to both groups, and division of land which had been requisitioned from 'fascists' to individual proprietors.

The CNT leaders refused these demands, arguing that there was a national agreement that only organizations which had existed before July 19 should participate in revolutionary committees, and the UGT branch had been formed after that date, that all arms were kept in one place under guard of the revolutionary committee, and that all requisitioned land should be cultivated collectively. As a result, on October 8, a deputation from the Communist Party in Barbastro came to consult with the CNT leaders of Esplus. While the consultation was in progress, a demonstration of the UGTers in front of the building broke up in a shooting spree. In the process, some 30 people, including the head of the local UGT, had been killed before it was over.

Two days after this incident, all of the UGT members applied for membership in the collective. According to an anarchist source, the application was at first rejected, but was finally agreed to.[58]

The Collectives and the War

Many of the Aragónese collectives were only a few miles from the front between the late summer of 1936 and March 1938, when the Franco forces began their Aragón offensive. They contributed to the militia both men and provisions. For instance, there were 145 young men from Graus who were in the CNT militia;[59] and in Binefar, with a total population of only 3,500, some 60 joined the militia; while in the Calanda collective, 500 of the total population of 4,500 were in the militia, most in the 26th Division.[60] In Mar de las Matas, the miller of the collective complained to Souchy: 'There are too many comrades at the front. We don't have enough workers.'[61]

Certainly most of the food supply for the Republican troops on the Aragón front was provided by the collectives of the region. In the case of the collecttive of Monzón, it sent vegetables to the soldiers, for which it was paid.[62] In the case of the Binefar collective, it sent 30 to 40tons of food each week to the front. At the height of the battle for Madrid, it sent 30-40 tons of provisions to the beleaguered city.[63]

Augustine Souchy reported another example of a collective – that of Albalete de Cinca – voluntarily helping to supply Madrid: 'In March there was an act of solidarity with Madrid. Ten live hogs, each with 115 to 120 kilograms; 500 kilos of pork, 87 chickens, 50 rabbits, two tons and a half of potatoes, 200 dozen eggs, beans and other vegetables, as well as dozens of goats, were sent to the unbeaten city. An evidence of generous solidarity of a village with the needy people of the capital. They wouldn't accept any payment, even by the Military Supply Department The Albalate Comarcal Committee sent, in addition, ten wagons of flour and other foodstuffs to Madrid. Also for this they refused compensation...'[64]

The General Characteristics of Aragón Collectives

Augustine Souchy described the general characteristics of the Aragón collectives as he saw them on his visits there in 1936 and 1937:

> The smallest unit of collectivism in Aragón is the labor group. It is composed of 5 to 10, and sometimes more members. They are formed by peasants who have friendly relations with one another; sometimes also the residents of a street. The former small proprietors, small renters, sharecroppers and laborers belong to them. They go out to work together. At their head goes the delegate. Often the delegate himself chooses his work companions. The collective distributes the work to the groups. When the group has finished its work, it aids another group...

If the labor groups go beyond this number of members, each member receives a producer's card. The delegate confirms on this the work of the member of the group. The utensils, machines and animals necessary for work are the property of the collective. The cultivation of the land, the carrying out of the work assigned to them, is the task of the group.[65]

Augustine Souchy also noted the way the products available to a collective were distributed among its members:

The distribution of the land, of work, of the tools and cattle, was the first thing that was done. The Collective had to be concerned, first of all, with assuring the material existence of its members. The products of the field were taken to a common warehouse; the most important foods, distributed equally among all. The surplus products were used for exchange with other communes or with the collectives of the cities. Their own products were distributed without charge. Depending on the richness of the collective, there was the bread and wine; sometimes also meat and other food, without limit, and free. What had to be gotten from outside, by exchange or purchase from other communes or from the city, or that which existed in insufficient quantities, was rationed. But everyone had what was necessary to live, to the degree that the situation of the collective permitted it to satisfy the needs of its members...

The satisfaction of needs was separated from the work capacity of each person. They no longer said *A good day's work for a good day's pay*, but rather the norm was: *from each according to his abilities; to each according to his needs.*[66]

This new system of distribution involved in most cases the partial or total suppression of money. Frequently, the individual collective established some kind of medium of exchange of their own for use within the organization. In other cases, all goods were either rationed or were freely available for the asking to members of the collective. There was considerable variety of procedure in this, but only rarely did the money of the Republic continue to be used within a particular collective – although, of course, it was frequently needed by collective members when they went 'outside'.

Perhaps as typical as any in so far as money substitutes were concerned was the situation described by Augustine Souchy in the collective of Mazaleón: 'The president of the collective of the village, Manuel Aranda, had an original idea. He proposed some tin plate tokens as a substitute for money ... There exist tokens worth twenty-five pesetas. But this money is not distributed as a wage: it serves only as a medium of exchange. Each member of the collective receives these tokens. He buys with them what he needs to live and what there is in the collective. One peseta a day for adults, 0.75 for those under fourteen years of age.'[67]

In retrospect, at least one group of Aragón collectivists concluded that the abolition of money had been one of the principal mistakes made by the Aragónese anarchists. Those who wrote up the study of the collectives of the *comarca* of Valderrobres in the province of Teruel, wrote that:

> We wish to place in evidence a tactical and psychological error, the total or partial suppression of money. Those who have participated in this all experienced that suppression. All can confirm, more than once, the discontent which those decisions provoked. Without doubt there still exist partisans of suppression of money, as there are those who support the system of 'free distribution'. We consider that these are very complex matters, good for philosophizing, but difficult to put into practice, at least in one or two generations. Man wishes to work, but he also desires to dispose as he wishes of the part to which he is entitled. And as is said, one cannot discuss tastes and colors.[68]

There is little or no indication that the family payment method of recompense for members of the collectives provoked any appreciable attempts by free loaders to take advantage of it. Félix Carresquer has insisted that the spirit of cooperation was great enough to prevent that, but added that social pressure from other members of a collective for each member to do his part was also great.[69]

Some Examples of Aragón Collectives

It would be impossible to try to describe in any detail all of the collectives about which information is available. However, to better understand the nature of the anarchist rural collectives in Aragón, a few examples may be given.

Certainly one of the most successful of the Aragón collectives, and one which has been most written about, not only by anarchists but by others as well, was that of Graus, in the northern part of the region. Socialist writer Abelardo Prats said: 'Those who wish to know the phenomena of creativity which have taken place in Spain, once the Revolution and the war were started, I recommend should visit Graus.'[70]

Gaston Leval, who visited Graus in June 1937, noted that that part of Aragón was very conservative, and of the 43 villages in the *comarca* of Graus, only one had been totally collectivized and 10 were partly collectivized.[71] However, in Graus itself, a village of about 2,600 people, collectivization had been extensive.

According to Abelardo Prats, 700 families in Graus had joined the collective, and only 160 had stayed out of it.[72] However, many of these were not peasants, since Graus, as Leval pointed out, had 'many small establishments serving the countryside'. As of July 1936, 40 percent of the population was engaged in commerce, the rest in industry and agriculture.[73]

Leval noted the process of collectivization in the town. The agricultural collective was organized on October 16 1936, and subsequently the CNT and UGT, working together, during the next two months collectivized transportation, print shops, shoe stores, medicine, pharmacies, horseshoers' and blacksmiths' shops, and carpenters' and cabinet makers' establishments.[74] Prats concluded: 'The village is an economic unity at the service of the common good and collective interests.'[75]

Prats, who visited Graus a month or two after Gaston Leval, was particularly impressed by the accomplishment of the rural part of the collective. He claimed that with the establishment of 'family compensation', the average peasant family was receiving at least half again as much as it had before the establishment of the collective.

He was particularly impressed by the efficient management of the collective: 'Everything is systematically organized. Each branch of production has its file with exact data on its development and its daily land hourly possibilities. In this way, nothing is lost and everything is at a maximum point of organization.'[76]

According to Gaston Leval, 'The collective's coordinating functions were conducted by an 8 member administrative commission. This was divided into 8 departments, each headed by a highly qualified secretary, delegated for no set term of office by the rank and file membership of the two unions. Both the CNT and the UGT were equally represented on the Commission – 4 for each union. All delegates were subject to instant recall by the General Assembly. The departments were: Culture and Public Health, Statistics and Labor, Industry, Transportation and Communications.'[77]

As a consequence of the decline of commercial activity as the result of the War, more attention in Graus had shifted to agriculture and animal husbandry. Among the accomplishments had been the establishment of a hog farm with 2,000 animals; each family to be provided with an animal for butchering in the fall. Prats noted that 'the animals have showers and all the care that scientific treatment of animals requires'.

The collective had also established a large poultry farm with its own laboratory. More than 10,000 birds were in it when Prats visited. He claimed that 'all is new and magnificent. Everything has been installed in accordance with the exigencies of technique.' The director of the establishment had invented a new kind of incubator 'with greater output than current ones'.[78]

The social needs of the collective's members had also been attended to: 'The children are objects of special care and permanent attention by the collective. They do not work until age fourteen for any reason or excuse. The exploitation of the child by his own family members, forced in other times in most cases by the misery of the homes in which they were born, has ended ... The mothers, and above all, the women about to become mothers, are also objects of special treatment, particularly during their nursing period. They are relieved of all need to work.'[79]

A new school of arts and crafts had been established. There was also a library, and the collective had a printing establishment and a bookstore. When Prats visited, there was a special installation for about 100 refugee children from Madrid and other war fronts.[80]

Graus was an exceptionally successful collective. According to Abelardo Prats, its success owed much to its secretary-general, Emilio Portella.[81]

Certainly a number of collectives were not able to supply the kinds of services for their members which that of Graus did. For instance, Augustine Souchy reported that, in the case of the Muniesa collective, 'culturally, this locality is worse than other villages. There is no teacher, 500 children cannot go to school, illiteracy is very extensive. There is no movie theater and, what is worse, there is no doctor in the village; two neighbors with some knowledge are those who handle this in a defective manner, naturally.'[82]

Perhaps more typical than either the Graus collective or that of Muniesa was the collective of Calanda in the valley of Guadeloupe in Lower Aragón. At the time of the Revolution in 1936, the land in the area was mainly in large landholdings although there were also some small properties. The land was worked in shares, and it was estimated that 40 or 50 families in Calanda took half of the income as owners of the land, and the other 5,000 people had the other half, most of them living in dire poverty.

With the army uprising, the large property owners joined the revolt. A revolutionary committee, composed of the CNT and Izquierda Republicana Party was formed. The CNT had had a Sindicato de Oficios Varios in the area, with some 800 members, mainly agricultural workers and sharecroppers, as well as some artisans. The revolutionary committee took the place of the municipal council, and in November 1936 was officially recognized as the municipal council.

An agrarian collective was formed, by about 2,500 of the 5,000 people of the municipality. The rest remained small proprietors. The one-time secretary of the collective admitted many years later that some of the peasants may have joined it out of fear, although he insisted that there was no basis for such fear.

The members of the collective were broken up into teams of 10 to 14 workers. Each team had its delegate, and every night the delegates met to decide what to do the next day, and who should do what. There was also a directive committee, which had general control of the collective, elected by the general assembly of the collective. The general assembly met every week, and the directive committee and delegates reported to it on what they had been doing.

The payment to members of the collective was on a *per capita* basis, so much given to each person, man, woman and child. Most of this was paid in kind. In its relations with the outside, the collective operated largely on the basis of barter exchanges. In some cases, it even ceased producing things which could be better produced elsewhere – as in the case of hogs, which it decided could better be produced by people on the mountainsides.

Relations with small individual cultivators were reportedly friendly. They had a cooperative in the town, separate from that of the collective. The collective's cooperative was sometimes able to get products, such as light bulbs, for instance, which the other one could not obtain, but provided the individualists' cooperative with these, for cash. Some of the individualist peasants were themselves members of the CNT.

There were various committees set up in the community. One looked at various landholdings to decide whether owners were 'fascists' or not. Another was to decide whether land which had been confiscated from 'fascists' should be given to the collective or to individualist farmers. On these and other committees, the various political groups in the community were all represented.

The collective took over a Dominican monastery. The buildings were turned into a school, with 19 classes. The teachers included six from the previous public school, five nuns from a nearby convent, half a dozen near-graduates of a nearby normal school, and several retired teachers. All children were in school, about 40 to a teacher. When the front moved near Calanda, the children were evacuated and the buildings were turned into a hospital. The land of the monastery was used as an experimental farm. The collective also organized a library and public baths for the community.

The collective at first supplied the food for its members who had joined the militia at the front, and whose place in the workforce was largely taken by women. After things got better organized, more regular channels for obtaining supplies for the military were established.[83]

An unusual collective was that of Cuevas Portal Rubio, not far from Teruel. For some time, it existed between the lines of the two fighting forces, consisting of 40 families, all those in the community, and produced principally wheat and sheep. On one occasion, the Francoites stole 250 of the collective's sheep, and shot one of the shepherds in charge of them. As was generally the case, goods were distributed to the families of the collective in proportion to the number of their members, and all got free medical care, a few serious cases being sent as far as Barcelona for hospital treatment. The collective was finally overrun by Franco troops in March 1937.[84]

The Communist Troops' Invasion of the Aragón Collectives

After the 'civil war within a civil war' in Catalonia early in May 1937, and the consequent fall of the government of Francisco Largo Caballero later in the month, anarchist domination of Aragón continued, so also did a determined effort to eliminate the anarchist rural collectives in the region.

Although the Communists were the strongest protagonists of the destruction of anarchist political and economic power in Aragón, and it was largely troops under their control which were to carry out the operation, they were by no means the only political element involved. Indeed, the Right-wing Socialists, and particularly minister of defense Indalecio Prieto, played key roles in the manoeuver, as we shall see in a later chapter.

Gaston Leval has graphically described the attacks by Communist troops – principally those of Lister's 11th Division and the 27th Division, the former Karl Marx Column: 'In the middle of June, the attack began in Aragón on a large scale and with methods until then unknown. Harvest time was approaching. Rifle in hand, the collectors, of Communist inspiration, detained on the important roads the trucks leaded with foodstuffs and took them to their own camps. A little later, the same guards went to the collectives, and in the name of the General Staff which had its headquarters in Barbastro, demanded that they turn over large quantities of wheat.'

Leval described the next step of the Communists and their allies against the Aragón collectives: 'There began the requisition of all trucks, then indispensable for transport of the harvested products, particularly wheat ... almost always the collectives had procured trucks through exchanges of their agricultural products, sometimes depriving themselves of foodstuffs. The trucks were one of the acquisitions of which they were most proud. But all were requisitioned, brutally, on the pretext of the war.'

Leval indicated still another way in which the Aragónese collectives were further undermined:

At the same time, and always in Aragón, they mobilized the recruits on the pretext of the next offensive. At the beginning of the harvest, fifty youths of Esplus were recruited... Almost all the other villages were deprived of their youths, but the same categories of recruits were not called up in Catalonia. They came later. In the meanwhile, the harvest was taken in in the worst conditions...[85]

Then came the open attack. Major Lister was in charge of it. It would take too long to give full details on the episodes. The final result was that 30 percent of the collectives were destroyed. In Alcolea, the Municipal Council which directed the collective was arrested; the inhabitants of the Home for the Aged were thrown into the street. In Mas de las Matas, in Monzón, in Barbastro, to a certain degree everywhere, there were arrests. There was sacking everywhere. The warehouses of the cooperatives, the deposits of wheat were robbed; the furniture was destroyed. The governor of Aragón, sent by the central government after the dissolution of the Council of Aragón ... protested. They told him to go to the devil.[86]

Later, at a CNT National Peasant Congress, on October 22 1937, the regional committee of Aragón submitted a report on what had happened there: 'More than 600 organizers of the collectives have been arrested. The government has named Management Committees which have taken over the food deposits and distributed their contents haphazardly. The lands, the draught animals and work instruments have been returned to the families or to the fascists whom the Revolution had treated without rigor. The harvests were distributed in the same way. The animals that the collectives had raised suffered the same fate. A large number of collective cages, stables, dairies have been destroyed. In some municipalities, such as Burdeos and Calaceite they deprived the peasants of the seeds which now are unavailable to till the soil.'[87]

The Communists rationalized this destruction of the Aragón collectives in their daily paper, *Frente Rojo* on August 14 1937,

In so far as the Collective are concerned we shall say that there is not a single Aragónese peasant who has not been forced to enter them. Anyone who resisted suffered in his flesh and in his small property from terrorist sanctions. Thousands of peasants have migrated from the region, preferring to desert than to support the thousand torturing measures that the Council of Aragón imposed. Their lands were seized, they were forced to work from sunup to sundown on their own lands, a debilitating task, receiving a wage of ninety-five centimos. Anyone who resisted was deprived of bread, soap and the most indispensable things for living. All private foodstuffs were seized. In the municipal Councils known fascists were placed; squadron chiefs of the Falange, owners of party cards, served as mayors, councillors...[88]

However, subsequently even the Communists, both those who remained in the party and those who dropped out, recognized that the dissolution of the collectives of Aragón had been a mistake. Burnett Bolloten cites José Duque, as saying that Lister's measures 'were more severe than they need have been'. Bolloten noted that the other Communist (and still a Communist), who served on the Consejo de Aragón, Manuel Almudi, said: 'Lister's measures in Aragón were very harsh. He could have acted with greater discretion. Great ill feeling was aroused as a result of his conduct.'[89]

Perhaps most decisive were the observations of José Silva, general secretary of the National Institute of Agrarian reform, and a Communist, who said:

When the government of the Republic dissolved the Council of Aragón, the governor general tried to allay the profound uneasiness in the hearts of the peasant masses by dissolving the collectives. This measure was a very grave mistake and produced tremendous disorganization in the countryside...

It is true that the governor's aim was to repair injustices and to convince the workers of the countryside that the Republic was producing them, but the result was just the opposite from that intended. The measure only increased the confusion, and violence was exercised, but this time by the other side. As a result, labor in the fields was suspended almost entirely, and a quarter of the land had not been prepared at the time for sowing.[90]

The Partial Restoration of the Collectives

If Gaston Leval is correct, about two-thirds of the Aragón collectives escaped the ravages of the Communist troops in August 1937. In addition, a number of those which had been disrupted by Lister's division, or one of the other Republican army units, were reconstituted once the campaign against them had been relaxed.

José Peirats has noted the change in the policy of the government and of the Communist Party. 'The collective farms were once again authorized. The prisoners were released. Collectivization got under way. The new sowings were prepared. But this time it was Franco who reaped the harvest... One cannot play the game of demoralizing a front and its rear with impunity.'[91]

No comprehensive information is available concerning the number of collectives that were reconstituted after the Communist invasion. However, details on a few of these cases can be given. For instance, in the case of the Calaceite collective in Teruel province, 'After the attack, the Collective was reorganized as well as possible. In the meantime, the so-called Communists had turned over part of the lands to those who had risen in arms against the Republic, that is to say, to the fascists. Naturally, the attack produced demoralization; the Collective was no longer the same as before, there was not the same enthusiasm.'[93] In the case of Cretas, in the same province, the collective apparently continued to exist, although after the Communist attack, there was reportedly 'certain demoralization' in its ranks.[93]

In the case of La Fresneda collective, the results were apparently less disastrous. That collective had been legalized by the ministry of agriculture, and when the leaders of the collective presented the document attesting to this to the invading Communist forces, the latter apparently hesitated in totally dissolving the organization. However, they did call a public meeting, where they announced that anyone who wanted to leave it was free to do so. 'Some discontented one', thereupon withdrew, including some people who had belonged to the CNT before July 19.

After this incident, it was reported that 'Cleaned of noxious elements ... the Collective rebounded with unexpected vitality. That was a true family...' In the groups there was only talk of the work to be done to increase production, to repair roads and irrigation facilities, to recondition houses; that is to say, about the future and progress...'[94]

In the case of the Calanda collective, it was reconstituted soon after the Lister Brigade had left. In conformity with a government decree, it received its legalization, with the help of a young man who had not quite finished his law studies. It persisted until the Franco forces' invasion of March 1938.[95]

The Ballobar del Cinco collective, near Huesca, which was broken up by the Karl Marx Division, was also reconstituted soon after the attack took place. One of the former members of the organization reported many years later that it was 'just as it had been before', once it had been reorganized.[96]

Conclusion

Certainly one of the most notable achievements of the anarchists during the Spanish Civil War was the reorganization of agriculture, along the lines of their doctrines, throughout most of Aragón during the first year of the War. There was obviously a considerable degree of diversity among the collectives which the anarchists established, but certain features they seem to have had in common.

It seems to have been universally true that the Aragón rural collectives adopted the principle of paying their members in terms of need rather than of production. They all seem to have done the work of the collective in groups or gangs of approximately ten people each, headed by a *delegado* chosen by the members of the group. Ultimate decisions within each collective were taken by the general assembly, made up of all of the adult members of the collective, a body which met in most cases with surprising frequency. Each collective had an administrative committee, elected by the assembly, to direct the work of the collective in between assembly meetings, but which had to report periodically to the membership. Members of such committees seem to have been subject to immediate recall, although there is little evidence that such actions actually occurred with any frequency. Finally, all of the collectives apparently bartered their surplus products with one another, as well as with outside organizations, usually through their *comarcal* federations.

Less universal, but still widespread, was the abolition of the use of money of the Spanish Republic for transactions within the collectives, although in many cases even those collectives which had abolished official government money for internal purposes, needed to use it in their dealings with organizations outside the collective or the *comarcal* federation. Substitutes for money varied from internal money created by the collective, to a pure rationing system, to at least a handful of cases, in which collective members merely asked for and received without charge from the cooperative store of the collective the things they needed. Probably in most cases there was a combination of rationing and free goods and services.

Great emphasis was placed on establishment of schools, or their expansion where they already existed. Many of these were organized along the lines of Francisco Ferrer's 'free school'. Other cultural organizations, particularly libraries, were also prevalent among the collectives. They also sought in most cases to provide medical care for their members, either in the collective or through connections with doctors or hospitals in neighboring towns and cities.

From a purely economic point of view, the evidence indicates that the collectives were very assiduous in establishing small industries to process their crops or manufacture things for the collective or for the *comarcal* federation. They also laid emphasis on extending electric and telephone lines, building or improving roads, constructing new installations and projects such as crop storage facilities, hogpens, cattle barns and the like.

Perhaps the most remarkable non-farming activity undertaken by one of the rural collectives was the lignite mine opened up by the Andorra collective, in Teruel province. The existence of the lignite reserves in the vicinity had been known long before the Civil War, but had been declared unusable by geologists. However, given the difficulties – and subsequently the impossibility – of getting coal from Asturias, whence it had previously been obtained, a coal shortage developed in Catalonia, and the need for new sources closer at hand become urgent.

The Andorra collective took the initiative in November 1936 of opening a mine in its vicinity. With the aid of seven experienced miners who were recruited for the purpose, the peasants of Andorra made up most of the work force. They dug a mine 50 meters deep, with three galleries. Their only instruments of labor were picks and shovels, although a motor was used to keep water out of the mine galleries. Finally, they were providing an average of 30 tons of coal a day. Gaston Leval noted: 'Various factories of Catalonia functioned thanks to this.'[97]

Available evidence would seem to indicate that the productivity of the areas in the collectives was at least as good during the existence of the collectives as it had been before, and in many cases notably better. Broué and Temime noted the anarchist claims 'that output increased from 30 percent to 50 percent between 1936 and 1937.[98] The collectives undoubtedly made a significant contribution in supplying provisions for the troops on the Aragón front, and to a less (but still significant) degree to Madrid under siege, as well as helping to supply the cities of Catalonia and the Levante.

The Aragón anarchists themselves not infrequently referred to charges by their critics that they were trying to construct a Utopia. To some degree that was certainly the case. One must conclude that, although their efforts did not clearly demonstrate that their particular vision of a just and equitable rural society was feasible in the longer run, neither did their slightly more than one year of experience with libertarian communism in Aragón definitively prove the contrary.

14

Rural Collectives in the Levante Region

After the Civil War, Spanish anarchists tended to look back upon their experience with agrarian collectives in the Levante region as their most successful agrarian revolutionary experiment. Some foreign anarchist observers, who were personally acquainted with the CNT's rural revolutionary efforts in various parts of Republican Spain, concurred in this assessment. Thus, the French anarchist Gaston Leval wrote: 'According to our opinion it is in the Levante – thanks to its natural riches and the creative spirit of our comrades – that the work of the agrarian collectives has been most vast and best carried out.[1]

There is no question about the fact that rural collectives sponsored by the CNT continued to increase in number throughout most of the War. It is also true that they generally maintained good relations with their counterparts affiliated with the Unión General de Trabajadores, which in that part of the country continued to be largely under the control of followers of Francisco Largo Caballero. Likewise, both the CNT and UGT rural union federations sought, throughout the War, to organize the agrarian economy of the region so as to give the most possible support to the war effort. Finally, during the first year and a half of the war, the two union groups mounted an interesting effort to organize under their own control the exports of citrus fruit and other products which were of major importance in providing foreign exchange for the hard-pressed Republican regime.

However, it would also seem to be the case that the anarchists tended to understate the continuing gravity of the conflict between the agrarian collectives and the small and medium-sized landholders who made up most of the rural population of the region, particularly of the three Valencian provinces, a conflict of which the Communists were quick to take advantage. The anarchists also considerably exaggerated, both at the time and in retrospect, their success in overcoming the exceedingly serious problems which the collectives faced, including in many cases an exaggerated parochialism, the low cultural level of their members, and the lack in many cases of a clear understanding of the philosophy and nature of the kind of collectives they were trying to bring into existence.

The Nature of the Pre-war Situation in the Rural Levante Region

The region which the Spanish anarchists designated as 'the Levante' consisted of the three provinces sometimes referred to as 'the Valencian country' (*el Pais Valenciano*), that is Valencia itself, Castellón de la Plana and Alicante, as well as the provinces of Murcia and Albacete to the south and west respectively, of the Valencia region. In much of this area, the pre-war rural situation was quite different from other parts of Spain, such as in Andalusia, Extremadura and Castille.

The Valencia region, in particular, was not generally characterized by latifundia. Large landholdings (those over 100 hectares or approximately 250 acres) occupied only about one quarter of the rural land in the three Valencian provinces, whereas those of 10 hectares or less accounted for 51.35 percent of the total land, and those between 10 and 100 hectares occupied 24.12 percent of the land. Small proprietors made up 56 percent of the total, medium-sized landholders 27 percent and large landholders only 16 percent.[2]

Dr Bosch Sánchez sums up the landholding situation before the Civil War thus: '... in the Valencian countryside, small and medium property rather than large holdings predominated, a large part of the coastal zone was dedicated to intensive truck gardening which required a specialized peasantry, and until the civil war there had never been serious discussion of an agrarian reform that would substantially alter the property structure.'[3]

Partly as a reflection of the landholding pattern of the region, the CNT, at the outbreak of the Civil War, 'had no specifically agrarian trade union organization in the Valencian Country, and its organizational weakness in the countryside was manifest.'[4] In contrast, according to Dr Bosch Sánchez, 'The Federación de Trabajadores de la Tierra (UGT) had been consolidated during the Republic, and it appears that it remained during the war the largest peasant organization' in the Valencia region.[5] According to one Communist source, the UGT federation had about 80,000 members during the conflict in the three Valencian provinces, compared to 30,000 in the CNT's federation. Another Communist, Jesús Hernández, claimed that at the outbreak of the war the UGT federation had 30,000 members, of whom 8,000 were under Communist leadership, the CNT had about 8,000 agricultural laborers, the Federación Regional de Colonos, 'influenced by the Communist Party', had 3,500, and the Catholic-controlled Federación Valencia de Sindicatos Agricolas, had 'more than 30,200 affiliates'.[7]

With its more than 3,000,000 people, this part of Spain was blessed with almost perpetual sunshine, a sub-tropical climate and was one of the richest agricultural areas of the peninsula. It specialized in citrus fruits, rice and truck gardening, and much of its output came from land which had been irrigated since the time of the Moors. With the early loss of other key rural areas to the Rebels, the Mediterranean coastal region became of particularly great economic importance for the Republic, not only to feed the armed forces and population of the Loyalist areas, but also to provide exports and foreign exchange.

From a political point of view, there were many different tendencies represented in the region. The two geographical parts of the area, and more hilly western part and the litoral along the Mediterranean coast, had diverged. In the former, where subsistence farmers had predominated, the very conservative Carlist, or Traditionalist, movement had long been dominant but, by the 1930s, the Republican parties had come largely to displace them, and both the CNT and the

Socialists' Unión General de Trabajadores, had developed some following.[8]

In the litoral, the Partido d'Unió Republicana Autonomista, a conservative but autonomist party, had extensive support. So did the two major Republican parties, the Izquierda Republicana and Unión Republicana, as well as the Socialists in the cities. The Popular Front parties supported the idea of Valencian regional autonomy, along the lines of what had been granted to Catalonia. In fact, in July 1936, before the outbreak of the Civil War, the Republican parties had drawn up a draft of a regional autonomy statute.[9] Soon after the War began, the CNT also drew up a similar document.[10]

Land Seizures Early in the War

With the outbreak of the Civil War the trade union organizations and new revolutionary authorities in the Valencia region and neighboring provinces seized substantial quantities of land. It was taken principally from two groups of people: large landholders and people who had shown sympathy with the Rebels. In the three Valencian provinces, 289,418 hectares were taken over, amounting to approximately 13.18 percent of the total landholdings of the region.

There was considerable difference in the amount of land seized in different areas. In the province of Alicante, for instance, 18. 94 percent of the pre-war holdings were taken, in contrast to only 5.53 percent in Castellón, and 14.89 percent in the province of Valencia. In Albacete, also part of the Levante, a much larger proportion of existing landholdings, 33.35 percent were taken over.[11] I have no figures for Murcia.

These land seizures were of particular significance in so far as the establishment of rural collectives by both the CNT and the UGT was concerned. It was principally on them that collectives were established. Dr Bosch Sánchez has noted that in 87 collectives in the Valencia region which she was able to study in some detail, in 93 percent of the cases, the land on which these collectives had been established was that seized early in the war, whereas in only three joint CNT–UGT collectives had both seized land and land belonging to members of the collectives been used, and only in two had the land been only that belonging to those who went to form the collective.[12] Also, she estimates that 31.58 percent of the 13.18 percent of the land seized in the three provinces of the Valencia country was organized in collectives.[13]

The Spread of CNT Rural Organizations

In the revolutionary atmosphere that followed the suppression of the Rebellion in the Levante region, CNT organizations spread rapidly in the rural areas. The anarchists quickly realized the need for establishing an overall federation of their rural groups. As a consequence, the first regional congress of peasants of the CNT met in Valencia from September 18–20 1936. It was claimed that there were present 146 delegations representing 41,347 members.

This congress established the Federación Regional de Campesinos de Levante (FRCL). It included within it CNT organizations from the three Valencian provinces as well as Albacete and Murcia. It proposed the establishment by the CNT rural unions of each *comarca*, of a *comarcal* federation, as well as five provincial federations.

This founding congress of the FRCL also set forth the agrarian policy advocated by the anarchists in the region. It supported the socialization of land which had been seized, but at the same time supported the right of smallholders to 'cultivate the land which they can cultivate with their own hands, so long as this doesn't obstruct or make difficult the orderly development of the nucleii which are socialized.' This motion was not passed without opposition from some of the delegates present. Some argued that 'it is a weakness in our position to respect the small proprietor, because this is a seed which can reproduce itself,' and proposed 'that each community operate in terms of its own possibilities'.[14]

Subsequently the FRCL held further congresses on a *comarcal*, provincial and regional level. Thus, a regional plenum of peasants met in December 1936, and urged more vigorous action in carrying out the Revolution in the countryside.[15]

By June 1937, the anarchist daily *Fragua Social* maintained that there were *comarcal* federations of the FRCL in 23 *comarcas* in Valencia province, eight in Alicante, eight in Castellón, ten in Murcia, and four in Albacete.[16] However, by June 1937, it had become clear to the leaders of the FRCL that there was need for a separate organization within the federation for the collectives affiliated to it. As a consequence, the second congress of the FRCL, in November 1937 called upon the collectives to form *comarcal* federations of their own.[17]

The Early Organization of Collectives

In the revolutionary euphoria at the beginning of the Civil War, both the CNT and the UGT began the organization of rural collectives. However, there was great diversity in nature and organization of these groups, particularly among those formed by the CNT.

At one extreme were Pedralba and Bugarra in the *comarca* of Campo de Turia in Valencia, where 'in general assembly, the people decided on total collectivisation. Lands, stores, workshops came to be run by the Committee, money was abolished, and the CNT flag waved over the town hall.'[118] On the other hand, at the other extreme, in many places nothing had changed, 'the landholders continued cultivating their land and turning over the product to the same private merchants.'[19]

Not all anarchists were pleased with the libertarian communism of the Pedralba collective. Terence M. Smyth cited a criticism of the CNT public utility workers union of Valencia which was published in the UGT's periodical *Corresponcia de Valencia* at the end of September 1936. It commented: 'libertarian communism will not resemble a convent or a barracks, will not be scarcity but abundance.' It then proceeded to cite scarcities of consumer goods and of raw materials for the textile plant which was also part of the Pedralba collective. The statement said that 'when libertarian communism is imposed by force on the people, they will sabotage it as much as they can, obviously secretly.' The criticism ended by saying that 'Pedralba, a community of great productivity is becoming one of consumption.'[20]

In between the establishment of libertarian communism and the maintenance of the status quo ante there was the greatest variety. Dr Aurora Bosch has noted: 'In some localities the CNT had not obtained control of seized land, in others only small quantities, and when the CNT organization did possess land, the local leaders and militants didn't really know what a collective was. If they succeeded in initiating collectivization, one case was different from another, some functioned well, others poorly, the CNT organization had no real control over them.'[21]

Undoubtedly, peasants joined collectives during the first months of the War from a variety of motivations. Right after the outbreak of the conflict, one major reason was the pressing need to take in the harvest. The War began just before the harvest season, and there was a great urgency to take in the crops on those lands which had been abandoned by their owners. Collectives were certainly organized for that purpose.

In many other cases, collectives were formed because of the ideological conviction of the peasants involved. I have described the proclamation of 'total collectivization' in Pedralba and Bugara, two communities where the anarchists had earlier proclaimed libertarian communism during the abortive CNT insurrection in January 1933.[22] There were many other localities in the five provinces of the Levante where the peasants who established collectives were similarly motivated by ideological considerations. Dr Bosch Sanchez has noted, for instance, the explanation of the leaders of the collective of Caudete de las Fuentes that 'on July 19 of 36 we workers believed that the hour of our total emancipation had arrived, and naturally, we began in Caudete de las Fuentes to make our economic revolution.'[23]

However, Dr Bosch Sánchez also suggested other factors which motivated some of those who joined collectives in the early phase of the Civil War: '...It is difficult to think that these various motives for voluntary adhesion to the collective influenced the decisions of those individuals who were neither in a situation of extreme misery, nor shared the collectivist ideology of the unions, but who at least at the beginning of the War entered en bloc in some CNT collectives. In these cases it was rather terror or mere subsistence which obliged them to enter the collective, since the CNT dominated politically the locality, had seized lands, houses and harvests, organized the supply and distribution of all products. Who could risk staying out of the collective?'[24]

The wartime editor of the anarchist daily, *Fragua Social*, in Valencia admitted that one of the most difficult jobs of the anarchist leaders in the region in the first period of the conflict was to prevent over-enthusiastic CNTers from seizing the land of the small peasants who were loyal to the Republic. He himself visited the countryside on that mission several times, and at least once was accompanied by Civil Guards to add to the impressiveness of his presence, although he told me that he had no intention of ordering the policemen to take any action. The peasants, after discussion, were usually amenable to reason on the subject.[25]

The exile anarchist periodical *CNT*, inadvertently showed the negative results excessive enthusiasm by anarchist militants had had in one municipality of the Levante province of Castellón, the village of Alcalá de Chiavert. It noted that after the February 1936 election some disaffected CNTers and Republican parties formed a local UGT. At the same time, the CNT reopened its headquarters, which had been closed by the previous rightest administration.

On July 19, with the outbreak of the Civil War, there was a roundup of 'reactionaries' in the village. 'To the unhappiness and against protests of the moderates, the seizure of factories, lands and buildings was undertaken for collectivization. The factories were put immediately to work, the expropriated land represented half of all, and buildings in the town were municipalized. A Revolutionary Committee 'with representation of all antifascist sectors' displaced the municipal council. A collective was officially established in January 1937 at a meeting of 2,000 people, including UGTistas, but the demand of UGTers that they be allowed to distribute land individually to their members was rejected by the CNT, which obviously was dominant.

In July 1937, the governor of Castellón sent in Assault Guards to Alcalá de Chiavert. Encouraged by nearby Communist militia, 'reactionaries' seized the food warehouse of the collective, and the headquarters of the Juventud Libertaria. Four leading CNTers were jailed. A Communist Party local was formed for the first time in the village, apparently by the UGTistas.[26]

The Expansion of the Collectives in the Levante

Whatever the original motives peasants had for entering the collectives, the fact is that the number of collectives in the Levante region continued to expand during most of the Civil War. This is attested to by virtually all sources, although there is wide disagreement over just how many collectives were in fact organized in the region.

The largest estimate that we have encountered of the number of collectives in the five provinces was given to the author by Rafael Esteban who, during most of the War, was secretary of Statistics and Control of the Federacion Regional de Campesinos de Levante, and claimed that there were either 922 or 932 collectives in all in the region.[27]

Gaston Leval, who visited many of the Levante collectives during the War, claimed in his 1972 book *Colectividades Libertarias en España* that there were 900 collectives.[28] However, in his somewhat earlier work *Ne Franco Ne Stalin* (1969), he wrote: 'In the Congress of the Federación de los Campesinos de Levante (21–23 November 1937) there were represented 430 organized collectives. Five months later, there were 500.' He added that there were collectives in 43 percent of the 'localities' of the Levante region.[29]

Limiting herself to the three Valencian provinces, Dr Bosch Sánchez has estimated that in that region there were 264 CNT rural collectives. In addition, there were 69 controlled by the UGT, and a further 20 which were jointly organized by the CNT and the UGT.[30]

It is notable that the number of rural collectives continued to increase between the spring of 1937 and the end of that year, during which period they were subjected to severe persecution (as we shall see subsequently) at the hands of the Communist Party and (after the fall of Largo Caballero) to the hostility of the government of Dr Negrín. This fact would seem to bear witness to the voluntary nature of most of the collectives which existed by the end of 1937.

According to Dr Bosch Sánchez, whereas in March 1937 the FRCL claimed to have 84 collectives affiliated with it, by August it reported that it had 180 legalized collectives, another 130 which were in the process of obtaining legal recognition, and 230 more 'in the process of formation' throughout the Levante region, while in November 1937, the FRCL reported having 340 legalized collectives and 75 more in the process of getting legalization. She indicated that the UGT in the Valencia region had also experienced some growth in the number of collectives associated with it.[31]

According to Terence M. Smyth, there were 84 collectives associated with the Peasants' Federation in March 1937, and some 360 collectives which had received legal recognition by October 1937. However, by April 1938, there were 437 collectives, of which 135 were not yet legally recognized.[32]

The Nature of the CNT Collectives

There was a great deal of variation in the organization and functioning of the CNT agrarian collectives in the Levante region. Bernabé Esteban, who for much of the War was secretary of the provincial federation of the FRCL in Alicante, told me that they included both good and bad ones, that some collectives were run by people without adequate education for the job, and a few were exploited by those who were in charge of them. However, on balance, he concluded that the agrarian collectives of the CNT in the Levante region had been successful under trying circumstances.[33]

Probably one of the most successful of the Levante collectives was that of Alfara del Patriarca in the province of Valencia. The peasants there were among the first groups to organize a collective in the region. They were lucky, in that a high official of the supply department (Intendencia) of the army was caught in the town at the time of the Rebellion. Although he was sympathetic to the Rebels, he none the less worked with the leaders of the collective in setting up the paperwork of the collective. He worked loyally throughout the War, although when it was over he returned to being an officer in the (Franco) army.

With this officer's help, the leaders of the Alfara del Patriarca collective quickly set up an extensive accounting system. They developed a variety of forms upon which to report the various activities of the collective, which were later used by a number of the other collectives of the area.[34]

At the other extreme, perhaps, was the agrarian collective of Alcoy in the province of Alicante. There, the collective came to be controlled by a committee, the members of which began to sell the collective's crops for their own account, and in addition ran up a large debt with the ministry of agriculture, which they were unable, or unwilling, to repay. After receiving complaints from members of the Alcoy collective, the secretary of the Alicante federation of the FRCL, together with the local representative of the Institute of Agrarian Reform went to investigate the situation. At a meeting of the members of the collective, the federation secretary recommended that all loyal CNT members of the collective should forthwith withdraw from it, and form another one. When this was done, the new CNT collective was soon able to pay off its share of the debt to the ministry, and it continued to function more or less normally until the end of the War.[35]

Gaston Leval has left some generalizations on how the collectives in the Levante region were organized:

Almost always the collectives were created on the initiative of the peasant unions of the locality, but they soon constituted an autonomous organization. There was maintained only an external contact with the union, which was the link between the collectivists and the individualists. In fact, the latter brought their products for exchange for others; thus, in practice, their isolation was diluted through the medium of the *sindicato*, which would be organized thenceforward on the basis of a structure which corresponded to the new situation...

Within it there had been created commissions for rice, oranges and truck gardening. The collective itself had its own store and its own commissions; but later, this useless duplication was suppressed; the stores were unified; the commissions were integrated with both collectivists and individualists being registered in the *sindicato*. Others founded mixed commissions, as for instance ones for the purchase of machines, seeds, fertilizers, insecticides, veterinary products, etc. All used the same trucks.[36]

The rural collectives of the Levante started out with different systems of payment of their members. However, by the end of the War, they had generally adopted the system of paying in accordance with the number of members in each family in the collective. This was, of course, in conformity with the ideological principles of the CNT.[37]

The POUMist leader Wildebaldo Solano has recounted the way a collective worked in the province of Valencia in which his parents took part, and which had been established voluntarily by a group of smallholders. There, he said, they virtually abolished th use of money within the collective, with the collective providing the food and other necessities for each family, and giving each family as much cash as was needed for things they absolutely had to get from the outside. Work was done in common, the collective sold the products. Solano remembered the collective as being 'a happy one', and recalled conversations with women in their sixties who stoutly defended it in later years, saying that it was a better, more efficient and more equitable way of organizing the local agriculture.[38]

According to Walther Bernecker, the abolition of the use of Republican money in the collectives of the Levante region was widespread: 'In a large part of the *levantine* collectives ... the monetary economy was either abolished or displaced to a position of secondary importance by the introduction of local money or of chits and the simultaneous reinforcement of the practice of the natural economy of barter. In less than half (31 of 75 collectives) is there indication of the monetary economy having been preserved.'[39]

The FRCL sought to get the collectives to adopt standardized statutes. Thus, the section of advice and statistics, reported to the November 1937 congress of the FRCL: 'To avoid the confusion created by different statutes in each Collective, which would materially impede knowing about the development of each of them and their norms because of their diversity, apart, it is clear, from the danger that the Ministry of Labor will not approve them, there was need to prepare a model Statute for all the Collectives. A statute which all those now constituted and those pending approval now have; Statute which is not all that the organization desires – why deny it? – but is the only one which can receive approval in the light of existing social law, inspired only in Marxist doctrines.'[40]

Perhaps the statutes of the collective of Alcorisa were more or less typical. They contain ten articles, dealing with the property of the collective, the use of that property, membership in the collective, procedure for admission to it, procedure for separation from the group, the role of the administrative *junta*, the function of the general assembly of the collective, 'the rights and duties of the collectivists', the way in which the collective might be dissolved (only when it was reduced to less than ten members), and what would happen to the property of the collective should it be dissolved.

A few comments on these statues are in order. New members could be admitted by the general assembly, upon receipt of an application. Three kinds of exit from the collective were foreseen: justified voluntary withdrawal, unjustified voluntary withdrawal, and expulsion; in the last two cases the member leaving would lose all of his share in the collective. As to the rights and duties of the members, 'the member of the collective will have the obligation of contributing with all his power and capacity to the benefit of the same', and 'the members of the collective will have the right to receive what they need from the collective in accordance with its possibilities'.[41]

However, by no means all of the rural CNT members in the Levante region wanted to belong to collectives; some chose instead to remain small proprietors. Franz Borkenau noted during his visit to the area in August 1936: 'In the village of Silla a few members of the local committee in my presence started an argument with my companions from anarchist regional headquarters about it; they not only regarded it as a matter of course that the peasant's land should remain intact, but considered that even the expropriated land of the executed fascists ought not to be collectivized, but distributed among the peasants . . .'[42]

According to Dr Bosch Sánchez, the leadership of the FRCL, as a result of this situation, 'had no choice but to recognize in the month of August 1937 that in addition to collectives, there existed within the union "communal exploitation, production and consumption cooperatives, and collective stores of those who live as small proprietors".' Furthermore, the second congress of the FRCL, in November 1937, passed a resolution 'to form cooperatives which would include the two forms of work, although in many cases this merely confirmed a situation of fact.' Dr Bosch added that this resolution 'represented a great step towards flexibility and realism in the CNT organization, which was reflected in numerous concrete cases quite far from libertarian orthodoxy.'[43]

The Educational Efforts of the Collectives

One of the most notable aspects of the CNT collectives in the Levante region was their efforts to provide education for their children. Walther Bernecker has noted that by 1938 all of the collectives of the Levante had their own schools: 'The literacy and technical training programs for the youths and the adults contributed to the raising of the general level of instruction of the rural population. At the same time, they achieved the most complete possible education for the children.'[44]

One person who spent most of the War as a child in the Torre a Juera collective in Murcia, of which his grandfather was secretary, has commented on the educational opportunities and difficulties in that group: all of the children were in school, whereas before the War many parents had not been able to forgo the small increase in family income which their working children had been able to provide. With the assurance of adequate support for each family from the collective, they no longer had reason to keep their children out of school.

However, as the War went on, the collective was faced with a serious labor shortage, since most of the young men went into military service. It thus became necessary to use child labor at orange and grape harvesting time. So they rotated the work among them, some children staying out of school to work each day. The children were all paid equally, regardless of how much time they spent at work.[45]

The preoccupation of the collectivists with the education of their children was illustrated by the statutes of the Jativa collective in Valencia province. Article 21 provided: 'No child can be sent to work until fourteen years of age, and they will be obliged to go to school from the age of six. Absences shall be the responsibility of the parents or the teachers, and for any unjustified absence, one day's pay, that is, six pesetas, will be deducted from them.'[46]

This provision was given practical application in the collective. Three school buildings were made available, as well as a building where the children could stay after school under some adult supervision, until their parents returned from work.[47]

The Work of the Federación Regional de Campesinos de Levante

The Federación Regional de Campesinos de Levante, formed a few weeks after the outbreak of the Civil War, played a leading role in the CNT agrarian collectivist movement in the Levante region. It sought to develop uniform procedures among the various collectives, as well as to provide them with a wide range of services. At the same time, it sought to organize the sale and distribution of the products of the collectives – and of other CNT peasants – both domestically and outside Spain.

The FRCL was supposed to be the top layer of a pyramid of organizations, starting with the local *sindicatos* and collectives at the base, and moving up to federations in each *comarca*, grouped in federations in each of the five provinces, culminating in the regional federation. Gaston Leval has said that there were in fact 54 *comarcal* federations and five provincial ones.[48]

However, there is evidence that the generalization of *comarcal* federations did not proceed as smoothly as the FRCL had hoped, casting some doubt on the number of such groups Leval claimed to exist. A resolution of a regional plenum of peasant *comarcal* groups in September 1937 said: 'We have said, and it is true, that there are many peasant *comarcal* groups established, but it is no less certain that there are many *comarcal* groups which function with great irregularity, since the differentiation of functions between the peasant organization and the rest of the confederation has not occurred ... Where *comarcal* Peasant Federations have not yet been created, they must be rapidly established and the accords for their functioning must be put in practice.'[49] Dr Bosch Sánchez maintains that she could find evidence of only four *comarcal* federations being formed in the three Valencian provinces.[50]

The provincial federations, on the other hand, did function more or less effectively. For instance, in the Alicante provincial federation, there were 20 accountants employed, who kept reasonably close track of the situation of the various collectives of the province.[51]

The FRCL was supposed to hold a congress each year, and in fact held two of these, in September 1936 and November 1937. In each case, the congress elected the regional committee, which directed the activities of the federation. According to Leval, this regional committee had 26 technical sections, dealing with the principal products of the region, and with such questions as transport, machinery, imports and exports, construction, and health and education.[52]

The FRCL had a sizeable corps of accountants working for it, who received financial reports from the collectives of the CNT in the region. The federation tried to keep track of how each collective was functioning, and when it became aware of one having difficulties, it sent someone out to investigate the causes. This man might suggest changes in the collective's organization or accounting methods, might suggest that they get a new accountant, which the federation would provide. However, the role of the federation was strictly advisory. According to Rafael Esteban, it could never impose its suggestions on a member collective, since that would be strictly against CNT principles.[53]

The federation also sought to help out those collectives which were financially or economically weakest. The FRCL objective was that the economic level of all members of all collectives be as nearly equal as possible. In line with this, the federation originally suggested establishment of a *banco sindical*. However, both the national and regional committees of the CNT turned down that idea, arguing that it was against CNT principles to establish a bank. So the federation set up a compensation fund of agrarian collectives (Caja de Compensación de Colectividades Agrarias). The surpluses of the wealthier collectives were supposed to go into this *caja*, and out of it were paid substantial sums to the poorer collectives, to help them get seed, machinery, or to cover other costs. These loans were generally not paid back, and in fact it was not intended in most cases that they would be. No interest was charged on these loans.[54]

There were examples of solidarity among the different collectives. At one time, Rafael Esteban, as statistical and control secretary of the FRCL, visited the collective of Polina del Jucar in the province of Valencia, a relatively prosperous organization of 800 families. At that time, there were being formed nearby two new collectives, whose land was much poorer and who very much lacked resources to get started. Esteban told the leaders of Polina del Jucar that the federation was going to finance these two new collectives. Esteban reported many years later that the leaders of the prosperous collective took this as virtually a personal insult, adding that they were perfectly able to help their two neighbors, and that it was shocking that they should not be allowed to do so. Of course, the federation was perfectly happy to have them do so, and reportedly the Polina del Jucar organization did help the two nearby collectives get established.[55]

However, there is evidence that not all of the better-off collectives showed the same kind of solidarity as that of Polina del Jucar towards their less fortunate neighbors. Horacio Prieto, speaking at the economic congress of the CNT in Valencia in January 1938, was critical of the 'permanent egotism of the workers who administer a collective'. Also, the Valencia anarchist newspaper *Fragua Social*, in August 1938, complained that 'the collectives until now, in spite of their evident success, have been autonomous economic formations, left individually to their fate. If the land was rich, the collective also was. If the land, on the contrary, was poor, the collective develops in the midst of the greatest penury.'[56]

Another function of the Federación Regional de Campesinos de

Levante was to improve the training of those administering the affairs of the collectives. To this end, the FRCL set up 'institutes' in each of the five provinces, where secretaries, accountants and other technical employees were given short-term training.[57]

The first of these schools was established in October 1937. It was set up in an old convent. Of the 120 applicants for admission, 100 were accepted. They were required to have fundamental knowledge of reading, writing, arithmetic and general culture. All male students had to be over 30 years of age, and thus out of the range of the military draft. This school was able to turn out a student with enough training to take over the secretaryship of a collective within one month. The graduates were eagerly sought after by the collectives belonging to the federation.[58]

In addition, two 'universities' for members of the collectives were established, one in Valencia, the other in Madrid. The students were chosen from the outstanding graduates of the institutes, and many were children of leaders of the local collectives. The students attended these universities – that in Valencia was called the Moncada University – for a whole year, with about 200 students at a time, both boys and girls, in each university. They were taught a wide variety of agricultural subjects. Each morning they worked in the experimental farm attached to each of the universities, learning by practice how to do what they were being taught. In the afternoons, they had classes in more theoretical material. Although emphasis was on agricultural subjects and accounting, there was also some general cultural education as well. Two classes were graduated from these universities, but the third had not ended its studies when the war concluded.[59]

Complementing its efforts to train accountants for the local *sindicatos* and collectives, the FRCL sought to get them to adopt a uniform system of book-keeping. It drew a standardized model system of accounting and urged its member groups to adopt this.[60] By November 1937, 60 of the 340 collectives belonging to the federation had adopted the uniform system.[61]

Another function of the FRCL and its provincial organizations was to try to improve both farming techniques and technology of the various collectives. The federation and its provincial groups and individual collectives had many of the best agronomists, veterinarians and agricultural engineers of Spain working with them. Rafael Esteban is witness to the fact that these people were generally loyal, and gave the federation their fullest cooperation.

One thing the agronomists of the federation did was to organize a number of experimental farms. When an agronomist made a suggestion to the federation for establishment of an experimental farm in a given area, the FRCL would contact the collective on whose land the agronomist wanted to set it up, asking the collective to cooperate. Although this request was not an order, since the federation had no power to order anything, Rafael Esteban reported that there was never a case when the local leaders of the collective refused to cooperate with the agronomist.[62]

Gaston Leval has sketched the principal functions of the technicians working with the various levels of the collectives:

> The agronomists proposed necessary and possible undertakings: planning of agriculture, changing of crops which individual property could not always adapt to the most favorable geological and climatic conditions. The veterinary organized scientifically the breeding of cattle; eventually he consulted with the agronomist on the resources available, and in accord with the peasant commissions, adapted crops to the best possible conditions...
>
> But the veterinarian also consulted the architect and engineer on the construction of collective pigpens, stables, and chick coops ... Thanks to the engineers, there were constructed a large number of canals and artesian wells, which permitted the better irrigation of lands which needed it.

Irrigation activities, Leval noticed, were particularly pronounced in the Murcia and Cartagena areas.[63]

Another innovation undertaken by the FRCL and its subordinate groups was the establishment of processing plants to elaborate derivatives of some of the region's major crops. This move was at least partly provoked by increasing difficulties in selling produce abroad, and the loss of markets for fresh commodities as Franco's armies advanced. Oranges, potatoes, tomatoes and vegetables were among the principal goods processed by new installations established by the collectivists. According to Gaston Leval, the principal plants for orange concentrates and other derivatives were set up in Oliva and Burriana, while vegetable canning installations were established in Murcia, Alfasar, Castellón and Paterna.[64]

Feeding the Armed Forces

The Federación Regional de Campesinos de Levante and its subordinate organizations played a major role in providing food for the armed forces, particularly those of the Army of the Center, based in Madrid, as well as for the civilians of Madrid. Rafael Esteban has described how this supply system worked. Colonel Casado, the military commander of the Madrid region during much of the War, would call up Esteban and tell him, for instance, that he was sending 200 trucks to get merchandise from the Levante area. In return, Esteban, who had information on what goods were available where, would tell Casado to send a given number of trucks to various collectives, and a certain number also to Valencia, where the FRCL had sizeable deposits. Thus, the truck drivers did not have to waste time and gasoline going to where food was not available.

Colonel Casado worked through the Federación Campesina del Centro, in the Castille area, in so far as paying for the goods obtained from Levante was concerned. Each truck would go with a manifest from the federation of the center, ordering so and so much produce from such and such a collective. The local collective would send this manifest to the FRCL headquarters in Valencia, where the federation would make up a single bill from all of these manifests, which it would forward to the Federación del Centro. That organization would collect the money from Colonel Casado, and remit it to the FRCL, which in its turn would pay each of the local collectives which had contributed goods.[65]

Export Problems of the Levante Collectives

One of the most interesting aspects of th agrarian activities of the CNT in the Levante during the Civil War was participation in management of the exports from that region, which exports provided a large part of the Republic's foreign exchange during the conflict. The principal products involved were onions, citrus fruits and rice, although the last of these was principally sold within Loyalist Spain.

With the collapse of government authority and disruption of most existing institutions in the Levante region during the first weeks of the War, the region was immediately faced with a crisis with regard to onion exports. The uprising had occurred when the onion harvest was about to be gathered and exported. However, in the confusion of the moment, the previously established channels of distribution of this very important crop had broken down.

As a consequence, the CNT and UGT in the area stepped in to handle the problem of collecting and shipping the 1936 onion harvest of the Levante region. They organized the Comité de Enlace of Productos-Exportadores de Cebollas CNT–UGT.[66] Its arranged shipment of the onion crop through some of the old exporting houses, which had been doing business with Great Britain for many years. The Comité de Enlace paid the people in those exporting houses wages rather than commissions, and in the beginning the exporters did not object. However, by the end of 1936, the export agents were demanding that they receive commissions as they had before the war. So long as the Comité de Enlace continued to handle the export of onions, however, it refused those demands.[67]

Terence M. Smyth concluded that before the setting up of the CNT–UGT organization, 'The first export campaign of revolutionary Valencia, that of onions, was not going to be a success ... The defects – defects of packing, change of established trademarks ... absence of control over the profits made abroad – were going to be strong arguments for those advocates of centralized trade union control, and of the traditional exporters subject only to political veto to use against their opponents.'[68]

After the fall of the Largo Caballero government, the new Negrín administration, in a decree of June 12 1937, established the Central de Exportación de Cebolla, to take the place of the CNT–UGT Comité de Enlace. The new organization had an administrative council, made up of three government representatives, and one representative each of the FRCL, the Federacion de Trabajadores de la Tierra of the UGT, and the Communist-controlled Federación Provincial de Campesinos (FPC). Although the CNT and UGT objected strongly to the establishment of the new organism, and particularly to representation on it of the FPC, which they claimed 'has in its ranks the majority of the exploiting employers', there was nothing effective that they could do to keep the government (and to a greater or less degree the Communist Party) from taking over the export of onions in the next two growing seasons.[69]

However, the most serious export problem was that of oranges, which were the region's largest crop and principal foreign exchange earner. At the outbreak of the Civil War, there existed a UGT union in the field, the Sindicato de Trabajadores, Exportadores y Similares, and a CNT organization, the Sindicato Unico Regional de la Exportación Frutera. After extensive conversations, the two unions decided, at the end of October 1936, to establish jointly the Consejo Levantine Unificado de Exportación Agricola (CLUEA), as the 'directing organ of orange exports', which enjoyed the formal delegation of responsibility in the field by the ministry of industry and commerce.

The council consisted entirely of CNT and UGT members, who represented the various aspects of the export of oranges. They included four peasants, one port worker, two administrative workers, two export technicians, one bank worker, two representatives of the provincial secretariat, one railroad worker, one truck driver, one commission agent, one maritime transport worker, and one packing worker. The council was presided over by a delegate of the Commission of Agriculture, Industry and Commerce of Valencia.[70]

It was the CLUEA which officially handled the export of oranges during the 1936–7 crop season. However, as Dr Aurora Bosch Sánchez has noted, 'in the 1936–1937 orange campaign improvisation dominated.' [71] It was exceedingly difficult for the CLUEA to organize an efficient export process. They encountered grave problems with the local organizations which collected the fruit and prepared it for shipment, with their agents abroad, and in their relations with the government. They also had to face strong opposition from the Communist Party and its Federación Provincial de Campesinos.

Some foreign observers at the time were favorably impressed with the CLUEA. Thus, Franz Borkenau wrote of it in February 1937: 'Technically, the CLUEA works fairly well. Oranges are sold and transported, partly by ship, but not, of course, in such quantities as in normal times. But the CLUEA is able to fulfill its contracts as to the delivery of oranges and is able to pay for its own buyings abroad cash down. There are only a few complaints as to the quality of the oranges.'[72]

On a local basis, the CLUEA operated through local councils for export of fruit (Consejos Locales de Exportación de Frutas – CLUEFs). These were established in 275 orange-producing localities. Dr Bosch Sánchez noted that 'the proprietors of orange groves, the collectives, the cooperatives, turned over the product to the local CLUEF, which processed and packed the oranges, and in their turn handed them over the CLUEA to be exported.'[73]

The CLUEA had major problems with these CLUEFs. According to Dr Bosch Sánchez, 'The local CLUEFs worked with excessive autonomy, to the point of competing with the export organism itself, selling directly abroad at lower prices, and provoking a consequent general fall in prices.' Dr Bosch Sánchez goes on, 'Many CLUEFs employed workers inexperienced in the selection and processing of oranges, simply because they were members of the two union groups; the results could be disastrous. Confusion in packing was frequent, they mixed up types and altered weights, packing boxes with one trade mark on the fruit, and a different one on the box.'[74]

In localities where the unions had not existed before the outbreak of the War, 'these were formed immediately to take over local power and control of the CLUEF.' As Dr Bosch Sánchez noted, 'thus there entered individuals over whom they had no type of political control. However, the CLUEFs needed politically doubtful people with rightist antecedents ... It was really the old merchants and exporters of oranges who took over direction of the CLUEFs; in cases where that did not occur, the result could be disastrous.'[75]

The CLUEA was quite aware of the weaknesses of the CLUEFs. In the spring of 1937, it made a survey of 53 of them. This study found that in 50 percent of the localities involved, 'The immorality of some members of the CLUEFs, the lack of culture and professional incapacity of others, were the principal causes of this deficient functioning.'[76]

The CLUEA also had serious problems at the other end of the export chain – in the countries in which the oranges were sold. With the onset of the Great Depression, Spanish exports of oranges had declined from 11,963 *quintales* in 1930 to 9,098 *quintales* in 1934. However, in spite of a decline of 50 percent in income from orange exports, during the 1931–5 period, they accounted for 11.07 percent of the total value of Spain's exports.[77]

After the Civil War began, Germany, which had been a large pre-war market, was closed to Republican Spain, because of the Nazi regime's support of Franco.[78] For some time, there were also problems in shipping to France, while in Great Britain, Spanish oranges were meeting increasing competition from those from Palestine, North Africa and South Africa.[79]

The need to improvise in its sales abroad, as well as in organizing production and collection of oranges in Spain, also presented serious problems. The CLUEA perforce had to use as its agents many of the representatives in England, France, Belgium and Holland of the old exporters. Not infrequently, these people turned out to be sympathizers with the Rebels, or were otherwise unscrupulous and worked in ways which discredited the CLUEA.[80]

The CLUEA also had problems with the Republican government. The government agreed to turn over to the CLUEA 50 percent of the value of the oranges shipped at the time they were exported, paying the other 50 percent after they had actually been sold abroad.[81] However, in fact, the government was exceedingly slow about paying the second half of what it owed to the CLUEA, with the result that the CLUEA itself was very tardy in compensating the local CLUEFs for the fruit which they had provided.[82]

Finally, the CLUEA had to face strong opposition from the Communist Party and its peasant group in the Valencia region. Jesús Hernández, in his tirade against the Spanish anarchists written after the Civil War was over, was perhaps typical of the kind of assaults on CLUEA which the Communists made during the War. He accused CLUEA of corruption, exploiting the peasants, working with Franco sympathizers, using the funds of the organization to subsidize the activities of the FAI, and even of selling oranges to the Franco side.[83]

Dr Bosch Sánchez has noted the Communists' campaign against CLUEA: 'The Federación Provincial Campesina, supporter of orange cooperatives, argued that freedom of export, and total freedom of trade marks would have brought greater economic benefits. It also accused the CLUEA of robbing the peasants, in not paying them fully for the oranges exported.'[84]

Shortly before the extinction of the CLUEA, the FPC denounced the CLUEA in the following terms: 'The CLUEA and the CLUEFs brought as a consequence the cases of violence which we all know. Naturally, we cannot think of using this organism, since it is, practically a cadaver.'[85]

In addition to denouncing the CLUEA, the Communist-controlled peasant organization also sought to undermine it economically. Terence M. Smyth has noted: 'The orange cooperatives organized by the Provincial Peasant Federation worked in competition with the CLUEA, and it had the advantage of the concession of credit by the Institute of Agrarian Reform and the Ministry of Agriculture.'[86] the minister of agriculture, of course, was a Communist.

However, apparently all peasant discontent with the CLUEA did not come from the Communist-led organization. Terence Smyth commented: 'The hostility of the peasants of the CNT *sindicatos* against the centralized export organization was going to continue, and the system whereby the CLUEA paid immediately only 50 percent of the value of the exports was badly received and badly understood.'[87]

As the CLUEA prepared for its second export season, that of 1937–8, it took steps to overcome the difficulties and errors which it had encountered during its first year. According to Dr Bosch

Sánchez, it was planning 'to end the competition among the CLUEFs and their autonomy, to unify trade marks into a single national trade mark differentiating quality, improving transport and using more appropriate packaging, and specially take care for the quality of the oranges designated for export.[88]

The End of CLUEA

However, in fact, the CLUEA was not to have a second export season. On September 6 1937, the Negrín government established under the ministry of finance and economy the Central de Exportación de Agrios (CEA). Its function, according to the decree, was to deal with 'all the problems of collection, preparation, transport and sale of citrus fruits, and also the products derived from them, when those are destined for export.'

Neither the CNT nor the UGT had any direct representation on the administrative council of the CEA. There were 'producers' representatives' on that council, elected by local agrarian committees or municipal councils if there were no such committees.[89] Presumably there were at least some CNT and UGT people among these. However, Frank Mintz has noted that the CEA was 'under governmental and Communist control'.[90]

As a result of the establishment of the CEA, the CLUEA disappeared. However, both the FRCL and the UGT's Federation of Agricultural Workers 'continued working as one more exporting entity within the state organ'.[91] Gaston Leval claimed that the *sindicatos* and collectives of the CNT in the Levante exported 51 percent of the citrus fruit shipped from the region during the War.[92] This judgment was confirmed by Walther Bernecker.[93]

Dr Bosch Sánchez summed up the significance of the substitution of the CEA for the CLUEA: '...the appearance of the CEA not only put an end to trade union collectivization of orange export, but closed the circle of state intervention in the principal Valencian agricultural products, and above all, put an end to a stage in which the trade unions had dominated key aspects of the Valencian economy. It was evident that also in the terrain of agricultural exports, the winners in the polemic of war-revolution/revolution-war, had been the central government and the Communist Party.'[94] The Party was reported to control 90 percent of the area's rice production.[95]

However, it was not only the export crops – onions and oranges – which were areas of contention between the anarchist–Socialist controlled rural groups and those aligned with the Communists. The same was true with rice, which was mainly consumed inside Spain. According to Frank Mintz, 'The Federación Sindical del Arroz was pro-Communist and enjoyed political privileges.[96] At the plenum of CNT peasants of the Levante, the secretary of the regional committee "reported on the question of rice and said that the War Commission, while buying more dearly from the Federación Sindical del Arroz, did not purchase from us, although we offered greater advantages..." The opposition reached such a point that the rice farmers near Silla refused to sell to a CNT collective which bought rice at 60 pesetas a *quintal*, and sold it to the Federación Sindical del Arroz which paid 40.'[97]

Some CNT *sindicatos* joined the rice federation.[98] The second congress of the CNT regional peasant federation in December 1936 saw its presiding officer saying: 'One cannot understand how there can be members of the CNT in organizations such as the Federación Sindical de Arrosseros, our adversary who opposes us with their defeatism.[99]

Relations of the CNT with the UGT in Rural Levante

Generally, relations between the CNT and the UGT in the rural areas of the Levante region remained good throughout most of the Civil War. As already described, there existed a number of rural collectives which were joint CNT–UGT enterprises and the anarchist and Socialist union groups collaborated in the first part of the war in establishing organizations to handle the region's principal agricultural exports.

The reason for the generally close collaboration of the CNT and UGT in the rural Levante was that the two organizations shared more to less the same vision of what the War was all about. The UGT was in most Levante areas controlled by Socialists associated with the Largo Caballero wing of the party, and shared with the anarchists the belief that winning the War and winning the Revolution were closely interdependent, that one could not happen without the other. With regard to agrarian issues, both the Federation of Land Workers (FETT) of the UGT and the CNT's rural federation believed in collectivization of agriculture, at least as the long-run objective. On the other hand, in their different ways, they worked out a compromise between the collectives and those in their own ranks and outside them who wanted to remain small proprietors.

The principal cases in which conflict developed between the CNT and UGT in rural Levante were where the local UGT was in the hands of the Communist Party. In addition, there were a few other cases in which on a local level there developed some conflict between the two organizations.

Like the FRCL, the socialists; FETT had to deal with the problem posed by the fact that many of their own members preferred to remain small landholders rather than to join in collectives. Very early in the War, the FETT developed an organism which made that possible, without splitting the ranks of the organization.

The FETT's method of uniting individualist and collectivist members of the federation was the Cooperative of Multiple Bases. Dr Bosch Sánchez noted: 'Many *sindicatos* ... didn't limit themselves during this period to forming cooperatives, but rather carrying out the agrarian policy of the FETT, formed sections of collectivists within the cooperatives of multiple cases, or, continuing a tendency begun in the first moments of the war, formed joint collectives with the FRCL–CNT...'[100]

One case of conflict between local CNT and UGT rural groups took place in Alicante, in the Valencia county. The Communists dominated the UGT in parts of that province. Although they agreed to join with the local CNT units to form joint collectives on seized land, they also agreed to the local Agrarian Reform Institute authorities' demand that in return for financial help to get them started, the collectives would turn over to the institute the sale of their crops.

However, when Bernabé Esteban became provincial secretary of the FRCL in Alicante in July 1937, he sought to separate the CNTers from the joint CNT–UGT collectives in the province. He got the CNTers to withdraw from those organizations, and with help from the FRCL, he got funds to pay off the anarchists' share of the former joint collectives' debts to the Agrarian Reform Institute. Finally, the CNT had some 60 collectives in the province of Alicante, of which more than 20 had been formed by secession from the CNT–UGT collectives.[101]

There were also two cases in the province of Valencia, those of Cullera and Carcagente, mentioned by Dr Bosch Sánchez, in which peasants withdrew from CNT collectives to form rival UGT organizations. In both instances, relatively small landholding peasants had been coerced into joining collectives, and when the opportunity presented itself they withdrew to form UGT-affiliated *sindicatos*.[102] Terence Smyth also noted bad relations between the CNT and the UGT in the town of Oliva, attributing it to the fact that 'both unions had proposed to establish their brand of revolutionary socialism in the areas they controlled.'[103]

These instances of dissidence between local CNT and UGT groups were apparently the exceptions which proved the rule. Generally, the anarchists' and Socialists' rural trade-union groups collaborated closely in the Levante area throughout the Civil War.

Relations between the Rural and the Urban Affiliates of CNT in the Levante

Relations were not always entirely smooth between the rural unions and collectives of the CNT in the Levante and their urban counterparts. There were several reasons for this.

On the one hand, peasants resented the measures which the anarchists and other Republican elements of the cities took particularly right at the beginning of the War to maintain the supply of food in the urban areas. During the almost two weeks in which the garrisons of Valencia and some other cities remained 'neutral,' while *de facto* new revolutionary authorities were set up, the normal functioning of the economy was greatly disrupted. On an emergency basis, the new revolutionary bodies, in which the anarchists played a major role, seized food from warehouses and stores for distribution among the civilian populace. In addition, both the CNT and UGT sent groups to the surrounding rural areas to requisition food, 'paying' for it with a kind of IOU, a *vale*, which declared that the union group seizing the produce would in time pay for it.

Such measures engendered resentment among many peasants. In addition, some of the more doctrinaire anarchists sought to establish these *vales* and a kind of barter system between the peasants' and workers' organizations in the cities on a more or less permanent basis. This idea was finally stopped in September 1936 when the local CNT in Valencia condemned the *vale* system as a means of obtaining 'the product of the work of another'.[104]

The peasants had other complaints. In an October 1936 regional peasant plenum, it was suggested that 'superfluous' industries be closed and their workers, together with the unemployed, be sent out to work in agriculture.[105]

For their part, some of the urban members of the CNT had their grievances against their rural comrades. The dim view which some of the urban union leaders took of the extreme measures establishing libertarian communism in some of the rural collectives, has already been described.

Some of the urban collectives also had more specific grievances. For instance, the *sindicato* of gas, water and electricity objected that many of the peasants were failing to pay their bills, in spite of the fact that the workers' collective in that field had reduced rates. In November 1936 the UGT–CNT coordinating committee of that collective issued a statement which said in part, 'They also protest against the numerous villages of the province who refuse to pay their electricity bills and won't permit the installation of controls by the committees to provide adequate administration.'[106]

The Communists' Federación Provincial Campesina

Throughout the Civil War, the Communists carried out an unremitting campaign against rural collectives of the anarchists and Largo

Caballero Socialists in the Levante region. In this campaign, they used every resource at their command. These resources included the fact that, from September 4 1936 until almost the end of the War, a Communist, Vicente Uribe, was minister of agriculture; as well as growing Communist influence in the military and police forces of the Republic, and unofficial violence.

In their campaign against agrarian collectivism in the Levante, the Communists were able to mobilize considerable popular support from small proprietors who were opposed to, or fearful of, the drive for collectivization in Levante agriculture. Indeed, illogical as it might appear from a theoretical ideological point of view, the Communists became the defenders *per excellence* of private farming in the Levante area.

The conflict between small proprietors and the collectives was real enough. Although CNT leaders undoubtedly favored only voluntary collectivization of small landholdings[107] as has already been indicated, there was certainly some forced collectivization of such holdings in the Levante region during the first weeks and months of the Civil War.

Furthermore, even leading figures of the CNT in the region admitted the importance of the 'individualist' proclivities of many of the peasants and agricultural workers in the Levante region. H. Noja Ruíz, a leading figure in the CNT in the area, recognized that to speak to many Valencian peasants of collectivization was the same as 'speaking to them in Greek'. He added that 'the plan which had most supporters in the Spanish Levante was that of subdivision' of seized land among the peasants.[108]

In the Levante area, as elsewhere in Republican Spain, the Communists interpreted, and sought to use, Communist Minister of Agriculture Vicente Uribe's October 7 1936 decree as a tool in defense of the small and medium-sized landholders. The fact was, as the Communist peasant leader in the Valencia area, Julio Mateu proclaimed, 'When the rebellion began, in the first moments of confusion, no organization except the Communist Party, dared to propose respect for the small proprietor.'[109]

Soon after the issuing of the decree of October 7 1936, the Communist Party in the Levante area undertook to strengthen its

position in the rural parts of the region, by sponsoring the organization of the Federación Provincial Campesina (FPC). The FPC proclaimed its objective to be 'to bring together all of the societies,
sindicatos, agricultural cooperatives and organizations of poor peasants, renters, sharecroppers and small proprietors, and in general all
those working the land with their own hands and those of their
family members.'[110]

The Federación Provincial Campesina was founded on October
18 1936, by elements of the Communist Party, but also had the
backing of the Republican parties of the region, whose support
came in considerable degree from the small agriculturalists. At its
establishment, the FPC claimed to have 68 peasant societies affiliated with it. A few months later, the FPC claimed 230 'peasant
sections', in addition to 80 cooperatives, and more than 50,000
members.[111]

The organizations which joined the FPC were not generally run by
the Communists. Rather, they had before July 1936 been members of
a network of Catholic agricultural unions, organized by a priest,
Padre Vicente. They had also been the electoral bulwark of the
Valencian regional right.[112]

Burnett Bolloten has described this situation:

In the rich orange- and rice-growing province of Valencia ...
where the farmers were prosperous and had supported right-
wing organizations before the Civil War, according to official
figures, fifty thousand had by March 1937 joined the Peasant
Federation ... 'The Communist party,' complained a Socialist,
'devotes itself to picking up in the villages the worst remnants of
the former Partido Autonomista, who were not only reactionary, but also immoral, and organizes these small proprietors
into a new peasant union by promising them the possession of
their land.' In addition to providing its members with fertilizers
and seed and securing credits from the ministry of agriculture –
likewise controlled by the Communists – the Peasants' Federation
served as a powerful instrument in checking the rural collectivization promoted by the agricultural workers of the province.
That the protection afforded by this organization should have

induced many of its members to apply for admission into the Communist party is understandable.[113]

The New York anarchist newspaper *Spanish Revolution* noted in August 1937: 'In Valencia ... the former regional secretary of the Gil Robles party, among others, is now a CP member.'[114]

Understandably, the Communists had to rationalize and explain their action of basing their own peasant organization on groups which had until the outbreak of the Civil War been a stronghold of the Right in the politics of the Levante region. To this end, Vicente Uribe, explained that 'it was not the fault of the peasants that they had not been well led, had suffered reactionary influence, the influence of clericalism which has used arms against the Republic,' and that the Communists were trying to convert them into 'a progressive democratic force', loyal to the Republic.[115]

The Communist leader of the Federación Provincial Campesina, Julio Mateu, explained that the Communists had two objectives in forming the FPC. On the one hand, they were seeking to end 'the economic war among the peasants'. On the other, they were trying to win to the side of the republic 'the principal lever of maneuver used by the leaders of the Regional Right to win elections'. Hence, the ranks of the FPC were to be open to any peasant who worked his own lands regardless of his political or religious convictions.'[116]

There can be little doubt about the important economic and political role the FPC played in the fight against the rural collectives in the Levante region. We have already noted the part they played in helping to sabotage the CNT–UGT effort to centralize the export of oranges from the region through the CLUEA, and in bringing about the substitution of the government-dominated (and Communist-controlled) CEA for the CLUEA. According to Dr Bosch Sánchez, by the end of the winter 1936–7, the CNT and UGT had come to consider the FPC 'the principal enemy of their agrarian policy'.[117]

The Use of Violence Against the Collectives of Levante

However, the Communists did not limit their opposition to the

Levante collectives to the mobilization of the political and economic weight of those individualist peasants belonging to the Federación Provincial Campesina. They used their growing influence on the Spanish Republican government to bring about the use of the Assault Guards and other police forces – and ultimately army units also – as well as civilian strongarm groups to attack many of the collectives physically.

In an earlier chapter the intervention by elements of the CNT's Iron Column in defense of collectives in Vinalesa, Moncada and Alfara del Patriarca, which were attacked by Assault Guards early in March 1937, was described. However, Dr Bosch Sánchez noted that these events 'were not isolated, and during the Spring of 1937, numerous CNT *sindicatos* and collectives denounced to the National and Regional Committees of the CNT attacks by the police ... the Ministry of Government, suspecting that similar uprisings might happen in other Valencia localities dominated by the CNT, undertook a forceful action of searching the *sindicatos* and collectives, seeking arms and arresting militants.'[118]

Gaston Leval stressed the carefully planned nature of these attacks:

Various attacks were planned. The offensive was turned over to the *carabineros* and assault guards, who were undoubtedly carefully selected ... The attack left from two centers (Murcia and Alicante) ...

Our peasant comrades, who were forewarned, decided to resist. They had no assault vehicles, but used rifles, pistols and two anti-tank cannon, undoubtedly provided by the Iron Column on the Teruel front ... As prearranged, church bells were rung as warnings and the comrades of important villages of the region rallied to help the attacked towns. There was ample use of hand grenades; two battalions of the Iron Column and two of the Confederal Column were from the front of Teruel towards Segorbe. The *comarcal* federations of Jativa, Carcagente, Gandia and Sueca joined forces and established the front of Gandia, while those of Catarroja, Liria, Moncada, Paterna and Burriana established that of Villanesa.

After four days or more of fighting, the national leaders of the CNT intervened, and succeeded in bringing it to an end. Most of the anarchists taken prisoner in the conflict were released. Leval concluded: 'There were dead and wounded, but the collectives were not destroyed; on the contrary, their number grew at an accelerated pace.'[119]

Dr Bosch Sánchez gives some specific examples of these police incursions. In Carcagente, 'on March 22, two trucks and four cars of the Assault Guards, after placing a machine gun in front of the headquarters of the FAI, blockaded all entrances to the village, took over the telephones and telegraphs and searched the houses of various CNTers, seizing 200 shotguns . . . A few days later, on March 26 1937, practically the same thing occurred in Benaguacil, where the Assault Guards, not finding arms in the headquarters of the CNT, left 50 to 60 of their number in the locality, assuring with their presence the establishment of the Municipal Council, by express order of the governor and political parties . . .'

As a consequence of these and similar events, the regional confederation of labor of Levante denounced the actions of the ministry of government and the police: 'They seek out the comrades who have carried out and are carrying out this social work of restructuring the new economy, and molest them when they don't jail them, thus disturbing the normal functioning of the new organisms so that they will fail.'[120]

The attacks on the collectives intensified after the May Days in Barcelona. However, according to Dr Bosch Sánchez, 'In this situation it is clear that the insecurity, confusion and demoralization that these attacks on the collectives provoked in wide sectors of Republican agriculture seriously menaced the harvests . . .' As a result, Minister of Agriculture Vicente Uribe issued, on June 8 1937, the decree of Temporary Legalization of Agricultural Collectives. That decree promised technical and financial aid to the collectives 'so that they can carry out as well and rapidly as possible, the agricultural harvests appropriate to the season.'[12]

Although the CNT–UGT leaders hoped that this decree would signal at least a truce in the attacks on the collectives, this did not in fact prove to be the case. Dr Bosch Sánchez noted: 'The enthusiasm of the trade unionists would last a short time, since when the summer of 1937 had barely begun, many collectives once again were denouncing the rounding up of their members and sacking of their property.'[122] The attacks continued through the fall of 1937, involving not only police but unidentified gangs of people who seized crops and destroyed property.[123]

Attacks on the collectives continued in 1938, although they were 'more sporadic', according to Dr Bosch Sánchez. She also noted a change in the nature of those attacking the collectives, saying that except in a few cases, 'the collectives no longer saw the Municipal Councils and Assault Guards as their principal enemies, but now saw their revolutionary work menaced by units of the army and refugees who were being massively settled in Valencian localities.[124]

The CNT collectives did what they could to defend themselves from these attacks. In at least some cases, they continued to have a system of ringing church bells to warn the peasants of a locality and neighboring localities of the approach of potentially hostile forces.[125]

Dr Bosch Sánchez concluded that 'the atmosphere of persecution described by the Information and Statistics Section of the CRTL existed.' Although not professing to have accounted for all of the cases of violence against collectives, she provided more or less detailed information on 42 of them between the spring of 1937 and the latter part of 1938. Her figures deal only with attacks in the Valencia region, and do not include information on Murcia and Albacete.[126]

The Question of Legalization of the Collectives

Understandably, the anarchists at first rejected out of hand the idea of seeking legal recognition for their agrarian collectives in the Levante or elsewhere. From an ideological point of view, the idea that these groups should have to seek legalization by the state was anathema to them – although not to the socialists in so far as the UGT collectives were concerned.

During the first year of the Civil War, there was also considerable impediment on the side of the government to recognizing the legality of CNT collectives. It has already been seen the October 7 1936 decree was at best equivocal about the subject.[127]

However, after the decree law of July 1937 temporarily recognizing the legality of rural collectives, the attitude of both the government and the CNT changed on the issue. Dr Bosch Sánchez has suggested that 'the menace of not receiving economic aid and the danger that the seized lands might be taken from them' were the principal factors influencing the collectives affiliated with the Federación Regional de Campesinos de Levante in the direction of seeking legal recognition.

In any case, after July 1937, the FRCL decided generally to have its affiliated collectives apply for legal recognition. By the second congress of the Federación in Nov ember 1937, it was reported that 340 collectives had been legally recognized, and 75 more were in the process of obtaining legal recognition.[128]

However, if the FRCL leaders thought that obtaining the government's legal sanction for their collectives would make them immune from persecution at the hands of the Communists and other opponents of collectivization, this certainly did not prove to be the case. Persecution continued until the last months of the War.

The Crisis of the Collectives in Last Part of the War

The last months of the Civil War were a period of growing problems, disillusionment and, in many cases disintegration, for the CNT's rural collectives in the Levante region. For one thing, the area, which had for the first two years of the conflict been securely in the rear of the fighting, no longer was so. On June 14 1938, Castellón, capital of one of the Valencian provinces, fell to Franco's forces.[129] Also, the Republic was then split into two separate areas, putting increasingly great pressure on the economy of the center, and thus upon the collectives.

One of the major problems which the rural collectives faced during the last part of the War was the inroads made on their more or less trained personnel by the increasing mobilization of men for the hard-pressed Republican armed forces. Thus, the UGT–CNT joint collective of Ademúz requested help from the FRCL in March 1938 to prevent its accountant from being drafted, 'because unfortunately the comrades who remain are not able to take his place, because they are illiterate.' Similarly, the *comarcal* federation of peasants of Alcoy informed the FRCL in February 1938 that it could not send anyone to the accounttants' training course, because 'those who might go must march rapidly to the front, and no one who remains has the least notion of accounting'.[130]

According to Dr Bosch Sánchez:

> Problems such as lack of workers, scarcity of fertilizer, difficulties of transport, which began to appear at the end of 1937, became the daily norm of the Valencian collectives during the year 1938.[131]
>
> For the first time in all the war, not only was the tendency to form new collectives and cooperatives halted, but many of these ended their days because of economic difficulties and lack of workers, occupation of their territory by the enemy army, or direct and indirect sabotage to which many saw themselves submitted, by those within the republican area who had been hoping since the beginning of the conflict for the triumph of Franco. This declining tendency of the collectivist movement would only increase precipitously during the final three months of the civil war.[132]

Conclusions

There is little question about the fact that one of the most interesting socio-economic experiments carried out in Loyalist Spain during the Civil War was that of the rural collectives in the Levante region. Not only did the anarchists' Federación Regional de Campesinos de Levante organize several hundred rural collectives in the region, but it also sought to develop patterns for their organization and functioning, to help train their leaders and officials and to extend to them technical and extenaion services. Together with the organizations belonging to the UGT's Federation of Land Workers, the anarchists made interesting efforts to try to organize the production, shipping and sales abroad of the region's major export products.

One of the principal problems which the anarchists faced was the preference of the majority of the rural population – including many of the CNT's own agrarian followers – for small proprietorship over collectivist agriculture. Although within their own organization they were able to arrive at workable compromises between the individualists and the collectivists, the existence of this problem on a broader scale in the region provided a basis for the Communist Party to organize a substantial part of the peasantry against the collectives and against the CNT itself. The Communists also made full use of the fact that one of their own principal national leaders, Vicente Uribe was minister of agriculture during most of the War. In addition, the Communists used their influence in the government – and outside of it – to mount scores if not hundreds of physical attacks on the collectives. In the end, however, it was of course, the loss of the War itself that put an end to the anarchists' agrarian collectivist experiment in the Levante.

Frank Mintz sought to sum up the rural collectivization effort in the Levante: 'It is difficult to draw general conclusions ... the export of oranges and of rice was faced with sabotage. But is it not a proof of economic vitality, of the possibility of success for the trade unions if it had not been attacked continuously? In the countryside, there were a total of four hundred and fifteen collectives, which is a certain sign of importance in that region, so populated and vital.'[133]

Dr Aurora Bosch Sánchez has also attempted to assess the balance of that experiment. On one level, she said that 'we know from information from the *sindicatos* that some collectives put under cultivation new lands, that others attempted to improve methods of cultivation, that many constructed cattle farms and that the great majority of them made every effort to maintain production until the end of the War, in spite of growing economic difficulties, scarcity of fertilizers and seeds and lack of manpower.'[134]

On another level, the same author noted: 'For those sectors of the poor Valencian peasantry who voluntarily entered the collectives and for the convinced sindicalists, the collectives brought a substantial change in their lives. It is undeniable that the collectives liberated them from extreme misery and forced unemployment, conferred on them unaccustomed economic and political responsibilities, permitted them access to education, leisure and to those prohibited territories which were the houses and lands of the richest part of the population, and finally, they fixed those years in their memories as the best in their lives.'[135]

I have little to add to this assessment.

15

Rural Collectives in Castille, Andalusia and Extremadura

The nature of the anarchist agrarian collectives organized in Castille, Andalusia and Extremadura was not fundamentally different from that of similar groups in the eastern parts of Spain. However, the conditions under which they were established did differ substantially from those in Catalonia, Aragón and the Levante.

Whereas the Mediterranean regions had a landholding pattern in which small peasant proprietors and long-term leaseholders were the predominant factor, Castille and Andalusia were the regions *par excellence* of latifundia. The large landholdings in the two regions were of ancient vintage. However, Franz Bokenau, visiting Castille and Andalusia in the second month of the Civil War, noted: 'There is little similarity between the wheat-growing, middle-sized estates of Castille, obviously of feudal origin, whose laborers, a few generations ago, were serfs, and the enormous olive-growing latifundia of Andalusia, unchanged in character since Carthaginian and Roman times, whose landless proletariat derives from slaves and still retains many features of a slave population helplessly dependent on its owners.'[1]

There was also a significant difference in the pre-war political and trade union inclinations of the peasants in the two regions. In the case of Castille, the Socialists had a long history of influence among the peasants, and the Federation of Land Workers (FETT) was already well established there before July 19. However, as we shall see, CNT influence spread rapidly in the region after the beginning of the War.

Although most of Old Castille was quickly occupied by the Rebels, most of New Castille remained under Republican control throughout the War. Gaston Leval commented: 'Two thirds of the provinces of Madrid, Toledo and Ciudad Real ... and all of the province of Cuenca' remained within the republican lines.[2]

In contrast to Castille, Andalusia had always been one of the principal centers of anarchist influence in Spain. Gerald Brenan has said of the spread of anarchism there in the last decades of the nineteenth century:

> In the farm laborers' gananias *or barracks, in isolated cottages by the light of oil candiles*, the apostles spoke on liberty and equality and justice to rapt listeners. Small circles were formed in towns and villages which started night schools where many learned to read, carried on anti-religious propaganda and often practiced vegetarianism and teetotalism. Even tobacco and coffee were banned by some... But the chief characteristic of Andalusian anarchism was its naive millennarianism. Every new movement or strike was thought to herald the immediate coming of a new age of plenty, when all – even the Civil Guard and the landowners – would be free and happy. Now when this would happen no one would say. Beyond the seizure of the land (not even that in some places) and the burning of the parish church, there were no positive proposals.[3]

Unfortunately for the anarchists – and the Republic – much of Andalusia fell early into the hands of the Rebel Army of General Queipo de Llano.

Land Seizure Between February and July 1936

In the pre-revolutionary effervescence which swept much of Spain between the Popular Front electoral victory of February 1936 and the outbreak of the Civil War in July, extensive seizures of land by the peasants, and the legalization of these seizures by the Institute of Agrarian Reform (IRA), took place in the regions of Castille, Andalusia and Extremadura.

On March 5, the Institute of Agrarian Reform was instructed to restore to peasants all land in certain provinces which had been taken from them in the period of reactionary 1933–6 government. The claims of some 40,000 peasants were reportedly to be restored within a week. On March 20, the IRA was authorized to take over any estates which it felt it 'in the social interest' to expropriate.

However, as Walther Bernecker has noted, 'Parallel with this, there occurred in many southern provinces (Seville, Cáceres, Badajóz), but also in Old Castille, Salamanca and Toledo, hundreds of illegal occupations of land to the cry of 'Viva la República!', occupations which in their majority were legalized on March 28 by the Azaña government...' He added that, 'The revolutionary coloration which the reform acquired came not so much from the measures of the new government as from the initiative of action groups of the extreme Left not institutionalized under its direction ... the agricultural workers and peasants occupied *fincas* on their own account...'[4]

Early Confusion in Rural Castille

With the outbreak of the Civil Wars there was initially a great deal of confusion in the Castillian countryside. Most of the large landholders sided with the Rebellion, and either fled or were executed by their workers. Their land was seized by the tenants and wage workers. However, there was a great deal of uncertainty on their part concerning just how to organize the landholdings once their owners had disappeared.

Franz Borkenau, passing through the area about six weeks after the beginning of the War, reported:

... The land-question is completely unsolved and the greatest uncertainty prevails about the problem of how to solve it. Where the whole land belongs to one or two aristocrats who are with the insurgents, the problem is relatively simple. There the land is automatically expropriated and remains in the hands of the committees and the trade unions, who have not changed anything in the mode of cultivation. The same hands work the same land, the divisions between the old estates are upheld, the old wages are paid, and the only difference is that they are no longer paid by the landowner's estate-agent, but by the committees and unions, and that the wheat is not sold to merchants, but somehow divided between the villages and the troops...[5]

Gaston Leval also attested to the initial confusion:

... Without waiting, in all the villages dominated by a social organization of past centuries, the Popular Front named administrators who confiscated not only the land but also the machinery and working animals. Simultaneously, the Unión General de Trabajadores named Committees of Administration to organize the exploitation of the expropriated land... The influence of this mixture of administrators without creative initiative was disastrous... But the work in the field needed constant initiative, in accordance with varying circumstances which could not be foreseen from the offices, and it was insupportable for the peasant to obey people who know nothing of their job. Instead of intensifying, they restricted their activities.[6]

In the face of those circumstances, the CNT, which reportedly had only 8,000 peasant members in Castille at the beginning of the War, set about propagating the idea of establishing rural collectives in Castille. A number of anarchists from Madrid, where the CNT had a strong nucleus, went out into the countryside to preach that solution to the problem, and about a thousand CNT peasants from the Levante region also spread out through the Castillian countryside with the same message.[7]

Other CNT activists fanned out from the city of Cuenca, where the anarchists also had a considerable organization. Many years later, Juan de Cuenca wrote that 'of the 298 *pueblos* ... which constituted the province of Cuenca, the CNT was only known in half a dozen of them...' In contrast, the UGT had organizations in almost 80 localities. Juan de Cuenca noted, however, that '...we went out to the province, without leaving one village or hamlet without a visit, to leave, with our acts and words the libertarian seed as a promise of a new world without slaves or masters.'[8]

In a few Castillian *pueblos* where there already existed at least some anarchist tradition, the establishment of collectives came about more rapidly than elsewhere in the region. This was the case in Membrilla, in the province of Ciudad Real where, at the outbreak of the War, only the CNT and the Left Republican Party had any significant following.

In Membrilla, a village and rural hinterland of about 8,000 people, when word was received of the Rebel uprising, the anarchists succeeded in calling an effective general strike, gathering the workers in the center of the town, where they soon overcame a handful of Falangistas who sought to seize the area. At that point, the mayor called together 'the responsible political and trade-union figures of the *pueblo*, to study the solution which could be given for the bad moment which they were experiencing.' As a result of that meeting, the incumbent municipal authorities 'declined all socio-economic responsibility in favor of the responsible men of the Confederación Nacional del Trabajo, who accepted, having the collaboration of Izquierda Republicana, since no other trade union or political party organizations existed.'

The new leaders then summoned a general assembly of the people. At that point, 'the prime need was to proceed with the harvest of wheat and barley, ready in the field ... and in danger of being lost as the result of any weather change.' The assembly agreed to this and elected a council of administration of ten CNT members and five of the Izquierda Republicana. Under this council, four commissions were established, those of agriculture, supply, housing and health, and defense, and they proceeded to organize virtually all aspects of the life of the community.

Thus was born the Membrilla collective, which lasted until the end of the War in March 1939.[9]

The Extent of the Collectives in Castille

Although it is clear that the number of CNT members and of collectives grew rapidly in rural Castille after the first few weeks of the War, there are no clear figures on just how many agrarian collectives the CNT had in the region. Gaston Leval estimated that a year after the War began, the CNT had 100,000 rural members in Castille and that there were then 200 agrarian collectives. He added that by the end of 1937 the number of collectives had risen to 300.[10]

However, Walther Bernecker concluded that Leval's estimates were very low. He seems to accept the estimate of 340 collectives 'in both Castilles'. Based on incomplete official figures, Bernecker estimated that there were 181 collectives in the province of Ciudad Real, of which 112 were UGT controlled, 45 were of the CNT, and 24 were mixed CNT–UGT, and they contained some 33,200 families. In Cuenca there were 102 collectives, of which 37 were UGT, 5 CNT, and 60 mixed, with 4,620 families; in Guadalajara some 205 collectives, 195 of which were UGT and only seven of the CNT; in Madrid province there were some 76 collectives, 56 of then UGT, 15 CNT and 5 mixed; and in the province of Toledo there were 100 collectives, 77 of the UGT and 23 of the CNT.[11]

The CNT leaders always maintained that the rural collectives in the Castille region were completely voluntary. Thus, Eugenio Criado, secretary general of the CNT Regional Peasants Federation of the Center, commented in July 1937: 'In Castille we have some two hundred thirty collectives. We never imposed one of them. We propagated them. We led the peasants with manifestos, lectures and meetings ... It is the peasants, without coercion or imposition of any kind who came themselves to ask us for orientation and the sending of militants to aid the constitution of peasant collectives...'[12]

Similarly, writing many years later in an anarchist exile periodical, F. Crespo noted that when the Membrilla collective was organized, the non-peasants of the vicinity were given the chance to choose whether they would join it. He observed that of the 122 who were eligible for membership, 86 decided to join, the rest stayed outside the collective.[13]

There is good reason to believe that, in contrast to what certainly happened in cases in Aragón and even in the Levante, coercion by the CNT was largely missing in the establishment of rural collectives in the Castille area. During the first weeks of the War, the CNT had little following in rural Castille, and the armed forces there were far from being dominated by the CNT, the anarchists had very little force at their command to coerce the peasants into collectives. Rather, the spread of CNT collectives in the region would seem to be almost completely the result of propagating anarchist ideas among the peasants, and convincing then of the virtues of rural collectivization.

The Internal Organization of the Castillian Collectives

The structure of the collectives in Castille did not differ markedly from that of their counterparts in the eastern regions. Gaston Leval has noted the general existence of an 'Administrative Commission named by the Assembly of the whole *pueblo* or the collective's Assembly, and responsible to it; groups of producers constituted according to sex and age diversity; delegates of the groups meeting periodically to plan the overall tasks and coordinate efforts.'

Generally, the administrative commissions had members assigned to particular tasks, such as 'agriculture, grazing, education, exchange, transport, health'. However, according to Leval, 'In small villages or in less important collectives, a single delegate frequently assumed various functions, without, almost always, ceasing to work...'[14]

The fact that some of the collectives were established on very large landholdings meant that they had to have a somewhat different structure from those in the Mediterranean regions of the country. Thus, 'certain properties were so large that with the personnel on them they constituted true economic units. Consequently, an isolated collective had great importance, and also in certain municipalities various dispersed collectives were joined by a Local Liaison Committee. In other cases, almost the whole municipality was collectivized, and it constituted a unified organization with a multiplicity of general activities.'[15]

A hierarchy (although the anarchists would not have liked that word) of organizations above the local or municipal level was developed among the anarchist collectives of the Castillian region. On the level of the *comarca* there was established a *comarcal* compensation fund. Its administrators were named by a general assembly of collective-delegates, and Gaston Leval noted that 'each collective, after having paid the wages . . . bought chemical fertilizers, seeds, machines, having paid school and health costs, sent the remaining money which it had' to the *caja*.

The major task of the *caja* was to meet the needs of less favored collectives. Leval noted that 'no community struck by hail, drought or frost and aided against the caprices of nature, had to repay the value of what it had received.'[16] However, in addition, the *caja* had some of the functions of a rural extension service. Leval has noted that with the help of technicians of the committee of the Federation of the Center, it studied the situation of 'isolated collectives which were regularly and involuntarily in deficit', and worked out ways of 'remedying these difficulties, improving agricultural productivity and organizing auxiliary industries'.[17]

Each *comarcal caja* was part of a *comarcal* peasant Federation. Those in turn were brought together in provincial peasant federations, and soon an organization for the whole region was established.[18]

The CNT Peasant Federation of the Center

The rapid growth of the number of peasants in the ranks of the CNT in the Castillian region, and the proliferation of collectives under CNT leadership, soon made it necessary to bring the rural CNT affiliates together on a regional level. As a consequence, in April 1937, the Regional Peasant Federation of the Center (Federación Regional de Campesinos del Centro) was established. At its founding congress in Madrid, some 480 delegations representing 87,895 members were reported as attending.

The founding congress of the Federación Regional expressed its desire to cooperate with the UGT's Federation of Land Workers in the region. Also, as Walther Bernecker has noted, 'From speeches of numerous participants in the congress it was ... clear that the regional federation not only had economic tasks, but also the defense of the interests of the CNT in the struggle against internal political enemies.' They stressed 'the usefulness of the regional connection of the collectives to constitute strong organizations capable of resistance'.[19]

In late October 1937 it was decided to merge the Regional Peasant Federation with its 97,843 members and the Distribution Union (Sindicato de la Distribución), which had 12,897 members. The reorganized organization was then called the Regional Federation of Peasants and Foodstuff Workers (Federación Regional de Campesinos y de la Alimentación).[20]

According to Walther Bernecker, the regional committee of the federation 'had to coordinate the economy of the region, coordinate the statistics of production and consumption, and aid in the constitution of collectives. The creation of numerous sections on all levels characterized the desire of the federation to organize the collectives – while safeguarding their internal autonomy – according to economic criteria, and in accordance with the most recent technical advances ... The regional federation had to coordinate the heterogeneous conglomeration of collectivist experiments and deprive the enemies of the CNT, who were always talking about the 'chaos' in the collectives, of any real arguments.'[21]

The regional federation had a variety of different activities. It established its own laboratories which studied soil samples sent in by the collectives, and gave advice on the seeds and crops which were most appropriate for them, what fertilizers they should use, and even how deeply the collectivists should plough. The fertilizer section of the federation undertook to obtain the chemical fertilizers which the various collectives needed.

The periodical of the federation, *Campo Libre*, among its other tasks, published 'precise indications about the method of cultivating and handling cereals, fruits, vegetables, grapevines, fruit trees, according to their varieties, the climate and the soil. It published technical instructions about the way to combat diseases, about how to conserve various products, the animal strains which were most appropriate for each region, their rational feeding, etc.'

Gaston Leval concluded that all of this 'contributed to the technical education of the peasants, and such efforts facilitated the rapid rationalization of agriculture, to which our engineers, agronomists, chemists and specialists of all types gave their enthusiasm.'[22]

Another feature of the work of the regional federation was that of aiding the less fortunate collectives. Thus, within a year, it spent 2,000,000 pesetas on providing chemical fertilizers and machines to poorer collectives, the money for this being provided by the sale of products of the wealthier ones.[23]

Particularly after the merger of the original Regional Peasant Federation and the Food Distributors Union, the federation became the principal institution through which the products of the CNT collectives in Castille were distributed. Gaston Leval recorded that, by the end of 1937, people coming from Catalonia or the Levante to the CNT collectives in Castille to obtain grain and other supplies were being regularly directed to the headquarters of the regional federation in Madrid, which was handling such matters, the local collectives being unwilling to sell directly.[24]

During at least part of the War, a CNT member of the Madrid city council was in charge of supply, that is, obtaining the consumption goods, particularly food, which the people of the city needed. The council had taken over the city's markets, and it was to these that the collectives of the region brought the food they provided for the people of the city.[25]

The federation was not without its difficulties. An article in *Campo Libre*, on November 6 1937, summed up complaints about the federation's problems:

The work done has not been sufficiently productive because of the insufficient number of workers, due to the fact that many joined the Popular Army. Although this Federación has been the source of our wealth, it has not been helped as much as necessary. So long as the trade unions have money in the bank, they have believed that the Federación should solve its own problems. The local CNT organization of Madrid, a few local unions and militia groups have helped economically; but this is not sufficient. Although some unions are rich, others are poor; there does not yet exist sufficient solidarity, and the Federación is virtually unable to help them... Note should also be taken of the difficulties which the State has put in the way of the development of the collectives...

Relations With the UGT

Relations between the CNT rural unions and collectives in the Castille region and those of the UGT tended to be cordial throughout the War. Gaston Leval has noted: 'The Federación de los Trabajadores de la Tierra, which formed a part of the UGT, also supported collectivization.'[27] Also, speaking particularly of the province of Cuenca, Juan de Cuenca wrote: 'The CNT–UGT pact smoothed over differences, avoided some shocks and had the virtue of invigorating the collective experiments in many villages of the province.'[27]

The pact to which Juan de Cuenca refers was signed by the CNT and UGT in that province in March 1937. Its preamble stated: 'In view of the constant differences which have arisen in the villages between components of the UGT and CNT concerning the problems created by the Revolution, the responsible elements of both organizations in this province, meeting to study and resolve these problems, agreed to subscribe jointly to the following norms for the development of the work and coexistence in the villages of the province where both organizations have representation and affiliates.'

The pact then set forth 21 points, establishing how collectives should be organized and managed. They provided for an administrative council in each collective 'elected in the assembly by the collective and with an equal number from each organization'. Each collective was to be organized into groups, according to the work to be done, and each group would elect a delegate, who would meet each day with the administrative council to plan the next day's work.

The pact provided that the delegates 'will attempt by all persuasive means to have the work done with the greatest efficacy, showing affinity and morality and teaching their comrades those jobs for which they do not have previous training.' The delegates could not punish anyone, but only bring charges of misbehavior to the assembly, 'and this will be what definitively resolves the question'.

The agreement provided that each worker would receive as an 'advance' an amount equal to the wage he had been receiving, as well as up to 28 centimos more for each minor child. The local exchange of products would be through a cooperative in each collective. Any profits after payment of costs and advances would be divided, 'in the following way: 25 percent for education, another 25 percent for acquisition and improvement of working materials, and the remaining 50 percent will remain for the benefit of all the collectivists, if they agree to this in the assembly.'

Point No. 20 of the agreement provided: 'Mutual respect must inflexibly characterize the relations among collectivists, in view of the fact that the collective is constituted to work together for the welfare of all. Consequently, any collectivist who attempts to abuse another, even though this other person is not a collectivist, or attempts to usurp returns to which he is not entitled, in the first place will be punished, and if it occurs again will be expelled, losing all rights which he might have acquired and without being able to reclaim anything which he may have contributed to the collective...'[28]

Relations With the Institute of Agrarian Reform

Many of the CNT rural collectives in the Castille region tried to have as little as possible to do with the government's Institute of Agrarian Reform (IRA). This is understandable not only because of the anarchists' general aversion to dealing with the government but also because, from September 1936 onwards, the minister of agriculture, under whose general orders the IRA was, was the Communist Central Committee member Vicente Uribe, an enemy of peasant collectives.

Juan de Cuenca noted that in the province of Cuenca, the UGT collectives often would turn to the IRA for financial aid in getting in their crops and adding to their equipment. As security for loans from the institute they would have to mortgage their crops and even in some cases control of their land.

This the CNT collectives sought to avoid. According to Juan de Cuenca, 'Not a single one of our collectives or councils of administration needed to mortgage their crops or asked the Agrarian Reform for anything which would authorize it to put their "noses" in the collectivist economy. Quite to the contrary, they increased and developed the agricultural and grazing wealth through a great spirit of work and sacrifice. The fronts were nourished with the youth, while the old, the women and even the children were employed with enthusiasm in all of the tasks, however hard they might be.'[29]

However, there were some cases in which CNT collectives in the Castille region did receive help from the Institute of Agrarian Reform. For instance, the Torija collective in the province of Guadalajara, which was established in March 1937, received loans of 7,000 pesetas from the CNT and 25,000 pesetas from the IRA. However, by October it had repaid the IRA loan, doing so in the form of 99,242 kilos of wheat which were reportedly worth 33,590 pesetas.[30]

Some Examples of Successful CNT Collectives

There were some CNT collectives in the Castillian region which did not function well and were not successful and we have seen that one of the functions of the Peasant Federation of the Center was to help those collectives which were having difficulties.

Understandably, the CNTers did not give wide publicity to those collectives which were not succeeding. However, they did provide considerable information, at the time and subsequently, about some of those rural collectives which were successful. It is worthwhile to look at a few of these.

The foundation of the Membrilla collective in the province of Ciudad Real right at the beginning of the War has already been referred to. It was one of the largest anarchist collectives in Spain, starting with about 1,000 members. It was also one of the most successful, in both economic and social terms.

One of the first decisions of the Membrilla collective was to tear down the fences which had separated the various private landholdings from one another. With the tractors, five large ploughs and other equipment, they set about to sow, cultivate and harvest a variety of different crops, principally wheat, barley, vineyards and saffron. Gypsum was also present in the collective, and some 50 workers (instead of the dozen formerly employed in that work) were assigned to scraping it from the earth and grinding it; gypsum became one of the most important products that the collective exchanged for other things it required.

Production on the collective grew substantially. Output of wine in 1937 was half again as great as it had been the year before. There were also increases in output of cereals and truck gardening crops. But the most spectacular increase was in the production of saffron, which became the largest source of return for the collective.

The Membrilla collective rehabilitated or established a number of industrial enterprises. A slaughterhouse which had been closed was reopened and in 1937 handled 1,000 sheep. A factory making *alpargatas* (typical Spanish sandals), as well as a shoemaking shop, were opened. They installed machinery to extract alcohol from wine, as well as an auto repair shop, a flour mill and a plant to extract saffron essence.

The Membrilla collective exchanged its excess products for things that it needed from outside. After the establishment of the CNT Peasant Federation of the Center, those operations were conducted through that organization.

At the same time, the Membrilla collective settled a substantial number of refugees from Andalusia as members of the collective. Reportedly, only about 32 percent of these 2,000 refugees were of working age.

The members of the Membrilla collective were perhaps most proud of the group's cultural activities. It opened not only a regular school but an arts and crafts school as well. Teaching materials were acquired in Madrid and Barcelona, and at various times both students and teachers from Madrid and Valencia came to observe the operation of these schools, which became models of anarchist educational institutions. In addition, there was an active *ateneo*, an adult education group, which presented frequent lectures and discussions of political, economic and trade union subjects.

A sad footnote to the story of the Membrilla collective was the fact that after the end of the War, 146 of its members were shot by the victors.[31]

Another collective of which the anarchists were proud was that of Brihuega, near Guadalajara, and the center of much of the fighting in the so-called battle of Guadalajara in March 1937. The Brihuega collective survived that battle, in which many of its members participated.

The Brihuega collective was established in September 1936 by 125 families, with a total membership of 600. It took over the large estates of the region, controlling 1,900 *fanegas* (1.59 acres per *fanega*) in the municipality of Brihuega, while 1,400 *fanegas* remained in the hands of small proprietors, some of whom left Brihuega with the retreating Italian troops in March 1937. The collective produced wheat, barley, oats, beans, potatoes, olives, honey, and various fruits and nuts.

When it was established, the collective lacked money. However, it soon sold the wheat crop from the expropriated land, which gave it its original working capital, to a baking cooperative in Madrid run jointly by the CNT and UGT.

The Brihuega collective apparently did not seek to establish libertarian communism. It continued to way 'wages' to its members, five pesetas a day per married couple, and 75 centimos additional for each child (although most children were evacuated at the time of the battle of Guadalajara). Wages were paid even on those days in which no work was done. A municipal cooperative was organized where all residents – whether in the collective or small farmers – bought goods for money.

The Brihuega collective had a flour mill, an electricity plant, as well as a textile and a chocolate factory. It likewise originally had three olive-oil extracting plants, but these were destroyed by enemy bombardment.

The ten members of the municipal council of Brihuega were

divided equally between the CNT and the UGT, which in that area was controlled by the Communist Party.

Brihuega was also the seat of the Federación Comarcal de Campesinos de Brihuega. That federation had in it, in addition to the Brihuega collective, 13 other collectives in that *comarca*.[32]

Certainly one of the most successful CNT collectives was that established on a large property, Miralcampo, formerly belonging to the count of Romanones in the province of Guadalajara. It consisted of an area of 12 square kilometers along the Henares river and produced grain, melons, hay and wine. There were some 600 people in the collective.

The Miralcampo collective added a number of other activities. By the end of the War, it had a herd of 41 milk cattle, 200 hogs, and a large bakery to provide bread for its members. At one point, when it became impossible to get soap from Valencia as had been the custom, facilities were set up on the Miralcampo collective to manufacture it.

The biggest project undertaken by the collective was that of diverting the flow of the Henares river, which went through the middle of the collective, and frequently overflowed its banks and flooded valuable agricultural land. This was done with the help of an engineer sent by the Peasants' Federation of the Center, and cost about 500,000 pesetas, some of the cost apparently being borne by the federation.

Output on the Miralcampo collective increased substantially. For example, its production of wheat more than doubled between 1936 and 1937, barley increased four times over, and wine output increased by 50 per cent from one season to the other.

The incomes of the members of the collective also rose markedly. Wages rose from four pesetas a day to 15, 'as well as the right to housing, light and fuel, medicines and doctor's services'. Finally, at the end of each year, some of the profits from the operations of the collective were divided equally among its families.

However, some of the surplus funds of the collective were turned over to the Regional Peasant Federation. Also, the Miralcampo collective regularly supplied hospitals in Madrid with free fruit and other foodstuffs, as well as milk. From time to time, it also made additional contributions, as in the winter of 1937 when there was a bread shortage in Madrid, and for two days and nights trucks from Madrid carried wheat from Miralcampo to the city,[33]

When the Count of Romanones returned after the end of the War, he was sufficiently satisfied with the way his land had been handled by the collective, that he intervened on behalf of some of its former members who were being persecuted by the Franco regime.[34]

Another collective was known as the Madrid collective, on the outskirts of the city, where trolley cars still were running, and within a short distance of the fighting during much of the War. This collective contained some 260 workers, who built an extensive irrigation system, using a river which had never been used before, at the cost of some 100,000 pesetas. The members of the collective also spent 100,000 pesetas on seeds and fertilizer during the 1937–8 season.

This collective was devoted to truck gardening. Most of the produce was sold at the collective itself, where soldiers from the front and civilians from the city came to buy. The collective also delivered directly to collectivized restaurants in the city and to the Comité Regulador de Hoteles (Hotel Regulation Committee).

The workers of the collective were earning some six pesetas a day before the War. Soon after the collective was established, the daily income of its members was raised to 8.50 pesetas and, by December 1937, had increased to 12 pesetas. In addition, the collective bought on a wholesale basis such things as rice, potatoes, oil and soap, which were given in equal proportions to all members.[35]

Communist Opposition to Castillian Collectives

As elsewhere in Republican Spain, the Communists were the most determined and ruthless opponents of rural collectives in the Castillian region. At the same time that they were mounting attacks on the collectives of the Levante, the Stalinists were also seeking to undermine and destroy those of Castille.

In April 1937, Mariano Vázquez, national secretary of the CNT, publicly accused the Communists of having 'assassinated dozens of Anarchosyndicalists in the province of Toledo'. In July of that same year, the general secretary of the Peasants Federation of the Center claimed: 'We have fought terrible battles with the Communists, especially with brigades and divisions under their control, which have assassinated our best peasant militants, and savagely destroyed our collective farms and our harvest, obtained at the cost of infinite sacrifice.'[36]

César Lorenzo has described some of the details of the operation of Communist troops in Castille against the collectives: 'The chief of Communist guerrillas "El Campesino" sowed terror in the area of Toledo and Ciudad Real. He surpassed Lister in ferocity; hundreds of peasant collectivists massacred, fields were devastated, houses burned. The CNT had to menace him with death and dispatch troops to confront him in order to attempt to put an end to the bloody excesses.'[37]

Burnett Bolloten has also commented on this situation: 'It was inevitable that the attacks on the collectives should have had an unfavorable effect upon rural economy and upon morale, for while it is true that in some areas collectivization was anathema to the majority of the peasants, it is no less true that in others collective farms were organized spontaneously by the bulk of the peasant population. In Toledo province, for example, where even before the war rural collectives existed, eighty-three per cent of the peasants, according to a source friendly to the Communists, decided in favor of collective cultivation of the land.'[38]

Extent of Rural Collectives in Andalusia

The part of Andalusia which remained most firmly under Republican control throughout the Civil War was the province of Jaén, where Socialist rather than anarcho-syndicalist influence had been dominant before the War. Most of Almería also remained in Republican hands. Part of the provinces of Granada and Córdoba also remained under Loyalist control, but the western portions of the Andalusian region (Cádiz and Seville) where anarchist influence had been strongest for the longest period of time were overrun quickly by the troops of Generals Queipo de Llano and Franco.

This perhaps helps to explain why the anarchist writers gave little prominence in their discussions, both during the War and afterwards, to the CNT collectives in Andalusia, in contrast to their extensive descriptions of those in Aragón, the Levante, Castille and even Catalonia.

However, in spite of this reticence on their part, there were certainly extensive CNT rural collectives in the region. As in other parts of Republican Sain, estimates of the number of collectives and of their membership vary widely. Walther Bernecker has noted that the claim of Antonio Rosado, secretary of the Regional Peasants' Federation, that there were 600 collectives in Andalusia was made 'without justifying the figure'.[39] Bernecker himself estimated, on the basis of incomplete official data, that in the province of Córdoba there were 148 collectives, all of them under mixed CNT-UGT sponsorship containing 8,602 families. There were 33 mixed collectives in Granada, with 20,000 families; 760 mixed collectives in Jaén with 33,000 families.[40]

However, there is reason to believe that at least some of the collectives in Andalusian provinces were purely CNT affairs. For instance, a report in the CNT–FAI *Boletin de Información*, late in 1937, about six rural collectives in the *comarca* of Gandia in Jaén indicates that these were 'ours', that is, of the CNT. From the beginning of the War, this report said, those collectives had been particularly active in providing food for the front, which was not far away.[41]

The Nature of Andalusian Collectives

As elsewhere in Loyalist Spain, there was a good deal of variation in the way the rural collectives on Andalusia were organized. Franz Borkenau presented a classic account of a collective he visited early in September 1936, near Pozoblanco, that of Castro del Rio (which was subsequently occupied by the Franco forces):[42]

The local anarchists had had time to introduce their anarchist Eden, which, in most points, resembled closely the one introduced by the Anabaptists in Munster in 1534. The salient point of the anarchist regime in Castro is the abolition of money. Exchange is suppressed; production has changed very little... The local *ayuntamiento* has not merged with the committee, as everywhere else in Andalusia, but has been dissolved, and the committee has taken its place and introduced a sort of Soviet system. The Committee took over the estates, and runs them. They have not even been merged, but are worked separately, each by the hands previously employed on its lands. Money wages, of course, have been abolished. It would be incorrect to say that they have been replaced by pay in kind. There is no pay whatever; the inhabitants are fed directly from the village stores.[43]

Borkenau was not favorably impressed with the libertarian communist organization of the Castro del Rio collective:

Under this system, the provisioning of the village is of the poorest kind; poorer, I should venture to say, than it can possibly have been before, even in the wretched conditions in which Andalusian *brazeros* are wont to live... I tried in vain to get a drink, either of coffee or wine or lemonade. The village bar had been closed as nefarious commerce. I had a look at the stores. They were so low as to foretell approaching starvation. But the inhabitants seemed to be proud of this state of things. They were pleased, as they told us, that coffee-drinking had come to an end; they seemed to regard this abolition of useless things as a moral improvement... Their hatred of the upper class was far less economic than moral. They did not want to get the good living of those they had expropriated, but to get rid of their luxuries, which to them seemed to be so many vices. Their conception of the new order which was to be brought about was thoroughly ascetic.[44]

There were apparently some other collectives which initially adopted libertarian communism, but subsequently modified it. Thus, a contemporary anarchist report of the collective of Iznalloz in Granada noted: 'The Committee of the people in the most natural way in the world gave in successive declarations all of the social and economic content of its development, beginning in those days by making money disappear and using the best commercial houses, converting them to common use. During about two months – high point of the Revolution – Iznalloz lived in Libertarian Communism. The economy did not suffer in consequence, nor did anyone make the least protest... Afterwards, it suffered various transformations as in all villages, imposing a moderating sense, carried out from power, in its economic life...'[45]

Luciano Suero Sánchez, who served as secretary of the Torreperogil collective in the province of Jaén from June 1938 until the end of the War, described something of the nature of the anarchist collectives in that province: 'There were collectives of the CNT in Baeza, Ubeda, Torreperogil, Cazoría, and Peal de Becerros, as well as the provincial peasant federation in Jaén... In all these villages the collectives were administered and were based on exchanges and in many cases the circulation of money for payment of the days of work to the comrades who made up the collective.'[46]

Suero Sánchez had formerly been secretary of the Damiel collective in Castille, and had apparently been requested by the Andalusia Regional Peasant Federation to help reorganize its affiliate in Torreperogil:

With my arrival ... the comrades changed a bit the form of administration of the collective, drew up formal documents of land seizure, set up accounting records and others covering the warehouse, and made an inventory of everything the collective possessed, naming in the General Assembly an administrative committee, and from then on drew up the lists and paid the comrades according to the lists of workers and the information of the delegates of the groups elected by them...

[All of the members of the collective] provided merchandise equally to the Supply Committee for the forces on the war front which was at Andujar, a city that suffered many and very heavy attacks of aviation and artillery until the moment the war ended.[47]

Reportedly, most of the anarchist collectives in Jaén continued to use money, but apportioned returns from the disposal of the crops on the basis of the family responsibilities of the collectives' members, rather than in proportion to the work done. However, in the collective formed on the largest landholding in the province, one of some 30,000 hectares, the use of money was abolished. On one occasion, someone came to that collective to buy something and offered to pay money for what he wanted. The peasants refused this, saying that they wanted to exchange products for those they had available. When the man insisted on paying in cash, the peasants pointed to a bag, said that if he was interested in money, they had a whole bag full that they did not want, but what they did want was products in exchange for the goods they had available.[48]

Antonio Rosado told Ronald Fraser many years after the Civil War: 'We appropriated no land, setting up collectives exclusively on estates that had been abandoned, and with any land that small-holders wished to bring in. Otherwise, the latter were left to continue working their own land as before and to sell their produce freely.' He added that there were 350 collectives with 60,000 members in the Loyalist sections of Andalusia by the end of the Civil War.[49]

Federación Regional Campesina de Andalusia

As in other parts of Republican Spain, the CNT peasant unions and rural collectives of Andalusia established a regional federation, the Federación Regional Campesina de Andalusia (FRCA). The first step in this direction was taken at a meeting of the CNT regional committee in Málaga late in September 1936, where a sub-committee of development, coordination and defense of the agricultural economy was established. Named to head this sub-committee was Antonio Rosado, a peasant leader from the province of Seville who, after his home was overrun by the troops of Queipo de Llano, had succeeded in getting to Madrid, and from there had gone to Málaga.

Rosado's basic job was to stimulate the organization of CNT rural collectives, and to try to assure that they would have as rational an organization as possible. To this end, his first act was to draw up a standard accounting system which, although it would provide all the absolutely necessary information about the economic and financial state of each collective, would be simple enough to be useful for the at least minimally literate peasants who would have to deal with it.

Rosado then undertook a wide trip through the areas of Andalusia still controlled by the Republic. He took copies of his accounting document with him, leaving them with the various rural unions and collectives which he visited. This trip gave the regional CNT the first more or less comprehensive look at the state of the part of the rural economy of the region then in the hands of their members.[50]

Although Rosado became ill and had to withdraw from activity for several months, work for the establishment of the regional peasant federation, which he had advocated from the beginning, went forward. It was finally established at a congress in July 1937, reportedly attended by representatives of 41 collectives, of which 23 were completely CNT, while 18 were joint CNT–UGT organizations.[51] At this congress in Guadix there were present two representatives of the national committee of the CNT and 'a delegation from the National Committee of the FNC' (National Peasant Confederation).

The Federación Regional Campesina de Andalusia (FRCA) founding congress adopted the new organization's statutes. One contemporary anarchist source noted: 'The Federation is constituted with the same structure as a Confederal Regional organization, that is, the *sindicato* to the *comarcal* Federation, from this to the Provincial Committee and from this to the Regional Committee of the Federation, and in addition as subsidiaries of these Committees will be created the necessary technical organs, regulators of the agricultural economy in the *comarca*, the Province and the Region, as well also in those zones which for the importance of their production it is necessary to create arteries of communication, etc.'

It was provided that each provincial federation should send two delegates to form jointly the regional committee. Antonio Rosado was elected secretary general of the regional committee. It also authorized the regional committee of the FRCA, in consultation with the regional committee of the CNT, to name two delegates to the National Peasant Federation.

The FRCA congress passed a resolution proclaiming 'its unbreakable faith in winning the war and also the revolution, for which they promise to mobilize all their energies.' It also passed a motion 'to intensify the relations with the peasant organisms of the UGT'.

The Guadix congress resolved 'to promote by all means the development of the collectives and the *sindicatos*, giving to these organisms the social content which will be the secure guarantee of the triumph of the revolution.'[52]

The federation which was established at the congress in Guadix covered organizations in a considerable part of southern Spain. The unions and collectives which were a part of it covered virtually all of the provinces of Jaén and Almería, and parts of Málaga, Grenada and Córdoba. There were also a few collectives and unions in the limited parts of the region of Extremadura which remained in Loyalist hands.

The heart of the federation was its secretary-general, Antonio Rosado. He had two assistant secretaries, as well as a young Catalan CNTer, who was in charge of accounting for the federation and its affiliates. Much of their time was spent in visiting the affiliates of FRCA, seeking to keep track of them and dealing with their particular problems. Much of the rest was taken up with writing reports on what was going on and discussing problems with the regional committees of the federation and the CNT.

Associated with the Federación Regional de Campesinos was the CNT's Comité Regional de Economía. The distinction between the two organizations was not entirely clear, but the Comité de Economía was basically in charge of the exchange of products between the collectives of the region and organizations in other parts of Republican Spain.

The federation had a variety of functions. First of all it sought to establish a certain degree of uniformity in the way in which the collectives operated. Thus, it tried to get them to draw up an inventory of what the collectives possessed, and then to adopt a simple but more or less uniform accounting system to reflect the current operations of the organizations. It sought to encourage them to get legal recognition for their collectives. It also tried to get the collectives to pay attention to the quality of the products they provided, particularly their olive oil.

The FRCA played a major role in exchanging the products of its affiliates for those of CNT organizations elsewhere, particularly in the Levante area. Antonio Rosado himself frequently arranged such exchanges on a more or less large scale.

The federation also sought to get financial help from the Servicio Nacional de Credito of the ministry of Agriculture. On one occasion, for instance, the federation arranged for a loan of 3,000,000 pesetas for the collectives of the region.[53]

The federation also helped its affiliates in problems they had with governmental authorities. Perhaps the most important case of this was an effort of the civil governor of the province of Almería to take over from the FRCA affiliates the sale of all of the province's grapes. Antonio Rosado intervened in the situation, and made arrangements with military authorities to accept the region's grapes from the CNT. At that point, the governor of Almería backed down, and allowed the FRCA to handle the disposal of the crop.[54]

Finally, the federation sought to get for the collectives a variety of inputs which they needed. These included machinery for their olive-oil mills, pesticides, fertilizers and various other materials. In a number of cases, the FRCA was able to arrange to obtain these in exchange for the products of the region's collectives.[55]

Antonio Rosado has himself borne witness to the difficulties faced by the collectives of Andalusia during the Civil War. One of these was the drafting into the army of the relatively few leaders who were capable of dealing with the complicated accounting and administrative problems of the collectives. The FRCA sometimes intervened to get exemption of key personnel of the collectives from the military draft. Other problems hampering their efficient operation included lack of sufficient transport facilities, and inadequate storage facilities for their products.

However, some of the difficulties were with the collectives themselves. Rosado wrote:

There were collectives which, paying attention only to the needs of their affiliates, forgot the combatants, and had established the system of dividing among themselves the products of the land which they cultivated, and everyone in the village, from the mayor to the man in charge of the cemetery, or the garbage collective, had his fat pig, and had in store the oil, grain, beasts, etc. they considered necessary until the new harvest, and what was needed for new sowing, with the rest being for sale or exchange for other products, which they didn't produce. It is true that there were few of these cases, but it is also true that they existed ... although it did not occur in the majority of the collectives, inspired and controlled by men of the anarchosyndicalist movement.[56]

The Agrarian Collectives in Extremadura

There were very few agrarian collectives in the eastern region of Extremadura, for the simple reason that most of that area fell into the hands of Franco's troops in the early weeks of the Civil War. However, apparently in those small parts of the region which remained for a longer or shorter period under Republican control, there were some collectives organized.

Certainly in the months between the Popular Front victory in February 1936 and the outbreak of the War in July, there was a great deal of discontent in the Extremadura region among the peasantry. Hugh Thomas noted: 'In Extremadura, villagers began to go out on to the large neglected estates, mark out their claims, assume ownership over a particular area, and then held a meeting in the village square on return, crying *Viva la República!* At the village of Yeste, where the Emperor Charles V had passed his last days in a monastery, there was a violent clash between Civil Guard and villagers...'[57]

Thomas also noted that there was a good deal of legal land redistribution in Extremadura during those same months: 'The Government also set to work to carry out the provisions of the Popular Front pact. The Institute of Agrarian Reform set to work once more. Between 50,000 and 75,000 peasants were settled (chiefly in Extremadura) with their own land under these auspices before the end of March.'[58]

However, the Extremaduran province of Cáceres fell to the Franco forces almost from the first day of the War. The province of Badajóz, in contrast, stayed loyal, but by the end of August most of it had been overrun.

Nevertheless, in the small part of Extremadura which remained in Republican hands there apparently was some move to establish rural collectives. Walther Bernecker, on the basis of incomplete official records, estimated that there were 23 collectives in the province of Badajóz, of which 17 were set up by the UGT, the other six being mixed UGT–CNT organizations. In all, he claimed that 2,650 families were members of those collectives.[59]

As we have noted, the CNT collectives of Extremadura were affiliated with the Regional Peasant Federation of Andalusia.

Conclusions

In the central and southern parts of Republican Spain, rural collectives spread extensively during the Civil War. Although in Castille and the main province of Andalusia which remained under Republican control, and that the small part of Badajóz in Extremadura which continued under the Loyalists, the anarchists had not been as important before the War in the rural areas as they had been in the Mediterranean parts of the country, CNT rural unions and collectives gained considerable consequence during the conflict.

With the help of CNT 'missionaries', particularly from the Levante, the idea of establishing rural collectives spread rapidly in Castille, and somewhat less rapidly in the Andalusian province of Jaén. Within a year and a half of the outbreak of the conflict, there were hundreds of thousands of peasants living in collectives, although probably a minority of these were in CNT–dominated or joint CNT–-UGT organizations.

The nature of the anarchist collectives did not differ markedly in central and southern Spain from those along the Mediterranean coast. They varied from those which established libertarian communism and those which continued the full use of Republican money for everything from payment of income to the collectivists to selling goods in the communal stores. Probably a majority of them established the system of compensating their members on the basis of their family responsibilities rather than of the work they did in the collective. Virtually all of them sought to provide schooling for their members' children (and some cases for the adult members themselves), as well as health care and other attributes of a modern society.

Certainly, there were collectives which were good, bad and indifferent among those in Castille, Andalusia and Extremadura. However, there were almost certainly fewer collectives in those areas which were imposed by force than in the eastern part of the country, and there were assuredly many which were a success from the economic and social point of view.

Part Four

Anarchist Urban Collectives

16

Overall View of Urban Collectives

In the days following the suppression of the military revolt, workers throughout much of Republican Spain–Catalonia, the Levante, New Castille (the center), Andalusia, Santander and Asturias – seized control of the industrial and commercial enterprises for which they worked. The only Loyalist area in which such seizures did not take place was the Basque region. The Basque Nationalists, who dominated the Basque government, did not permit the kind of seizures which took place elsewhere. The son of one Basque factory owner, who in the Franco period was himself the owner of the plant, told me that the family metallurgical firm remained in the hands of a man to whom the owner had given power of attorney, while the owner and his son spent most of the War in France.[1]

Spontaneity of the Collectivizations

The first thing that is clear about the workers' seizures of their places of employment is that these were spontaneous, without any incitement or direction from the CNT or from any other higher authority. Victor Alba, who at the time was a journalist and a leader of the youth movement of the Partido Obrero de Unificación Marxista in Catalonia, has attested to this.

According to Victor Alba, the key reason for the establishment of what soon came to be called 'collectives' was the abandonment of their enterprises by their legal owners. 'One must insist on the exceptional phenomenon which was unexpected and had little probability of being repeated ... the massive abandonment of their enterprises by the owners of firms of some importance, because it helps us to understand the situation without which the collectivizations would not have occurred.[2]

Enrique Marco Nadal, who was the CNT leader of the Valencia railroad workers during the Civil War, has written: 'The collectives were begun with the taking over (incautación) by the workers of the industries abandoned by those owners who sympathized more with the Rebels than with the Republic, and left them, to flee the Republic, or by others who without being unsympathetic with the Republic, had a bad conscience about how they had treated their workers, and also fled to avoid being victims of reprisals.'[3]

However, Victor Alba, speaking particularly about the elimination in Barcelona, argued: 'The owners, without leadership from their organizations, allowed themselves to be carried away by fear, and didn't examine the situation. Had they done so, the majority would have returned to their firms when the fighting in the streets was over, and although they would have had to make many concessions, possibly they could have succeeded in maintaining the principle of private property in them. In any case, there was a strong possibility that they would have succeeded in this. But they didn't even try. They resigned before their resignation was asked for. And it is not certain that it would have been asked for.'

Alba argued that if the owners had returned, there would have been strong elements to support them within a short time. The middle class, which was extensive, would have rallied to back them, as would the government once it had to some degree been re-established. However, when the owners had disappeared they made it impossible for anyone to support them.[4]

Both Marco Nadal and Victor Alba agreed that after a short while a substantial number of employers of smaller firms did return, but only after the collectivization process was in full swing. Marco Nadal, continuing his description of the advent of collectives in the Valencia region, noted: 'Others, surprising in their number, came into existence due to understandings of workers and owners ... and the workers, with good tact, in those cases gave the owner the function which he wished, or made him Technical Adviser to the Comité de Fabrica, instead of assigning him to a position in front of a machine...'[5]

Victor Alba also commented with regard to Catalonia: 'With time, some owners, possibly as many as 30 percent, in middle-sized firms but in none of the large ones, reappeared and what had been their firms gave them employment as technicians, accountants and even directors, and as such, they earned a wage. There were no cases of conflicts of importance between those salaried ex-owners and their new working comrades.'[6]

In some cases, the workers even called back the former employer to manage his former firm under the general supervision of the workers' Comité de Empresa. This happened in the case of one of the principal foundries in the Barcelona area which was converted to making aerial bombs.[7]

Victor Alba has also suggested that there was an alternative to workers' seizure of their factories, workshops and commercial enterprises. This was the intervention of the Generalidad in those firms in Catalonia, and of other governments, including the Republican one, in other parts of the Loyalist area.[8] However, since immediately following July 19, no government in Loyalist Spain had the prestige and power to permit it to take such a step, even if any of them in fact contemplated it, this alternative was not resorted to. (One exception to this was the takeover of all Catalan banks by the government of the Generalidad a few days after the Civil War began.)

Given the abandonment of their enterprises by the owners of industries and other firms, and the immediate failure of the governments to provide a substitute for the entrepreneurs, the workers undertook to act on their own accord. Victor Alba has insisted that in part at least the workers were motivated by worry about how they would get their wages on the following Saturday.[9] July 19 was a Sunday, and by a couple days later, this had become a problem which required resolution.

Victor Alba has described what happened:

Everything was up in the air. Things were clarified on Tuesday, the 21st. In the majority of the large firms there was not present the owner, or the manager, and sometimes not even the engineers. If the firms were not functioning what would happen?

The doors were opened, because it was not the owner or manager who appeared, keys in hand, but some night watchman... They were there. The people walked around disoriented. Each was on his own. In some cases, the factories began to work, but in most cases, the workers formed little groups, commenting, listening to someone who had participated in the fighting. In the middle of the morning, after a few phone calls or visits to the union, the workers met in an assembly in the workplace.

The initiative was taken sometimes by a trade union steward, in other cases by rank-and-filers. In those assemblies, after exchange of known information (that the owner or manager wasn't in his home, and his whereabouts were unknown), it was agreed to name a committee which, for the time being would make plans to be submitted to another general assembly... That same day, there were other assemblies in many places. In others, they were held early in the following day, Wednesday the 22nd... In all these assemblies – in Barcelona, in some industries of Valencia, in the factory cities of Catalonia ... it was agreed that the workers would take charge of the firm, that the elected Committee would direct it and that contact would be maintained with the union.[10]

The Ideological Background of Moves to Establish Collectives

It is clear that the national and regional leaderships of the CNT had little or no part in the workers' decisions to take over their industries. Indeed, in most cases, even the local union was at most consulted, but did not lead the process, although there were some instances, in Badalona and other provincial cities, in which the *sindicatos* as such did take the lead.

The Partido Obrero de Unificación Marxista publication *The Spanish Revolution* pointed out this lack of central direction of the collectivization process by the CNT at the time: 'The CNT or Anarchist trade unions, representing the most radical workers, do not succeed in giving the director necessary [*sic*] to face the problems of the revolution. Confronted with concrete tasks their utopianism reveals its incapacity. Burdened with the weight of old conceptions and trying at the same time to face the realities of daily problems, it leaves practically all decisions in the hands of certain comrades and local committees. This has led to confusion and the appearance of isolated initiatives which need to be organized.'[11]

However, the failure of the anarcho-syndicalist leadership to direct the process of collectivization does not mean that the anarchist nature of the Confederación Nacional del Trabajo was of no significance in the process. As Victor Alba has said, the absconding of the employers, 'created an exceptional opportunity to carry out an old trade union aspiration. It is necessary to insist ... on this. Without the desire – sometimes unconscious – to be owners, without the survival of collectivist traditions in the countryside, without the aspiration of the anarcho-syndicalists to transform society through the *sindicatos* and convert them into the administrators of the economy, the workers, to resolve their problem, would have chosen one of the other possible alternatives, all simpler and less charged with responsibility than the formation of Comités de Empresa.'[12]

It is interesting to note that at least some of the anarchist national leaders did not approve of the collectivizations. This was the case with Horacio Prieto, who was secretary of the national committee of the CNT when the War began, at which point he was in the Basque area, where there were no such seizures of firms by the workers. Upon his return to Catalonia, he expressed shock and distress at what had occurred there.[13]

The Short- and Long-term Significance of Collectivization

Even the opponents of the anarchists have paid tribute to their role in getting the Republican economy going again after the suppression of the Rebellion in those parts of Spain in which it was overcome. For instance, Rodolfo Llopis, the Socialist leader who was Prime Minister Francisco Largo Caballero's principal lieutenant during the time he was prime minister noted that, after July 19, the State had virtually disappeared, and that thanks to the existence of a strong trade union movement, the trade unions were able to take over industries, set up collectives and get the economy going again. He commented that in doing this the anarchists made a great contribution. However, he had doubts about whether the collectives were sufficient to serve the purpose of fighting the war.[14]

Luis Portela, the leader of the Partido Obrero de Unificación Marxista in Valencia during the Civil War, has also said that the collectivization saved the economic situation of the Republic at the beginning of the War.[15]

Anarchist students of the role of the anarchists in the Civil War, although they agreed with the importance of the collectives in putting the economy of Republican Spain back into operation, did not agree with the reservations of Rodolfo Llopis on their subsequent role. Thus, Gaston Leval has claimed: 'The industrial collectivizations, the sindicalizations of industry and public services, agrarian socialization, which all permitted resistance during almost three years, and without which Franco would have triumphed in a few weeks, were the work of the libertarians, who created and organized, without paying attention to the minister or the ministries.'[16]

Anarchist Treatment of the Middle Class

Some observers, who were basically friendly to the Revolution which the anarchists and their Left Socialist and POUMist allies had brought about in the early phases of the Civil War, and who subsequently wrote extensively about it, felt that the revolutionaries had made a fundamental error in their handling of elements of the middle classes. Two such observers may be cited.

Burnett Bolloten was a United Press correspondent in Loyalist Spain from 1936–8, devoted much of the rest of his life to collecting materials on the War and Revolution, and wrote two books on the subject, dealing particularly with the struggle between the anarchists and the Stalinists during the conflict:

> To the dismay of thousands of handicraftsmen, small manufacturers, and tradesmen, their promises and their equipment were expropriated by the labor unions of the anarchosyndicalist CNT and often by the somewhat less radical unions of the Socialist UGT... In short, the labor unions impinged upon the interests of the middle classes in almost every field. Retailers, barbers and bakers; shoemakers and cabinetmakers, dressmakers and tailors, brick makers and building contractors, to cite but a few examples, were caught up relentlessly by the collectivization movement in numberless towns and villages.
>
> It is no wonder then that in the first shock of these revolutionary events the small-scale producers and businessmen looked on themselves as ruined; for even when the anarchosyndicalists respected the small man's property, some among them made it clear that this was only a temporary indulgence while the war lasted.[17]

Victor Alba was a journalist of the Partido Obrero de Unificación Marxista (POUM) during the War and had a chance to observe at first hand the collectivization process. He has written two extensive manuscripts about that process, from a friendly point of view. However, he agrees with Bolloten, and has spelled out the consequences of the anarchists' treatment of the middle classes.

Alba has written that it was a fundamental error of the anarchists 'not to have attracted the middle class. Without the middle class, the Communists would not have found any echo for their campaigns against the collectivizations, would not have been able to persuade Negrín (because he would have seen no advantage in it for himself) to send the gold to Moscow and they would not have had the personnel or the means to impose Soviet policy.'

Alba argued that the anarchists could have carried out:

> ...a policy of attraction of the middle class. They should have

done so – it was perfectly possible without prejudicing the workers' interests, and even benefiting them. They could have incorporated in their ranks a good part of the middle class, to establish permanent relations between the private enterprises – small and middle class – and the collectivized economy, using the services of the professionals.

On balance they didn't do so, perhaps because they identified the middle class with the worst elements in politics and because it has been the middle class in power which – for very complex reasons – persecuted the labor movement during the Republic.[18]

The anarchists were certainly not oblivious to the problem of trying to gain the backing of the lower middle class. John Langdon-Davies, the British journalist, cited in this connection an appeal addressed by the CNT to the petty bourgeoisie early in August 1936:

It is inexplicable, this fear that the petty and modest bourgeoisie has of us – that the capitalists, the millionaires, the plutocrats, the land-owners should fear us is logical, because they are the incarnation of injustice and represent the privileged classes. But the modest bourgeois, the small business-man and small industrialists, should clearly see that we are not their enemies... In Catalonia the *petite bourgeoisie* is a large proportion of the community. We do not want to underestimate their social function. We believe that in the building of the new society which is being born, this group will be a most important piece of the powerful mechanism that the workers have been forging since the very moment that capitalism passed away on July 19th...[19]

However, too often, the anarchists in practice did not pay attention to the interests and opinions of the middle class and this had a negative impact, particularly in political terms, in so far as the anarchists were concerned.

Innovations in the Collectives

There was considerable technological and organizational innovation carried out by the collectives. The most striking example of the former was the quick mounting of a war industry, to provide arms and equipment for the militia and the new republican army.

Organizational change largely took the form of converting what had been workshop industries into factory ones, particularly in Catalonia. Within a few months there were in existence some 36 of these 'general' collectives in Catalonia, formed by bringing together the machinery, equipment and personnel of small workshops into large enterprises, which could be organized more efficiently. Among these were organizations in the wood industry, milk, truck gardening and furniture. There was some resistance to the policy from within some of the smaller collectives which had been set up right after the beginning of the War. The workers in collectives which were doing well financially sometimes did not want to be merged with some which were having financial difficulties.[20]

This tendency to consolidate and rationalize the industries under workers' control was not confined to Catalonia. In Valencia a plenum of CNT unions in December 1936 resolved: 'The idiosyncrasy of the majority of the manufacturers, determined by the lack of technical-commercial preparation, has prevented them from carrying out the last experiment: grouping of large industries to achieve better technology and more rational exploitation. Therefore ... the socialization proposed by us must correct the defects of system and organizations within each of the industries...'[21]

Internal Structure of the Collectives

Although there was some variation from one collective to another, a more or less general pattern of internal organization soon emerged. Victor Alba has described this, particularly in Catalonia:

The assembly of all the manual and white collar workers of an enterprise elected members of the Comité de Control or Comité de Empresa, which consisted of five to ten workers. Theoretically, the two central labor groups were represented in the committee, proportionate to their number of members in the enterprise. But in the majority of the firms, before May 1937, there were no members of the UGT, or so few that they had not established a trade union branch. Things changed after the events of May 1937, when, because of the victory in the streets of the adversaries of the CNT, the UGT succeeded in forming traces of union branches in many enterprises, consisting of the more timorous or less politicized workers who before the war had been indifferent or bootlickers of the employers.

On this point, the situation was substantially different in the Levante region. The UGT was much stronger there than it was in Catalonia at the outbreak of the War, and most of it was under the control of the Largo Caballero Socialist faction. As we shall see in the following chapters, the UGT there often collaborated enthusiastically with the CNT to set up collectives.

Victor Alba's description of the organizational structure of the collectives continued:

In the committees there had to be represented all of the departments of the enterprises: office, warehouse, different manufacturing sections, shops, etc. The *sindicatos* insisted on this, seeing in it not only a means of interesting in trade union life elements before outside of it – like white collar workers – but also because among these elements there were people who had knowledge which was indispensable in a Comité de Empresa, such as accountants and technicians. As a result, many committees had a majority of members who were recent or lukewarm CNTistas, but the coordinating force and the 'soul' of the committee were the old trade union militants.

The committees generally had few people younger than 30 years of age; the younger people were soon at the front. This deprived many enterprises of the imagination, enthusiasm and devotion of youth.

It was the committee that elected the director of the firm. That individual, however, worked under the close supervision of the Comité de Empresa, and had to submit all major decisions to it.

The selection of a manager was often difficult, because those who had had administrative positions before were often not trusted by the workers. However, where relations between the workers and such administrators had been good, an ex-administrator might be selected. Often white-collar workers, accountants or others with necessary knowledge and experience, were chosen. In some cases, where relations between former employers and their workers had been friendly, the former owner was elected as manager.[22]

Alba concluded his description of the internal organization of the collectives by noting: 'The administration of the majority of the enterprises was not very complex, because of their smallness. It was logical that the workers with certain experience in the leadership of their unions concluded that they also could administer the enterprise in which they worked.'[23]

Cipriano Damiano, a CNT journalist during the Civil War, who was well acquainted with the collectives of Barcelona at least, noted that all important decisions were taken by the general assemblies of the workers, and that these were widely attended and regularly held. Damiano said that if an administrator did something which the general assembly had not authorized, he was likely to be deposed at the next meeting. He added that the *sindicatos* still existed and were there to advise the administrators.[24]

Wartime Problems of the Collectives

The anarchist urban collectives were faced with a wide number of problems which were created by the peculiar circumstances which existed after July 19 1936. There were also other kinds of difficulties which arose from the process of collectivization itself.

One of the major problems which faced the worker-collectivized industries of Loyalist Spain was the fact that when the Civil War began the country was still suffering from the effects of the Great Depression. One of the most obvious effects of the Depression, and one with which the various collectives had to deal, was unemployment. Gaston Leval has estimated that there were at least 200,000 unemployed workers in Catalonia alone.[25] As we shall see in subsequent chapters, the collectives were able to put back to work a number of these people by restarting firms, or parts of firms, which had until then been closed down. But in many other cases, following their egalitarian principles, the collectives felt themselves forced to pay their unemployed comrades their regular wages even though they were not working.

Gaston Leval presented as an example of this problem the case of the construction workers of Barcelona. As a result of the Civil War, there was little employment in that sector after July 19. But the government of Catalonia decided to pay the construction workers their wages even though they were not working. When the CNT construction union decided that this should be ended, and began to try to place its members in other economic activities, the Stalinist-controlled Unión General de Trabajadores established its own construction workers union and promised that its members would continue to receive their wages without having to work, which ended for the time being at least, the CNT union's attempt to deal with the problem.[26]

Josep Maria Bricall has noted that in Catalonia '...the problem of the struggle against unemployment lost importance at the end of 1937, because of the decrees of mobilization.' In September and October 1937, the Catalan government – of which the anarchists were no longer a part, and in which Stalinist influence was marked – issued decrees providing that workers in industry and commerce who until then had been receiving what amounted to unemployed benefits from the Regulating Office for the Payment of Wages, were to be 'civilly mobilized at the disposition of the president of the Generalidad'. They were to be assigned 'to those jobs for which they were qualified, especially fortifications and other war objectives'. Those who would not submit to such mobilization would no longer receive payments from the Regulating Office.[27]

Another difficulty presented by the situation in which the new collectives found themselves – in this case, the Civil War – was the need to convert many of the industries of Loyalist Spain to war production. Diego Abad de Santiallán commented: 'The necessity of dealing with ... a war which every day assumed larger importance and used up the largest part of production, completely absorbing the energies of the most conscientious and trained members of the proletariat.'[28]

A related problem was the shortage of raw materials, which quickly appeared in Republican Spain. It arose from their relative paucity in the Republican area and the growing blockade of Loyalist Spain, not only by the part of the Spanish fleet which the Franco forces had been able to capture, but also by the fleets of Fascist Italy and Nazi Germany.

The anarchist leader Diego Abad de Santillán described this problem: 'We faced from the first day the alarming lack of raw materials, in a region which is not rich in them. For example we lacked totally coal for industry and transport. The normal consumption of Catalonia was five or six thousand tons a day, and the only mines which were exploited, of paper-grade coal, even with intensification of production, produced only three hundred tons.'[29]

Another problem which the collectivized industries faced was that of lack of markets. At the outbreak of the Civil War, the most industrialized parts of Spain remained in the hands of the Republic. Until July 19 1936, the market of industries had included all of the nation. However, after the Rebel forces had taken control of about half of the country, that part of Spain was cut off, and the industries of Catalonia and the Levante found that much of the output of their manufacturing firms had no market. Increased unemployment and financial problems are only two of the resulting difficulties which those collectives encountered.

Still another problem arising from the War was the physical destruction of part of the economy of Republican Spain. The Franco air force, composed largely of Italian Fascist and German Nazi planes and aviators, more or less heavily bombarded Barcelona, Valencia and other Loyalist cities. Some of these air raids damaged industrial establishments as well as railroad centers, and residential areas.

As early as January 1937, CNT National Committee member M. Cardona Rossell noted the extent of this damage: 'There are hundreds of factories, workshops, stores, etc. in various zones of the country which are either destroyed or partially destroyed, bombarded by the enemy. And in these factories etc. the workers receive their wages without working. Take account of the fact that there are hundreds and thousands of workers involved.'[30]

The general economic situation of Republican Spain deteriorated as the Civil War progressed. The splitting of the country in two by the conflict resulted in shortages of all kinds, not only of raw materials and markets, but of food as well. The results were mounting inflation, depreciation of the Republic's currency (which intensified the inflation in so far as imported goods were concerned), and a growing black market. Ronald Fraser has noted that in Catalonia prices went up 47 per cent in the first six months of the War, and an additional 49 per cent in the following six months.[31] These were the problems with which the collectives and the CNT itself had to try to deal with.

Problems Arising from Collectivization

Aside from these problems arising from the War and the general economic situation of the country, there were innumerable difficulties which came from the very process of collectivization. These included the unpreparedness of the CNT, in terms of its own organization, to deal with the sudden appearance or thousands of collectives established by its rank and file members; the rise of what we shall call 'factory patriotism', the problems of labor discipline; the lack of trained personnel; the frequent lack of sufficient means of financing the collectives; the problem of relations of the collectivized part of the economy with the still existing private sector, and with the government sector. Another serious question was that of the attitude to be taken towards foreign-owned firms. Finally, the collectives were faced with constant and growing opposition from the enemies and opponents of the anarchists, most notoriously of the Stalinists, seconded by some elements of the Socialists and the UGT, and by the middle-class parties and organisations.

Inadequacy of CNT Organizational Structure

As we have seen, the sudden appearance of collectives formed by rank and file CNTers, which took over most of the larger industrial plants, much of the commerce and various other economic activities, was totally unexpected in so far as the national and regional leaderships of the Confederación Nacional del Trabajo were concerned. More serious was the fact that the CNT's existing organizational structure was totally unprepared to handle this situation.

For the most part, the CNT was organized on the basis of a local, regional and national hierarchy. At the base was a group of workers in a factory, commercial firm or artesans' shop. Workers in the same industry or other activity were brought together in a local union or *sindicato*. These *sindicatos* were joined in local federation.

In some cases, the local federations were joined to form a *comarcal* federation; in others, the next step in the hierarchy was the provincial federation. The provincial and *comarcal* federations were brought together into regional federations, or confederations, which were the organizations which together formed the Confederación Nacional del Trabajo.

What was lacking in this structure, in so far as the handling of the sudden appearance of the collectives was concerned, was a series of national industrial unions (*federaciónes nacionales de industria*). The establishment of such organizations had been a subject of strong, and sometimes bitter, debate for more than a decade and a half within anarchist ranks.

The first attempt to establish national federations was defeated at a CNT congress early in the 1920s. Although the 1931 congress of the organization adopted the idea, little had been done to put that decision into practice by the time the Civil War broke out.

Had there existed a series of national industrial unions, bringing together on a national level all of the local unions of particular industries or other branches of the economy, these could have more or less quickly provided local, regional and national groupings of the collectives established by their members. However, in the face of the lack of national industrial unions, each collective had to operate more or less on its own, except in those cases in which local unions coordinated them. There was, so far as I know, no case in which the urban collectives were brought together on a regional basis, except possibly in Asturias.

The leadership of the CNT soon became acutely conscious of this weakness in the structure of their movement. For instance, in January 1937, M. Cardona Rossell, in a speech in Barcelona, said: 'Collectivization is a forced step, a beginning of socialization; and now the proletariat in the large and small cities are busy with the great and difficult task of constituting in a complete way their federations of industry, on both a regional and national basis. The federations of industry are certainly a necessary step, an indispensable measure to arrive at socialization ... it is very pressing to establish the federations of industry ... it is a requirement of the Revolution, and all the needs of the Revolution are pressing.'[32]

In March 1937, a regional congress of the CNT of Catalonia adopted a resolution providing for the setting up of industrial unions on a regional level. It set forth the establishment of 12 such organizations.[33] We shall see in a later chapter that the National Economic Plenum of the CNT, which met in Valencia in January 1938, finally set forth a plan for the national grouping of the collectives under the aegis of the national industrial unions. By then, however, it was too late.

Factory Patriotism

One result of the lack of sufficient local, regional and national coordination of the collectives was the quick appearance of factory patriotism. Both anarchists and non-anarchists have described this phenomenon.

Victor Alba noted in October 1937: 'We have occasion to see how in some workers' sectors, to collectivize a factory or an industry consists only of appropriating it without consideration of the needs of the war and of the general organization of production, nor of whether the raw materials they possess are needed by other branches of production. There have been *sindicatos* which have believed that collectivization consisted of appropriating the private property of an enterprise... The taking over or socialization of an industry should never be for the benefit of a *sindicato* or of a labor sector but for the benefit of the whole proletariat.'[34]

The French anarchist Gaston Leval noted the same phenomenon. He wrote: 'Many times in Barcelona and in Valencia – the workers of each enterprise took possession of the factory, of the workshop, of the machines, of the raw materials, and taking advantage of the fact that there still existed the monetary system and the mercantile economy characteristic of the capitalist system, supported by the government, organized production for their own advantage, selling for their own benefit the production of their labor... This practice didn't create a true socialization, but a species of workers' neo-capitalism...'[35]

M. Cardona Rossell described two other aspects of this problem, which he called 'professional sense' and 'localist vision'. He said that some workers tended to think only in terms of what was good for their particular branch of the economy to the exclusion of the economy as a whole. There was also a tendency for workers of one part of the country to think primarily, if not exclusively, in terms of what was good for that region rather than what was good for the general welfare of Republican Spain, or the workers as a whole.[36]

Horacio Prieto, the former national secretary of the CNT, was even sharper in his criticism of what we have called 'factory patriotism'. Speaking in January 1938, he said: 'The collectivism we are living in Spain is not anarchist collectivism, it is the creation of a new capitalism, more inorganic than the old capitalist system we have destroyed... Rich collectives refuse to recognize any responsibilities, duties or solidarity towards poor collectives... No one understands the complexities of the economy, the dependence of one industry on another.'[37]

Clearly, the problem of factory patriotism was made worse than it might otherwise have been by the lack of a mechanism within the CNT for coordinating the operation of the dispersed collectives. It was also more of a problem in some parts of the economy than in others. In some cases, local unions succeeding in limiting if not eliminating the phenomenon, as appears to have occurred in the Badalona textile industry.

The Problem of Labor Discipline

Inevitably, the workers elected to lead the collectives were faced with the problem of labor discipline. With the disappearance of the owners and old managers of the enterprises, as well as of their methods of imposing and maintaining labor discipline, some worker members of the collectives would interpret this to mean that they could do more or less as they pleased, without consideration for the effect of their actions on the well-being of their fellow workers and the collective as a whole. On the other hand, given the traditional anarchist argument that solidarity was sufficient to assure that there would be no labor discipline problem in post-revolutionary society, some of the workers in charge of coordinating and directing collectives had an understandable reluctance to impose rules and regulations – and punishments – on their fellow workers.

Victor Alba noticed that, in the first few weeks at least, the initial enthusiasm of the workers for the collectivization and their conviction that they were building a new society minimized the problem of labor discipline. However, after that period, the question was 'How to maintain discipline without diminishing enthusiasm, without the workers ending up saying that they had only changed bosses...?' Alba explained what happened:

> Different methods were used, according to the criterion of each committee and in accordance with the conscience of each committee with regard to this issue. There were those who didn't worry about this, and who in fact acted like a new owner; they were the minority, and sometimes the workers removed them when they found that vapors had risen to their heads or that they had sacrificed everything to efficiency.
>
> The most common thing was to convoke frequent assemblies, to tell the workers of the situation, to ask them for suggestions and discuss with them the problems and their possible solutions.

The most active and youngest elements of each enterprise had gone to the front. There remained, then, the old militants ... and the majority who were not active. The old militants, it is clear, exercised a decisive influence.

Alba observed that it was hard to know whether the effectiveness of such assemblies would have continued if the War had ended with Republican victory and there were no longer the pressures of war to reinforce the appeal for voluntary labor discipline.[38]

Ronald Fraser has presented an interesting example of labor discipline recounted to him by Luis Santacana, a leader of the España Industrial textile collective in Catalonia. A worker was caught stealing a spanner, and Santacana reasoned with him, explaining that he was no longer robbing the boss, but his fellow workers, and appealed to him not to steal again. However, when a couple of weeks later the same man was caught stealing a second spanner, Santacana told him: 'The collective ... would not sack him because he had children and needed his weekly wage. Instead, they were going to move him to a new section, the cleaning department. But that would require public notification.'

Santacana thereupon told the worker: 'You will write your full name on the blackboard, underneath it that you have stolen two spanners, and that is the reason for your move to a section where you will have no chance of further theft.' Although the worker appealed against what he considered an indignity, he was forced to do as Santacana demanded. As a consequence, according to Santacana, 'There were no more cases of indiscipline; the threat of the blackboard was sufficient.'[39]

In a later chapter, we shall see that in the national economic plenum of the CNT in January 1938, considerable attention was paid to the problem of labor discipline, and it adopted somewhat more draconian resolutions of the problem than might have been expected from an anarchist organization.

Lack of Trained Personnel

One handicap, which was more serious in some industries than in others, was the lack of sufficient trained personnel. One cause of this was the fact that not only the former employers had disappeared, but in some cases the technically trained higher-echelon personnel in the plants taken over by the workers did not choose to participate in the collectives.

Gaston Leval wrote: 'Our impression is that, taking into account the nature of the work in metallurgy, where technology is much more important and is more often involved than in other industries (wood, for example), there was a lack of sufficient engineers or specialists capable of adequately assuming organic responsibilities. Competent specialists were lacking in the armaments industry, in construction of important machines. Proletarian enthusiasm could not make up for the use of mathematics.'[40] And José Brincall has noted: 'The continuous pleas in favor of the technicians launched by *Solidaridad Obrera* because of the lack which Catalan industry began to experience.'[41]

In some cases, the problem was resolved by keeping the former owner as manager of the collective. This was particularly the case in relatively small firms. Ronald Fraser cited Joan Ferrer, secretary of the CNT commercial workers' union in Barcelona, who attended many workers' assemblies to urge them to take care of their enterprises, to the effect that: 'Very often the owner would also address the assembly, practically bringing tears to everyone's eyes with the story of the sacrifices he had made to build up the firm – only now to see it threatened with collectivization. In these cases, I always suggested to the assembly that he be made the managing director, since the works council had to appoint one anyway. My idea was that the former owner was the most suitable person because, with his capitalist egoism, he would watch over the enterprise and make sure everything functioned as well as possible; he no doubt would one day be hoping to regain possession. My proposal was almost always accepted.'[42]

This subject, too, got some attention at the National Economic Plenum of the CNT, Various suggestions for the establishment of technical training schools were adopted there.

Wage Policies

One of the problems which the collectives had to face was the nature of the wage payments to their members. The *a priori* prejudice of the anarchist trade unions was for payment on the basis of family responsibility, with a high degree of equality of payment. However, as we shall see in the chapters which follow, there was a widespread tendency to leave in place, at least to a considerable degree, the wage and salary disparities which had existed before July 19 1936. The collectives found that this was particularly necessary to gain the collaboration of technical and white-collar personnel.

In Catalonia, the Generalidad, perhaps with a view to winning the sympathy of the anarchists who clearly dominated the region, issued decrees late in July 1936 providing for the 40-hour week and a wage increase of 15 per cent for all those with income below 6,000 pesetas a year.[43] However, these moves by no means won universal approval from the anarchists. Juan Peiró, writing in the newspaper *Llibertat* of Mataró on August 9 1936, opined that the reduction of working hours 'could not be more inopportune'.[44] For its part, the CNT Barcelona federation 'recommended the increase of production and not solicitation of new increases in wages or diminution of the work day since the problem was not achievement of partial improvements but that of attacking the basic problem through socialization of wealth.' As José Maria Bricall noted, a number of unions rejected the decrees, particularly that one reducing working hours.[45]

After the elimination of the anarchists from the Catalan government, it established in October 1937 the Wage Regulating Commission, under Juan Comorera's department of economy. This sought to establish minimum wages, maximum wages and establish a system of wage differentials.[46] However, it is not clear the degree to which the Catalan government was in fact able to intervene in the fixing of wages in the workers' collectives.

Lack of Financing Facilities

One of the most serious problems faced by the collectives was derived directly from the anarchists' own ideology. This was the lack of any kind of financial network to serve them.

The Spanish anarchists before the Civil War certainly regarded banks and credit as 'capitalist' devices, not appropriate to a libertarian economy. Therefore, they had paid little attention to organizing bank workers, and had no plans for banks in their view of the post-revolutionary economy. At the beginning of the War the only bank workers' union was that of the UGT, which Burnett Bolloten has described as 'a fief of left-wing Socialist Amaro del Rosal, a Communist supporter'.[47] Although the CNT subsequently organized its own bank workers' union, it was too late.

These attitudes continued for some time after the beginning of the Civil War. Thus, M. Cardona Rossell, speaking in January 1937, claimed: 'To the same degree that socialization is realized and the capitalist order is abandoned, to that same degree, institutions, which are fundamentally capitalist, will face substitution or total modification and they will have to be substituted by other organisms.'[48]

In Catalonia, where the anarchists, through their unions and the militia council took over most of the economy in the first phase of the War, they left the banking system in the hands of the government of the Generalidad. Less than a week after the War began the Generalidad issued a decree intervening all of the banks. The government's Comisaría General de Banca and the UGT's Bank Workers' Federation were challenged to exercise that control.[49]

Ronald Fraser has commented on this problem:

In their revolutionary surge to take over the means of production ... the Catalan libertarians had overlooked one very 'material' element of power: finance. The Generalidad never lost control of Catalonia's banking and financial institutions, which were under the control of the UGT bank employees' union. From the start, the Generalidad appointed delegates in each bank, with the union's agreement, to control operations and prevent the flight of capital. The union carried out to the letter all the instructions issued by the Generalidad financial councillor and the central government...

Paraphrasing the views of Joan Grijalbo, who had been a prominent member of the UGT bank workers union during the War, Fraser noted:

The Catalan libertarians' 'oversight' was perhaps less important than was often supposed. Pre-war Catalonia had never been able to 'cash in' its industrial weight for the political direction of the Spanish state; the bourgeoisie lacked one requisite for it: banking and finance capital. Now, for much the same reason, the Catalan revolution could not 'cash in' its specific weight; it did not control the country's financial resources; Madrid did. Nevertheless, the 'oversight' reveals something of the ambiguity of the libertarian revolution; for banking gold are to capitalism what organized coercion – the police, judiciary, army – is to the state: the ultimate power. The republic had temporarily lost the use of the second, but retained the first. The libertarian revolution has gained neither.[50]

However, virtually from their beginning, some of the collectives were faced with financial problems. Not a few of the enterprises taken over by their workers were already bankrupt or near to it, as a result of the Depression. Others soon ran into financial difficulties for a variety of reasons, and needed credit from banks or some other source. Had there been general coordination of the collectives and some kind of CNT financial institution, these problems would not have presented any menace to the individual collectives and the collective system as a whole. However, the lack of these things constituted a danger to the whole collective experiment.

Those opposed to the collectives used the lack of a CNT institution to finance them to try to undermine or destroy the workers' controlled enterprises. Foremost among these enemies of the collectives was Juan Negrín, who both as minister of finance in the government of Francisco Largo Caballero and as Largo Caballero's successor as prime minister, did his utmost to keep them from functioning well and if possible to destroy them.

Victor Alba said of Negrín's work against the collectives:

> There is no doubt that the Ministry of Finance ... could have organized a monopoly of foreign trade, not against, but in accord with the collectives, thus gaining foreign exchange for the country and stimulating the workers to augment production, by provoking in them the sensation that they were working for themselves and for the country, and not for the owners. It could have attempted to do what the Generalidad did with the collectivization decree of 1936, that is, to coordinate the collectives, to give the *sindicatos* part in this coordination and, at the same time, reserve for the State certain superior functions. It could have facilitated credit to the collectives... But Negrín was not interested at all in this ... he was interested in undoing what the workers had done...[51]

This financial sabotage by Negrín was extended after the Republican government moved to Barcelona in October 1937. He forced the not entirely unwilling government of Catalonia, by then to a large degree dominated by the Stalinists, to turn over to the government the funds from the profits of the Catalan collectives, which had been deposited in the Caja de Credito Industrial y Comercial, which had been established under the Catalan collectivization decree. According to that decree, these funds were to be used for investment in the collectives.[52]

This problem, too, was dealt with by the CNT National Economic Plenum of January 1938. That meeting approved the idea of setting up a CNT bank, the Banco Sindical Ibérico, to finance the collectives. But, once again, by then it was too late.

Relations with the Private Sector

Although the workers took over a substantial part of the urban economy of Republican Spain, another important segment of it remained in the hands of private firms. Victor Alba cited an estimate that even in Catalonia, where the urban collectives were most widespread, almost half of the workers continued to be employed by private enterprises.[53]

The workers who took over many of the industries and other economic firms had to continue to do business with many of the existing private firms. Often, the private firms were either the collectives' customers or they were suppliers of some of the inputs which the collectives used.

Contacts with the private sector were also of some importance in another connection. With the growing economic difficulties of the Republic, the black market became extensive. The collectives sometimes dealt with it either as suppliers of their inputs or customers for some of their products.

The National Economic Plenum of the CNT dealt with this black market problem also. It resolved to establish distribution centers in the Republic's cities and towns to try to control the country's inflation and fight its black markets. But time was too short for these decisions to be very effective.

Problems with Foreign-owned Enterprises

The taking over of Spanish-owned firms by their workers did not present any particular international problems for the Republic in terms of damaging powerful interests in other countries. However, this was not the case with collectives set up in enterprises which were owned by foreign firms or investors after July 19.

The seizure of such companies by their workers involved at least two kinds of problems for the Republic. On the one hand, such actions would assure that the foreign firms, whose Spanish subsidiaries had been taken over by their workers, would be mobilized in opposition to the Loyalist cause in the Civil War.

Of more immediate damage to the Republic's economy was the likelihood that any of the output of seized foreign firms which might be sent for sale abroad might be the subject of lawsuits claiming that the collective's output in fact belonged to the 'mother company' in Great Britain, France or some other country. Such cases are discussed in the chapters which follow.

The CNT leaders were not oblivious to the general problems of the foreign-owned firms which had been seized by their organization's members. In fact, as early as July 28 1936, *Solidaridad Obrera* published a list of British firms in Barcelona which it urged its members not to seize.[54] Several months later, M. Cardona Rossell, in his speech in January 1937, suggested that the answer to the problem was that, in cases where the workers had taken over a foreign firm, the former owners should be compensated for their investments in Spain.[55]

However, no such general principle was adopted by the CNT. Usually, the CNT workers did not proclaim the total seizure of foreign-owned enterprises, but rather established elected committee to 'control' the operation of the firm. However, as will be discussed in the subsequent chapters, in some cases foreign-owned enterprises were totally taken over by their workers even though this was not the workers' original intention.

Problems with the Opponents of the Collectives

Finally, there were the problems which the collectives faced as the result of the impediments presented by those elements in the Republic who were totally opposed idea of workers' control of their enterprises. We have already noted the efforts of Juan Negrín, as minister of finance and prime minister, to undermine and destroy the collectives. However, Juan Negrín was only one element in the opposition to the CNT workers' controlled enterprises.

The Stalinists of the Communist Party of Spain (PCE) and the Partido Socialista Unificado de Catalonia (PSUC) in Catalonia were absolutely opposed to the anarchists' collectivization of a substantial part of the economy. They made this clear not only in action, but also often in words. Perhaps typical was an attack on the urban collectives by Dolores Ibarruri in a report to a Communist Party plenum in May 1938. After admitting that 'what happened in industry was a necessity imposed on the workers by the owners, who abandoned all the Enterprises'. Ibarruri went on:

> The Spanish proletariat has given proof of a marvelous spirit of initiative and organization in taking in its hands the factories, making them function ... Experience has demonstrated that the collectives, badly oriented, fomenting particularism, make more difficult for the workers themselves the vision of the general interests of their own class. On the basis of the present collectives it is impossible to construct a solid economic regime or a new form of State. Under the direction of the State itself, in a regime of democracy, the present situation must be corrected and modified in many ways, nationalizing a part of production, centralizing and coordinating another, and also, if it is necessary, returning a part to private initiative...[56]

The Catalan Stalinist party, the PSUC, was from its inception at the end of July 1936 adamantly opposed to the seizure of control by the workers of their factories and other centers of employment. One of the first documents issued by the PSUC, on September 9 1936, proclaimed: 'We demand an economy liberated from the influence or pressure of so many new-born committees, manifestation of the pseudo-revolutionary pullulation which is strangling Catalonia's magnificent vitality...'[57]

Juan Comorera, head of the PSUC, also made clear the Stalinists' opposition to workers' control of the economy. In addressing the first national conference of the PSUC a few weeks after the formation of the Negrín government, he said:

> Our party considers that in the new situation of war and revolution, the syndicates have the following essential duties to carry out: 1. Betterment of the position of the working class, and help the workers to organize their lives on better lines. Create for the workers all the commodities compatible with the interests of the war; fight against speculation, and the hoarding of primary necessary articles, and raise the new culture of the workers. 2. Cooperate with the Govern-

ment in the better organization and rationalization of production...

We believe that the syndicates have a great part to play in the common struggle, but we consider it an error that the syndicates should direct the economic and political life of the country...[58]

Allied with the Stalinists in the UGT and general politics was the Right wing of the Socialist Party (PSOE), although the Left-wing Socialists and UGTers, particularly in the Levante and Asturias, cooperated with the anarchists. Understandably, the various national and regional Republican parties, which had as their main constituency the middle class, including a lot of proprietors of small industries, artisan workshops and family-farm agriculturalists, also were generally aligned against the anarchist collectives, whether urban or rural.

The only party which joined the CNT in support of the collectives was the Partido Obrero de Unificación Marxists, the dissident Marxist–Leninist party with its major strength in Catalonia. It did not believe that this was the best way to bring about the establishment of Socialism, but did believe that the collectives were a first step in that direction and, as such, supported them.[59]

Gaston Leval has noted the importance of the opposition of Juan Comorera, head of the Stalinists in Catalonia, once he had come to be in charge within the Catalan government of the region's economy:

As much as he would have desired to do so, it was impossible to wipe out in the industries, in the various factories, the organizing influence and preponderance of our *sindicatos*. To have tried it would have paralyzed production... As a result, he resorted to two procedures which were complementary. On the one hand, he deprived the factories of raw materials, or saw to it that they were delivered late, after which he criticized them, especially those in the armaments industry. On the other, he held up payments for merchandise received, which had an effect on the material life of the workers because, since the wages were paid under trade union control, the discontent of the workers were directed against the militants and delegates of the CNT, and as a result, against the CNT itself.[60]

From the beginning of the Civil War, the Stalinists were opposed to the workers' collectives. In those parts of Spain in which they controlled the Unión General de Trabajadores, they mobilized it against the collectives also. This was the case particularly in Catalonia where, from the beginning of the Civil War, they controlled the CNT's rival. There, as the CNT leader Felipe Alaíz recalled many years later, the UGT 'made it known in a manifesto that it proposed that abandoned industries be organized as cooperatives, "labor control" be established in the rest of large industry, and small industry and commerce should be protected from seizure.'[61]

Were the Collectives Economically Successful?

There is little question about the fact that, as a result of the seizure of most of manufacturing, public utilities, and many commercial enterprises by the workers, the economy of Republican Spain began functioning as normally as wartime conditions permitted a few days after the suppression of the Rebellion there. It is also clear that the workers' collectives quickly created a war industry where none had existed before, an industry which was able to provide a substantial part of the weapons, vehicles and other military equipment which was used throughout the War by the Loyalist armed forces. At the same time, essential consumers goods such as textiles continued to be available from the factories run by the collectives. In these senses, the collectives were an economic success.

Victor Alba has argued: '...the Spanish collectivizations, as they were, short-lived and conditioned by the war, constitute a lesson, in that they proved that the workers could administer the means of production as well as, or better than, their private owners.'[62]

Elsewhere, Alba has said: 'The collectives of 1936 not only didn't fail, but they were a success. Given the circumstances, they demonstrated the principle that the workers can administer enterprises with equal or more efficiency than their employers.' He went on to say that this result arose 'not only from their desire to be owners, but also from the tradition of education, trade union training, militant spirit which the labor movement had given the workers. The workers of 1936 not only wished to be the bosses, but were prepared to be such.'

However, Victor Alba was not willing to speculate beyond that. No one will know, he said, whether, if the Civil War had been won by the Republic, the workers would still have wished to be the owners, or whether conflicts might have arisen within the collectives which the pressures of war kept from appearing during the 1936–9 period.[63]

Another observer of the collectives, Ramón Trías Fargas, who by the early 1960s was a professor of economics in the law school of the University of Barcelona, was also on balance favorably impressed with how the collectives there had functioned. He concluded that many of them did well, and observed that he knew a number of employers who found their firms in good condition when they returned after Franco's victory in the Civil War. Some of those plants had raw materials on hand, goods in their warehouses, and there had been improvements made in the plants and machinery.

Similarly, Geronimo García, a CNTer who served during the first year of the Civil War as assistant to the head of military transport of the Consejería de Guerra of Catalonia, from which vantage point he was able to observe both the CNT-controlled military transport system and the civilian collective organized by the CNT transport workers union, concluded that at least in the Catalan transport sector the collectivization had been successful. He maintained that the experience showed that the unions could run economic organizations and run them efficiently.[64]

However, not all those who had supported the collectives while they existed thought, in retrospect, that they had been successful. José Marín Salto, a one-time member of the National Committee of the CNT, with whom we talked in 1951, felt that they had been a complete failure or almost a failure. This was true in part because too many of the technical people had left the collectives. He thought that their replacements were able to do a good job in purely administrative terms, but not on the technical side, where the workers lacked the necessary know-how. However, he noted that there were some exceptions to this, where there had been capable administrators, and where consequently the plants were in good condition once the War was over.[65]

Employers and management people with whom I talked years after the Civil War had varying views about the collectives. One of these, who had been an engineer in a plant that was converted to war production, concluded that from what he had seen the collective under workers' control had been a 'disaster'.[66]

Another man, who had been in charge of collective bargaining for a Barcelona textile firm before the Civil War, had fled soon after the War began, and by 1960 was manager of that same firm, was by no means so sure. He commented that the state of the collectivized firms by the end of the War varied a great deal from case to case. He noted that in some of the collectives there had been people in charge in the Comités de Fabrica who were loyal to the old owners and who took good care of their property, and who left a large inventory on hand when the War was over. In other plants, there was no inventory left, which was the case in his own firm. However, this manager noted that in most cases the machinery was well taken care of even in plants where no inventory was left – the major exceptions being plants which had been subject to bombardment during the War.[67]

The director of another Barcelona textile firm claimed that for the most part the factories were handed back to the original owners in bad shape. Because they had been under war tension for three years, there were practically no raw materials available, and there was a shortage of skilled workers. He conceded that there were a few instances in which the workers had done a pretty good job administering the industries, and they were turned back to their original owners in fairly good shape. However, he added, very few good administrators were developed during the war period.[68]

A man who served for a short while on the Comité de Control of a Barcelona factory making turbines as representative of the technicians, but who quit because, he said, he saw that workers' control was going to be disastrous and who, years later, was an official of the employers' side of the *sindicato* system of the Franco regime, claimed that the people elected to the *comités* in the collectives were chosen not because of their competence but because of their personal popularity. He added that the workers had the idea that anyone was capable of directing a factory, which was not in fact the case.[69]

Finally, even official Francoite sources admitted that at least some of the collectives had functioned efficiently. The Falangista periodical *Sindicalismo* in 1965 published an article which said: 'For my part, I have collected direct accounts from persons (engineers, administrators and workers) who participated in the job of running collectivized firms such as the Trolleycar Company of Madrid; 'Mengemore', producing and distributing electric energy; the still existing 'Material y Construcciones', making locomotives, wagons, etc., of Valencia. The three, according to versions received from honorable people, were well administered, maintained labor discipline, defended the interest of the firm and even introduced improvements which later benefited the old owners upon recovering the full use of their rights.'[70]

Conclusion

During the Civil War there took place in Republican Spain a unique experiment of workers' control of the great majority of the larger enterprises in the Republic's economy and many of the middle-sized and smaller ones. Committees elected by the workers managed these enterprises, in most cases under the close control of periodical general assemblies of the workers.

Much was accomplished by these workers' collectives, which were established by the spontaneous action of the workers employed in them. They organized a sector of the economy which produced a substantial part of the arms and equipment used by the Republic's military during the conflict. They maintained supplies of most manufactured goods needed by the civilian population throughout the War.

The workers' collectives were faced with innumerable difficulties, some of them resulting from the remnants of the Great Depression, others from the Civil War. In addition, they had problems which arose from the very fact that the workers had taken over control of their former employers' enterprises.

The question remains open as to how effectively the collectives operated their various enterprises. There was a great deal of difference on this score between one collective and another. However, it can certainly be asserted that the war was not lost by the Republic because of the revolutionary establishment of worker-controlled collectives in a large part of the urban economy of Republican Spain. Certainly in many cases, the collectives made significant contributions to the military and political struggle. They simulated the workers' desire to work for the victory of the Republican cause. There is reason to believe that the attacks on the collectives by the Stalinists and other enemies of the anarchists served to undermine the morale of the workers, and therefore the cause of the Republic, particularly after the May Events in Catalonia, subsequent to which the anarchists were fighting a bitter battle to defend the collectives and other elements of anarchist strength in Republican Spain.

The Catalan Consejo de Economia and Collectivization Decree

During the period in which anarchist influence was still largely predominant in the government of Catalonia, that government became the only one in Loyalist Spain not only to recognize legally the workers' expropriations of industries, public utilities and other enterprises, but to seek to generalize the process throughout the region. The instrumentality through which this was achieved was the Consejo de Economia (Economic Council), and the law which was passed was the Decree of Collectivization of October 24 1936.

Spontaneous Collectivizations in Catalonia after July 19

César Lorenzo has described the process by which, immediately following the suppression of the military insurrection on July 19–20, the workers of Catalonia seized control of their places of employment:

> During the three weeks that followed July 19 there began, then was prodigiously developed, a vast movement to take possession of the mines ... quarries, workshops, factories, railroads, means of transport in general ... public services ... by the workers themselves ... General assemblies of workers, workers councils,

control committees, enterprise committees, technico-administrative commissions, local industrial committees, sectional committees, liaison committees, central directive committees, unions and industrial federations were the new organs which took charge of the branches of activity... This occurred in Barcelona as well as, for example, in Hospitalet de Llobregat, Tarrassa, Blanes, Granollers...[1]

Lorenzo stressed the spontaneity of these developments: 'It must be stressed that this had not been imposed by any organization but was the fruit of spontaneous action of the masses moved by revolutionary enthusiasm. In fact, capitalism had been overthrown and there was implanted a socialist economy based on worker self-management.' He concluded: 'This social revolution, perhaps the most radical of all time ... had broken out *in spite of the CNT* ... although the CNT later defended it with ardor against all those who sought to liquidate it.'[2]

Lorenzo also noted that some of the CNT leaders were appalled by what had happened. His own father, Horacio Prieto, then national secretary of the CNT, who was caught in Bilbao at the time the Civil War erupted, later wrote that when he got news of what had occurred in Catalonia, 'I was filled with consternation... While it gave an indication of what was the power of the Movement in Catalonia, I couldn't keep myself from declaring: That seems impossible; you have gone too far and we shall pay very dearly...'[3]

José Peirats confirms the spontaneity of the workers' movement to take control of the economy: 'It is clear that the constructive revolutionary impulse sprang from the People, from the *sindicatos* of the CNT and from its rank and file militants. The movement of requisitions, seizures, and collectivizations was a *fait accompli* that the Committees had to confront...'[4]

Getting the Catalan Economy Moving Again

Understandably, normal economic activity had come to a halt in Catalonia during July 19–20. Not only was there extensive armed conflict in Barcelona and many of the other Catalan cities and towns, but a general strike had been declared against the attempted military coup.

Once the rebellion had been suppressed, the unions ordered their members back to work.[5] But the economy of the region faced a serious and potentially catastrophic crisis. The normal machinery for supplying the population with food and other necessities had broken down.

A booklet published by the CNT in 1937, and republished various times by the CNT in exile, described what happened immediately after July 19. 'The unions undertook above all to solve the most pressing problem, which was the provision of food for the population. Popular eating centers were opened in all of the wards, in the union headquarters. The supply committees, created for the purpose, took foodstuffs from the wholesale warehouses of the city and also from the countryside. Payment was made in bonds guaranteed by the unions. All members of the unions, the women and children of the militiamen, and the population in general, received food free of charge... The moneyless economy of the antifascists lasted about two weeks. When labor then resumed and economic life revived, there was a return to the money economy.'[6]

However, the new revolutionary authority, the Comité Central de Milicias de Cataluña, sought to organize supply on a more orderly basis. For this purpose, it established the supply committee (Comité de Abastos or Comité de Abastecimientos), with representatives from all of the parties and trade union groups on the Comité de Milicias. José Domenech, of the CNT, was the secretary and *de facto* head of the Comité de Abastos. Later, when the CNT entered the Catalan regional government, Domenech became the supply councillor of the Generalidad.

Many years later, José Domenech recounted that he had had no preparation for this post. He had not the slightest notion of how a big city was supplied, where they got their eggs, their chickens and all of the other things. However, he said, he learned very quickly. He consulted merchants and others with experience in these matters and soon found what the normal channels of supply were.

One of the first orders issued by the Supply Committee provided:

1. Retail food shops are obliged to replenish their shops in the way they did before the fascist insurrection. They must go to Via de Layetana 16 to have their requests stamped by the Comité de Abastos. The shops must be supplied. 2. The responsible comrades of the antifascist organizations need not preoccupy themselves about supplying the population which shall be done in the normal manner, only seeing to the feeding of the militia. 3. It is necessary that the organizers of all collective kitchens for Militias or groups which function under the control of the antifascist organizations inform the Comité de Abastos ... of the number of rations they serve and can serve. 4. The food warehouses, flour mills and coal warehouses must be open for business. The Comité de Abastos will take over on Monday all those which don't obey these orders.[7]

Some foodstuffs for Catalonia came from abroad. Domenech quickly sent a member of his committee to the Netherlands to obtain eggs and chickens, which had largely come from there. He sent one Communist member of the Committee with a shipload of oranges, lemons, onions and other goods to Russia, and in Odessa that man exchanged these for a ship load of foodstuffs which Catalonia needed.

There were particular supply problems within Catalonia. Each new agrarian collective, and each municipality had set up its own supply committee, and immediately following July 19, these groups sought, largely through barter, to obtain the goods they needed. Some even sent truckloads of goods to France for this purpose. The result of this was chaotic.

Domenech finally called a meeting of the heads of all the Consejos de Abastos of the Catalan localities. After explaining the need to centralize the exchange of supplies, he told the local leaders to come to the Catalan Comité of Abastos for anything they needed, and to bring there anything they had to sell or exchange. Since most of the local supply committee heads were CNTers, and the minority who were Republicans favored a centralized supply system in principle, Domenech was soon able to establish such a system.[8]

Valerio Mas, a CNT representative in the Comité de Abastos, has said that within a month the supply system for the Catalan region was stabilized and assured. There were still some organizations which were operating outside the *comité*'s system, but most of the needs of the region were being met through it.[9]

Domenech organized several large central warehouses in Barcelona. One was for feeding the civilian population at large, and merchants, cooperatives and others went there to get what they needed, paying for it in money. The second was the armed forces warehouse, where Domenech tried to have an even wider range of goods than were available for the civilians. These were also paid for. The third central warehouse was for beneficent organizations – hospitals, asylums, orphanages etc., which received what they needed free of charge. All of these warehouses handled not only foodstuffs, but clothing and other consumer goods.

When the Comité de Abastos was set up, the Generalidad provided it with a sum of money to get it working. Thereafter, Domenech was able to make the operation self-financing, by charging slightly more than its costs to those using its services.

One of the operations of the Comité de Abastos of which Domenech was most proud was an experiment in inter-regional barter, in conformity with anarchist principles. He circulated an announcement that Catalonia had certain goods in excess which it was willing to exchange for other goods from other regions. During the period of his control of Abastos, his committee exchanged goods worth 300 million pesetas.[10]

One problem on the retail level during this period was handled directly by the CNT. This was sudden proliferation of street vendors soon after July 19. Many of these were unemployed people. A CNT source noted: 'This spread like an epidemic. All of the streets of the capital were flooded with merchandise, sold on the sidewalks and even in the middle of the street. The whole city had a new appearance...' Many store owners, facing this competition, hired their own street vendors.

The CNT, which had a union of street vendors, first sought to limit their number by closing the books to new members; which resulted in the UGT organizing its own union for them. Finally, the Barcelona municipal federation of the CNT made a decision which 'had the effect of a decree', limiting the number of vendors, and assigning them particular areas in which to operate.[11]

One purpose of the supply system organized by Domenech was to limit the increase in prices. The CNT source I have been quoting noted: 'Wholesale commerce passed into the hands of the unions. Retailers acquired their goods from the *sindicato*. The retail prices were fixed for the merchants... At the head of the "monopoly" was the Consejería de Abastos... Unified prices were fixed in the collectivized communes, in the fishermen's unions and other food industries, in agreement with the distributing organism. The end sought by this economic policy was to prevent the rise in the price of food. Speculation and usury were to be done away with.'[12]

According to Josep Maria Bricall, 'One can say that from the creation of the Department until the middle of December 1936, the policy of supply was to establish an administrative monopoly of domestic commerce, to determine the maximum price of foodstuffs, to charge the *sindicatos* or their representatives with the organization of distribution and to replace the old entrepreneurs with workers' committees.' He also noted that on October 13, the Generalidad decreed the establishment of a rationing system in Barcelona, although this was not in fact begun until the councillorship of supply had passed from the hands of the anarchists to those of the PSUC.[13]

Sometimes the CNT unions took a direct hand in this process. Soon after the outbreak of the War, there began to be a shortage of eggs in Barcelona, and their prices rose sharply. The egg supply section of the CNT's Food Workers Union called a general membership meeting to which it summoned all of the wholesalers and the larger retailers. At that meeting, 'a comprehensive plan of workers' control was worked out ... and under the circumstances the employers could not but accept it.'

The union then undertook 'a large-scale purchasing operation, backed up by the financial resources of the egg dealers. Results showed immediately. Prices came down...'[14]

Inflation remained a serious problem in Catalonia and throughout the Republic throughout the Civil War. According to the Central Statistical services of the Generalidad, the prices of food, clothing and shelter in Barcelona rose from an index number of 100 in July 1936 to 453.3 in October 1938.[15]

Josep Maria Bricall has noted three factors related to this inflationary spiral. One was the substitution throughout the Civil War of inferior quality goods for better ones, due to the exigencies of the war and the general economic situation. Another was the increase in barter, rather than purchase and sale of goods for cash, about which Bricall has written: 'The cornering of certain productions by some functionaries of the Supply Service and also by peasants, who hid some of their crop without reporting it, gave rise to barter, which to large degree took the place of the mechanism of prices and sales.'

A third factor, according to Bricall, was the growth of the black market. Naturally, the official price statistics did not take into account goods sold in the black market.[16]

The CNT's control of the Catalan supply system lasted only until the middle of December 1936. Then, on the occasion of a crisis in the Catalan cabinet, the CNT regional committee, at a meeting Domenech was unable to attend, decided that it wanted to exchange his post for the positions of councillors of defense and public services. Although Domenech was furious at this, arguing that for the CNT to control the way to the people's stomachs was more important than even to control the regional military, he had to accede to the decision. His post was taken by Juan Comorera, principal leader of the Stalinist Partido Socialista Unificado de Catalauna.

The Consejo de Economía

Meanwhile, less than a month after the suppression of the military uprising in Catalonia, the Comité Central de Milicias had established a body to reorganize the general regional economy. Diego Abad de Santillán explained:

As the Comité de Milicias, at first obliged to deal with and resolve everything, was being increasingly converted into a

Ministry of War in time of war, to take care of functions which might otherwise interfere with its fundamental job we created a Committee of the Economy of Catalonia, whose decisions could not be rejected by the Councillor of the Department of Economy. It functioned under the presidency of the Councillor of that branch in the Government of the Generalidad, and was made up also of representatives of all the parties and organizations. From it came all the legislation of an economic character during the war and the revolution in the autonomous region...[17]

This Consejo de Economía was established formally by a decree of the Generalidad dated August 13 1936. After a preamble stressing the urgent need for such a body, the decree stated that the *consejo* would have 'competence throughout all Catalonia and will constitute the ordering organism of Catalan economic life'. It was empowered 'after obtaining the advice it considers necessary' to establish the norms adequate for the establishment of economic normalcy in all the territory of Catalonia'.

The decree charged the council to prepare a plan for the Socialist transformation of the country, which should include eleven points:

1. Regulation of production according to the needs of consumption. 2. Monopoly of foreign commerce. 3. Collectivization of large agrarian property and obligatory unionization of individual peasants. 4. Partial devaluation of urban property through taxes and reduction of rents. 5. Collectivization of large industries, public services and common transport. 6. Confiscation and collectivization of abandoned enterprises. 7. Extension of cooperatives in distribution of products. 8. Worker control of banking operations leading to nationalization of banking. 9. Trade union control of private enterprises. 10. Rapid absorption of the unemployed. 11. Suppression of indirect taxes and establishment of a single tax.

Josep Bricall noted: 'The Government which took office on the 26th of September used this program as the starting point for revolutionary legislation.'[18]

A statement of the CNT–FAI announcing formation of the Consejo de Economía said: 'To consolidate the triumph of the revolution, it is necessary to create with energy and rapidity a series of very fundamental institutions. That with greatest importance is without doubt control of the economic factor. Without it, in these difficult moments, the development of the life of the city would be impossible.'[19]

After noting that the president of the new body would be the councillor for economy and public services of the Generalidad, the decree named its other members. Three were from the Esquerra Republicana Party, one from Acción Catalana, three from the CNT, two from the FAI, three from the UGT, one from the Unió de Rabassaires, one from the POUM and one from the PSUC.[20] Those who were for a longer or shorter period of time to play the most important roles in the Consejo de Economía were Martin Barrera of the Esquerra Republicana, Ramón Peypoch of Acción Catalana, Juan P. Fabregas and Andrés Capdevila of the CNT, Diego Abad de Santillán of the FAI, Andrés Nin of the POUM and Estanislao Ruíz Ponsetti of the PSUC.

Not all anarchists were pleased with the establishment of the Consejo de Economía. The Italian anarchist Camilo Berneri, who was then working with the CNT–FAI in Barcelona, wrote on November 5 1936, that 'The Consejo de Economía is basically nothing else than "The Economic Committee" established by the French Government. It doesn't seem to me that it is sufficient compensation for the ministerialismo of the CNT and the FAI...'[21]

Alberto Pérez Baró, a one-time member of the CNT and still an anarchist sympathizer during the Civil War, who headed the major sub-committee of the Consejo de Economía during most of the Civil War, has criticized the way the anarchists participated in the *consejo* and the councillorship of economy of the Generalidad. 'After the 26th of September and for nine months, it was the CNT which controlled the Councillorship of Economy and the post was held by Juan P. Fabregas, Abad de Santillán, J. J. Domenech, Andrés Capdevila and Valerio Mas... Evidently there was good faith in the men of the CNT ... but the constant change of people was certainly counterproductive.'[22]

Soon after the anarchists entered the government of Catalonia in

September 1936, with the CNTer Juan P. Fabregas as councillor of economy, the Catalan Regional Confederation of Labor of the CNT named Andrés Capdevila, until then a member of the enterprise council of the Fabra y Coats textile firm in Barcelona, to be delegate president of the Consejo de Economia, on behalf of Fabregas, who by law was to preside over it, or to name a delegate to do so. Capdevila has left a record of the early meetings of the council which he attended, which indicate the kinds of things which it then dealt with.

On his first appearance as delegate president, Capdevila, after expressing his doubts about his capacity to do the job, wrote:

> Having recovered my nervous equilibrium at seven in the evening I entered the meeting room of the Consejo Económico, accompanied by the Councillor of Economy who formally presented me ... The minutes of the last meeting being read and approved, some industrial groups, presented by the members dealing with construction and food industries, were approved without discussion. The rest of the session was spent in seriously discussing some questions presented by the reporter on agriculture related to the agrarian problem of Catalonia. When the session ended at nine-thirty in the evening, I was favorably impressed, and giving free play to my good faith, I believed that all the political parties and the UGT which were represented in the Council ... were disposed to collaborate loyally and honorably in the organization of the collective economy which was born in the heat of the revolution.
>
> We had several sessions without discussing any project of importance and without any change in the good relations among the parties and organizations which made up the Council. However, I waited impatiently the discussions of the Decree of Collectivization which a commission was finishing to present to the President, and so for discussion and approval by the Consejo de Economía.[23]

Meanwhile, pending discussion of the collectivization decree, Andrés Capdevila as *delegado presidente* of the *consejo* dealt with some other urgent problems. One of these was that of the foreign trade of Catalonia. Capdevila found a rather chaotic situation, in which the Economic Council, the Supply Council and the CNT itself were all engaging in foreign trade. This resulted in a situation in which many individuals were able to exploit it to their own benefit, and the foreign exchange earned from exports was not centralized so that it could be used to the best advantage of the economy as a whole. He succeeded in centralizing most Catalan foreign trade in the Consejería de Economía, and reached agreement with the central government in Valencia, recognizing Catalan autonomy in foreign trade but also agreed that all foreign exchange earned from Catalan exports would be turned over to the Republican government's institution for handling foreign trade.[24]

The Genesis of the Collectivization Decree

Certainly the most important activities of the Consejo de Economía de Cataluña during the first part of the Civil War were the enactment of the Decree of Collectivization of October 24 1936, and its subsequent application and modification. This was not the first effort of the government of the Generalidad to intervene in the process of collectivization of firms by their workers. Although Josep Maria Bricall noted that, 'initially, the posture of the Government of the Generalidad consisted of accepting the facts, waiting and watching',[25] that attitude soon changed. Councillor of Economy José Tarradellas issued a number of decrees during the month of August. These, on the one hand, largely legalized the seizures by the workers, and on the other hand, sought to establish a key role in the collectivized enterprises for representatives of the Generalidad. According to these decrees 'interventor delegates' representing the government were to have a place on the control committees of the collectives.

According to Bricall, these interventors were, among other things, to 'control the income and expenditure of funds, and documents, approve the daily account of income and expenses, control the technical advising, assure contact between official organs and the

Workers' Committee of Control ... to inform the Councillor of Economy weekly about the progress of the firms...'[26]

Almost certainly, the role of the government interventors was honored more in the breach than in the execution in that early period. However, with the reorganization of the Catalan government late in September, and the entry of the CNT into it, serious efforts to legalize the collectives on a permanent basis began. There has been considerable disagreement about the origins of the Decree of Collectivization which resulted from these efforts.

Frank Mintz has stated: 'the decree was the work of a CNTista, Juan P. Fabregas, "the illustrious unknown, even by the old militants before the 19th of July".' Mintz added: 'It was presented as a worker victory, although it was exactly the opposite.'[27] Gaston Leval has made much the same claim in relation to Fabregas.[28]

Although it is certain that the Decree of Collectivization bore the signature of Juan P. Fabregas, as economic councillor of the Generalidad of Catalonia, his responsibility for it was at best quite secondary. The details of the decree were worked out within the Consejo de Economía, among the various political tendencies represented there.

According to José Peirats, there were three basic elements in the Consejo de Economía, in so far as the discussion of the Decree of Collectivization was concerned. The Stalinists of the PSUC favored outright nationalization of most of the region's industries, and their organization and coordination by a highly centralized national planning hierarchy. The CNT–FAI representatives, on the other hand, favored collectivization by the workers of individual enterprises and their coordination through a federalist system, organized by industry and geographical region. For their part, the middle-class Republican parties' representatives sought as much as possible to defend the rights of the small and middle-sized entrepreneurs to continue to own and manage their enterprises.[29] Peirats further noted that the decree went through 'a laborious process of elaboration, in which the representatives of the workers' organizations, the Marxist parties and those which represented the petty bourgeoisie had to confront one another, more or less violently, in the heart of the Catalan government.'[30]

Andrés Capdevila, who presided over the process, described the way in which final version of the Decree of Collectivization was drawn up:

> Finally on the 22 of October of the year 1936, at seven in the evening ... I presented for discussion of the Council the historic Decree of Collectivizations which so aroused Spanish and foreign public opinion. The discussion of the preamble and the articles of the Decree were difficult, the representatives of the political parties and the UGT fought desperately to reduce the number of collectivized firms to the minimum. The representatives of the CNT and of the FAI defended energetically the most radical possible provisions for obligatory collectivization of the firms.'
>
> At three in the morning, after heated discussions and mutual concessions, there was definitively approved the much discussed Decree of Collectivizations, which was subsequently passed to the Councillor of Economy, so that he could that same day in the afternoon present it for approval by the Government of the Generalidad ... As the trademark of the historic session, all political and trade union sectors which made up the Council, solemnly promised to respect and be loyal to the spirit and the letter of the Decree of Collectivizations, which was approved by the Governmeant of Catalonia and was officially inserted in the Official Bulletin of the Generalidad on October 24, of year 1936.[31]

Alberto Pérez Baró has also emphasized that, in its final form, the Decree of Collectivization was a compromise among all of the political and trade union elements represented in the Consejo de Economía. It was 'a common denominator of the different action programs of the various parties and trade union organizations which spontaneously had formed a common front as a result of July 19,' and the decree was 'the collective work of the Consejo de Economía'.[32]

Even after the collectivization decree was finally adopted and put into execution by the Catalan government, important anarchist leaders remained opposed to it. Thus, Diego Abad de Santillán, who for a short while succeeded Juan P. Fabregas as councillor of Economy, wrote to Alberto Pérez Baró in 1971: 'I must make clear, however, that I was an enemy of the Decree because I thought it premature. You know that I was then absorbed day and night by the militia and its problems and I didn't follow what was happening in other spheres of activity . . . It was when I went to the Councillorship of Economy it was not to fulfill the Decree, but to ignore it, and not take it into account or to allow our great people to work according to their inspiration and good sense; there would be plenty of time some day to convert into law the necessary regulations.'[33] However, Abad de Santillán did not remain in the councillorship post long enough to provide any significant interference with the application of the decree.

The Contents of the Collectivization Decree

The 39-article Decree of Collectivization and Workers' Control consisted of several distinct segments. First came a longish and 'revolutionary' preamble, then a section setting forth which parts of the Catalan economy should be compulsorily collectivized, and how the enterprises involved should be organized. Another part of the decree spelled out the role of the 'workers' control committees' in those firms which remained private enterprises, followed by provisions for coordination of both collectivized and private firms on a regional and industry level, and by a final section providing in various ways for the implementation of the decree.

The preamble of the decree, after noting that the suppression of the military revolt of July 19 'has provoked a profound economic-social transformation' in Catalonia, proclaimed: 'The accumulation of wealth in the hands of an increasingly smaller group of persons had been followed by an accumulation of misery in the working class, and the former group, to save its privileges has not hesitated to provoke a cruel war in which the victory of the people will be the equivalent of the death of capitalism.'

The preamble went on to say, 'It is necessary to organize production, to orient it so that the only beneficiary will be the collectivity, the worker, to whom will correspond the directing function in the new social order. The concept of income which is not associated with work will be suppressed.'

The document then set forth the basic principle on which the reorganization of the Catalan economy would be based. 'The substitution of private property by collective will be achieved by the Council of the Generalidad by collectivizing the property of the large enterprise, that is to say, capital, while allowing private property to persist in consumers' goods and small industry.'

Finally, the preamble provided for the ultimate establishment of what amounted to a bank to finance the collectivized sector of the economy. It 'charged the Consejo de Economía to study the basic norms for the establishment of a Caja de Credito Industrial y Comercio [Fund for Industrial and Commercial Credit], which will provide financial aid to the collective enterprises and to group our industry in large concentrations which will assure the largest return and make possible the largest transactions for our foreign commerce.'

The first enumerated article of the decree provided that there would be 'collectivized enterprises in which the direction will fall to the workers who make them up, representea by a Consejo de Empresa' (enterprise council), and 'private enterprises, in which the direction is in the hands of the proprietor or manager, with the collaboration and fiscalization of the Comité Obrero de Control' (Workers' Control Committee).

Article two provided that all firms which, on June 30 1936, had 100 employees or more were to be compulsorily collectivized, as well as all firms with less than that number of workers the owners of which had been declared by the popular tribunals to be Rebels. Other firms with less than 100 employees could also be collectivized if a majority of the workers and the employer agreed, and in the case of firms with from 50 to 100 workers, there would be collectivization if three-quarters of the workers voted in favor of it.

Articles 10–20 of the decree dealt with the enterprise councils. These were to be elected by general assemblies of the workers of the collectivized firms, and should have not less than five members and not more than 15. The councils should have representatives of the production, administrative, technical and sales parts of the firm, and should also have representatives of the central labor groups (CNT and UGT) in proportion to their membership among the workers of a particular firm.

The enterprise councils were to have all the powers of management, although they were to conform to the general policies of the General Council of Industry set up in their particular branch of the economy. The enterprise council was to appoint a director, to whom it could entrust some or all of its powers. However, in firms with more than 500 workers, with a capital of over 1,000,000 pesetas, or which were part of a war industry, the appointment of the director must have the approval of the Consejo de Economía of Catalonia.

In each collectivized enterprise there was also to be an interventor of the Generalidad, who would serve as a member of the Consejo de Empresa, and would be named by the Consejo de Economía,' in accord with the workers'.

The enterprise councils were to keep minutes of their meetings, and to inform their respective Consejo Genral de Industria of any decisions they made.

Finally, the members of the enterprise councils, who normally were to serve for two years, and could be re-elected, could be removed by the general assembly of the workers, or by the appropriate Consejo General de Industria 'in case of manifest incompetence or resistance to the norms' of the Consejo General de Industria. In case of workers' opposition to removal of the director by the Consejo General de Industria, there could be an appeal to the Consejo de Economía de Cataluña, the decision of which would be final.

Articles 21–23 of the decree dealt with the committees of control in private enterprises. Such committees were required in all private firms. Their number could be decided by the workers, but they should have representatives of all the different kinds of workers in the enterprise, and have representation of the central labor groups in proportion to the membership of those groups in the enterprise. The Comités de Control Obrero were to have supervision of all labor relations matters, to see to it that all labor laws were enforced in the enterprise. They were also to have 'administrative control, in the sense of keeping track of all income and outgo, whether in cash or through the banks, to make sure that they conform to the necessities of the business...' The employer was required to present a copy of the firm's annual accounts to the Comité de Control. The committee was also to 'control production, meaning to work closely with the owner to perfect the process of production'. Also, the committee of control 'will seek to maintain the best relations possible with the technicians, to assure the progress of the work'.

Articles 24–28 dealt with the proposed Consejos Generales de Industria, and Articles 29–31 established a process to allocate sectors of the Catalan economy to the various *consejos*. Each member of the Consejo de Economía was to preside over one or more of the Consejos Generales de Industria.

Each *consejo general* was to be made up of three different categories of people. First, there were to be four representatives from the various enterprise councils 'elected in the manner that will opportunely be determined'. In the second place, there were eight representatives of the central labor groups, 'in proportion to the affiliates of each ... as determined by common accord'. Finally, four members of each *consejo general* would be 'technicians named by the Consejo de Economía'.

The *consejos generales* were given broad powers by the decree. According to Article 25 they, 'will formulate plans of work of their respective industry in a general way, orienting the Enterprise Councils in their functions, and will have charge of: regulating total production of the industry; unifying costs insofar as possible, to avoid competition; studying the general needs of the industry; studying the needs of the consumers of its products; examining the possibilities of peninsular and foreign markets...' The councils could also 'propose the suppression of factories or their increase, in accordance with the needs of the industry and of the consumers, as well as the merger of certain factories; propose the reform of certain methods of work, credit and circulation of products; suggest modifications of tariffs and commercial treaties.' They were empowered to establish research facilities, keep statistics on production and consumption, and 'study and adopt the measures they think necessary and useful for the better development of the task which is confided to the them'.

The Consejo Económico de Cataluña was instructed within 15 days of the issuance of the decree to indicate the classifications of industries which should be included under different *consejos generales*. As we shall see, these instructions were not followed.

The final articles of the decree dealt generally with the possibility in certain cases of compensating those whose industries were nationalized. However, the criteria for this remained vague.[34]

Alberto Pérez Baró has pointed out that one provision, which had been adopted by the Consejo de Economía, was missing when the decree was finally promulgated by the Generalidad. This had to do with the problem of foreign-owned or partially foreign-owned firms which might be collectivized, and the possibility of compensating those firms: 'It has not been possible to localize the project of the decree as it emerged from the Consejo de Economía, but we can say from memory, and we do not think that we are mistaken, that the part that was not published referred to recognizing the liquid value, after technical considerations, of the businesses passed to the collectivized industries voluntarily; recognizing on the part of the Generalidad that the Caja de Crédito Industrial, through special titles of debt which would be amortized with part of the profits which the collectivized enterprises would have to turn over to that fund.' He attributed the elimination of this part of the decree to the anarchist and POUM members of the Genetalidad,[35] and this judgment is confirmed by Victor Alba.[36]

The Application of the Decree of Collectivization and Workers' Control

For more than two years after it was enacted, the Catalan collectivization decree was applied, modified and sabotaged by varying elements in the region's government, political spectrum and trade unions. Generally, the anarchists and their friends defended and sought to enforce and expand upon the decree, the Communists and their Republican allies sought to undermine it.

Much of the application of the decree was placed in the hands of a Commission of Interpretation of the Decree of Collectivization, composed of one anarchist, one Stalinist and one Republican. Alberto Pérez Baró, a one-time CNTista and still an anarchist sympathizer, was secretary of that commission throughout most of its existence.

Pérez Baró has described this commission and its role: 'The mission of this organism, which was like a permanent committee of the Consejo de Economía, which met twice a week with the president of the Consejo, had two functions: on the one hand, to give its opinion sometimes orally, otherwise in writing, on the problems presented by the enterprises affected by the decree, and on the other, to propose to the Consejo de Economía the solution or solutions it suggested to problems which could affect the various enterprises, or simply the progress, development and application of what had been legislated.' Pérez Baró noted that the commission dealt with 1,400 individual questions dealing with a single enterprise, and about 50 cases 'of general or collective nature...'[37]

Elsewhere, Pérez Baró gave a number of examples of the kinds of problems with which the commission dealt. A sample of these will indicate their range.

At one of its earliest meetings, the commission was asked. 'What are the attributions of the Interventors of the Generalidad in the collectivized enterprises?' To which it replied: 'At the moment, and until practice shows to the contrary, it must be understood that the Interventor must be the one who assures the strict fulfillment of the Decree and its complementary dispositions, as well as those issued by the General Councils of Industry, serving as the liaison between the collectivized enterprise and official organisms ... and to exercise the right of veto of certain accords contrary to those dispositions which the Consejos de Empresa might take.'[38]

Another issue presented to the commission was 'Can the Consejos de Empresa name one of their members as Director? On the contrary, can the Director attend the meetings of the Consejo de Empresa? In any case, does he have a vote and voice in the meetings or only a voice?' To which the answer was: 'The Director can be a member of the Consejo de Empresa or not; in the first case, he will have voice and vote and in the second only voice. Always he must attend meetings of the *consejo*.'[39]

On another occasion, the commission was asked, 'Can Control Committees be organized in government dependencies?' The answer was: 'The functionaries of the Generalidad don't have the right to organize Control Committees. The spirit of the Decree of Collectivization is that the legal text will be applied to industrial and commercial enterprises, which implicitly indicates that official organisms are excluded. Furthermore, the functionaries of the Generalidad have their own class organizations, fully recognized by law and the government organs.'[40]

In particular, the commission was presented with problems from foreign firms and investors, whose enterprises were collectivized under the October 24 decree. Some 103 foreign enterprises officially complained against the collectivization of their investments in Catalonia. Almost half of these were French firms, and the rest were firms in Great Britain, Argentina, the United States, Switzerland, Cuba, Austria, Belgium, Denmark, Sweden and the Netherlands.[41]

Alberto Pérez Baró, who dealt with this problem continuously, felt that it had been a serious error not to include compensation for foreign firms (in one form or another) in the original collectivization decree. He noted that his commission was forced to keep promising the foreign firms that there would be a supplementary decree issued to deal with the problem, which did not come to pass. Quite a few of the foreign firms were not satisfied with promises and on occasion lodged court suits in other countries when goods produced by their former Spanish branches were exported there, to claim those goods as belonging to them.

Another problem that the commission faced frequently was that of the behavior of Comités de Control in remaining private enterprises. The commission generally held that the Comités de Control should confine themselves to seeing to it that the provisions of the law were applied, and that there was no flight of capital. But in many cases, the trade unionists, particularly those of the CNT, behaved as if such firms were in fact collectivized. There were many cases of this kind of controversy.[42]

However, there were other kinds of problems facing those who were trying to put fully into effect the Decree of Collectivization and

Workers' Control. Whereas, many if not most of the collectivized firms had already been taken over by their workers when the decree was issued, the General Councils of Industry and the Fund for Industrial and Commercial Credit remained to be created when the decree became law.

Although the Consejo de Economía was supposed to define the sectors of the Catalan economy which would be organized under the General Councils of Industry within two weeks, it was December 26, 1936 before a decree defined the 14 parts of the economy for which these institutions should be established.[43] Furthermore, it was July 9 1937 before a new decree spelled out the details for the organization of the Consejos Generales de Industria. It is not clear how many of these councils were actually established.

The fulfillment of the provision of the collectivization decree calling for the establishment of an Industrial and Commercial Fund, to serve as a bank for the collectivized industries, took more than a year. However, a decree of the Consejo de Economía of January 30 1937, establishing a model statute for collectivized enterprises, provided that 50 per cent of the profits of such firms should be deposited in the Industrial and Commercial Fund (which did not yet exist) and be used to finance the financially weaker firms, and new ones which might be created.[44]

However, according to Alberto Pérez Baró, 'All of the economic life of the collective organisms, as directors of the new collective economy, was in fact subordinated to the creation and functioning of the Caja de Credito Industrial y Comercial, but its creation was postponed more and more.'[45]

It was not until November 10 1937 that a decree was finally issued establishing the Caja de Credito Industrial y Comercial.[46] It provided for a directing council made up of a president named by the councillor of economy or someone designated by him; a vice-president named by the councillor of finance, two 'technical delegates' named by each of those councillors; four representatives of the General Councils of Industry and chosen by the Council of Economy, of whom at least two were to be members of enterprise councils of collectives; two banking technicians, one named by the UGT, the other by the CNT; a representative of the Permanent Committee of

Industry named by the councillor of economy, and one representative of the Superior Cooperative Council.[47]

However, as Pérez Baró has commented, by this time 'there had begun the fall in the revolutionary spirit which had inspired the collectivizations.[48] Furthermore, by the time the *caja* was established, the overall supervision of the Catalan economy was in the hands of Councillor of Economy Juan Comorera, the head of the Stalinist PSUC party, who was determined as much as possible to thwart the original objectives of the Decree of Collectivization. As a result of this fact, and of the declining fortunes of war of the Republic, the *caja* never really came to perform the role of a general bank for the collectivized sector of the economy for which it was originally designed.

The Merging of Collectivized Firms

One important aspect of the collectivization decree was its provisions for legalizing the merger of collectives into large enterprises, known in Catalan as *agrupaments*. We shall note in our discussion of specific collectives a number of instances of this type. Josep Maria Bricall has written: 'On balance, the number of *agrupaments* authorized was quite high. The *agrupaments* sought to promote a reconversion of the sections involved and some of them were going to get economies of large-scale production, closing down the poorer production units and concentrating on the better ones...'[49]

In the early months of the collectivization decree a considerable number of those concentrated enterprises were legalized. Thus between December 16 and 30 1936, 14 were approved, and in January 1937, 35.[50]

These unified enterprises involved various industries, and various parts of the region. Some in the metallurgical industry spread throughout Catalonia. The collective of construction of Catalonia involved 30,000 workers, the bleaching, stamping and tinting collective of Barcelona involved 70 firms with more than 8,000 workers and a capital of 150 million pesetas.[51]

A number of the unified firms which had been established by the workers of the CNT had not achieved legal recognition from the Catalan government even by the end of the war in the region. Several sessions of the Consejo de Economía in August 1938 dealt with this problem. After extensive and apparently bitter discussion, the suggestion of the CNT member of the consejo, Andrés Capdevila was accepted, to allow these illegal *agrupaments* to continue to operate for the time being, and study ways of giving these provisional legalizations.[52]

The Sabotage of Collectivization Decree by Juan Comorera and Others

As a result of the prolonged Catalan governmental crisis following the May Events of 1937, Juan Comorera became councillor of economy, in a new cabinet in which the anarchists were no longer represented. He used that post extensively to undermine not only the Decree of Collectivization, but the workers' collectives themselves.

In the early months of the War, the Stalinists did not openly oppose the collectivization decree. Thus, the English-language news bulletin of the Partido Socialista Unificado de Cataluña contained in February 1937: 'By a decree of the Generality of Catalonia, a committee of control has been elected in each factory or firm. Five of the workers are elected democratically to compose a committee of control. One is concerned with questions of work, one in the technical section, a third in the commercial department, one economic, and the fifth deals with social questions... The committee of control is invested with considerable power but without the approbation of the personnel they cannot take any important commercial or social decision.'[53]

However, the process on the part of the opponents of the CNT–FAI of seeking to frustrate the fulfillment of the Decree of Collectivization had begun long before Comorera became councillor. This was particularly evident in the Consejo de Economía in so far as final legalization of the collectives was concerned. The collectivization law and supplementary legislation provided that the collectives would request legalization from the *consejo*, which would assign one of its members, whose job it was to deal with the branch of the economy in which that collective was, to report on it. However, very early the *consejo* members from the PSUC, UGT, and bourgeois parties began procrastinating in their presentation of the *consejo*'s requests for legalization which were their responsibility.

On a related issue, not only new collectives, but mergers of old ones to form larger economic units, had to obtain legal authorization from the council in the same way. Generally, the non CNT–FAI members of the *consejo* engaged in similar dilatory tactics with regard to such mergers.[54] (In spite of this procrastination, some 36 general collectives were established during the first year of the Revolution.)[55]

The Stalinists and their allies used their position in the machinery established under the collectivization decree to try to sabotage rather than support the collectivization process. J. Esperanza, who was a CNT member of the Consejo General de la Industria Quimica (General Council of the Chemical Industry), described, many years later, how they did so in the chemical industry. The *consejo* had several supposed functions. One was to distribute raw materials equitably among the enterprises in the chemical industry. However, to participate in this distribution, a collective was supposed to be legally recognized by the *consejo*. According to Esperanza, the four representatives of the UGT (members of the PSUC), and the representative of Acción Catalana who served as its president consistently opposed giving such legal recognition, over the vigorous but futile Protests of the four CNT members of the *consejo*.

Another function of the *consejo* was to ascertain the relative strength of the CNT and the UGT among the chemical workers of Catalonia. On the basis of such a census, the membership of the *consejo* itself was supposed to be altered to reflect the relative strength of the two organizations. However, the five-man majority of the *consejo* saw to it that such a census was never carried out.[56]

However, it was when Juan Comorera, became Catalan councillor of Economy in the wake of the May Events, with PSUCer Ruíz Ponsetti as his *éminence grise*, that a massive campaign was undertaken by the Catalan government to undermine the Decree of

Collectivization, culminating just before the Franco forces invaded Catalaonia in an effort to abolish it entirely. Comorera started this campaign by completely transforming the nature and function of the Consejo de Economía.

Until the advent of Comorera as councillor of economy, the Consejo de Economía had functioned in conformity with the decree under which it had originally been established. According to Valerio Mas, Comorera's immediate predecessor and an anarchist, the influence of the CNT within the Consejo de Economía had been largely predominant until that time.[57]

As originally created in August 1936, the Consejo de Economía was given executive authority, that is, the Generalidad was required to put into legislation the decisions of the *consejo*. On August 14 1937, Comorera issued as an internal regulation of the council, a document which completely changed that relationship with the Catalan government.

This document defined the Consejo de Economía as 'the high consultative and advisory organism of the Government of the Generalidad in economic matters'. It was thus deprived of its executive functions, and was made totally subordinate to the government, in which the region's major labor organization, the CNT, was no longer represented.

But Comorera's 'regulation' went still further. It deprived the working-class organizations (CNT, FAI, UGT, PSUC) of the formal majority which they had heretofore in the Consejo de Economía, by adding five representatives of government ministries, as well as one each from the Unió de Rabassaires and the confederation or cooperatives.

Alberto Perez Baró underscored the impact of this change: 'It is from that moment that there began the fall of the revolutionary movement.' He went on to say: 'Accords already approved many times by the Consejo de Economía on the grouping of industries were definitively shelved; the task of putting under way the Decree on the constitution of General Councils of Industry was postponed; the idea was adulterated and the implementation was enormously retarded insofar as the Caja de Credito Industrial y Comercial, the real cornerstone of the whole collectivist edifice, was concerned.'

But the process went much further. After August 14, 'projects were reiteratedly presented which tended to disfigure the basic norms which had been adopted in October 1936, with the acquiescence of everyone, ending with the project of Ruíz Ponsetti to convert the collectivizations into cooperatives... The representatives of the CNT had to fight basically to defend the Decree as it had been established...'[58]

Andrés Capdevila pointed out other actions by Comorera to undermine the collectivizations: 'Taking advantage of the fact that there were numerous ex-owners and technicians who because of their fascist maneuvers had not been admitted by the workers in the collectivized firms, the Councillor of Economy, Juan Comorera, ignoring the authority of the *consejo*, claiming irregularities in the enterprises, every day put orders in the Official Bulletin of the Generalidad, naming on his own authority, interventors of doubtful political antecedents, on the condition that they enter the Party. This policy, contrary to the interests of the workers and the morals of the antifascist cause, provoked protest and discontent among the workers of the collectivized enterprises.'

Comorera also proposed a new regulation governing the establishment of new enterprises, 'which would be directed and administered in the Soviet style with an Administrative Technical Council composed of representatives named by the Councillor of Economy, the Councillor of Finances and the Caja de Credito Industrial y Comercial. The workers could have a Committee of Control without any role in the technical administrative direction of the enterprises.' Capdevila noted that the CNT and FAI members of the Consejo de Economía were able to prevent the enactment of this project.

However, he also observed: 'By action of the Councillor of Economy, without reference to the Consejo, there was inserted in the Official Bulletin of the Generalidad a Decree creating the Technical Council of Enterprises, an organism given attributions for examining whether the directors and interventors proposed by the workers of the enterprises had sufficient knowledge and capacity.' He added: 'The directors and interventors proposed by the workers of enterprises to the Technical Council ... if they were PSUC–UGT affiliates were rapidly approved. In contrast, if they declared that they belonged to the CNT, they were submitted to such a rigorous examination that none of them was accepted.'

In some cases, as in the potassium mines of Suria and the public spectacles collective in Barcelona, in which the Communist-controlled PSUC had a very small minority, Comorera published orders in the official bulletin suppressing the elected Consejos de Empresa, and substituting for the administrative technical councils made up of people named by Comorera himself.[59]

For its part, the Republican government under Prime Minister Juan Negrín did its share also to undermine the Catalan collectives. For one thing, the ministry of finance threatened to fine collectivized firms if they did not pay stamp taxes applicable to corporations – in this case the Commission on Application of the collectivization decree advised the collectives to pay the stamp tax, but also to lodge a formal protest both with the Republican ministry of finance and the Generalidad, on the grounds that they were not corporations in the terms of the stamp tax law.

The ministry of finance also sought to interpret application of the Republican wartime excess profit tax, as being levied on gross profits of the collectivised firms. Since the Decree of Collectivization had provided that 50 percent of gross profits had to be paid to the Caja de Credito Industrial y Comercial, and the Republican tax was as high as 80 percent, that would mean that virtually nothing could be paid into the *caja*, thus depriving the *caja* of virtually all resources.

Finally, the Republican government interpreted an early decree seizing real property of Rebels for the Republican government as entitling it to seize property of Catalan collectives which had been formed in whole or in part on the basis of firms formerly belonging to Rebels. A number of collectives were seriously crippled by this maneuver.[60]

Finally, the Communists and their allies did not limit attacks on the Catalan collectives to legal or administrative maneuvers. According to Pérez Baró:

The press campaign attributing to the Enterprise Councils and Committees of Control the increase in the cost of living a singularly violent campaign on the part of dailies controlled by the Communists...

Remember also that in the Third Congress of the UGT of Catalonia in November 1937 in Lerida, the Bank Workers Union of Barcelona ... and the Office Employees Union of Lerida presented proposals affirming the failure of the collectivizations, in spite of the fact that the experience was only a year old, and demanding the return to unipersonal direction of enterprises. These worker representatives denied their own comrades' capacity and right to direct the economy, attributing to them all of the defects inherent in any revolutionary situation, above all in the process of a civil war.[61]

Banking and Finance Arrangements in Catalonia

One key sector of the Catalan economy over which the anarchists had little influence was that of banking and finance. This lack of anarchist input reflected to a large degree their ideological position. In their pre-Civil War schemes for the reorganization of the Spanish economy, they had had little room for banks, and even for money. Although in the latter part of the War, as we shall see in a later chapter, they put forward the idea of establishing a trade union bank, to coordinate the CNT's collectivized sector of the Spanish economy, it was by then too late to put that plan into execution.

One result of the anarchists' ideological bias on this subject was that when the War broke out, only the UGT had a federation of bank workers in Catalonia. As a consequence, it was the units of that body which took over control of the banks of the region, and on a micro basis they continued to manage the banks throughout the Civil War.

But on a region-wide basis, the control of banking and financial matters fell to the government of Catalonia. More specifically, that sector of the Catalan economy was largely in the hands of José Taradellas, of the Esquerda Catalana party, who served throughout most of the War as councillor of finance of the Generalidad, as well as being prime minister. After March 1938, Taradellas was to a large degree pushed aside by the Republican government of Juan Negrín, which by then was located in Barcelona.

A major drawback facing Taradellas was the lack of a Catalan central bank. However, soon after the beginning of the War, the Catalan government 'intervened' all of the branches of the Bank of Spain (the Republic's central bank) in Catalonia, as well as taking control of the Spanish treasury organs in the region. The Barcelona branch of the Bank of Spain thereafter served some of the functions of a central bank, at least in discounting and rediscountation paper from the other Catalan banks. However, in March 1938, the Negrín government cancelled the Generalidad's 'interventions' in the Bank of Spain and the Republican treasury.

In taking over the Catalan branches of the Bank of Spain, the Catalan government also seized their gold supply. For some months that gold had served the needs of Catalonia for foreign exchange with which to buy abroad raw materials, equipment for the new war industries, and other purposes. However, when these reserves were exhausted, the Catalan government had great difficulties in getting further grants of gold or foreign exchange for these purposes from the Republican regime. (It is not clear whether Taradellas and others were aware of the fact that most of the Spanish gold had been shipped to the Soviet Union.) The Catalan government established its own office of foreign commerce.

The Generalidad set up several new financial institutions which were in large part financed, at least initially, by the treasury of the Generalidad. These included the Regulating Office for Payment of Wages. During the first half of the War, at least, this organization made 'loans' which were in fact grants, to collectives and other enterprises whose financial situation did not permit them to pay the wages of all of their workers. It also provided a kind of *de facto* unemployment insurance payment to workers who, because of raw material shortages or other causes, were forced into whole or partial unemployment.

Other important new institutions were the Official Fund for Discounts and Hypothecations, the Fund for Deposits and Consignment, and the Fund for Repairs and Aid. The first two helped to maintain the liquidity of the private banks and to provide funds for capital investment. The third was a special fund to help in the repair of buildings destroyed by enemy aerial bombardment, and to help those injured or displaced by those air attacks.

Another financial problem faced by the Catalan regime was the scarcity of low denominational currency which, before the War, had largely consisted of metal coins that disappeared from circulation with the onset of the War. The Catalan regime itself issued small-denomination currency, as did many of the municipalities of the region. In addition, numerous non-governmental organizations issued paper which served as currency, at least on a local basis. A fair proportion of this was various kinds of tokens and bills issued by the anarchist collectives, both urban and rural. Over time, the Catalan government tried to recall much of this 'money', and after March 1938 the Republican government 'forbade' it, although it is not clear how effective this measure was in practice.

These emissions of currency, and more importantly, the wide extension of credit by the Catalan government's new financial institutions, were important factors in stimulating the inflation which was a characteristic of wartime Catalonia. Of course, the growing scarcity of raw materials, the dismantling of the original supply system by Juan Comorera in the early months of 1937 and the continuing Stalinist sabotage of the workers and peasant collectives were also important contributing factors to inflation.[62]

The Anarchists' Resistance Against the Repeal of the Collectivization Decree

Shortly before the fall of Catalonia to the Franco forces, the anarchists had to resist an effort to abolish the Decree of Collectivization entirely. Many months earlier, they had succeeded in thwarting a manoeuvre which might have meant an early end to that legislation.

That earlier incident had occurred in May 1937, when the Consejo de Economía was discussing the issue of the official listing of the legally recognized workers' collectives in the mercantile register, in which their privately owned predecessors had been enrolled. A majority of the *consejo* tentatively accepted a proposal to make a formal inquiry of the Republican government as to whether Catalonia had the faculty under its autonomy statute to enact such a law as the Decree of Collectivization, and as to whether the Decree itself was constitutional.

Valerio Mas, the CNTer who was then councillor of economy in the Generalidad, rejected the idea of making such a submission to the Republican regime. In a letter to the Consejo de Economía dated May 21 1937, he admitted that 'It is evident that the Decree of Collectivizations has gone beyond the faculties which the Generalidad had according to the Statute and, perhaps, the provisions of the Constitution, but that is nothing new, and it was done in full understanding, since for that reason it is a revolutionary work. Is it perhaps unknown that there was a revolution in Catalonia? Is it perhaps being suggested to ask the Central Government to debate everything which the Generalidad has done which goes beyond the limits of its Statute?' He reminded his readers of the unfortunate precedent of an appeal by the 'most Catalan' Catalan League, a conservative group which had succeeded in 1934 in getting the Republican Tribunal of Constitutional Guarantees to declare unconstitutional a law passed by the Generalidad to help the region's tenant farmers.

Mas went on to say: 'Let's not, then, deceive ourselves. We have a Decree of Collectivizations. It has been put into force and now almost all enterprises are in conformity with its precepts. It is a work of the Generalidad and we are obliged to carry it forward, correcting its defects, if that is desirable, but always within our own house. We cannot and must not appeal to anyone if we wish to be proud and respected.'[63]

As a result of Valerio Mas's strong stand, the suggestion of approaching the Republican government about the Decree of Collectivization was abandoned.[64]

However, the most overt attempt by the non-anarchists in the Consejo de Economía to put an end to the Decree of Collectivization took place during the final weeks before the fall of Catalonia to the Franco forces. Valerio Mas, who was also a member of the Consejo de Economía during most of its existence, has left an extensive report on this. It is of sufficient importance for us to deal with it at length:

> In the middle of October ... the representative of Acción Catalana presented to the *consejo* three draft decrees for its discussion which derogated the Decree of Collectivization and its complementary decisions, purely and simply. To justify the presentation of the three mentioned decree projects, the representative of Acción Catalana said: 'Clearly manifest is the hostility of the democratic nations to the republican cause. This is stimulated by the fact that we have gone too far in economic legislation of collective-social type, so in view of the extremely unfavorable turn of military operations, realism counsels us to step back, repealing the Decree of Collectivization, and saving what we can without raising fears and doubts in the countries with liberal regimes...'

Mas noted the attitude of other groups within the *consejo*: 'The representatives of Esquerra Republicana said that they were completely in accord with the exposition of the representative of Acción Catalana, and that they supported the draft decree presented by him. The representatives of the PSUC and the UGT indicated some reservations with an eye to the gallery; but basically indicated that they were in accord with the statements by the representative of Acción Catalana, and with the need for discussing the draft decrees presented by him.'

The CNT representatives' reaction was far different:

> When we approved the Decree of Collectivization we solemnly promised to be loyal to the spirit and letter of it; we all recognize that the social advantages obtained by the workers were not a charitable gift of the state, but were conquered in the street, fighting against criminal fascism and its principal collaborator, capital, and now, using the pretext of the hostility of the democracies against the social advances won by the Spanish workers, it is proposed to erase everything without taking account of the struggles, the sacrifices and the blood spilled by

the Spanish proletariat, The governments of the democratic countries which are submitted to the control of capitalist monopolies don't care what decisions we take, they are not going to give us any aid to triumph over Falangista fascism and the Italo-Germany invaders.

The CNT–FAI delegation ended its argument by saying: 'For the reasons we have given, the representatives of the CNT and of the FAI protest and reject totally the draft projects presented, and if the other delegations persist in this discussion, we shall retire from the *consejo*. We shall carry out our responsibility in public meetings by informing the workers of the betrayal of which it is being attempted to make them victims.'

As a result of the attitude of the CNT–FAI members, the draft resolutions were tentatively withdrawn, and a sub-committee was appointed to bring in a substitute draft. The next day, the CNT–FAI members of the Consejo de Economía met in the CNT regional committee headquarters, and decided that there was no compromise possible on the issue. Thereafter, negotiations went on for six weeks in the *consejo* sub-committee, but no compromise was reached.

Andrés Capdevila reported on the upshot of the negotiations:

The last meeting of the sub-committee took place at the culminating moment of the Rebel offensive against the Catalan front. The representative of Acción Catalana Republicana, with the support of the other political groups and the UGT, insisted with energy that it was the moment for the sub-committee to work positively...

In reply, the representatives of the CNT intervened, saying, 'It is lamentable that party interest and the desire to destroy the industrial collectives which cost the workers so much effort and sacrifice, so obfuscates your brain, that you don't even pay any attention to the tragic moment in which we are living. The Rebel Army ... advances rapidly through Catalan lands, and it is probable that in few short days the *mercenarios* of Franco will triumphantly enter Barcelona.'

Is it that we take no account of the responsibility which we have before the Spanish people and before history, if on the eve of losing the war we repeal the Decree of Collectivization? If so, then the traitor general and his accomplices can say to the workers of the collectivized enterprises, 'It is not we who return the industries to their old and legitimate proprietors; it is yours, the Reds, who before leaving for abroad have decreed dissolution of the collectives. We have done nothing than put into practice these decrees.'

The CNT–FAI delegates prevailed. Capdevilla noted: 'Due to the energetic and blunt attitude of the representatives of the CNT and the FAI in the Consejo de Economía de Cataluña, we could avoid the shame before the universal conscience which the Catalan region would have had if it had repealed the Decree of Collectivization a few days before the Franco troops entered Barcelona.'[65]

Conclusions

The enactment and application of the Decree of Collectivization and Workers' Control was one of the most interesting experiences of the anarchists during the Spanish Civil War, both from a practical and a theoretical point of view. It was virtually the only case in which a government gave legal approval to the workers' seizure of urban enterprises and their organization of them into self-governing collectives. On the other hand, it certainly raised theoretical questions about how it conformed to anarchist doctrine.

Clearly, the collectivization decree was legislation by a government, albeit a government in which the anarchists were represented and in which, probably, their influence was still predominant. As legislation by an established government, the decree was certainly not in conformity with orthodox anarchist anti-State ideas and philosophy.

However, the enactment of, and anarchist support for, the collectivization decree did not arouse the degree of controversy and opposition among the anarchists, at the time or subsequently, as did their entry into the governments of Catalonia and the Spanish Republic. Such criticism as there has been has been relatively muted.

Gaston Leval, who had long experience with, and participation in, the Spanish anarchist movement, has been one of those to express doubts about the collectivization decree, which 'tended to control the situation and mortgage the future'.[66] Also, noting that after the revolutionary actions of the workers right after July 19, middle-class elements sought to 'regain lost ground'. Leval said: 'One cannot affirm that the decree of collectivization of Barcelona (this concerned only Catalonia) was a conscious first step in that direction. But with that initiative, legalized and encased in the law, the State had put in its hand, and arrogated to itself the right to direct it, sooner or later, in its own way.'[67]

However, in spite of the incursion of the State in the whole process, the anarchists may well have felt that, given the circumstances of the War and the necessity for working with the other forces opposing the Franco insurrection, they had been able to establish a framework in the collectivization decree upon which (having won the War) a future economy and society more or less in conformity with their philosophy and ideas might be organized. The base was the enterprise run by people chosen by the workers. The enterprises, in their turn, were to be 'federated' in Consejos Generales de Industria, controlled basically by delegates from the worker-controlled enterprises. At the top of the regional economic organization was the Consejo de Economía, also made up (during the first year) predominantly of delegates from workers' organizations. Even the banking institution, which Pérez Baró insisted was the heart of the structure but which did not fit in very well with traditional anarchist ideas, was to be governed fundamentally by delegates from the workers' organizations (had it been established as originally conceived).

Diego Abad de Santillán has confirmed this interpretation of the Catalan anarchists' view of the Consejo de Economía and the collectivization decree.

From the Consejo de Economia legal form had been given to the new economic creations, and structuring the coordination of the enterprises by industries to which they belonged. The ideal was the transformation of each industry, regionally and nationally, into a large enterprise directed by the workers and technicians. This process was too slow. The Spanish workers were not sufficiently prepared to carry it out without vacillations and without equivocations and we had to combat energetically the proprietary sense of the Control Committees, which felt themselves absolved of their revolutionary mission by the sole fact of having taken possession of the industry or the enterprise of the old owner.[68]

Certainly the Consejo de Economía de Cataluña and its Decree of Collectivization and Workers' Control illustrate the quandaries which faced the Spanish anarchists throughout the Civil War. On the one hand, because of the Civil War and the need to cooperate with other political and trade union groups which were on 'their side' in that conflict, the anarchists had to compromise extensively with the pristineness of their ideas in setting up both the *consejo* and in enacting its principal decree. On the other hand, they tried to use their influence in the *consejo*, and in enacting and applying its principal decree, insofar as the wartime circumstances permitted, to lay the basis for the future organization of the economy, society and polity along the lines of their philosophy and ideas.

18

The Case of the War Industries

One of the major achievements of the anarchists during the Spanish Civil War was the establishment and maintenance of extensive war industries in Catalonia, Valencia, Madrid and elsewhere in the Republic. However, like many other aspects of the anarchists' role in the Civil War, this aspect has either been overlooked or denied by those who have written about the conflict.

Perhaps typical are the observations of David Cattell, the historian of the Communist Party in the Civil War. 'The Anarchists in their efforts and rush to collectivize and carry out the revolution had failed to develop any munition or war industries in Catalonia.'[1] Cattell goes even further, giving credit to the Communists rather than the anarchists for whatever war industry was created in the Catalan region. 'The Communist pressure, particularly that from the "friendly advisers", as the Russian technicians were called, was just the impetus needed to put industry on a war footing. It is difficult to measure in figures exactly the increased industrial war Production, but from an economy which in 1936 produced a negligible amount of arms there developed a steady flow of munitions.'[2]

What actually occurred in Catalonia and other parts of the Republic was markedly different from what was suggested by David Cattell.

The Situation at the Beginning of the War

Upon the outbreak of the Civil War, the principal center of heavy industry in Spain was the Basque region, around Bilbao. In the other major industrial area, Catalonia, textile production was the predominant form of manufacturing activity, and the metallurgical and chemical industries, which were to be the core elements in production of goods for the Republican military, were only of secondary importance. In addition, there were scattered metallurgical plants and workshops in the Levante, in Asturias, and in and around Madrid. Finally, the Spanish army had had its own arms production facilities on a modest scale, and during the first months of the War one of these, that of Toledo, remained in Loyalist hands.

Once the War commenced, one of the most urgent tasks of the Loyalists was to mount an industry which could provide the material needed by the Republican armed forces. The arms and munitions seized from defeated Rebel military units were soon exhausted, and although it was possible at first to acquire some military supplies from France, this became increasingly difficult. Substantial military supplies from the Soviet Union did not begin to arrive until October 1936, and those were distributed, as we have seen, along very partisan lines. Much of the Republican military had to be supplied by sources within the Republican territory.

Toledo was soon lost. The metallurgical plants of the Basque region might have been adapted to supply much of what was required but, cut off as that area was from the rest of Loyalist Spain, it was difficult to get arms and munitions from there to the eastern and central parts of the Republic, and Basque arms went mainly to supply the northern Front. Within a year of the beginning of the War, even that source was cut off when the Franco forces overran the Basque territories.

It thus fell to Catalonia, and to a secondary degree, the Levante and Madrid, to provide the bulk of the domestically produced arms and munitions for the Republican forces. Although this task was undertaken almost immediately by the workers who took over the industries of Catalonia late in July 1936, its success was limited not only by economic factors, such as a lack of raw materials and appropriate machinery, but also by bitter political conflicts.

This political strife centered on at least two issues. One was the control of the war industries largely by the CNT, and the efforts of the Communists and others to wrest that control away from the anarchists. The second was the fact that during the first year or the War, and even for some time after that, such government control as there was over Catalan war industries was in the hands of the Catalan, not the Republican, government, and that was resented by the Madrid (and then Valencia and still later Barcelona) Republican authorities, who for two years or more sought to remove that control from the Catalan Generalidad.

The Early Establishment of Catalan War Industries

Many years after the Civil War, a Stalinist history of the conflict claimed: 'Paying no attention to the vital needs of the antifascist war, the anarchists did nothing serious to establish a war industry; the immense possibilities that existed were not taken advantage of.'[3] However, the truth of the situation was quite different.

While the fighting in Barcelona to suppress the Rebellion was still in progress, the work of converting industries to war production had already begun. Some months later, *Solidaridad Obrera* described this process:

On July 21, the Sindicato de la Metalurgía, in accord with García Oliver, chose [Eugenio] Vallejo to organize the war material factories. From July 19 on, various factories of Barcelona had turned spontaneously to the construction of tanks, with more good will than technique. Vallejo went throughout the neighborhoods to recruit all the comrades useful for this task. Within six days several tanks were already delivered to the Comité de Milicias. There were lacking all kinds of facilities, and particularly designs, because war material had never been constructed in Catalonia...

We lacked technicians and designs at the beginning of the

War. García Oliver presented Vallejo two technicians who had worked in the factories of Oviedo. At the same time we obtained the valuable help of Artillery Colonel Jiménez la Veraza, former director of the arms factory of Oviedo... We captured some designs as well as specialized machines which were hidden in a certain factory of Barcelona. The first thing that was done was to centralize the activity of Hispano Suiza, as the most important of Catalania and which had the best material and personnel. It and seven or eight other plants resolved in the first instance the most urgent manufacturing problems.[4]

There were many small metallurgical workshops in Barcelona, with 10 or 15 or so workers. The Metal Workers' Union of the CNT centralized many of these into about 50 large factories with 500 to 2,000 workers each. Not all of the metal union leaders favored this, fearing that it robbed the workers of direct control of their plants, but the exigencies of war made it necessary.[5]

Catalan President Luis Companys explained the hitherto diverse nature of these workshops: They included 'factories of office equipment, factories of electric material and metal propaganda articles which were adapted to produce casting for bullets.'[6] In all, according to Josep Maria Bricall, there were 'some eight hundred factories or workshops of some importance' in the metallurgical industry, as well as chemical plants making 'fertilizers, mineral acids, colorants, synthetic ammonia, chlorine, soda ash, explosives for mines, etc.' But, he added that 'this structure was not designed to confront a situation such as this'.[7]

In the early phase of the Catalan war industries, production was stimulated and rationalization and innovation were encouraged, according to the wartime head of the Metal Workers' Federation of Catalonia. He cited an instance: the fabrication of one part of a Mauser had taken seven operations, but the number was reduced to five by changes suggested by the workers in the plant. He added that the initiative of the workers was generally very much stimulated by the collectivization of the industry, and many workers knew their jobs and the industry well, and were able to make good contributions to its improvement.[8]

The Organizational Structure of Catalan War Industries

Perhaps the Casa Riviera is as good an example as any of how the process of organization of the war industries was undertaken by the workers in Barcelona. It was an enterprise with three factories and a central office staff. Six brothers had owned the enterprise, five of whom fled to France, and thence to Franco territory, the youngest, aged only 19, was captured, and put on 'trial' by the workers, but was freed upon the urging of one of the members of the control committee.

With the suppression of the Rebellion in Barcelona, a control committee (Comité de Control) was named by the Barcelona Metal Workers' Union to take over temporary control of the enterprises. All employees had to join either the CNT or the UGT; most of the manual workers already belonged to the CNT, and the office workers in their great majority opted to join the UGT.

A few weeks after July 19, there was the first general assembly of the firm's workers, including both manual and office employees. It elected an enterprise committee (Comité de Empresa) to take control of the firm on a more permanent basis. That committee chose as its president the man who had been secretary of the personnel manager before the Revolution. Another white-collar worker was chosen as secretary of the Comité de Empresa, and both of these people served throughout the War.

Each of the four sections of the firm – the three factories and the office staff – held their own general assemblies at least once a week. There they discussed matters ranging from the most important affairs to the most trivial ones.

Financially, the firm worked at first on the basis of the funds it had in its bank account. The Generalidad had almost immediately issued instructions to the banks to honor checks signed by members of the Comités de Control. A bit later, the Generalidad gave liberal credits to this industry to assure its normal operation.

Within a few months, the Metal Workers' Union of Barcelona wanted to take over control of the enterprise from the Comité de Empresa. However, a rather raucous meeting of the general assembly of the workers of the enterprise rejected that notion.

In one way, perhaps, the Casa Riviera enterprise was not entirely typical. It did well financially during the War, perhaps due to the capacity of the president of the Comité de Empresa. It paid off debts acquired before July 19, and added some new machinery, so that the capital equipment of the firm was as good when Franco troops marched into Barcelona as it had been on July 19 1936.[9]

Another example of a collectivized metal plant in Barcelona was that of Fabrica Torres Pueblo Nuevo. It had about 800 workers, of whom about 40 percent had belonged to the CNT before the outbreak of the War, and 80 percent were members of the CNT during the War, the rest belonging to the UGT.

This factory was collectivized as soon as the War began. A Consejo de Control was elected, which had under it a subsidiary Comisión de Produccion, to direct the actual operation of the plant. There was also a Comisión Sindical, which functioned as a regular trade union, handling any grievances which the workers had. Most technicians, engineers and former supervisors remained on the job. The workers' leaders explained to them that they, just like the manual workers had been employees, and that now the boss was gone (who was not needed) and the workers were taking over control of the plant. There were apparently no notable conflicts of these people with the workers elected to control the plant.

The collective paid those of its members who went into the army their full wage, at least in the beginning, which their wives or other dependants collected. Full health insurance for all workers was also established. Workers who had to go to the hospital were sent to the CNT's Hospital de Sangre.

In the Fabrica Torres Pueblo Nuevo, they maintained the wage system existing before the War. Wages were increased about 30 percent within a few months. The CNT leaders would have liked to establish the system of paying workers in proportion to their families' size, but they felt that they could not do so because of the necessity of dealing with the non-CNTers in the plant, who were opposed to this system.[10]

A few of the small metallurgical plants in Barcelona were not taken over by their workers. These included a plant belonging to a Czech Jew, who stayed on throughout the War. It employed 29 people, of whom 20 belonged to the CNT and the others to the UGT. The CNT union was headed by a young woman.

More or less normal collective bargaining relations continued in that plant during the War. At one point, when the employer was particularly resistant to demands for a wage increase, the young CNT leader called a strike, which lasted for three days, and was successful.

However, on other occasions, the CNT union came to the aid of the employer. He was having great difficulty in obtaining the steel he needed. The plant's CNT leader got in touch with the CNT Metal Workers' Union of Barcelona, and succeeded in getting through them the steel the plant needed, but on condition that it shift from making zippers to producing war material.[11]

In contrast to what was occurring in the Barcelona textile industry at the same time, the CNT's Metallurgical Union of Barcelona began almost immediately to carry out a coordinating role among the metal plants and workshops which had been taken over by their workers. According to Gaston Leval, '... the union succeeded in exercising a rigorous administrative control over the functioning of the firms whose committees accepted an administrative discipline, discipline which strengthened the spirit and practice of the methods used. The Catalan government demanded the establishment of this discipline, which could only be brought about thanks to the traditional labor organization.'

Leval was asked by the union to prepare a plan for the 'syndicalization' of the Barcelona metal industry. He did so, but the political complexities of the time prevented putting into practice the total organization of the industry by the Metal Workers' Union.

Leval has noted one serious problem of the collectivized war industries: 'Our impression is that, taking account of the nature of metallurgy, where technical matters are much more important and arise much more frequently than in other industries ... there was lack of an adequate number of engineers and specialists capable of duly assumed organic responsibilities. Competent specialists were lacking in the armaments industry, in the construction of important machinery. Proven proletarian enthusing couldn't take the place of the manipulation of mathematics.'[12]

Certainly all of the collectives in the war industries sector were not successful, either in technical or financial terms. This seems to have been the case with La Maquinista, which before the War had been Spain's largest locomotive works.

Three and a half decades later, Joan Roig, a Catalan nationalist who had been assistant manager of the plant collective, wrote:

> The workers' committee and later the works council was never able to impose an efficient order of production; the original members, whose first president was a laborer – a great orator in the CNT style – weren't technically qualified to run the factory, let alone convert it to arms manufacture. Too much was left to luck, too much depended on the individual will of a few people rather than on the combined effort of the whole workforce. The majority of technicians weren't sympathetic to collectivization... All in all, I don't think production ever reached 50 per cent of its potential...
>
> The factory, moreover, never received orders for the sort of war material it was best suited to produce – large tanks, for example. No new machine tools were brought in; the factory's existing press forge, its milling machines and lathes were not suited for producing shells, grenades and anti-submarine depth charge...

Nor was La Maquinista a financial success during the War. Roig noted that upon the return of the plant to its previous owners at the end of the War, they calculated that it had incurred a loss of 9,000,000 pesetas, nearly 50 percent of the firm's subscribed capital.[13]

General Accomplishments of Catalan War Industries

On August 7 1936, the government of Catalonia established the Commission of War Industries. This council consisted of representatives of the councillors of defense, economy, finance and internal security, and was presided over by prime minister José Taradellas in his capacity as councillor for finance. There were no direct representatives of trade unions or political parties. Soon after its inception, the commission had only two anarchists in it, Francisco Isgleas of defense and Diego Abad de Santillán of economy.[14] The commission named CNTer Eugenio Vallejo as its delegate, to coordinate the establishment and direction of the new war industries of the region.[15] José Peirats commented on 'the close collaboration and solidarity between the Esquerra and the CNT' in the activities of the commission.[16]

Diego Abad de Santiallán said of this commission that 'to it belonged technicians such as Jiménez de la Pereza, enterprising spirits such as José Taradellas, members of the Comité de Milicias, outstanding workers such as Eugenio Vallejo of metallurgy and [Manuel] Martí of the chemical industry...'

Abad de Santillán added that under its guidance 'hundreds of metallurgical and chemical factories were destined to produce in an orderly way the most urgent material, artillery pieces, aviation bombs, bullets, gas masks, ambulances, armored cars, etc., etc.'[17] By mid-September 1936, 24 factories and workshops were under the general orientation of the commission but, by July 1937, this number had risen to 290,[18] and by October 1937 there were 500 factories with 50,000 workers, and an additional 30,000 workers in 'auxiliary enterprises'.[19]

This intervention of the Catalan Generalidad aroused some resistance on the part of the CNT workers, fearful that it would weaken the workers' control of the war industry sector of the regional economy. President Companys himself explained this situation. The establishment, he said, of the commission:

Met some resistance, to some degree understandable, on the part of those Committees which from the beginning had taken over the factories and believed in good faith that only they could push forward the fabrication of war material. However, in spite of all these difficulties, some of them of certain seriousness, the Generalidad was coordinating this great effort ... and the task at first looked at with suspicion, soon gained the confidence of the working masses of our people and the technicians and that permitted us to establish an industry which, if not becoming as large as we would have wished, let us say, at least, with real satisfaction that we have achieved what Catalonia and the Republic needed, within the means and possibilities which we had.[20]

Colonel Jiménez de la Veraza headed an inspection service of the War Industries Commission. He had his aides visit the war industries factories regularly, and frequently made suggestions to the local control committees of the plants, suggesting improved methods of operations. According to Juan Manuel Molina who, as sub-Councillor of defense of the government of Catalonia between November 1936 and May 1937, was closely associated with the War Industries Commission, there was little if any friction between the Comités de Control and the commission during that period.[21]

President Companys, in a letter to Indalecio Prieto, then minister of national defense, dated December 13 1937, recounted what the war industries of Catalonia had achieved. He based his information largely on a report of the Commission of War Industries of October 1937. Both documents were published after the end of the War.

In his letter, Luis Companys summarized some of the accomplishments of Catalonia's war industry:

> We have been able to send, for example, more than two million hand grenades to the fronts; 30 million meters of barbed wire; 71,619 aviation bombs; to be repaired in our workshops, between coaches and trucks, 3,200 vehicles; to provide replacement parts for the innumerable weapons which our army uses... I want to underscore that almost all the machinery to carry out this effort has been made in Catalonia; it is enough to say, as one of the many pieces of data, that under our direction, there have been constructed 119 presses, and 214 lathes, many of them never fabricated in Spain, milling machines, perforating machines ... an endless number of small and large machines which it has been necessary to construct, particularly all the machinery complementary to the cartridge equipment bought in France, have been made in our shops and foundries.[22]

The report of the Commission of War industries went into considerable detail not only concerning what each of 15 large factories produced, but of materials which had been produced for the first time in Catalonia, and in all of Spain. Included among those were naval artillery grenades, mortar and cannon projectiles, 1937-version Mauser muskets, a large number of different parts for Hotchkiss machine guns, pieces for Colt machine guns, and pieces for Russian rifles.[23]

Aside from weapons, various kinds of explosives were necessary. President Companys wrote of this that in face of threatened shortage of gunpowder in the winter of 1936–7, 'Catalonia made possible ... the adaptation of the factory of Murcia for greater production, providing rapidly the machinery needed to increase it... But the factory of Murcia was not enough, and we thought that we could resolve this problem with the rapid installation here of a powder factory.' Although faced with a shortage of technicians and the need to construct the necessary machinery, by July 1937 the factory was completed. Companys added that in the following months the plant had turned out only 30,000 kilograms of powder, and told Indalecio Prieto that although the plant had a capacity of 1,000 kilograms a day, its low output was due to the fact that 'a person who had had important positions of responsibility at your side, indicated to us three months ago that it was not necessary for us to manufacture powder, since the Subsecretariat of Arms and Munitions had a more than sufficient quantity... However, the Catalans had been producing large quantities of natamita and fuses.'[24]

One of the largest projects undertaken by the Comisión de Industrias de Guerra was the rehabilitation of the Artillery Park of Barcelona, which assembled munitions and repaired guns of various kinds. President Companys noted that the number of employees in the park was increased between July 1936 to August 1937 (when it was taken over by the Republican government) from 30 to 1,000, adding that 'the Generalidad of Catalonia had provided the Park all the machinery and equipment necessary so that these thousand workers could do the work entrusted to them.'

The park had been attacked on July 19 and half destroyed. So the first task was 'to reconstruct it, adapt it, and undertake construction of special machinery for putting in place the cartridge shell, and filling it with powder, linking machines, installation of machines to load the projectiles for cannon and add fuses, etc.' They also gathered together some 6,000,000 empty shells found in various barracks of Catalonia, and reloaded them.[25]

Although Companys and Tarradellas do not seem to have mentioned the fact, the British observer Frank Jellinek, who was not over-friendly to the anarchists, writing in 1937, maintained: 'By March 1937 Catalan factories were turning out three airplanes a day.'[26]

Both President Companys and Prime Minister Taradellas paid tribute to the role of the workers in establishing and maintaining the war industries of Catalonia, during the period in which they were under the general supervision and orientation of the Generalidad. Companys wrote to Prieto that there was reason to be proud of 'the discipline in our factories and workshops during the time that they were intervened by us. The enthusiasm and abnegation of all the workers and technicians was enormous and there should be no confusion about this, and one must realize that if sometimes some factory has not been working it has not been due to lack of willingness to work, but to lack of raw materials or problems of a technical order ... Proof of this is the fact that during the time that we have controlled more than 300 workshops and factories devoted to the production of war material, there was not a single conflict, or problem, either of a social nature or in production...'[27]

Companys also noted: 'The working masses of Catalonia have always offered the greatest effort without any haggling, most workers laboring a 56-hour week, others working extra hours without collecting for them, and others meriting the greatest tribute – such as those workers of the Griona, Riviera, Elizalde plants, among others – who in spite of bombardments and the victims they caused in their factories, continued working with their usual enthusiasm.'[28]

Juan Andrade, the POUMist leader, writing early in 1937, described the working conditions in the Catalan war industries:

The workers in the war industries are, in reality the anonymous

heroes of our civil war. They work giving all that they have ...
They work seven days a week, and the trade union organization,
understanding the extremely grave moments in which we live,
imposes on them a severe labor regimen. The smallest fault is
gravely punished. It is necessary to maintain strong labor
morale. On the other hand, since the war industries depend
directly on the State and this has to deal with tremendous costs
which create enormous economic difficulties for it, principally
the onerous and disloyal bureaucracy, wages of the workers
cannot be improved. These workers, almost anonymously, are
carrying out an extraordinary job, without so far having been
able to receive directly the benefits of the revolution through
which we are living. Because, for example, after ending their
exhausting day of work, they have to continue to live in unheal-
thy homes, while there are magnificent buildings still occupied
by the bourgeoisie.[29]

Even the Soviet journalist Ilya Ehrenburg was impressed with the
intensity of the work in the Catalan war industries which he visited
early in the conflict: 'The workers of Barcelona are accustomed
to work without any great hurry. Now they have acquired a new
rhythm. No one pressures them, no one animates them. In spite
of the noise of the machines, they hear the noise of the steps of
the Moroccans as they approach the suburbs of Madrid. That
stamping teaches them a standard which workers of Spain have never
known.'[30]

Ehrenburg also praised the inventiveness of the workers in the
General Motors collective: 'In the factory of General Motors they
had never done anything before except make machines. When the
workers took over the firm, they decided to make the first thousand
trucks, 'Marathon' type by the first of April. The engineers of
Barcelona gave their approval to the projects drawn up by the old
worker Carrero ... Now they are making in 145 factories and
workshops with twelve thousand workers, the different parts for the
Marathon trucks.[31]

However, the Stalinists generally tended to deny the efforts of the
Catalan workers, led by the anarchists, to establish a war industry.

More typical of their position than Ehrenburg's comment was that of the United States Communist leader Steve Nelson, in his memoirs of participation in the International Brigade: 'The syndicalists ... ignored the central, all-important fact of the war. lhey ran the factories "for the benefit of the workers of those factories". They continued to turn out goods for export, rather than for the armies fighting the fascists. In the Hispano–Suiza factory, producing trucks and cars in Barcelona, they established a one-shift, six-hour day; and Communists who advocated three shifts were shot.'[32]

For his part, José Taradellas in his prologue to the October 1937 report of the Commission of War Industries noted: 'Catalan industry, during these fourteen months has carried out a truly epochal job of work and profound intelligence, and Catalonia will have to always thank all these workers who with their enthusiasm, with their efforts, and many times with the sacrifice of their lives, have worked to aid our brothers who fight at the front, to make possible the victory which our people wish and deserve. To all of them, our gratitude and our homage.[33]

During the period which Taradellas referred to, the war industries of Catalonia remained largely under the control of their workers, although working under the general guidance of the Generalidad's Commission of War Industries, and fulfilling contracts from either the government of Catalonia or that of the Republic, through the mediation of the Commission of War Industries.[34]

José Bricall presents index numbers of production of the metallurgical and chemical industries of Catalonia, the two principal parts of the economy involved in the war industries. These indicate much oscillation from month to month in 1936 and 1937, but with a general tendency for output to decline, particularly after April 1937. However, there is no indication of the degree to which this decline was reflected in those parts of those sectors which were converted to war purposes, or whether it principally showed the closing down of parts of the industries which had been devoted to civilian production.[35]

War Industries Outside Catalonia

Although the bulk of the Republican war industries was in Catalonia, there were more or less important installations elsewhere in the Republican area. As in Catalonia, in most cases, during the first year of the War at least, these were also largely under the control of their workers. The great exception, of course, was in the Basque area, the one part of Loyalist Spain which did not experience a major social revolution with the onset of the Civil War.

In Madrid, Lorenzo Iñigo, who represented the Juventudes Libertarias on the Junta de Defensa of Madrid, was placed in charge of the war industry of the city. He had as technical secretary of War Industries another anarchist, Francisco Calvillo Pineda, a leader of the local CNT metal workers' union.[36]

At that point, Madrid was not a major Spanish industrial city. The *Boletín de Información* of the CNT–FAI noted: 'The characteristics of metallurgy in Madrid had been, until July 19, more than rudimentary, primitive. Its radius of action was extraordinarily poor; there only existed a few workshops of relative importance ... which all were devoted to metallic construction and repair work; there existed other small workshops which were devoted to making pipes, lamps and heating equipment.'[37]

One of the few more or less substantial firms in the war industries category was the Standard Electric plant. The existing CNT committee in the plant was enlarged to bring in UGT members, and that committee took control of the enterprise. They dismissed the manager, and put the assistant manager in his place. The rest of the administrative force stayed on. The plant functioned much as before, except that ultimate control was in the hands of the CNT–UGT committee, and it was converted to production of war material.[38]

Most of the metal plants and other operations which could be considered as war industries were small, and for the most part belonged to people of Republican and Socialist sympathies. Iñigo and his advisers wanted to establish a larger scale operation, bringing together the machinery and workers of the various plants in one place. After extensive consultation with these industrialists, most of them agreed to his proposal, and he in turn promised to give each of them an inventory of all the machinery which they had made available. Afterwards, Iñigo was proud of the fact that none of the industrialists involved ever brought any kind of charge against him, although the Franco government invited them to do so.

There was obviously a problem in the war-torn city of Madrid in finding some place large and secure enough to house the kind of operation Iñigo had in mind. He soon found out about the existence of a long tunnel running the length of La Castellana Boulevard in the center of the city, which had been dug for a railroad line but never completed. With the help of the CNT Construction Workers' Union, they soon got the water out of it, and made the tunnel watertight.[39]

Ronald Fraser has said of this Madrid war industry: 'Technically and administratively, the "tunnel" was controlled by Iñigo's department, which also paid the workers. "A sort of self-management from above." For Pedro Gómez, a UGT turner, working in the "tunnel" was like working in a state factory. 'Production norms came from above, from the workshop committee and the technicians. Work conditions were excellent. Wage differentials existed but they were not large. There were no strikes. Once things were organized, work continued around the clock in three shifts.'

Fraser quoted Pedro Gómez as saying: 'The norms needed no enforcing. If the night shift produced 300 shells, the day shift would do its utmost to beat it. We never had to stop work for shortage of materials, or for electricity cuts as the war went on. Above us we had six metres of earth; there was no fear of bombing or shelling. There was only one problem – not enough unity at the top. We were united enough on the shop floor, there were no great problems between UGT and CNT workers. But it needed someone to prevent all that bickering and dissent at the top if we were to win the war...'[40]

In February 1937, General Miaja, who had supported and financed Iñigo's project suddenly refused to sign a voucher for wage payments, saying that the Valencia government had ordered that there be no more war industry in Madrid. Lorenzo Iñigo then hurried to Valencia, where he talked with Indalecio Prieto, who assured him that there had been no such government order, and saw to it that wage payments were resumed. However, he refused to allow transfer to this installation in Madrid of certain machinery needed to make artillery shells, still fearing as he did that the city would soon fall.[41]

This tunnel industry continued to operate until the end of the Civil War. It produced a variety of different kinds of shells, bullets, shell casings and a number of other things needed by the troops who were fighting in the streets above the tunnel factory.[42]

In Valencia, too, there was a small war industry. With the outbreak of the War, the workers under CNT leadership set up a collective of the metal industry. In the early period of the conflict, that collective set up six or seven war factories, one of which produced the first machine guns for the Republican army, and others produced rifles, grenades, ammunition and other things.[43] According to Stanley Payne, the ammunition output of factories in the Valencia region had in several categories surpassed that of Catalonia.[44]

One of the Valencia metallurgical plants about which we have information is the Industria Socializada Torras CM, which was on the outskirts of the city, and employed 103 workers. It was jointly taken over upon the outbreak of the War by the CNT and the UGT. The workers elected a 12-person committee, which included two representatives of the administrative workers, two of the technicians, and the rest manual workers from various parts of the enterprise. That body chose an executive committee of four which was in charge of day-to-day operations.

At least during the first year of the War, the Industria Socializada Torras CM was a financially successful enterprise. This was indicated by the fact that the capital value of the firm rose from 1,157,000 pesetas when it was taken over, to 1,195,000 pesetas by the end of 1936, and 1,265,000 by the end of March 1937. This was accomplished while the enterprise continued to amortize the machinery and other equipment, wrote off some bad debts, and substantially raised wages.

In that collectivized enterprise, as in many others, the workers chosen to run the collective took special care to improve working conditions of the members of the collective. New toilet and shower facilities were constructed, and a library was established. Full medical care was provided for the workers use after their day's labor was over with; arrangements being made, too, for the water from the pool subsequently to be made available to nearby truck gardening farmers to irrigate their holdings.[45]

There were several other more or less important war industry enterprises in the Levante region. For instance, the former Andreu Mateu firm, collectivized exclusively by the CNT, was assigned by the ministry of defense to produce cartridges for rifles. However, in addition, the directive- administrative committee of the collective also undertook on its own initiative to produce a sub-machine gun similar to the American Thompson weapon modified by them to prevent its overheating. This weapon was christened the Naranjero (orange) because of its production in Valencia, famous for its oranges. That collective also produced two of Spain's first tanks, which were sent to the Teruel front.

The former Miguel Davis firm, which had made railway locomotives, also became a CNT collective. It was converted to produce artillery shells, and the former Maquinista Valenciana, which before the War produced industrial machinery, was converted to the production of rifles. In the case of the Miguel Davis firm, when it was returned to its former owner at the end of the War, he 'needed skilled workers and not the inept Falangistas recommended by the authorities'. So he agreed to employ the workers of the North Spain Railroad machine yards in Valencia, who had been dismissed by the Franco regime authorities, because they had the skills he needed, and 'it was enough to promptly get a job in the Casa Davis ... that one had been dismissed by the Railroad.'

The Altos Hornos de Sagunta, the only blast furnace in Republican Spain outside the Basque area, with 6,000 workers, was also collectivized by its workers. It produced armor for trains and other vehicles[46]

There were also a few war industries in the Asturias region: about which Ramón Alvarez has written: 'In our power we only had the Santa Barbara Factory, in Trubia (near Oviedo). It was a heavy industry where particularly cannons were made. That industry was totally militarized, although there was UGT–CNT workers' control.

Then, especially in Gijón and La Felguera, the metallurgical industry could be considered as supporting the war, making armored trucks and munitions for the front, but it was not properly speaking a war industry.'[47]

Early Republican Government Sabotage of Catalan War Industries

In spite of the strategic importance of the new war industries of Catalonia, they received very little encouragement or help from the government of the Republic. The quickly achieved and rapidly growing influence in the Republican armed forces of the Communists, who were more interested in trying to undermine the CNT's control of the Catalan metallurgical and chemical industries than they were in having those industries provide arms for the Republic, was one factor in this situation. Another, even under the government of Prime Minister Francisco Largo Caballero, was the Republican regime's unwillingness to strengthen the position of the autonomous Catalan government, which admittedly had assumed powers going far beyond those bestowed on it by the relatively modest Catalan Autonomy Statute.

An early example of the unwillingness of the Republican government to help the development of Catalan war industries was its refusal to transfer any of the machinery and equipment of the Toledo cartridge-making installations to Catalonia, in spite of the fact that from the earliest weeks of the War, the Republic's ability to continue to control that city was quite doubtful. Diego Abad de Santillán said of this incident:

> The State had in that city three cartridge factories. Two of them were working; the third had been paralyzed for several years because it was antiquated arid its productive capacity was limited... We didn't ask for either of the factories which was working, although we saw them in danger and they would have been more productive if transferred, together with their specialized and technical personnel, to a place such as Catalonia; we

asked only for the one which had been paralyzed and wasn't being used. The hatred and jealousy of Catalonia were so great that they categorically refused us that paralyzed factory, and a few weeks later, Queipo de Llano could boast that the factories which they had not wished to turn over to Catalonia were producing cartridges for the Rebels.[48]

In more general terms, José Peirats has noted: 'The Generalidad suffered from the first moments the effects of the financial policy of Madrid, which amounted to the internal blockade of foreign exchange, which deprived Catalonia of the ability to take care of its needs.'[49] Peirats concluded: The incomprehension of the central government, its lack of confidence about the good and sincere intentions of the predominant sector in, Catalonia, wasted the military and industrial possibilities of this important region, which greatly influenced the destinies of the war.'[50] 'Of course, 'The predominant sector in Catalonia' to which Peirats referred is that of the anarchists.

Luis Companys also complained of the unwillingness of the Republican government to work with that of Catalonia in building up the region's war industries. He wrote to Indalecio Prieto:

We always had the great illusion of believing that the efforts of Catalonia would be understood, and that the Government of the Republic, putting aside political questions or an inefficacious centralist criterion which has often demonstrated its incompetence, would give Catalonia the facilities for coordinating its industry with the needs of the war. But, although I am not talking about you, but of another person, I cannot fail to note and to remind you that in the month of September of 1936, we offered the then President of the Council of Ministers and Minister of War, everything which Catalonia had and could do with its industry. This attitude of ours was answered with a negative, a negative which upon remembering it, we doubly lament, because our offer was sincere, was loyal... Never can anyone show that Catalonia has denied anything, absolutely anything, none of the requests, none of the suggestions which have been made...[51]

One problem which the war industries throughout the Republican area faced was the drafting of their young workers into the armed forces, once conscription had become general. In November 1937, a statement of the CNT's National Federation of Steel-Metallurgical Industries elaborated upon this problem: 'We all agreed that the most important factor in the good development of an industry is that it have good manual workers. In this case, how can one understand it when specialized workers are sent to the front, while in automobile repair shops there are men of 25 to 30 years entering who have the pompous name of apprentices. It has also happened that some workers for whom we have submitted regular requests for exemption from the draft, and have not received it, have sought the influence of some political party and have achieved what they were seeking... Are the political parties better acquainted than we are with the skills of those workers?'[52]

For their part, the Stalinists, both the Partido Comunista de España and the Partido Socialista Unificado de Cataluña, carried on an unremitting campaign against the Catalan war industries. The nature of the Communists' attacks can be seen in a reply by *Solidaridad Obrera* to a charge by the Catalan secretary-general of the United Socialist Youth, to the effect that 'in that region there existed factories for war industry, magnificently equipped, which are used only to make munition capsules for pistols.'

Solidaridad Obrera answered, saying:

First, it is a Councillor who affirms something he knows nothing about, and on being confronted and invited to prove what he says, makes no reply. Then it is a lieutenant-colonel operating on the Aragón front, who undertakes to claim that the war material fabricated in Catalonia has caused more victims than the bullets of the fascists. He is invited to prove that, and the man of words and responsibility offers no reply. Later, in view of the same charge, material is returned from the front, and a Commission composed of military technicians and civilians, signs a document in which they say that this material has been returned although it is in perfect condition. Another shipment, and another, all from the same place and with the same result...

Then, a note in the periodical defender of unity talking about honesty in the war industries, and trade-union competence...[53]

Juan Comorera, addressing the first national conference of the PSUC a few weeks after the formation of the Negrín government, made clear what the Stalinist objectives were with regard to the war industries:

The war industries have to be placed under control of the Republican Government. Naturally in the direct organization of the Catalonian war industry, the Generalitate cannot be eliminated. There exists, then the necessity of the reorganization of the war industry, from the bottom upwards. This reorganization will be carried out in a specialized and disciplined manner; with a plan of production, a knowledge of basic materials, responsibility for the quantity and quality of production, a single superior and technical administration, and no factory committee. Foremost of all this will mean the centralization of the war industry, and the militarization of the factories and transport services...

At the same time we will have to get down to the security of all our industries. To the reorganization of the economic life of our country, destroyed by the committees, and most of all by the uncontrollables...[54]

He could not have stated more clearly the intention to destroy all workers' control over the war industries.

Indalecio Prieto and the Catalan War Industries

With the fall of the government of Francisco Largo Caballero, and the installation of the Right-wing Socialist Indalecio Prieto as minister of defense in the succeeding government of Prime Minister Juan Negrín, the Republican government began to assert extensive control over the Catalan war industries. Prieto had first suggested the establishment of a separate Republican ministry of war industries when still a member of the cabinet of Largo Caballero, and the latter rejected the idea.[55]

Although Prieto apparently did not revive the idea of a separate ministry of defense industries, he did establish a sub-secretariat of munitions and armaments within the ministry of national defense. It was this organization which began to try to exercise extensive control over the defense industries of Catalonia.

Of course, the Negrín government came to power in the aftermath of the 'May Days', the severe fighting between anarchists and POUMistas on the one side and Communists and police on the other during the first week of May 1937. These events severely weakened both the government of Catalonia and the CNT–FAI. The former was deprived by the Republican government of control of the police and military forces of the region. The anarchists were removed from both the Catalan and Republican regimes, and put strongly on the defensive, a posture they were forced to maintain throughout the rest of the Civil War. These facts facilitated the Republican government's seizure of Catalan war industries.

One major Catalan war industry installation, the engine factory of Elizalde, had already been impounded by the government of Largo Caballero in February 1937. In August, the Sub-secretariat of munitions and armaments also took over the Hispano Suiza factory and the Artillery Park.[56]

The first approach of the sub-secretariat of munitions and armaments was to appoint 'delegations' in each part of the Republic in which some war material and arms were being produced. However, this system only sowed confusion in the war industries of Catalonia As Eugenio Vallejo subsequently explained to the sub-secretary of munitions and armaments, 'To justify the employment of a certain number of individuals without technical preparation, those people limited themselves to coercing the factories controlled by the Commission and which lacked raw materials, saying that if they worked for Valencia, they would be given a payment in cash on signing the contract, and they would be given all the materials they needed, which they would not receive so long as they were working for the Commission of War Industries.'[57]

Consequently, the sub-secretary invited the Catalan Commission of War Industries to send someone to Valencia, to discuss with him the coordination of the Catalan armaments sector with that of the rest of Republican Spain. Eugenio Vallejo was sent on that mission, arriving in Valencia on September 1 1937. That first meeting went smoothly, Vallejo giving the sub-secretary and extensive report on the state of the region's war production, and the sub-secretary reportedly admitting 'that the War Industry of Catalonia had done ten times more than the rest of the Industry of Spain', and agreeing with Vallejo that 'this production from the month of September could be increased ten times over if Catalonia was provided the means needed to acquire the raw materials that did not exist in Spanish territory.'[58]

One frankly political issue was dealt with in the meeting. This was the fact that PSUC leader Juan Comorera, upon becoming Catalan councillor for the economy, had dismissed the five members of the Commission of War Industries who had served since the beginning of the War. It was agreed that Comorera's substitute members should remain, but that José Tarradellas, as councillor of finance, should name five others – and he named the five who had been dismissed by Comorera.[59]

The first meeting in Valencia reached agreement that the general staff would draw up a list of things which it needed, which it would send to the Catalan War Industries Commission through the sub-secretariat. For its part, the sub-secretariat agreed that when it signed contracts, with the advice of the War Industries Commission, with Catalan armaments firms, it would undertake to provide them the necessary raw materials. On the other hand, it was agreed that the War Industries Commission would not make any contracts with Catalan industries without the approval of the sub-secretariat.[60]

However, a further meeting, this time in Barcelona, of the sub-secretary with the members of the Catalan Commission of War Industries, did not turn out so well. The sub-secretary arrived with several assistants, including not only Spaniards, but a 'Russian armaments technician, Sampters; three other Russians who were called technicians and another two or three who belong to the Department of the Subsecretary'. At the first of three meetings, spread over two days, the sub-secretary presented the general staff's list of armament needs in so far as Catalan industry was concerned. Although the list was long, the War Industries Commission did not reject it.

However, after the second of the three meetings, 'the Russian escorts began to visit the war material factories and took advantage of the attention shown them by the people who wanted to reach a definite accord and didn't think that anyone would abuse this circumstance. In these visits, these individuals limited themselves to asking the trade-onion affiliation of the majority of the workers in the said factories, and particularly of the Committees, and in a brazen manner asked if they wouldn't prefer to work for Valencia instead of working for the War Industries Commission.'[61]

In the third meeting with the War Industries Commission, the sub-secretary, who had obviously been under great pressure from the Stalinists, suggested that, in addition to the arrangements which had been made in Valencia, he would name another delegate to manage the work of the War Industries Commission, alongside of and with equal authority to that of Eugenio Vallejo, the CNT trade unionist. He suggested a certain Senor Izquierdo, a Communist, for this new post. Vallejo objected strongly to this, arguing that it would disrupt the work of the War Industries Commission, fomenting dissension, with CNT-controlled factories seeking to work through him, while the minority of plants and workers controlled by the PSUC would try to work through Izquierdo.

While rejecting the idea of sharing power in the War Industries Commission with a hand-picked Communist colleague, Vallejo suggested as an alternative, that the sub-secretariat of munitions and armaments take over complete control of Catalan war industries, 'Signing the contracts, providing the raw materials, paying the wages, warehousing the products, verifying them and sending them to the front. That is to say, that the War Industries Commission would be abolished.'

However, 'this, which was to cede everything, was rejected in an energetic way by the sub-secretary, who said that he didn't want the industry, since neither he nor the people around him were prepared to take charge of the direction of all the industry...'[62]

After this third meeting, which ended in a deadlock, the sub-secretary met several times with José Tarradellas, the head of the War Industries Commission, but no solution to the impasse was reached. He also conferred extensively with Juan Comorera. Finally, when the sub-secretary was asked why he had not reached an agreement with the War Industries Commission, he replied,' They won't let me do so.'[63]

Although he left Barcelona threatening to return shortly to take over complete control of Catalonia's war industries, the sub-secretary did not do so. The move to completely absorb Catalan war material production had to await a further turn in the political wheel.

Meanwhile, the National Federation of the Sidurergical-Metetallurgical Industries of the CNT protested against what was happening. Perhaps typical was a statement of the federation, substantially censored by the authorities, which appeared in the CNT–FAI *Boletín de Información* of November 4 1937. After objecting to the fact that skilled workers whom the unions recommended for draft exemptions were denied such exemptions, it noted that in some workshops 'there have been put in charge personnel who don't have the least notion of what metallurgy is, while, in the Unions we have personnel who are very competent to direct this production, as we have demonstrated during the time that those workshops were under its direction.'

The federation's statement pledged 'enthusiastic collaboration' with the government 'to achieve the victory over fascism', and said it 'accepts government control of war industries', but demanded the abolition of the sub-secretariat of armaments, and urged its replacement by a National Council of War Industries, made up of representatives of the CNT, UGT and the government.[64]

The Negrín Government's Total Control of War Industries

It was not until August 11 1938 that the cabinet of Juan Negrín issued the decree 'militarizing' all of the Republic's war industries (naturally including those of Catalonia). That decree probably had more political than economic or military significance, since it was never put fully into effect, and to a greater or less degree, CNT-controlled war industries remained in the hands of the workers until the end of the War. On the same day, two other decrees 'militarized' the nation's ports and reorganized the commissariat.

Part of the political significance of the August 11 decrees was that they were issued by a cabinet in which, after being out of the Republican regime for more than a year, the anarchists were again represented – Asturian CNT leader Segundo Blanco being minister of education. The decree and the reaction to it of lower-ranking CNT trade unionists reflected the growing schism within anarchist ranks at that time (and which will be discussed at greater length in a subsequent chapter).

Another political consequence of the August 11 1938 decrees was that they provoked a significant political crisis. Jaime Ayduade and Manuel de Irujo, representing respectively the Catalan and Basque Nationalist parties in the Negrín cabinet, both resigned from the government in protest.[65] In spite of the nominal participation of the CNT in the Negrín regime, the exit of the two regionalist parties represented a serious narrowing of the political base of that regime.

The workers who were directly affected by the decree 'militarizing' the war industries reacted strongly in opposition to the measure. Although the Executive of the Unión General de Trabajadores (GT), by then largely controlled by pro-Communist Socialists and real Stalinists, almost immediately issued a statement endorsing the August 11 decrees and the national committee of the CNT apparently had little to say formally about the matter, that was not the case with the metal and chemical workers' unions which were directly involved in the question.

One of the earliest reactions came from the workers in the war industries of Madrid, which were largely under CNT control. When, soon after the signing of the August 11 decrees, the delegation in Madrid of the sub-secretariat of munitions and armaments sought to take over the CNT-controlled war industries there, 'The workers paid no attention to the orders and documents and declared publicly their refusal to turn over their workshops, unless they first received a guarantee: the constitution of the National Council of War Industries.'[66]

On August 27 1938, there was a meeting of the CNT metal workers of Madrid. Minutes of that meeting reported: 'It was announced that the *Sindicato* had taken steps to defend its interests in the face of the decree, and aside from other things that may be done and for which preparations have been made, has published a manifesto in which it admits the principle of militarization, but demands trade union intervention and respect for the gains made during the war. The assembly agreed unanimously to approve the attitude of the *sindicato* and the continuation of the steps to resist the application of the decree.'[67]

José Peirats does not indicate what further steps, if any, the government took to try to take over the arms industry in Madrid. However, the anarchist who was in charge of that industry, Lorenzo Iñigo, has indicated that the CNT continued to control the war industries of Madrid until the end of the Civil War.[68]

The nature of the proposed National Council of War Industries, which the CNT–FAI had already presented, was formally ratified in a plenum of regionals of the libertarian movement which met early in September 1938. As part of a resolution urging the establishment of a Ministry of War Industries, that plenum called for a 'Superior Council of War Industry: In everything relating to war production in Loyalist Spain the adviser and decision maker will be this Council, made up of trade union and technical representatives of the following Industrial Federations: Power and Light, Combustibles, Chemicals, Iron and Steel, Transport, and Construction of the CNT and the UGT.[69]

It was mid-November before the sub-secretariat of munitions and armaments ordered its Delegation in Valencia to take over CNT-controlled war industries there. José Peirats has noted: 'On the 21st, the delegates of the Sub-secretariat tried to execute an order of seizure of the Schmaissers factory, which the workers and other responsible people opposed. A few days later, a meeting of the metal workers of the CNT and of the UGT of Valencia agreed not to turn over any socialized workshop until the government had taken over the privately run workshops, and particularly, until the National Council of War Industries had been established.'[70]

The controversy over the government's taking over the war industries in the center-south part of Loyalist Spain (by this time the Republican-held area had been split in two by the Franco forces' push to the Mediterranean Sea), continued until the final attack of the Rebels on Catalonia. Late in November 1938, at a meeting of the Joint CNT–UGT Metallurgical sub-committee, Pascual Tomás of the UGT 'indicated his conviction that the application of the decree was an attack on the workers and damaged war production, but that he had orders of the Executive of the UGT to proceed with turning over factories and workshops without conditions.' He reiterated this position at a further meeting on December 3.

Meanwhile, at a meeting on December 2 of the metallurgical sub-committee and the national sub-committee of the CNT for the center-south region, it was agreed to formally ask the delegate of the sub-secretariat to suspend further seizures until he had received 'concrete instructions' from the government, then located in Barcelona. It was also agreed that in view of their inability even to get a reply to their appeals for help on the issue from the Barcelona-based CNT national committee, they would send a delegate to Barcelona, to meet with the national-committee and with Segundo Blanco the CNT member of the Negrín cabinet.

In the face of continued UGT insistence on its willingness to see the center-south war industries turned over without conditions to the sub-secretariat, the CNT in the region kept insisting that it would not agree to this. Apparently the last statement of the center-south national sub-committee of the CNT before the beginning of the battle of Catalonia, noted:

The workers need to have the maximum guarantees that in turning over the industries, for the expansion of which they have been solely responsible, the revolution will not stagnate...

The CNT in all its decisions puts the war first before any other consideration, not forgetting that for any material or moral concession guarantees are needed which serve to stimulate the workers to continue their participation with the same enthusiasm they had before the concession, and in doing this, we feel we have fulfilled our duty, both for the war and for ourselves.

According to José Peirats, 'That is where the question stood on the eve of the last and most tragic phase of the revolution and of the war.'[71]

As we have seen, the process of the Republican government's taking over at least some of the Catalan war industries had begun as early as the first half of 1937. It was somewhat intensified during the period that Indalecio Prieto was minister of national defense. It is not clear whether the decree of August 11 1938 changed the Catalan situation fundamentally. Diego Abad de Santillán, in his account of the Catalan war industries, does not mention the decree. However, he does say: 'To avoid conflicts and satisfy the ambitions of command and administration, Catalonia ceded the war factories, with the exception of those established as new plants by the Generalidad, and even some of them, since also part of the new factories were ceded to the sub-secretariat of armament...'[72]

It is doubtful that there was time, between August 11 1938 and the beginning of the Franco invasion of Catalonia in December, for the Republican government to take over control of all of Catalonia's war industries. It is clear that at least in many cases, the workers continued largely to run the plants, regardless of which branch of government had formal title to them.

It is also clear that their constant campaign against workers' control of the war industries did not win the Stalinists any degree of support among the workers in those industries. In May 1938, Dolores Ibarruri reported to a plenum of the Communist Party: 'We have very few comrades in the war industry factories, and the Provincial Committees of the Party don't do much about this situation, which should and must be corrected.'[73]

Results of the Government's Absorption of the War Industries

The advantages which were presumably supposed to flow from centralization of control of the Loyalist war industries in the hands of the Republican government were those of coordination, simplification and rationalization. In theory at least, the top military authorities, who knew best the arms and munitions their forces needed most urgently, could pass that information to the civilian branch of the government which controlled all the enterprises in Republican Spain manufacturing and distributing those items. Through centralizing orders, supplies of raw materials, and financing, that agency supposedly could allocate orders to those plants best able to produce particular arms or material, avoiding such duplication of effort as undoubtedly had existed when different military organizations often sought to get particular plants to produce what they needed, regardless of what might be happening in other similar factories or workshops. Also, specialization of particular production in particular plants might be supposed to lead to certain economies of larger scale production, as to those due to greater concentration of expertise on the part of managers and technicians.

However, in the protracted struggle over control of the Republican war industries, few of those advantages would seem to have been achieved. Entirely aside from the disorganization and confusion arising from the Negrín government's efforts to take control of the war industry plants away from the workers, and the workers' resistance to those efforts, few of the touted advantages of centralized control seem to have been forthcoming in those segments of the war industries which, at one point or another, were taken over by the sub-secretariat of munitions and armaments – or directly by one or another branch of the armed forces.

Often what occurred was the multiplication of bureaucracy rather than output. Frequently, considerations of party affiliation were more important than those of technical or administrative competence in the selection of government-appointed managers. In at least some instances, the 'militarization' of a plant brought the imposition of draconian systems of 'labor discipline' on the part of the new authorities. Almost universal was the demoralization of the workers – admittedly resulting in part from the growing hardships of a war which was being lost, but certainly greatly intensified by the workers' conviction that what had been 'their own' industries in the first half of the War, now belonged to 'them', whether those involved were unapproachable government bureaucrats or Communist Party aparatchiks.

Space does not permit the presentation of more than a few examples of these effects of 'militarization' of the war industries. But there can be little doubt that these are only particular cases of phenomena which were very widespread within Republican Spain.

In writing to Minister of National Defense Indalecio Prieto, Luis Companys said that under the Catalan War Industries Commission, 'We have been able to carry forward our job with great austerity, without bureaucracies and without that accumulation of Directors, Inspectors and Interventors, the result of which often is to asphyxiate what they are seeking to give more life.[74] However, the assumption of control by the Republican sub-secretariat resulted in just that kind of multiplication of bureaucratic posts and paperwork which Companys said the Catalan war industries had been able to avoid.

In December 1937, the CNT issued a protest against 'the cloud of bureaucratic parasites fallen on them, and which grab hold of privileges, as molluscs cling to a rock.'[75] There is considerable specific evidence of the bureaucratization of those parts of war industry taken over by the central government.

The workers of the Elizalde factory, one of the first Catalan industries taken over by the Republican authorities, submitted to the defense section of the CNT National Committee on April 10 1938, a report on how the plant had fared since being taken over by the Republican authorities. Part of this report noted: 'To satisfy each of the needs of the factory requires such a quantity of steps, to obtain so many "approvals" that what is needed never comes in time. This is even true if the matter is urgent. "Following regulations" is ahead of everything else. Gentlemen who have never been near the factory have to approve one or another material, machine, allotment, accessory or lubricant as being necessary. And these approvals require three, four and even six months. To that must be added the time necessary to actually acquire them.'[76]

The workers of another Republican government-controlled plant also wrote to the CNT national leadership, in March 1938. They had similar complaints about the bureaucratization of their enterprise under central government control. They gave an example: 'We need electric motors. They are available. One of them is for the Kellembartgert machine... We asked for them at the beginning of January, and don't know whether they have been approved. By direct negotiation they could have been obtained the next day.'[77]

A document of the CNT, introducing the October 1937 report of the Catalan War Industries Commission, and published in Buenos Aires after the end of the War, commented on the politicization of the management of war industries taken over by the sub-secretariat. Posing the question, 'Results of the intervention by the central power?' it responded, 'Appointments of a political type for the technical jobs of greatest responsibility; creation of a bureaucracy of Interventors, Inspectors, Directors, etc., whose most outstanding merit was their affiliation with a particular party or their absolute subjection to it... pernicious influence of the so-called "proselytism", which has been the "art" of placing elements loyal to the party, of forcing the weaker or more unscrupulous, with only skin-deep antifascism, to enter the party; "art" which was characterized by the elimination, by whatever procedures, of workers and technicians not addicted to the party or manipulable by it.'[78]

Although working conditions in the plants appropriated by the Republican government undoubtedly varied considerably, there were at least some cases of the worst kind of oppression of the workers. One of these is shown by an order issued by the general political commissar of the sub-secretariat of aviation, about discipline in factories controlled by the air arm, and dated August 11 1938.

Of a decree of the sub-secretary of aviation dated July 29 1938, 'militarizing' all personnel in factories under its jurisdiction, the general political commissar observed that both the men 'militarized' under this decree and for women employees who were not covered by it, infraction of labor discipline would be divided into those considered 'light', and those which were 'grave'. Among the former were: 'Lack of care or negligence in conservation of industrial equipment and machinery; failure to fulfil the obligations imposed by the labor required of those workers; indications of displeasure or lukewarmness in the service; faulty reasoning or discourteous answers to the Superior; absence for a period which comes to constitute a grave indiscipline or crime; contravention of the labor norms and good government within the military factories, and whatever is not punished under any other heading, as grave faults or crimes, involving undermining of good labor behavior or the functioning of the factories . . .'

The decree then went on to list the punishments for such 'light' offenses. These included: 'Private repression, public repression, loss for up to five days of half the payments of whatever kind received by the militarized workers, and . . . expulsion from the factory, and if it is a worker of less than 45 years, assignment to build fortifications.'

Those guilty of 'grave' labor offenses would be immediately sent for trial under the military code of justice. This draconian decree ended with an irony of which the commissar general perhaps was unaware: 'I underscore the importance of this because one must contribute to the strengthening of labor discipline, since the primordial obligation of the Commissars is to work for Justice and the application of the norms which are established.'[79]

There can be no doubt that the Republican requisition of worker-controlled defense plants severely lowered the morale of the workers in those plants. Such evidence is clearly available in the case of the Elizalde factory SAF in Barcelona. According to a report to the CNT by the workers of that plant, 'of their own free will and after working eight hours a day and 56 a week, and apart from their habitual shift, they worked before the requisition, without hope of retribution, a number of hours which varied according to the possibilities of getting to work of each one.' The report cited one of the sections of the plant selected at random, where the 58 workers in the five weeks from August 15 to September 18 1936, worked a total of 2,688 hours, an average of 9.2 extra hours a week per worker.

However, the report added: 'After the requisition, the enthusiasm in production declined so much that no one – with a few exceptions – has worked more than the normal hours. On the contrary – and this is sad – generally work ends a few minutes before the hour fixed to terminate...'

The effect of the decline in workers' morale was further indicated in this report by the comment that 'it has been possible to determine that the average increase of time used to make a particular piece has risen by 21.33 percent.'[80]

Conclusion

It is clear that the problem of the war industries of Republican Spain was much more a political problem than an economic one. The workers of Catalonia, as well as in some parts of the Levante and in Madrid, after taking over metallurgical and chemical plants, had brought into existence a war industry which had not existed before. Within a year, it was producing a wide range of small arms, tanks, cannon, air and naval bombs, hand grenades and even airplanes, as well as a great variety of other war material. In addition, the workers and the technicians cooperating with them had engaged in prodigies of innovation and improvisation, not only in turning out equipment for the armed forces, but also in developing and making much of the machinery which was required to make the arms and munitions they were providing to the Republican armed forces.

With wider access to raw materials, and with greater technical skill, the worker-controlled – largely CNT-controlled – war industries could have done more than they did. Perhaps the organizational structure of the Catalan War Industries Commission and the plants and workshops working under its general supervision could have been improved with time.

However, the main problem with the Republican war industries during the year in which they were created, was that on a plant-by-plant basis throughout virtually all of Loyalist Spain they were under the inspiration and control of workers of the Confederación Nacional del Trabajo, and that the government which was coordinating the largest part of the war industries effort was that of Catalonia, not that of Madrid (and later Valencia). Hence, for many of the politicians leading the Spanish Republic – and this was overwhelmingly the case with the Communists of both Spain and Catalonia – the removal of workers' control from the factories, and the destruction of the Catalan Generalidad's general supervision of the major part of the war industries, became matters of much greater importance than any effort to build an arms industry in Spain which could have partially freed the Republic from dependence on foreign arms sources. Of course, had that been achieved, the basis of Communist influence within the Republic would have been largely destroyed. Also, the strategic position of those Socialist and Republican politicians, who were more or less the allies – when not the servants – of the Communists, would also have been undermined.

19

The Collectivization of Transport and Public Utilities

Most of the infrastructure of the economy in Loyalist Spain was more or less collectivized by the unions during the Civil War. The initiative for this came principally for the CNT, although there was usually cooperation, and sometimes enthusiastic cooperation, on the part of the Unión General de Trabajadores.

Not only were the railroads taken over and to a large degree administered by the unions, but the same thing was true of municipal transport – trolley cars, subways, buses – in Barcelona, Valencia and other major cities. In addition, to a varying degree in different parts of the country, bus and truck transport were also collectivized. Peculiar circumstances deriving from the war made this process more difficult in so far as maritime transport was concerned. Finally, public utilities such as gas, electricity and water supply were also widely collectivized by the workers' organizations.

Collectivization of the Railroads

Although the railroad systems in different parts of Loyalist Spain were immediately taken over by the railroad workers unions of the various regions, it was some time before a National Railroad Council was finally established, with six Republican government representatives and three each from the UGT's Sindicato Nacional Ferroviario (SNF), and the CNT's Federación Nacional de la Industria Ferroviaria (FNIF). This council sought to coordinate and supervise generally the operation of the railroads in the parts of the Republic which remained under Loyalist control.

One of the accomplishments of the council was the establishment of a single railroad enterprise, in place of the considerable number of private firms, many of them foreign-owned, which had existed before July 19. This single rail system was maintained after the Civil War by the Franco government in the form of the Red Nacional Ferroviaria (RENFE).

The National Railroad Council had four sections, dealing with commercial, personnel, accounting and technical questions respectively. Each of these sections was run by a sub-council, consisting of one government representative as chairman, a secretary from one of the unions, and a third member drawn from the other union.

The influence of the anarchists was at least to some degree shown in the functioning of the personnel sub-committee of the Railroad Council, of which Francisco Diezhandino, who had been head of the FNIF at the outbreak of the War, was secretary. It sought, and generally succeeded, to standardize wages of workers throughout the country, with the same kind of worker getting the same wage, usually at the highest prevailing wage for that category of employee. They also established paid vacations for all the workers, and established the principle that illegitimate spouses of railroad workers had the same right to social security payments – old age and survivors' insurance – as legitimate wives.

Some of the National Railroad Council's most difficult problems came from outside Spain. For one thing, the Spanish Republican railroads depended in large part on imports of coal from Great Britain, since electrification was relatively limited and most of the coal mines of the country fell more or less quickly into the hands of the Franco forces. The council felt that there was considerable sabotage from the British side of their efforts to get sufficient coal. Messages were frequently garbled, for minor reasons the British refused to cash checks of the council, and finally, the British would not sell any coal without full payment in advance. However, when the National Railroad Council turned to the Soviet Union as a source of coal, they found that there, too, they had to pay for it in advance of shipment.

Another kind of foreign difficulty was reflected in an incident which occurred in April 1937. The council sent a mission to Holland, to negotiate a number of cars which had been ordered from a Hungarian factory through a Dutch firm before the beginning of the Civil War. The government set up by General Franco had tried to claim control of those machines, but the National Railroad Council's mission was successful in getting them shipped to Loyalist Spain.[1]

Other problems arose from the fact that a number of the 17 railroad enterprises taken over had belonged to foreign firms. One such instance was the Central Railroad of Aragón, which had been Belgian-owned. Belgian Foreign Minister Paul Spaak, a Socialist, officially protested the seizure of that enterprise, and asked Spanish Prime Minister Francisco Largo Caballero, also a Socialist, for compensation for the seized property. Largo Caballero argued that the road had been taken over to help the war effort, and that the issue of compensation could be settled after the War was over. Actually, when Franco won the war, he did not compensate the Belgian company, and the line remained part of the centralized railroad system maintained by the Franco regime.

There were also political problems faced by the National Railroad Council. The Communists opposed consolidation of the railroads, claiming that any such decision should be taken by an assembly of the workers involved, not by the National Railroad Council. However, this attempt to make demagogical use of anarch-syndicalist arguments apparently did not seriously hamper the council's efforts to establish a single rail system in Republican Spain, since the Communists' influence among the railroad workers was minimal.[2]

The anarchist railroaders clearly looked upon the wartime arrangements for the organization and running of their industry as temporary, for the duration of the conflict, and to be replaced after the War by a fully collectivized form of organization. A national plenum of the Federación de la Industria Ferroviaria in March 1937 adopted a resolution setting forth in some detail the CNT proposals for ultimate workers' control of the country's railroads.

The resolution had 24 articles setting forth the Bases of Collectivization. The first of these proclaimed: 'All of the rail lines of Spain must form part of a single Collective and its organization and administration must be ratified by the workers themselves.' The second article Provided: 'There will pass to the Collective all assets and liabilities of the former firms, but financial charges will be nullified, such as debts before July 19 to non-collectivized firms, although foreign traffic arrangements will be respected.'

Most of the other articles of this resolution dealt with the internal organization of the railroad collective. The overall ruling body would be the national committee of the federation, elected by a national plenum, and below it would be regional committees, chosen by regional plenums. On each level, too, there would be 'professional committees'(the exact nature of which is not clearly spelled out), the members of which would be members of the regional and national committees of the federation, with voice but not a vote. On the national professional committee there would also be three delegates of 'the organism regulating the life of the nation' (presumably the government), one each from 'the departments of industry and commerce, finances, and public works'. They, too, would have a voice but not a vote in the national professional committee.

The resolution provided for the profitable parts of the national railway system to finance those which were not so profitable, and said also that if the railroad system as a whole had a deficit 'it will be the organism which regulates the life of the nation which is obliged to make up the deficit'. Any profits the overall operation of the railroads might render were to be used 'to improve the railroads' services and material'. There would be 'total unification of tariffs, regulations, signals, rights and duties, etc., etc.'

In accepted anarchist fashion, the resolution provided: 'Each comrade who enters the Collective will be assigned to the work for which he demonstrates preference and ability, taking account always of the best use of their energies for the benefit of the Collective.'

The railroad collective would also work towards the establishment of a coordinated transport system throughout the nation, including railroads, over-the-road transport, maritime services and air services.[3]

Several years after the Civil War, Fernando de los Rios, the Socialist leader who had been the Republic's ambassador to the United States during the conflict, concluded that the overall handling of the railroads by the unions during the War had been successful: 'The exploitation of the railways was entrusted to a committee in which the unions were the prevailing force. Considering the circumstances and the difficulties of management, the result was favorable.'[4]

The Catalan Railroads Under Workers' Control

In spite of the formal establishment of a single railroad system for all of Republican Spain, the railwaymen's unions in the various regions of the country continued to have a wide degree of autonomy in running the railroad system in their areas. This was particularly the case in Catalonia, Aragón and the Levante region.

An early issue of the *Boletín de Información* of the CNT–FAI described the first moves of the Catalan workers to take over that region's railroads. It reported that on Monday, July 21st, the workers took over the MZA (Madrid–Zaragoza–Alicante) and Norte lines:

> They constituted Revolutionary Committees and organized the defense of the stations with guards of riflemen and machine-gunners. On the MZA it is the comrades of the *sindicato* of the CNT who were the first to come and confront the task of reorganization of the service. However, room was made in the Revolutionary Committee of the stations for the UGT in equal proportion. On the Norte line it is also the *sindicatos* of the CNT which took the initiative in the occupation, later making room also for the UGT in equal proportion...
>
> By railroad telegraph it was communicated to all the stations that the *sindicato* of the CNT had taken over the firm. This news is received everywhere with satisfaction. A Station Committee of the CNT was named, at the disposal of which was placed the

Police and all the dependencies. There proceeded the naming by circular, ratifying the orders transmitted in the first moment, of revolutionary subcommittees in the most important stations: Sabadell, Terrasa, Manresa, Granollers, Vich and Ripoll. Relations were established with Lérida, where the comrades had constituted a committee.

This same article noted that one of the first actions of the railway workshop in San Andrés was to place armor on two locomotives and two cars, which were used almost immediately to take militiamen to the Aragón front. Also, on the request of the Central Militia Committee a hospital train was made ready.[5]

While action was being taken in each locality to place the local railroad facilities under CNT (and later CNT–UGT) control, the same kind of move was occurring in Barcelona to take over the general management of the railroads of the region. Gaston Leval has described this process in the case of the Madrid–Zaragoza–Alicante enterprise:

On the 20th of July, when the battle was still going on, the hierarchical personnel of the company were summoned. The interview, which took place in the room of the Council of Administration, had dramatic characteristics. The worker delegates had been in this room many times, to present problems on behalf of their comrades. The administrators had received them with insolence, without even asking them to sit down. Now there were together some thirty technicians and administrators, standing, not able to believe what they saw. Three workers – three members of the *sindicato* – seated on the chairs until then reserved for the hierarchy, and supported by a group of workers armed with rifles who were in the corridor, spoke to them firmly:

'We have called you to demand your resignations, as well as renunciation of all rights which you may have acquired in the company.' Emotion took hold of almost all those who had until then been arrogant bosses. Some began to weep, particularly when the director, who as always was late, appeared and saw the situation. They had to resign themselves and sign. The workers took over the direction of the railroad network.[6]

A few days later, legal cover was given to the workers' seizure of control of the Catalan railroads. On July 31, a document addressed 'To All the Personnel', signed by the councillor of government of the Generalidad of Catalonia, and by representatives of the CNT and UGT railroad workers organizations announced this fact. It noted that the two union groups had 'informed the Generalidad of Catalonia' of their seizure of control of the railroads, and the Generalidad, 'taking note of that, had no objections and accepts the fact of seizure', on four conditions. These were that an inventory of what had been taken over be made within ten days, that there be an accounting of the funds in the safes of the firms, that anything else belonging to the seized firms also be inventoried, and that the Generalidad 'reserves the right to an intervention in the seizure'. This 'intervention' should consist of a 'delegate ... whose mission will consist exclusively of keeping track of the exploitation and the income received from all phases of the same, with the basic objective that the latter be used for payment of the personnel and its improve- ment, as well as taking care of the costs of exploitation and amortiza- tion, it being well understood that the obligations corresponding to the former rights of stock and bondholders under no circumstances will be included.'

Finally, the document said that the Generalidad de Catalonia 'recognizes the right of the aforementioned trade union organizations to organize all of the services, technical and industrial as well as bureaucratic, in the way they think most appropriate for the best operation...' while at the same time promising to give 'all the advice and counsel which it deems useful in the technical aspect, when this is requested.'[7]

During the first weeks after the outbreak of the Civil War, there was a certain amount of confusion on the Catalan railroads, which I actually experienced. Arriving in Port-Bou about a month after the outbreak of the conflict, I asked members of the local militia com- mittee (after finally being authorized to proceed to Barcelona) how much it cost to go to the Catalan capital. To my surprise (and pleasure) I was informed that there was now no charge for travelling on the Catalan railroads. There wasn't, at least not on the Port–Bou–Barcelona line in August 1936.

Gaston Leval has confirmed the decentralization and improvization characteristic of the Catalan railroads during the first months of the War: 'Until the middle of 1937, orientation did not come from the Central Committee of Barcelona. On the one hand, the manual workers who made it up could not replace rapidly the former administrators, and on the other, such replacement had not been necessary. The work went on simply as it had always done. The personnel of each section continued simply to do its job. The members of the Central Committee contented themselves with keeping track of the general activity and coordinating the lines. They slowly united the parts of the organism and prepared for better future cohesion.'[8]

Finally, there was established a regional central committee which was in charge of all rail lines in Catalonia. It consisted of a president, secretary, a representative of each of the three divisions of the system–traffic, technical services and administration – and one from the sub-sections dealing with various aspects of work of the enterprise.[9] The central committee had equal representation of the CNT and UGT railroaders' unions.[10]

Workers' control worked on all the levels of the Catalan railroad system, according to Leval:

> All of the divisional committees were made up of equal numbers of representatives of the CNT and the UGT. For the organization of traffic, there were established zones of demarcation with committees, whose members, representing the services, work on their jobs, and meet after work. They control the general activities and send the divisional committees their observations and initiatives. They are named directly by the workers of these zones, or by the central committee, with the approval of the divisions concerned. Each demarcation committee elects someone responsible for the administrative function of the local office.
>
> In each dependency, station, workshop or brigade, the workers

freely name a responsible delegate charged with directing and coordinating the services. The sections of each line who think it necessary establish a control committee. In localities where there are sections of different lines, they establish a liaison committee...[11]

The workers' (and particularly CNT) control of the railroad lines of Catalonia was weakened after the May Days of 1937 and a few months later, the movement of the national government to Barcelona. At some time thereafter, Rafael Hernández, a Socialist railwayman from Asturias, who had succeeded in escaping to Barcelona, was appointed '*comandante* of the Barcelona transport commission'. He told Ronald Fraser several decades later that he found the Catalan railroads not working well because 'no one was in charge'. He added: 'The stationmasters were no longer in charge of their stations. Instead, there was a station committee, made up of guards and representatives of other railway personnel, and an engine drivers' committee. If the latter decided against the former's decision to run a train to the frontier, for example, it didn't run.'

Consequently, according to Fraser, 'He summoned stationmasters and sub-masters and told them it was their task to run a scheduled train service under his command. Anyone who opposed them would be thrown in jail. If they failed in their duty it would be on their heads...'[12]

The Catalan railroads had serious problems arising from the War. These included the difficulty in obtaining coal. Although some came in from the Asturias region in the early months, as well as from Great Britain, efforts were made to increase local sources in Catalonia. Existing coal mines, which provided a poor type of coal, were expanded. In addition, as a result of the initiative of people in a town about 60 kilometres from Barcelona, a deposit of low-grade coal was found there. The railroad workers themselves exploited it, although it was very difficult, since none of them were miners, and they did not have adequate equipment.

To try to counteract the shortage of coal, those in charge of the Catalan railroads drew up extensive plans for electrification of the lines in the region.[13] Although the exigencies of war made it impossible to carry out most of these plans, José Bricall has noted that the Catalan government spent some 480,000 pesetas on railroad electrification.[14]

In addition, after the fall of Bilbao to Franco, the railroads in Catalonia didn't have the iron and steel parts which they needed, particularly replacements for axles of cars which were damaged or which wore out. So they resorted to cannibalizing discarded railway cars which had axles which were still usable, and putting them on functioning cars.[15]

The railroads in the part of Aragón recovered by Loyalist forces were also under the control of the Catalan regional central committee. There, the workers of the MZA line 'with the collaboration of the collectives of some Aragón villages and with the dynamic direction of Comrade Engineer Vila, constructed a branch line in record time, from Puebla de Hijar to the coal mines of Utrillas.'

One of the most serious problems faced by the union administration of the Catalan railroads was the great inequality of payment among various groups of workers. On the one hand, those who had been employed on some of the financially weaker railroad firms, received close to starvation wages. It was decided to establish a wage of 10 pesetas a day for all workers in the system.

In addition, there was a problem of many temporary workers, particularly in the maintenance of way section. Many years later, the anarchist exile newspaper *CNT* noted: 'So that they could not cease being temporary, which prevented them from making any demands and from receiving small concessions made to permanent workers, the foremen had permanent instructions to dismiss them after three months, and curiously, they were dismissed today and given work again the next day.'

It was decided that all of these workers would become permanent workers on the unionized railroads. The Catalan CNT railroad workers also demanded that the same thing be done for the temporary workers on the railroads in other parts of Republican Spain. To their surprise, not only the government representatives on the Republican rail administration but also the UGT representatives on that body at first opposed this. However, after some time the temporary workers on all of the Republican railroads were given permanent status.[16]

The Valencian Railroads Under Workers' Control

In the morning of July 18 1936, the secretary of the Valencia branch of the CNT railroaders' federation was informed by phone from Madrid that the military uprising had begun there, that a general strike had been declared in Madrid, and that the decision had been taken by the CNT to take over the railroads, to prevent the army from moving. He was told to have the local committee of the railroad workers go through all sections of the railroad in the city and dismiss any managers who were of doubtful loyalty. At that point, the head of the UGT railroad workers local union informed the CNT leader that he had gotten a similar message from Madrid UGT head-quarters. They then worked together to remove doubtful management officials.

One such official was a Basque Catholic, Sr Zañártu, head of maintenance of way, who was very conservative politically. However, when the workers in his department vouched for him and urged that he remain in his post, the union leaders agreed. Subsequently the local CNT leader supported his admission to the CNT union, when it was decreed that all the employees of the railroad had to belong to either the CNT or the UGT. Ultimately, most of the dismissed managerial people were restored to their previous positions, under the continuing scrutiny of trade union leaders.

The Valencia railroaders faced a particular problem with railroad workers who had fled from Franco-occupied areas and who, according to the previously existing collective agreements, had the right to employment in the Valencia region and to special payment as transferees. This double payment to railroaders from other areas aroused considerable resistance among the Valencian workers. The local CNT railroad workers leaders finally were able to work out a compromise on the issue, by which the double payment was made only until the transferees had been able to settle into new jobs and housing. This was one aspect of the more general problem of the stream of refugees which continued to pour into remaining Republican areas, as the Franco armies advanced.

Under workers' management, steps were taken to reduce the inequality of compensation among the Valencian railroad workers. Whereas, before July 19, the lowest paid workers, the gatekeepers, got only two and a half pesetas an hour, while locomotive engineers received 1,000 a month, the minimum wage for all workers was raised to 10 pesetas an hour – the same wage received by soldiers in the Popular Army.[17]

Railroads and Other Transport in the Cantabrian Regions

As elsewhere in Loyalist Spain, the pre-existing railroad companies in Asturias were merged into a single system in January 1937 by the Consejo Interprovincial de Asturias y León, the new Loyalist administration in that region. In the following month, the *consejo* proposed to its counterparts in Santander and the Basque country the establishment of a single railroad system for the three Republican areas of the north. However, it was not until July, when the final campaign of the Franco forces to liquidate the northern front was well under way that the formal approval of the establishment of such a unified rail system was received from the National Railroad Council.

The National Railroad Council's decree provided for unification of the railway system in the north as part of its general scheme for establishing a single railroad network for the whole country. It also provided that in the body charged with running the railways in the north, there should be representation of both the CNT and UGT railroad workers' unions. Although concrete information about how the railways were run during the War in the North is lacking, it is presumed that the actual management of them, particularly in Asturias, was in the hands of the two unions.

More difficult in the north than the railroads was the problem of road transport. On the outbreak of the War, local revolutionary committees had commandeered buses, trucks and even private cars. The Comité Provincial of Asturias issued orders to the local committees to put all vehicles under their control at the disposal of that *comité*'s provincial department of transport, but apparently there was considerable resistance to this measure on the part of the local committees.

The Comité Provincial took over at the beginning of October, the largest road transport company of Asturias, the Automoviles Iuarca SA, which maintained bus services and carried the mail. It was reconstituted as Omnibus ALSA, which was run by a directive committee, consisting principally of representatives of the CNT and UGT unions, directly elected by the manual and white-collar workers.[18]

Urban Transport Collectives in Barcelona

One of the collectivization efforts of which the anarchists were most proud was that of urban transport in Barcelona and its environs. By all odds, the most important part of the transport system consisted of the trolleycar lines, some 60 in all, with about 7,000 workers, of whom 6,500 belonged to the transport and Communications Workers' Union of the CNT. In addition, there were smaller subway, bus and taxi transport sections.[19]

The trolleycar system had been particularly disrupted by the fighting in Barcelona on July 19–20, because of the construction of barricades across streets, and the knocking down of dozens of posts carrying the electrical wires used by the system. According to an article in *Solidaridad Obrera*, reviewing the trolleycar workers' collective, the workers had been out even before the fighting had completely ceased, clearing streets and replacing the posts.[20]

On July 20, when the fighting was still underway in Barcelona, the trolleycar section of the union sent a seven-man delegation to take over the headquarters of the trolleycar company. That committee then summoned a meeting of delegates of the various sections, such as the electrical plant, repair shop, transit, etc., and at that meeting it was decided to reorganize the trolleycar enterprise.

The next day, all members of the staff – both manual workers and technical personnel – were summoned to a general assembly. This meeting ratified the decision to take over the control and management of the trolleycar system. Within five days of the end of fighting, the trolleys were circulating once again, newly painted red and black and emblazoned 'CNT–FAI'.[21]

Even non-anarchists were impressed with the speed and efficiency with which the workers got the public transport system back in operation. Andrés Nin, leader of the Partido Obrero de Unificación Marxista during the first part of the War, compared the slowness of reestablishment of public transport after the Bolshevik Revolution in Russia – a matter of months – and the rapidity with which that was accomplished by the anarchist workers in Barcelona.

Gaston Leval has described the way in which the worker-controlled enterprise was organized: 'Each section had at its head an engineer named in agreement with the union, and a representative of the workers. At the second level, the assembled delegates constituted the local general committee. The sections met separately when they were dealing with specific activities. And when general problems were involved, all the workers of all kinds met in general assembly. From the base to the top, the organization was federalist...'[22]

During the period of workers' control of the trolleycar system, a number of improvements were made in it. A new system for hanging the cables used by the trolleycars was installed which eliminated many if not most of the metal posts which, in many of the narrow streets of Barcelona, were a frequent cause of accidents. In addition, in collaboration with the water, gas and electricity *sindicato* a number of electric transformers which had been located in such a way as to cause the trolleys to make brusque turns and were also the cause of accidents, were 'more rationally' located.

Equipment of the workshops of the enterprise was substantially improved. A new lathe, of US origin, costing 200,000 pesetas was purchased in France. Two new drills, costing 80,000 pesetas, were also acquired, as was an electric furnace used to make shaft bearings, and a variety of other machines.[23]

The result of these acquisitions was to make the workshops of the enterprise much more self-sufficient than they had been. In March 1938, *Solidaridad Obrera* announced that the workshops now provided 98 percent of the equipment needed by the trolley cars, in comparison with only 2 per cent before the enterprise had been taken over by the workers. It said that the only things the enterprise's workshops could not produce were foundry products.[24]

From the point of view of the services rendered to its customers, and even in financial terms, the trolleycar workers' collective was successful. *Solidaridad Obrera* noted in March 1938 that, whereas the trolleycars had carried 97,937,748 passengers between January 1 and July in 1936, and 85,605,516 between July 24 and December 31, for a total of 183,543,361 for the whole year, in 1937 it had carried 233,557,508, an increase of more than 50,000,000 passengers.

That same article noted the financial difficulties faced by the workers' committee of control when it took over the enterprise, and the way it overcame them. Pay day fell on July 20, so they immediately had to pay out 295,535.65 pesetas in wages, and also had to pay bills for materials which were owed by the old company, amounting to 1,272,322.18 pesetas. It not only met these immediate drains on the enterprise's treasury but, by the end of 1936, had some 3,313,594.70 pesetas in its coffers. *Solidaridad Obrera* concluded:

> A triumph of will and intelligence had been achieved. That balance sheet, which in the last days of July of 1936 might have predicted a financial failure for insufficiency of funds due to the evident abnormality of the service, produced by such exceptional circumstances, had been resolved without the least official aid, to the satisfaction of all: of the public, which saw assured the continuation of the trolleycar and other urban transport services so essential for the life of the city, due to the creative capacity of the organization of the workers themselves; and the workers, who had confirmed that their efforts had been compensated for by such excellent results, and with natural satisfaction of a duty fulfilled.[25]

The system of payment for travelling on the trolleycars was simplified. Before July 19, fares had ranged from 10 centesimos to 40, depending on the length of one's trip. A 20 centesimo fare was instituted for all trips. This was not changed for almost two years.[26]

At the end of December 1937, the Comité de Control announced that as of January 1 1938, all schoolchildren of 15 or under would be given free passes to go to and from school.[27]

The Barcelona urban transport collective was officially legalized under the collectivization decree of the Generalidad de Catalonia on June 28 1937. Thereafter, according to Walther Bernecker, there was a tendency for the authority of the *sindicato* to gain more power in the collective, *vis-à-vis* the local control committees in its various sections. Even before that, the *sindicato* had taken most of the profits of the enterprise, and had used them to subsidize the financially weaker lines, as well as to pay taxes to the Generalidad. After the establishment of the Caja de Credito Industrial y Comercial late in 1937, it received most of the profits of the collective.[28]

The trolleycars were only the largest part of the Barcelona transport system. One reason for the growth of their patronage was certainly the increasing difficulty of getting gasoline for internal combustion vehicles, particularly the taxis, but to a less degree also the buses.

Fortunately, there exists a manuscript about the collective organized by the workers of the former Compañía General de Autobuses SA de Barcelona, which took the name of Autobuses G after the workers took it over, and was by far the largest bus workers' collective in Barcelona, written by J. Barconi, a member of the collective's control committee. It indicates that the company was seized by the Sindicato del Transporte y Comunicaciones (Sección Autobuses) before fighting had completely ceased in the streets of Barcelona.

A six-man group of workers constituted the temporary control committee for the enterprise, in which position they were apparently confirmed by a general assembly of the workers. When they opened the documents of the former management, they found, among other things, lists of the 'dangerous' and 'very dangerous' union leaders, from the company management's point of view, as well as lists of company spies.

Although top officials of the firm had disappeared, most of the technical personnel remained. The new worker leaders of the collective invited them to continue to work, and dismissed only three as of dubious loyalty to the new regime. According to Barconi, the technicians were enthusiastic participants in the collective, since they were given much more freedom of action than they had had before, and their suggestions for improvement of the operation of the enterprise were taken seriously by the worker leaders of the collective.

The clerical workers of Autobuses G were brought together in one large office, where they had much closer contact, were able to work more efficiently and in a more sociable atmosphere.

New machinery was soon installed in the workshops, and the repair shops of the enterprise were consolidated. The collective began for the first time to construct complete buses, and subsequently also made some war material.[29]

For some time, the repair shops of the bus system were apparently one of the show places of the CNT. Visiting Barcelona about a month after the outbreak of the Civil War, I was taken to visit that installation, after I had asked to see one of the worker-controlled enterprises in the Catalan capital. After more than half a century, the only thing I remember about this visit is the claim of the workers there that they had substantially increased the output of the repair shops, including the construction of new buses.

At about the same time, Franz Borkenau was also taken to see this same part of the Barcelona transport collective:

> Only three weeks after the beginning of the civil war, two weeks after the end of the general strike, it seems to run as smoothly as if nothing had happened. I visited the men at their machines. The room looked tidy, the work was done in a regular manner. Since socialization, this factory had repaired two buses, finished one which had been under construction, and constructed a completely new one. The latter wore the inscription 'constructed under workers' control'. It had been completed, the management claimed, in five days, as against an average of seven days under the previous management...'
>
> Things could not have been made to look nice for the benefit of a visitor, had they really been in a bad muddle. Nor do I think

that any preparations were made for my visit. Still, one must certainly not generalize from this one experience.[30]

Various changes were made in the bus service of Autobuses G. A number of new bus routes were established, particularly in areas formerly without service. Also, free passes were provided for members of the collective as well as for schoolchildren (who were given little badges of identification in their schools), soldiers and the handicapped. Also, it was decided that those who would stand in the front of the buses should travel free.

There were also various work changes made by Autobuses G. Three suits of clothing were given each year to the chauffeurs and fare collectors. Regular rations of milk were given to workers in the workshops doing the hardest work. Differentiation in pay was maintained, but the number of pay categories was greatly reduced. Also, as a result of the exigencies of war, women increasingly took the place of men who entered the armed forces, throughout the enterprise.

Changes were also made in fringe benefits. Pensions for widows of white-collar workers were eliminated (since manual workers' widows did not receive them), but the women were offered jobs in the collective. Financial aid was offered to all of the children of the members of the collective who maintained their standing in school. The collective maintained a hospital for its ill and recuperating members.

In the beginning, there were frequent meetings of the six members of the control-commission of the collective with their counterparts in other collectives of the *sindicato*. However, subsequently, a delegated body consisting of two members of each collective was established. However, Barconi insisted that it was a 'federal' body, and the autonomy of the various collectives was maintained.

After Juan Comorera of the Stalinist Partido Socialista Unificado de Catalonia became councillor of commerce in the government of Catalonia, he launched an attack on all of the CNT collectives, including that of Autobuses G. Attempts to undermine the collective included the procedure of having large numbers of police board a bus, take seats and refuse to pay their fare. Comorera refused to provide the foreign exchange the collective needed to import equipment it needed for its workshops. A one point, the headquarters of the collective was raided late at night, and its papers were strewn around. Finally, the PSUC members of the municipal council pushed it into resolving to 'municipalize' the city's public transport system, obviously to transfer control of it from the CNT to the Stalinists. However, when a *pleno* of the Barcelona CNT unanimously rejected this idea, no further move was made to dispossess the CNT collectives before the fall of the city to the Franco forces.[31]

Another aspect of transport which was collectivized was trucking. This sector was divided into two parts, civil and military, both of which were controlled by the CNT, at least during the first year of the Civil War. The CNT had taken over all of the trucking firms and organized them into a collective, which served the needs of the civilian population.

In addition, the Consejería de Defensa of the Generalidad had its own military transport operation. At least until the ouster of the anarchists from the Catalan government, this, too, was headed by officials of the CNT transport workers' union, and it collaborated closely with the civilian collective.

From time to time the military transport system of the Catalan government needed to use some of the trucks controlled by the civilian collective. At least during the first year of the War, it was the practice of the collective to lend to the Consejería de Defensa the trucks which it needed, rather than renting them to the government.[32]

Collectivization of Urban Transport in Valencia

In Valencia, too, the municipal transport system was collectivized. The Unidad Sindical de Auto-Tranvias was founded, including the 1,514 workers who had been employed by the Trolleycar and Railroad Co. of Valencia and the Valencia Bus Co., including 1,300 of the trolley company and 214 bus employees. The great majority of these had belonged to the CNT before the outbreak of the War, and at a general assembly of the workers it was agreed that a poll would be taken, and whichever union had a majority would accept into its ranks those belonging to the other organization. Thus, all joined the CNT.

The workers' council of the Unidad Sindical de Auto-Tranvias consisted of seven members, five from the trolleycars and two from the bus workers. Each part of the council had various sections, dealing with traffic, workshops, maintenance of way, and technical and administrative services. Each section had its own council to deal with specific problems, elected by the workers of that section.

One of the first problems which the workers' collective had was that the great majority of passengers refused to pay their fares, whether on the trolleycars or the buses. The Consejo Obrero running the enterprise finally got in touch with all of the trade union and political organizations of consequence in the region, and got their support. As a result, by the end of 1936, the enterprise was generally collecting their regular fares.

The workers' enterprise expanded the workshop of the trolleycar system. It also spent resources on projects to take care of refugees from Franco-occupied parts of the country, as well as on the construction of several schools and a sanatorium. Finally, the collective established a retirement and illness fund for its members and their families.

The collective increased workers' wages from an average of 10 pesetas a day, to 13.50 to 14.50 pesetas. But at the same time, it appropriated 200,000 pesetas for the support of the 100 members who had joined the militia forces at the various fronts.[33]

Other parts of the transport system of Valencia were taken over and organized by the CNT's Sindicato del Transporte de Levante. Those in this transport collective included 2,350 stevedores who loaded and unloaded ships in the harbor, 1,700 freight loaders who worked in railroad stations, the port and in warehouses, 1,300 horse-drawn cart drivers, who had 800 horses and 1,500 different kinds of carts, 200 bus chauffeurs and collectors, 425 taxi-drivers, who had 315 vehicles, and various groups of auxiliary workers.

The general assembly of the union elected a committee in charge of the whole operation. It maintained a central secretariat, in which each part of the union was represented, to coordinate transport in the city and its environs. It established a special service with the railroads, 'to transport in the capital and outside it all kinds of merchandise ... which enormously facilitates the work, ending obstacles in this class of service ... which is rigorously controlled and nothing has been lost or gone astray.' The taxi-drivers established an emergency service, available night and day. In general, the collective saw to it that its various services functioned seven days a week.[34]

Collectivization of Other Land Transport

Throughout most of Republican Spain, the unions, particularly those of the CNT, took control of other kinds of land transport, such as inter-urban bus lines, and trucking concerns. There are no precise figures on the extent of this type of collectivization, although the indications are that it was widespread.

In the northern region of Santander, it was the Socialists' Unión General de Trabajadores which took over the local privately owned trolleycar system. The president of the UGT trolleycar workers' union became president of the collective and other members of the executive constituted themselves the directors of the firm. The trolleycar system there reportedly worked well under union control and was quite prosperous. One reason for this was the elimination of the competition of small family-controlled buses, whose drivers did not belong to any union. As soon as the War began, the buses were seized and were sent with the militiamen to the front.[35]

Many, if not most, of the rural collectives in various parts of the country had at least a few trucks under their own control, as did some of the collectivized urban industrial enterprises. Elsewhere in this volume, I describe how the anarchist-controlled Council of Aragón organized a bus service which went from one end of the region to the other. But aside from these, local *sindicatos*, and *comarcal* and regional federations of transport unions had their own collectives.

As was the case in farming areas and in the cities, the transport unions of the CNT sought not only to maintain the service needed for the war effort and the service of the civilian population, but also to organize their sector of the economy on a long-term basis, as nearly in conformity with anarchist ideas as was possible under the circumstances. This was reflected in resolutions adopted at a regional plenum of transport unions of the center, which met in Madrid in the middle of March 1937:

> To structure the economy of the socialization of the Transport Industry, there will be created economic councils which will be charged with regularizing the contracting of the services provided and at the same time satisfying the needs of the industry, such as conservation of materials, organization and payment of wages of those participating in the socialization, and finally the uninterrupted progress which the industry needs to become larger every day. These councils, in the regional, provincial and *comarcal* federations and in the *sindicatos* will have close mutual relations, so as to know the needs of each, with the objective that when one of the organisms needs solidarity, it can be provided by those which are in a better situation.

This plenum also took steps to assure greater equality among the various groups making up the regional transport federation. Although not at the moment trying to establish total wage equality among the members, it did resolve to work towards establishment of such equality. It also provided that the profits made by the more prosperous *sindicatos* or local or *comarcal* federations should go to the regional federation, which would use them to help those units which were less well-off. Similarly, it agreed that those local groups which had more trucks or buses than they needed should make them available to units which had shortages of equipment – although it also provided that those groups receiving the use of equipment from other parts of the Regional Federation should bear the costs of operating them.[36]

The Issue of Militarization of Transport

One problem with which the CNT's transport collectives were faced was the threat of the 'militarization' of transport by the Republican government. The CNT was strongly opposed to that, although expressing its perfect willingness to make transport facilities available to the military in emergencies.

The National Committee of Transport Unions of Spain, representing the regional federations of those unions in the Center, Levante and Catalonia, addressed a document 'To the Antifascist and Revolutionary People' in June 1937, arguing against militarization of transport:

> For some time there has been talk of militarization of transport, but without a solid basis, without firm arguments which can convince us. Civilian transport has another different mission from that of war transport; although they have some relationship, it is not enough so that there should be taken from the *sindicatos* that which for reason and logic belongs to them. To militarize civilian transport is equivalent to creating an army corps, where the workers will be simple functionaries of the State, at the service, and without the right to give their opinions, but only to obey. If the State takes over the exploitation of this industry, the workers will completely lose their personality, being submitted to a rigid discipline, being reduced to the condition of automatons...
>
> The militarization of transport is one more maneuver of those men who embody and defend authoritarian centralism, and consequently the complete annulment of man as the directive element of production and consumption, and as the principal factor in the economic development of the State...
>
> The Regional Transport Federations signing this manifesto, together with the National Committee of the same, are not disposed to tolerate the militarization of civilian transport, believing that only the *sindicatos* are competent to exploit these services, and not the Ministry of Public Works or any other official organism.[37]

By November 1937, the CNT transport workers' unions had considerably modified their attitude. A plenum of the transport federations of the Levante, the Center and Catalonia in that month adopted a resolution which, among other things, stated:

> In the various parts of the transport industry and particularly in animal and mechanical transport, the transport *sindicatos* of the CNT will not oppose any resistance, so long as their personality is respected, to the requisition of material, garages, etc., always provided that the personnel of these is employed by the Government, which will pay them the wages which are their due...
>
> The Transport *sindicatos* will accept and will offer to the antifascist cause, adjusting themselves to the decrees published by the ministry of National Defense, the personnel which because of its physical condition and technical competence will be qualified to carry out the job for which it is called.

The last part of this resolution sounded an almost plaintive note. It pledged the regional federations 'to maintain as much as we are able, the collectives already created and those which may be created, always providing that to do so is not a drawback to the economy or doesn't prejudice the war effort.[38]

Workers' Control in the Maritime Industry

Workers' control of the Spanish Republican merchant marine did not go by any means as far as it did in land-based economic activities. Although the unions moved in the first days and weeks following the suppression of the military rebellion in much of litoral Spain to take over the headquarters of the country's major shipping lines, the Republican government also moved rather quickly to try to get control of as much of the merchant marine as possible. Furthermore, almost from the outset of the War, units of the Loyalist merchant fleet were subject to military action by not only those segments of the Spanish Navy which the Rebels seized, but also from foreign, particularly Italian, warships, particularly submarines. As a consequence, the maintenance of shipboard discipline and the need to keep the services of experienced merchant marine officers was peculiarly acute.

The upshot of this was that on board ships, and even in the ports, a modified form of collective bargaining, along pre-July 19 lines, seems to have largely prevailed. This was supplemented by a modified system of union delegates whose jobs were to help assure the efficiency of the shipping services and to keep a wary eye on captains and other officers about whose loyalty there might be some doubt. On a national level, the maritime unions of the CNT and UGT tried to exert as much influence over the functioning of the merchant navy as wartime conditions would permit.

In the port of Barcelona, the principal change after July 19 was the elimination of labor contractors and other middlemen who had thrived there before. Augustine Souchy has described the situation both before and after July 19: 'At the expense of the low wages and poor working conditions for longshoremen, the racketeers dominated the waterfront before July 19. 'The waterfront reeked with graft, waste and stealing. The racketeers and the ship agents, ship captains and longshore bosses were all in collusion...'

Souchy goes on to say: 'After July 19th, the port and maritime unions got rid of the racketeers and their agents. They decided to deal directly, without go-betweens, with the ship captains and the ship companies. This led to the takeover of labor operations by the newly formed port workers' collective. While contracts already made between foreign ship companies and their agents could not be cancelled, the unions closely supervised the financial operations of the Spanish agents of the foreign ship companies.'[39]

A CNT publication of the period noted an agreement between the CNT union and the shipping firms operating in the port:

[The union's] Junta Administrativa will receive the payments for loading and unloading in accordance with existing rates, it will organize the groups of workers and will pay the wages. The warehouses, ship owners, and agents will not recognize any other agency than the Sindicato Unico del Transporte of the

CNT. With this fact, the Confederation, in addition to taking a large step towards the socialization of wealth, imposes absolute control...

This collective contract will permit easy knowledge of movement in the port of Barcelona: entry and exit of ships, tonnage and types of merchandise, etc., since that control resides entirely in the hands of the Sindicato del Transporte.[40]

Souchy noted: 'These changes brought much higher wages and better working conditions for the longshoremen. By setting aside a certain sum for each ton of cargo handled, unemployment, health and accident protection and other benefits were provided.'[41]

The headquarters in Barcelona of the CIA Transatlantica, one of the principal Spanish overseas shipping lines, were taken over first by members of the UGT. However, soon afterwards a joint UGT–CNT central committee was established, with three members for each union, as well as representatives of the Catalan and Republican governments. This Committee took over not only the ships of the company but its cash and bank accounts.

The central committee dismissed all of the top officials of the firm. However, all of the technicians of the company stayed on the job.

The workers' committee agreed to the request of the Catalan Comité Central de Milicias to make two of the company's ships available to be used as jails, and one as a hospital ship. The rest of the vessels were put back into normal operation. It was recorded that, 'The old shipboard committees continued to carry out their functions, as technical committees, subordinate to the Central Committee'. At least at first, the sailors refused to accept the 40-hour week decreed by the Generalidad de Catalonia, and continued to work 48 hours. Also, they rejected the 15 percent wage increase decreed by the Generalidad.[42]

During the period of extended Catalan autonomy between July 1936 and May 1937, ships and boats operating out of Catalan ports were under the general jurisdiction of the councillorship of public services of the regional government. According to a report of CNTer Juan Domenech, when he held that councillorship, there were six ships of 16,000 tons or more, and 'hundreds' of vessels of between 180 and 300 tons operating out of Catalan towns and cities, with a total overall tonnage of some 600,000.[43]

Although relatively little information is available about the organization of that part of the Republican merchant marine which operated during the first year of the War out of the northern regions of Vizcaya, Santander and Asturias, the maritime workers of that part of the republic issued a declaration of May 1937, shortly before the Franco army began its all-out attack on that part of Loyalist Spain. It announced the formation of an Inter-Regional Committee of Maritime Transport, by 'the UGT and CNT organizations of Bilbao, Santander and Gijón and Solidarios Vascos of Bilbao'. The last group was the trade union organization closely allied with the Basque Nationalist Party.

This proclamation particularly stressed the need for seamen loyal to the Republic in the struggle with Spanish, Italian, German and Portuguese fascism, to continue to sail in spite of the military menace from enemy naval forces, and to be vigilant against anyone in their own ranks whose loyalty might be doubtful: 'We draw tighter and tighter our union; we shall sacrifice what we have to sacrifice to crush in Spain the international fascism which attempts to invade our country. Above Spain in ruins, we shall develop the society which we have dreamed of, where there do not exist the exploiters and the exploited.'[44]

Late in 1937, after the fall of Vizcaya, Santander and Asturias, the Federación Nacional del Transporte, Pesca e Industrias Maritimas of the CNT and the Sindicato Nacional del Transporte Maritimo of the UGT established a liaison committee, 'with executive character' and with equal representation of both unions. The proclamation announcing the establishment of this organization said: 'Both trade union organizations accept, as a first step towards socialization of the maritime transport industry, as well as for the best and most immediate reorganization of the general economy, and the greatest efficiency in the use for war purposes, the total takeover of the industry by the Government of the Republic.'

The document then pledged that both organizations: 'will support and cooperate in the purging and reorganization of the General

Directorate of the Merchant Marine ... organizing their direction and administration in accordance with ... the necessities of the national economy.' It proposed the establishment of a body to study and draw up such a reorganization.

There were then interesting indications of the way the merchant marine was organized and functioning at that time: the structure of shipboard committees would continue to be 'the present one', and that 'during the permanence of the ship at sea or in port, the functions of the Committee will be limited to internal questions, 1. Control of administration and cooperation in the shipboard work, 2. moral and intellectual training of the crew through newspapers, books, instructive lectures...'

The document continued to describe how union members on each ship would elect a 'trade union delegate', to be a link between the crew and the unions, who would inform the unions at the end of each voyage, concerning what had occurred during the trip. Also, 'in case of difficulties arising at sea, these should be known by the trade union delegate.'

Evidence of the situation on board the ships of the Republican merchant marine was outlined: 'The organization of labor on the ships will be the responsibility of the captain, provided his support of the cause has been proven...' The captain could delegate his authority to 'the first officer above deck and the first machinist in the engine room... The political commissars who are active on the ships, as a result of the decree of June 12, will be elected on the proposal of the maritime trade union organizations, with equal representation of the UGT and the CNT.'

The last segment of this document dealt with the 'shipboard bonus' to be paid to those who went to sea in the face of enemy action.[45]

Clearly, there was no general collectivization of the merchant marine such as took place in the national railroad system, and in various parts of the industrial sector of the economy of Republican Spain. However, the Spanish merchant navy was by no means entirely immune from the revolutionary wave which spread over the Republic at the beginning of the Civil War-Revolution.

591

Collectivization of Catalan Public Utilities

The public utilities – gas supplies, electric power and water supply – were collectivized to a greater or less degree by the workers in Republican Spain. As in other parts of the Republican economy, there was considerable diversity in these workers'-controlled experiments.

The POUMist leader Juan Andrade, in his general discussion of workers' collectives early in 1937, noted that in the public utility area the organization on a trade union rather than local shop basis had predominated: 'Syndicalization in these industries has been relatively easy. One can say that the workers of the unionized public service industries are today those who enjoy a situation of greatest privilege in so far as security of income, and hence, of payment of wages. Since they have not only been able to maintain their wages, but have augmented them in many cases, they have appreciated directly the benefits of the change in the situation. As they continue to receive benefits, it has been possible to absorb all those formerly unemployed, whereas in other areas not only did unemployment not decrease, but it increased. The lack of competition permits the regulation of prices.'[46]

In Catalonia, since 1927, the CNT had had a union covering the workers in electricity, gas and water supplies of the region. It was this organization which took over control of these three industries once the military uprising had been suppressed.

On July 20 1936, while the fighting in the streets of Barcelona was still under way, a group of workers of the three activities met to take measures to ensure the continuation of service once the battle had been won. Soon afterwards, general assemblies of the workers of the various services met and decided to keep them operating more or less as they had done before July 19. It was not until late in August that the CNT and UGT formally decided to take possession of electricity, gas and water throughout the region. Shortly thereafter, the Generalidad de Catalonia officially sanctioned this action.

Throughout Catalonia there were 610 electrical installations, including two large hydroelectric projects at Tremp and Camarsa, and many tiny ones centering on a single transformer or other installation. Many of these were organized before the Revolution as separate companies. Within six months of the beginning of the War, 70 percent of the firms with 99 percent of the output of electricity had been centralized in a single one.

After the ouster of the anarchists from the government of Catalonia, when the PSUC leader Juan Comorera was councillor of economy, the CNT-controlled Serveis Electrics Unificats de Catalunya was intervened by the Generalidad in October 1937, and placed under a commission 'of three delegates of the Generalidad and an advisory body made up of workers serving as a Control Committee'. Then in April 1938 the Republican government created the general commissariat of electricity and placed the Catalan electric system under it. This was done 'on the proposal of the Minister of National Defense', who happened to be the fellow-travelling prime minister, Juan Negrín.

The gas workers' collective was also taken over by the Catalan government in October 1937, apparently under conditions similar to those governing electricity.[47] Similar to the case of electricity, the pre-revolutionary enterprises in the gas industry had been united into a single operation. In contrast, the provision of water had been largely in the hands of one privately owned Spanish firm before the outbreak of the conflict, and so was taken over as a unit.

Most of those employed in these three industries were skilled workers. So, in the trade union reorganization, the lowest hierarchical unit was a section composed of 15 or more workers of a particular skill. When no one specialty had that number of workers, two or more more or less similar ones were joined to form a section. Each section elected two delegates, one a technician, the other a person designated to direct the work of the section.

These section delegates chose a 'building committee', to direct the operation of the local installation. Usually this committee consisted of a manual worker, a technician, and an administrative worker, although sometimes a fourth member was added, to maintain parity between the CNT and the UGT. The first of these delegates dealt with any problems that might arise among the different sections, received suggestions of the workers concerning the employment and dismissal of personnel. He also 'serves as intermediary between the base and the general council of the industry, and called periodical general assemblies of the sections.'

The technicians' delegate kept trace of production of the various sections, sought ways to increase productivity, inspected power lines, and kept statistics on production. The administrative delegate was in charge of most of the paperwork, ordered and saw to the warehousing of raw materials and handled correspondence.

The third step up in the hierarchy consisted of the industry councils, one each for electricity, gas and water. Each of these consisted of eight members, four from the CNT, four from the UGT, and half of each council was elected by general assemblies of the members of the CNT and UGT in the industry, the other half being chosen by the delegates of the technical sections, so as to ensure that there would be adequately trained people in the council.

At the top of the hierarchy was the General Council of Electricity, Gas and Water, also with eight members, equally divided between the CNT and the UGT. According to Gaston Leval, 'This council coordinates the activity of the three industries, harmonizes the distribution of production and raw materials from regional, national and international points of view; in sum, takes and applies all of the initiatives referred to it by the producers as a group, for production and various needs. But always it must submit its activities to the control of the trade union assemblies.'[48]

Various modifications were made in the three industries. Standard prices were introduced in each, for electricity, gas and water, instead of different prices in different areas, as had existed before. Also, rental charges for meters were abolished. Adolfo Bueso has claimed that the collective controlling the Barcelona water supply 'doubled its capital, completely improved all installations, as well as constructing low cost housing for its personnel.'[49]

As in the case of the railroads, the gas industry in Catalonia faced a serious shortage of coal, due to the fact that the Franco forces controlled most of the country's coal mines. The industry got most of its coal from Great Britain, delivered via transshipment to and from Oran, Algeria.[50]

Regular service was maintained from the beginning of the Civil War until Catalonia was finally overrun by Franco's troops. Even bombing attacks by Rebel aircraft only caused temporary interruptions of electricity and gas.[51]

One of the most famous public utilities in Barcelona to be taken over by its workers was the telephone system, belonging to the Compañía Telefónica Nacional de España, a subsidiary of the International Telephone and Telegraph Corporation. Burnett Bolloten has noted that it 'was placed under the control of a joint CNT–UGT committee, with the consequence – according to the testimony of the anarchosyndicalists, who were the dominant influence on that body – that the management was left with practically no other function but to keep an account of income and expenses and was powerless to withdraw funds without the committee's consent.'[52]

Of course, it was the attempt of Civil Guards under Stalinist orders to seize La Telefónica which set off the May Days of Barcelona in May 1937. After the virtual surrender of the anarchists at the end of the May Days, control of the telephone system in Barcelona and throughout Catalonia passed out of the hands of the workers, and into those of the government.

Workers' Control of Public Utilities in Valencia

As in Barcelona, the CNT in Valencia had a regional union covering the water, gas and electric industries, founded in 1930 at the end of the Primo de Rivera dictatorship. After July 19, it took over the public utilities of Valencia and nearby areas, the most important of which were Electra Valenciana, Energia Electrica de Mijares, Dynamis, Gas Leblón, Aguas Potables and Gas Valencia.

The administrative board of the union was converted into the Trade Union Council. Under it were established a number of sub-secretariats, including the technical–industrial, technical administrative, trade union, juridical, culture and education units, dealing with different aspects of the work of the collective.

The CNT noted in its *Boletín de Información*: 'The Consejo Sindical is everything, after the General Assembly, and has as organisms delegated to the administration and government of the industries' technical administrative councils for each one of the specialties ... there were also committees of each factory, locality and building...'

The trade-union administration of the Valencian public utilities kept prices of its products at the same level as before July 19, for more than a year after it had taken over the enterprises. This was in spite of the fact that the cost of its inputs had increased substantially, and in some cases dramatically. This was particularly the case with coal, the principal raw material for the gas plants, but was also true of transport costs – and the union administration complained strongly about the fact that the CNT unions controlling transportation in the area had doubled its prices during the first year of the Revolution.

Some of the public utility enterprises apparently produced appreciable profits under worker management. The union appropriated substantial parts of these profits to help the ministry of war's health services, and also provided 406,000 pesetas to send several score truckloads of food during the battle of Madrid.[53]

The gas sector of this collective was particularly profitable during the War. Some of its profits were made available to the electricity section, to help finance extension of service to some of the less populous parts of the province.

This collective sought to use the technicians of the old firms. Thus, the head of the control committee of the gas sector insisted over the opposition from some of his colleagues, on maintaining in his post the chief engineer. However, the control committee chief later had reason to believe that the chief engineer was injecting impurities into the gas. When he sought to flee, the chief engineer was arrested and jailed – and after Franco's victory turned in the former head of the control committee to the police of the new regime.[54]

The CNT in the Communications Industry

Unlike most other public utilities in pre-Civil War Spain, the communications industry outside Catalonia was largely in the hands of the government. This severely limited the practical possibilities for establishing trade union-dominated collectives in that part of the economy. Rather, the CNT's role was mainly confined to collective bargaining and lobbying.

This was reflected in the decisions of the first national plenum of the Communications Unions of the CNT in January 1937. The only part of the major resolution of that meeting which reflected the general collectivist policies of the CNT was its passage urging: 'There be constituted a National Council of Communications, presided over by a representative of the Government and with an equal number of members of the two trade union organizations, which will study and propose urgently the most immediate reforms of the services and the organic transformation of the corporations which have control of the public functions of national communications. It is also solicited that there be established, with identical purposes and composition regional and provincial communications councils.'

Most of the rest of the provisions of this resolution were those of a collective bargaining agent rather than of an organization seeking to control and administer a part of the national economy. They dealt with increases in the compensation of the workers in the industry, and the strengthening of their rights to negotiate with the authorities in control of various parts of the communications industry.[55]

Conclusion

Much of the infrastructure, as well as the agricultural and manufacturing sectors, of the Spanish Republican economy was taken over by the trade unions, particularly those belonging to the Confederación Nacional del Trabajo, in the wake of the suppression of the military insurrection July 18–19 1936. There is considerable indication that under workers' control, those industries were

managed successfully, that various innovations were introduced, and
certainly that the working conditions of those employed by these
industries were improved.

20

The Collectivization of the Textile Industry

The largest industry in Loyalist Spain at the onset of the Civil War was that of textiles and garments. It was heavily concentrated in Catalonia, where a few years before the War it employed 56.5 percent of the industrial workers,[1] but there were also textile plants in the Levante region and scattered ones in other parts of the Republic. During the War, it was one of the most generally collectivized parts of the economy of Republican Spain.

General Characteristics of Pre-War Textile Industry

The textile industry in Mediterranean Spain, and particularly in Catalonia, has a long history, dating back to the Middle Ages. However, the modern industry dates from the early decades of the nineteenth century. Eduardo Comín Colomer has noted that as early as December 1836 the first organization of textile workers, the Asociación Mutua de Obreros de la Industria Algodonera was established in Barcelona, which event he considered the beginning of the modern labor movement in Spain.[2]

The industry which developed during the following century had certain peculiarities. It grew behind a high wall of government protection from foreign competition. Much of the struggle of the early Catalan autonomists of the Liiga Catalana early in the twentieth century centered on their efforts to assure protection for the Catalan textile industry. As a consequence of the pressure of the Catalan textile manufacturers, as Walther Bernecker has noted, protective tariffs 'reserved the Spanish market almost completely to the Catalan industry'.[3]

However, although the Spanish textile industry was extensive, it was anything but modern. According to Bernecker, 'Because of technically backward equipment and deficiently organized entrepreneurial management, the textile industry provided until the Civil War mainly products of mediocre quality; because of using the most varied raw materials and of the enormous dispersion of the sector, it produced an almost infinite variety of different articles. The unfavorable structure of the firms in the textile sector and the high cost of production it brought about, the aging of the machinery and technological backwardness, made Spanish textiles unable to compete internationally...'[4]

The production of cotton goods was predominant. Shortly before the Civil War, there were reportedly 266 cotton spinning plants in the Catalan textile industry, and 632 cotton weaving installations, together employing 115,000 workers. The wool sector of the industry consisted of 133 spinning mills and 175 weaving plants, with a total of 26,850 workers. There were also much smaller numbers of plants producing linen, hemp, jute and silk products. In all, there were at least 174,850 workers employed in the Catalan textile industry.[5]

The textile industry had suffered severely from the Great Depression. By late 1935, it was reported that one quarter of the spinning plants and a third of the weaving factories had closed down.[6]

Strongly unionized even before the Civil War, a report of the CNT textile union of Barcelona a few months after the outbreak of the conflict indicated that it had 40,000 members. The same report said that 70 percent of the textile workers of Catalonia were CNT members, and 30 percent belonged to the UGT.[7]

The surprising thing about these figures is not the predominance of the CNT, but the fact that the UGT had nearly a third of the textile workers in its ranks. This is probably explained by the fact the

Catalan government had decreed right after the War broke out that all workers mast belong to either the CNT or the UGT; and there was a tendency after this decree for previously unorganized office workers to opt for the UGT. In the particular case of the textile unions, this same decree had forced unions under control of the Partido Obrero de Unificación Marxista to join the UGT, and at least until the early part of 1937, the influence of the POUM continued to be strong in the UGT textile workers' unions.

The Generalized Nature of the Textile Industry's Collectivization

Soon after the outbreak of the War, the textile industry in Catalonia and elsewhere was nearly completely taken over by the workers. A major reason for this was that the great majority of the employers had disappeared. According to the CNT's Textile Union of Barcelona, some 40 percent of them had been 'eliminated from the social scene', while 50 percent has fled abroad or gone into hiding. Only 10 percent of the employers 'stayed in their factories, laboring as simple workers'.[8]

There were a number of textile firms that belonged to foreign companies. In these cases, there was some hesitation on the part of the workers in declaring the firms 'seized' and 'collectivized'. However, even in some of these cases, as will be indicated in one of the examples we look at below, the workers ended up doing so.

One of the principal exceptions to general collectivization involved three textile plants in the Catalan border town of Puigcerda in the Pyrenees. The workers there opted to establish a workers' control, to keep tabs on the owners, but leaving the plants in their hands. Bernecker attributed this to the fact that the workers there belonged to the UGT, and were under the control of the Stalinist Partido Socialista Unificado de Catalonia, which was an avowed enemy of collectivization.[9]

Major Problems of Textile Industry

The textile industry was particularly plagued with problems arising from the war situation, quite apart from any which the installation of workers ownership might have provoked. As we have seen, the textile firms of Catalonia and Levante produced for the whole Spanish market. But they were deprived from the outset of the War of nearly half of that market, which lay behind Franco's lines. That situation got worse, as the Rebel forces conquered more territory.

The result of all this was that much of what the textile firms were producing went into inventory, rather than being sold. An early example of that was that of the large España Industrial in Barcelona, where a report of the administrative committee to a general assembly on October 25 1936 indicated that, as of August 8, the enterprise had 48,213 pieces of material in its warehouses, and by October 24, this had risen to 50,321.[10]

In some cases, this problem was alleviated by increase in demand for military purposes from the ministry of defense. However, in terms of the civilian sector, the shrinkage of that market remained a problem until the end of the War.

A quite different problem presented by the War was that of growing shortages of raw materials. Most of the cotton used by the Spanish textile industry came traditionally from the United States, with supplementary amounts from India and Egypt.[11] But once War broke out, import of cotton became increasingly difficult. On the one hand, a growing blockade by the Rebel fleet, supplemented by ships of both the Italian and German navies, made overseas sources of raw cotton increasingly difficult to obtain.

In addition, particularly in the early phases of the War, the situation was complicated by quarrels between the central government and that of Catalonia over control of foreign exchange. Particularly Minister of Finance Juan Negrín was exceedingly reluctant to make foreign exchange available to Catalonia, and although so long as the CNTer Juan Peiró was minister of industry, he did succeed in getting some credits for the Catalan textile industry, the lack of sufficient foreign exchange was a growing difficulty for the workers' collectives in that industry, particularly in turning out goods for the civilian market. It was further complicated, as the fortunes of war increasingly turned against the Republic, by the falling international exchange rate of the Republic's peseta.[12]

There were also severe problems with other kinds of raw materials. Although the wool used in the textile industry had come from other parts of Spain, much of the region of Andalusia, Extremadura and Castille where sheep were most prevalent, early fell into Franco hands.[13] Customary sources of coal were also disrupted by the War.

Thus, one of the major challenges facing the workers' collectives in the textile industry was that of improvising new kinds and sources of raw materials and other inputs. In at least some cases, as we shall see in that of the textile collectives of Badalona, the workers had some degree of success.

Finally, it should be noted that the War created other direct problems. There was heavy bombing of the Barcelona area, starting as early as 1937. Sometimes the bombs fell on textile plants, in others they disrupted the free flow of electricity which was essential.

The combination of shrinkage of markets and interruptions with sources of supply of inputs brought about the somewhat anomalous wartime situation of both declining production and substantial unemployment in the collectivized textile industry. Bernecker presents figures showing that the woollen sector output fell to an index number of 65.30 by the end of 1936, to 47.92 in July 1937 and 53.71 by the end of 1937 – all based on the January 1936 output as 100. The Catalan textile production overall fell more than 50 percent during 1937.[14]

As production fell, a considerable number of the textile workers in fact became unemployed. But in many cases they continued to come to their factories and to get their pay. Of course, this considerably increased the costs of production.

However, in another sense, the continuing shrinkage of the territory under the control of the Republic ironically made the fall of output of the textile industry less important than it might otherwise have been as far as the overall economy of the Loyalist region and the consumer needs of its people were concerned. This point was made by a leader of the wartime collective in the España Industrial plant in

Barcelona, when he told Victor Alba: '... the truth is that there was never lack of textile products in the market. Perhaps there were not the variety or abundance of before, but no one who wished to make a suit or dress found himself unable to find the cloth for it.'[15]

Problems of Collectivization in the Textile Industry

Apart from the difficulties brought upon the textile industry by the wartime situation, there were problems arising from the collectivization of that industry. Certainly a major one was that of insufficient coordination of the industry on a Catalan regional basis, or even on a citywide basis in Barcelona. Although the Barcelona textile union set up a committee which was supposed to allocate raw materials, allocate orders for goods on the basis of the technical capacity of various enterprises, assign labor among the various enterprises, and coordinate financing so that the profits of financially successful firms could be used to help those less well off, [16] there is considerable indication that that effort was a good deal short of successful.

There was a marked tendency on the part of the workers of each collectivized firm to develop a kind of 'enterprise patriotism'. Collectives, particularly those which were more fortunate and/or more prosperous, not only fought against elements which were opposed to collectivization (as might have been expected) but not infrequently resisted efforts of their fellow workers in other collectives to get help, in terms of raw materials, finances or other matters, not indeed evidencing the solidarity upon which the anarchists tended to pride themselves.[17]

Juan Andrade, the second most important leader of the Partido Obrero de Unificación Marxista during the Civil War, who was basically sympathetic to the collectives, sketched this situation in the industry:

Many collectives have been converted *de facto* into private enterprises of the workers employed in them. Not being joined to the general economic process, it was natural that this occurred. They function by themselves and at their own risk, and in the majority of cases without liaison with other collectivized factories or workshops of the same industry. Precisely because of this there are established among the workers themselves different categories, which depend exclusively on the reserve funds the capitalists of the collectivized firms possessed or upon the greater or less need for their products during the War. As an example, we could note the textile industry.

With the advent of the revolution, the workers proceeded to collectivize the factories. The interior economic situation of these was very different, as is characteristic in capitalism. There were some in which the owners had abundant bank accounts, over which the workers naturally took control. Some had, when the revolution began, more raw material than others and more goods in their warehouses. The same could be said with regard to machinery, since there were factories where it was very old and others where is was very modern, with high productivity. But all were equally collectivized through their corresponding workers organizations...

Because of these circumstances, in the textile industry there are great differences in the level of living, in the midst of the revolution, of different workers groups, that is to say, it depends on the economic situation which the owner had had... As a permanent phenomenon, this system of collectivizations would create irritating inequalities and new categories of workers. It would establish *de facto* a new model of private property, enjoyed by social groups instead of individuals.[18]

A serious effort was made by the CNT and the UGT in February 1937 to develop coordination of the whole industry in Catalonia. However, as we shall see, it was ineffective.

In some cases, there was coordination of the textile industry at least on a citywide basis. This apparently was particularly successful in Badalona and Alcoy.

A related problem to that of coordination was that of finances. Had there been real coordination among the textile collectives they might together have largely dealt with the financial difficulties of the weaker firms in the industry. However, lacking that, quite a few collectives which were having financial problems turned to the government of Catalonia for help. Particularly in the beginning, the Generalidad was quite willing to extend financial aid. However, although this provided short-tern benefits, it generated longer-term difficulties for those collectives. It gave the Generalidad, particularly after it fell under the control of the Stalinist Partido Unificado Socialista de Catalonia, which was absolutely opposed to the collectives, the possibility of using the financial lever to undermine them.

There were also internal problems in a number of individual textile collectives. One of these was opposition, on the part of skilled technical and managerial personnel who continued on their jobs, to the 'levelling' propensities of the general assemblies of the collectives.

There were certainly cases in which this kind of disagreement took on a political coloration. The Stalinists, who were trying to build up a middle-class base in Catalonia and elsewhere, were undoubtedly quick to come to the defense of those unhappy about the egalitarianism of the anarchist workers.

Another problem was labor discipline. There were certainly those workers who interpreted workers control of their industry to be a license to take it easy, or worse. However, there is little indication that this was a major problem in the textile collectives, particularly in the early phases of the War, in which workers' morale was generally high.

Examples of Textile Collectives in Barcelona

Data does not exist upon which to base an enterprise-by-enterprise survey of the textile collectives. Even if it did, such an effort would not be appropriate to this book. However, there are more or less extensive details available about a limited number of plants which were taken over by their workers. It is perhaps logical to start with the city of Barcelona, the largest single center of the textile industry. Three of the plants we shall look at were among the largest in the country, the others were more modest in size and importance.

The Hilaturas Fabra y Coats, engaged in spinning cotton yarn, had four factories in Catalonia, two of them in Barcelona, one in

Badalona and another in Torello. Its largest plant, in the San Andrés section of Barcelona had 2,000 workers of both sexes. It had begun in 1905 as a Spanish enterprise of the Fabra family, the major figures of which were the Marqués of Alella and the Marqués of Masnou, but had merged with a branch of the Coats firm from Great Britain, and at the time of the outbreak of the Civil War, 70 percent of its stock belonged to the British firm. It was a modern factory in terms of its equipment and technology, and had had a relatively enlightened labor policy, providing a nursery for the children of its women employees, some health care for them, and a retirement system for those workers who had been employed for 45 years.

Because it was a largely British firm, the workers did not immediately collectivize it. At the suggestion of the management, they did elect a control committee, to collaborate with the managers. However, within a few weeks, most of the British employees of the firm had returned to their native land.

During the first three months, the control committee functioned largely as a grievance committee. However, it did bring about one major change in working conditions, the abolition of piecework, a long-sought aspiration of the CNT. In negotiating this with the management, the control committee conceded that the abolition of piecework would probably result in a decline in output, and it was agreed that a 25 percent decline would be acceptable. But at the end of the first week, production had declined by 40 percent. The control committee then called a general assembly of the workers of the four plants and explained the situation, insisting that it was necessary to increase production as a contribution to the Revolution. The result, as Andrés Capevila, then the principal figure in the control committee, wrote many years later, was that 'after two weeks of stimulating with our efforts the sense of responsibility of the worker comrades, without the use of any coercion or applying any sanctions, we were successful in stabilizing the production at the normal level which we had established.'

At the end of three months the firm faced a financial crisis. Sales, which before the War had averaged 4,000,000 pesetas a month, had fallen to two and a half million, because of the loss of markets in the Franco-held territory. As a consequence, the management announced a three-day work week, with three days' pay, a proposal which the control committee 'flatly rejected'.

The control committee asked the local management to have representatives of the British firm meet with a delegation of the workers in Marseilles. There, the control committee presented four alternatives: 'First – the workers of the four factories … would work three days and be paid for the entire week. Second – they work a full week, and the excess production would be warehoused. Third – they would work all week, and the excess would be shipped to Britain. Fourth – the company would accept any of the three previous propositions to assure a full week's pay to the workers so long as the abnormal conditions persisted in Spain.'

The representatives of the Coats firm totally rejected all of the suggestions of the workers' representatives. Many years later, Capdevila asked one of the directors of Coats why they had taken this position, which led directly to the collectivization of the plant, and he replied:

> The management of the Coats company recognized the justice of the propositions presented for its consideration by the Control Committee. But in the light of the revolutionary events in Spain, they considered that this did not involve a dispute between the workers and the Company, but was a question of life or death for international capitalism, the Company thus participating in the accords which the great monopolies of all the countries made to make the Spanish Revolution fail, was loyal to the policy of boycotting the Red zone and giving unconditional help to Franco, who represented the continuity of the capitalist regime.

When the workers' delegation returned to Barcelona, the control committee was faced with the alternative of giving in to management or proposing collectivization of the Fabra y Coats plants. They decided on the latter course, called a general assembly of the workers of all four plants, and the decision of the assembly to collectivize the enterprise was virtually unanimous.

Andrés Capdevila summarized the result of collectivization thus:

The Control Committee, with ample freedom of action, suppressed the payment of dividends, ended useless jobs, and with efficacious methods reestablished rapidly the finances of the Firm, thus assuring the weekly wage of the workers. A circulating library was organized, a Monthly Review was published, courses were organized in grammar, arithmetic, geometry; in a word, the social and cultural structure which we were giving the factories of the Firm gave excellent results, and each day we came a bit closer to the fulfillment of our beloved ideals. It must be pointed out that, in spite of a lack of raw materials and of electricity during the last months of our resistance to fascism, the workers always had their wages assured.[19]

Another of the largest textile plants in Barcelona and Catalonia was España Industrial. It was a spinning and weaving plant, with 2,000 workers, of whom 1,500 were women.[20]

With the end of the fighting in Barcelona 'the managers and a large part of the administrative personnel gave no signs of life'. So the CNTers in the plant called a general assembly of the workers, which was attended by almost all of them. That meeting decided to collectivize the plant, and elected a committee of 12 people, drawn from manual workers, technicians and administrative personnel, to run the enterprise.[21]

This Comité de Empresa ran the España Industrial plant during the rest of the War, until Franco's troops overran Catalonia at the beginning of 1939. After enactment of the collectivization decree by the Catalan government there was also a delegate-inspector, representing the Catalan Consejo de Economía, who in this case was also a member of the CNT. Although he was entitled by the decree to receive a salary equal to the highest salary in the firm, this delegate-inspector foreswore that right, and receive the same pay which he had gotten before the War. That was also the case with the members of the Comité de Empresa. Also, only four of the 12 members of the Comité de Empresa spent full time in work of the to *comité*, the rest continuing at their old jobs, and being engaged in *comité* work only after their regular working hours.[22]

Each section of the enterprise had its local supervisor, who was elected by the workers in that section.[23] Also, when on three occasions it was necessary to replace a member of the Comité de Empresa, the replacement was elected by the general assembly of all of the workers in the enterprise.[24]

A former member of the Comité de Empresa, interviewed by Víctor Alba 40 years later, was asked how the system of having managers and supervisors who were elected by the workers worked out in practice. He replied: 'The comrades felt responsible for having to live with those who had elected them, that they had to respond for their actions to those who had elected them. If the chief of a section had been named by the Comité de Empresa, he would not have had sufficient moral authority. But he was elected by his comrades, and with his election they were committed automatically to respect his decisions and to support him.'[25]

This man argued that there were no particular problems of labor discipline arising from having the managerial and supervisory people chosen by the workers themselves: 'Those elected people could maintain discipline, organize the work, etc., better than when they were named by the management. People, particularly workers, can only be moved by coercion – even if this only consists of having to earn one's living – or by stimuli which we might call spiritual. We believe that the stimuli of the latter kind incite one to work more, to maintain discipline, than do fear, coercion. The facts proved us right.'[26]

To a limited degree, the egalitarian principles of the anarchists were put in practice in España Industrial. This was reflected in the fact that those who were chosen for supervisory positions continued to receive the same pay as they had gotten while working on the shop floor or in the office. It was also shown in the decision of the general assembly of the workers to eliminate the Christmas bonuses formerly received by the directors and technicians of the enterprise, and in a move to reduce the highest salaries paid to managerial and technical personnel. But as the Comité de Empresa member interviewed by Victor Alba commented, 'The very high salaries of some were reduced although there was much resistance and, to calm them because we needed them, the reduction was limited to only 20 percent.'[27]

However, interestingly enough, anarchist egalitarianism did not extend to the elimination of wage differences between men and women workers. Víctor Alba's interviewee commented that 'the disparities of wages between men and women were maintained. Some of the latter asked for equal wages, but couldn't do anything, in spite of the fact that in the assembly they had a majority to approve this idea.' He explained this with the somewhat lame argument that 'this depended on the Consejo de Economía and on the CNT. It should be a general measure and not one of a single enterprise.'[28]

The technicians and former supervisory personnel obviously presented some problems to the workers elected to run the industry. Víctor Alba's interviewee noted: 'Although the manager left, the technicians all stayed, including the supervisors. There was no need to replace anyone, since the Comité de Empresa occupied the position of the manager. The only thing was, and this is very important, that the technicians were deprived of the command which they had had over the personnel and retained only their technical functions.'[29]

This former member of the Comité de Empresa admitted that the technicians and supervisors 'were not satisfied. I think that most of all they resented the loss of their privileges, not only their economic ones ... but also those of command. They liked to command and they didn't pardon us that we didn't allow them to command. But they understood that there was nothing they could do, that they could not change things, and they adapted.'

However, these people showed their resentment in small ways. 'For example, the *comité* would call one and he was late in arriving, or he had to be called several times. Or he would lose papers and only find them when they were no longer needed. This kind of thing, infantile, didn't amount to sabotage, but showed their bad humor, bad disposition.'[30]

The España Industrial collective confronted the common problems provoked by the War. They were faced with shortages of cotton, of dyes (formerly obtained from Germany), of the coal from Asturias (which forced them upon occasion to use wood as a substitute.[31] Shortages were particularly acute for the production of civilian goods. In the case of fulfilling orders from the ministry of defense, the ministry usually provided the necessary raw materials.[32]

However, as the former member of the Comité de Empresa told Víctor Alba, 'On balance, there were some imports of raw materials, other imports were substituted by goods from the country, dyes were made, coal from mines in the Republican zone was used. One can say that in the three years of the war, no worker was left without his wages.'[33]

However, there were times when raw material shortages virtually closed down the plant. In some of these instances, the CNT's textile coordinating organization made arrangements with the ministry of defense for some of the workers who were physically able to do so to work on the building of fortifications and bomb shelters in nearby areas.[34]

Working conditions in the factory were improved by the collective. The workers themselves constructed new showers, washrooms, places to keep their clothing. Workers over 65 years of age were allowed to retire with a pension.[35]

However, the oft-cited ex-member of the Comité de Empresa of España Industrial admitted: 'The lack of raw materials resulted in there not being profits and that the standard of living of the workers didn't improve very much in a material sense, although it improved in the moral sense, because there was good treatment, the initiatives of the workers were taken into account in organizing the work, the firm provided cultural materials for the workers.'[36]

A third Barcelona textile plant of considerable size was the weaving enterprise, Fabrica de Tejidos Casacuberta. *Solidaridad Obrera*, the Barcelona CNT daily, reported upon it on the occasion of a visit there by the Mexican ambassador early in 1938. The enterprise had five separate units, employing about 2,000 workers, the largest unit having 600 workers. At the time of the visit, this largest unit was working with three shifts, and it was reported to the ambassador that output was considerably larger than before the War.

The Casacuberta collective had established a school, with two teachers. A lending library to which 300 workers belonged was associated with the school. The library had some 700 books.

The Mexican ambassador also visited a clothing enterprise established by the CNT after the outbreak of the War. This was the Talleres Confederales de Sastrería. It produced mainly goods for the military.

It had 950 workers, who were working a 44-hour week. Early in 1938, it was producing about 2,000 pieces a day, although its installed capacity would have permitted the production of 4,000.[37]

Finally, we may note the experience in a much smaller collectivized enterprise in Barcelona. This was a small plant employing between 50 and 60 workers. After July 19, it was collectivized by the workers, although the owner did not flee or hide. In fact, the new Consejo de Administración, elected by the workers, asked the ex-owner to preside over the *consejo*, which he continued to do until the end of the War in Catalonia. Almost 25 years later, the son of the wartime owner recounted this experience with a more or less favorable view of what had occurred. How widespread this experience of workers inviting the ex-owner to preside over – or at least participate in – the workers' own management of collectivized firms was, is not known. However, it is to be presumed that this was not an isolated case, particularly in small enterprises in which pre-war relations between the owner and his workers had been more or less friendly.

Textile Collectivization in Badalona

The approach to collectivization of the textile industry in Badalona, a city just to the north of Barcelona was different from that in the Catalan capital. Instead of the workers of each textile enterprise in the city going more or less on their own, the whole process was carried out under the leadership, and more or less control, of the CNT textile workers' union of the vicinity. Throughout the War there was a relatively high degree of coordination among the collectivized textile plants of the city.

There were 37 textile plants employing about 8,000 workers in Badalona at the time of the outbreak of the Civil War. At that time about half of the workers belonged to the CNT. Soon after the start of the War, a union affiliated with the Unión General de Trabajadores was formed. But throughout the conflict the CNT union continued to be strongly dominant, its rival never having more than 1,500–1,600 workers in its ranks.[38]

The UGT union was formed in part by workers who previously

had been members of the CNT, but who were affiliated with one or another of the parties which joined to form the Partido Socialista Unificado de Catalonia a few days after the War began. However, there remained within the CNT union, and in some cases with positions of responsibility, many other workers who had belonged to the Catalan branch of the Socialist Party, as well as members of the Partido Obrero de Unificación Marxista.[39]

On July 19, there was virtually no fighting in Badalona. The CNTers immediately seized the city hall, and a group of them participated in a successful attack on an army barracks some miles from the city. The police did not come out on the streets on July 19. A general strike closed down even those economic activities which would normally have taken place on a Sunday.[40]

On July 22, the union (the Sindicato de Industrial Fabril, Textil, Vestir y Anexos de Badalona y su Radio) issued a manifesto signed by its president, Ramón Martínez González, and secretary, José Costa Font, asking the textile workers to return to work, to the same jobs they had had before July 19. It also announced that a general assembly of the union would soon be held.[41]

The union leaders immediately called a meeting in the city hall of all of the technical and supervisory personnel in the industry in Badalona. Most of the people involved attended the meeting. There, the union leaders informed them that the workers were for the time being taking over the control of the industry in the city. They urged the technicians and former supervisory personnel to return to their jobs, assuring them that they would be treated like fellow-workers, and that they would be able to carry on their jobs, but under the supervision of people elected by the workers. They were given 24 hours to consider the situation. Most of them returned to their jobs by the next day.[42]

A week after the return to work, the Junta Central of the union issued another communique, calling for the workers of all of the textile plants of the city to elect control committees. Regarding the workers' seizure of the factories as a temporary measure only for the duration of the War, which they thought would not last for long, the union did not in the beginning foresee the organization of a permanent system of workers' control. It was not until late in December, a couple of months after the Catalan collectivization decree, that the union decided to have the workers formally assume ownership of the enterprises. At that point, the Comités de Control were renamed Consejos de Empresa, in conformity with the collectivization decree.[43]

There were three exceptions to this general collectivization. Two of these were foreign-owned enterprises which were kept 'under the control of the *sindicato*'. The third was a firm in which the majority of workers belonged to the UGT and decided to maintain the control committee instead of collectivizing the enterprise.[44]

Later, the CNT textile union proposed that there be a complete consolidation of the textile plants in badalona, creating effectively a single workers-controlled enterprise. However, they didn't go through with the idea because of strong opposition from the city's UGT union, apparently following the directions of the Catalan Stalinists of the PSUC.[45]

In the meanwhile, the duties of the Comités de Control were set forth in the union communique which called for their election, dated July 29. They were supposed to make a thorough survey of all aspects of the firm's operation, physical, commercial, financial and tax liabilities, and report those details to the union. In addition, the Comités de Control were to report weekly to the union on all aspects of their enterprises' operations.

The union communique noted: 'With the fulfillment of these instructions and with the first phase completed, the Committees of Control will exercise the technical and administrative functions, being charged on their own responsibility, and together with the Management, with the organization and direction of work, deciding on the process of fabrication which is most convenient for the collectivity at this time.'

The same communique provided for two other elected workers groups in each plant. These were the Comités de Fabrica and the Delegados de Cotización. The former were the union grievance committees which had existed before July 19, and their tasks would continue as before, except that they were also to 'keep order within the factories, seeing to it that all the workers fulfill their duties'. A member of the Comité de Fabrica would attend all meetings of the Comité de Control. The Delegados de Cotización were to collect union dues from all of the workers of the enterprises.[46]

Another early measure taken by the union was to decree the abolition of piecework, and to establish the 40-hour week. However, before long, because of raw material shortages and other difficulties, there had to be a further reduction of the work week to 32 hours.[47]

The union also set up a Consejo de Control y Economía de la Industria Textil y Derivados. The communiqué of July 29 said that the *consejo*, 'in accordance with the general lines indicated by the *sindicato* ... will have full authority to organize the control of the textile firms of the zone, in the best conditions possible, assuming the task of coordinating the various organs of control of all the factories and workshops. This *consejo* will consult with and provide each Comité de Control of each enterprise all the details which are requested.'[48]

Costa Font and Martínez González have described the role of the Consejo de Control y Economía: 'Aside from the job of knowing the conditions under which we were working, its principal work was that of orientation, if one could orient towards carrying out a program, more or less concrete, which was that of maintaining industrial structures with the capacity of production adequate for the needs of the War, and to meet in so far as possible, the growing demand for textile manufactures.'[49]

Among its functions was that of transferring financial resources from those firms which were more or less profitable to those which were not. Profits of enterprises were put in the *consejo*'s account in a local bank, and were then transferred by the *consejo* as required.[50] In addition, the *consejo* 'contracted with the Ministry of National Defense, and followed a policy of commercial interchange and barter ... strengthening the union ranks and the spirit of solidarity among the workers.'[51]

Immediately after July 19, the CNT ordered the blocking of all accounts in the banks in Badalona, to avoid capital flight. They reached agreement with the Bank Workers' Union to make this measure effective.[52] As far as the textile industry was concerned, the Consejo de Control y Economía was charged with seeing to it that the Comités de Control of the various enterprises drew from their accounts only what in fact they needed to conduct their business.[53]

The union's Consejo de Control y Economía undertook to reorganize the textile industry in Badalona. This was done on the basis of the surveys which the union had asked each local Comité de Control to make of the conditions of its enterprise. Costa Font and Martínez González have said: 'We had in our hands complete statistics, including skilled workers and technicians, machinery, lubricant needs, electric power, raw materials, dyes, economic status firm by firm, as well as the possibilities of commercialization and demands for products. That was a marvelous job, which enthused those who developed it ... which gave us a broad vision that made it possible to know which seas it was possible to navigate.'[54]

The Consejo de Control y Economía sought to make the textile industry in Badalona more efficient. They closed some small and particularly unproductive plants, and transferred their machinery, technical people and some of their workers to more efficient ones. Where there were not positions for all the workers of the closed plants, they found jobs in other parts of the local economy. Costa Font and Martínez González claimed: 'Unemployment was soon completely ended, at least in the textile industry. We had little, but we distributed the little there was equitably.'[55]

The clothing industry, which also came within the scope of the textile workers' union, soon had special difficulties. It was organized on the basis of small artisan shops, and was particularly faced with raw material shortages. The Consejo de Control y Economía undertook to organize a cooperative among those artisans, using for the purpose a factory which had been closed down before the War began. It was financed by the union, and the Consejo de Control y Economía sought to provide the members of the cooperative with sufficient raw materials.[56]

The Consejo also sought to come to grips with the general problem of raw material shortage. One partial solution was to sign contracts with the ministry of defense for clothing and other products needed by the armed forces; the ministry undertaking to provide the raw material needed to fulfill those contracts.[57] The union also undertook a number of experiments with substitute raw materials, and although they were not able to mass produce substitutes, they were able to provide some replacements for goods which were increasingly difficult to obtain from abroad.

Costa Font and Martínez González explained: 'The experiment consisted in transforming hemp from Alicante, which has always been of high quality, into fiber, bleached and worked on the same machines for spinning and weaving cotton. With these threads were formed the warp and woof; several meters were woven, and the cloth obtained was submitted to tests of resistance and quality, which showed a textile which was totally satisfactory for clothes for common use, although with a tendency to shrink a bit more than that made of cotton.'[58]

With agreement of both the CNT and UGT textile unions of Badalona, the *consejo* issued, on November 2 1936, a new wage schedule for the textile workers of the city and vicinity, with equal pay for men and women workers. This same document provided that women workers were to have two months of paid leave before and after giving birth, at 75 percent of their regular wage, and that while they were breastfeeding their children, they were to have two half-hours a day for that purpose.[59]

On April 22 1937, the CNT textile union issued a further modification of the wage scale for workers in the industry in and around Badalona. Although the UGT union was not happy about this, it did not seriously challenge the move.[60]

The Consejo de Control y Economía also established a kind of social security system for the textile workers of Badalona. On the one hand, it told retired workers to return to their factories where, if they wanted to, they could get work which was in conformity with their capacity. In any case, they would get the same wage which they had gotten before leaving employment. Previously, they had not received any regular income at all.[61]

It was also provided that the families of textile workers who had joined the militia and gone to the front were to receive the wages which the militiamen would have received had they continued working in the industry. Some 500 textile workers from Badalona had left to join the militia in the days following July 19, headed by the union president, Ramón Martínez González who subsequently returned.

The *consejo* levied a war tax on the rich firms under its control, to finance the purchase from local retailers of textile products which they were hoarding, which were sent to the union's members at the front.[63] However, as the War dragged on and the militia were converted into a more or less regular army, the textile workers of Badalona were no longer able to maintain this kind of direct contact with their members at the front.[64]

One of the aspects of the collectivization of their industry of which the textile workers of Badalona were most proud was the healthcare system established by the Consejo de Control y Economía of the CNT union. Once it was established, the UGT union asked to participate, and a joint CNT–UGT liaison committee was established to deal with the health system.[65]

The system was established by contracts signed between the CNT textile union of Badalona and two sections of the CNT health workers' union of the city, those of doctors and pharmacists. A special commission within the textile union's Junta Central was established to supervise the health system. Each worker was given an identification card, which he/she presented, together with his/her union card, in order to get the health care they needed.[66]

There were two large clinics in Badalona which were the heart of the system, The workers were free to choose which of these clinics they wanted to patronize.[67]

The health service was free to the individual workers and their families. In addition, workers who were confined to bed received, in addition to full medical care, their full wages during the first month of confinement, 75 percent for the next three months and 50 percent from then on. The regulations sought to prevent workers from taking unfair advantage of the system.[68]

The health system was financed from two sources. On the one hand, each textile enterprise contributed towards it, and in addition, a part of the union dues payments also went into it.[69]

Other Cases of Collectivization in the Textile Industry

There were textile and garment industry collectives in many other places in addition to Barcelona and Badalona and there was great diversity in the way those collectives were organized and conducted their business.

One of the larger CNT collectives was that of the garment workers of Valencia. It was established right after the War began, bringing together the machines and the 3,000 or so workers – 80 percent of them women – who had been employed in many small shops, in one large establishment. They were able to get a number of electric sewing machines, something of a novelty in the garment business of Valencia at that time, which operated mainly with the foot-pedalled type of machine. They produced clothing both for the armed forces and for civilians.

The Valencia garment collective had a cooperative, where they made available goods which they got as a result of swaps with other industrial collectives and with agrarian collectives. The products in the cooperative store were made available to the members of the collective in conformity with their needs, that is in proportion to the number of members in their families. Wages were also paid, and the worker had the alternative of taking his/her income in money wages, in goods, or in a combination of these. The union was active in promoting classes and other activities for the members of the collective.[70]

Most of the textile industry in the Levante region was located in the province of Alicante. Enrique Marco Nadal has written: 'During the period of existence of the militia, it was dedicated to alternating production of goods for the civilian population with that of blue fabric which was later transformed by the women of the Clothing Collective in Monos for the militiamen; after the militarization of the militia to the production of khaki colored fabric which was used to make the uniforms which the soldiers wore.'[71]

One rather unusual case was that of the Roder de Ter textile plant near Vich in Catalonia. It had been closed, due to the Depression, for a year before the War began. After July 19, the workers opened it, cleaned up the place, and put it back into full operation. For the first three months they agreed to work without a wage, and for eight months at half pay. Reportedly, they were very successful in running the enterprise. It had a 10,000,000-peseta deficit in 1936 but, at the end of the War, there was 14,000,000-pesetas' worth of textiles in the warehouse, and a large amount of cash in the bank.[72]

In Hospitalet de Llobregat, near Barcelona, the collectivization effort of the textile workers suffered from the same drawbacks as it did in the Catalan capital. The plants there were collectivized individually and the CNT union of textile workers in the city had little control over how each one of them functioned. As a consequence there developed a considerable spirit of rivalry among the various plant collectives, and there was little cooperation among them.[73]

However, there were other towns in Catalonia and the Levante where the collectivization model in the textile industry was more similar to that of Badalona than that of Barcelona. One of these was Igualada, also in the province of Barcelona. Textiles constituted the principal industry in the town, and all of the factories were taken over by the workers. The CNT had about two-thirds of the workers in its ranks and the UGT the other third. The two unions established a liaison committee with representatives of all of the factories in the town, headed by the CNTer Jaime Casellas. It supervised the running of all of the factories, and according to Casellas, there was no 'enterprise patriotism' in Igualada. Raw materials were apportioned by the liaison committee. It also established a common wage scale for all of the factories, and although this brought about some degree of levelling of wages, skilled workers and supervisory people did receive higher wages than the average worker. Pay for the same kind of work was the same in all of the plants.

Those employers and managers, who had not been physically eliminated or had not otherwise disappeared, were invited to participate in the collectivization of the Igualada textile industry. They were frequently incorporated into the Comités de Empresa which were established in each factory. In the large plants, these *comités* consisted of workers elected by each section of the plant; in smaller ones, they were elected 'at large'.

According to Jaime Casellas, the workers left most of the plants in Igualada in better condition by the end of the War than they had been when they took them over. The obvious care with which the workers treated their plants served to encourage a number of the ex-managers to collaborate with the collectives. Indeed, one became so closely associated with his collective that he was jailed by the Franco forces when they overran Catalonia.[74]

The most thoroughgoing, example of coordination among collectivized textile plants was in Alcoy, the second city of the province of Alicante. Gaston Leval called Accoy 'the most complete example of "syndicalization of production" in all of Spain'. Virtually all of the economic activities of Alcoy, one of the earliest centers of the anarchist movement in Spain, were taken over by the CNT's union there. The 6,500 CNT textile workers in Alcoy first set up control committees in each factory. But then, on September 14 1936, the textile union officially took over '41 textile factories, 10 spinning mills, 4 dye works, 5 processing factories, 24 linen works, and 11 carding shops'. The union's commission of control thereupon became 'the organ for the overall administration of the textile industry in Alcoy'.

Each textile factory was divided into five sections, and the workers in each section elected someone to the Comité de Fabrica of the factory. Members of the Comités de Fabrica, together with an equal number elected by the general assembly of the union became the body in charge of administering the Alcoy textile industry.

Gaston Leval commented on this structure of the collectivized textile industry in Alcoy: 'We are not therefore facing an administrative dictatorship but rather a functional democracy in which all the specialized workers play their roles which have been settled after general examination by the assembly...'[75]

Finally, although in most instances the initiative for collectivization of the textile industry came from the unions of the CNT, there were apparently at least a few cases in which they were organized and run where the majority of the workers belonged to the UGT. This seems to have been the case in at least two factories in the town of Valls in the Catalan province of Taragona. The *Boletín de Información* reported on these in December 1937.

One was a small garment factory, the Empresa Hispano Colectizada, which at the time of the report had two male workers and 30 women workers laboring inside the factory, in addition to 30 others who worked in their homes but turned their output over to the firm. The workers had collectivized this enterprise when, in July 1936, its owner disappeared, leaving a bankrupt company. The CNT textile unions lent the collective enough money to get it started again, and the collectivized firm had thereafter been able to earn enough to pay its workers and acquire necessary raw materials. It was run by a Comité de Empresa of 12 workers elected by a general assembly and a three-person permanent committee.[76]

The second case in Valls was that of the Hilados y Tejidos Esteve, Colectivizada. A small spinning and weaving enterprise, with three separate plants, with a total of about 100 workers, almost all of them female, it was collectivized by the workers at the beginning of January 1937, and was legalized under the Catalan collectivization decree, in July of that year. It, too, was in dire financial straits when the workers took it over, but they had been able by the end of the year to at least break even, although the difficult economic situation kept the work week at only three days. The collective ended the piecework system, and substituted payment of 36 pesetas a week for all members of the collective. The report on this enterprise stressed that 'all accords and decisions are taken in majority vote in assemblies'.[77]

Efforts to Coordinate the Collectivized Textile Industry

There were, therefore, at least two alternative models for the collectivization of the textile industry. One was that prevalent in Barcelona, in which each collectivized plant operated on its own, with relatively little coordination of the industry as a whole; and the alternative, in such places as Badalona and Alcoy, in which it was the local textile union which took over general coordination of the plants collectivized by its members.

Costa Font and Martínez González have described the Barcelona situation: 'In Barcelona there was collectivization by enterprise. The consejos in them had wide independence from one another. There did not exist an economic organ of the union to bring together the enterprises to work in common. Some functioned well, others with enormous difficulties, and the majority had to mortgage their industrial properties to the Government of the Generalidad de Catalonia to obtain the funds necessary to be able to pay the wages of their workers. The Union limited itself to intervening in problems among the workers of a single enterprise, or those of different *consejos*.'

These authors noted the existence of a commission of relations which was supposed to help coordinate the various Barcelona textile collectives. It tried to obtain raw materials for firms which were lacking them. However, as Costa Font and Martínez González concluded: 'Our Textile Union of Barcelona was mentally conditioned to practice solidarity in the class struggle, but not in the other one, the economic, resulting from having the means of production in our hands.'[78]

A few months after the beginning of the War, the commission of relations of the Barcelona textile union sought to bring more order out of this rather chaotic situation. It issued an elaborate plan for the establishment on a citywide and even Catalonia-wide basis of coordinating committees, and specified the form of organization and the tasks of the various departments into which these committees would be divided.[79]

However, this effort was a failure. As Costa Font and Martínez González commented, 'This Commission sketched a project to gather general statistics of the means of production and to try to control them; it published questionnaires, but not a single one was filled out; each enterprise worked by itself and for itself.'[80]

In February 1937, an even more ambitious attempt to coordinate the Catalan textile industry was made at a conference held in the headquarters of the CNT textile unions of Barcelona, This was a meeting of Catalan textile unions of both the CNT and UGT. At that point, the Partido Obrero de Unificación Marxista still had considerable influence in the UGT's textile unions, and several of the principal participants in the meeting were members of the POUM.

This conference called for a total reorganization of the textile industry in the Catalan region. It proposed the immediate setting up of a Consejo General de la Industria Textil, to be charged with this reorganization and coordination. This *consejo* was to seek the consolidation of the industry into a relatively small number of large enterprises, in which both the machinery and personnel could be more efficiently organized. It was to standardize products, while at the same time seeking to determine more efficiently what kinds of products the consumers wanted. It was to establish research laboratories to seek out new raw materials, and was to develop relations with peasant collectives and other agricultural producers to stimulate the domestic production of raw materials. It was to centralize the distribution of the industry's products, both to gain more efficiency and to eliminate exploiting middlemen.[81]

However, all of the plans of the February 1937 conference came to nought. As explained in a report on the conference given to Víctor Alba, 'All of the planning proposed, which we have amply summarized, existed only on paper. The truth is that not the least attempt was made to put it into practice... The enormous political differences which existed in those days among the forces which had opposed the military uprising, couldn't have any other result than sterilization of all efforts.'[82]

Conclusion

The textile industry was one of the most thoroughly collectivized sectors of manufacturing in Republican Spain during the Civil War. It was also one of the segments of the economy which was most afflicted by wartime circumstances, both because of the loss of established markets and the increasing difficulties the industry had in obtaining necessary raw materials.

The record of workers' control in the textile industry, in both social and economic terms, is so diverse that it is difficult to draw generalizations from it. The textile collectives showed, in different areas, both the weaknesses and the strengths of the anarchist experiment with workers' control of segments of the national economy. On the one hand, in areas in which there was no coordinating role played by the local union, there often tended to develop a kind of 'enterprise patriotism' or 'working-class capitalism' which was not consistent with the anarchists' belief in class solidarity, On the other hand, in places like Badalona and Alcoy, where the local unions did undertake seriously the role of coordination of the textile workers collectives within its jurisdiction, the results appear to have been distinctly more positive, both in terms of economic efficiency and social solidarity.

One thing that the experience of the textile collectives demonstrates is the handicaps faced by the CNT workers, when they suddenly had the role thrust upon them of running their own enterprises, resulting from the incompleteness of the structure of the CNT itself. Before the outbreak of the Civil War, there did not exist any national federation of textile workers, or even strong local textile trade union structures in many parts of the country. Had there been such structures in place, the CNT textile unions, local, regional and national, could have seized the opportunity to organize the whole textile industry of Republican Spain on the basis of direct control of each enterprise by elected representatives of the workers, but supplemented by strong coordinating bodies made up also of workers directly or indirectly delegated by the workers of the individual enterprises. Such a structure would have conformed more closely to the anarchist ideal of local autonomy, combined with solidarity among the autonomous workers' collectives, than what actually developed.

This lack of adequate structure within the CNT textile sector also weakened the anarchist workers and their organizations in the face of those elements within Loyalist Spain who were opposed to the whole idea of workers' control. Without the resources under their own control to meet the financial difficulties with which many of the textile collectives were faced, they were often forced to turn to the government – particularly the government of Catalonia – for financial assistance. Although the situation varied a good deal from case to case, that often meant that the price of such help as they received from the Catalan government, particularly after it came to be dominated by the Stalinists subsequent to the May events, was subordination of the individual collectives to that government, and evisceration of the experiment of workers' control.

The dogmatism of the pure anarchists, and their opposition to the establishment of strong national unions in the pre-Civil War period, thus served the anarchist movement poorly following July 19, when they finally got an opportunity to put their ideas into practice.

21

Miscellaneous Urban Collectives

The collectivization of urban enterprises by their workers during the Spanish Civil War was by no means confined only to transport and public utilities, the war industries and textiles and garments. Indeed, José Costa Font and Ramón Martínez González estimated that in Catalonia some 80 percent of all firms were taken over by their workers, that in the Levante area 60 percent were collectivized, while in Madrid 30 percent were taken over by the workers.[1]

The establishment of workers' collectives took place in the most diverse kinds of economic activity. They ranged from public entertainment to merchandising, to a wide range of manufacturing industries. Even the barbering trade of Barcelona was collectivized. In this chapter I shall describe and discuss a few samples of those very diverse experiments with worker control.

In most cases, the initiative was taken by the workers belonging to the CNT. However, in other instances, particularly in the Valencia region, where the Socialists continued to be largely aligned with the Largo Caballero faction of the Socialist Party, the UGT was a full partner in these experiences.

Collectives in the Wood Industry

One of the collectivized industries about which the anarchists talked a good deal was that of the wood industry of Barcelona. That industry included cabinet makers, furniture plants, saw mills and construction work. There were a few relatively large wood product enterprises in the city and a large number of comparatively tiny ones. The latter were quickly in financial difficulties with the onset of the War, and they borrowed considerable amounts of money from the Catalan government, but this did little to resolve their problems.

The larger wood enterprises were generally collectivized by their workers after July 19. They remained throughout the War under the guidance of their elected Comités de Control or Comités de Fabrica, apparently with some general orientation from the CNT's Sindicato de la Madera.

But the innovation in the wood industry of Barcelona was the union's move to bring together all of the owners and workers of the small, mainly bankrupt, enterprises, after a general assembly of the union had apparently agreed on this course, and announced to the people of these small firms, ordinarily not subject to the Catalan collectivization decree, that they were all to be merged into a single enterprise. That firm then established a number of plants with 200 or more workers in each, and all the machinery and workers (including ex-employers) from the small firms were moved to those new plants.

There were at least three bodies which ran Madera Socializada, as the CNT consolidated wood enterprise was known, which had 12,000 workers. Overall, there was the Economic Council of Socialized Wood, headed by Manuel Hernández Rodríguez, who had for many years been head of the Sindicato Unico de la Madera of Barcelona. Another was the Comisión Tecnica, composed of as many members as there were specialities in the industry, which met twice a week 'to study the necessities of all the specialties which existed'. There was also an administrative commission in charge of the financial and administrative details of the enterprise.

As was true of many collectives, the Madera Socializada was faced with difficulty in obtaining raw materials. The economic council of the enterprise succeeded in substituting local Spanish woods for those that were formerly imported.

In the plants of Madera Socializada there were established recreation areas and swimming pools for after-work relaxation for the workers. There were also libraries, vocational training courses and at least some schools set up.[2]

Gaston Leval described the result of this unionization rather than collectivization of the Barcelona wood industry: 'The authority of the *sindicato*, that is to say, of the assemblies whose decisions were unappealable, imposed itself. Where there were superfluous workers, they were directed to other enterprises, which made objects useful for the new situation, for example, simple furniture instead of luxury furniture. The use of raw materials was rationalized and in so far as conditions of war permitted there was a return to the practices of our kind of unionism.'[3]

Madera Socializada was relatively prosperous. It also had a strong sense of labor solidarity. Thus, on one occasion it made a substantial loan to the trolleycar workers' collective of Barcelona, when that enterprise was having financial difficulties.[4]

In nearby Hospitalet de Llobregat, the wood industry was collectivized as it was in Barcelona. The collective was controlled by the wood workers' *sindicato* of the CNT, which brought together all of the small workshops which characterized the industry in that city, concentrating all of the available machinery in a few large enterprises. The wood collective of Hospitalet was reportedly prosperous and successful.[5]

In Valencia there was a wood workers' collective of a rather different sort. It was a joint enterprise of the CNT and the UGT of Valencia province, and involved the workers who made the boxes and containers for the citrus fruit which was the main product of the region. After July 19, the CNT and UGT unions set up a joint regularizing committee to reorganize that industry, which employed 1,500 workers in the province.

Before the War there existed a situation which the CNT described as 'chaotic' in which a number of the employing firms were on the point of bankruptcy. The regulating committee took over all of the enterprises, standardizing prices, wages and working hours throughout the province, and in the beginning acquired new machinery, and distributed all of the machinery available so as to get, in its judgment, the most efficient output for the industry as a whole.

As was true in most of the collectivized industries, in this case a system of medical care for all members of the collective and their families, and pensions for retired workers, were established. There were also more unspecified cultural improvements made.

By the latter part of 1937, the principal problem facing the Comité Regularizador was that of getting adequate transport to bring the wood which the industry required from the other parts of Spain. The Comité Regularizador made a special appeal to the ministry of transport to make available the facilities which were needed.[6]

The Paper Collective of Urgel

In the Catalan provincial city of Urgel there were two paper manufacturing plants, which before the Civil War belonged to the Sociedad Anónima La Forestal de Urgel. For some time they had been subsidized by the government, but shortly before the outbreak of the War they had been closed down, apparently as a result of a strike.

Soon after the defeat of the Rebels in Catalonia, the workers of the two plants in Urgel decided to open them, in view of the threat of a scarcity of paper in the region. The financial situation of the new collective was an unhappy one. One report on the collective late in 1937 noted: 'There were 19,000 pesetas in the bank and an enormous debt. It was necessary to pay five weeks of strike. The collective put its greatest efforts in normalizing things. Within three months we had paid the five weeks' wages, and during the year the debts had been reduced by seventy percent. At the present time there are enough funds to deal with all the needs.'

Between January and September 1937, the two plants in Urgel had produced 5,600 tons of paper. This compared with a comparable period just before the closing of the plant in 1936 when they had turned out 4,800 tons.[7]

Collectivization of Housing

A good deal of housing stock was taken over during the first days and weeks of the Civil War by the various organizations which participated in the Revolution. According to the anarchist writer, Lazarillo de Tormes:

> In addition to having taken over the most urgent things, such as automobiles, palaces and industries, the people also seized the homes whose owners had fled abroad or who had been judged to be fascists. These seized houses served to have the people cease to live in infected slums and begin to live as persons. Afterwards they were used to give refuge to the many who fled the territory invaded by the rebels ... The families of those who fought in the trenches, as well as others whom the fascist barbarism had forced to flee towards us in search of help, had a perfect right to be housed and a special right to be housed in the homes of the enemy. It is not necessary to say that this housing was absolutely gratis.[8]

There is no information concerning how or by whom such housing was apportioned to those who presumably needed it. However, it is clear that as the State recovered at least some of its authority, it sought to control the housing which had been seized. The Negrín government decreed that, as of August 1 1937, rent would have to be paid to the government by those occupying buildings which had been seized. This applied not only to housing accommodation but to edifices which had been taken over by various parties and union groups. As Lazarillo de Tormes commented, 'There was lacking only the small detail of whether the people would agree to pay...'[9] There is no data available on how successful the government was in collecting its rents.

Two Mining Collectives

Most of the mining industry of Spain lay in the regions of Vizcaya (Basque country), and Asturias, which were with the Republic in the first part of the Civil War, and in León and Andalusia, regions which quickly fell into Rebel hands. However, there were some mines of various kinds in Catalonia and the Levante. In two of these, the experience with collectivization had contrasting results, more for political than for economic reasons.

The more successful of the two involved pyrite mines in the vicinity of the town of La Unión, some nine kilometers from Cartagena, in the province of Murcia in the Levante region. Due to the Depression, those mines had been closed down before the outbreak of the War, and most of the miners were unemployed. However, there continued to exist unions affiliated with both the CNT and the UGT.

With the outbreak of the War, the workers took control of the mines, and proceeded to put them back in operation, both the CNT and UGT miners participating in this. In the beginning, each mine was collectivized separately.

However, the CNT soon proposed that all of the mines be 'socialized', that is, be organized as a single collectivized enterprise. They met stiff opposition to this from the UGT, which was controlled in that area by the Communist Party, which in principle was against collectivization. So, in six of the mines where the CNT had a majority, they decided to carry out the policy of socialization on their own.

However, they were immediately faced with financial problems. The new socialized enterprise did not have the funds necessary to modernize the installations. So they turned to the CNT Chemical Workers' Union of Badalona in Catalonia for help. It responded favorably, on the condition that the miners send their output of pyrite to the chemical collectives of Badalona. With the 50,000 pesetas received by this arrangement, new machinery and equipment for washing the mineral, was installed. The miners also solved the problem of lack of sufficient transport facilities to get the mineral to a shipping point by mounting a long cable along which large containers full of mineral could be rapidly lowered from the hills in which the mines were located to their destination.[10]

Less happy was the fate of a collective formed by potassium miners at Sailent in Catalonia. Those mines belonged to a foreign company with its headquarters in Paris, but shortly before the outbreak of the War the foreign managers and technicians had left Spain. So, after

July 19, the workers seized control of the mines, and elected a control committee, which invited Juan Farre, a leader of the CNT's Commercial Workers' Union of Barcelona to be manager of the enterprise.

Things seemed to be going well until the collective began to ship the products of the potassium mines abroad. Before the War, 90 percent the output has been for sale abroad, and Spain produced about 30 percent of the potassium then being sold in the world market. However, now, as soon as the product reached French soil, the French company, Potasas Ibéricas SA, instituted a court suit, claiming that the mineral belonged to it.

Several such suits were brought. Facing the claims of the French company, lawyers for the workers' collective argued that what the company had had was a concession from the Spanish government, authorizing it to mine potassium; and that when it abandoned that concession as it in effect had done when its representatives left Spain just before the outbreak of the War, the company had forfeited its concession. At least some French courts accepted this argument, provided that the Spanish government formally declared the concession forfeit, and transferred it to the workers' collective.

The workers then approached Juan Peiró, the CNT leader who was then minister of industry, and he brought this proposition before Largo Caballero's cabinet, where Finance Minister Juan Negrín strongly objected, saying that it would cause 'international problems'. Thereupon, Prime Minister Francisco Largo Caballero suggested to Peiró that he issue the transfer of the concession in a ministerial order, not requiring full cabinet consent. Peiró did this, and it appeared in the *Diario Oficial* a few days before the fall of the Largo Caballero government.

One of the first things that Juan Negrín did when he shortly afterwards became prime minister was to cancel Peiró's ministerial order. The workers of the mines then held a general assembly and developed a series of conditions under which the company would return to Spain and the workers would again become its employees. A delegation was sent to Paris to negotiate with the French company. After two meetings with the company's representatives, the workers' delegation was told flatly that the company had no intention of returning to Spain until the establishment of 'conditions of personal and legal security'. The company representatives added that they could afford to wait the two years they expected it might take for the Franco forces to win the war and re-establish such conditions.

In the face of this situation, the workers had no alternative but to close down production in the mines. A small group of workers was named to keep the mines in condition to reopen as soon as the opportunity presented itself. The rest of the workers either went into the army, or found employment with the government of Catalonia on various public works projects in the vicinity.

Juan Farre concluded telling Víctor Alba his account of the fate of the Sailent miners' collective by noting: '... The war over, the mines were in perfect condition, and the company, upon returning, could begin to exploit them immediately.'[11]

The Oil Refining Collective CAMPSA in Catalonia

Before the Civil War, the refining and distribution of petroleum products was the monopoly of a predominantly government firm, known by its initials as CAMPSA. Although apparently this did not happen everywhere in the Republican area, in Catalonia CAMPSA was taken over by the workers with the outbreak of the War. The workers in general assembly elected a six-person central committee of management, while the workers of six different sections of the petroleum operation – except the refineries – elected their own people to supervise those parts of the enterprise. Apparently, the five refineries in the region were taken over separately by the CNT's Sindicato Regional del Petroleo.[12]

Many years later, the Socialist who had been secretary of the Republican government's petroleum council indicated to me that he had not been favorably impressed with the CNT's control of the Catalan oil industry. He claimed that at least in the first months of the War, although the collectives in the various oil refineries sold the oil they produced, they did not pay the national government for the crude oil which it had provided, and for other things which it owed the Republican regime.

Finally, according to Sr Martínez Perera, the Socialist official, he went on an inspection tour of the Catalan oil industry, soon after the May Days. When he went to the refinery at Sabadell, which produced aviation gas, he was met by workers armed with machine guns. Only after much persuasion did they take him in to see the head of the workers' council which was running the refinery. He did concede that that gentleman was 'A fairly reasonable person'.[13]

Collectives in the Gastronomic Industry

One of the largest collectives formed during the Civil War was that in the hotel and restaurant industry of Barcelona, referred to in Spanish as the 'gastronomic' industry. It had 114 different establishments under its control, and was organized as a single enterprise, the Agrupamiento de la Industria Gastronómica (AIG). The AIG controlled 30 hotels, boarding houses and pensions; three luxury restaurants and five 'of second category', five large café-restaurants and brasseries, 52 café-bars, and various other establishments. Some 3,000 men and 1,000 women belonged to the collective.

The AIG introduced a number of innovations. It established five large warehouses, two for food products, two for utensils and one cold-storage house. It also had a sausage plant, an ice-cream plant and another for making 'preserves in general'. It established a plant nursery, where it experimented with the growing of some of the products used in the industry.

Early in November 1937, the AIG opened a number of 'popular restaurants', which provided cheap meals. By the end of the month, those were serving some 6,000 meals a day.

As in most collectives, the AIG sought to improve the working conditions of its members. It was reported that 'the majority of the kitchens had to be reformed', to make them more healthy, and showers were installed for the workers of a number of the enterprises.

The gastronomic collective of Barcelona also provided the equivalent of social security for its members. Those who were sick were given their full wage, those who were retired or invalided got 50 percent of their former wage, and women workers received five weeks off with full pay when they were giving birth. There was a clinic, with various specialties for the members of the AIG free of charge to them.

This collective was run by a councillor delegate, an interventor of the Catalan government, a permanent committee and a Consejo de Empresa, all elected by a General assembly of the workers. In each unit of the AIG there was a director delegate named by the Consejo de Empresa and two councillor delegates named by the workers of the unit.

The AIG was a joint enterprise of the UGT and the CNT, in which the former was the majority. This fact was reflected in the Consejo de Empresa, which consisted of the interventor of the Catalan government, and ten councillors of the UGT and five of the CNT.[14]

In the neighboring city of Hospitalet de Llobregat much of the food-dispensing industry was also taken over by the workers. In this case, it was the local Sindicato de Alimentación of the CNT which took over all of the food markets except three cooperatives, which were allowed to remain separate after a bitter controversy. It also took over many of the bars and restaurants of the town. However, they did not force the small bar and restaurant owners who did not want to join the collective to do so, and among some of those who did join, they were allowed to continue to run their establishments as managers on behalf of the *sindicato*.

The city of Hospitalet de Llobregat, which was largely dominated by the CNT during the War, had its own supply secretariat, headed by a young CNT member, Gines Alonso. He had his problems with the Sindicato de Alimentación, particularly on the setting of prices. On several occasions, he had to engage in very hard bargaining with the *sindicato* leaders to get them to sell at prices which he did not consider to be exorbitant.[15]

In Valencia, the gastronomic *sindicato* controlled almost all of the hotels, cafés and bars of the city, most of them by agreement between the former owners and the workers. In addition, the *sindicato* established (as in Barcelona) 'public restaurants' to serve the refugees who had swarmed into Valencia.

In the case of one of the bars which had been collectivized by agreement of owner and workers, the Bar Balanza, where the former owner continued as cashier in the collective, the firm was turned back to the owner by the Franco authorities. But when he refused to point out to them those who had been active in the collective, he was sentenced to 30 years in prison on the charge of 'collaboration with the Reds'.[16]

Another food-related collective was Fabricas de Harina Socializadas de Valencia y Provincia. This was formed on October 1 1936 by the workers of the grain mills of the Valencia region. It was led by a *consejo obrero*, made up of members of both the CNT and UGT unions in that sector. The Consejo Obrero had under it several sections, dealing with grain purchases, allocation of flour, and general administration.

Representatives of the grain-purchasing section scoured the countryside for all the sources of wheat which it could encounter. According to Gaston Leval, its agents upon occasion even penetrated areas controlled by Franco's troops.

The allocations section received orders from all of the bakeries of the region on a daily basis. It then arranged for the distribution and sale of the flour available based on 'the needs of each baker and people, making a just and equitable distribution'.

As the War progressed, the problem of providing enough flour became more and more complicated. On the one hand, there was a certain decrease of other kinds of food, with consequent increase in the demand for bread. On the other, the population of Valencia was increased substantially as the result of the arrival of refugees from parts of the country occupied by the Franco troops.

In addition, the Fabricas de Harina Socializadas faced the hostility of the communist minister of agriculture, Vicente Uribe. Gaston Leval claimed: '...the available wheat was rapidly monopolized by the Minister of agriculture ... who should have calculated and foreseen the situation, but on the other hand procrastinated a great deal about establishing an agreement with Molinos Socializados: kill the revolution if you can't dominate it...'

In November 1937, the Valencia milling collective sent a memorandum to the ministry of agriculture suggesting four steps: '1. Monopoly by the State of the existing wheat in the loyal territory of the

Republic. 2. Equitable distribution of the same to the provinces, in conformity with the needs of each of them. 3. Issuing of price ceilings on wheat of not more than forty-four pesetas a metric quintal... 4. Immediate importation by the State of wheat from other countries (Russia and Argentina, etc.) to assure the present needs.'

According to Leval, 'The government gave silence for an answer' to these suggestions. 'It was enough for it to make daily proclamations announcing the imminent defeat of fascism. There came the moment in which wheat and flour were lacking.' He added, 'But, while it was possible to make bread in Valencia, the population owed this to the Fabricas Socializadas.'[17]

The Public Entertainment Collective of Barcelona

Like most of the rest of the economy of Barcelona, the public entertainment industry was collectivized, first spontaneously by those employed in each part of the sector, then decision of the general assembly of the CNT's Sindicato de Espectáculos Públicos. The collectivization involved the movie houses, legitimate theater, music (including opera), bull fighting, the circus, jai alai *frontons* and dog-racing enterprises.

Right after the beginning of the War, the CNT union was presented with a moral problem: whether to continue in operation those public spectacles which involved betting – the dog races and jai alai games. It was finally decided to continue them in operation, in part to preserve the jobs of the workers involved, and in part because public demand for them continued. The union was encouraged to keep these open, too, by the government of Catalonia, which received considerable income from taxes on betting.

Public entertainment activities during the first part of the War were coordinated by an economic commission of the *sindicato*. It was in charge of transferring funds from those public entertainment sectors which were prosperous to those which had deficits. The continuously prosperous segments of public entertainment were the motion picture houses, and the activities involving betting. Funds from them were used to subsidize the legitimate theater, musical and operatic performances and the circus, all of which tended to have deficits.

The *sindicato* sought to make more widely available to the public both the legitimate theater and musical and operatic performances. Decisions about what plays should be performed, what concerts should be given and what operatic performances there should be, were not taken on the basis of whether they would pay for themselves.

José Robuster, head of the dog-racing section of the *sindicato*, who described the public entertainment collective to Víctor Alba, sketched the way in which decisions were made by the economic committee of the *sindicato*: 'The Economic Committee received the suggestion, a commission of actors, musicians, authors was gotten together which reported on the work or project, and if the report was favorable, means of financing it were sought, even if a deficit was foreseen. Authors' copyright continued to be paid as usual...' Robuster also insisted that ideological and political considerations did not enter into these decisions, and that no 'war plays' were offered.

Before the War, because of the effects of the Depression, there had been extensive unemployment among actors, musicians and the like. However, there was little if any during the War.

One of the most controversial decisions made by the general assembly of the *sindicato* right at the beginning of the War was that everyone in the public entertainment field should get the same wage, 15 pesetas a day, which was five pesetas more than Republican militiamen at the front were receiving. Although this was more than the lowest wage paid in the sector before the War, it was also far from the highest.

Those who were most upset by the egalitarian wage system were the actors, musicians and bull fighters. Although most of the actors and musicians joined the CNT when compulsory unionization was instituted, a minority of actors formed a UGT union. Also, the employees of the *fronton*, most of whom came from Madrid and there had belonged to the UGT, continued their UGT affiliation in Barcelona.

The bull fighters presented a special problem. There were relatively few bull fights during the War, but the bull fighters, like everyone else in the entertainment industry, received their 15 pesetas a day. However, when it came time to put on a bull fight, they demanded the much higher pay to which they were accustomed – but did not get it.

Few of the employers in this part of the economy fled, went into hiding or otherwise disappeared. They were incorporated into the collective, getting the same wage as everyone else. In some cases, they continued to manage the particular enterprise that had been theirs before the conflict, in other cases they were given other tasks.

Within each entertainment enterprise, there continued to exist the trade-union grievance committee, which functioned more or less as before. In case of a disagreement between such a committee and the workers elected to run the particular enterprise, the matter went to the executive committee of the *sindicato*, not to the economic committee, which was relatively in the position of the employer.

After the May Events in Barcelona, the government of Catalonia, largely influenced by the Stalinist Partido Socialista Unificado de Catalonia, named an economic committee of public spectacles, which insisted on taking the place of the economic committee of the *sindicato*. Although the *sindicato* protested strongly, they finally conceded, upon the urging of the Catalan regional committee of the CNT.[18]

Collectivization in the Glass Industry

The glass industry of Barcelona and its environs was also collectivized. With the outbreak of the War, the workers in each enterprise took over the individual workshops. However, the industry was made up mostly of artisan shops and for the purposes of war production there was need for larger and more efficient enterprises. So the Glass Workers' *sindicato*, in its general assembly decided that all but two or three of the larger enterprises should be closed down, and the machinery and personnel from the rest should be moved to these. However, the last word on such closings was taken by the assembly of the workers of each individual plant. Apparently no plant collective voted against the move.

In each plant in the glass industry there was an assembly of the workers of that plant. The *sindicato* also had general assemblies at least every three months, and more often if required. But, in addition, each plant assembly had a delegate to the *sindicato*, and when the *sindicato* had to take some decision – such as a plant closing – the executive of the *sindicato* met with the appropriate plant delegates about it. Then, if necessary, plant and *sindicato* assemblies were called to make the final decision on the issue.

The workers in the glass industry made many innovations during the period of collective ownership. Thus, the secretary of the *sindicato*, when he went back to work after the end of the fighting in Barcelona in July 1936, found that the workers in the plant in which he worked had already decided to switch from production of perfume bottles – their pre-war work – to the making of little bottles to contain drinks for the militiamen at he front. The secretary, many years later, said that this was typical of the kind of changes that the workers made.

There were cases in which the former owner of the plant continued to serve as manager when the workers took over. One of these was the Unión Vidriera No. 7 plant, in San Vicente del Sols, run by a man described by the CNT union ex-secretary as 'a fervent Catholic, but in spite of that a very decent man', who had treated his workers well before the War. (More than 45 years later, the man's grandsons were still running the enterprise.[19]

One part of the glass industry to which the CNT gave some publicity was that of optical glass. The workers in that industry apparently had not been unionized before the outbreak of the War, but then they decided unanimously to join the CNT's glass workers' union. There were almost 4,000 workers in that segment of the industry.

There was not immediate collectivization in the optical glass industry. However, control committees were established in each enterprise, and a Committee of Relations of the Optic Section was established 'to unify prices, fix the distribution of stocks and resolve difficulties and conflicts which developed'.

At the beginning of November, a meeting of the workers and owners decided upon the conditions upon which collectivization would take place and, on November 6 1936, these conditions were accepted by a separate meeting of the employers. A central distribution committee, presumably as a subsidiary of the Optic Section of the glass union, was set up to plan for the whole industry in the Barcelona area.

The collective also instituted a number of innovations. Among these was the opening of shops to make leather and celluloid glasses cases, and the establishment of a furnace to make optic glass, something which had never been undertaken before.

The need for innovation was spurred by the fact that most of the raw material of the optic glass trade had been imported from abroad before the War. It was necessary to try to supplant exports by domestic production where possible. Even so, the industry was plagued with raw material shortages throughout the War.

Before the War, wages had ranged from 70 to 80 pesetas a week for manual workers, and from 350 to 500 a month for white-collar workers, with a few managers getting from 700 to 800 pesetas a month. Also, there were in some enterprises long working hours and payment by piecework. Right after the outbreak of the War, the weekly wage was set at 400 pesetas a month, for both men and women workers, with an extra payment for each family member supported by the worker. By January 1938, the monthly wage had risen to 700 pesetas. Piecework was eliminated.[20]

The CNT glass workers' union in Valencia also 'socialized' their industry in April 1937. This was done, the CNT–FAI reported, as the result of a 'pact' with the employers of the industry. There were two relatively large plants, and a number of smaller ones. Those smaller installations which were deemed uneconomic were closed down and their equipment transferred to other enterprises, with a record being kept of what had been transferred, with an eye to ultimate compensation of the former owners. There were some 230 workers in these plants, and 100 others who had been employed in them were at the front at the time of socialization.

Under workers' control, there was the general assembly which was the ultimate authority. There were also a workers' council, an accounting committee, a technical committee and local committees in each enterprise. Within the first six months of operation, improvements were made in the industry which brought its original value of 100,000 pesetas to some 225,000 pesetas. At the same time, the socialized industry continue to pay off debts incurred by the former employers.

Wages were increased substantially, from an average of 65 pesetas a week, to 90 pesetas. Also provision was made for pensions for some workers who had retired. Finally, 'like so many other socialized industries ... it was in the most lamentable state in so far as hygiene was concerned, the workers not having an adequate place to dress and serve other needs. Today, these comrades have magnificent showers, individual wardrobes and places to change clothes, as well as medicine chests for first aid in each workshop, factory or section...'[21]

Collectivization of the Barcelona Milk Supply

One of the collectives of which the CNT was most proud was that which was organized to provide milk for Barcelona, which had been primitive before the outbreak of the War. Firms which sold the product used to send trucks to pick up milk cans from farmers in the countryside, without much attention being paid to the sanitary and health conditions involved. Upon the outbreak of the War, the companies were three months behind in their payment to the farmers.

After July 19, the milk section of the Sindicato de Industrias Alimenticias of the CNT took over a large part of the milk distribution business. The union built seven refrigerating centers throughout Catalonia, to which the peasants in the vicinity brought their milk each day. By late 1937, one of these, the Franquesas milk station, was receiving milk regularly from about 600 peasants in the vicinity, and handled about 25,000 liters a day.

The union also dealt with the problem of transporting the milk from those milk collection centers to Barcelona, for pasteurization and subsequent distribution. It secured 16 new chassis, upon which it constructed refrigerated trucks capable of carrying 3,000, 5,000 or 6,000 liters. Once the liquid was in Barcelona, it was taken to the nine centers – there had been 60 reception centers before the War – where it was pasteurized, and then put into bottles, which were sealed mechanically, and then were refrigerated again.

From these pasteurization centers the milk was distributed to centers throughout the city which had their own refrigeration facilities, and which had been established by the union. The milk provided by the *sindicato* was destined principally for the sick, the hospitals and children under two years of age. It distributed some 45,000 liters of milk each day, but in addition there were about 10,000 liters sold by private firms operating under the pre-war circumstances.

As part of the milk workers' collective, there was a plant in Puigcerda in northern Catalonia, which before the War had mainly produced condensed milk. However, during the War, it had difficulty in obtaining the sugar necessary for turning out the product. As a result, it shifted to production of butter and cheese, principally for the army.

The CNT claimed that infant mortality decreased significantly during the War as a result of the improved provision of milk for children by the CNT's milk industry collective.[22]

The system of collecting, processing and distributing milk in Barcelona which the CNT had organized was largely maintained after the conflict was over – but naturally without the CNT.[23]

The Chocolate Workers' Cooperative of Torrente

Another collective project to which the anarchists gave considerable publicity was that of the chocolate makers of Torrente, a small town in the province of Valencia. Before the War, there had been 45 small enterprises, each with a few employees, turning out chocolate products of various kinds. On September 1 1936, the local CNT called a meeting of both workers and employers in this small industry. That meeting decided unanimously to establish the Cooperative of Chocolate Workers of Torrente. The new organization began immediately the construction of a single large plant, near the railroad line. Forty machines were installed in the plant, some brought by the former employers, others purchased by the cooperative. They turned out in the new plant considerably more products than the small scattered workshops had been able to do before, and there was greater quality control than in the past. Some new lines of product were initiated.

At a general assembly of the cooperative soon after the plant began to operate, someone proposed that there be a substantial increase in wages. However, the overwhelming sense of the meeting was that this was unwise, at least until the cooperative had begun to be profitable.

The chocolate cooperative was directed by a labor council of six members, elected by the general assembly of all of the members of the organization.[24]

Some Shoe and Leather Workers' Collectives

The leather and shoe industry was a significant part of the economy of the Mediterranean coastal areas of Loyalist Spain, particularly in the Levante. It had been badly hit by the Depression in the years preceding the Civil War.

Perhaps the single most important center of leather and shoe manufacturing was in and around the city of Elda (25,000 inhabitants) in the province of Alicante. Aside from Elda itself, in which there were 7,500 shoe workers (of whom 4,500 were in the CNT), in the nearby towns of Petrel, Monovar, Novelda and Sax there were also shoe and leather plants. In Petrel, there were 3,500 workers, and in Monovar, Novelda and Sax together there were an additional 2,000.

During the War, the CNT and UGT, working together, had two different approaches to collectivization in the shoe and leather industry of Elda and its vicinity. On the one hand, in Elda itself there were 12 factories, employing 2,800 workers which were totally collectivized. Each was run by a six-person committee elected by the general assembly of its workers. The CNT union coordinated the statistics of these 12 plants, and handled the disposition of their products. These plants worked mainly on the basis of orders from the ministry of defense.

On the other hand, the rest of the shoe and leather factories of the region were ostensibly left in the hands of their owners, with a control committee of workers keeping a watch on the management in each plant. But these plants, 80 in number with 12,500 workers, were brought together on August 1 1936 to form what was called the Sindicato de Industria de Calzado de Elda y Petrol (SICEP). It was formed at first on the initiative of the private owners, but the CNT and UGT unions soon demanded 60 percent representation in the organization and, according to Gaston Leval, it was in fact dominated by the workers.

The SICEP coordinated the shoe industry of Elda and vicinity. It bought and distributed the raw materials, it sold the output, developing an extensive sales network, not only in both segments of Loyalist Spain, but also in Algeria and Morocco. Its operations were financed in the beginning by loans (on the basis of mortgages on the privately owned plants) from local banks and a 7,000,000-peseta loan provided by Juan Peiró, the CNT leader who was then minister of industry.[25]

A somewhat similar approach to that used in Elda was adopted by the shoe and leather workers of Valencia, some 1,000 in number in 30 different plants. The CNT and UGT unions to which these workers belonged intervened and did not collectivize the industry in that city. Intervention took the form of establishing a Consejo Local de la Industria de la Piel y Calzado CNT–UGT, which undertook to coordinate the operation of the industry, while ostensibly leaving it in the hands of the private owners. The *consejo* took charge of obtaining and distributing raw materials, as well as of selling the output.

Although before the outbreak of the War there was substantial unemployment and part-time employment in the shoe and leather industry of Valencia, it was reported 15 months after the War started that all of the workers were fully employed. Wages were half again as high as they had been before July 19, and there were numerous improvements in working conditions, including installation of showers and clothes cabinets for the workers.[26]

In the case of one of the shoe plants in Valencia, the Ernesto Ferrer firm, which was also collectivized by agreement between the former owner and the workers, in which the owner served as adviser to the directive-administrative committee of the collective, he was a member of a mission which was sent on business to Paris by the Comité de Fabrica, and there told the other members of the mission that he would not return to Spain. After the War, although he emerged as a captain in the Falange he did not denounce or dismiss any of his workers. However, he did counsel some of those who had had major responsibility in the collective to 'retire from circulation' to protect themselves. Also, when some Falangista came to the factory looking for a particular worker, he always had the man wait in his office until an aide had 'looked for' the worker involved, and reported back that the worker had not come in to work that day.[27]

Soon after the outbreak of the Civil War, the CNT leather workers' union in Barcelona decided in a general assembly to collectivize the whole industry in that city, including large, small and middle-sized plants. The employers were called together and informed of what was to take place. This collective was the first one to be registered under the Catalan collectivization decree.

The workers decided to merge the smaller workshops into larger establishments. Some 40 small enterprises thus disappeared, and there were 27 plants under the control of the collective. In addition, it had six warehouses, for both raw materials and finished products. One sector of the collective was in charge of both wholesale and retail sale, and an extensive system of accounting was set up to keep track of both raw material needs and ultimate disposal of the collective's products.

During much of the War, the collective was able to purchase in France the raw materials which it needed to supplement what could be purchased in Loyalist Spain. However, the Negrín government finally prohibited this, as one of the measures designed to destroy the collective.[28]

A much smaller collective enterprise in the shoe industry was that in the Catalan city of Lérida. Right after the War began, a group of workers, together with the owner of a small shop and his son, joined to establish the Colectividad de Zapateros de Lérida. By the latter part of 1937 there were in all 38 workers, most of them employed in one large establishment. The collective was managed by a committee of six members, three of the CNT and three of the FAI, elected by an assembly of the workers.

Virtually all of the members of the collective had worked by hand before the War. But the collective acquired machines and, in November 1937, had 23 of these, of which all but four (which were rented) belonged to the collective. In one three-week period late in 1937, the collective produced nearly 500 pairs of footwear. They also did a lively shoe-repair business.

Early in November 1937, the city of Lérida was bombed by Franco aviation. This made it necessary for the plant to close for two weeks, but the workers received their pay during this period.

In the establishment of the wage scale in the Lérida collective, the anarchists certainly did not put fully into practice their egalitarian ideas. The scale provided for payment of 90 pesetas a week to male workers, 45 to 65 pesetas a week to female workers, and 20 pesetas to apprentices.

Most of the output of the Lérida collective consisted of boots for the armed forces, and was sold to the Catalan government. However, according to Gaston Leval, near the end of the existence of the collective, the Stalinist Councillor of Economy Juan Comorera refused to pay for the boots that the Catalan government had received. The collective was forced to get along on relatively limited civilian sales, which income the workers supplemented with the products of their gardens, according to Leval. Shortly afterwards, the Franco conquest of Lérida put a definitive end to the collective.[29]

The Unión Naval de Levante Collective

The Unión Naval de Levante was a ship construction and repair yard in Valencia, employing 1,400 workers, about equally divided between the CNT and the UGT. It was taken over by the workers soon after the War broke out. A Comité de Fabrica with two representatives from each of the 21 sections into which the enterprise was divided was elected. That group chose a *comité obrero* of seven, together with two administrators to have day-to-day charge of the Unión Naval.

At the time the workers took over the enterprise, three ships were under construction, a Mexican gunboat, and two oil tankers for CAMPSA. The gunboat, which was almost completed, was turned over to the Mexican authorities in August 1936. Work was suspended on the two tankers, with the enterprise concentrating on ship repairs and construction of smaller vessels.

The Unión Naval was running at considerable financial loss at the time the workers took it over. By the end of the second semester under workers' control, it was making a small but appreciable profit. Also by the end of the first year, the collective had succeeded in replacing a number of worn out machines and other installations.

Working conditions had been considerably improved, including installations of showers and wardrobes for the workers' use. The collective also installed a clinic, attended by two doctors, where the workers could receive a variety of treatment, including operations.[30]

Collectivization of Commerce in Valencia

The CNT's Sindicato Unico Mercantil collectivized a substantial part of the commerce of Valencia. The union was divided into various sections, which took over a considerable amount of the trade in various kinds of products. Together with units of the UGT, the Sindicato Unico Mercantil also reorganized the city's principal large food market.

The food section of the *sindicato*, which consisted largely of proprietors of small grocery stores, most of whom had no employees, decided to collectivize these enterprises. A year after the War began, that collective controlled more than 80 percent of such stores. It had closed down 70 which were deemed unsanitary, but to meet the needs of people served by them had opened up 29 new branches in different parts of the city, which according to the CNT 'in addition to meeting the needs which they were designed to fulfill, are equipped with all the modern improvements'. This section of the Sindicato Unico had 950 members, all of whom received wages from the collective.

The 75 members of the meat section of the union also formed a collective. A CNT source stressed that, with the workers of this section receiving a regular wage, they had less incentive than before to try to cheat their customers. Other groups which established collectives were sections made up of merchants selling eggs and chickens, and a section of people selling garlic and limes.[31]

A major section of the Sindicato Unico was that which sold coal. A meeting at the end of September 1936 of its members decided to socialize the distribution and sale of coal in the city. As in many other spheres of activity, the CNT unionists sought to rationalize coal delivery. On the one hand, small merchants who had had coal delivery as a sideline, while they worked most of the time in some other line of endeavor, were asked to decide which work they wanted to concentrate on and, if coal delivery, to become part of the collective; if on the alternate occupation, to turn over their coal business to the collective. On the other hand, a number of inefficient businesses were closed down, and were supplanted by larger, and presumably more efficient, outlets. In addition, the collective took special care to make coal available to outlying parts of the city, where delivery had been at best sporadic in the past, using a small fleet of its own vehicles for this purpose.

The coal collective also established a central distribution point to which the coal was first brought. There and elsewhere, facilities were installed in which the workers kept their street clothes while working, and where they could bathe once their day's work in a rather dirty occupation was completed.

More than a year after the establishment of the coal collective, its members were proud of the fact that the price of coal distributed in Valencia had not risen since the commencement of the War. This was in sharp contrast to the situation in Barcelona, Madrid and other Loyalist cities.

Finally, the Federación de los Trabajadores de la Distribución took over the management of the principal wholesale food market of Valencia, on February 1 1937. In that new federation, there was participation of the commercial and transport workers' unions of the CNT and UGT in the city, as well as of the regional agricultural workers' federations of the CNT and UGT. According to CNT sources, the workers' administration of that market laid particular stress on preventing price gauging of retailers who obtained their products there, on cutting out traditional fraudulent practices, and on physically cleaning up the market. The CNT claimed that prices in this market had been kept substantially below those in a smaller but competing private wholesale market which was still in operation.

The Federación de los Trabajadores de la Distribución had also improved the working conditions of the members of the collective. It had built new and more modern offices, as well as installing new showers and toilet facilities for the workers.[33]

The Lorqui Canning Collective

One of the collectives which the anarchists at the time cited as a model of workers' control was that of a canning enterprise in Lorqui, a town some 30 kilometers from the city of Murcia. This plant had belonged to the Count of La Cierva, who had won certain fame for bad labor relations and reactionary politics. In 1934, he had closed down the enterprise due to the Depression.

At the beginning of the War, the workers, both of the CNT and the UGT, occupied the plant and began to put it into operation once more. There were plenty of fruits and vegetables grown in the vicinity, and initial shortages of sugar and of cans, into which to pack the product, were apparently overcome by the collective. By February 1938, it had turned out some 80,000 boxes of canned tomatoes, and 40,000 boxes of canned orange pulp and preserves of various kinds.

Although the government officially intervened this plant, in fact it continued to be run by a committee of control elected by the workers. The collective was a joint enterprise of the CNT and the UGT.[34]

Collectivization in the Printing Industry

At least some of the printing establishments in Barcelona were taken over by the workers. This was the case with the Grafica Rieusset, a plant owned by a Frenchman. After the workers took over the enterprise, the ex-owner turned up, dressed like a worker. However, the new committee of control did not permit him to take over, but instead facilitated his getting out of the country to return to Toulouse, where he had another printing plant. The committee of control dismissed the manager of the plant, who was unpopular with the workers.

One of the first things the collective did was to cut drastically the pay of the managerial employees, which did not win them to support the Revolution. The collective also decided to maintain the inequality of pay between men and women workers, although Antonia Fontanillas, daughter of an editor of the anarchist newspaper *Solidaridad Obrera*, who emerged as the leader of the women employees, succeeded in obtaining a substantial wage increase for the women. Although there was some discussion of setting a single wage for all of the workers, this was never done, seniority wage differentials particularly being maintained. Miss Fontanillas also represented the plant union in the CNT printing trade union of Barcelona.

On the *Solidaridad Obrera* it was decided after the War began to introduce the same wage for everyone, from the editor down to the lowliest worker. They had not had this system before the War, editors and the other administrative employees getting substantially higher salaries than the average workers received.[35]

Barcelona's Barbers' Collective

One of the collectives which some people at the time thought of as bordering on the ridiculous, but of which the CNT was quite proud, was that of the barbers of Barcelona. On July 19, there were approximately 11,00 barber shops in the city, many of which had quite unsanitary conditions, and paid very low wages. An appreciable number of barbers were unemployed.

So, at a general assembly of the CNT barbers' union soon after the outbreak of the War it was decided to collectivize the barber trade. The owners of the shops were not consulted, and apparently there were a certain number who strongly objected. Others, on the other hand, became members of the collective.

There was considerable rationalization of the industry. The number of barber shops was reduced from 1,100 to 235, and equipment from those which were closed was used to increase the service in the shops that remained open, or to replace worn-out equipment in those shops.

Under the new regime, the *barberias* remained open from eight in the morning until nine in the evening, with two shifts of barbers, each working six and a half hours. In each barber shop there were two *delegados*, whose job it was to take the day's earnings to the headquarters of the union and to pick up the pay of all of the workers in their enterprise each Saturday noon.

The considerable savings on rent, light and other costs of the shops which were closed down were used to increase the pay of the members of the collective. Everyone in the collective received the same pay.

The collective eliminated unemployment among the barbers of Barcelona. The ranks of the collective included not only the former employees who had worked for a wage, but also the ex-employers, and widows of union members, who were given jobs in the various shops.[36]

Frank Jellinek, the British observer, writing in August 1937, maintained that even the brothels of Barcelona had been collectivized, citing as his source Eduardo Barriobero, the CNT lawyer who reorganized the courts and administration of justice in Catalonia in the early weeks of the Civil War. Jellinek first noted the anarchist campaign against prostitution, which included 'horrifying anti-venereal posters' put up by the Mujeres Libres, and observed that the anarchists tried to approach the problem from two angles, 'the reform of the Society which had produced prostitutes and made them pariahs, and the "psycho-therapic re-education" of the prostitutes themselves.'

However, Jellinek goes on to say: 'The brothels were actually collectivized. Eduardo Barriobero has explained how this happened. One night the Generalidad sent him a commission of girls who wanted him to fix a proper tariff. "Love," he said, "cannot be an article subject to a tariff. Let us be more practical. Let us create the Love Union, and then you can expropriate the industry and throw the Madame out." "The odd thing," Barriobero notes, "was that these Unions were really seriously controlled – by the Caterers' Union!" '37

Some Examples of Communalization

In some parts of Loyalist Spain – particularly in a number of smaller cities and towns, the anarchists were able not only to collectivize particular industries, but to establish a degree of planning and coordination of the whole local economy through the labor movement. In those instances, they were able to come closer than in the major cities to their ideals of the union as the base of the reorganization of the economy and the local commune as the basis of the polity of the revolutionary society.

There is no information available concerning how many of such experiments took place during the Civil War. However, as I have indicated in an earlier chapter, they were quite widespread during the first year of the War in the parts of Aragón controlled by the anarchists. In the present chapter, I will consider one case in Catalonia and two in the Levante region.

In the Catalan town of Rosas everything was collectivized. The most important occupation was fishing, and a fishing collective was one of the first established. The previous wage earners formed it as well as the owners, not all of the latter doing so willingly. On the outskirts of the town there was an agrarian collective, including all of the farms in the area. In both the fishing and agrarian collective each member was paid the same basic income, with additional amounts for each family member dependent on the collective member.

In addition to these collectives, there were others of bakers, mechanics, woodworkers and a few other groups. All of the collectives were represented in an economic council, which coordinated the economy of the whole town, helping those collectives which were financially weaker from the funds of those in a better fiscal condition.

All were created by CNT members. Members of the CNT and the Catalan Left Party, the only important political groups in town, made up the town council, which was in charge of supply. It abolished all private stores, and set up a number of cooperative distribution centers, where the workers bought with special tickets. Part of the workers' pay was in these tickets, part was in money.[38]

A somewhat similar development occurred in the city of Villena de Valencia, with between 25-30,000 people. Here the commune was established to cover the whole *comarca* of which Villena de Valencia was the center. At the time the War broke out, the UGT tended to dominate among the agricultural workers of the area, the CNT among urban workers.

Most landowners disappeared with the outbreak of the War, and their lands were reorganized as collectives, although small land-owners who stayed and did not want to join the collectives were not forced to do so. Aside from agriculture, there were reportedly 14 urban collectives organized. These included those in the wood, metal, leather, baking, wine and alcohol, and textile industries. All of these had representatives in the Consejo Regulador de Economía, set up jointly by the CNT and UGT. This organization had complete charge of the economy of the *comarca*. It was the only seller outside the *comarca* of goods produced there. All wages of all industries were paid by the *consejo*; all profits went to the *consejo*.

Conditions throughout the economy were equalized. The *consejo* used the profits from those industries doing well to help those doing badly, wages were equal for all – fixed at first at the wage of a soldier at the front, they were later raised significantly.

The great majority of the industries in the area reportedly did well financially and economically. In the wood industry, for instance, all firms were doing badly at the outbreak of the War; most of them had heavy debts. The collective paid off those debts, and at the end of the War all the firms were reportedly in better shape than they had been when it began.

In most cases, the ex-employers were incorporated into the collectivized industry as workers. In the wood industry, for instance, a CNTer was president of the collective, while an ex-employer was secretary, the treasurer was a member of the UGT, and there were four other members of the elected executive, of which three were ex-employers.

The ex-employer who was secretary of the wood collective told a story in later years: he said that he had had an anaemic cat, which someone stole. The thief fattened the cat up until it was in fine condition, then returned it. He was grateful for the cat's being fattened up, but he still insisted that the cat had been stolen. The 'cat', of course, was his firm.

There were no moves in Villena de Valencia to rationalize the various industries, such as occurred in many other places. However, in the local textile industry which had been quite small when the War began, the plants were increased considerably in size. They supplied shirts and underclothes for the army.[39]

The communization of which the CNTers were most proud, and about which they subsequently wrote a good deal, took place in Alcoy, with a population of 45,000, the second largest city in the province of Alicante.

Although there existed unions of the UGT, with a total membership of about 3,000, principally among civil servants and small merchants, it was the CNT, with 6,500 members, which 'controlled the essential economic functions necessary to social life'. The CNT unions in the town included those of workers in food, paper and cardboard manufacturing, construction (including architects), hygiene, transport, public utilities, cobbling and bootblacking, textiles and clothing, metallurgy, professions (teachers, painters, writers), and truck gardeners on the outskirts of the city.

In this ease, it was the CNT unions which undertook the collectivization of their respective parts of the local economy. Gaston Leval insisted on the anarcho-syndicalist and anti-bureaucratic nature of the economic organizations in Alcoy in the years of the Civil War: 'Everything was controlled by the syndicates. But it must not therefore be assumed that everything was decided by a few higher bureaucratic committees without consulting the rank and file members of the union. Here also libertarian democracy was practiced. As in the CNT there was a reciprocal double structure: from the grass roots at the base – the mass of workers, unionists and militants – upwards and in the other direction a reciprocal influence from the federation of these same local units at all levels downwards. From the source back to the source...' At all levels, the administrators are chosen by the appropriate general assembly of the workers.

At the apex of the wartime economic structure in Alcoy was the Syndical Administrative Committee. Each industry had representatives on this committee. Leval described its functions: When an order is received by the sales section it is passed on to the production section whose task it is to decide which workshops are best equipped to produce the required articles. While settling this question, they ordered the required raw materials from the corresponding section. The latter gives instructions to the shops to supply the materials and finally the buying section receives the details of the transaction so it can replace the material used.'[40]

Urban Collectives in Asturias

Little has been published about the collectives established in the Asturias region. However, it is clear that in the early days and weeks of the Civil War, there was widespread taking over of both industries and commerce by their workers. The CNT chose to regard this process as provisional, pending the successful conclusion of the War, after which final decisions would be taken.

Ronald Fraser has noted: 'In the ... steel town of La Felguera, a traditional CNT stronghold, the anarcho-syndicalists made no attempt to collectivize the Duro-Felguera iron and steel works, which employed nearly 4,000 workers. As in October 1934, a workers' control committee was set up, composed entirely of CNT militants, who soon discovered that production was impeded by the loss of engineers who had fled or gone into hiding. Two politically uncompromised engineers from the works were found in Bilbao and returned when asked to be on the workers' committee, which did not technically manage the works but exercised considerable weight on those who did.'[41]

The post-Franco regional CNT newspaper *Acción Libertaria* reported: 'The CNT sought to put under the professional and economic administration of the *sindicato* the industries which were originally seized; it suggested that the labor organization could take care of the industries, stores, cafes, restaurants, etc., until the end of hostilities, postponing until then the solution of the problem in conformance with legislative norms established for the whole country.'[42]

Ramón Alvarez has noted that 'industries were centralised in the Councillorship of Industry, headed by Segundo Blanco.'[43] Blanco issued instructions to bring together in larger and more efficient units, the small industries. He recommended that the owners affected be incorporated in the productive process, providing them with a labor position and means of livelihood the same as the rest of the work force.'[44]

A regional congress of the CNT in May 1937 called for the establishment of local, regional and national economic councils, structured along the lines of the CNT. These councils would have varied tasks of coordinating the economic activities within their jurisdictions: 'In summary: to promote and stimulate all the initiatives assuring greater knowledge of the needs of the country, and rational control of the vast field of productive activities.'[45] The final crisis in the War, in so far as Asturias was concerned, came only a few weeks after the CNT regional congress, so there was little chance of putting into effect the congress' resolutions.

Ramón Alvarez has briefly sketched the organization of the wartime food distribution industry: '...The first labor controls were established in the food industry after it was taken over and put back into operations; contacts were established to guarantee the provisioning of an isolated zone. We had to organize a network of distribution posts in the neighborhoods. There was formed the General Cooperative Council and then there was instituted the family card to be used at the distribution posts. There was established the Councillorship of Commerce and Fishing (I was Councillor of this) which assured the supplies for the civilian population and the army.'[46]

There was widespread 'syndicalization' of the industries in the Asturias region. CNT leader Segundo Blanco, as councillor of industry in the Consejo Interprovincial de Asturias y León issued a decree to the effect that 'the social revolution having triumphed, all industries, their working equipment, will be turned over to the *sindicatos* for them to direct and administer as property of the workers.' The more or less official Stalinist history of the Civil War claimed: 'Each *sindicato* made of the firms which it controlled a fiefdom and hindered the efforts towards establishing a joint plan for war production.'

However, contradicting this statement, the same source noted: '...The principal metallurgical factories, especially those of Trubia, Moreda, Laviana, Metales Lugones, Duro Felguera and others commenced to produce, although in small quantities, artillery projectiles, cannons and armored vehicles and carried out production of ammunition for rifles.'[47]

The fishing industry of Asturias, of major importance in the region, was collectivized on the initiative of the fishermen's unions. Included in this collective were also the fish-canning plants and fish markets. According to José Peirats, 'During the first months of the experiment, money did not circulate among the fishermen. Family supplies were provided through presentation of a producer's and consumer's card. The fishermen turned over their catch and received these cards in return.'[48]

Apparently, many industries were not in fact taken over by their *sindicatos*, The system of workers' control committees was adopted for those firms which were not collectivized. These were set up jointly by the CNT and UGT, and members of the control committees had to have belonged to one or the other of the trade union groups before July 19 1936.

The role of the Control Committee was defined by a joint document of the regional CNT and UGT of January 1937:

The Comités de Control are that: Comités de Control. CNT and UGT promise to popularize among their affiliates the mission of these Comités de Control, which is not the administration or the absorption of functions of the technical administrative bodies. Their principal role is collaboration with the management; aiding the administration with all kinds of initiatives and suggestions, working for exact fulfillment of production, in the organization of which they will remain informed, denouncing to the administration anomalies and defects so as to correct them and surpass the conditions of labor and production. These same obligations the direction, administration and technical bodies will have towards the Comités de Control.[49]

Conclusion

There was the widest range of experiments with workers control of sectors of the urban economy in Loyalist Spain during the Civil War. Usually, the initiative for these came from CNT workers, or workers at least influenced by anarchist preachings. However, notably in the Levante and Asturias regions, there was frequent participation by UGT workers as well.

For the most part, the workers' control was on an enterprise-by-enterprise basis. However, there were other instances in which a particular union sought to coordinate all of the worker-controlled plants within its jurisdiction. Finally, there were an unknown number of experiments with union coordination of the whole of a local economy, a few examples of which we have looked at. Only in the Asturias region was there apparently an effort to coordinate the collectives on a region-wide basis, and this was carried out under the aegis of two CNT members of the wartime Asturias government.

22

Anarchist Educational, Health and Welfare Efforts

In previous chapters, we have considered the propensity of the wartime anarchist rural collectives to establish or expand schools in their respective areas. We have also looked at the almost universal tendencies of the urban collectives to provide for the medical needs of their members (including the extensive system established by the textile workers of Badalona) as well as to provide for pensions for retired members of the particular work groups establishing the collectives. In this chapter, we shall look at more general educational, medical and related activities of the anarchists during the Civil War, which were not specifically associated with a particular collective.

Traditional Spanish Anarchist Attitudes Towards Education

The Spanish anarchists had traditionally had an ambivalent attitude towards education. To sum this up in perhaps over-simplified terms, they believed passionately in the need for education, while at the same time tending to be suspicious of the educated.

Gerald Brenan speaking of the first decades of the twentieth century, described the passion for education of the rank and file anarchists: 'A movement for founding Anarchist schools ... grew up in various parts of the country. At Barcelona the *Escuela Moderna* was founded by Francisco Ferrer. At this children were brought up to believe in liberty, social equality and so on, and above everything else to hate the Church which taught false and "perverted" doctrines. There were also night schools for adults and a printing press which turned out a continuous stream of Anarchist books and pamphlets ... Other schools were founded in Andalusia. Working men were taught to read and to abjure religion, vice and alcoholism...'[1]

Gaston Leval at one point estimated that before the outbreak of the Civil War there were between 50 and 60 of these anarchist schools in various parts of Spain.[2] Elsewhere, he gave the larger estimate of 50 to 100.[3] 'To maintain this school I have seen the peasants of a certain village of the province of Valencia derive themselves of their sole pleasure, tobacco, to be able to give a *duro* (five pesetas) a month. The teacher was always a self-taught comrade who, in spite of the lack of a diploma was much more competent than the great majority of the official teachers.'[4]

Even some of the anarchists' opponents have paid tribute to their educational aspirations. For instance, Gabriel Pradel, who after the War was editor of the Socialist exile paper *El Socialista*, noted that although most CNTers were manual workers, many of them had a real thirst for education and read wisely although not necessarily in an organized and disciplined fashion, and had knowledge in a great number of fields.[5]

Germinal Esgleas, the companion of Federica Montseny and long-time national secretary of the CNT in Exile, who taught for many years in one of the anarchist 'rationalist', schools, in Mataró, near Barcelona, has described that institution. He drew a distinction between a 'rationalist' school and the Escuela Moderna of Francisco Ferrer. Whereas Ferrer's school sought to indoctrinate its pupils in anarchist ideas, the rationalist schools, as a matter of principle, did not try to indoctrinate the students in anything. Rather, they tried to give the students all the information and material they needed to make up their own minds.

In the school in which Esgleas taught, there were five teachers, only one of whom had been a teacher in a state school. The other four did not have official teaching qualifications. There were from

250 to 300 students, from the age of six to 16. Esgleas said that the school had as good equipment as the state schools of the time. The institution taught regular subjects such as reading, writing, arithmetic, geography, history, literature, mathematics up through algebra, which all students took, and there were other more advanced subjects for specially selected students.

Esgleas said that the CNT had such rationalist schools in most of the Catalan towns and cities where they had any significant following. They thought that they were important not only for the development of young people with inquiring minds, but also because of the poor quality of the other existing schools, Church and state run.[6]

The other side of the anarchists' attitude towards education was attested to by a number of anarchist leaders themselves, to whom we talked many years after the Civil War. For instance, Fidel Miró, the wartime leader of the Libertarian Youth, noted that a large part of the anarchist following in Andalusia and Murcia were illiterate, but that even in Catalonia, where illiteracy was less prevalent, most of the anarchist workers were self-taught, and that their ideas were 'rather disordered'. He noted that many of these self-taught workers were anti-intellectual. On the other hand, the extreme egalitarianism of the anarchists, symbolized by their use of the intimate *tu* instead of *usted* (you) when addressing even people they had never met before had the effect of offending the 'dignity' of many university-trained people.

Fidel Miró added that a few idealistic intellectuals were attracted to, and became part of, the anarchist movement. However, he also concluded that with certain important exceptions, the anarchists had been unfortunate in those intellectuals who did join their forces.[7]

Javier Elbaille, a leader of the exiled CNT, also emphasized the tendency of the anarchists to be suspicious of intellectuals, regarding them as 'bourgeois'. He noted that one result of this was that the CNT tended to have a shortage of trained personnel for administrative work when much of the economy was thrown into their hands, at the beginning of the Civil War.[8]

Salvador Gurrucharri, a leader of the Libertarian Youth in exile after the Civil War agreed with this analysis. However, he also noted that during the Civil War a 'remarkable' group of intellectuals who had never belonged to the organization, worked closely with the CNT in various aspects of its work.[9]

Some of the anarchist leaders had recognized the drawback presented by the limited part of the intelligentsia which it had associated with it. For instance, Gabriel Sesma, head of the metal workers' federation of Catalonia before and during the War, had sought to have the CNT develop a program for sending children of anarchist families to the university at CNT expense to obtain the training which would be useful after the Revolution. This proposal was turned down by the CNT, for fear that the young people so trained would become 'bourgeois'. Sesma noted that one result was that during the war, the CNT felt a considerable lack of adequately trained people in its own ranks.[10]

The CNT's suspicions of people with advanced education is perhaps reflected in the fact that the organization did not have a national teachers' federation until the Civil War was quite advanced. Only in July 1937 was the Federación Nacional de Sindicatos de la Enseñanza established. Its establishment was due to the initiative of the teachers' union of Madrid, which in September 1936 proposed the setting up of a national organization. Their suggestion received strong support from the CNT teachers' federations in the Valencia region and Catalonia. When the national federation was established, it had 22,300 members, and its largest affiliate was in Barcelona, with 9,228 members, followed by Madrid, with 2,284. The federations in Levante, Andalusia, Aragón and Extremadura were the other affiliates of the national federation. According to F. Cardona Rossell, Secretary of the Regional Federation of Teachers' Unions of the Center, the Madrid branch group was the most completely organized part of the national federation, with subsidiary groups in each of the provinces of Castille.[11]

Consejo de la Escuela Nueva Unificada in Catalonia

Aside from Aragón, where during the first year of the War, control of the Republican part of the region was almost completely in the hands of the anarchists, their influence on education was most notable in Catalonia. On July 27 1936, about a week after the suppression of the Rebellion there, a decree was issued creating the Consejo de la Escuela Nueva Unificada (CENU), which continued to function until the end of the Civil War in Catalonia.

Diego Abad de Santillán summed up the accomplishments of the CENU: 'The efforts of the CENU have produced precious fruits, carrying out in a few months a job which the Republic was not able to achieve in the five years of its existence. The children attending the official schools of Barcelona before the 19 of July were 34,000; five months after the revolutionary movement there were 54,758 attending school. The creation of schools has continued at a rate never before equalled. The school population of Catalonia has almost tripled, without taking into account the improvement of materials and of the pedagogic orientation.'[12]

Anarchist influence in the CENU was extensive, although not exclusive. The *consejo* was composed of equal numbers of representatives of the CNT and the UGT, as well as government nominees.[13] It was presided over by Professor José Puig Elías, an anarchist, who set to work immediately to establish short courses of three months, for emergency training of teachers for the new school year. Within six months, the CENU appointed 4,707 new teachers.[14] Emma Goldman the Russian-American anarchist, wrote of Puig Elías that he 'is one of the most outstanding modern pedagogues in the world, a man of wide culture, a profound psychological understanding of the life of the child.'[15]

There was relatively little conflict within the council between the CNTers and their opponents. The only serious opposition to the anarchists came from a woman representing the UGT, who had once been a CNTer. However, after the May Events of 1937, one UGT member of the council, who was a member of the POUM, was murdered by the Stalinists.[16]

In addition to the CNT, UGT and Catalan government members in the CENU, there were also representatives of the University of Barcelona, the Industrial University and the region's Fine Arts Commission.[17]

Miguel Cabra, the wartime secretary of the teachers' section of the CNT Sindicato de Profesiones Liberales in Barcelona, has noted that although the *consejo* sought to set up a common program for the schools of the region, one of its basic principles was that teachers should be allowed wide leeway for experimentation in teaching methods. Its most immediate objective was to have classrooms and teachers for all Catalan children of school age by the time the 1936–7 school year opened in October. Cabra said that although it did not achieve this for the whole region, it did achieve it largely in Barcelona. Eight hundred new classrooms were opened in Barcelona in the fall of 1936; which was not all net gain, because the religious and private schools were closed.[18] According to Gaston Leval, whereas before the War began only 4,000 of the 8,000 school-age children in Hospitalet were attending school, with the opening of the 1936–7 scholastic year, there were 6,500 in class.[19]

The CENU obtained teachers from a number of places. First, they put all unemployed teachers – of whom there were a substantial number – back to work. They also incorporated those from the private schools in the schools of the *consejo*, as well as the lay teachers from the Church schools. Those teaching nuns who were willing to work under the new circumstances were also given posts, although, of course, they could not come to work in their clerical garb or teach the Catholic religion.

The existing anarchist schools were incorporated into the new system. At that time there were seven such schools in the Barcelona area. These were the Escuela Moderna, originally founded by Francisco Ferrer, and in 1936 still functioning under the aegis of the CNT factory workers' union; a school of the metal workers' union, and neighborhood schools in Barrio Hospitalet, Barrio Carmelo, Barrio Barceloneta and Barrios Sta Coloma and San Andrés.[20] Félix Carresquer noted that the anarchists directly organized 20 new schools in Barcelona during the War.[21]

There were some special schools as part of the system. Four or five resident schools were established for children of militiamen at the front, whose families could not take care of them.

The Ribas Orphanage was also incorporated into the CENU

system. Before July 19, the children there had had to wear uniforms and lived a highly regimented existence. Under Miguel Cabra, uniforms were abolished, and steps were taken to try to eliminate the conflicts between the orphaned kids and children from the nearby area who also attended the orphanage's school. The school was reorganized to provide a lower school which was held in the orphanage building, and was attended by both orphans and neighborhood children; and a higher school which was set up in a nearby church building which had been taken over, and where both kinds of youngsters also were in attendance.

When Cabra took over the Olphalanato Ribas, there were 70 children there. However, this number rose to 300 resident students, 500 day students and 50 adults in a night school which was organized.[22]

Generally, the Catalan schools during the War tried to serve the needs of both youngsters of primary and secondary school age, and those of adults who wanted to learn to read and write or to study more advanced subjects. Classes for these adults met in the evenings after the children had gone home.

Félix Carresquer, FAI Peninsular Committee member who taught in one of them, has commented on the teaching methods used in the anarchist-directed schools. He said that they were organized along libertarian principles, with the basic idea being that the children should guide their own learning; it should not be imposed on them. The initiative schools are their descendants.

Carresquer said that quite a few of the entering students were already able to read and write, and they would be encouraged to read good literature of different kinds. The schools had no textbooks, but the children had available a wide choice of books, which they could read, and they were given freedom to choose what they wanted to read.

In the case of children who didn't yet know how to read, the teacher would ask them to say some simple thing, anything that came to mind. Then the teacher would spell it out on the blackboard. The children had printer's type available, and they would be allowed to find the letters, and then they took them to a young man who ran a little press, and he would print what they had gotten together, and they would proudly take this home.

Even arithmetic, which needed a somewhat more structured approach, was tied to the children's learning from their own experience. They were encouraged to ask their own questions about addition and subtraction, and the teachers sought to avoid forcing anything on them.

Carresquer claimed that this more voluntary approach to learning, based on the children's desire to know, their feeling of the necessity of knowing, rather than having something forced upon them, was reflected in the attitude of the children themselves. Their spirit was one of cooperation instead of competition, he said, and there was never fighting among the children, the selfishness which is the cause of fights not being present in these schools.[23]

Perhaps more generalized than the libertarian approach to education in the anarchist-oriented schools were some other reforms in the educational system carried out by the CENU. For the first time in many cases, schools were set up in towns and villages outside the provincial capitals. There was general introduction of coeducation in the Catalan schools. An effort was made to establish libraries in each school, something which had been comparatively rare before the War. Often these libraries were stocked with books contributed by the citizenry.[24]

'Popular universities' were also organized in Barcelona and a few provincial towns. The University of Barcelona could not function regularly during the War, and the popular university was established by the CNT in the buildings of an ex-seminary. Its teachers included many from the faculty of the University of Barcelona, as well as many from the schools which the anarchists ran before (and during) the War. The popular university offered a wide range of courses, including the sciences, social sciences and humanities. There was particular emphasis on economics.

The popular universities did not try to preach anarchism. Juan Pintado, who in later years became a leader of the CNT in exile, recounted that as a student in the popular university of Barcelona, he never heard a lecture on anarchism, although he 'did hear much said about liberty'. There were courses in comparative religion.

Any student who was recommended by a teacher in the popular university of Barcelona could attend courses. There were no tuition or other charges, and in the case of students for whose families their attendance represented a financial hardship, the students were actually paid a small sum.[25]

Specialized Schools

There were various specialized schools organized under the aegis of the anarchists during the War. One such institution was the school established in the maternity hospital of Barcelona, during the six months that the anarchist leader Félix Carresquer was director of the hospital. Carresquer brought in young men and women teachers – mainly Socialists, he said – who gave classes after dinner to the nurses and the prospective (or already actual) mothers 'on child care, the nature of the revolution, the progress of the war and similar things'.

The school also prepared young people to be nurses. Associated with the hospital was a group of youngsters known as Children of the House (Hijas de la Casa). Those were youngsters, who at the age of ten, were supposed to go to an orphanage, but instead had stayed on at the maternity hospital to aid the nurses. Carresquer organized classes to teach these girls how to be nurses, and although he left the hospital before their training was completed, he was told that all of the students in the course had become nurses.

Carresquer was also involved in another specialized school, this one in Binefar in Aragón. This was an institution he organized for the CNT 'to prepare men with an adequate social ethic to prepare to be administrators of the collectives, which were very much needed, and secretaries of municipalities...' The school started out to serve only the *comarca* of Binefar, but subsequently was extended by the regional organization of the CNT to cover all of Republican Aragón. Each local community sent two or three young people, 15 years or older to the school.

During each day there were three or four formal classes, given by Carresquer himself, because 'the youngsters knew nothing of grammar, almost nothing of arithmetic, and nothing of geography, history, or accounting'. In addition, there were three hours of work a day in gardens of the school, which provided most of the money for maintaining it.

Carresquer had been much influenced by the ideas of John Dewey and the Frenchman Frainet. Following the notions of the latter, Carresquer formed voluntary groups of students to do research in physics, agricultural chemistry, sociology and photography. 'The school had a library. The youngsters ran these groups themselves, Carresquer's role being that of a consultant, if they ran into problems which they could not resolve.

Carresquer told Víctor Alba that the youngsters in the school reacted very positively to the kind of program it offered. He said that although upon arrival, most of them 'were more accustomed to fighting and gossiping than studying, upon encountering a new kind of school, they responded with such enthusiasm that at ten oclock at night I had to be very firm about their going to sleep.'

After eight months, the school began to provide secretaries to collectives and municipalities. However, when the military draft began to be applied to teenagers, a number of the students were taken into the army.

When the Consejo de Aragón was dissolved by the Negrín government and the Communist troops moved against the Aragón collectives, the new governor of Aragón, Monzón, ordered the school closed. However, in fact it was moved to a place near Caspe, where it continued to function more or less surreptitiously until Aragón was overrun by Franco troops in 1938. It was then moved to Catalonia, where it continued to operate for several months, until that area too fell under Franco's control.[26]

The CNT's Federación Local de Sindicatos Unicos de Barcelona established a special school made necessary by the sudden entry into the factories of many women workers, as the men were increasingly taken into the armed forces. This was the Escuela de Adaptación Profesional para la Mujer, the purpose of which was to allow the 'female workers to acquire the preparation necessary to be able to replace those who, continuing the mission of workers, exchange their tools in order to be able to combat fascism in the most crucial way.' The Mujeres Libres was given the task of organizing and running this school.

After the Stalinists' influence had become predominant in the Catalan government, following the May Events, the Generalidad decided to establish an Instituto de Adaptación Profesional to do what the CNT's school was already doing. The CNT said that it had no objection to the Catalan government's idea, but that all that was really necessary to carry out the Generalidad's objective was to include representatives of the UGT in the management of the school which was already functioning under the aegis of the Mujeres Libres.[27]

One specialized school established by the CNT during the War, the training school for militants of the *confederación*, was a failure, according to Juan García Oliver, although he gave few details of its failure. It was established in the CNT regional headquarters in Barcelona during the period of the Comité de Milicias, and had an extensive curriculum in both theoretical and more practical terms.

Among the subjects covered were the various schools of interpretation of history, the evolution of trade unionism from the medieval guilds to 'revolutionary syndicalism'; public speaking; the theories of socialism, both anarchist and Marxist; the evolution of anarchist ideas; and the structure and functioning of the CNT and its unions.[28] Little publicity was apparently given to this militants' training school and the exact nature of, and reasons for, its failure are not clear.

The CNT and FAI of Catalonia held a joint conference on October 8 1936 to discuss educational issues and problems.[29]

Anarchist Doctors and Other Health Personnel

In addition to expanding educational facilities, the anarchists were also active during the War in expanding health services. Among the intellectuals in the anarchist movement before the outbreak of the Civil War, there were several distinguished doctors. Gaston Leval mentioned five in particular. Pedro Vallina was perhaps the outstanding anarchist leader in the region of Andalusia, and Leval described him as the 'personification of the anarchist apostle and heroic combatant, whose influence extended to all of Andalusia'. Isaac Puente 'exercised great influence in the regions of Aragón, Rioja and Navarre, being one of the active personalities, collaborator in our press, author of excellent orientation pamphlets, and secretary of the FAI'. Amparo Poch y Gascón was 'the most cultured woman of our movement'. Roberto Remartínez is described by Leval as 'of encyclopedic culture, one of the maestros of the libertarian generation which flourished during the revolution'. Finally, Félix Martí Ibáñez was the 'personification of the group of doctors–sociologists which appeared in those years, humanist, specialist in sexual and psychoanalytical problems, excellent writer.'[30]

In the years before the Civil War, the anarchists had themselves established some health service institutions. Most notable was the Sociedad de Socorros Mutuos de Levante. According to Leval, it 'had numerous doctors and specialists. Being more than a simple mutual benefit society in the traditional mold, it was an association which extended through the Levante...' (It survived the Civil War and still existed in the early 1970s.)[31]

During the War, the CNT described the nature of the Mutua de Levante. It had 50 doctors at its service. There were specialized services to deal with accidents, as well as surgery, radiology, pediatrics, gynaecology and a variety of other specialties. The services of the Mutua were available to the workers affiliated with it as well as to members of their families.[32]

However, the incompleteness of the CNT pre-war organizational structure was evident in the health field, as in so many other sectors. In Barcelona – and presumably elsewhere – there did not even exist a separate union of health workers, but only a section of the Union of the Liberal Professions.[33] It was not until September 1936 that the Sindicato de la Sanidad, which apparently covered all of Catalonia, was established by the CNTers.

In February 1937, the new union had 7,000 members, including 1,020 doctors, 3,206 nurses, 330 midwives, 603 dentists, 220 veterinarians and members with various other specialties.[34] The Catalan UGT also organized a health workers' union, but it was much smaller than that of the CNT, and Gaston Leval estimated that it had less than 100 doctors in its ranks.[35]

A national Federación de los Sindicatos Unicos de Sanidad of the CNT was not established until February 1937. It drew up extensive plans for the reorganization of medical and health services throughout the country, once the Civil War had beer won.[36]

Reorganization of Health Services in Catalonia

In Catalonia during most of the first year of the Civil War, the anarchists worked in the medical-health field on two levels, direct union activities, and through the Catalan government. When the anarchists entered the Catalan government in September 1936, one of the posts they received was that of councillor of health, which went to Antonio García Birlán, another leading doctor in the anarchist ranks. García Birlán named Felix Martí Ibáñez as director general of health services and social assistance. From then until the anarchists finally were excluded from the Catalan government a few months after the May Events, government involvement in health matters was in the hands of the anarchists.[37]

However, even before the anarchists entered the Catalan government, they had become involved in controlling and expanding the regional healthcare system. Such intervention frequently arose – as did the establishment of industrial and other collectives – from the peculiar circumstances of the first weeks and months of the Civil War.

One such case was that of the Barcelona maternity hospital. A few weeks after the beginning of the War, Félix Carresquer received a hurried call from anarchist friends living in the vicinity of the maternity hospital, asking for his help.

The problem at hand was that the Catalan government had ordered the nuns who ran the maternity hospital to be suddenly removed, and had sent a truck with Assault Guards to take them away. This would have left no one to take care of the women and children in the institution. Upon arriving with several armed militiamen, Carresquer ordered the guards to return whence they had come, after asking the nuns, who had already boarded the truck, to return to their work in the hospital.

Carresquer took over the supervision of the maternity hospital immediately. He was confirmed in that post by the Barcelona local committee of the CNT a few days later, and the Catalan government named his second-in-command. Carresquer remained director of the maternity hospital for six months.

That hospital dealt principally with unwed mothers. It had been customary for them to leave the hospital a few days after giving birth, frequently leaving their children behind them, where they would stay for ten years and then be transferred to an orphanage. Carresquer sought to change all that. He ordered that no new mother should have to leave until her baby was weaned. While they were there, the women were given classes in childcare, and two workshops were established on the premises where, it was hoped, they could learn a trade at which they could work when they left the institution.

Carresquer hoped that, with extended experience with nursing their children, the mothers would not want to abandon them when they themselves left the hospital. He reported to Víctor Alba that, in fact, not a single mother did abandon her child during the six months that he was in charge.

In so far as the nuns were concerned, Carresquer told them that they were welcome to stay, but if they wished to leave they could do that too, but only when someone was available to take their place. He instituted a training program to give teenage girls knowledge of the rudiments of nursing, and in time those took the place of most of the nuns.

Carresquer applied his egalitarian anarchist convictions while at the hospital. Although it had been customary for the director to eat with the doctors, who were served better food than the nurses, mothers and children, he soon quit doing so. Instead, he ate with the children, so that he could see what they were given to eat and could observe how they were treated.

Also, Carresquer refused to accept any salary as director, although the Catalan government sent him a form, on which he was to name the salary he wanted. He informed the Generalidad that he was a bachelor, had at the hospital a place to live and the food which was about all that he required, and so did not need a salary.[38]

Meanwhile, the CNT Sindicato de la Salud had reorganized and substantially expanded health services throughout Catalonia. The region was divided into nine geographical sub-regions, under which there were 26 secondary centers. Gaston Leval has written: 'Together, 35 more or less important centers totally covered the four provinces, so that no town, no village lost in the mountains nor any distant farm, no man, woman or child, was isolated, without health protection, without medical help.'

In each of the centers there were clinics, where most cases were dealt with. Intensive care and more specialized treatment was provided in Barcelona, to which patients were brought by ambulance.

During the first year of the War, six new hospitals were built in Barcelona. At the same time, six new sanitariums were constructed in other parts of Catalonia. By June 1937, there were 18 hospitals in Barcelona controlled by the Sindicato de la Sanidad, six of which it had built. There were 22 clinics, six psychiatric facilities, the maternity hospital and various other institutions under the union's supervision.

Those who were in charge on the various levels of the system were elected by the appropriate general assemblies of workers. Once a week, the central committee of the *sindicato* met with delegates from the nine primary subdivisions of the system, to coordinate activities.

The *sindicato* sought to overcome the tendency for medical personnel to be concentrated in Barcelona and a few other large cities and towns. When a request for the services of a doctor was received by the *sindicato*, the central committee, taking into account the particular need and the qualifications of the doctors in the system, would ask an appropriate doctor to go to answer the request the *sindicato* had received. Gaston Leval noted that 'To refuse the post offered, it was necessary that the person designated have very good reasons.'

The *sindicato* did not itself have the financial resources to maintain this system. Much of the money came from the municipal governments, which usually financed the clinics in their areas, and from the government of Catalonia.

Doctors in the system were paid 500 pesetas a month, for three hours a day service – which compared with 350 to 400 pesetas a month (and eight hours' work a day) received on the average by workers in Catalonia in that period. Private practice of medicine was not abolished, but the fees which doctors could charge were regulated by the *sindicato*, which kept fairly strict control.[39]

Hospitals Established by Anarchists

In various parts of Loyalist Spain, there were new hospitals organized by the anarchists during the War. One of these was what was originally established by the CNT's Railroad Workers' Federation as the Hospital Confederal Modelo, but which later became Military Hospital No. 20.

When the War began, this institution was in the planning stage. However, Pedro Rodríguez, of the Railroad Workers' Federation was placed in charge of it by his union, which also put up several hundred thousand pesetas to complete and equip it. Within a short time, it owned extensive operative and other equipment, and the patients' rooms were made as bright and cheerful as was possible.

According to the CNT–FAI there was extraordinary dedication on the part of those who were working in the hospital. Many of the nurses and other workers in the hospital were recruited from among the railroad workers and their families. The dedication of the workers in the hospital was exemplified, according to the CNT–FAI by Dr Franco, the radiologist, who continued to work even after he had been adversely affected by the x-ray machines in his charge.

Most of the patients treated by this hospital were people who had been wounded in the War, particularly in the fighting in the Madrid area. However, it also handled a considerable number of civilian patients. Even after the hospital had been officially taken over by the armed forces as a military hospital, the railroad worker Pedro Rodríguez was left in charge of it.[40]

Concluding Observations on CNT Health Work During the War

Most of the information available about the anarchists' work in the medical and health field during the Civil War has to do with Catalonia. However, Gaston Leval has written:

> Everywhere that we were able to study the towns and little cities transformed by the revolution, the hospitals, the clinics, the polyclinics and other health establishments have been municipalized, enlarged, modernized, put under the safekeeping of the collectivity. And where they didn't exist, they were improvised. The socialization of medicine was a work for the benefit of all. It constitutes one of the most notable accomplishments of the Spanish revolution...[41]
>
> It is the unions which undertook – together with the specialists of the army – to organize the emergency hospitals behind the lines on the front. It was they who forced fascist and semifascist pharmacists to open their shops, or who took them over when the proprietors had abandoned them. It was the *sindicatos* of the CNT which organized also, together with the corresponding units of the military apparatus, the evacuation of large numbers of the aged, women and children, menaced in the war zones. It was they who founded anti-gas brigades, and in cooperation with the municipalities took part in construction of bomb shelters. And we know, although we don't have statistics on the matter, that thanks to them numerous hospitals, dispensaries, clinics and rest houses were established in Levante, Castille, Asturias, etcetera.[42]

CNT Orphan Asylums

Another social service activity of the CNT during the Civil War was the establishment of refuges for children who were forced to flee with the advance of the Franco forces. There were many of these institutions, but I have information about only three of them.

The first is the Spartacus Refugee Children's Colony, established by the CNT's Railroad Workers' Federation in Arnus in the municipality of Argentona, 30 kilometers North of Barcelona. In well-provided quarters on the estate of a banker, Sr Gari, who had fled with the onset of the War, this was financed with the voluntary contributions of the railroad workers all over Republican Spain.

This colony was established, in October 1936, to provide refuge for some of the children who were evacuated from Madrid, as the war approached the capital city. It housed children aged from three to 12. In ten days, it was organized, with the railroad workers making some of the furniture and other equipment to supply its needs.

The children were housed in rooms with from six to ten beds. There were adequate bathing facilities for the children. A dining-room, various workshops and an infirmary were part of the installations. There was also a school, with three teachers, as well as personnel to take care of the pre-school children. All of those working in the colony were paid.[43]

Another similar CNT institution was the Farm School in the provincial Catalan city of Sabadell. This was established by the local CNT Union of Liberal Professions, and was also described as serving refugee children, particularly those from Madrid.

The Sabadell institution maintained a rationalist school, which provided teaching in basic subjects, but also encouraged the children to conduct their own studies in subjects and fields which particularly interested them. There was a 500-volume library. It also provided a wide variety of sports, including soccer, swimming, tennis and others. There were carpentry and electrical workshops, as well as chicken coops and rabbit hutches where the children 'studied theoretically and practically these disciplines; consulting books, exchanging ideas, preparing feed, studying formulas, taking care of the animals, keeping track of the eggs...'

The children were given regular medical examinations. Close attention was paid to both their physical and psychological conditions.[44]

Emma Goldman reported on her visit to another orphan refuge established by the anarchists, the Durruti–Ascaso colony near Figueras in Catalonia, She said that it had ample facilities for the 200 children housed in it, most of whom were refugees from Madrid. She found the food 'ample and wholesome', and the dormitories 'surprised me by their space, air and sunshine'.

The anarchists had established a school in the children's refuge, organized in accordance with their educational ideas, and although when she visited the place in December 1937 it had officially been incorporated in the Catalan government's educational system, she said that the government had 'not yet succeeded in changing the splendid educational plans' of the anarchists. There were only three teachers, but Emma Goldman reported that 'the most gratifying impression was that the children are free and easy going and that there was no cringing before their elders. Perfect good fellowship and comradeship prevailed between our comrades at the head of the colony, the teachers and the children...'[45]

Conclusion

The anarchists not only took over much of the rural and urban economy of Republican Spain, they also had great influence over the educational system and the social welfare institutions of the Loyalist half of the country. For the first year of the Civil War, they directed the educational activities of the Catalonian government, as well as continuing to conduct the schools which they had organized before the War began, and establishing many new ones under their direct union control. Even after the Stalinists had launched their drive for complete control over the Spanish Republic, the anarchists were able to continue to control a substantial part of the Republic's educational system.

The anarchists' approach to education was quite different from that of either the Church or State schools before the Civil War. They were much influenced by the doctrines of John Dewey and other educational reformers, and they put these ideas into practice when much of the educational system of the republic fell into their hands.

The anarchists also played a major role in establishing a social security system in Loyalist Spain. This effort was most notable in

Catalonia, where they established a region-wide system of healthcare for all of the people of the area. However, on a more piecework basis, they established provision for healthcare and old-age retirement for workers in other parts of the economy which they controlled.

Finally, the anarchists undertook many special projects for helping those elements of the population of Republican Spain who were most disabled and disadvantaged. Their efforts to take care of the children who were victims of the War were particularly outstanding.

Many of the innovations of the anarchists in the educational and social fields were undertaken because of the peculiar situation which they faced with the collapse of governmental and virtually all other authority with the outbreak of the Civil War. However, what they did – aside from their collaboration with the established government – generally conformed to their basic philosophy. Also, in the special economic plenum of the Confederación Nacional del Trabajo in Valencia in January 1938, they sought to provide for the establishment of more organic and long-term structures for the soviety which they hoped they would be able to establish after the Civil War.

23

The CNT Economic Plenum

The anarchist collectives, both rural and urban, which were established early in the Civil War were virtually spontaneous. They arose from
the disappearance of landlords, owners of industries, commercial
firms and other enterprises in the first days and weeks of the War;
from the fact that it had been largely the workers, particularly the
anarchists, who had suppressed the insurrection of the regular army;
and the general collapse of governmental authority in Republican
Spain at the beginning of the War.

There was no central direction from the Confederación Nacional
del Trabajo to the movement to establish collectives. In some cases,
local unions took the lead in organizing their industry in their area,
as in the Badalona textile industry; while in Alcoy and some other
cities and towns, the local CNT undertook to organize all of the
economic activities within their jurisdiction.

However, it was a year and a half after the beginning of the Civil
War before the CNT developed plans for a national framework for
the parts of the economy which had come under its control. It did so
at the national economic plenum of the organization held in Valencia
in January 1938.

General Characteristics of the Economic Plenum

José Peirats has indicated that the idea of having a national meeting to try to coordinate the economic work of the CNT was first proposed late in 1937. It was first scheduled for the beginning of January 1938, but was postponed until the middle of the month:

> The proposition was, then, the most ample possible discussion of the economic problems within the competence of the *confederación*... The Plenum would deal with certain fundamental questions: demonstrate the maturity acquired by the organization during 18 months of constructive experiences in the economic field (production, technical matters and administration) and resolve with 'precision, clarity and positivism' these problems, to demonstrate that the workers are capable of resolving the problems presented by the situation, imposing on themselves the necessary sacrifices, and overcoming existing deficiencies, orient for the collective interest of the working class people the problems which fundamentally affect them, to study, apart from politics and the war, the economic situation and the most pertinent and rational solutions.[1]

This plenum was the nearest approach to a national congress which the CNT held during the Civil War. According to Peirats, some 800 delegates met in the Serrano Theater in Valencia. The delegates represented the local and *comarcal* federations of the CNT, and there were also representatives from the regional committees of Catalonia, the Center, Andalusia, Levante and Extremadura. José Peirats noted that the national industrial federations were not directly represented in this meeting.[2]

Voting in the meeting was staggered, with each delegate casting a vote in proportion to the size of the organization he/she represented. At one extreme, the representative of an organization with 500 or less members had one vote; at the other, one from a group with 200,000 members had 20 votes.

Peirats noted one peculiarity of the economic plenum. The national committee of the CNT presented draft resolutions relative to each of the appropriate items on the agenda of the meeting. In all previous gatherings of the CNT, draft resolutions had always been developed by committees of the meetings themselves.[3]

In this case, all but three of the proposals put forward by the national committee were basically accepted unanimously. One was defeated, and a motion presented from the floor of the meeting was accepted in its place, the other two were accepted, but on a split vote.[4]

The economic plenum reflected the changes which had come about during the War in the relationship of the CNT and the national economy, and changes within the anarchist labor organization itself. It set forth a program for the reorganization of the economy under the aegis of the CNT. An almost total lack of discussion of the autonomy of the constituent parts of the *confederación* was one of the most notable indications of the changes within the *confederación*.

The resolutions adopted by the economic plenum can be divided into two categories. The first group dealt with immediate problems presented by what had happened since the beginning of the Civil War. The other consisted of the plenum's outline of the nature of the post-war and post-revolutionary structure of the national economy which the anarchists hoped to establish. However, there was necessarily certain inter-relationship between these two kinds of resolutions.

Nature of Resolutions Arising From Experience of War and Revolution

Those resolutions of the economic plenum which were clearly responses to problems which had arisen as a result of the War and Revolution were of different kinds. Some arose from crisis situations in the War. Others, although also coming from the CNT's experiences since July 19 1936, were of more long-term significance, both in terms of the traditional ideology of the Spanish anarchists, and their vision as of January 1938 of the kind of permanent reorganization of Spanish society that they wanted to bring about.

Two resolutions were clearly political. One of these sent greetings to the 'antifascist prisoners' then in jail in the Republic, and promised to do all the CNT could to bring about their release.[5] The other was a message sent to Prime Minister Juan Negrín demanding the immediate release of such prisoners.[6]

In a somewhat similar category were messages sent to various foreign trade union bodies. Those addressed included the (Socialist-dominated) International Federation of Trade Unions, the British Trade Union Congress, and the French Confederation Géneral du Travail. No such message was sent to the anarcho-syndicalist International Workingmen's Association, although one was dispatched to the IWMA's Swedish affiliate, the SAC.[7]

Two other resolutions were at least in part provoked by wartime conditions, rather than by the Revolution. These dealt with the establishment by the CNT of distribution centers for consumer products, to try to combat the black market and price gauging, and one decreeing a reduction of the number of publications of the CNT.

Other resolutions of the meeting arose from the CNT's experience with rural and urban collectives since July 19, rather than from the War situation, properly speaking. These included documents on the establishment of a system of labor inspectors, one establishing a pattern of wage differentials, one providing for the justification for, and nature of, disciplining workers in the collectives, one providing for establishment of a Banco Sindical Ibérico, one treating with problems of social security and insurance, and several short ones dealing with the establishment of schools to train the skilled personnel the collectives needed.

Finally, there was a motion concerning the number of national industrial unions which the CNT should have, at least for the present.

Resolution on CNT Distribution Centers

By the time the national economic plenum met, the economic situation in Republican Spain was growing serious, in terms of inflation, shortages of some kinds of goods, particularly food, and unemployment. Chilean Ambassador Agustín Edwards reported to President Arturo Alessandri, in October 1937, that he had been informed by the leader of a Barcelona union which had taken over a British company that 'for three months there has been no meat in Barcelona; the last mule was eaten a long time ago. There is no bread of any kind and the food supply is reduced to a few vegetables from the garden of Valencia, rice and sweet potatoes.'

This same union leader had commented: 'Catalan industry is dying for lack of markets; in all of the territory occupied by General Franco, Catalan products, which before sold without any difficulty, have been replaced by German and Italian merchandise.'[8]

Although there was nothing the CNT economic plenum could do about the loss of territory to the Rebel forces, it did pass a resolution designed to bring about more equitable distribution of what food was available in the Loyalist region: 'The Distribution Sections of the *sindicatos*, together with the Local and *comarcal* organizations will proceed immediately to create in all population centers large distribution warehouses...' Each local, *comarcal* and regional economic council of the CNT should organize a statistics section, the purposes of which should be: 'To gather statistics daily of the goods available in the warehouses, for equitable distribution in the localities according to their needs... Intervene in the operations of wholesale marketing... To fix sale prices, taking into account the general costs, transport, etc. etc. which will vary according to the place of origin of the articles and the characteristics of the locality where they are sold... In establishing these distribution warehouses it must be taken into account that their services will be for the people in general.' Finally, all purchases of products abroad should be carried out by an organ of the national CNT.[9]

Reduction of CNT Publications

One surprising resolution of the CNT economic plenum was that calling for a drastic reduction in the number of publications of the CNT itself and the collectives and other institutions under its control. This may well have had political as well as economic motivations.

In the pamphlet presenting the resolutions of the plenum, the CNT leadership noted that since the beginning of the War, the number of publications of all organizations and parties had increased tremendously, in spite of difficulties in obtaining paper: 'In this also, the CNT has the honor of putting itself in the vanguard and has elaborated a plan, imposing restrictions on itself... An enormous quantity of publications will disappear with this agreement; dozens of periodicals, a multitude of bulletins; a great quantity of reviews, suppressed voluntarily to save paper.'[10]

However, in fact, the resolution calling for the cutting back on CNT publications listed three reasons for the action. The first was the shortage of paper. The second was 'the need to have in charge of each publication a comrade of absolute confidence, from being an old militant of the Movement, while at the same time having the competence needed to bring out a good publication,' and the scarcity of such people.

The third reason for the cutback 'is the need to give homogeneity to the orientation of our publications, the only way to get a return from the potent arm which the press is. It is necessary to end the public contradictions in the Movement.'

By the beginning of 1938 there was beginning to be considerable discontent within anarchist ranks over the degree to which the CNT had compromised with what, until July 19 1936, had been its basic principles. This discontent was to result a few months later in a virtual split between the leadership of the CNT and the leadership of the FAI. It is to be presumed that many of the publications about which the resolution complained were organs which were critical of the line of the CNT national committee.

In any case, the resolution provided that in Barcelona, Valencia and Madrid there should be two anarchist papers, one in the morning and one in the evening; that other dailies should appear in the Catalan cities of Gerona, Lérida, Tarragona, in the Levante cities of Castellón, Albacete, Alicante and either Murica or Cartagena (with suppression of the paper in one other city). In Andalusia there should be papers in Almería and either Ubeda, Jaén or Baza; in Extremadura only in Cabez de Buey; in the center only in Cuenca, Toledo and Ciudad Libre (formerly Ciudad Real). In Aragón there should be a daily only in Alcaniz.

All kinds of bulletins had also proliferated after July 19. The resolution provided that only national industrial federations should henceforward publish such periodicals and that 'That Bulletin will be for the exclusive use of the *sindicatos*, and not deal at all with political or military affairs, those being the exclusive province of the dailies.'

Similarly, reviews were to be issued only by the national industrial federations, and were to be quarterlies, except that of the Peasants' Federation which was to appear each month. The resolution said: 'The reviews will circumscribe their contents to technical study and orientation, abandoning absolutely political and trade union orientation, which are now the exclusive competence of the Press in one case and the bulletins in the other.'[11]

The content of this resolution would seem to indicate that it was at least as much motivated by the national committee's desire to maintain its concept of discipline within the ranks of the organization as it was by the shortage of paper. Surprisingly, it was not one of the national committee's draft resolutions which was challenged from the floor, and was passed unanimously.

Enrique Marco Nadal, a leader of the CNT in Valencia during the Civil War, and subsequent to Second World War one of the major figures in the CNT clandestine leadership, has insisted that this resolution on publications was not adopted 'with the intention of eliminating the opposition which was being mounted from them against the National Committee ... but to limit the confusion created within the organization arising from propagation of personal points of view which no one prevented being expressed in General Assemblies which had to be held upon convocation of every Plenum or Congress.'[12]

Resolution Establishing a System of Labor Inspectors

Although available sources do not provide any information about what was said in the debates on the various resolutions of the economic plenum, one gathers from the vote on the motion to establish a labor inspectorate that there was substantial opposition to the idea. The motion passed with 516 votes in favor, but with 120 against, and 82 abstentions.[13]

The text presenting this resolution by the national committee of the CNT is more eloquent about what was involved than the resolution itself. 'The war makes us consider the labor front as the complement of the combat front. For that, the discipline indispensable in the trenches must have its repercussions in the centers of production.'

The national committee went on to say: 'We know perfectly that the immense majority of the workers and of the militants, have complied with their duty since the 19th of July, tried in every way to intensify production. However, the existence of a minority has been recognized who, with full irresponsibility and lack of conscience, have not given in the rearguard the output which should be expected.'

Therefore, the national committee (and the plenum) came to the conclusion 'to establish technical delegates, who will inspect and orient the economic units under their jurisdiction, and when the case requires it, will proceed to punish both the workers and the Consejos de Empresa or the Technical-Administrative Councils which are rot capable of rising to the circumstances, and sabotage through their lack of experience, incapacity or reluctance, the normal process of production.'[14]

Apparently, the resolution was not in fact implemented. Enrique Marco Nadal has noted: 'Inspectors of Labor in the Anarchosyndicalist Collectives were not established ... since it was felt that no one was better able to carry out such Inspection than their Directing Committees made up of a representative of each Workshop or Factory Section...'[15]

Resolution on Wage Differentials

Another resolution of the economic plenum which differed substantially from the traditional positions of the Spanish anarchists was that which they entitled 'Form of Retribution of Labor'. The national committee of the CNT explained: 'Of importance was the problem that the Spanish proletariat had and has with the payment of labor. Different scales, divergent types, multiple systems. In the same kind of work and in the same locality, differences exist within specialized categories.'[16]

The resolution itself said that it did not want 'to negate the basic principles which our Organization has always had, and accepting that the family type wage is more in consonance with those principles, we propose that there be adopted this payment procedure, with the percentage and form presented in the resolution, or the Industries, National Federations etc., which cannot put into effect another system of family payment on a wider basis.'

The resolution then set forth the wage differentials which should be standard for the CNT-controlled industries. Whatever the basic wage in a firm or industry might be, various more skilled workers or managerial personnel were to receive from 20 percent to 100 percent more than the minimum.

However, there was some concession to the anarchist principle of workers being paid in conformity with their family responsibilities. The resolution provided that each CNT-controlled enterprise should set up a fund for family compensation, and that each national industrial federation should decide what the basis of the distribution of funds to workers in accordance with their family responsibilities should be in its sector.[17]

Obviously, this resolution was a serious compromise with the idea that workers' income should be based on the number of family members they had to support. As we have seen in earlier chapters, many rural collectives and a few urban ones had adopted that principle. However, the CNT economic plenum's resolution seemed to want to bring that to an end. It is doubtful that there was enough time for the resolution to have much effect on the existing collectives. I have not come across any case of a hierarchically superior organization of the CNT trying to enforce it on a collective.

Resolution on Workers' Discipline

Another resolution of the economic plenum which would certainly not have been contemplated by the pre-war CNT was that which was entitled 'General Labor Norms', and in fact dealt with the problem of labor discipline. It too was passed unanimously, and reflected the evolution of the thinking of many anarchists as a result of war pressures and the fact that they had had *de facto* placed upon them the responsibility for running much of the economy of Loyalist Spain.

In its explanation of this resolution, the CNT national committee observed:

> The CNT has the responsibility of indicating labor norms; a regulation which indicates to everyone his rights and duties. Clearly in establishing rights and duties one cannot eliminate sanctions since all and everyone is obliged to give the most possible in collaboration in the great work in which we are engaged, maintaining a war and overcoming an economy broken as a result of the conflict...'
>
> ...[However,] the CNT is not proceeding in accordance with the old bourgeois norms, but rather, based on our principles of exercising moral coercion on the individual, the sanctions are scaled to achieve a reeducation or a reform in the defects and vices of the producer.[18]

The reader can judge for him or herself to what degree the CNT norms differed from those of a bourgeois society.

In its rather long preamble, the resolution claimed:

> The Libertarian Movement has never been the enemy of organization... The other vanguard schools sought, on the one hand, to place all wealth under the control of the State, so that, from it, taking advantage of its absorbing nature, to monopolize the means of production and of commerce; and on the other hand, negating all unifying tendency, leaving to improvisation and the instinct of sociability the free use of the resources of labor and exchange. No sociological school set forth what the organization to administer things should be, either because it appeared to them that the proletariat would be incapable of methodical

construction, and so there was needed one single executive thought and voice; or because they considered it premature to establish previous norms, which implied tyranny, and it was necessary to leave it to chaos to produce the miracle of the birth of order through a providential free will of the revolutionary masses...

The Confederation's libertarian ideal opposes these false systems ... the formula of RESPONSIBLE ORGANIZATION, acting in each historic period, in each country, in accordance with the possibilities, and with a discipline voluntarily recognized and accepted. This conception which is anti-state and enemy of all individualism, represents the real application of democracy in all the social life of the people.

The operative parts of the resolution started by providing that technical administrative committees in each collectivized firm, and CNT economic councils in localities and regions and in the national industrial federations, 'will be the organisms responsible for the conduct of work. They will plan, contract, direct and carry on the work, movement of productive units, acquisition of materials, financial management, etc., naming and adding to the Consejos de Empresa in accordance with the workers of the industrial units.'

Within each enterprise, each craft group will have 'a distributor of tasks', and that person 'will be responsible for the quantity and quality and conduct of the workers'. Over these individuals each enterprise would have an official responsible to the technical administrative committee, 'enjoying an authority which can only be limited by the Consejo de Empresa or the Trade Union Control Committees.'

These were the officials to administer labor discipline. In contrast to the situation which existed in many of the urban collectives, there is no mention of the idea that these people should be elected by the workers of the collective.

The resolution lists a number of breaches of labor discipline which might justify sanctions. These were 'unjustified absence, habitual tardiness, failure to carry out the kind of production indicated, those who with defeatist tendencies organize confrontations with the task distributors...' Disciplinary action could be appealed by a worker to the local union executive committee, with which the collective was associated. It, in consultation with the technical administrative committee of the collective, would make the final decision.

The major punishment for infringement of discipline provided for in the resolution was dismissal. However, if this was the first case that a worker had been sanctioned, the union executive committee had the obligation to get the worker employment in some other collective in the municipality. In case of a second dismissal, the union executive was to get the worker a position in some other locality. The third time, a record of the worker's offenses would be put in his workbook, and the union would be free to choose between temporary suspension from work or final dismissal.

Perhaps the most uncharacteristic provision of all in this resolution, from a traditional anarchist point of view, was that concerning the workbook. It read: 'Since the employment of all personnel will be reported to the Technical Administrative Council of the *Sindicato*, all workers will have a document in which will be listed the main characteristics of his professional and social personality. The Technical-Administrative Council will receive personnel information from the respective sections of the *Sindicato*, and they will certify as to the morality and professional aptitudes' of the worker.

The resolution further provided that in each enterprise there would be a trade union control committee. According to the resolution, it 'will assist the Consejo de Empresa and will keep track of the scrupulous fulfillment of work. It will be a collaborator and will seek always to aid in the perfection of work methods, in quantitative and qualitative improvements. The Control Committee will keep the union informed of the details of the enterprise. It will facilitate the discovery of negative elements, denouncing cases of incompetency which are revealed. It will seek to improve the material conditions of the worker...'

The control committee and the principal employment official of the enterprise were supposed to investigate each work accident. In case they found injuries from labor accidents to be fallacious or self-imposed, they were to report this to the technical-administrative committee. In other cases, the injured worker was to receive full pay and necessary medical expenses from the collective.

A final paragraph of the resolution stated: 'In all cases, the Confederation Organization is absolutely authorized to decide about norms, sanctions, transformations of all kinds and all disputes arising among chief labor officers, Technical-Administrative Councils and Local Economic Councils.'[19]

Apparently this resolution remained more or less a dead letter. Marco Nadal has written: '...NO DISCIPLINE OF LABOR was established ... it would have been an offense against those making up the workforce of each Workshop or Factory, due to the enthusiasm and seriousness with which all of them carried out their jobs, all having the same workday as before, since that established in the time of the Bourgeoisie was not modified.'[20]

Resolution on the Banco Sindical Ibérico

One of the most striking breaks with its own past made by the CNT in the economic plenum of January 1938 was the decision to establish its own large bank, under the name of Banco Sindical Ibérico. The resolution authorizing this was apparently one of those arousing most debate in the meeting. It was one of the three which was submitted to a recorded vote. It was passed with 581 delegates voting in favor, with 60 voting against, and 74 abstaining.[21]

In the past, the Spanish anarchists had paid little attention to the banks and the whole problem of credit. Before the Civil War, they certainly saw no place for banks in the post-revolutionary society which they hoped to create; and in so far as credit was needed, it would be made available on the basis of solidarity between one part of the post-revolutionary economy and another.

César Lorenzo has noted this lack of understanding of, or concern for, the banking system before the Civil War: 'The libertarians did not understand the importance of the banking system and its long-term impact on socialization; they paid no attention to this fundamental sector of the economy.'

Lorenzo also quotes the German anarchist Souchy on the same

point: 'Collectivization would not have remained partial, it would have included all economic life. The process of collectivization could perhaps be compared with the construction of a group of buildings: the stones are brought from numerous locations and small independent buildings are constructed. Thanks to the collectivization of the banks, the construction of all of them could have been carried out in accordance with a general architectural plan. Unhappily, it was not done that way and time was lost.'[22]

César Lorenzo also observed that when the anarchists entered the Catalan government in September 1936, they took over most of the key posts, but did not take that of finance: 'The fact is of importance, because it is witness to the political ingenuousness of the men of the CNT or, if one prefers, of their romanticism: uncomfortable with low questions of money, they put first revolutionary purity, and lacked interest in the financial network, which they would have been hard pressed to control because of lack of technical competence (we have already said that the bank employees, unfriendly if not hostile to libertarian ideas, were part of the UGT).'[23]

However, by the end of a year and a half of the Civil War, the anarchist leaders had certainly become clearly aware of the importance of banking in the national economy, and of the dangers which their lack of any substantial influence in that sphere represented for their collectives, particularly the urban ones. We have noted in earlier chapters that many collectives had had to turn for financial aid to the Catalan and Republican governments. So long as José Taradellas was councillor of finance in the Generalidad of Catalonia, and José Peiró was minister of industry in Largo Caballero's government, such help was available, at least to some degree, on acceptable terms.

However, once the anarchists had been forced out of the Catalan and Republican governments, and the strength of the sworn enemies of the collectives, the Stalinists, had become very great if not predominant in the two regimes, such financial help was not available, and the Stalinists and their allies used the indebtedness of many of the collectives as a tool to try to transfer effective control from the workers of the collectives to the State.

To a minor degree, the collectives had tried to solve this problem on an *ad hoc* basis, with financially stronger ones helping those with fiscal difficulties. The loan given by the chemical workers' collective in Badalona to a miners' collective has already been mentioned. But such *ad hoc* arrangements were far from being an adequate answer to the problem. The result was this resolution of the economic plenum.

The national committee of the CNT explained it thus:

> The operations which the BSI will be able to carry out will bring about an efficacious stimulation to an infinity of industries whose precarious development is leading them towards ruin. The peasantry can also, through the BSI, obtain the loans, at the appropriate moments, to save them in difficult periods...
>
> To sum it up, the mobility of capital which is deposited in the BSI will not only provide benefits to the Sindical Organizations, but – and this is most important – will increase production, will help put into practice rational industrial planning; it will bring about a progressive advance in economic reconstruction, to provide under honest conditions the economic means which at the moment the Collectives and industries lack.[24]

The resolution itself called for the establishment of the Banco Sindical Ibérico, as a joint enterprise of the CNT and UGT – but provided that the participation of the UGT was not necessary to get it started. It also provided for the establishment of a special commission which would nominate the president, vice-president and general manager of the bank, as well as determining the amount of necessary capital and spelling out what role the CNT unions would play in the bank on all levels, from local branches to the national organization of the bank. All of these decisions were to be ratified by a national plenum of regional organizations of the CNT.

The special commission was to consist of the secretary of the CNT national committee, who would preside over it, as well as the economic secretary of the national committee, the secretary of the banking sub-section of the national CNT bank and insurance workers' union (Federación Nacional de Trabajadores de Banca, Seguros y Afines), the secretary of the CNT economic committee of Barcelona, and one delegate each from the CNT regional federations of Catalonia, the center, the Levante, Andalusia, Aragón and Extremadura.

Finally, the resolution provided that those parts of the CNT located in the places where it and its branches would first be established should provide the capital for those local bank branches.[25]

This decision of the CNT to establish its own bank certainly came too late in the War to be effective. The loss of Aragón to the Franco forces only a few weeks after the economic plenum, followed shortly by the Franco forces' breakthrough to the Mediterranean, splitting the Republic in two once again, followed a bit later by the Republic's last great military offensive, the battle of the Ebro, together with the deteriorating economic circumstances in the Loyalist area, and the growing influence of the Stalinists in the Negrín regime, all militated against the effort to establish a CNT bank to finance the collectives.

Resolution on Insurance

Insurance was another aspect of the economy to which the Spanish anarchists had paid little attention. Like banking, it had seemed to be quintessentially capitalist, and totally irrelevant to the kind of economy and society which the anarchists hoped to bring into existence.

However, by January 1938, the exigencies of the War and the defense of the anarchist collectives both forced the CNT to take a serious interest in the problem of insurance. The result was a further resolution of the economic plenum.

In its explanation, the national committee of the CNT said:

> The creation of those organisms of our own which in our environment carry out the arduous and very useful job of coordinating, inspecting, orienting and when necessary controlling the various mutual aid societies, established by workers to

cover the risks of illness, temporary or permanent invalidity by work accidents, pensions or retirement, etc., cannot be postponed, so as to prevent these social security functions being carried out by organisms which in spite of being animated by the best intentions lack the necessary resources and the technical and administrative guarantees which are indispensable to be able to offer and facilitate the best results and the greatest perfection possible in the services...[26]

This long preamble noted that hitherto the CNT had not concerned itself particularly with problems of social security and insurance. It said that it had been taken for granted that 'security would make insurance unnecessary' in libertarian society, and that therefore the anarchists had not dealt with the insurance sector of the economy.[27]

The resolution provided for the creation of an administrative trade union agency for insurance. It was charged with a variety of different tasks.

One problem facing the CNT collectives was that in spite of the fact that most of them gave their members much wider social security than was provided for by the official government institute of social security, which covered only modest workmen's compensation, retirement and birth benefits, many collectives were being sued by the institute for failure to pay the social security taxes provided for in the law. So one of the major tasks given to the new agency was to negotiate with the institute for dropping these suits. It was also charged with seeking exemption of the collectives from the provisions of the law establishing the institute.

The agency was also supposed to try to standardize as far as possible the social security provisions of the CNT collectives. It was also to be the organization through which any collectives which signed contracts with either the government's institute or with still existing private insurance companies would negotiate, so as to obtain some degree of uniformity in such agreements.

The Resolution on National Industrial Federations

A final resolution of the economic plenum dealing particularly with questions raised by the Civil War and Revolution which had followed the uprising of July 19 1936 was that on the number of national industrial federations (equivalent of national industrial unions) which the CNT should have. This was another resolution on which a recorded vote was taken.

This was the only case in which the draft resolution presented by the CNT national committee was rejected by the plenum. A motion presented from the floor was passed, by a vote of 352 in favor, 266 against, and 115 abstentions. However, since there had been no absolute majority, the issue had to be submitted to the membership of the CNT. We have no information as to whether such a referendum was held, or what its results were.

The issue of establishing national industrial unions, or *federaciones industriales nacionales* had long been a matter of controversy within the anarchist movement. It had first been proposed in the early 1920s, but it was not until the 1931 CNT congress that the idea was approved. However, shortly afterwards there occurred the split in the CNT between the FAIistas and the Treintistas, and the people of the FAI, who remained in control of the majority CNT, were opposed to the idea of national industrial federations and did little to establish them, César Lorenzo noted that there were only four such organizations in existence at the outbreak of the Civil War.[28]

After the Civil War began various new national industrial federations were established. According to José Peirats, at the time of the national economic plenum, there were 13 in existence: agriculture, fishing and food; steel; transport; health and hygiene; construction and wood; water, gas, electricity and fuels; public spectacles; banking and insurance; education; communications; paper and graphic arts; chemical industries; public, administrative and judicial employees.

The draft resolution submitted to the plenum by the CNT national committee proposed to establish seven additional national industrial federations, by splitting several of the existing ones. However, a

blood OR whiskey

EIRE
RECORDS
PRESENTS

& GUESTS

Album Launch   Sat. 26th May
EAMON DORANS
8pm   adm. £5

P—

WHY NOT SUPPORT THE
NATIONAL FEDERATIONS?

counter-proposal, sponsored by the regional delegations of Catalonia and the Center, provided for maintaining the 13 national federations as they then existed. As we have noted, that motion received the support of only a plurality of the delegates, and so had to be submitted to a referendum.[29]

Resolution on the Organization of CNT-Controlled Economy

The resolution of the economic plenum which, if the Loyalists had won the Civil War, would have had greatest long-term significance was that setting forth the anarchists' plan for organizing that part of the Republican economy under their control. The proposed structure was supposed to include not only the economic institutions over which the anarchists had complete control, but also those in which they shared control with the UGT.

Perhaps the most striking thing about the plan adopted by the economic plenum was that it had no relationship at all to the resolution on the post-revolutionary society adopted by the Confederación Nacional del Trabajo in its Zaragoza congress a short two months before the outbreak of the Civil War. The experiences of the war and the Revolution which had quite unexpectedly been thrust on the anarchists only a little while after their delegates returned home from Zaragoza would seem to have convinced them of the utopian nature of the proposals adopted there.

In an earlier chapter, I sketched briefly some of the ideas about the reorganization of the Spanish economy and society which had been put forth in the decade or so preceding the War by Spanish anarchist thinkers and by Gaston Leval, a Frenchman with long association with the CNT. There are elements of the thinking of some of those people in the document accepted by the economic plenum. Certainly, the emphasis of several of them on the crucial role of the national industrial unions or federations in the post-revolutionary economy is apparent in the Valencia document. So, too, is Leval's dismissal of the excessive nature of the traditional emphasis on autonomy. The model of economy adopted in Valencia in January 1938 also bears a strong resemblance to the plan for the post-revolutionary economy adopted by the Industrial Workers of the World, of the United States, a generation before.

The preface to this document by the national committee of the CNT in its pamphlet on the economic plenum sets forth the immediate background for this resolution:

> Many were the workers and the places of production taken over by the workers on July 19, as a result of the abandonment of their former owners. And many were the workers who thought that there had been simply a change in the form of property. Thus they functioned, when the industries were prosperous, with absolute autonomy...
>
> However, it became necessary and is necessary to make them understand that on the 19th of July it was not just a few who triumphed but the collective forces of the proletariat that won so it was not admissible that the benefits be concentrated on a small nucleus. Common effort to fight and triumph; common benefits which victory provides; benefits tending to improve the wellbeing of the people. Furthermore, the CNT has understood that there cannot exist a prosperous economy, collectively speaking, without a control and a centralized coordination in terms of administration.[30]

The backbone of the CNT plan for organization of its part of the national economy was the then current organizational structure of the CNT itself. It had groups of workers in particular plants; local *sindicatos* bringing together workers of a particular industry in a locality; provincial, regional and national industrial federations. It also had local federations of all CNT unions in a locality, and similar structures on a provincial, regional level, topped by the national CNT itself. To this basic structure certain new institutions were to be appended, according to this resolution of the economic plenum.

The plenum resolution (which was entitled 'Administrative Centralization of the CNT Economy') were described as: '1. The economic organs which a Federación National de Industria will have, and 2. The Economic Councils.'

On each level of the organization, Technical-Administrative and Statistical (TAS) Councils were to be established. Within each plant, a general assembly of each specialized group of workers would elect such a body; in a given locality, a general assembly of each specialized group of workers of all of the plants of a given industry would also elect one; and a general assembly of all of the workers of a given industry in a locality would also elect a secretary, treasurer and technician, who together with representatives of the technical-administrative and statistical council of each specialized group in local industry, would constitute the TAS council for the local union.

Above the local level, there would be plenums of representatives of the TAS councils of each zone (apparently, each province) which would choose members of the zonal committee, and this same procedure would apply on the regional level; and a plenum of regional representatives would choose the TAS council for the national industrial federation.

The exact function of those technical-administrative and statistical councils was not made entirely clear. Certainly, they were to collect statistics on the functioning of the collectives on each level, but they were also on the lower levels at least 'to direct the progress of work in all aspects', and they were 'to seek always to have a good technical orientation'.

Alongside these technical-administrative and statistical councils, there were to be economic councils (Consejos de Economía). The TAS councils of each industry in a locality, meeting together, were to name two members of the permanent commission of the local economic council. They, together with two representatives from each local industry, and one representative from the local federation of industrial unions were to constitute the local economic council. These bodies were to have the duties 'delegated to them by the superior organization'.

Similar economic councils were to be established in each region, Catalonia, the Levante etc. Finally, all of the national TAS councils would name eight delegates each, who would make up the CNT National Economic Council. It 'will have technical administrative and statistical control of all the industries, mercantile centers and cooperatives belonging to the CNT as well as also the banking organizations, the Administrative Trade Union Agency for Insurance, the Fund for Family Compensation,' and other organizations which exist or might be created in the economic field.

Finally, the resolution provided that all of the members of permanent commissions had to have the approval of the trade union federations on local, regional and national levels. Also, 'The Trade Union Committees parallel to the local regional and national economic organs will designate the comrade who will carry out the functions of secretary of the Economic Councils.'[31]

Since the beginning of the Civil War, the CNT had been urging the establishment of a national economic council with participation of the CNT, UGT and appropriate governmental groups. Thus, for example, Juan Fabregas, the first anarchist councillor of the economy in the Catalan government, had written early in April 1937: '...if to win the war and the revolution military mobilization and single command is asked for incessantly, we understand that to win our war and our revolution it is essential also to have mobilization of the rear guard and establishment of a single direction of the economic front; that is to say, a brain which conceives and determines and others that obey and carry out the directives and watchwords of those with maximum responsibility ... without coordinated work, with both mobilizations at the same time, failure will be inevitable...'[32]

CNT national committee member M. Cardona Rossell, in a speech in Barcelona in January 1937 was more explicit in sketching the kind of national economic council which the CNT wanted. He described it as a body in which the CNT and UGT together would have a majority, the rest of its members representing various economic branches of the national and regional governments. He also sketched the way in which the council should be organized and should function.[33]

However, neither the Largo Caballero government nor that of Juan Negrín had set up such an economic council as the anarchists advocated – one in which the two union groups presumably would have had the major voice. Consequently, the CNT decided in its national economic plenum to move to set up such a body for the part of the economy which was under its control, and to set forth the general form of organisation that that sector of the economy would follow.

Conclusions on the National Economic Plenum

Some of the lessons, which the CNT leadership had drawn from the experience of the year and a half following the spontaneous seizure by the workers and peasants of a large part of the economy of Republican Spain, are clear. It concluded obviously that some kind of general direction and planning were needed in the CNT economy. They concluded that some facility under CNT control was needed to provide for the financial needs of the several thousand collectives. It had come to feel that within the collectives, as well as among them, there was need for instruments to enforce labor discipline. There was need, they concluded, to standardize the social security aspects of the system of collectives, in so far as possible without the interference of the state.

Missing from the resolutions of the economic plenum were some of the traditional beliefs of the Spanish anarchists. Gone was the insistence on the complete autonomy of every unit of the libertarian economy. Gone was the trust in spontaneous solidarity, both among the workers within each collective and among all of the collectives, as being sufficient to assure the smooth functioning of the system as a whole.

The decisions of the economic plenum, had the Civil War been won and the anarchists been in a position to carry out the decisions of January 1938, would almost certainly have resulted in a degree of bureaucracy in the anarchist economy which they had always abhorred, and before the War had always tried to avoid in practice within the CNT and its affiliated organizations. One can only speculate on whether such modifications in anarchist doctrine were the inevitable result of trying to run a large part of a more or less modern economy or were the consequence of a group of people for the first time in their lives having considerable power, liking it, and seeking to expand it.